HANDBOOK OF BUILDING MAINTENANCE MANAGEMENT

Mel A. Shear

A RESTON BOOK
PRENTICE-HALL, INC., Englewood Cliffs, New Jersey 07632

Library of Congress Cataloging in Publication Data

Shear, Mel A.
Handbook of building maintenance management.

Includes index.
1. Buildings—Maintenance—Management—Handbooks, manuals, etc. I. Title.
TH3361.S45 1983 658.2'02 82-21577
ISBN 0-8359-2729-6

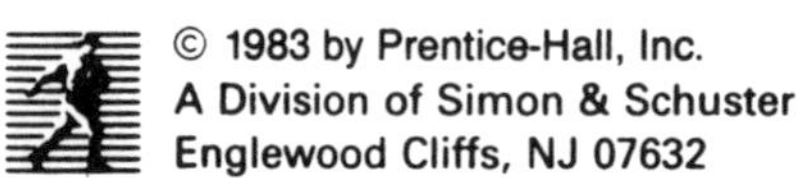

A Division of Simon & Schuster
Englewood Cliffs, NJ 07632

10 9 8 7 6 5 4

Printed in the United States of America

CONTENTS

Preface, 11

Chapter 1 Maintenance Programming, 1

1–1 An Overview, 1
1–2 Life Cycle Costs, 2
1–3 Management Theory, 5
1–4 The Planning Function, 8
1–5 Budgeting, 20
1–6 Inspections, 25
1–7 Organizing Work and People, 29
1–8 Management Decisions and Policy Formulation, 37
1–9 Biological Fouling and Corrosion, 39
1–10 The Benefits of Efficient Operation, 51

Chapter 2 The Building Profile, 53

2–1 Why A Building Profile? 53
2–2 Takeover Inspection, 54
2–3 Metric Conversion, 55

2–4 Important Information About A Building, 56
2–5 Exterior Elements, 57
2–6 Interior Elements, 62
2–7 Electrical Services, 68
2–8 The Fire Control System, 68
2–9 The Air Conditioning System, 70
2–10 Plumbing and Drainage, 78
2–11 Tools, Equipment, and Inventory Control, 83
2–12 The Importance of Records and Statistics, 86
2–13 Summing Up, 92

Chapter 3 Security, Safety, and Fire Protection, 93

3–1 Introduction, 93
3–2 Security, 94
3–3 Safety, 97
3–4 Fire Protection, 107
3–5 Life System Audit, 131
3–6 How to Budget for the Necessary Funds, 135

Chapter 4 Housekeeping Services, 137

4–1 An Overview, 137
4–2 Special Housekeeping Jobs, 138
4–3 Floors, 145
4–4 Floor Care, 152
4–5 Carpet Care, 164
4–6 Pest Problems, 170
4–7 How to Budget for the Housekeeping Services Funds, 179
4–8 Housekeeping Services Terminology, 182
4–9 Summing Up, 184

Chapter 5 Groundskeeping Services, 185

5–1 Planning, 185
5–2 Soils, Chemicals, and Fertilizers, 188
5–3 Pruning Trees, Shrubs, and Hedges, 197
5–4 Lawn Care, 199
5–5 Watering, 199
5–6 Equipment, Plants, Tools, and Inventory, 205
5–7 Grounds Maintenance Inspection Check List, 215
5–8 Preparing a Groundskeeping Budget, 215

Chapter 6 Structural Services, 219

6–1 An Overview, 219
6–2 Principles of Diagnosis, 221
6–3 Basic Building Construction, 223
6–4 Causes of Defects, 227
6–5 Change in Size, 229
6–6 Cracks, 230
6–7 Plaster Problems, 233
6–8 Dampness in Buildings, 235
6–9 Asphalt Paving Maintenance, 245
6–10 Painting, 247
6–11 Windows, 250
6–12 Roofing, 251
6–13 Building Hardware, 269
6–14 How to Budget for the Necessary Funds, 280

Chapter 7 The Plumbing and Drainage System, 285

7–1 An Overview, 285
7–2 Hot and Cold Water Distribution, 287
7–3 Plumbing Maintenance, 293
7–4 The Drainage System, 304
7–5 The Swimming Pool, 317
7–6 Budgeting for the Necessary Funds, 321
7–7 Glossary of Plumbing Terms, 322

Chapter 8 The Heating System, 325

8–1 An Overview, 325
8–2 What Is Comfort? 326
8–3 What Is Heat? 329
8–4 Forms of Energy Used to Heat A Building, 330
8–5 Boiler-Burner Efficiency, 335
8–6 The Burner, 342
8–7 The Boiler, 349
8–8 Heat Distribution, 358
8–9 Home Heating, 374
8–10 Temperature Control, 382
8–11 The Operator's Responsibility, 385
8–12 Handling Heating Complaints, 387
8–13 How to Budget for the Necessary Funds, 390
8–14 Terminology, 392

Chapter 9 Air Conditioning Systems, 399

9–1 An Overview, 399
9–2 Humidity, 403
9–3 Air Requirements, 404
9–4 Air Pressure Problems, 405
9–5 The Ventilation System, 406
9–6 Air Distribution, 411
9–7 Balancing the System, 422
9–8 Balancing Home Air Conditioning, 428
9–9 The Refrigeration Cycle, 434
9–10 The Cooling Tower, 441
9–11 How to Budget the Necessary Funds, 447
9–12 Terminology, 447

Chapter 10 Electrical Services, 451

10–1 An Overview, 451
10–2 Understanding the Wiring Service, 460
10–3 Understanding the System, 461
10–4 Lighting, 475
10–5 Troubleshooting the System, 480
10–6 Timers, Motors, and Their Controls, 490
10–7 Electrical Appliances, 497
10–8 How to Budget the Necessary Funds, 502
10–9 Safety Tips, 502

Chapter 11 Mechanical Services, 507

11–1 An Overview, 507
11–2 Elevators, 508
11–3 Overhead Doors, 523
11–4 Garbage Compactor Maintenance, 524
11–5 Motors, 525
11–6 Fans, 531
11–7 Maintenance of Air Handling Equipment, 534
11–8 Lubrication, 545
11–9 Bearings, 547
11–10 Pumps, 551
11–11 Equipment Noise Problems, 556
11–12 Valves, 556
11–13 Budgeting the Funds, 561

Chapter 12 Energy Management, 563

12–1 An Overview, 563
12–2 A Building Energy Analysis, 567
12–3 A Building's Weather Sensitive Components, 570
12–4 A Building's Occupant Sensitive Components, 578
12–5 Domestic Hot Water, 590
12–6 Monitoring Efficiency, 596
12–7 Summing Up, 602

Index, 609

This book is dedicated to my wife Shirley, my children, Neil, Randy, Ellen, Heather, and my daughter-in-law Suzann, who put up with me over the years while I spent my time gathering the information and writing the book.

It is also dedicated to all the people who ever were a part of the residential maintenance and operations teams at Cadillac Development and Cadillac Fairview, and who worked out of 55 St. Regis Crescent North, Downsview, Ontario, Canada.

Without their help and encouragement, the book would never have been written.

PREFACE

In 1961, I was offered a job in property management which, after much thought, I declined. I was concerned with my lack of knowledge about building structure and electrical/mechanical equipment, and I wondered how, without any training, I would cope with the complaints from tenants who lived in the buildings twenty-four hours a day, seven days a week. When I finally began my career in the real estate industry three years later, however, I soon discovered that managing real estate was similar in many ways to my previous occupation. I found in all of my management positions that management was really faced with two basic problems. The first one was dealing with the economic problem of competition, changing markets, and so forth. The second problem concerned maintaining a team spirit that would allow individuals to satisfy their own desires through working together. In short, I found that "management is management."

Nevertheless, my experience did not adequately prepare me for the structural and electrical/mechanical problems I faced in the buildings I was managing. Problem-solving was difficult because the people who designed and erected the buildings didn't realize the problems they were building into the structures. Furthermore, the builders only built the structures; they weren't exposed to the operational problems.

Even many of the troubleshooting tradesmen lacked the training in diagnosis and analysis required for the problems I was experiencing. Often, their services only compounded the initial problems. When I looked for suitable training programs to teach me the property management business, I found none.

So I started from the beginning. I subscribed to all of the trade magazines, as they often published meaningful, up-to-date information about the technical problems I encountered. I gathered around me people who became specialists in housekeeping, groundskeeping, structural, and electrical/mechanical services. In the beginning, we all needed the support of each other, and as we worked together, our skills seemed to complement each other and we all benefited. By concentrating their responsibilities on specialities, they all became better and better.

Eventually, I developed an in-house school. The specialists provided on-site training and I put together a manual to complement the hands-on education. Over time, we upgraded the maintenance staff and learned to provide tenants services that were the envy of the industry. As the operation staff improved and we were able to build a preventive maintenance program into our plans, the emergencies were reduced, unscheduled maintenance was reduced, and the benefits were increased. In 1982, we saved approximately $1.8 million in maintenance expenses for the 17,000 apartment units that we were managing. Moreover, we also reduced our energy costs by $1.9 million. THE BIG BENEFIT OF AN EFFECTIVE MAINTENANCE AND OPERATIONS PROGRAM IS THAT, AS PRICES GO UP, THE SAVINGS ALSO INCREASE AUTOMATICALLY.

It was only in the last few years that I decided to put all the information I've accumulated into a book. I received encouraging cooperation from the suppliers and manufacturers to whom I turned for assistance and suggestions. It is my hope that this book will encourage the development of desperately needed training programs for maintenance staff.

The information in this book is meant to be used by property managers of all types of buildings: commercial, residential, and institutional. It is not exclusive, however; the new technology involved in the building of sophisticated high-rises will require you to seek maintenance information designed specifically for such buildings. Still, *Handbook of Building Maintenance Management* will serve as a good foundation on which to establish a comprehensive maintenance plan for all buildings.

If the information helps you understand and resolve many of your problems; if it helps you find a new way of doing jobs; if it improves your diagnostic ability; and if it results in a better way of handling your responsibilities, then it will have served its main purpose.

Chapter 1

MAINTENANCE PROGRAMMING

1–1 An Overview

The design, appearance, and quality of construction of residential and commercial buildings usually determine the character of a building during its life span. A building's location and design usually attract compatible people and businesses. To maintain this compatibility, it is necessary to keep up the appearance of the structure, to operate the electrical/mechanical systems efficiently, and to keep the interior clean and safe.

To achieve this goal it is essential that the building is properly staffed with people who handle their responsibilities professionally. It is also essential that all prospective tenants are screened and that undesirable tenants are kept to a minimum. These criteria form the basis of competent management.

When a building is allowed to deteriorate the desirable tenants move out and the undesirable tenants move in. The deterioration of a building does not happen overnight; it is usually not noticed until an increase in vandalism, in emergencies, and in vacancies triggers an awareness, along with a decrease in cash flow and an increase in operating and capital expenditures. Reversing deterioration is difficult and costly. In some buildings this negative trend is never overcome.

After World War II, most countries experienced a serious housing shortage and resourceful development entrepreneurs quickly saturated the market with a less than desirable product. We have never really been able to overcome many of the built-in problems. The skills required by the developer, builder, manager, and operator were never fully identified, which led to an ad hoc development of training programs that lacked the needed scope. The most serious problem is that the various activities were never synchronized into a team effort—communications between the developer, designer, builder, manager, and operator have been practically non-existent.

When we analyze the traditional concept of real estate management, we find that most people believe that the management of a building begins after the building is built. The people that build the buildings are usually called project managers and the people who manage the buildings are usually called property managers—which automatically leads one to believe that there is no relationship between the two responsibilities.

In reality, any profit-making venture can be called a "project" and in the real estate industry it should mean the management of a building project through its life cycle stages of development, design, construction, and operations.

The people who are a part of the "project's management team" need to be skilled in marketing and administration (the paper and people function) and others need to be skilled in various technologies (the physical functions). The physical function people include specialists in design, development, construction, and operations troubleshooting activities. These would include the housekeeping, groundskeeping, structural, and electrical/mechanical services specialists, as well as the troubleshooting tradesmen who are qualified to resolve problems.

If we use an individual building as the smallest complete unit and its components as a basis for organization, the following "physical function" classifications emerge: housekeeping, groundskeeping, structural, electrical, and mechanical services, plumbing, drainage, heating, ventilation, air conditioning, and fire control systems.

This means that all planning, organizing, staffing, directing, and controlling of a building's maintenance program would revolve around these classifications. It also means that the finance, administration, and marketing people would function as a resource support for the developers, designers, builders, and operators. It is not uncommon to find that the roles are often reversed. To make the efforts of this "project management team" work, the "physical function people" must have exactly the kind of information they need to help them do their job. The ability to monitor their own efficiency must be a prime requisite of the system.

1-2 Life Cycle Costs

The "project management team" concept also means that when decisions are made by the team of design, construction, and operations specialists, consideration would be given to the operating costs of a component, as well as the initial cost.

This approach is needed because many problems and unnecessary expenses are created when purchased equipment is not suited to the intended application. This ad hoc decision process wastes energy, maintenance, and utility dollars, and many components eventually have to be replaced as energy costs soar or as they wear out before their expected life cycle.

Before making a decision about equipment or structural material during construction, the operational costs over a fifty-year life span should be added to the initial cost. The cost of replacement could be three to ten times more than the initial cost. This de-

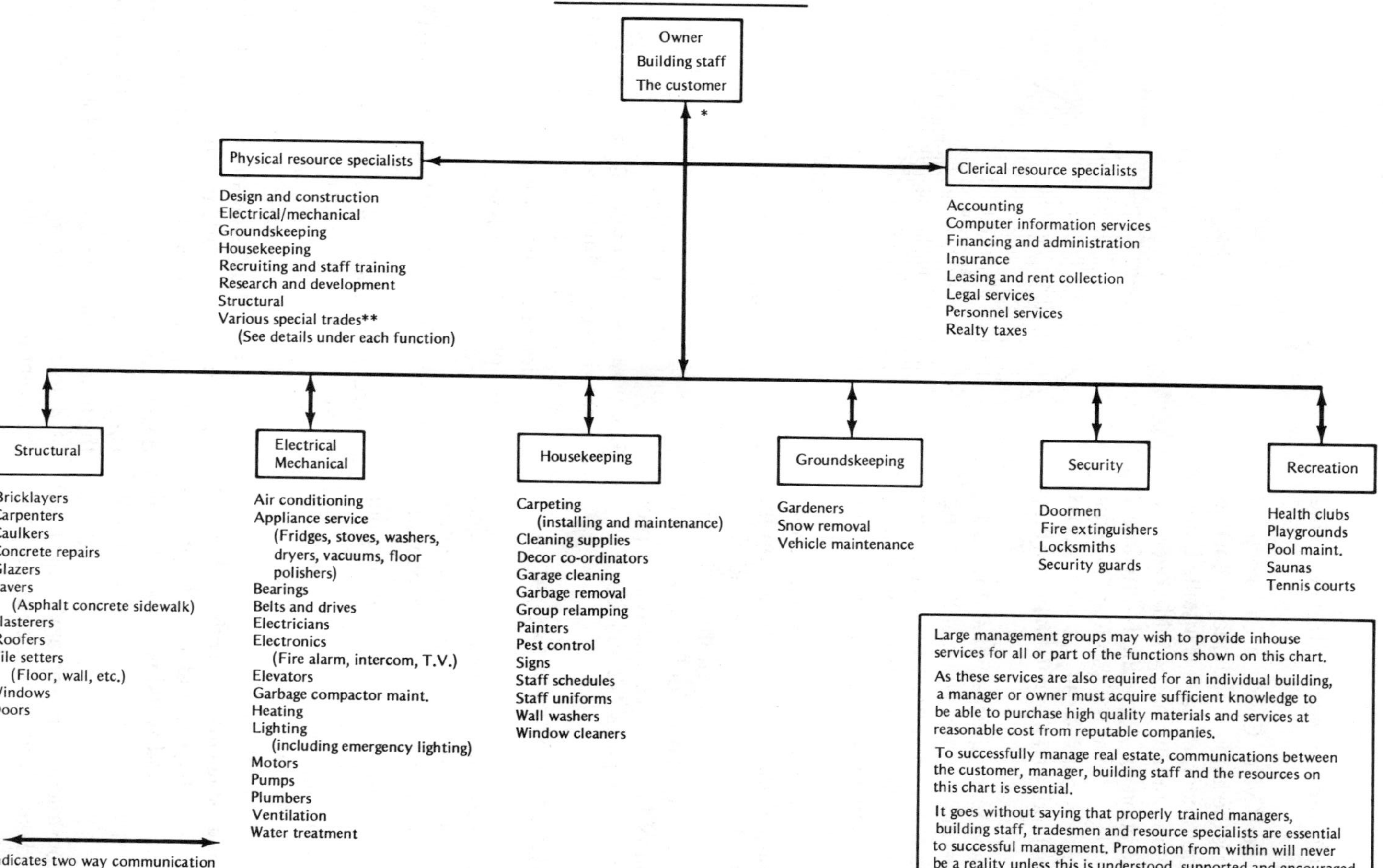

FIGURE 1-1 The project management team.

cisionmaking process is called "Life Cycle Costing."

The "Life Cycle Cost" of a piece of equipment is the amount of money needed to buy the equipment, to have it installed, and to provide an annuity that would cover the cost of operation for a specified "life time." The life cycle cost would also identify what components or parts wear out and would provide the funds to replace them before they fail.

Up to now many use the initial cost as the main criterion when designing and building. There was not a great need to evaluate life cycle costs in the past when energy was plentiful, and maintenance was paid for with uninflated dollars.

Research would indicate that cheap equipment and materials always ate up the cash flow. The energy shortage and rising inflation have merely driven this fact home with a vengeance. Let us look at an excellent illustration of life cycle costing over a project's time span (Figures 1-2 and 1-3).

THE LIFE SPAN OF A PROJECT

First, let us look at the life span of a project. It should be noted that the conception, design, and construction may be maximums.

1. The conception step—including the purchase of land, financial arranging, leasing, selling, renting space, and gaining approval for the project—could take a minimum of *three years*.
2. The design stage may consume *one or two years*. This stage would include preliminary design and working drawings, estimates, specifications, and contract documents.
3. The construction time on any project will depend entirely upon the size and scale of the project. However, it may take up to *four years to complete*.
4. Operating the building is usually projected over a time span of forty to fifty years; thus maintenance and operations are nine or ten times longer than the initial creation of the project.

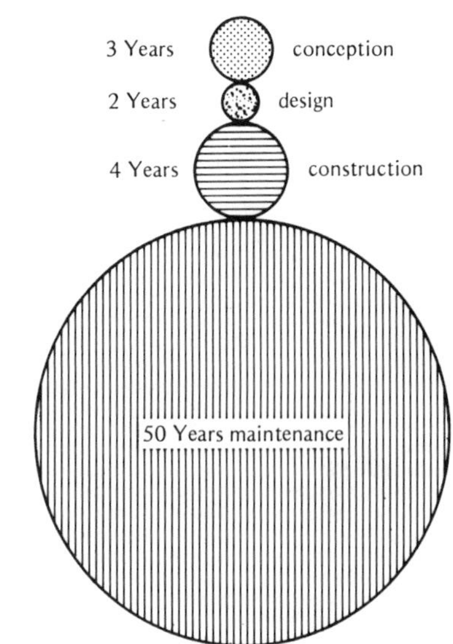

FIGURE 1-2 A project's time span.

PERCENTAGE OF LIFE CYCLE COSTS

Figure 1-3 shows that maintenance and operations expenses account for the major portion of the life-time cost of any project. The relative importance and impact of efficient operation is clearly indicated when comparisons are made to other costs.

The importance of evaluating various design and construction decisions against life cycle costs is thus self-evident. Converting the time and life cycle costs to dollars instead of years and percentages would surely make the point more startling.

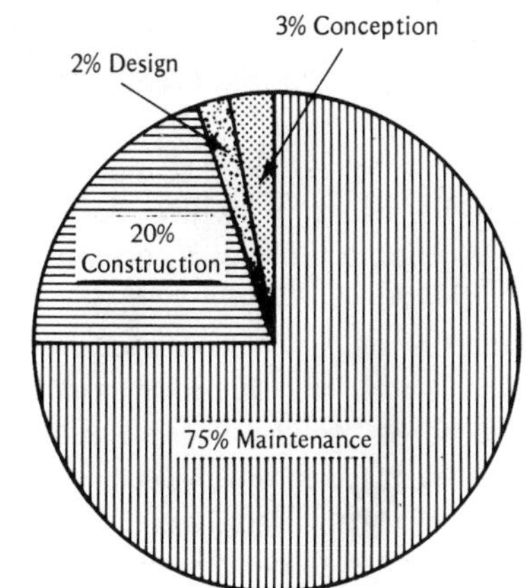

FIGURE 1-3 Percentage of life cycle costs.

A LONG-TERM INVESTMENT

It is essential that designers, planners, builders, and managers develop a more sophisticated method of determining the life expectancy of a building's components. A proper accounting system, using a computer, will gather the statistics about operating expenses, store them, and eventually provide accurate life span costs for all the components. Without this information decisions can only be based on assumptions.

It should be pointed out that a proper maintenance program would ensure a full life cycle for the components. Experience has shown that with a good program we can add 50 percent to the life span expected by the manufacturer. Funds should always be allocated for replacement so that time will not be wasted when a component's time for replacement has arrived. Proper planning and budgeting are essential.

Most of us have seen worn carpets or chipped, unsightly paint. Maintenance programming will assure full value for the investment dollar, but when an item's time has come, change it. Funds must be available for these specific items. Never defer maintenance as a means of improving profit and cash flow.

From the foregoing one can see that decisions about development, design, construction, and operations are crucial and are all interrelated. Real estate development is a long-term investment and thus dictates the necessity for long-term thinking; we should organize our actions and recordkeeping so that we have the necessary funds for the original purchase, for ongoing maintenance, and for replacement when things wear out.

1-3 Management Theory

UNDERSTANDING MANAGEMENT THEORY

If we accept the concept that "Project Management" is managing a building through its "life cycle" stages of development, design, construction, and operations, then it will be necessary for everyone on that team to acquire the necessary human, conceptual, and technical management skills required to operate the building comfortably and profitably.

Although the Greek and Roman Empires employed excellent managerial systems, it wasn't until the dawn of the twentieth century that administrative methods were formalized into some semblance of "management theory." A good example of project management would be the Pyramids in Egypt, whose life cycle has not been determined. In fact, the Pyramids are still one of the major attractions that provide tourist dollars for Egypt. This is still a productive project.[1]

THE THEORY OF SCIENTIFIC MANAGEMENT

In the early 1900s, Fredrick W. Taylor, an American engineer, observed that management had no clear-cut concept of its role relative to its employees, that motivation of the worker in the context of positive leadership was non-existent, and that excellent performance on the part of the worker was to management's benefit. This was the beginning of modern scientific management. Working from the Midvale steel plant, Taylor developed four basic principles which were incorporated in his theory of scientific management:

1. Workers should be scientifically selected and trained, and placed in work situations that best suit them physically and mentally.
2. The work process should be analyzed on a methodical basis, given to scientific evaluation rather than rule of thumb.
3. Management and labor should cooperate closely, thus ensuring that work follows in accordance with the developed scientific analysis.
4. Management and labor should share equally in task fulfillment, with each doing the work for which it is best fitted.

Uniquely, Taylor separated *mental work from manual work,* laying great emphasis on the planning process. His observation, which is even more valid today, was *that planning was the most important function in developing efficiency and profit.*[2]

A recent example of project management was the NASA program, which culminated with the landing on the moon and the return to earth of the Apollo Space Vehicle.

The success of the NASA program was achieved by hundreds of project managers who coordinated the efforts of thousands of people, united by a common goal.

It is not our intention to dwell too long on the subject of management theory. For those who wish to improve their management skills there are many books that cover this discipline in depth.

THE PRINCIPLES OF MANAGEMENT

One of the basic principles of management is to define the purpose of the enterprise. Many people, organizations, and profit-making ventures fail because they don't know their purpose or the nature of their business. The temptation is to deny reality. In the real estate business, when a company develops, designs, builds, and manages, the tendency is to believe that they are in the development business. If we consider a building's life span as fifty years and the development construction stage spans only nine years, it logically follows that we would be managing the building for fifty-nine years and that professional management is the key to success, even though good location, quality of design, sound construction, and proper financing are still very important.

[1] Project Management Theory—Professor K. R. Blowatt, Brock University—St. Catharines, Ontario.

[2] F. W. Taylor; "A Piece Rate System on the Art of Cutting Metals"; ASME, 1907.

THE GOAL OF THE PROJECT MANAGEMENT TEAM

The goal of the project management team is to acquire the skills needed to adequately plan, organize, staff, direct, and control the resources required to effectively manage real estate property through its stages of development, design, construction, and operations.

Success is evident if they provide safety, comfort, and convenience for the lessee, resident, patient, or student while maintaining the owner's reputation for quality and integrity, maximizing their cash flow, and protecting the investment in the property.

These goals apply whether buildings are publicly or privately owned, and whether they are commercial, residential, or institutional buildings.

Management is often defined as the management of *"agreed upon goals"* using a minimum of resources. Management is also *"getting the right things done right."* It involves the coordination of manpower, machinery, money, and materials. It involves delegating, motivating, communicating, evaluating, and improving. It doesn't matter whether you are managing a hot dog stand or a multimillion dollar development. "Management is management." The differences are the products, the goals, and the people.

BASIC MANAGEMENT ACTIVITIES

Although we will not include an in-depth study of management it is important that you understand that successful project management hinges around six basic mangement activities. A brief outline of these activities should help you.

Planning Establish clear-cut, well-defined organizational goals and strategic plans that provide the basis for systematic planning at the lowest level of the company.

Organization Should be structured on the basis of task identification and work specialization.

Job specifications and channels of communication should be identified by vertical lines in a tiered structure and should be defined by an organizational chart which is backed up by procedures and regulations. The organizational chart should show patterns of authority, work flow, and feedback.

Staffing Involves the manning, training, and when necessary, firing, of the people filling the organizational positions.

Directing The success of this function depends on the style, nature, and skill of top, middle, and first-line managers. They must be skilled and endowed with the necessary conceptual, human, and technical skills. Successful managers must be able to lead, motivate, and give direction to their staff.

Controlling Controls are a means of measuring performance, identifying problem areas, and redirecting them to conform with corporate purpose.

Controlling is a means of measuring the inputs of information, energy, and materials against the output from the system of products or services.

The system should inform, appraise, and support the managers who could then intelligently react and correct or redirect problem situations.

Feedback Feedback is the only way to test whether the assumptions on which a decision has been made are still valid, or whether they are becoming obsolete. Organized information is needed for feedback and it must be accurate if effective results are to be achieved.

A POSITIVE TAKEOVER AND MANAGEMENT APPROACH

1. The completion of a new structure should be considered as only the beginning, not the end of the project.
2. The transition from construction to management of the structure and electrical/mechanical systems should be formalized and the turnover executed professionally.
3. The architect and engineer should participate in the turnover and should ensure that adequate instruction and information is made available for future management personnel. If necessary, factory experts should be available to explain more sophisticated equipment.
4. Project managers, on-site construction staff, property managers, and building and office staff must receive suitable training.
5. Management should receive the necessary drawings and operations manuals soon after the structure is built and equipment is installed.
6. Management should develop the necessary inspections required to properly take over and manage the building and operate the equipment.
7. Management should develop workloads, hire suitable staff, establish duty schedules, and provide detailed job descriptions in writing.
8. Suitable preventive maintenance programs should be developed and the necessary funds should be available in a repair and maintenance budget (see Figures 1-4 to 1-15).
9. The symptoms of abnormal conditions should be identified and the operating staff should be instructed about how to troubleshoot problems and correct them.
10. The operating staff should be instructed about when to call for help and who to call. A suppliers and services manual should be developed and made available (Figure 2-21).
11. The operating staff should have all the necessary tools and spare parts.
12. Equipment and shut-off valves should be tagged.
13. Logs to monitor operations, maintenance, and energy consumption should be developed.
14. The idea that operating expenses are an investment, and not an expense, should be emphasized.
15. All of the operating costs should be included in a zero-base budget—repair and maintenance, fuel, hydro, water, staff salaries, taxes, insurance, and other management expenses. The owner will then be able to understand and approve or reject an item before the money is spent. A summary of these maintenance and operations expenses follows (Figures 1-4 and 1-15).

1-4 The Planning Function

MANAGEMENT'S ACTIVITY AREAS

In real estate management there are seven strategic areas of activity that repeat them-

CAPITALIZED EXPENDITURES	ACCOUNT NUMBERS	ACCOUNT TOTALS
BUILDING ADDITIONS	20	
BUILDING REPLACEMENT	21	
CONSTRUCTION DEFICIENCIES	22	
EQUIPMENT ADDITIONS	23	
EQUIPMENT REPLACEMENT	24	

FIGURE 1-4 Summary of budget expense schedules, repair and maintenance categories; master list.

selves each month and must be controlled.

1. Leasing
2. Occupant turnover (move-ins and move-outs)
3. Rent collection and bad debt recovery
4. Inspections
5. Purchasing of services and supplies
6. Accounts receivable, payroll, and other necessary recordkeeping
7. Daily, weekly, monthly, semi-annual, and annual maintenance tasks

HOW THE SYSTEM WAS DEVELOPED

Reviewing how this system of maintenance programming was developed will help you understand the need for planning and organization and how the system breaks down into realistic, logical project management needs.

1. It is necessary to identify each area of specialized services required to operate the building (housekeeping, groundskeeping, structural, electrical, and mechanical). A team of resource specialists for each of these services must be developed. As these people are absolutely essential, suitable training programs must be given top priority.
2. Under each of these specialized areas a listing of all of the key expense items should be developed. Skilled trouble-shooting tradesmen will be required to ensure that all maintenance problems are corrected and that preventive maintenance programs are completed as planned. The decision to use in-house or outside services will be based on quality of workmanship and need.
3. A suppliers and services manual should be compiled around the key expense items (Figure 2-21). Specifications and guidelines are needed to ensure quality of the services and supplies. These specifications would apply when using either in-house or outside trades or suppliers.
4. It is essential that a proper reporting system is developed to ensure that accurate records are kept of all activities.
5. The key expense items are used as a basis for zero-base budget expense working

HOUSEKEEPING SERVICES	ACCT. NOS.	ACCOUNT TOTALS	TOTAL
CARPETING	25		
CLEANING SUPPLIES	26		
OUTSIDE CLEANING SERVICES	27		
INTERIOR DECORATING	28		
PEST CONTROL	29		
SIGNAGE	30		
WASTE DISPOSAL	31		
WINDOW CLEANING	32		

GROUNDSKEEPING SERVICES	ACCT. NOS.	ACCOUNT TOTALS	TOTAL
GARDENING	33		
SNOW REMOVAL	34		
VEHICLE MAINTENANCE	35		

FIGURE 1-5 Summary of budget expense schedules, repair and maintenance categories; master list.

schedules and form the control points of the budget. Each schedule includes input from inspections, maintenance programs, and other repair and maintenance activities. This is the base on which the system is built.

TYPES OF MAINTENANCE

When we refer to maintenance programs we should understand that there are actually four types of maintenance:

1. Breakdown maintenance or fixing things as they fail.
2. Corrective maintenance or improving repairs and conditions as they exist.
3. Maintenance or redesigning existing conditions to eliminate failures.
4. Preventive maintenance—a system of periodic inspections of existing facilities to uncover conditions leading to break-

STRUCTURAL SERVICES	ACCT. NOS.	ACCOUNT TOTALS	TOTALS
BRICKWORK & STRUCTURAL CONCRETE	36		
BUILDING HARDWARE	37		
CAULKING	38		
COUNTER TOPS & CUPBOARDS	39		
DOORS	40		
EXTERIOR PAINTING	41		
FLOORS	42		
PAVING (CONCRETE & ASPHALT)	43		
ROOFS	44		
WALLS & CEILINGS	45		
WINDOWS	46		

FIGURE 1-6 Summary of budget expense schedules, repair and maintenance categories; master list.

down or harmful depreciation and the correction of some of these conditions while they are still minor.

THE BOTTOM LINE

Many industries measure their success or failure by the bottom line of their financial statement. The only problem with this approach is that by the time they see the bottom line figure, it is past history and the problems require drastic action to correct.

In real estate, a measurement of success is often high occupancy and gross rental collections. Many overlook the control of operations as a key element of successful management. Control of this expense can provide significant opportunities for profit improvement. In fact, an opportunity missed automatically becomes a loss.

HOW TO CONVERT OPERATIONS EXPENSE TO INCOME

Because maintenance is a service and supporting function, maintenance is often ignored as an area of potential cost reduction or as a means of producing revenue. Lack of a professional approach normally results in excessive costs.

To emphasize this point we could assume that a 10 percent return on a real estate investment annually is considered a fair return. If this is true and operations expenses were

ELECTRICAL SERVICES	ACCT. NOS.	ACCOUNT TOTALS	TOTAL
APPLIANCES	47		
WIRING DISTRIBUTION	48		
FIRE PROTECTION SYSTEM	49		
TELEVISION SYSTEM	50		

MECHANICAL SERVICES	ACCT. NOS.	ACCOUNT TOTALS	TOTAL
COOLING SYSTEM	51		
ELEVATORS	52		
HEATING SYSTEM	53		
PLUMBING & DRAINAGE SYSTEM	54		
POOL OPERATIONS	55		
VENTILATION SYSTEM	56		

FIGURE 1-7 Summary of budget expense schedules, repair and maintenance categories; master list.

$10,000,000 per year, then a 10 percent reduction of this amount would be $1,000,000. It should also mean that we would have to invest $10,000,000 in a new venture to make this amount of money. To put it another way, we would have to increase the rental income by over $1,000,000 per year to make up for the loss caused by a 10 percent increase in maintenance expenses.

PROTECTING THE INVESTMENT

Most owners of real estate believe that revenue is only earned from rental income. They should be reminded that owning a building represents a sizable investment and that proper maintenance is the only way to protect their investment.

The ultimate goal of a maintenance program should be to keep the property at its

MISCELLANEOUS	ACCOUNT NUMBERS	ACCOUNT TOTALS
COMMUNICATION MATERIALS	57	
GENERAL	58	
RECREATION	59	
SECURITY SERVICE (SEE CHAPTER THREE)	60	
TELEPHONES	61	

FIGURE 1-8 **Summary of budget expense schedules, repair and maintenance categories; master list.**

	ACCT.NO.	SUB	TOTAL
COMMUNICATION MATERIALS	57	TOTALS	

PRINTED MATTER	571	
POSTAGE	572	

			TOTAL
GENERAL	58	SUB TOTALS	

ADVERTISING FOR STAFF	581	
CREDIT CHECKS	582	
DECORATIONS	583	
MEMBERSHIP IN TRADE ASSOCIATIONS	584	
MOVING BUILDING STAFF	585	
NUSIANCE CLAIMS	586	
SHELVING	587	
TOOL KITS	588	
UNIFORMS	589	

FIGURE 1-9 **Summary of budget expense schedules, operations categories; miscellaneous.**

	ACCT. NOS.	SUB TOTAL	TOTAL
RECREATION	59		

ARTS & CRAFTS SUPPLIES	591	
ENTERTAINMENT	592	
EQUIPMENT RENTAL	593	
EQUIPMENT REPAIRS	594	
NURSERY SUPPLIES	595	
PLAYGROUNDS	596	
REFRESHMENTS	597	
SAUNAS	598	
TENNIS COURTS	599	
TOWELS & LINENS	5910	

	ACCT. NOS.	SUB TOTAL	TOTAL
TELEPHONES	61		

ANSWERING SERVICE	611	
BUILDING OPERATOR	612	
ENGINEER	613	
EXTENSION - ELEVATOR	614	
EXTENSION - POOL	615	
LONG DISTANCE	616	
MANAGEMENT OFFICE	617	
RENTAL OFFICE	618	

FIGURE 1-10 **Summary of budget expense schedules, maintenance and operations categories; miscellaneous.**

EMPLOYEE'S NAME	CURRENT SALARY				NO. OF PAYS	TOTAL ANNUAL SALARY
	HRS. WRKD.	RATE	PER	TOTAL		
1.						
2.						
SUPERINTENDENTS					TOTAL ACCOUNT	62

1.						
2.						
DAY HELP					TOTAL ACCOUNT	63

1.						
2.						
ENGINEERING					TOTAL ACCOUNT	64

1.						
2.						
GARDENING					TOTAL ACCOUNT	65

1.						
2.						
RECREATION					TOTAL ACCOUNT	66

1.						
2.						
RENTAL AGENTS					TOTAL ACCOUNT	67

FIGURE 1-11 Summary of building operations staff salaries, budget expense schedules.

ACCT. NOS.	DESCRIPTION	PREV. YEAR ACTUAL	CURRENT YEAR ACTUAL	PRESENT BUDGET	OVER OR UNDER	NEW BUDGET	YEAR TO DATE
	CAPITALIZED EXPENDITURES						
20	BUILDING ADDITIONS						
21	BUILDING REPLACEMENT						
22	CONST. DEFICIENCIES						
23	EQUIPMENT ADDITIONS						
24	EQUIPMENT REPLACEMENT						
	HOUSEKEEPING SERVICES						
25	CARPETING						
26	CLEANING SUPPLIES						
27	OUTSIDE CLEANING SERV.						
28	INTERIOR DECORATING						
29	PEST CONTROL						
30	SIGNAGE						
31	WASTE DISPOSAL						
32	WINDOW CLEANING						
	GROUNDSKEEPING SERVICES						
33	GARDENING						
34	SNOW REMOVAL						
35	VEHICLE MAINTENANCE						

FIGURE 1-12 Summary of maintenance and operations accounts (suggested computer print-out).

highest level of maintenance. While achieving this goal, the owners should enjoy an increase in cash flow and a reduction in repair and maintenance expenses, as well as satisfying the needs of their customers.

The value of real estate has always been considered as one of the few hedges against inflation. A good example of this theory is the Empire State Building and the Rockefeller Center, which celebrated their fiftieth birthdays in 1981. These properties look like they were just built, but more important is their present value. The return on these investments must be staggering.

SOLICITING SUPPORT

Maintaining real estate is a constantly changing activity. Because structures and equipment change and wear, the maintenance program must be flexible enough so that it can be constantly improved.

The dedication of the staff to the objectives of the plan must be developed. Resistance to

ACCT NOS.	DESCRIPTION	PREV. YEAR ACTUAL	CURRENT YEAR ACTUAL	PRESENT BUDGET	OVER OR UNDER	NEW BUDGET	YEAR TO DATE
	STRUCTURAL SERVICES						
36	BRICKWORK & CONCRETE						
37	BUILDING HARDWARE						
38	CAULKING						
39	COUNTERS & CUPBOARDS						
40	DOORS						
41	EXTERIOR PAINTING						
42	FLOORS						
43	PAVING (CONC.&ASPHALT)						
44	ROOFS						
45	WALLS & CEILINGS						
46	WINDOWS						
	ELECTRICAL SERVICES						
47	APPLIANCES						
48	WIRING DISTRIBUTION						
49	FIRE PROTECTION SYST.						
50	TELEVISION SYSTEM						

FIGURE 1-13 Summary of maintenance and operations accounts (suggested computer print-out).

change must be overcome through constant communication and education. Support must be solicited and obtained from building owners.

IDENTIFYING THE ROUTINE FUNCTIONS

All clerical and physical management functions must be included in the budget, thus ensuring availability of the necessary funds to complete them. Preparing a master action plan will help organize all of these activities and identify the routine functions. (See page 19.)

As stated previously, the plan's primary attitude is towards "preventive maintenance." Proper planning and execution help to ensure that these functions are carried out in an efficient manner.

Each year the plan should be outlined on a monthly calendar. This will eliminate the possibility of overlooking an item and allows a program to be scheduled at the most favorable time. An example: The fine tuning of the boiler burners must be done during the heat-

ACCT. NOS.	DESCRIPTION	PREV. YEAR ACTUAL	CURRENT YEAR ACTUAL	PRESENT BUDGET	OVER OR UNDER	NEW BUDGET	YEAR TO DATE
	MECHANICAL SERVICES						
51	COOLING SYSTEM						
52	ELEVATORS						
53	HEATING SYSTEM						
54	PLUMBING & DRAINAGE						
55	POOL OPERATIONS						
56	VENTILATION SYSTEM						
	MISCELLANEOUS						
57	COMMUNICATION MATERIAL						
58	GENERAL						
59	RECREATION						
60	SECURITY SERVICE						
61	TELEPHONES						

FIGURE 1-14 Summary of maintenance and operations accounts (suggested computer print-out).

ACCT. NOS.	DESCRIPTION	PREV. YEAR ACTUAL	CURRENT YEAR ACTUAL	PRESENT BUDGET	OVER OR UNDER	NEW BUDGET	YEAR TO DATE
	STAFF SALARIES						
62	SUPERINTENDENTS						
63	DAY HELP						
64	ENGINEERING						
65	GARDENING						
66	RECREATION STAFF						
67	RENTAL AGENTS						
68	FRINGE BENEFITS						
	UTILITIES						
69	FUEL OIL						
70	ELECTRICITY						
71	WATER						
72	NATURAL GAS						

FIGURE 1-15 Summary of maintenance and operations accounts (suggested computer print-out).

The Master Action Plan

Revenue

—rental fee

Marketing

—surveying the competition
—advertising
—leasing

Administration

—setting and maintaining a rental roll
—moving people in or out
—parking and key control
—rental collections
—issuing work and purchase orders
—accounting and recordkeeping
—managing an insurance program
—payroll records
—budgeting records

Planning-Organizing-Controlling

—conduct building takeover inspection
—detail interior and exterior elements
—tag electrical/mechanical equipment
—detail equipment records
—prepare building maintenance work loads
—assign duty schedules for staff
—prepare job descriptions for staff
—staff the building
—supply maintenance tools, equipment, and inventory
—develop an emergency procedure
—follow up construction guarantees (if necessary)
—decide on trades, services, and suppliers
—arrange service contracts
—arrange ongoing inspections
—prepare annual budget
—inspect individual units annually

Security

—set up a security system
—test and service the complete fire control system annually

Electrical / Mechanical Services

—conduct annual preventive maintenance inspection of service panels and emergency lighting and service where necessary
—lubricate equipment as required
—change filters regularly
—service pumps and motors

Plumbing & Drainage System

—clean drains
—service domestic hot water storage tanks
—service pressure regulating valves
—service plumbing fixtures

Heating System

—service controls
—service burners
—inspect boilers
—service fan coil units
—service hot air furnaces
—add and monitor water treatment
—inspect and top up glycol ramps and heaters
—daily monitoring of system

Ventilation System

—clean housing as required
—change filters as required
—align and replace belts

Cooling System

—service chillers
—service cooling towers
—add and monitor water treatment
—service incremental units
—service fan coil units

Housekeeping Services

—sweep underground garages seven times a year
—clean inaccessible windows annually
—steam clean carpets every two years
—wash walls every three years

Groundskeeping Services

—schedule all gardening chores (service all equipment; order flowers, fertilizers; replace dead trees, perennials, salt and sand, sprays, tools)

Recreation Facilities

—opening and closing and maintenance (pools, tennis courts, playgrounds, and recreation centers)

Structural Services

—inspect walls, roofs, sidewalks, parking lots, door closers, common area locks and the appearance of the buildings
—schedule all maintenance activities

ing season, while carpet cleaning and wall washing can be used as a filler job for companies in this business during their slack months. This allows you the opportunity to negotiate a better price for this type of maintenance. Work and purchase orders can be issued from the calendar in advance, allowing the trades time to plan and schedule their actions.

Owners of buildings should be made aware of all planning activities and given copies of the building profiles, staff requirements, and budgets. They should be encouraged to formally inspect their building once a year.

1-5 Budgeting

THE IMPORTANCE OF RECORDKEEPING

Recordkeeping is the watchdog of the maintenance system. Without records, there is no information, and without information, planning is merely guesswork.

A variety of problems are created when situations are not properly recorded and followed up. The following six problems may be encountered when proper written records are not maintained:

1. Problems are reported on the phone or through a personal meeting and are not recorded on a maintenance request.
2. Building operating staff are not given the opportunity to investigate the problem and, where possible, to effect the repair themselves.
3. Tradesmen are called in, but are unable to identify a problem because detailed instructions are not available, or the problem was other than the one assumed.
4. Invoices do not match purchase orders.
5. Tradesmen arrive to find that a job has already been taken care of because of confusion over work assignments.

MAINTENANCE REQUEST 89167

BUILDING ADDRESS | FLOOR NO. | HOME PHONE NO.

RESIDENT'S NAME | SUITE NO. | BUSINESS PHONE NO.

REQUEST

REQUEST RECEIVED BY | TAG NO

RESIDENT'S CONSENT

I WISH TO HAVE THE ABOVE MAINTENANCE ATTENDED TO AND I HEREBY AUTHORIZE CADILLAC PROPERTY MANAGEMENT TO ENTER MY APARTMENT. SHOULD IT BE NECESSARY TO USE A SERVICE AGENCY OTHER THAN CADILLAC PROPERTY MANAGEMENT OR SHOULD MORE THAN ONE VISIT BE REQUIRED FOR CORRECTION, I ALSO SIGNIFY MY CONSENT.

RESIDENT'S SIGNATURE | DATE

COMMENTS (C.P.M. USE ONLY)

REQUEST INVESTIGATED BY | DATE

REQUEST CORRECTED BY | DATE

DESCRIBE WORK TO BE DONE ON W.O. OR P.O.

P.M. TO CHECK TO INDICATE DOCUMENTS REQUIRED

✓		SUPPLIER	DATE ISSUED	OP COST NO
	WORK ORDER NO.	MAINTENANCE DEPT.		
	PURCHASE ORDER NO.			
	INSURANCE CLAIM NO.	RESIDENT TO BE INVOICED? NO ☐ YES ☐		

WORK AUTHORIZED BY | P.M.

SUPERINTENDENT - RESIDENT'S FILE

FIGURE 1-16 The maintenance request. (Courtesy of The Cadillac Fairview Corporation, Limited.)

6. Wrong tradesmen are called due to confusion over the nature of the situation.

Resident Service Requests

A sizable portion of the maintenance workload is composed of problems reported by residents. It is important that all such requests be efficiently recorded. A properly designed Maintenance Request form will serve several useful purposes:

1. It specifies the exact location and nature of the problem.
2. It obtains the necessary permission to enter the apartment to do the work.
3. It organizes the subsequent recordkeeping by providing space to record work order numbers, purchase order numbers, and related information.
4. It records the procedures eventually used in correcting the situation.
5. It obtains feedback from employees who become involved in the situation.

The Work Order

If a request has been evaluated and the problem not corrected, a work or purchase order is issued. The work order is used as a means of communicating a problem not corrected by the building operator. In essence, it is an internal purchase order requesting "in-house" specialized service from a maintenance department. A purchase order would be used for outside service.

A work or purchase order form

—Refers to the initial maintenance request, providing the manager with a flow record.

—Identifies the problem and where it is located.

—Allows for clarification by the tradesman.

—Gives a record of labor costs, materials used from inventory, materials purchased, and total cost to repair.

Preparing duplicate copies of the form allows the following additional advantages:

—It follows up a problem.

—It aids in cost distribution.

—It calculates charge backs to residents.

—It helps budget more efficiently.

—It helps monitor results.

—It isolates a special problem.

—It helps keep an inventory control.

—It provides keypunching statistics for a computer program.

THE BENEFITS OF THE RECORDKEEPING SYSTEM

These expense schedules (see figures 1-4 through 1-8) were initially developed by keeping copies of every work and purchase order for an extended period. This information helps in the following ways:

1. It indicates the resource specialists required.
2. It provides a breakdown of the repair and maintenance classifications.
3. It outlines the type of training required.
4. It forms the basis for this zero-base budget.
5. It helps include the funds in the budget for all the preventive maintenance programs. The details explaining the information needed and what was included can be found in each chapter of this book.
6. Once established, the information provides accurate, compatible year-to-year comparisons.
7. It is easy to summarize and total. The information is useful when arranging to pur-

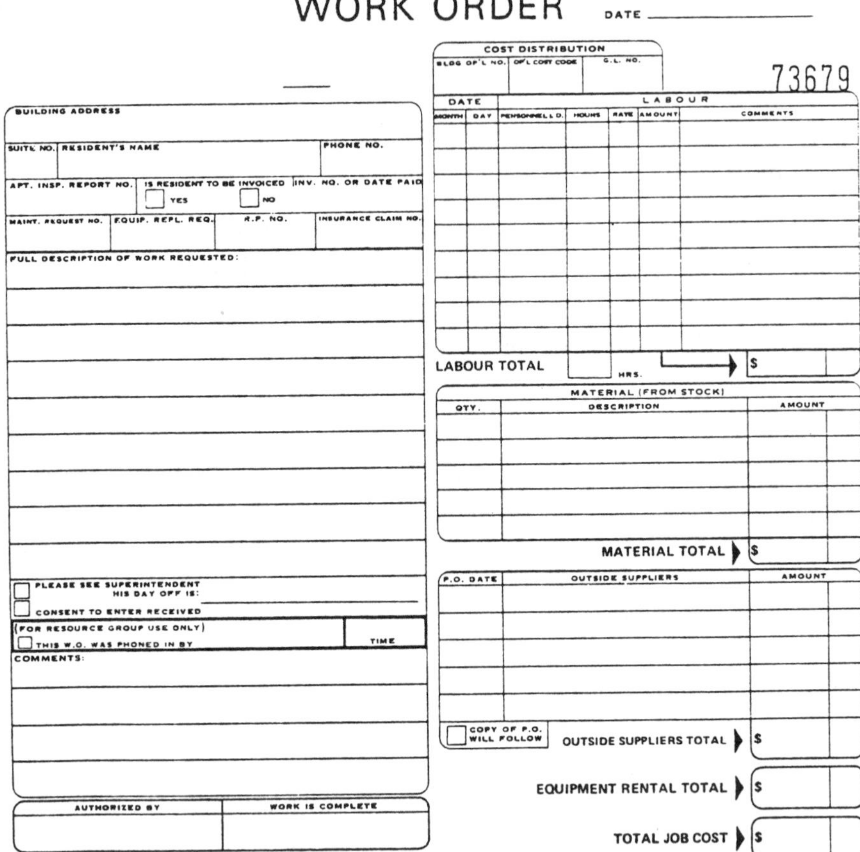

WORK ORDER DATE ____________

73679

BUILDING ADDRESS

SUITE NO. | RESIDENT'S NAME | PHONE NO.

APT. INSP. REPORT NO. | IS RESIDENT TO BE INVOICED ☐ YES ☐ NO | INV. NO. OR DATE PAID

MAINT. REQUEST NO. | EQUIP. REPL. REQ. | R.P. NO. | INSURANCE CLAIM NO.

FULL DESCRIPTION OF WORK REQUESTED:

☐ PLEASE SEE SUPERINTENDENT HIS DAY OFF IS: ____________

☐ CONSENT TO ENTER RECEIVED

(FOR RESOURCE GROUP USE ONLY)

☐ THIS W.O. WAS PHONED IN BY | TIME

COMMENTS:

AUTHORIZED BY	WORK IS COMPLETE

COST DISTRIBUTION		
BLDG OP'L NO.	OP'L COST CODE	G.L. NO.

DATE		LABOUR				
MONTH	DAY	PERSONNEL I.D.	HOURS	RATE	AMOUNT	COMMENTS

LABOUR TOTAL ____ HRS. → $

MATERIAL (FROM STOCK)		
QTY.	DESCRIPTION	AMOUNT

MATERIAL TOTAL ▶ $

P.O. DATE	OUTSIDE SUPPLIERS	AMOUNT

☐ COPY OF P.O. WILL FOLLOW

OUTSIDE SUPPLIERS TOTAL ▶ $

EQUIPMENT RENTAL TOTAL ▶ $

TOTAL JOB COST ▶ $

FIGURE 1-17 The work order. (Courtesy of The Cadillac Fairview Corporation, Limited.)

chase maintenance contracts or when purchasing supplies, parts, tools, or equipment in bulk.

8. It provides an excellent feedback for monitoring the results of all of our efforts.

THE BUDGET AS THE CONTROLLING FUNCTION

The most commonly used mechanism in management control is the budget. In fact, a budget is the integral tool of the planning process. Once the plan is activated it becomes the control point of the system.

The controlling function is that of monitoring results initiated by the planning process. It implies the measurement of activities and compares their values against a predetermined standard. The purpose is to ensure that the goals and objectives for the enterprise are being attained or have been accomplished.

A suitable system allows you to plan actions in advance, which when completed would assure you of a reasonable chance of success in achieving the agreed upon goals and objectives.

THE ZERO-BASE BUDGET

The program is built into the budget using the "zero-base" format, which is the perfect means of doing this. Records must be kept to monitor the results of the program. These records become an important communications tool, and help overcome resistance from owners and building operating staff when the problems are studied and reviewed.

The budgets are built around inspections and preventive maintenance programs. These programs cover routine maintenance (lubrication, filter changes, belt changes, and alignment), continuing preventive maintenance, service requests, and non-routine repairs.

The first step is to organize all the pieces of the puzzle. Not all aspects of maintenance operations can be foreseen and thus non-routine repairs must be estimated. An additional problem arises because all maintenance needs are not the same from one year to the next. This is especially true in the area of renovating and replacing building components.

Nonetheless, a large portion of maintenance tasks are routine items which must be performed on a daily, weekly, monthly, or seasonal basis in each year of the building's operational life. These items can be listed and organized into the Master Action Plan. The purpose of the plan is to organize management and staff functions. The Master Action Plan is the first step toward establishing a comprehensive program where specific projects are translated into detailed work schedules.

The Budget as a Planning Tool

It specifies objectives and basic policies.

It specifies courses of action to accomplish objectives.

It reflects plans and includes preventive maintenance and energy conservation programs.

It allows us to look ahead.

The Budget as a Control Tool

It provides a basis for comparison with the Master Action Plan.

It provides a means whereby variances with the plan can be pinpointed.

It motivates those that use the system.

The Budget as a Communications Tool

It plans ahead and thus requires communication at all levels of the organization.

Its reports compare budgets with actual performance and it provides a basis for communication concerning the activities listed.

Its reports provide the opportunity for communication about possible revisions to plans, programs, and budgets.

Advantages of this Budgeting System

It allows for planning activities in detail.

It promotes communication concerning plans and objectives.

It promotes participation of all maintenance and operations personnel at all management levels of the project.

It provides for a means of analyzing all the preventive maintenance and non-routine activities and their costs on a systematic basis. It should naturally provide factual information for feedback to development, design, and construction staff.

It helps promote efficient allocation of resources and thus improves itself by concentrating on specialties.

It helps planning and control at all levels by providing information in an organized manner.

It provides flexibility which allows problem areas to be pinpointed and actions to be adjusted accordingly.

Once the preventive maintenance activities have been executed as planned, costs and firefighting problems will decrease drastically.

If the preparation of the budget includes inspections, review of previous expenditures, and inclusion of preventive maintenance programs, the budget will closely balance the actual expenses.

Disadvantages of this Budgeting System

It is very time consuming to plan and organize.

It is difficult to sell because it is easier to average expenses over several years than to detail the activities.

Implementing all the preventive maintenance programs and catching up on activities that may have been non-existent may initially appear very costly.

It creates human relations problems if it is not understood and implemented.

Achievements of this Budgeting System

Experience has shown that this budgeting system produced the following results:

—Problems are constantly identified, attacked, and eliminated.

—Work assignments are easily delegated to people skilled in a particular field.

—Necessary resource specialists are identified.

—A recruiting and training program was consequently developed. Through these programs the knowledge and performance of the entire project management team is continually being upgraded.

—From these specialists future leaders will emerge; the important aspect is that they will develop from within the organization.

The ultimate goal of the budgeting system is to identify every opportunity to improve the staff, the building, and the operating equipment. These actions allow every potential for savings to be activated without allowing the building and equipment to deteriorate.

Complete and ultimate success will only be achieved when no further opportunities to save are evident and the electrical / mechanical systems are all operating efficiently.

BENEFITS OF PLANNING AND ORGANIZING

An organized effort inevitably allows opportunities for improvement to surface. They just seem to show up as a natural course of events.

Once all of this effort is organized and put into motion, the cash flow from the real estate investment automatically increases. The properties attain a high level of maintenance, the owners, and their tenants are properly serviced, and most important of all, the staff achieves a high level of satisfaction.

In contrast, an unorganized, hit and miss approach will eventually eat up the cash flow. When this happens the owners and managers use rent controls, escalating utility costs, high taxes, over-building, the declining economy, and a lot of other "beyond-our-control" excuses for a lack of return on investment.

MOTIVATION BY PARTICIPATION

People are motivated by participation, involvement, and opportunity for personal growth. By planning, organizing, delegating responsibility and authority, and evaluating performance against realistic goals set by the individual, it is possible to have a system of management that is highly effective and efficient, and at the same time, very human and satisfying to the individuals involved.

It is also possible to devise a system that will improve as it grows and develops. The two main ingredients are *communication* and *cooperation.*

1-6 Inspections

CONTROL OF PROBLEMS BY INSPECTIONS

Studies by F. J. Roethlisberger and William J. Dickson in 1939 established that an enterprise is constantly confronted with two sets of major problems:

1. *Problems of External Balance:* These generally are assumed to be economic—problems of competition, adjusting the organization to meet changing markets, and so forth.
2. *Problems of Internal Equilibrium:* These are chiefly concerned with maintaining a social organization in which individuals and groups can satisfy their own desires through working together.

Both of these problems are interrelated and interdependent; the social organization within a concern is related intimately to the effectiveness of the total organization. Likewise, the success with which the concern maintains external balance is related directly to its internal organization.

Inspections help the manager control the problems of "External Balance" and are directly related to planning, organizing, directing, and controlling the operations of the properties managed. The result of this action, in turn, is assessed by cost, profit, and technical efficiency.

Inspections also help the manager control the problems of "Internal Equilibrium" by affording him the opportunity to personally see and speak to the residents or lessees and the building staff. To accomplish this action it is necessary to organize the daily workload into a routine which allows the management team the time to inspect.

Firsthand knowledge of problems, while communicating with the residents and building operating staff, helps improve the manager's performance by upgrading the competence of his staff. Feedback to the people who develop, design, and construct new buildings could be very valuable when deciding future investments. Feedback information is developed from these inspections and from the repair and maintenance expense records.

There is a direct relationship between inspections and the responsibilities of building managers and operators. Everyone in real estate management seem to agree that inspections are important, but few people take the trouble to organize formal inspections, to detail them in writing, or to properly follow up the results. Inspections, in fact, form the basis for all maintenance programs and are vital to the upgrading of management effectiveness.

The question is often asked "you look, but do you see?" Just as with other skills we must train ourselves to comprehend what we see. Because we are creatures of habit, a problem may appear to be normal because we are accustomed to its appearance or sound. Developing technical skills so that we know what to look for and how to follow up will make our inspections and observations more productive.

An effective property manager must know

—when to inspect

—how to inspect

—how often to inspect

—who should inspect

—what to inspect

—where to inspect

The most important question is what to do with the results of the inspection? First, building operating staff inspections should include basic preventive maintenance such as recording the information detailed on the operating logs, changing filters, or lubricating and wiping down equipment.

Second, the inspection would also correct many minor problems. Last, but not least, it helps managers identify weaknesses and strengths of the building and their staffs, which can be useful in helping improve every facet of management's performance. This is accomplished by highlighting the problems with housekeeping, groundskeeping, structure, and the electrical / mechanical systems, and correcting them before they become serious.

BUILDING TAKEOVER INSPECTIONS

Through inspections of newly built or acquired properties, useful information about the physical characteristics of the exterior or interior of the building and the electrical / mechanical systems can be acquired. This very valuable information forms the basis of a historical record of the building for its life span. The information must be revised and updated so that it forms a source of continuing reference on the building and provides valuable information for preparing annual or long-range budgeting projections.

BUILDING OPERATING STAFF

Time must be allowed in their schedules of duties for following up all maintenance requests. Time to correct problems and time to report them must also be included.

Inspections must be a daily routine conducted by knowledgeable, competent people. Inspections of each occupied unit, leased or sold, are certainly an essential part of management's responsibilities.

"Takeover" of a new building begins with the inspection of the models. The complete "takeover" of a building occurs when the last unit "sold or leased" is inspected and management completes a preventive maintenance inspection on all of the electrical / mechanical systems. While conducting inspections of the structure and systems, records must be made of all of the components and identifying tag numbers affixed to each piece of equipment. These records form the basis of the building's history.

Having a form helps lead you through inspections or other functions in an orderly, uniform manner. The forms are then used as a follow-up tool for correcting deficiencies and collecting damages when units are vacated. Other forms such as maintenance requests, work orders, purchase orders, equipment records, and operational logs are also essential management tools. They help to organize routines and to gather information necessary to the professional management of a property.

Another important benefit of the orientation inspection is that it familiarizes the manager and operator with every aspect of the building. Whether the building is new, or whether the manager or operator is taking over the responsibility for an existing building, the orientation inspection is an essential basis for successfully managing and operating the property. This must be done as soon as possible after takeover and repeated, if necessary, until the manager is thoroughly familiar with the building and its equipment.

WORK MEASUREMENT STANDARDS

If inspections are the basis of effective, competent real estate management, a building's workload must be organized in such a way to allow the staff the time to complete them. Few managers realize how important it is to evaluate the time and staff needed to maintain buildings. Few take the time or make much effort to determine and standardize an accurate measurement of the building's maintenance and operations needs. An accurate assessment of these needs produces the following results:

1. The buildings are properly staffed.
2. The staff has the tools, inventory, and equipment to perform its jobs efficiently.
3. The skills needed for the job are identified and everyone on the team is trained to perform those job functions.
4. All daily routines, non-routine repairs, and preventive maintenance are included in realistic annual budgets and they are performed according to plan.

TYPES OF INSPECTIONS

The building operator must be trained to carry out a daily routine inspection that should be a "look, listen, and touch" inspection and should include making entries on equipment logs, as well as lubricating and wiping down equipment. The inspection should include many other preventive maintenance chores once a week.

The building manager should complete a regular inspection of the buildings managed, recording all deficiencies and positive aspects of the building. This information should be relayed to the operator and all deficiences should be corrected as soon as possible. These inspections should be completed in the spring, summer, fall, and winter.

Written inspections are a valuable reference for budget preparation and for long-term planning. The inspections also are an important learning experience. Results of all inspections should always be communicated to the building operating staff and when warranted, specific information about a problem should be fed back to the developers, designers, and builders.

Inventory and Equipment Inspections

On a regular basis, inventory and equipment should be physically checked. The equipment should be matched to equipment records and tested to assure the inspector that such equipment is well-maintained and operating properly.

A visual inventory stock check should be made at least four times a year. Control of parts and supplies inventories by comparing the actual inventory to the stock records is an essential requirement indicating professional management. (See Chapter 5 for typical equipment, plants, tools, and inventory lists.)

Inspections as a Communications Tool

Communication is the dialogue between the customer, the building operating staff, the property manager, the administrative staff, and other in-house or purchased resource services. Dr. Harvey Silver defined management as "the achievement of agreed upon goals using a minimum of resources." He explained resources as "time, dollars, tools, equipment, ideas, people and space." He also explained the importance of communications by commenting that "The effectiveness of management to make decisions depends on the quality of the ideas and the acceptance of the group that has to implement them. If either of these factors are low, then effectiveness will be low." In short:

—Communication is the instruction that results in action.

—Communication is the ability to listen, ask, and understand.

—Communication should include recommendations for improvement in any area or task.

—Communication should include the cooperation of line/staff efforts that result in the formation of objectives and policies.

—Communication is vital to successful project management.

Housekeeping Inspections

Fair work loads, as well as a productive housekeeping routine, depend on organization. Responsibilities should be detailed in writing so that the staff knows what it is responsible for and how the tasks interrelate. Proper training will teach the staff how to perform efficiently and effectively.

It is essential that persons performing any given task understand, in detail, all the procedures that are involved, such as

—what is to be accomplished

—how to perform the task

—standard of cleanliness

—frequency

—equipment and supplies needed and how they are used

—safety or other considerations

To ensure that the work is satisfactory, close supervision, inspections, instruction, and correction are essential. The philosophy behind inspections is to help everyone do a better job. If the staff is experiencing difficulties in carrying out any of its responsibilities, it should be encouraged to ask for assistance.

Performing housekeeping tasks in a professional manner is the only way to assure that the money spent on housekeeping will be wisely used. Conducting on-site clinics to overcome problems spotted during inspections is an ideal way to upgrade the performance of the staff.

Electrical/Mechanical Systems Inspections

All electrical and mechanical equipment are energy users. The ever-increasing cost of energy dictates that this equipment must always be in top condition. Furthermore, nothing upsets lessees and residents of buildings more than the failure of electrical and mechanical equipment.

For these reasons, an effective maintenance program for all equipment must be established. All the equipment must be tagged and records made of each major component in the electrical/mechanical systems.

These records should include couplings, bearings, seals, belts, starters, fuses, wires, valves, filters, and controls. A proper preventive maintenance program keeps the equipment in good order so that the incidence of failure is minimized.

All equipment, particularly motors, bearings, belts, and starters, is vulnerable to dust, moisture, friction, vibration, and overload. Therefore, all equipment rooms should be painted, color coded, and clean. Housekeeping is the basis of a sound maintenance program and indicates that the building operator is a professional.

The building operators must organize their daily workload so that they are able to perform all of the inspections and preventive maintenance assigned to them. This workload should include housekeeping, lubrication, troubleshooting, and "look, listen, and touch" inspections. Records of the maintenance and operations of these systems must also be maintained.

Efficiency can only be measured by monitoring the results of these efforts. The monitoring should include equipment maintenance records and parts inventory. The competence of the building operating staff is measured by the professional way they carry out their operational assignments, their control of the equipment efficiency, and the eventual cost to maintain and operate such equipment.

1-7 Organizing Work and People

WASTE IN LABOR PRODUCTIVITY

In project management the control of *on-going expenses,* such as energy and staff salaries, is vitally important. The *waste of energy or inefficient use of staff creates continual on-going losses.*

If the expense dollars for a building's operating costs are analyzed, you will find that operating staff salaries are one of the biggest individual expenses (Figure 1-11). Thus, accurate measurements for staffing a building and determining costs involve large amounts of money. Added to the salary expenses is the further loss from lack of productivity.

If the waste in labor productivity is an expense that accumulates at an inflationary spiral of 10-15 percent per annum, this waste will accumulate to a staggering percentage over the fifty-year life span of a building. To overcome this waste, the staff must know precisely what it is expected to do. The first step is to develop a maintenance workload for the building. The second step is to suitably train the staff so that it will complete the workload tasks efficiently.

OVERCOMING WASTE BY POSITIVE DIRECTION

Everyone responds favorably to strong and positive direction. This can be achieved by identifying precisely what is to be accomplished.

All members of the staff should know in advance

—what to do

—when to do it

—how it should be done

—how long it should take

—the equipment, materials, and supplies in the desired quantities

—what the end results should be

A systems approach leaves nothing to chance and simplifies work objectives. Organization and training ensure success.

When people know what is expected of them, they generally will respond accordingly. If a person knows that he has "X" amount of hours to do the work, and "Y" amount of dollars for supplies, he knows what to base his organization and effort on, and generally he will do just that.

Because the maintenance of a building is so closely tied with keeping the occupants happy, a qualified staff, which carries out its functions in an efficient and organized manner, will markedly improve the image of the company. The benefits of such a staff are as follows:

1. It contributes to the team effort.
2. It results in efficiency.
3. It results in effectiveness.
4. It develops people with knowledge and skills.
5. It improves the "bottom line":
   —less costs or more cash flow;
   —satisfies the basic needs of individuals for achievement and fulfillment.

FEEDBACK AS A CHANNEL OF COMMUNICATION

Often an individual may have an unclear view of his own strengths and weaknesses in work situations. Through feedback each individual learns about himself in an objective fashion. Feedback must be a two-way communication if sessions are to be meaningful. Without feedback, management will not be effective.

There are four things that must be kept in mind if feedback sessions are to be productive:

1. Employees should feel free to express true feelings and perceptions without fear of retribution. Feedback is most useful when it is voluntary.
2. Informal communication should be encouraged. Management should encourage feedback, but should not make it an employment requirement.
3. The habit of really listening to people should be developed.
4. The habit of giving out facts and straightforward answers should be developed. This creates confidence when giving or receiving verbal feedback.

THE ORGANIZATION PLAN OF ACTION

The critical actions required to properly organize maintenance and operations are

1. *The Organization of Work*

   This involves detailing the workload and establishing priorities so that critical tasks receive attention first. It establishes the proper sequence of activities necessary to complete these tasks and the time frames in which the work can best be performed.

   The mechanical services workload includes the daily, weekly, monthly, quarterly, and annual inspections to ensure that the fire control system, plumbing, drainage, heating, ventilation, and cooling systems are all operating efficiently. It includes the on-going maintenance required on the motors, the bearings, belts, and filters of the air handling equipment. It also covers the maintenance of the piping, valves, pumps and their bearings, and includes the water treatment program needed to keep the water systems pure and unfouled. These routine inspections ensure that there are no hazardous conditions developing in the electrical system and that the elevators, garage doors, garbage compactors, and security systems are all operating efficiently.

   An inspection of the structure should be completed in the spring to determine the extent of damage done to the roofs, caulking, and brickwork by the freeze-thaw cycles over the winter. After problems are corrected a further inspection should be completed in the fall to ensure the soundness of the structure before facing another winter.

   The housekeeping workload includes garbage removal, dusting, sweeping, damp mopping, stripping, waxing, glass cleaning, spot removal from walls and carpets, vacuuming, and replacing light bulbs and cleaning fixtures.

The groundskeeping workload includes picking up litter, sweeping sidewalks and parking lots, grass cutting, edging, sodding or seeding, fertilizing, spraying, cultivating, planting, pruning, and watering.

2. *The Organization of People*

   The classification of functions and the specification for each should indicate the qualifications required to perform the workload. This can be achieved by

   —developing a plan that will enable the programmed workload to be completed in an organized manner;

   —developing job descriptions for the people who will be responsible for the work and communicating their responsibilities to them;

   —recruiting and training people to carry out efficiently and effectively their assigned responsibilities.

STAFFING TO FIT THE HOURS

Once a building manager knows how many hours are required to maintain the building, he has things under control.

As an example, by using the going trade cost and payroll costs, which are always available, the manager can now calculate the labor cost for the maintenance and operations of each building.

Another thing for the manager to consider at the time a facility is staffed, is whether to use full-time or part-time people, or a mixture of both to cover the hours required to maintain the building. The manager might hire only full-time (eight-hour day) people. Other managers find it advantageous to use full-time people as well as part-time people for four or five hours each day.

The value of knowing how many people are needed, and how much it will cost should not be underestimated. A manager with that kind of information will have complete control.

To give a maintenance person eight hours to complete four hours of real work is a disaster. Soon the employees are induced to laziness, become disgruntled, and begin to feel overworked. Remember that ongoing expenses such as energy or staff salaries become losses when employees are unproductive.

HOW TO DEVELOP WORKLOADS AND SCHEDULE THE DUTIES

When developing a workload and schedule, a lot of information will be required if the building is to be staffed properly and the structure, housekeeping, groundskeeping, and electrical/mechanical systems well maintained.

Gathering this information for existing buildings would be more difficult than it would be for buildings under construction.

Developing a workload requires the following information:

1. The original plan of the structure, the electrical/mechanical systems, and the grounds.
2. The "as-built" drawings for the building after it is finished.
3. The room schedules showing the square footage for each area; these schedules should include specifications for all floor and wallcoverings.
4. The interior and exterior design drawings of the building, with specifications.
5. The door and window schedules, includ-

ing all the recommendations and specifications to ensure that the needs of the building are satisfied.

6. The manufacturer's literature relative to the
   (a) interior and exterior elements
   (b) tools and maintenance equipment
   (c) electrical / mechanical systems.
7. The lessee and unit mix for the proposed building.

Armed with this information, a manager can plan the staffing and maintenance of a building as soon as the plans are available. It is not necessary to build the structure before a workload is prepared. While preparing these schedules of duties you should feed back to the designers recommendations for management's requirements, such as office, storage areas, and work and utility rooms. Most important, meaningful budgets for staff and maintenance requirements can be prepared.

How to Develop a Workload

There are several ways to establish workloads:

—Asking contractors to bid and carry out the maintenance tasks.

—Detailing everything that must be done daily, weekly, monthly, semi-annually, and annually and determining the time it will take to complete these tasks.

—Comparing like buildings.

—Establishing square footage costs.

—Calculating the square footage of each common area in a building.

The following is one way to develop a workload:

1. Gather the following information:

—time needed to complete a structural, electrical / mechanical systems, "look, listen, and touch" inspection

—time needed to cover all the scheduled maintenance and unscheduled tenant requests

—number of suites, or square footage of the building

—type of building (adult or family, commercial, residential, or institutional)

—number of square feet of carpet

—number of square feet of terrazzo
   (a) laundry room
   (b) lobbies
   (c) entrances and exits
   (d) corridors, stairwells, or other common areas

—number of square feet of vinyl tile or other hard floor covers

—number of flights of stairs

—number of garbage rooms

—garbage removal procedure

—unusual design of building (extra work)

—number of elevators

—recreation facilities

—groundskeeping

2. Divide each classification into the maintenance programs required to service the area or equipment according to specified standards. This classification is called a workload.

3. Divide the workload into daily and weekly schedules of activity, indicating the specifications and time involved in each activity. The investigation of maintenance requests and the daily electrical / mechanical workload would be covered by allotting a period of time in the schedule. These schedules should be typed and available in an "easy to read and follow" format.

GROUND FLOOR FINISH SCHEDULE

ROOM NAME	ROOM NO.	FLOORS			WALLS			CEILING			
		FINISH	BASE	SQ. FT.	MATERIAL	FIN.	SQ. FT.	MATERIAL	FIN.	HT.	REMARKS
VESTIBULE	G1	Q.T.	Q.T.		DRYWALL			CONC.	S.C.S.	8'0"	To interior design drawings
LOBBY	G2	Q.T.	Q.T.		DRYWALL					8'0"	To interior design drawings
ELEV. LOBBY	G3	Q.T.	Q.T.		DRYWALL			CONC.	S.O.S.	8'0"	To interior design drawings
MAILROOM	G4	Q.T.	Q.T.		DRYWALL	P.T.		S.D.	S.O.S.	8'0"	
GARBAGE	G5	V.A.T.	R.		DRYWALL	P.T.		CONC.	S.O.S.	8'0"	
STAIR NOS. 1, 3, 4, 5, 6, 7	G6	V.A.T.	R.		DRYWALL	P.T.		CONC.	S.O.S.	8'0"	
CORRIDOR	G7	CARPET	W.D.		DRYWALL	W.P.		CONC.	S.O.S.	8'0"	
STAIR NO. 2	G8	V.A.T.	R.		DRYWALL	W.P.		CONC.	S.O.S.	8'0"	
STORAGE	G9	V.A.T.	R.		DRYWALL	P.T.					

TYPICAL FLOOR AND CEILING FINISH SCHEDULE

ROOM NAME	ROOM NO.	FINISH	BASE	SQ. FT.	MATERIAL	FIN.	SQ. FT.	MATERIAL	FIN.	HT.	REMARKS
ELEV. LOBBY	T1	CARPET	W.D.		DRYWALL	W.P.		CONC.	S.O.S.		
GARBAGE	T2	V.A.T.	R.		DRYWALL	P.T.		CONC.	S.O.S.		
STAIR NOS. 1, 3, 4, 5, 6, 7	T3	V.A.T.	R.		DRYWALL	P.T.		CONC.	S.O.S.		
STAIR NO. 2	T4	CARPET	R.		DRYWALL	P.T.		CONC.	S.O.S.		
CORRIDOR	T5	CARPET	W.D.		DRYWALL	W.P.		CONC.	S.O.S		
OFFICE	T6	CARPET	W.D.		DRYWALL	P.T.		CONC.	S.O.S.		
STORAGE	T7	V.A.T.	R.		DRYWALL	P.T.		CONC.	P.T.		
STAIR	R1	CONC.	P.T.		CONC. & C.B.	P. T.					
MECH. RM.	R2	SEALED CONC.			CONC. & C.B.						

BASEMENT ROOM FINISH SCHEDULE

ROOM NAME	ROOM NO.	FLOORS			WALLS			CEILING			
		FINISH	BASE	SQ. FT.	MATERIAL	FIN.	SQ. FT.	MATERIAL	FIN.	HT.	REMARKS
UNDERGROUND PARKING GARAGE	B1	CONC.			CONC.	P.T.		CONC.	P.T.		COLUMNS AND CEIL. PAINTED WHITE
AIR LOCK	B2	V.A.T.	R.		DRYWALL	P.T.		S.O.S.			
HALL	B3	V.A.T.	R.		DRYWALL	W.P.		S.T.		8'0"	
ELEV. LOBBY	B4	CARPET	R.		DRYWALL	W.P.		S.T.		8'0"	
LAUNDRY	B5	C.T.	C.T.		C.T.			S.O.S.			
WASHROOM	B6	C.T.	C.T.		DRYWALL			S.D.	P.T.	7'6"	
GARBAGE	B7	SEALED CONC.			CONC. & C.B.						HOSE BIB
TRANSFORMER	B8	SEALED CONC.			CONC. & C.B.						
ELEV. MECHANICAL	B9	SEALED CONC.			CONC. & C.B.						
CORRIDOR	B10	SEALED CONC.			CONC. & C.B.						
JANITORS RM.	B11	SEALED CONC.			CONC. & C.B.						
MECHANICAL	B12	SEALED CONC.			CONC. & C.B.						
TELEPHONE	B13	CONC.			CONC. & C.B.						
ELECTRICAL	B14	SEALED CONC.			CONC. & C.B.						
EMERGENCY GENERATOR	B15	SEALED CONC.			CONC. & C.B.						
TRANSFORMER VAULT	B16	SEALED CONC.			CONC. & C.B.						
CHANGE ROOM	B17	V.A.T.			DRYWALL	P.T.					
JANITOR STORAGE	B18	SEALED CONC.			CONC. & C.B.	P.T.		CONC.	P.T.		

KEY TO ABBREVIATIONS

CONC. – Concrete
V.A.T. – Vinyl Asbestos Tile
Q.T. – Quarry Tile
P.T. – Paint
C.T. – Ceramic Tile
S.T. – Stiple Ceiling
R. – Rubber
S.O.S. – Sprayed on Stipple
C.B. – Concrete Block

FIGURE 1-18 Maintenance programming.

FLOOR OPERATIONS

Sweeping	1000 sq. ft.
Halls & corridors	10 min.
General rooms	20 min.

Mopping	1000 sq. ft.
Dust mop (unobstructed)	5 min.
Dust mop (obstructed)	10 min.
Damp mop (unobstructed)	16 min.
Damp mop (obstructed)	30 min.
Wet mop and rinse (unobstructed)	35 min.
Wet mop and rinse (obstructed)	50 min.

Scrubbing	1000 sq. ft.
Hand scrub 12" brush	300 min.
Deck scrub	100 min.

Machine scrub	1000 sq. ft.
Machine scrub 12" diameter	48 min.
Machine scrub 14" diameter	40 min.
Machine scrub 16" diameter	36 min.
Machine scrub 18" diameter	31.5 min.
Machine scrub 19" diameter	30 min.
Machine scrub 21" diameter	27 min.
Machine scrub 23" diameter	25 min.
Machine scrub 24" diameter	24 min.
Machine scrub 32" diameter	18 min.
Machine scrub 36" diameter	16 min.
Automatic scrub machine (24")	6 min.

Vacuum pick up	1000 sq. ft.
Vacuum pick up (unobstructed)	20 min.
Vacuum pick up (obstructed)	30 min.

Wax	1000 sq. ft.
Wax	30 min.
Machine polish (19" machine)	15 min.
Rectangular machine (48" plate)	3.5 min.
Buff with steel wool	20 min.
Strip and rewax (1 person)	150 min.
Dry strip and rewax (1 person)	120 min.

Spray buffing	1000 sq. ft.
Spray buffing (unobstructed)	30 min.
Spray buffing (obstructed)	45 min.

Carpeting	1000 sq. ft.
Vacuuming (unobstructed)	20 min.
Vacuuming (obstructed)	30 min.
Spot vacuuming	16 min.
Shampoo (dry-foam)	60 min.
Pile lift	30 min.

FURNITURE & FIXTURES OPERATIONS

Dusting	1000 sq. ft.
Air conditioners	.30 min.
Ash trays (desk)	.25 min.
Book cases (3-tier sect.)	.30 min.
Chairs	.30 min.
Cigarette stands	.40 min.
Couch	.25 min.
Desks	.80 min.
Desk trays	.15 min.
File cabinets (4 drawer)	.40 min.
Lockers	.20 min.
Radiators	.30 min.
Tables (medium)	.50 min.
Telephones	.15 min.
Towel dispensers	.12 min.
Towel disposal cans	.40 min.
Typewriter & stand	.50 min.
Wash basin (office)	.60 min.
Waste basket	.50 min.
Window sill	.20 min.
Venetian blinds std. size	3.50 min.

WASHROOMS

Cleaning	
Cleaning commode	3.83 min.
Door (spot wash both sides)	.83 min.
Mirrors	.66 min.
Sanitary napkin dispenser	.16 min.
Urinals	3.00 min.
Wash basin--soap dispenser	3.00 min.

General washroom cleaning	
General cleaning per 1000 sq. ft.	120.00 min.

MISCELLANEOUS OPERATIONS

Wall washing	1000 sq. ft.
Painted walls (manual)	240 min.
Painted walls (machine)	150 min.
Marble walls (manual)	92 min.

Ceiling washing	1000 sq. ft.
Ceiling washing (manual)	300 min.
Ceiling washing (machine)	180 min.

Window washing	1000 sq. ft.
Single pane	125 min.
Multi-pane	170 min.
Frosted single pane	190 min.
Opaque glass	50 min.
Plate glass	35 min.
Office partitions (glass)	110 min.

Dusting lamps & light fixtures	
Wall fluorescent fixtures	.13 min.
Desk fluorescent lamp	.30 min.
Table lamp & shade	.58 min.
Floor lamp & shade	.58 min.

Washing fluorescent light fixtures	
Ceiling fixture (egg crate) 4' ea.	9 min.
Ceiling fixture (egg crate) 8' ea.	12 min.

Fabric upholstery cleaning	
Whisk or vacuum armless chair	.50 min.
Whisk or vacuum armchair	1 min.
Whisk or vacuum couch	2 min.
Shampooing armless chair	4 min.
Shampooing armchair	7 min.
Shampooing couch	20 min.

Stairway cleaning	
Sweep and dust 1 flight 15 steps	6 min.
Damp mop 1 flight 15 steps	5 min.
Scrubbing (hand)	20 min.

These cleaning time estimates represent average cleaning times. Layout, obstacles, maintenance level desired, environmental conditions, etc., will affect cleaning time.

FIGURE 1-19 Housekeeping time estimates.

BUILDING ADDRESS ____________________

EMPLOYEE ____________________

FROM ____________ TO ____________ WEEK # ____________

JOB	MON.	TUES.	WED.	THURS.	FRI.	SAT.	SUN.	TOTAL
Clean up litter								
Sweeping walks,parking lot,etc								
Litter in garage/ stairwells								
Garbage Removal								
Office /meetings								
Ground inspection								
Grass cutting								
Edging lawn areas								
Sodding /seeding								
Fertilizing								
Lawn Spraying								
Digging /cultivating								
Planting annuals								
Planting (other)								
Spraying								
Pruning								
Watering								
Sprinkler repair								
Machinery maintenance								
Obtaining supplies								
Trimming lawn areas								
Lawn sweeping								
TOTAL HOURS								

FIGURE 1-20 Groundskeeping work load diary. There are times when it is advisable to keep a diary of activities to help study the time required to handle things that are difficult to fit into a time frame. The diary can then be used to analyze the activities and efficiently include them in a schedule.

INSPECTION OR MAINTENANCE TASK	SQUARE FOOTAGE	TIME NEEDED	HOUR TOTAL	BY WHOM	COMMENTS
Moving people in or out					Unit inspections
In-suite preventative mtce.					Includes cleaning vacant suites
Structural inspection					
Garbage removal					Includes each floor
Vacuuming corridors					
Vacuuming other carpets					
Sweeping stairwells and garage entrance					Includes all hard floor surfaces equipment and locker rooms
Dust mopping					As above
Damp mopping					As above
Cleaning commercial areas					
Cleaning lobby glass					
Mechanical mtce. inspec.					
Log reading					
Maintenance requests					
Showing vacant units					
Collecting rents					
Administration					Ordering supplies & materials Communicating with mgmt. office
Cleaning lobby					
Cleaning elevator cabs					
Replacing light bulbs					

(a)

PERSON TO WHOM DUTIES ASSIGNED ____________________

DATE ____________________

TIME TO COMPLETE	AREA INSPECTION OR MAINTENANCE TASK	FREQUENCY	WEEKLY HOURLY TOTAL	TOTAL

(b)

FIGURE 1-21 Maintenance programming. (a) Daily/weekly work load summary (Note: Emergencies cannot be scheduled but would take precedence over routine tasks.); (b) Schedule of duties.

1-8 Management Decisions and Policy Formulation

IN-HOUSE VERSUS OUTSIDE CONTRACTOR

Many property managers satisfy their various maintenance needs by using a combination of in-house staff and outside contractors. The decision as to which method to use for a particular function should only be made after comparing the advantages and disadvantages of one method over another. Contracts offer the manager a greater convenience and a freedom from certain supervisory functions. However, these features are reflected in the cost of using contractors and the manager must be knowledgeable enough to know if he is getting what he wants. Many managers abdicate their responsibilities when they use contractors.

Using in-house staff offers the opportunity for cost savings, *provided* that the manager is able to effectively assume the contractor's managerial role. The advantages of having in-house staff are as follows:

1. Quicker response to emergency situations.
2. Greater flexibility.
3. Greater familiarity of workers with building systems and with expected standards.
4. Potential for better worker motivation, since workers are more closely identified with the quality of the building.
5. Better opportunities for obtaining statistical data relating to cost control.
6. Better opportunity to train and upgrade.

The disadvantages of having in-house staff are as follows:

1. Risk of incompetent technicians.
2. Difficulty in keeping full-time in-house staff busy at all times.
3. Lack of competition may lead to overly-inflated prices or half-hearted performance efficiency.
4. Need for greater workmen's compensation and liability insurance.

Some managers find that it is actually cheaper to contract for conventional unskilled labor than to use in-house labor. The present trend is to move away from the "jack-of-all-trades" handyman in favor of specialized technicians such as electricians or mechanics.

If a manager concentrates his "in-house" staff on specialties and uses them to carry out the preventive maintenance programs, tremendous benefits result. Not only do the in-house technicians become more expert in their field, but problems seem to disappear and costs level out. Successful managers must upgrade their own management skills as well as their human and technical skills if they are to effectively recruit, direct, motivate, and improve their staffs.

PERFORMANCE EVALUATION

Because there is no objective unit of production related to most maintenance functions, performance evaluation involves a large degree of subjectivity. No single measure of productivity can be applied without limitations. However, by combining various measures and supplementing them with on-the-job spot checks and time studies, a manager can gain a fairly good idea of the relative productivity efficiency of his in-house crew and of their operating methods.

The following are basic ways in which aspects relating to productivity can be calculated:

1. Man hours per job (useful where jobs are very similar).
2. Cumulative comparison of estimated hours required for a job and those actually consumed. Workmen who continually exceed time estimates may be functioning inefficiently.
3. Feedback from residents or building operating staff.
4. Studying work orders (Figure 1-17). Using a work order for each job will allow the manager to assess performance.

Records should be kept to determine the amount of time lost waiting for materials, receiving instructions, or traveling. The manager should also analyze how much time is spent on supervisory functions, in revising schedules, or in dealing with problems.

QUALITY CONTROL

A manager who cuts maintenance standards or defers maintenance in order to reduce costs will eventually downgrade a property and increase future maintenance costs. Such a strategy reveals that the manager does not have sufficient understanding of the importance of maintenance relative to long-range cost factors.

Managers can be assured of quality control by systematically concentrating their efforts on the following:

1. Selecting reputable contractors and qualified employees.
2. Providing suitable working conditions.
3. Giving clear instructions which adhere to acceptable specifications.
4. Timing supervisory inspections to coincide with the beginning of each crucial stage of the work.
5. Inspecting both incoming materials and outgoing scrap.
6. Following up personally on every complaint.
7. Continually evaluating and improving the operation of the department.

THE USE OF CONSULTANTS

From time to time, maintenance problems arise whose solutions are beyond the expertise of even the most seasoned project manager. Often totally unexpected problems alert a manager to the fact that he needs the advice of skilled structural or electrical/mechanical experts. Finding people with the needed skills can be a problem and educational institutions must recognize the need for suitable training programs to fill this serious void in management needs.

Some large companies do provide this expertise within their own staff. By educating themselves, project managers can improve their technical skills so that they will know which resources are needed to overcome the specialized problems.

There is no doubt that a reputable contractor can advise the manager effectively on a wise range of situations. Sometimes contractors are willing to serve as consultants, and will advise project managers on the best methods for undertaking a task, even if the actual work will not be given to their company.

However, a manager should remember two things about contractors. First, their practical knowledge is often limited to the situations they encounter on a day-to-day basis and that knowledge may be limited and based on guesswork. Second, contractors may tend to gear their advice toward services which they hope to sell to the manager.

There will be times when it is in the manager's best interest to seek the assistance of a professional consultant. Such a person is paid to provide advice, not to provide services. As a result, it is to the consultant's benefit that he give the best advice possible, so that the manager will seek his advice again in the future. The following is a partial list of types of consultants available to the manager and the areas in which they can provide assistance. The ones indicated with an asterisk may also sell corrective services in addition to their advice, a factor which the manager should bear in mind while evaluating their proposals.

*1. Architects—design problems, repairing major damage, rebuilding, or enlarging.
2. Mechanical Engineers—various mechanical systems, including heating and air conditioning.
3. Electrical Engineers—major electrical problems or renovations.
4. Structural Engineers—structural damage or deterioration; advice on the feasibility of modifications or extensions to existing structures.
5. Landscape Architects—problems relating to maintaining the desirable appearance of the grounds; problems with erosion or drainage.
*6. Tree Specialists—death or decay of trees and shrubbery, partial or complete removal of trees that are unwanted or causing safety hazards.
7. Soil Consultants—problems related to poor quality of soil.
*8. Pest Control Companies—infestations of insects or rodents.

*May also sell corrective services.

The following criteria should be examined before using a consultant for the first time:

—His reputation and reliability should be confirmed by requesting and checking references.

—His specific areas of competence should be determined.

—His degree of experience in buildings of similar age and structure should be considered.

Consultants can be especially helpful at those times when a major maintenance cycle is approaching. Though they are often expensive in terms of their hourly rates, the proper advice at a crucial time can be a wise investment.

1-9 Biological Fouling and Corrosion

The need for water treatment and cathodic protection becomes evident as one researches and develops a maintenance program. Problems such as corrosion, biological fouling, algae, bacteria, and other pollutants can only be overcome by introducing chemicals and utilizing cathodic protection.

There is no such thing as a universal corrosion inhibitor, but each blend of inhibitor must be tailored to the type of equipment or cooling water that it is designed to protect. An inhibitor that may provide excellent protection for one system may fail to protect another system and may even aggravate the corrosion. In buildings, water treatment is required in heating systems, cooling systems, swimming pools, and decorative fountains.

pH—A MEASURE OF HYDROGEN ION

As mentioned previously, water treatment must be tailored to the type of equipment which it is designed to protect. One important factor which must be understood when treating and testing water is the pH measure of a sample. This is defined as the measure of hydrogen ion concentration (activity) of the sample.

The pH of the water must be accurately determined because the adjustment of pH is usually very important in the control of biological fouling and corrosion in heating and cooling systems, as well as swimming pools and fountains.

A simple definition of pH is that it is a number between 1 and 14, denoting the intensity of acidity or alkalinity of a water.

The pH number of water of any solution indicates whether the liquid has an acid or an alkaline reaction. A neutral liquid, such as pure water, is neither acid nor alkaline and has a pH value of 7.

When water or any aqueous solution contains a surplus of hydrogen ions, it has an acid reaction. Conversely, an excess of OH^- ions will produce a basic or alkaline condition. The H^+ ions, liberated by the dissociation of the solution, attack metal, causing it to dissolve. The greater the hydrogen ion concentration, the more rapid the attack and vice versa.

A neutral liquid such as pure water is neither alkaline nor acid and has a pH of 7. Water treatment must achieve this neutrality if it is to be effective. A good example of this water treatment would be in swimming pools. To maintain a proper pH balance, the lifeguards are constantly testing the water and introducing chlorine to control algae or other chemicals to maintain the water chemistry. Sunshine and heavy use of the pool constantly upset this balance.

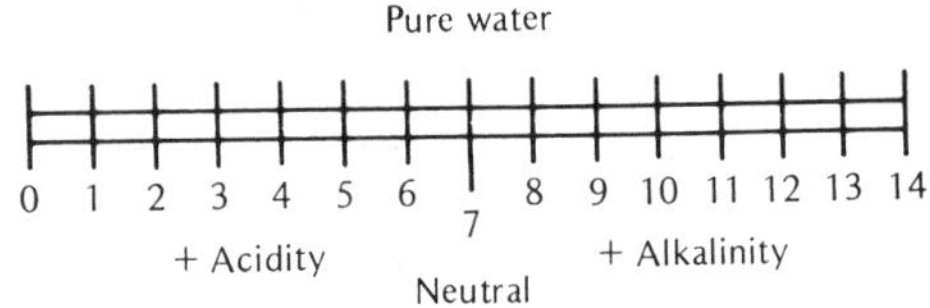

FIGURE 1-22 The pH scale of H-ion concentration. By measuring the Hydrogen-ion concentration in a sample of water, it can be determined what corrective measures to take to counteract the corrosive characteristics of the water.

The heating and cooling system water must also be kept in balance chemically if corrosion of the boilers and the heating piping or biological fouling of the condenser tubes is to be overcome.

Water is a chemical combination of hydrogen and oxygen—two atoms of hydrogen to one of oxygen. Actually, one of the hydrogen atoms associates itself with the oxygen, and their combination, OH^- (hydroxyl ion), has a negative charge. The other hydrogen H^+, has a positive charge. If these ions are present in the same number, they neutralize each other, so the water has no charge. When the concentration of hydrogen ions exceeds that of hydroxyl ions, however, the water has an acid reaction, and if hydroxyl ions are in greater concentration than hydrogen ions, the reaction is alkaline or basic.

In general, acid solutions are more aggressive to metals than alkaline ones, although some corrosion may take place even in neutral or alkaline media. For this reason, it is essential to control the pH of heating and cooling systems. pH will also influence scaling and biological fouling.

FACTORS INFLUENCING CORROSION

The principal factors influencing the corrosion of metals in water systems are the types and concentrations of impurities in the water, plus the temperature and rate of water flow. If the rate of flow is restricted by scale or other substances generally found in return water lines, the corrosion will accelerate as the impurities have a better chance to attack the metal. Proper rate of flow moves the impurities before they can cause a problem. These are periodically flushed out of the domestic hot water lines through a blow down by-pass at the return line to the domestic hot water storage tank (see Chapter 7, Figure 7-5).

The chief chemical variables controlling the characteristics of water are

—dissolved oxygen concentration

—carbon dioxide content

—pH

—dissolved solids

—presence of free mineral acid

—sulphide

—sulphur dioxide

Increased dissolved solids, particularly chloride and sulphate, enhance the corrosive effect of oxygen and carbon dioxide.

There are basically three types of corrosion: (1) physical corrosion, (2) chemical corrosion, and (3) electrochemical corrosion. It is important that you acquire a basic knowledge of these types of corrosion so you will understand the problem and know how to control the situation.

Physical Corrosion

In discussing corrosion, it is unfortunately necessary to use technical terms. One can almost say that corrosion has a language of its own. These terms will be explained in as simple a form as possible.

Unfortunately, many people often accept corrosion as inevitable. Actually, something can and should be done to prolong the life of many metals exposed to corrosive environments. It costs money to replace deteriorated material. Thus corrosion control becomes a very important factor in the very important area of "dollars and cents." The cost, in terms of dollars, for corrosion and corrosion control in the United States in 1975 was estimated to be in excess of ten to fifteen billion dollars per year. Inflation will compound these figures dramatically.

Most people are familiar with corrosion, particularly the rusting of an iron fence, or a "tin can," and the corrosion of steel pilings or boats.

When undertaking a study of corrosion it may be natural to think that corrosion is a simple single reaction, and that it can be turned off like a spigot. Unfortunately, this is not the case.

Corrosion is the deterioration of a substance (usually a metal) or its properties because of a reaction with its environment. The deterioration of wood, ceramics, plastics, and other substances must also be included in a study of corrosion.

Chemical Corrosion

The action of oxygen increases corrosion. Furthermore, if iron is placed in two similar flasks filled with water and nitrogen is added to one and oxygen to the other, the iron in the flask with the oxygen will begin to rust, while the iron in the flask saturated with nitrogen, which helps eliminate the dissolved oxygen, remains bright.

This is significant because in domestic water and cooling systems we continually evaporate or use the water (H_2O) in the system and thus are continually adding fresh water, which perpetuates the corrosion problem by adding fresh oxygen.

Electrochemical Corrosion

There are many theories regarding the cause and mechanism of corrosion. The electrochemical theory is the most widely accepted, and states that a potential must exist between two or more points and current must flow for corrosion of metals to occur.

Metal corrosion is caused by electrochemical reactions in which metal at one location (the anode) corrodes while, at another location (the cathode), hydrogen ions are reduced or discharged. The cathode and anode can be miles apart, or can be so close together that they may be considered to be coincident, but at any one moment, oxidation is taking place at one spot while reduction is progressing at another. There are millions of both kinds of reactive areas operating on a piece of metal simultaneously. This action requires four components: anode, cathode, electrolyte, and a metallic path for electrons. Anodes and cathodes are caused by differences in the surfaces of metals, which are created by metallic inclusions, metallographic discontinuities, different grain orientation, different stress, or different temperature.

If two different metals are in electrical contact in an aqueous environment, a large difference in electrolytic potential is established, resulting in severe corrosion of the more anodic metals. For example, the combination of copper and steel is a bad one for steel. The electrolyte (water) influences the severity of the corrosive processes. The more dissolved salts water contains, the better the conductor it is, and the greater will be the corrosion. The quantity of dissolved oxygen is most important because it is oxygen which keeps the cathodes functioning. A completely deaerated water with a neutral or slightly alkaline pH is almost non-corrosive—as in a heating system in which the oxygen has been all used up by superficial corrosion. If one area has access to dissolved oxygen while another is shielded, corrosion of the metal under a deposit can occur.

In heating and cooling systems there are two causes of electrochemical corrosion:

1. Difference in the concentration of dissolved oxygen at one point compared to another.
2. The use of dissimilar metal.

Bimetallic corrosion can occur when two dissimilar metals are brought into electrical contact in the presence of an electrolyte such as the water in the system.

Corrosion of metals in aqueous media, such as the water in heating systems, occurs by a combination of both anodic and cathodic reactions.

This corrosion does not happen in heating systems unless there is a leak or air is sucked into the system at the pumps. By introducing and controlling the needed chemicals into the water, the pH balance of the system can be maintained and the corrosive electrochemical action can be stopped. To maintain this balance all leaks *MUST* be corrected immediately. The water in the heating and cooling systems must be regularly tested and chemically maintained by correcting any imbalance noted as soon as possible.

WHY METALS CORRODE

Metals corrode through sheer cussedness. They want to corrode. This stems from the fact that it is more natural for a metal to exist in the form of a compound, since compounds such as oxides contain less energy than metals and are therefore more stable.

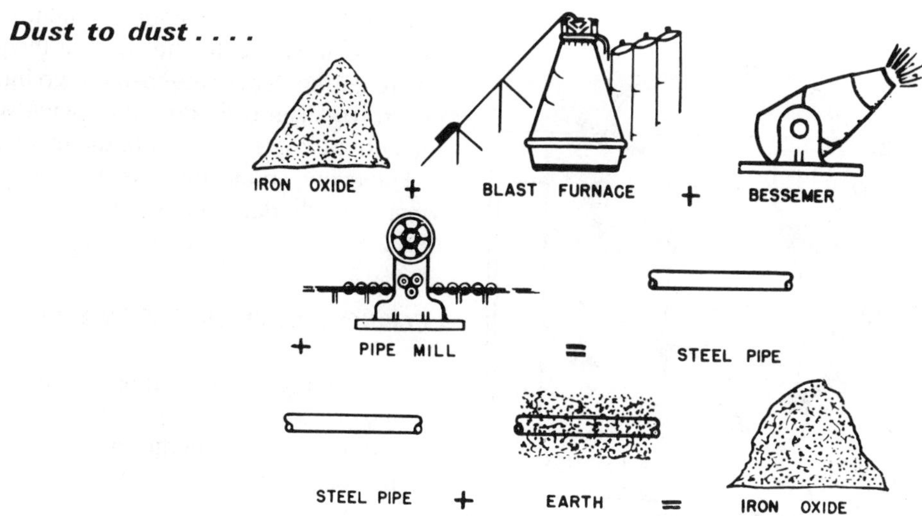

FIGURE 1-23 Why metals corrode. (Courtesy of Mr. T.R.B. Watson, Corrosion Services Company Limited.)

In making steel, when iron is divorced from its associated oxygen in the blast furnace, a lot of energy is added in the form of heat. As long as it remains metallic, a piece of steel retains a portion of this energy, bound up within itself, always urging the metal to corrode back to the ore from which it was unwillingly derived. This energy supplies the power to drive the various corrosion reactions, and provides the incentive to corrode. When steel rusts the latent energy is released and the metal, relieved of its uneasy hypertension, reverts to a stable oxide, and the cycle is complete.

When steel rusts the union with oxygen does not take place directly but by a rather roundabout series of reactions in which the passage of an electric current plays an important part. It is often stated that corrosion is caused by electric currents. It is perhaps more accurate to say that in most cases the electric current is caused by the corrosion, but the two forces are as interdependent as the chicken and the egg.

Corrosion Cell (Galvanic Activity)

Battery Action (Galvanic Cell)

A good example of the way current is generated by corrosion is the galvanic cell. The ordinary dry cell battery, which consists of a zinc can holding a moist paste which constitutes the electrolyte, has a graphite rod in its center which acts as the cathode of the cell. Because the zinc has more stored-up energy than the graphite and is thus more anxious to corrode, a potential of about 1½ volts exists between the zinc and the graphite, and if the external terminals are joined with a wire, current will flow in the cell from the surface of the zinc, through the electrolyte, to the cathode and back again through the wire. If a flashlight bulb is put in the external circuit it will light, and it is interesting that the electrical energy which lights it is the energy of corrosion of the zinc, and the same energy which was put into the zinc when it was refined from its ore. As the zinc

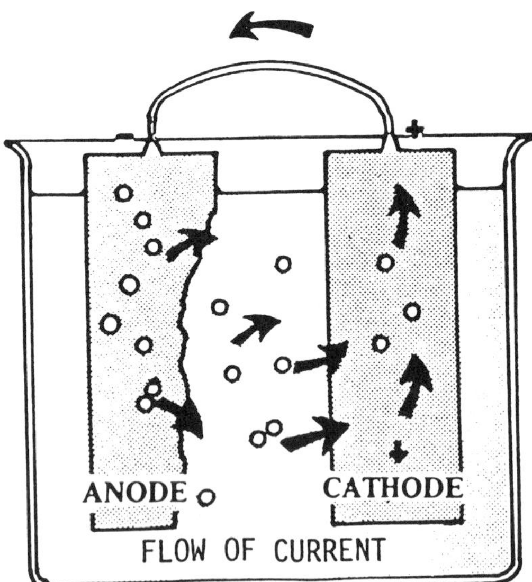

FIGURE 1-24 Corrosion cell (galvanic activity). The term "anode" is used to describe that portion of the metal surface that is corroded and from which current leaves the metal to enter the solution. The term "cathode" is used to describe the metal surface from which current leaves the solution and returns to the metal and a chemical reaction takes place. (Courtesy of Mr. T.R.B. Watson, Corrosion Services Company Limited.)

corrodes, it releases into the electrolyte small charged particles of itself, called ions, and these charged particles travel across the cell to the cathode where they discharge. The passage of ions constitutes an electric current. The more current flowing in a cell, the more zinc is corroded. After the battery has been used for some time, corrosion will eat a hole in it, and the cell will leak. Many people have had the experience of having a flashlight battery leak inside the case.

If the wire is disconnected from the external terminals the current is interrupted and the ions released at the surface of the zinc have nowhere to go, and accumulate in such numbers that corrosion is virtually stopped. This demonstrates that for corrosion to take place there must be a complete circuit.

Note that only the anode is attacked in every electrolytic cell. The anode is the place where current leaves the metal to go into the electrolyte. The cathode is the place where the current flows back out of the electrolyte.

For every anode there is always, somewhere, a cathode. *Anodes corrode; cathodes don't.*

CORROSION PROBLEMS IN BUILDINGS

In buildings, iron piping is the major source of corrosion. Heating pipes, domestic hot water pipes, underground piping, and heating pipes for ramps give the most trouble. Corrosion in boilers and in reinforcing steel rods in underground garage slabs also contribute to the problem.

The costs to correct the corrosion problems are staggering because walls or concrete usually must be broken to replace galvanized pipe with copper or plastic pipes.

Corrosion Due To Dissimilar Metal

In actual practice, the behavior of a bimetallic combination, such as a brass or

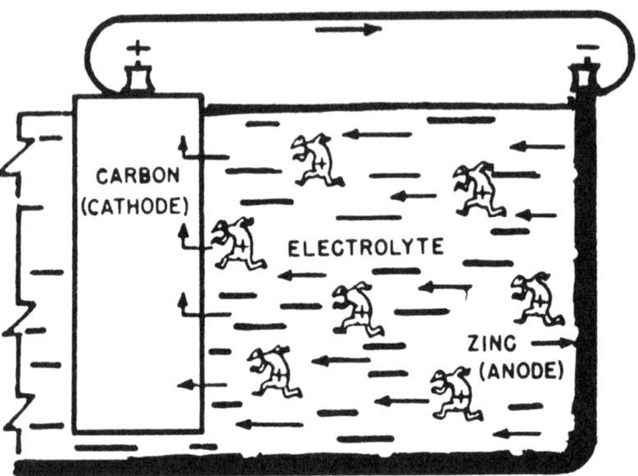

FIGURE 1-25 Battery action (galvanic cell). For corrosion to take place, there must be a complete circuit. (Courtesy of Mr. T.R.B. Watson, Corrosion Services Company Limited.)

bronze valve or copper convector in an iron pipeline, usually does not result in rapid failure of the pipe. Corrosion undoubtedly takes place, but the ratio of the amount of iron to that of the brass, bronze, or copper appears to be the governing factor. Corrosion is distributed over the surface of the iron to such an extent that penetration is generally negligible. If for some reason, such as turbulence, temperature, or oxygen distribution, corrosion of the iron is confined to a small area near the more noble metal, the attack will be serious and rapid, resulting in perforation.

A bimetallic galvanic cell is always established when two different metals in electrical contact with each other are buried adjacent to each other. In a home supplied by a steel gas service line and a copper water service, the metallic circuit between the two metals is completed through the water heater. The steel in this case will be corroded by the influence of the copper pipe, which acts as a cathode.

For every ampere-year of current, 20 pounds of metal are dissolved, and the rate of penetration depends on the area from which this metal is taken. If the pipe is coated and subject to electrolysis from stray currents, the coating can, in some cases, cause more rapid penetration of the pipe because the areas from which metal can be taken are confined to pinholes or cracks in the coating.

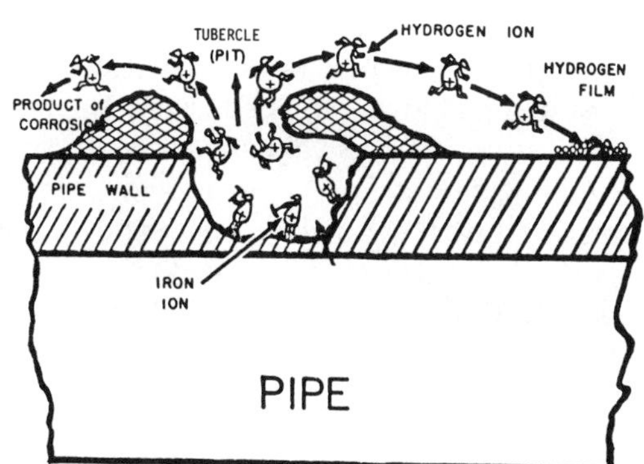

FIGURE 1-27 Pit action. Here we see a well advanced corrosion cell in which the anode has corroded to form a pit. The corrosion product has built up over the top of the pit to form a tubercle. This rust deposit is soft and quite permeable, and offers no resistance to the passage of the current through it and, in fact, aggravates the situation. Once a pit is started, the voltage of the corrosion cell goes up and the action is intensified. (Courtesy of Mr. T.R.B. Watson, Corrosion Services Company Limited.)

Problems Caused By New and Old Pipe

In the battery, the voltage was set up by the fact that the anode and cathode were made of different materials. In fact, it is always some difference of metal or soil which causes current flow and its associated corrosion. The greater the difference, the more severe will be the attack. Pipeliners say that pipes today are not as good as they used to be. The example is often cited of the line that lasted many

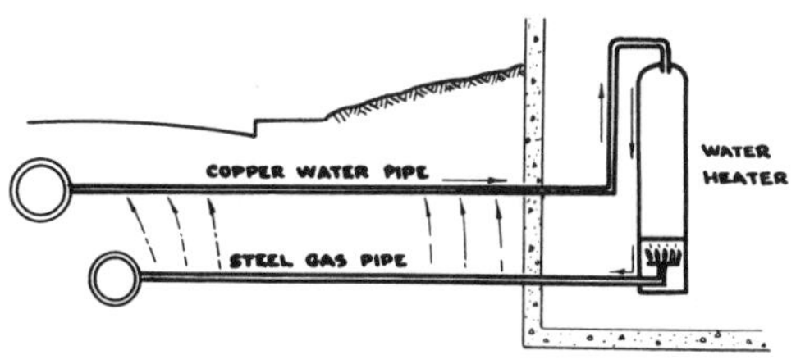

FIGURE 1-26 Corrosion due to dissimilar metal. (Courtesy of Mr. T.R.B. Watson, Corrosion Services Company Limited.)

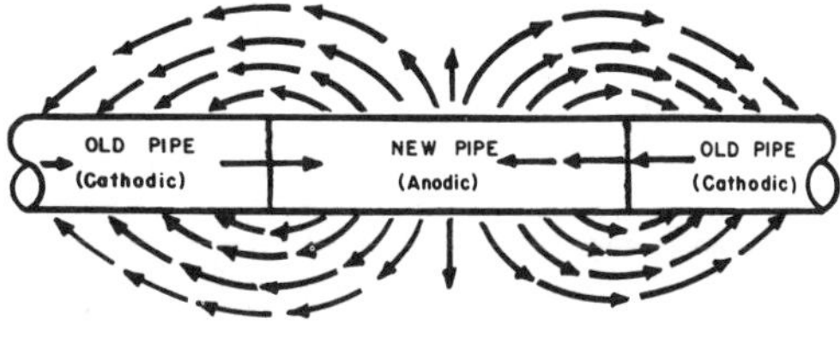

FIGURE 1-28 Corrosion due to dissimilar metal. It is always some difference of metal or soil which causes current flow and its associated corrosion. (Courtesy of Mr. T.R.B. Watson, Corrosion Services Company Limited.)

years until one short section had to be replaced. The new pipe lasted only a few years before it had to be replaced again. The trouble was not a defective new pipe, but that in coupling new and old pipe, a cell of different materials was set up, in which the new clean pipe was strongly anodic to the old rusty pipe, and it corroded as a result of the currents.

Corrosion Caused by The Nature of Soil

Take the case of a bare steel pipe buried in moist earth. Because of slight differences in metal composition or surface condition, and because of slight differences in the nature of the soil touching the pipe, small potentials or voltages are set up between some areas of the pipe surface and other adjacent areas. (This is analogous to the battery action described earlier.) From the more negative areas, current will flow into the soil (which acts as the electrolyte) and through it to the more positive or cathodic areas and back again through the metal of the pipe. At the negative, or anodic, area metal will dissolve. At the adjacent cathodes no corrosion will take place. This accounts for the common action of pitting: The pits are anodes where the metal is corroding, and the unaffected areas around the pits have been acting as cathodes and thus have been protected. Nevertheless, because every anode needs a cathode, the uncorroded areas were necessary to the reaction.

Current is conducted through the moist earth by a stream of hydrogen ions. Where these ions arrive at the cathode areas they are discharged and result in a film of hydrogen. This usually reacts with oxygen dissolved in the soil, and is not evolved as a gas. This little corrosion cell is representative of millions of similar ones on the surface of any pipe. The length of the current path may be anywhere

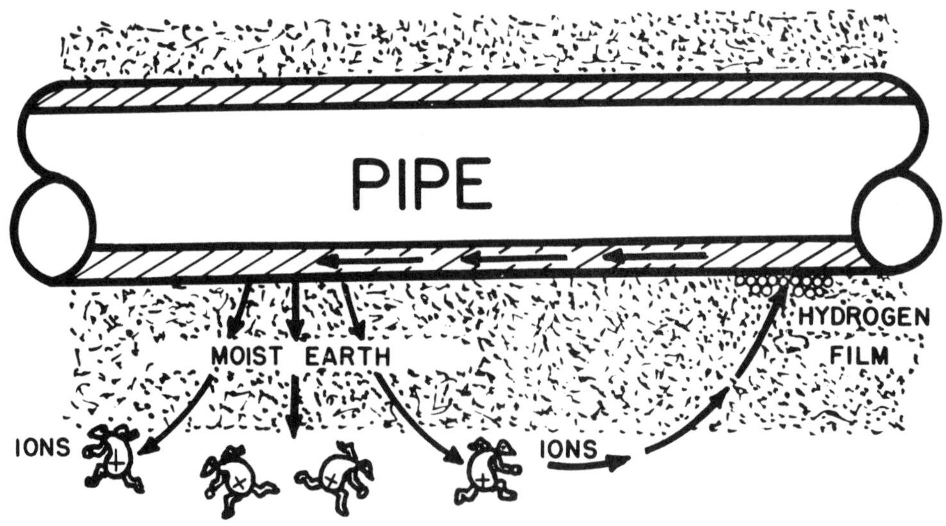

FIGURE 1-29 The hydrogen-ion. (Courtesy of Mr. T.R.B. Watson, Corrosion Services Company Limited.)

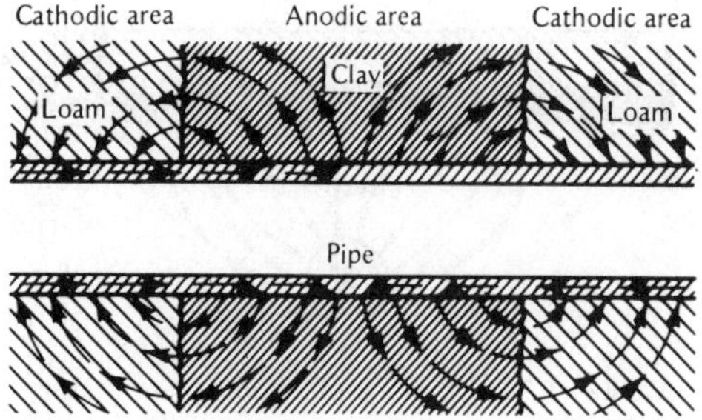

FIGURE 1-30 Corrosion caused by dissimilar soils. Differences in the nature of the soil in contact with a metal pipe can also form galvanic cells. The lighter, more porous soils are most likely to become cathodes. The metal in contact with the more impervious clay will suffer. (Courtesy of Mr. T.R.B. Watson, Corrosion Services Company Limited.)

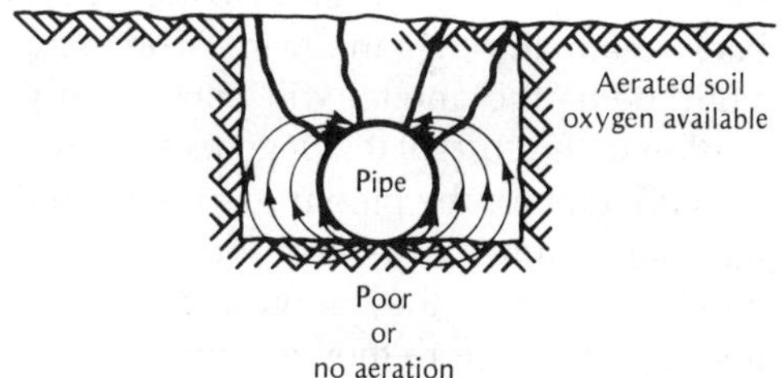

FIGURE 1-32 Corrosion caused by aeration of soil. (Courtesy of Mr. T.R.B. Watson, Corrosion Services Company Limited.)

from a millimeter or smaller to several miles, but the strength of the current is always proportional to the corrosion rate. One ampere, flowing for one year, will dissolve 20 pounds of steel.

Corrosion Caused By Aeration of Soil

If one surface of the pipe has more access to oxygen than has another surface, a similar cell will be set up. This accounts for a familiar condition when the bottom of the pipe, in contact with undisturbed, poorly aerated soil at the bottom of the trench, is subject to more corrosion than is the top of the pipe, which has an ample oxygen supply through permeation into the loose backfill.

CATHODIC PROTECTION MAGNESIUM ANODES

A current may just as easily be produced by galvanic action from the energy of corrosion of a magnesium anode. In this instance a piece of magnesium is connected to the pipe with a wire and buried some 10 ft away from it. Because the magnesium is much more active than the steel, a considerable voltage is established between the two metals and protective current will flow from the

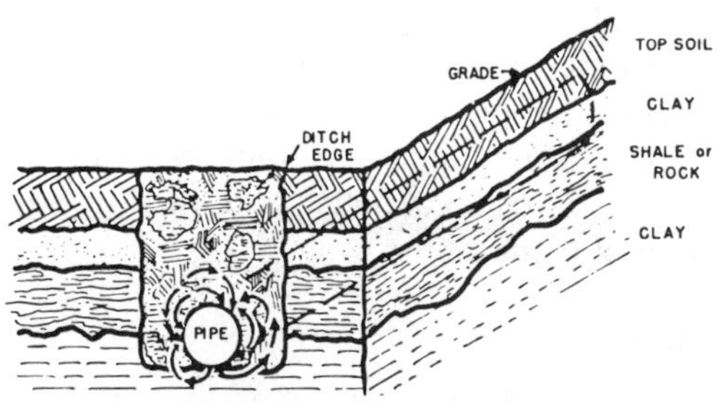

FIGURE 1-31 Corrosion caused by a mixture of soils. Such a condition often exists when a trench is backfilled with a mixture of lumps of different kinds of soils, as shown in Figure 1-31. (Courtesy of Mr. T.R.B. Watson, Corrosion Services Company Limited.)

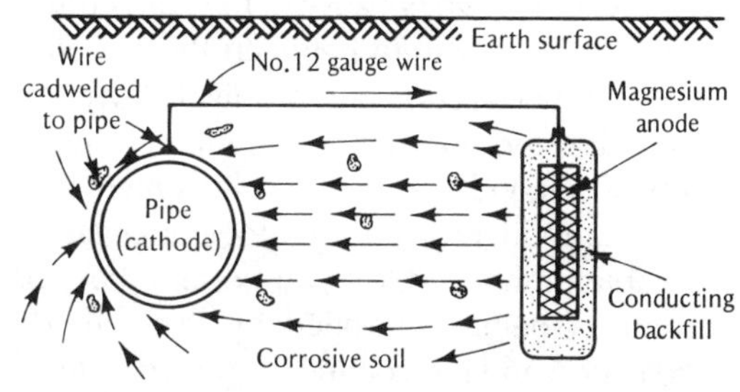

FIGURE 1-33 Cathodic protection magnesium anodes. A current may just as easily be produced by galvanic action from the energy of corrosion of a magnesium anode. (Courtesy of Mr. T.R.B. Watson, Corrosion Services Company Limited.)

magnesium through the earth to the pipe, and back again through the wire. The magnesium, being the anode, will corrode in proportion to the current that it generates. In fact, the corrosion of the pipeline is transferred to the magnesium. Wherever these protective anodes are used they should be inspected and replaced before they disappear.

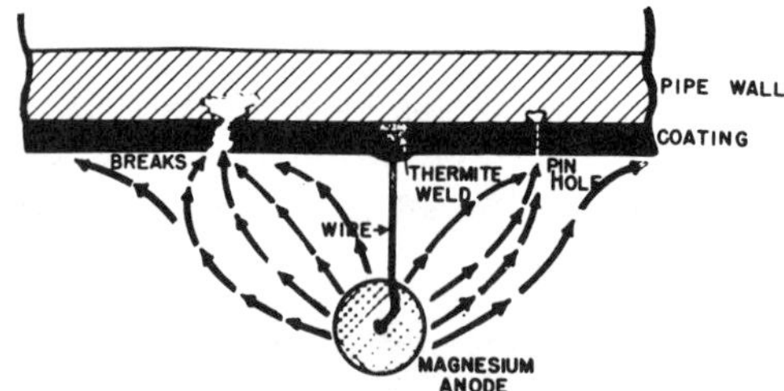

FIGURE 1-34 Pipe protection with coating and anodes. The current at the pinholes, although they are small, causes a high protective current density at the minute breaks in the coating. (Courtesy of Mr. T.R.B. Watson, Corrosion Services Company Limited.)

PIPE PROTECTION WITH COATING AND ANODES

Fewer mangesium anodes are necessary to protect a coated structure than are necessary to protect a bare one, since the available current has only to go to the breaks in the coating instead of having to cover a large bare area. The current at the pinholes, although very small, causes a high protective current density at the minute breaks in the coating.

Today, the vast majority of long buried pipelines are coated with an organic coating, because experience has shown that corrosion can be controlled more cheaply on a coated structure. Corrosion may be stopped in two ways: (1) by maintaining a perfect coating, and (2) by impressing a protective cathodic current density on a bare line. The first measure is impossible, since there is no such thing as a perfect coating and the second is unduly expensive because of the high current demand. Somewhere between the extremes of coating perfection and prodigal power demand lies the optimum economic combination of a good coating supplemented by a little cathodic protection to look after the inevitable pinholes. Or it can be said that corrosion is being controlled by the cathodic protection and the coating is applied to make the cathodic protection cheaper.

Corrosion control is an economic measure and the cheapest way to achieve it is the best. The choice is easier if you know why metals corrode.

CONTROL OF OBSTRUCTIVE GROWTH (BIOLOGICAL FOULING)

Biological fouling is the result of excessive growth and development of different members of the lower forms of plant life, namely algae, bacteria (slime), and fungi. The main function of these microscopic life forms is to restore the natural balance of life cycles when they are disrupted. As long as the microscopic life forms remain isolated as single cells, they present no problem. However, when the balance of nature is disturbed by constructing systems to store and conserve water, an ideal breeding place for microbiological growths is provided. Examples of breeding places are cooling towers and swimming pools. These growths can foul pipelines and interfere with heat transfer, cause corrosion of metal, and the disintegration of wood.

Algae

Algae are defined as a group of water plants that make their own food and that have chlorophyll but not true stems, roots, or leaves. Algae are able to accomplish this because they contain the green pigment chlorophyll, and thus utilize a process known as photosynthesis. Algae cannot survive without air, sunlight, or water. When pools and cooling towers are exposed to direct sunlight, they are plagued with the problem of algae growths.

Bacteria

Bacteria can be defined as very tiny and simple plants, so small that they can usually be seen only through a microscope. Bacteria consist of single cells, have no chlorophyll, and multiply by fission (splitting apart). In general they are unicellular, rod shaped, coccid, or spiral in form. Bacteria cause diseases such as pneumonia and typhoid fever, among others.

Slime-forming bacteria are the most common bacteria found in recirculating cooling water systems. The basic function of these bacteria is to form a gelatinous capsule which entraps other materials, and which protects the bacteria against the action of chemical and physical agents.

Problems Caused by Bacteria

Slime deposits on processing equipment retard heat transfer on cooling equipment and thus cause a serious loss of efficiency. Slime deposits on metal surfaces create local cell action and aggravate pitting tendencies.

Aerobic sulphur bacteria oxidize sulphur or sulphides to sulphuric acid. Some species of sulphur bacteria are commonly present in water containing dissolved hydrogen sulphide. These specific colored (red or purple) sulphur bacteria are similar to the chlorophyll-bearing plants in their ability to manufacture their food photosynthetically and to develop only in sunlight.

Iron bacteria precipitate ferric hydroxide (rust).

Chlorine

Many different chemical agents are employed for microorganism control in recirculating water systems. The primary purpose of the chemical agent is to kill and/or inhibit the growth and accretion of organisms.

Unless the chemical agent is present in sufficient quantity or is highly toxic, it is not uncommon for the chemical agent, in extremely dilute concentrations, to actually stimulate the growth of microorganisms.

Chlorine is probably the agent most widely employed for control of microorganisms. In the absence of substances that cause a high chlorine demand, chlorine is usually the most economical method of treatment.

It is not satisfactory to feed chlorine without first chemically testing the water to determine the residual of free chlorine that is present. Not only is chlorine one of the most effective slime control agents, but it is also one of the most damaging materials to cooling tower lumber and other vulnerable areas. *Consequently, the use of chlorine must be carefully controlled.*

TESTING CONTROL

A system of control testing ensures that chemical balances are maintained in recommended ranges so that deposits, delignification (destructive action on wood), and electrochemical corrosion are controlled.

Establishing a reliable water test program requires qualified personnel and proper facilities for testing. The personnel must be attentive to results that indicate deficiencies. They should bring them to the immediate attention

SAMPLE NO.______ DATE ______________

BUILDING ADDRESS ________________________________

HEATING WATER TEST

TEMPERATURE OF WATER SAMPLE	______	°C
pH (MEASURE OF HYDROGEN IONS)	______	pH
Fe ++ FERROUS IRON OXIDE	______	ppm
CONDUCTIVITY	______	mm
CORROSION INHIBITOR	______	ppm

COOLING WATER TEST

TEMPERATURE OF WATER SAMPLE	______	°C
pH (MEASURE OF HYDROGEN IONS)	______	pH
CHLORIDES	______	ppm
CONDUCTIVITY	______	mm
CORROSION INHIBITOR	______	ppm

COMMENTS

SAMPLE DRAWN BY ______________ DATE ______________

TEST LAB TECHNICIAN ______________ TEST DATE ______________

DATE FOLLOWED UP ______________ BY WHOM ______________

FIGURE 1-35 Water test control.

of those responsible for corrective action.

A control chart listing recommended ranges should be available for ready reference. The testing area must be secluded to prevent contamination from dust, smoke, and fumes.

Results should be recorded immediately on record sheets (see Figure 1-35), and circulated to those responsible. Problems should be followed up, corrected, and properly filed for future reference.

1-10 The Benefits of Efficient Operation

Maintenance and operations activities that are properly planned and executed result in benefits far beyond the dollars and cents savings.

1. The input of a resource specialist should be available when purchasing structural and electrical/mechanical components for new buildings and for recommending improvements, repairs, or replacements of components in existing buildings.
2. Savings on investment are maximized.
3. Optimum efficiency of operation is ensured.
4. Emergency breakdowns are prevented; if a breakdown occurs the down time will be minimized.
5. Replacement costs are saved as the life of building components and equipment is extended. The life cycle may be extended by 50 percent or more.
6. Occupant comfort is improved.
7. Engineer's design criteria are achieved.
8. Energy is saved. These dollars are a "free bonus" because they require no capital outlay.
9. Confidence and satisfaction is instilled in the management team. This spirit helps recruit, develop, and retain competent specialists, so important for the future of the enterprise.

Chapter 2

THE BUILDING PROFILE

2–1 Why a Building Profile?

If "Project Management" is the management of a building through its life cycle stages of development, design, construction, and operations, then it would be wise to specify the quality of the major components required for a project at the development stage, but certainly no later than at the design stage of a new or proposed project.

The ideal way to do this would be to use the suggested building profile statistics included in this chapter as a means of organizing the building's components.

Because the budgeting and accounting records are matched to the building's structural and electrical/mechanical systems, any forms used for projections should be organized to match the repair and maintenance classifications listed in Figures 1-4 through 1-15 in chapter one.

If a company is managing several projects, including residential, commercial, or institutional buildings, and its accounting system matches these classifications, it can now include the cost of operations in the decision process. This information is even more valuable if the operations statistics are kept for an extended period of time.

If the records are categorized by building structure, electrical/mechanical equipment, tenant-mix, use, and geographic area, the information would not only provide the original cost, but also the cost of operations.

This can be a manual or computerized system. The secret is the manner in which the information is organized. The computer is, of course, the ideal way to go. The detail needed to obtain the required information is very time consuming to gather manually. The computer allows a project to be simulated by mixing and matching components and supplys the operational costs for more realistic projections relevant to life cycle costs.

Recordkeeping would include the original costs for every component in the building: the structure (roofs, walls, brickwork, windows, parking lots, driveways, doors, floor coverings, etc.), the plumbing and drainage system, the heating system, the ventilation system, the air conditioning system, the cooling system, the recreation facilities, and the interior or exterior landscaping.

During the life of the building, expenditures for building additions, building replacement, equipment additions or replacements, staff salaries, and the costs for fuel, electricity, and water would also be recorded and made available.

The energy crisis and inflation have escalated the costs for building and operating a project to the point where this type of sophisticated system is the only way to realistically decide about new development investments and to control the operation of existing projects.

The value of the information gathered as a "building profile" is self-evident. The rapid escalation of costs to build have dramatically increased the value of existing buildings. These existing buildings are too valuable to be allowed to deteriorate through an ad hoc crisis system of management. The management system must feed back information to the designer and builder from the operations specialist. To be effective, the feedback must be based on facts and figures that support their recommendations. The building profile is the foundation for this type of action.

Each building being managed should have its own building profile available in a looseleaf binder.

2–2 Takeover Inspection

A building takeover inspection is necessary if the building is new, if the manager or superintendent is new, or if the owner has purchased or intends to purchase the building.

These inspections familiarize the owner, the manager, and the operating staff with the structure and the building's electrical/mechanical equipment. This action is the basis for a successful building management program. The results of such a program show in the maintenance of the structure, the efficiency of the electrical/mechanical equipment, the planning for the housekeeping and groundskeeping services, and the satisfaction of the lessees or residents. In addition, it helps organize, direct, and control the building operating staff.

Management is a continuous decision-making exercise. Performing inspections and gathering facts about the structure and the electrical/mechanical systems will qualify a manager to make intelligent decisions regarding the housekeeping, groundskeeping, and operations of the building.

Inspections quickly point out that owning a building represents a sizable investment, and that proper maintenance is the only way to protect this investment.

When engineers design heating, ventilating, and air conditioning equipment, they are confronted with demands for maximum air delivery at low power consumption as well as economical and quiet operation.

The housing, the wheel, the pumps, and other equipment require special engineering treatment to obtain maximum operational efficiency for the completed assembly.

To confirm that the equipment is operating efficiently, the technical data of all the components—fans, pumps, starters, overload relays, heaters, motors, sheaves, belts, filters, etc.—should be recorded on standardized record forms similar to those included in this chapter. The layouts shown are merely guides for recording information, and a better way to record the information may be developed according to individual situations.

The performance of blowers and pumps should follow established laws that make it possible to calculate the expected performance of an air moving, or fluid flow system, after changes within the system have been made. The information gathered should confirm the efficiency of the electrical/mechanical systems.

When one or more conditions are changed by known amounts, certain other conditions will vary in accordance with these laws. Therefore, it is apparent that properly designed and installed systems must be professionally set up, balanced, and maintained if maximum efficiency is to be achieved; only skilled technicians can properly perform these tasks. Owners, managers, and operators should be qualified to confirm this, to recognize problems with the systems, and know when to call in experts.

WHY GATHER BUILDING PROFILE INFORMATION?

1. It allows the people involved to become familiar with the structure, the mechanical systems, and the housekeeping and groundskeeping needs.
2. It improves the knowledge of the people involved by hands-on inspections.
3. It teaches them to recognize each piece of equipment and encourages them to learn more about its operation. Eventually this will qualify a person to check out and report on the efficiency of all new installations and to troubleshoot systems that are already in operation.
4. It provides information needed to develop workloads for a building. From these workloads, work schedules for the operating staff can be developed.
5. It teaches management to keep records about the structure, the equipment, and the maintenance activities in a building. This, in turn, helps plan the necessary programs, budget for the funds needed to carry out the programs, and thus manage successfully.
6. It provides historical data for the people who manage the building in the future.

2-3 Metric Conversion

Measurements of flow, volume, pressure, and motion may be shown in inches, feet, gallons, fahrenheit, or celsius. The following table will help you to convert to metric, which will eventually be the common measurement.

	Multiply	*By*	*To Obtain*
Length	Inches	25.4	Millimeters (mm)
	Inches	2.5	Centimeters (cm)
	Feet	0.305	Meters (m)
	Feet	30.5	Centimeters (cm)
	Yards	0.914	Meters (m)
	Miles	1.61	Kilometers (Km)
Energy	Btu	0.252	Kilogram-calories (Kcal)
	Btu	107.6	Kilogram-meters (Kcm)
	Tons (12,000 Btus)	3.024	Kilocalories/hour (Kcal/h)
Area	Square Inches	6.5	Square Centimeters (cm^2)
	Square Feet	0.092	Square Meters (m^2)
	Square Yards	0.836	Square Meters (m^2)
	Acres	0.405	Hectares (ha)
	Square Miles	2.59	Square Kilometers (Km^2)
Flow	Cubic Feet/Minute	1.7	Cubic Meters/hour (m^3/h)
	Cubic Feet/Minute	472.	Cubic Meters/second (cm^3/sec)
Volume	Gallons/minute	0.0631	Liters/second (l/s)
	Fluid Ounces	28.4	Milliliters (ml)
	Quarts (Canadian)	1.14	Liters (l)
	Gallons (Canadian)	4.55	Liters (l)
	Cubic Inches	16.4	Cubic Centimeters (cm^3)
	Cubic Feet	0.028	Cubic Meters (m^3)
	Cubic Yards	0.765	Cubic Meters (m^3)
Pressure	Pounds/square inch	0.0703	Kilogram/square millimeter (Kg/mm^2)
	Feet of Water	0.0304	Square Centimeter (Kg/cm^2)
Motion	Feet/minute	0.005	Meters/second (m/sec)
	Feet/minute	0.508	Centimeters/second (cm/sec)
	Feet/minute	1.6903	Kilometer/hour (Km/h)
	Temperature	$°F = \frac{9}{5}(°C + 32°)$	$°C = \frac{5}{9}(°F - 32°)$

2-4
Important Information About a Building

DISTRICT AMENITIES

MAJOR INTERSECTION ____________________

NEIGHBORHOOD SHOPPING ____________________

REGIONAL SHOPPING CENTER ____________________

PUBLIC TRANSPORTATION ____________________

HIGHWAY ACCESS ____________________

NURSERY SCHOOL ____________________

SEPARATE SCHOOL ____________________

PUBLIC SCHOOL ____________________

DISTRICT AMENITIES (Continued)

SR./JR. PUBLIC HIGH SCHOOL ______
HIGH SCHOOL/VOCATIONAL ______
COMMERCIAL SCHOOL ______
ANGLICAN/EPISCOPALIAN CHURCH ______
UNITED CHURCH ______
PRESBYTERIAN CHURCH ______
LUTHERAN CHURCH ______
ROMAN CATHOLIC ______
SYNAGOGUE ______
SUBWAY CONNECTION ______
HOSPITAL ______
PARK ______
THEATER/CINEMA ______
UNIVERSITY ______
ANY OTHER SPECIAL FEATURES ______

______

______

______

2-5
Exterior Elements*

AREA OF SITE: ACRES ______ SQ. FT. ______

CLADDING

TYPE ______ NAME OF CONTRACTOR ______

BALCONY PANELS

TYPE ______ NAME OF CONTRACTOR ______

WINDOWS (See window and door schedule on the drawings for detail.)

DOUBLE GLAZED: YES ______ NO ______

SASH TYPE ______ NAME OF CONTRACTOR ______

BALCONY DOORS

TYPE ______ NAME OF CONTRACTOR ______

ROOF (See as-built landscape plan for details.)

TYPE ______ AREA ______ NAME OF CONTRACTOR ______

*It is a good idea to take pictures of the building's exterior—typical window detail, entrances and exits, landscaping, parking.

GARBAGE REMOVAL

COMPACTOR ______ INCINERATOR ______ NAME OF CONTRACTOR ______

NO. OF BINS PICKED UP ______ HOW OFTEN ______

NO. OF BINS ______ COST ______ OWN ______ LEASE ______

FROM WHOM ______

LANDSCAPE AREA

AREA: ACRES ______ SQ. FT. ______

RECREATION FACILITIES ______

PARKING: AREA ______ NO. OF SPACES ______

GUEST PARKING: YES ______ NO ______ NO. OF SPACES ______

SWIMMING POOL: YES ______ NO ______ INSIDE ______ OUTSIDE ______

GALLONAGE ______ WHO SERVICES ______

TENNIS COURT: YES ______ NO ______

BLDG. NO. PROJECT NO.	BLDG. NAME
BLDG. ADDRESS	DATE COMPLETED

CONSULTANTS	NAME	ADDRESS & PHONE
ARCHITECT		
STRUCTURAL ENGINEER		
MECHANICAL ENGINEER		
ELECTRICAL ENGINEER		
LANDSCAPE ARCHITECT		
CONTRACTOR		
DEVELOPMENT OFFICER		
PROJECT MANAGER		
JOB CAPTAIN		
CONSTRUCTION FOREMAN		

FIGURE 2-1 Project consultants.

BLDG. NO.	PROJECT NO.	BLDG. NAME
BLDG. ADDRESS		DATE COMPLETED

DATE RECEIVED	TYPE OF RECORD	BY WHOM	WHERE KEPT
	AS BUILT ARCHITECTURAL DRAWINGS AND SPECIFICATIONS		
	ELECTRICAL/MECHANICAL DRAWINGS AND SPECIFICATIONS		
	MANUFACTURERS' EQUIPMENT MAINTENANCE AND INSTRUCTION MANUALS		
	INTERIOR AND EXTERIOR DESIGN AND COLOR SCHEDULE		
	INSIDE PARKING LAYOUT		
	AS-BUILT LANDSCAPE DRAWINGS		
	MICROFILM OF ALL PLANS		
	SERVICE AND OTHER CONTRACTS MADE DURING CONSTRUCTION		

FIGURE 2-2 Plans and other important records.

When a structure is built, the plumbing, drains, power cables, and gas lines are buried underground. Everyone plans to remember where they are located, but when faced with an emergency, everyone is left guessing at their location.

Searching for these services in later years can be avoided by charting their exact location initially. By strategically locating metal field markers or metal lines during construction, a metal detector (mine detector) will locate uncharted power or sprinkler lines.

All walks, parking lots, flower beds, contours, roof areas, swimming pools, and tennis courts should also be clearly marked. Listing all of these areas will help detail all maintenance and renovations, showing the areas and the cost.

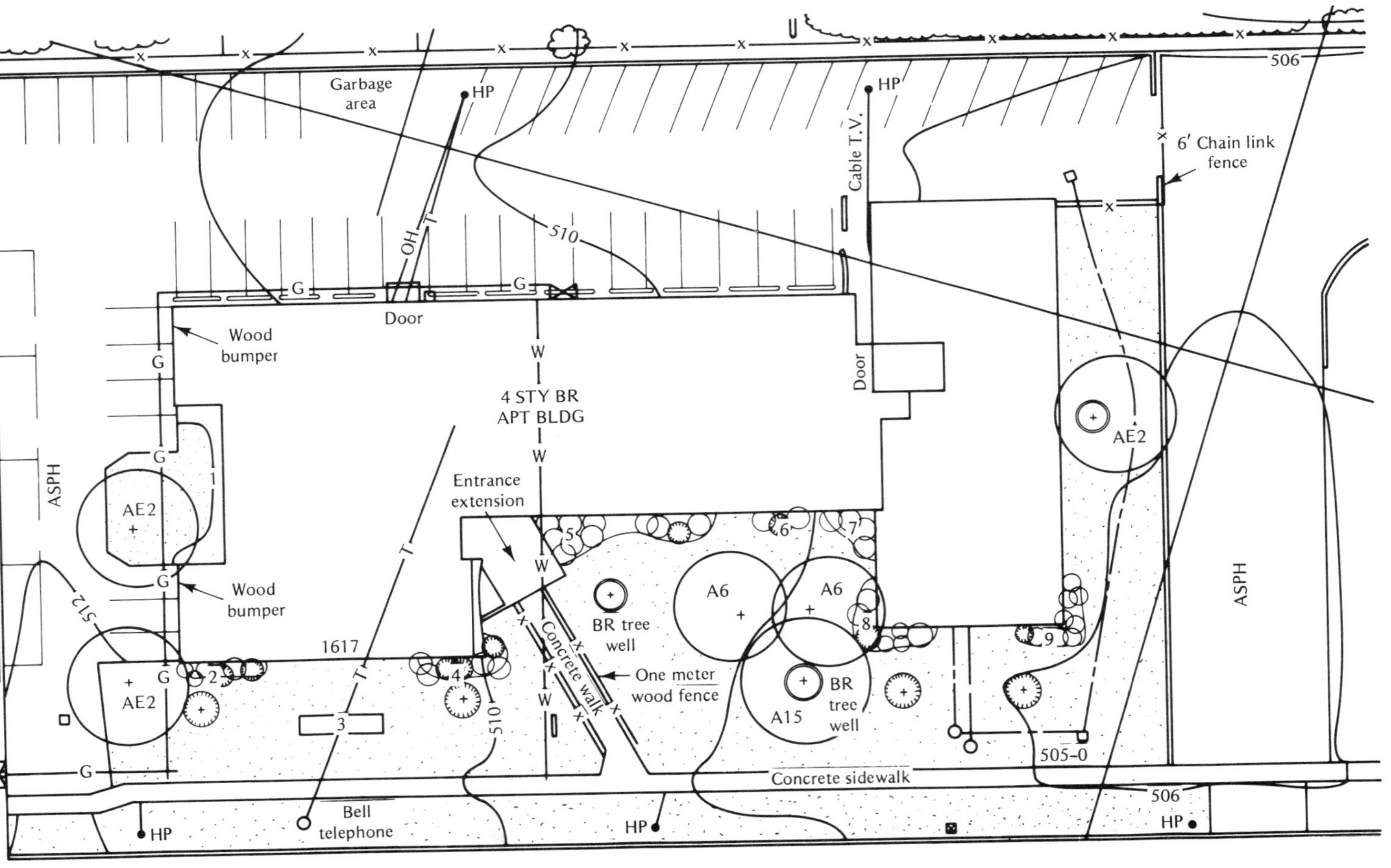

FIGURE 2-3 Typical landscape "as built" plan. (Courtesy of The Cadillac Fairview Corporation, Limited.)

Legend

Symbol	Description
——W——	Water main
	Water valves
	Sprinkler valves
——G——	Gas main
	Consumers gas shutoff valves
	Consumers gas emergency shutoff valves
——OH——	Hydro overhead cable
——H——	Hydro underground cable
——T——	Telephone underground cable
	Electric outlet
	Light standard
	Light standard and electric outlet
	Street light
	Spotlight
	Sanitary sewer
	Storm sewer
	Catch basin
	Manhole
	Hydrant
	Sign
	Sprinkler head
	Underground garage lock

Symbol	Description
486	Contours
	Property line (see plot plan)
——x——	Fences
	Line of basement below
	Sand
	Sodded areas
	Deciduous trees
	Evergreen trees
	Deciduous shrubs
	Evergreen shrubs
	Hedges
	Deciduous groundcover
	Evergreen groundcover

FIGURE 2-3 (Continued.)

2-6
Interior Elements*

FLOORS

NO. ______ HEIGHT OF BUILDING ______ AREA: ______

NO. OF FLIGHTS OF STAIRS ______ NO. OF STEPS IN EACH ______

(See room finish schedule and interior design drawings for details. Pictures of actual details are also wise.)

QUARRY TILE
LOCATION ______
AREA ______
INSTALLER ______

MARBLE
LOCATION ______
AREA ______
INSTALLER ______

TERRAZZO
LOCATION ______
AREA ______
INSTALLER ______

PARQUET
LOCATION ______
AREA ______
INSTALLER ______

CERAMIC
LOCATION ______
AREA ______
INSTALLER ______

VINYL
LOCATION ______
AREA ______
INSTALLER ______

CARPET
DESCRIPTION ______
LOCATION ______
SUPPLIER ______ DATE INSTALLED ______
AREA ______ HOW OFTEN VACUUMED ______
HOW OFTEN CLEANED ______

LOCKERS

NUMBER ______ LOCATION ______

MAIL DELIVERY

CENTRAL ______ EACH SUITE ______ OTHER ______
DESCRIBE ______

*As with the exterior elements, it is wise to take pictures of all the interior elements and include them with these records.

COMMERCIAL UNDERGROUND PARKING

NO. OF SPACES ________ NO. OF LEVELS ________

NO. OF GUEST SPACES ________ LOCATION ________

NO. OF SPACES LEASED TO OUTSIDERS ________

WALLS

HOW FINISHED ________

CORRIDOR PAPER—MFG. NO. ________

SIZE OF WALLS ________ HOW OFTEN WASHED ________

CEILINGS

HOW FINISHED ________

WHICH FLOORS HAVE DROP CEILINGS ________

NAME OF CONTRACTOR ________

DOORS

(See in-suite and service door schedules for details.)

NAMES OF SUPPLIERS

SUITE ENTRANCE ________

CLOSETS ________

BALCONY ________

BUILDING ENTRANCE ________

GARAGE DOORS ________

METAL CLAD DOORS ________

BLDG. NO.	BUILDING NAME
BLDG. ADDRESS	AREA

PARKING NO.	UNIT NO.	TENANT'S NAME	LICENSE NO.	MAKE OF CAR
1.				
2.				
3.				

FIGURE 2-4 Summary of parking allocations.

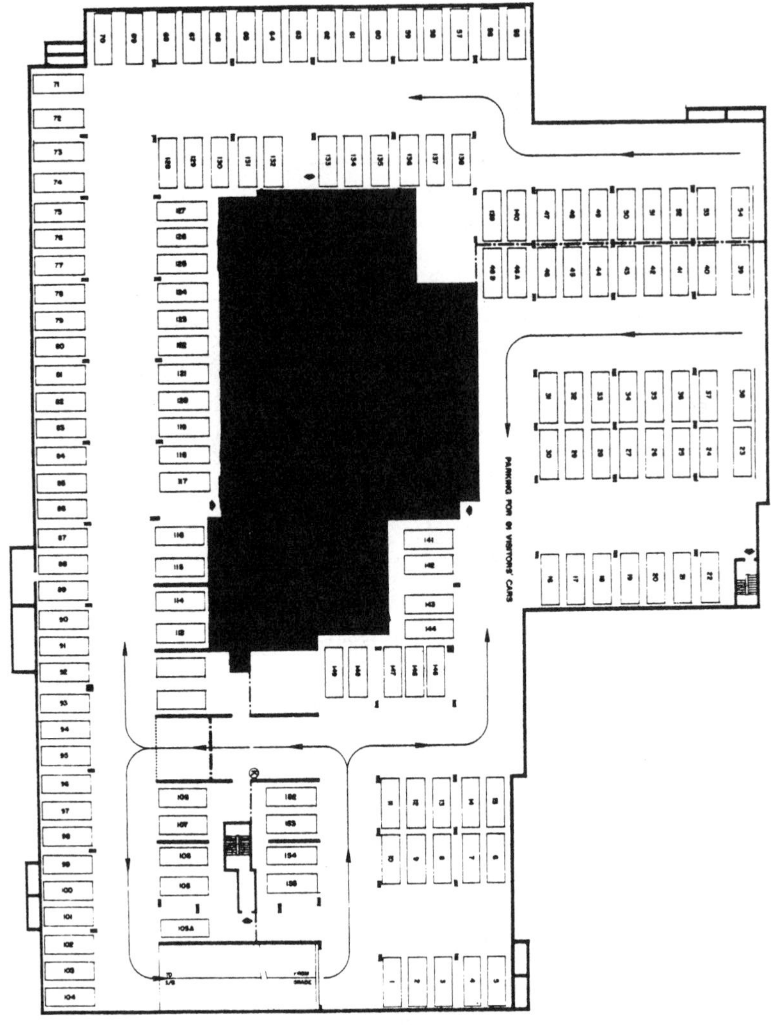

FIGURE 2-5 Typical underground parking plan showing direction of traffic. (Courtesy of The Cadillac Fairview Corporation, Limited.)

ROOM NAME	ROOM NO.	FLOORS FINISH	BASE	SQ.FT.	WALLS MATERIAL	FIN.	SQ.FT.	CEILING MAT.	FIN.	HT.	REMARKS
UNDERGROUND PARKING GARAGE	B1	CONC.			CONC.	P.T.		CONC.	P.T.		COLUMNS AND CEIL. PAINTED WHITE
AIR LOCK	B2	V.A.T.	R.		DRYWALL	P.T.		SOS			
HALL	B3	V.A.T.	R.		DRYWALL	W.P.		S.T.		8'0"	
ELEV.LOBBY	B4	CARPET	R.		DRYWALL	W.P.		S.T.		8'0"	
LAUNDRY	B5	C.T.	C.T.		C.T.			S.O.S.			
WASHROOM	B6	C.T.	C.T.		DRYWALL			S.D.	P.T.	7'6"	
GARBAGE	B7	SEALED CONC.			CONC. & C.B.						HOSE BIB
TRANSFORMER	B8	SEALED CONC.			CONC. & C.B.						
ELEV.MECHANICAL	B9	SEALED CONC.			CONC. & C.B.						
CORRIDOR	B10	SEALED CONC.			CONC. & C.B.						
JANITORS RM.	B11	SEALED CONC.			CONC. & C.B.						
MECHANICAL	B12	SEALED CONC.			CONC. & C.B.						
TELEPHONE	B13	CONC.			CONC. & C.B.						
ELECTRICAL	B14	SEALED CONC.			CONC. & C.B.						
EMERGENCY GENERATOR	B15	SEALED CONC.			CONC. & C.B.						
TRANSFORMER VAULT	B16	SEALED CONC.			CONC. & C.B.						
CHANGE ROOM	B17	V.A.T.			DRYWALL	P.T.					
JANITOR STORAGE	B18	SEALED CONC.			CONC. & C.B.	P.T.		CONC.	P.T.		

KEY TO ABBREVIATIONS

CONC. - Concrete
V.A.T. - Vinyl Asbestos Tile
Q.T. - Quarry Tile
P.T. - Paint

C.T. - Ceramic Tile
S.T. - Stiple Ceiling
R. - Rubber
S.O.S. - Sprayed on Stipple

FIGURE 2-6 **Basement room finish schedule.**

ROOM NAME	ROOM NO.	FLOORS FINISH	BASE	SQ.FT.	WALLS MATERIAL	FIN.	SQ.FT.	CEILING MAT.	FIN.	HT.	REMARKS
VESTIBULE	G1	Q.T.	Q.T.		DRYWALL			CONC.	S.C.S.	8'0"	To interior design drawings
LOBBY	G2	Q.T.	Q.T.		DRYWALL					8'0"	To interior design drawings
ELEV.LOBBY	G3	Q.T.	Q.T.		DRYWALL			CONC.	S.O.S.	8'0"	To interior design drawings
MAILROOM	G4	Q.T.	Q.T.		DRYWALL	P.T.		S.D.	S.O.S.	8'0"	
GARBAGE	G5	V.A.T.	R		DRYWALL	P.T.		CONC.	S.O.S.	8'0"	
STAIR NOS. 1,3,4,5,6,7	G6	V.A.T.	R		DRYWALL	P.T.		CONC.	S.O.S.	8'0"	
CORRIDOR	G7	CARPET	W.D.		DRYWALL	W.P.		CONC.	S.O.S.	8'0"	
STAIR NO.2	G8	V.A.T.	R		DRYWALL	W.P.		CONC.	S.O.S.	8'0"	
STORAGE	G9	V.A.T.	R		DRYWALL	P.T.					

(a)

ELEV.LOBBY	T1	CARPET	W.D.		DRYWALL	W.P.		CONC.	S.O.S.		
GARBAGE	T2	V.A.T.	R		DRYWALL	P.T.		CONC.	S.O.S.		
STAIR NOS. 1,3,4,5,6,7	T3	V.A.T.	R		DRYWALL	P.T.		CONC.	S.O.S.		
STAIR NO.2	T4	CARPET	R		DRYWALL	P.T.		CONC.	S.O.S.		
CORRIDOR	T5	CARPET	W.D.		DRYWALL	W.P.		CONC.	S.O.S.		
OFFICE	T6	CARPET	W.D.		DRYWALL	P.T.		CONC.	S.O.S.		
STORAGE	T7	V.A.T.	R		DRYWALL	P.T.		CONC.	P.T.		
STAIR	R1	CONC.	P.T.		CONC & CB	P.T.					
MECH.RM.	R2	SEALED CONC.			CONC & CB						

(b)

FIGURE 2-7 **(a) Ground floor finish schedule; (b) Typical floor and ceiling finish schedule.**

BLDG. NO.	BUILDING NAME
BUILDING ADDRESS	

LOCKS

MANUFACTURER
KEYWAY
GARAGE KEY NUMBER

CLOSERS

ENTRANCE & EXITS
STAFF & COMMON AREAS
GARBAGE ROOMS

HARDWARE (TYPE)

BATHROOM
BEDROOM
SUITE ENTRANCE
PATIO DOORS
HALLWAYS
LOCKER ROOMS
COMMON AREAS
SERVICE ENTRANCE
STAFF AREAS

COMMENTS

FIGURE 2-8 **The building hardware.**

2-7 Electrical Services

Understanding the equipment and knowing exactly how much electricity it consumes is very useful information. It could help minimize billing demand charges, help calculate savings when equipment is shut down, and help determine equipment maintenance workloads. Above all, information about the equipment and its operating costs could help "design for efficiency."

ELECTRICAL SERVICES INFORMATION

NAME OF CONTRACTOR ____________________
PRIMARY VOLTAGE ____________________

*APPLIANCES**

REFRIGERATOR
MAKE __________ SIZE __________ COLOR __________
MODEL __________ HANDING OF DOORS __________

STOVES
MAKE __________ SIZE __________ COLOR __________
MODEL __________

*(See inventory and parts lists for spare parts information.)

ELEVATORS MAKE __________ HOW MANY __________ TYPE __________
SERIAL NUMBERS __________
WHO HAS MAINTENANCE CONTRACT __________

TELEVISION CABLE __________ ANTENNA __________
CABLE CONTRACT WITH WHOM __________
CHANNELS AVAILABLE __________

INTERCOM MAKE __________ MODEL __________

2-8 The Fire Control System

ANNUNCIATOR PANEL MAKE __________

LIGHTS TYPE __________ FUSE SIZE __________
HOW IT FUNCTIONS __________

TROUBLE SIGNAL CHECK __________
REMOTE SIGNAL CHECK __________
CONTROL PANEL LOCATION __________

STANDBY BATTERIES HOW MANY __________ TYPE __________ SIZE __________

CHARGER MAKE __________ HYDROMETER ON SITE: YES __________ NO __________
HOW TO CHECK OPERATION __________

SPRINKLER HEADS RATING __________ WHERE SPARES KEPT __________

FUSIBLE LINK RATING __________ WHERE SPARES KEPT __________

PULL STATIONS SPRING TYPE __________ GLASS ROD SIZE __________
WHERE SPARE RODS KEPT __________

BELLS MAKE __________ VOLTAGE __________

HEAT SENSORS MAKE __________ RATING __________

SMOKE DETECTOR MAKE ______________ HOW POWERED: BATTERY _____ ELECTRIC _____

STANDBY GENERATOR MAKE ______________ FUEL ______________
HOW TO TEST OPERATION ______________

FIRE PUMP TAG NO. __________ MAKE __________ SERIAL NO. __________
RPM ______ HEAD ______ GPM ______ NORMAL PRESSURE ______
MOTOR
MAKE ________ HP ________ AMPS ________ VOLTS ________
FUSE LOCATION ____________ SHUT OFF ____________
FRAME SIZE ______________

BLDG. NO.	BUILDING NAME
BUILDING ADDRESS	

AREA	BULB TYPE	WATTAGE	TOTAL
BOILER ROOM			
COMMERCIAL			
COMPACTOR ROOM			
CORRIDORS			
ELECTRICAL ROOM			
ENTRANCES			
EXIT LIGHTS			
GARAGE PARKING			
GARBAGE ROOMS			
GUEST SUITES			
LANDSCAPING			
LAUNDRY ROOM			
LOBBY			
LOCKER ROOMS			
MAIL ROOM			
OUTSIDE PARKING			
PENTHOUSE ROOMS			
PUMP ROOM			
ROOF			
STAIRWELLS			
STORAGE			
	Incandescents	25	
	Incandescents	60	
	Incandescents	100	
	4' Fluorescents	40	
OTHER			
OTHER			
OTHER			

FIGURE 2-9 Lamp bulb inventory.

BLDG. NO.	BUILDING NAME
BUILDING ADDRESS	FLOOR NO.

LOCATION	EXT. TYPE	TAG NO.	SERIAL NUMBER	LAST SERVICED	DATE OF HYDROSTATIC TEST	HOSE SIZE	NOZZLE TYPE

*Indicates when hose or extinguisher was replaced.

S/A SODA ACID; C/D CARBON DIOXIDE; M/P MULTI-PURPOSE; P/W PRESSURED WATER; D/C DRY CHEMICAL; R/H REHUNG HOSE

FIGURE 2-10 The fire hose cabinet equipment record and maintenance inspection.

2-9 The Air Conditioning System

THE HEATING SYSTEM*

NAME OF INSTALLING CONTRACTOR __________
TYPE OF SYSTEM __________
LOCATION OF BOILER ROOM __________
DATE SYSTEM FLUSHED __________ BY WHOM __________
DATE HEAT ON __________ BY WHOM __________
FUEL: NATURAL GAS ______ OIL ______ ELECTRIC ______ COAL ______
DATE WATER TREATMENT ADDED __________ TYPE __________
BY WHOM __________ WHO IS TO TAKE SAMPLES __________
WHO TO TEST __________ FOLLOW UP __________
CONTRACTS: ELECTRONIC CONTROLS: WITH WHOM __________
TYPE OF CONTRACT __________
WHO NEGOTIATED __________ DATE __________
HOW OFTEN RENEWED __________
BURNER SERVICE: WITH WHOM __________
WHO NEGOTIATED __________ DATE __________
HOW OFTEN RENEWED __________

*(See burner, boiler, pump, and fan equipment lists for details about equipment records and tag numbers; see inventory and parts lists for information about spare parts.)

THE VENTILATION SYSTEM*

TYPE OF SYSTEM ____________________
CONTRACTOR ____________________
DATE STARTED ____________________ BY WHOM ____________________
DATE BALANCED ____________________ BY WHOM ____________________

* (See burner, boiler, pump, and fan equipment lists for details about equipment records and tag numbers; see inventory and parts lists for information about spare parts.)

THE COOLING SYSTEM*

NAME OF INSTALLING CONTRACTOR ____________________
DESCRIPTION OF SYSTEM ____________________
____
LOCATION OF EQUIPMENT ____________________
MAKE OF CHILLER ____________________
MAKE OF REFRIGERATION COMPRESSOR ____________________
WHO IS SERVICING THE CHILLER ____________________
MAKE OF COOLING TOWER ____________________
WHO IS SERVICING THE TOWER ____________________
IF CONTRACT, HOW OFTEN RENEWED ____________________
DATE WATER TREATMENT ADDED ____________________ TYPE ____________________
BY WHOM ____________________ WHO IS TO TAKE SAMPLES ____________________
WHO TO TEST ____________________ FOLLOW UP ____________________
DATE SYSTEM STARTED ____________________ BY WHOM ____________________
TYPE OF PACKAGED UNITS ____________________ MAKE ____________________
MAKE OF INCREMENTAL UNITS ____________________
MAKE OF FAN COIL UNITS ____________________

* (See pump and fan equipment records for details about records and tag numbers; see inventory and parts lists for information about filters and spare parts.)

HEATING AND COOLING SYSTEMS

The schematics illustrated (Figures 2-13 and 2-14) are examples of heating and cooling systems found in some buildings. Operating these systems efficiently requires knowledgeable, dedicated personnel. The components of these cooling systems must be added to the equipment lists so that proper maintenance programs can be established and so that the operators can communicate intelligently when ordering parts or service.

Figure 2-14 shows an air conditioning system where the units are installed around the outside wall of a building. These units are complete with casing, fans, water coil filter, and fan motor. In the back or bottom of the unit is an opening which connects to the outside through the wall. This opening is a supply for outside ventilating air.

BOILER №		1	2	3	4	5	6	7	8	9	10
PURPOSE											
MAKE											
DATE STARTED											
MODEL №											
SERIAL №											
WATER PRESSURE RATING											
OPERATING PRESSURE											
HORSE POWER RATING											
LOW WATER CUT-OFF	MAKE										
	MODEL №										
SAFETY VALVE	MAKE										
	MODEL №										
	SIZE										
	PRESSURE SETTING										
	TEMPERATURE RATING										

FIGURE 2-11 **Boiler data records.**

Burner No.		1	2	3	4	5	6	7	8	9	10
Make											
Date started											
Type	Forced draft / Btuh output										
	Atmospheric										
Fan motor	Make										
	H.P.										
	Frame number										
	Amps										
	Volts										
	Model and serial no.										
Burner Atomizor Compressor	Yes or No										
Fuel	Gas										
	Oil (type)										
Tank	Location										
	Size										

FIGURE 2-12 Burner data records.

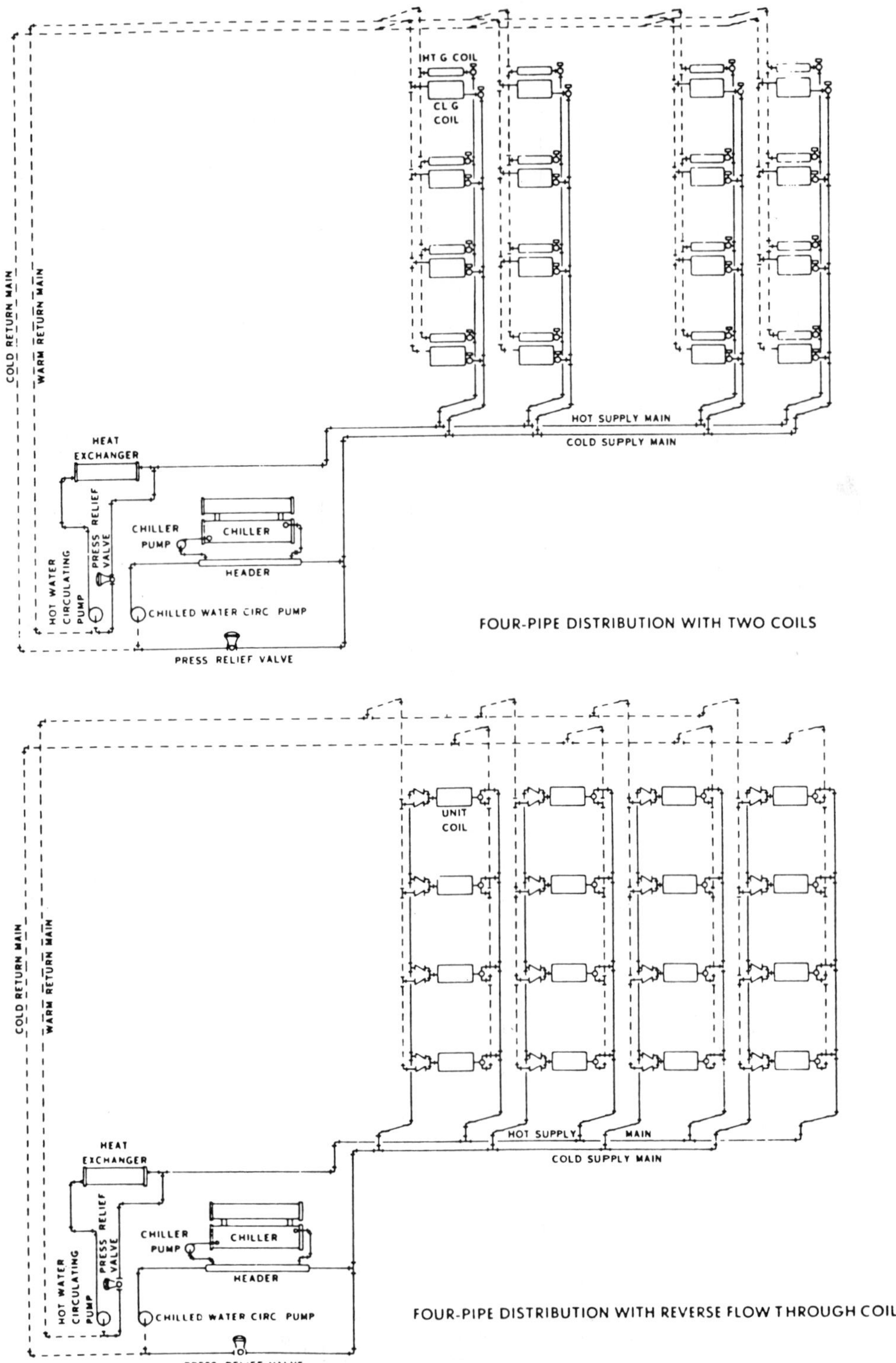

FIGURE 2-13 Examples of heating and cooling systems. (Courtesy of The Trane Company.)

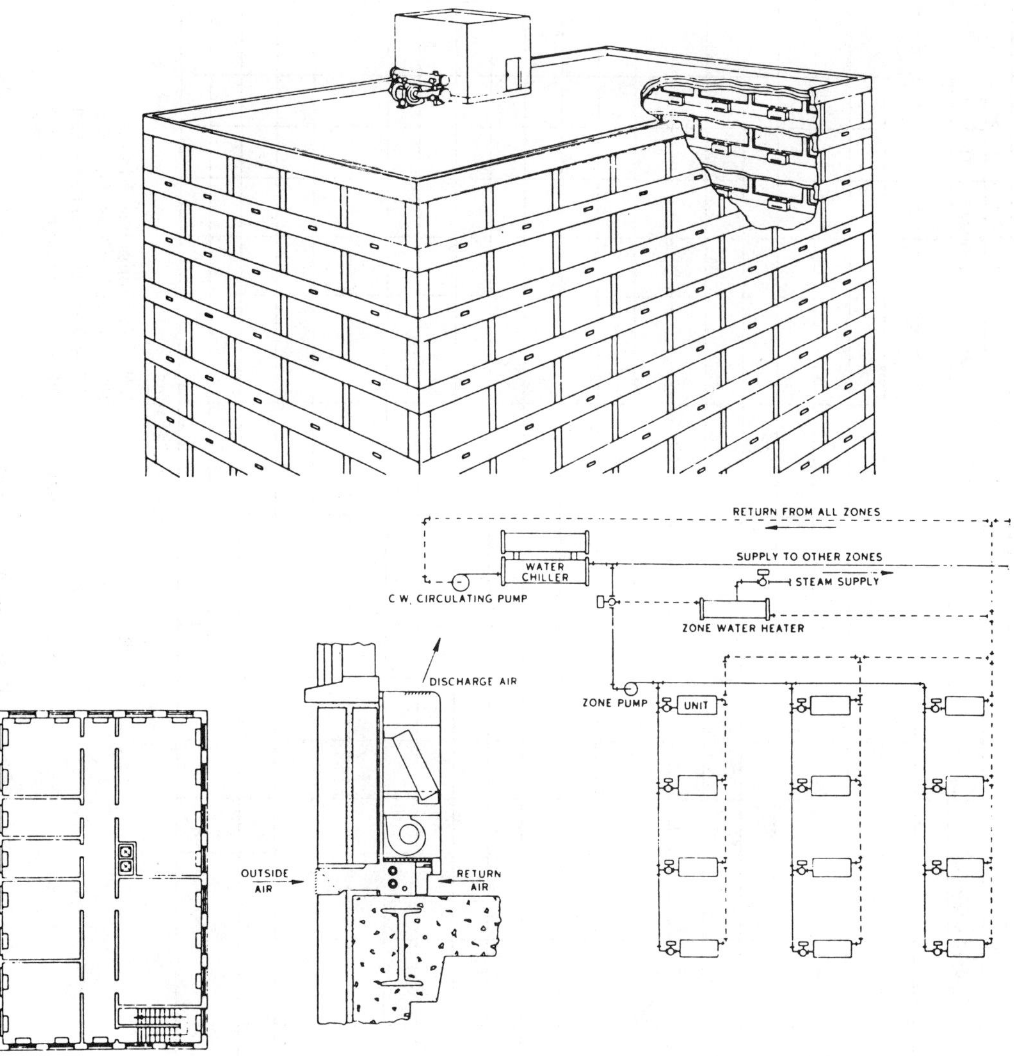

FIGURE 2-14 An air conditioning system with fan-coil-filter units. System with fan-coil-filter units in each conditioned space; water piping to each unit; refrigeration unit for supplying chilled water; chilled water circulating pump; water heater for each zone; circulating pump for circulating hot or cold water in each zone; and an outside air intake on each room unit with controls. (Courtesy of The Trane Company.)

PUMPS									STARTERS		MOTORS						
NUMBER	TYPE	MFG	SERIAL NUMBER	MODEL NUMBER	GPM	HEAD IN FT.	RPM	LUB	MFG	HEATER NUMBER	MFG	VOLTS	AMPS	TP	HP	FRAME SIZE	LUB

Pump Number Preceded By:

B = Booster
D = Dom. Hot Water
H = Heating
S = Sump

Abbreviations

LUB - Lubrication
O - Oil
G - Grease
SB - Sealed Bearing

GPM - Gallons Per Minute
RPM - Revolutions Per Minute
TP - Thermally Protected
HP - Horsepower

FIGURE 2-15 **Pump equipment records.**

FAN					STARTERS		MOTORS							BELTS AND SHEAVES			FILTERS	
NUMBER	MAKE	CFM	RPM	LUB	RELAY MFG.	HEATER NO.	MFG.	VOLTS	AMPS	TP	HP	FRAME SIZE	LUB	BELT SIZE	SHEAVE SIZE	ALIGN	TYPE	SIZE

Fan Number Preceded By:
E = Exhaust
S = Supply
K = Kitchen
B = Bathroom

Abbreviations

LUB - Lubrication
O - Oil
G - Grease
SB - Sealed Bearing
CFM - Cubic Feet Per Minute
RPM - Revolutions Per Minute
TP - Thermally Protected
HP - Horsepower

Notes:

1. Indicate "A" or "B" Before Belt Size
2. The Size of Both Sheaves Should be Stated
3. Make Any Comments On A Line Below The Appropriate Fan Number.

FIGURE 2-16 Fan equipment records.

There is another grilled opening in the front of the unit for drawing in return or room air. The coils in the units are supplied with chilled water from a refrigeration plant in the summer and with hot water from a hot water heater or heat exchanger in the winter.

TYPICAL SHUT-OFF VALVE CHART

Directional control valves are used to stop, start, check, and throttle the flow of fluids under pressure in pipes. In plumbing, heating, and cooling systems, the fluid is usually water, but piping could contain air, gases, vapors, solids in suspension, and other liquids. These are controlled by valves strategically located in the piping system.

Color Coding and Tagging Valves

All valves should be accessible, color tagged, and marked for easy identification by the operator during an emergency. Familiarity with the location of the valves, along with minimum maintenance, can save thousands of dollars in valve replacements.

What to Look for When Inspecting Valves

Valves that are usually left open should never be left completely open. The stem should be turned at least a half-turn shut so that corrosion will not seal it in the open position.

The major problem encountered with valves is leaking. A valve can leak internally by not shutting off completely. More obvious are external valve leaks at various connections, such as where the pipe joins the valve or flange, around the stuffing box, or where the body and bonnet connect.

Therefore, frequent and regular inspections are the best valve maintenance. When a leak is found it should be corrected immediately, because time will only make it worse.

Note: A closed valve should be opened slowly. Surge pressure or rapid temperature change can easily damage piping or equipment downstream of the valve (water hammer). When valves are closed they should be tagged until they are opened.

2–10 Plumbing and Drainage

NAME OF CONTRACTOR ____________

(See parts list for details—Figures 2-18, 2-19, 2-20.)
(See pump equipment list for equipment details—Figure 2-15.)
(See riser schematic for details of piping.)

GALVANIZED ____________ COPPER ____________
DRAIN CLEANING: HOW OFTEN ____________ COST ____________
CATCH BASIN CLEANING: HOW OFTEN ____________ COST ____________
DATE SYSTEM FLUSHED ____________ BY WHOM ____________
LAUNDRY MACHINES: NO. OF WASHERS ____________ NO. OF DRYERS ____________
TYPE OF SHOWER HEAD ____________
RUBBER STOPPER SIZE ____________ COLOR OF BATHROOM FIXTURES ____________
WATER CLOSET: MANUFACTURER ____________
TYPE OF FLUSH VALVE ____________

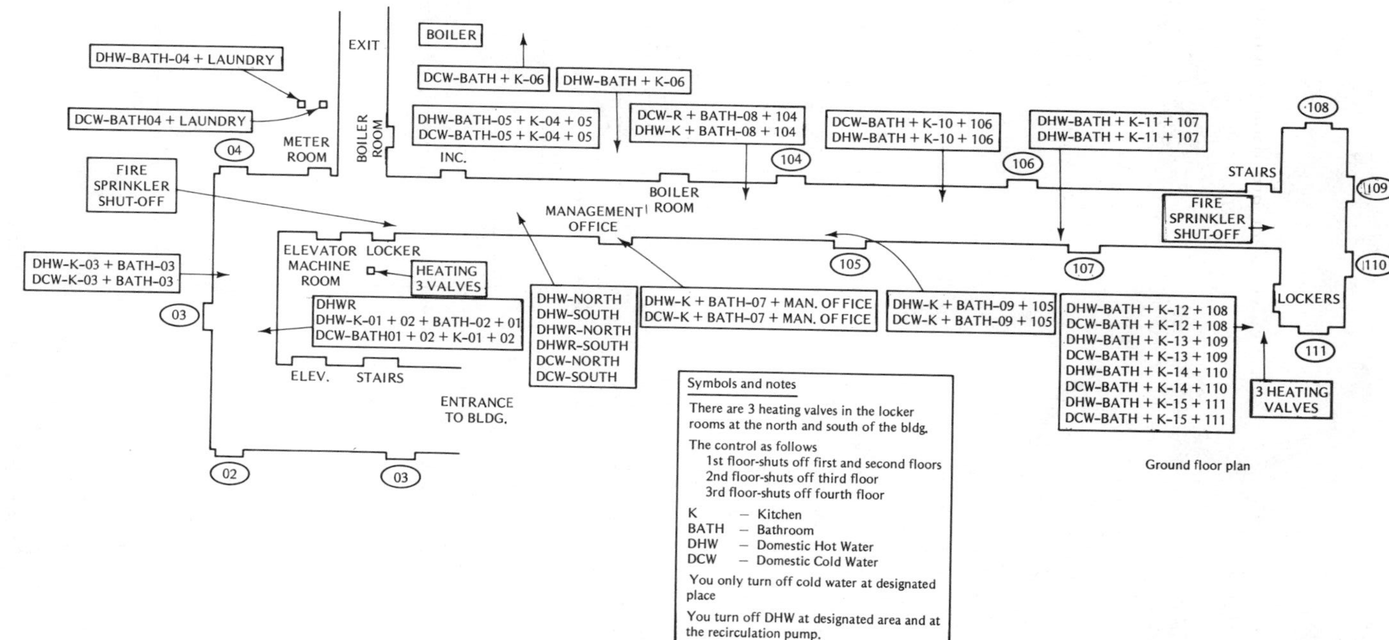

FIGURE 2-17 **Typical valve shut-off chart.** (Courtesy of The Cadillac Fairview Corporation, Limited.)

HANDLES

MANUFACTURER	MAX. INV.	KITCHEN MFG. NO.	BATHROOM BASIN MFG. NO.	BATHROOM TUB & SHOWER MFG. NO.
Hot	2			
Cold	2			
Screw	10			
INDEX BUTTONS				
Hot	2			
Cold	2			
Diverter	2			
CARTRIDGE				
Hot	2			
Cold	2			
Washer (Flat Bevelled)	50			
Washer Screw	10			
"O" Ring	50			
Washer (Fiber Plastic)	50			
Seat	10			
Deck Faucet Spout	1			
Aerator	2			
Hot & Cold Stem	2			
Diverter Stem	1			

FIGURE 2-18 Identifying the faucets.

MFG.	COLOR
DESCRIPTION	PART NUMBER
FLUSH VALVE	VALVE
	DISC
FLOAT	

BALLCOCK PARTS

FLOAT ROD ARM	
ADJUSTING SCREW	
ARM PIN	
PLUNGER	
BONNET	
BONNET SCREW	
DIAPHRAM	
SEAT	
REFILL WIRE	
REFILL TUBE	
BAFFLE PLATE	

BALLCOCK

BRASS	
REPAIR KIT	
PLASTIC	
REPAIR KIT	

HANDLES AND ARMS

BRASS	
PLASTIC	
URINAL VALVE	
TOILET SEAT	

FIGURE 2-19 Water closet tank fittings.

CAT. NO.	DESCRIPTION	MAX.INV.	ILLUSTRATION
90N	Olsonite	3	
	Sink Strainer Rep. Washer	3	
	Standard Type Stainless Steel Sink Strainer	3	
	Universal Type Stainless Steel Sink Strainer	3	
	Shower Curtain Hold Back Hook and Chain	3	
	Shower Curtain Pins (12 on a card-Blister Packed)	24	
	11" Beaded Chain	6	
	15" Beaded Chain	6	
	Rubber Stopper - (3 of each req'd. size)		
	"Aqua-Flo" Shower Head with Adjustable Spray Control	3	
	"Vari-Seal" Tank Ball	3	
	Polystyrene Toilet Tank Float	3	
	Upper & Lower Lift Wires - Brass	3	
	8" or 10" Float Rod - Brass	3	
	9" Refill Tube - Brass	3	
	3' Closet Tube Auger	1	

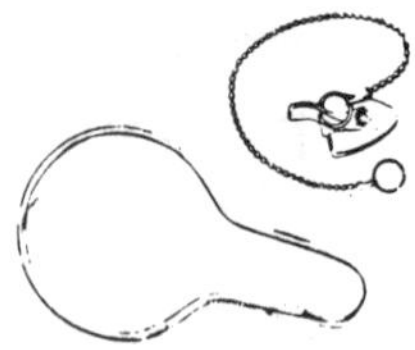

FIGURE 2-20 Accessories.

2–11 Tools, Equipment, and Inventory Control

Project management, or "getting the right things done right," involves the coordination of manpower, money, and materials.

One cannot visualize a successful building management program without controlling the purchase of tools, inventory, equipment, and the activities of the building operating staff. For this reason, typical inventory lists follow.

When we consider the value of the building, the cost of the operating inventory, and the cost of the staff salaries, we soon realize that we are spending a lot of money. To guarantee a fair return on this investment, the staff must be professionally trained, they must have the proper tools, spare parts, and materials, and management must conduct regular inspections and stock checks. Weaknesses should be identified and training initiated to overcome them.

Because modern buildings have various types of hard and soft floor coverings, and more sophisticated electrical/mechanical systems, they dictate that each building is competently staffed, and that they have the tools and equipment they need to carry out a successful maintenance program.

Intelligent decisions must be made about what to buy, how to use, operate, and maintain the equipment and tools, and what material and parts to stock.

USING A SUPPLIERS AND SERVICES MANUAL

To help coordinate and control all the maintenance and operations activities we recommend using a "services and suppliers" manual organized in the same manner as the repair and maintenance expense categories. The cost numbers used for each classification are then used as a reference number in the manual. Finding the information needed is easy if the numbers are kept simple.

Each page in the services and suppliers manual should have the following information:

- An explanation of who to call or where to find answers to problems related to a specific item (such as carpets, roofs, and refrigerators).
- The accounts payable vendor number, name, address, postal code, phone number, person to contact, terms of payment, and discounts allowed (Figure 2-21).
- Rates for services and trades.
- Specifications as developed by the company.
- Copies of any service contracts (filed in the appropriate section).
- Totals of all the inventory lists (filed under the appropriate cost code classification).

HOW IMPORTANT IS QUALITY?

Do not be tempted by cheap equipment, tools, supplies, or services. Look for the name of a reputable manufacturer and make sure that what you buy will do what you expect it to do. Do not rely on salesmen for your information. Develop specifications to identify exactly what you need and do not compromise when making your decisions.

THE EQUIPMENT LIST

Details about materials, specialized tools, plumbing parts, belts, and filters will

EXPENSE CLASSIFICATION AND COST CODE NUMBER			COST NO.
ISSUED BY	DATE ISSUED	DATE REVISED	
			PAGE OF

VENDOR'S NUMBER	VENDOR'S NAME & ADDRESS	SERVICES PROVIDED & CURRENT RATES	TERMS & DISCOUNT

FIGURE 2-21 Suppliers and services manual (a typical page).

A Typical Tool Kit

SAFETY GOGGLES
WORK GLOVES
PUTTY KNIFE
1″ AND 2″ PAINT BRUSH
CENTER PUNCH
AWL
ADJUSTABLE WRENCH (6″ AND 10″)
ALLEN WRENCH (5/64″ to ½″)
CHANNEL-LOCK PLIERS (12″)
LOCKING GRIP PLIERS (10″)
LONG-NOSE PLIERS
RETRACTABLE UTILITY KNIFE
OIL CAN—FLEXIBLE SPOUT (NOT A TRIGGER TYPE—TENDS TO OVER OIL)
WIRE BRUSH
STEEL TAPE RULER (12′ × ¾″)
WHETSTONE
TROUBLELIGHT
FLASHLIGHT
HEAVY DUTY EXTENSION CORD
VOLTAGE TESTER
RECEPTACLE CIRCUIT TESTER (LEXITON-75-49-E-Z CHECK)
FUSE PULLER
MEASURING CUP
CROSSCUT SAW (26″-8 POINT)
HACKSAW
GREASE GUN
FUNNEL
UNI DRIVER SCREWDRIVER SET
FLAT-TIPPED SCREWDRIVER (⅛″-3/16″-¼″-5/16″)
PHILLIPS SCREWDRIVER (#1 AND #2)
OUTSIZE SCREWDRIVER (FOR 12 AND 14 GAUGE SCREWS)
PLUNGER
PLUMBER'S AUGER
TAP SEAT WRENCH
TAP HANDLE PULLER
TUB AND SHOWER SOCKET SET
ALUMINUM LADDER (2′)
CURVED CLAW HAMMER (20 OUNCES)
FLAT FILE
HALF-ROUND FILE
ROUND FILE
TOOL BOX
FIRST AID KIT (SUITED TO THE PROBABLE NEED)

BLDG. NO.	BUILDING NAME
BUILDING ADDRESS	

*TAG NO.	DESCRIPTION	MODEL NO. & SIZE	SERIAL NO.	DATE WARRANTY EXPIRES	COST
	FLOOR MACHINE				
	VACUUMS				
	MOPPING UNIT				
	JANITOR CART				
	LADDERS				
	APPLIANCES				

FIGURE 2-22 The equipment list. * Tag numbers should be attached to each piece of equipment. Appliances should be classified by suite numbers on a separate listing for each appliance. If laundry rooms have washers and dryers, they should be tagged in sequence.

BLDG. NO.	ACCT. NO.	BUILDING NAME
BLDG. ADDRESS		EXPENSE CLASSIFICATION

DESCRIPTION	PART NO./SIZE	ON HAND	YRLY. USAGE	QTY REQ'D.	COST	TOTAL COST

FIGURE 2-23 A typical parts and inventory form.

be found in the chapters explaining the electrical/mechanical systems. It is important to establish the quantities of consumable items used annually. This information can be used to prepare budgets and to back up information entered on expense schedules.

Once this information is available on a building-by-building basis, the annual requirements can be estimated. These figures can be used to negotiate and to take advantage of bulk purchasing discounts. The building summaries indicate the quantities that will be drop shipped when needed at individual buildings.

CARING FOR TOOLS AND EQUIPMENT

There are several basic rules that apply to the care of tools and equipment.

1. Have a place to store each item and make sure it is in place when not being used.
2. Keep tools and equipment clean, lubricated, and rust-free. Allow enough time for cleaning up after a job.
3. Keep tools sharp.
4. Protect power cords from oil or solvent, and keep them coiled loosely for storage to prevent damage to the inner wires. Never carry a tool by its cord.

2-12 The Importance of Records and Statistics

It is not necessary to mention again the importance of cost control and its relationship to the successful management of a project. By establishing a format for gathering and organizing the statistics about a building, important information about a particular operational expense can be isolated. (Fig. 2-24.)

On a day-to-day basis, decisions are constantly being made that involve expenditures of money. In order to "do the right things right," specific major operations expenditures should be summarized:

- water treatment for plumbing, heating, and cooling systems
- roof repairs
- paving repairs
- overhead door repairs
- brickwork and other structural repairs
- supplies and parts inventory
- garbage chute repairs
- piping replacements for ramp heating
- boiler repairs
- fuel, water, and electrical energy consumption and costs
- drain cleaning costs
- pipe replacement charts and replacement costs
- pool maintenance costs
- vehicle maintenance costs
- service contracts

SUGGESTED MAJOR EXPENSE RECORD FORM

It is necessary to keep a summary for each of the items detailed above (for all buildings managed).

If you are managing a variety of buildings you should keep a separate list by building structure, electrical/mechanical systems, tenant use, and geographic areas. Be sure to keep "apple-to-apple" statistics, if the information is to be meaningful.

The information will become more and more useful as the buildings become older and especially when a new manager takes over a property.

These records and summaries will allow you to

1. Calculate your needs when you make bulk purchases, negotiate contracts, prepare annual budgets, or plan a new building.
2. Keep year-to-year repair and maintenance costs, plus lists of all renovation proposals (Figure 2-25), which detail specific expenditures of $________ or over. This information includes

EXPENSE CATEGORY________________________

DATE	BUILDING ADDRESS	DESCRIPTION	CONTRACTOR	COST

FIGURE 2-24 Suggested major expense record form. It would be necessary to keep a summary for each of the major expense categories listed previously. The summary would include all the buildings being managed.

- description of the problem;
- recommendations and specifications to correct the problem;
- quotes received and the recommended contractor to use;
- signatures of those approving the expenditure.

Having year-to-year expense summary comparisons allows you to measure your successes or failures. (Figures 1-12 through 1-15)

3. Prepare workloads and schedules for all building staff, and know what operations staff you require and their annual salaries.
4. Summarize the tools, equipment, and inventory on hand at the building and evaluate the annual cost to maintain and replace them.
5. Have reference records of the following:
   - a landscape plan showing all roof areas, outside parking, pools, fountains, and landscape details (Figure 2-3);
   - all underground piping, hydro, and telephone cable;
   - all utility shut-off valves;
   - all fire hydrants;
   - property lines and fences;
   - pumping equipment (Figure 2-15) for plumbing, heating, and air conditioning; pump records include tag number, type, manufacturer, serial number, model number, GPM pumped, head in feet, revolutions per minute, type of lubrication required, switch and starter manufacturer, and fuse or heater;
   - motor records, including manufacturer, volts, amps, thermal protection, horsepower, frame size, and type of lubrication (Figure 2-15);
   - electrical system, fire control equipment, intercom, television, elevators, garbage compactor, and other electrically-operated equipment;
   - burner data (Figure 2-12);
   - boiler data (Figure 2-11);
   - building hardware parts list showing manufacturers' numbers (Figure 2-8);
   - air handling equipment (Figure 2-16);
   - renewal statistics including month-by-month listing of expirees, move-ins,

1. For any individual expenditure of over $______,
   other than an on-going maintenance expense.
2. For any capitalized expense.

BLDG. NAME	BLDG. ADD.		
RECOMMENDED BY:	OP'L.BLDG.NO.	CODE NO.	R.P.NO.
DATE:			
BUDGET YEAR	BUDGETED $______	NOT BUDGETED___	

REASON FOR THE PROPOSAL AND PROBLEM TO BE CORRECTED

DESCRIPTION OF WORK TO BE DONE
(ATTACH ALL QUOTATIONS AND SPECIFICATIONS)

NAMES OF CONTRACTORS AND/OR SUPPLIERS RECOMMENDED	RECORDS OF EST. & ACTUAL COST		
	ESTIMATE	INV. DATE	COST
1.			
2.			
3.			
4.			

COMMENTS

AUTHORIZATION TO PROCEED

APPROVED BY	DATE

Prepare in duplicate and present all copies for approval

1st copy - Accounting 2nd copy - Originator

FIGURE 2-25 Renovation proposal form.

move-outs, suites to paint and clean, and floors to sand;

plumbing hardware parts lists (Figure 2-18 to 2-20) showing manufacturers' stock numbers.

6. Calculate the Btu requirements for each building so the energy management goal of 24°C inside temperature can be achieved. Consumption records should confirm the achievement of these goals or alert you to any problems (see Chapter 12—Energy Management).

SUGGESTED CONTENTS OF A BUILDING PROFILE

1. *General*

Purpose of a Building Profile

Building Takeover Procedure

Summary of the Building's Contract Services

Preventive Maintenance "Master Action Plan"

Typical Major Expense Record Summary Form

Typical Services and Suppliers Manual Page (Figure 2-26)

Summary of Typical Repair and Maintenance Account Classifications

District Amenities

Plan Locations

Color Code Chart

Summary of the Tools Issued to the Building Staff

2. *Energy*

Thermal Characteristics of the Building

Building's Energy Analysis

Heat Loss Values
- Roof Component's "R" Values
- Wall Component's "R" Values
- Window "U" Values

Utility Consumption Records
- Annual kWh per Square Foot Electrical Consumption Records
- Annual Water Consumption Records in Gallons
- Annual Heating Per Degree Day Fuel Consumption
- Annual Fuel Consumption

3. *Budget and Actual Expense Summaries*

Renovation Proposal Summaries

Summary of Repair and Maintenance Accounts (Figures 1-4 through 1-8)

Summary of Staff Salaries for the Building (Figure 1-11)

4. *Housekeeping*

Annual Housekeeping Expenses (Figure 1-5)

Housekeeping Equipment List (Figure 2-22)

Housekeeping Parts and Inventory List (Figure 2-23)

Room Finish Schedules (Figures 2-6 and 2-7)

Copy of Housekeeping Contracts

Copy of Building Staff Housekeeping Workloads and Schedule of Duties

Copies of All Renovation Proposals (Figure 2-25)

5. *Groundskeeping*

Annual Groundskeeping Expenses (Figure 1-5)

Groundskeeping Equipment List (Figure 2-22)

Groundskeeping Parts and Inventory List (Figure 2-23)

Annual Flower Planting List

Annual Trees and Shrubs List

Annual Chemicals and Fertilizer List

Copy of As-Built Landscape Plot Plan (Figure 2-3)

Summary of Outside Parking (Figure 2-4)

Summary of Inside Parking (Figure 2-5)

Copies of Any Groundskeeping Contracts

Copy of Groundskeeping Workloads and Schedules of Duties

6. *Structure*

Annual Structural Expense Summaries (Figure 1-6)

Building Hardware List (Figure 2-8)

Other Parts and Inventory List

Details of the Exterior Elements

Details of the Interior Elements

Plan of the Roof Area (Figure 2-3)

Plan of the Sidewalk and Outside Parking Area (Figure 2-3)

Copies of All Completed Renovation Proposals (Figure 2-25)

Summaries of All Major Expenditures (Figure 2-24)

7. *Electrical Services*

Annual Electrical Expense Summaries (Figure 1-7)

Lamp Bulb Inventory List (Figure 2-9)

Other Parts and Inventory List

Information About the Building's Electrical Services

Typical Unit's Electrical Circuit Layouts

Copies of All Completed Renovation Proposals (Figure 2-25)

Summaries of All Major Expenditures (Figure 2-24)

Information About the Elevators

Copies of All Service Contracts

8. *Fire Protection*

Annual Fire Protection Expense Summary (Figure 3-31)

Information About the Building's Fire Protection System

Equipment Records

Fire Hose Cabinet Records (Figure 2-10)

Parts and Inventory Records

Copies of All Service Contracts

Copies of All Completed Renovation Proposals (Figure 2-25)

9. *Plumbing and Drainage*

Annual Plumbing and Drainage Expense Summaries (Figure 7-41)

Information About the Plumbing and Drainage System

Pump Equipment Records (Figure 2-15)

Valve Shut-Off Chart (Figure 2-17)

Faucet Parts Record (Figure 2-18)

Water Closet Parts Record (Figure 2-19)

Other Parts and Inventory List (Figure 2-20)

Summary of Major Expenses (Figure 2-24)

Copies of All Completed Renovation Proposals (Figure 2-25)

Copies of Service Contracts

COMPANY NAME	TYPE OF CONTRACT	ACCT. NO.	COST
	AIR CONDITIONING	511 TO 514	
	BURNER SERVICE	314 - 532	
	CABLE TELEVISION	501	
	COMPACTOR SERVICE	313	
	ELEVATOR SERVICE	525	
	GARBAGE BIN RENTAL	311	
	GARBAGE BIN SERVICE	311	
	PEST CONTROL SERVICE	291-292	

SERVICE COMPANY	PRODUCTS OR SERVICES	ACCOUNT NUMBER
	APARTMENT CLEANING	271
	CARPET CEANING	251
	CLEANING SUPPLIES	261-262-263
	PAVING	431 TO 434
	COUNTER TOP REPAIRS	391
	FILTERS	516-535-563
	FIRE ALARM SYSTEMS	491 TO 497
	GARAGE CLEANING	272
	LIGHT BULBS	483
	PAINTER - INTERIOR	283
	PAINTER - EXTERIOR	411 TO 415
	PLASTERER	451 - 452
	PLUMBER	541 TO 547
	ROOFER	441 TO 444
	WALL WASHING	284
	WINDOW REPAIRS	461 - 462- 463
	FLOOR SANDING	422
	CLEANING CONTRACTOR	271
	SNOW REMOVAL	341

FIGURE 2-26 Summary of contracts, services and suppliers.

10. Heating, Cooling, and Ventilation Systems

Annual Expense Summaries for Each System

Information About Each of the Systems

Boiler Equipment Records (Figure 2-11)

Burner Equipment Records (Figure 2-12)

Pump Equipment Records (Figure 2-15)

Fan Equipment Records (Figure 2-16)

Valve Shut-Off Charts (Figure 2-17)

Parts and Inventory Lists

Summary of Major Expenses (Figure 2-24)

Copies of All Completed Renovation Proposals (Figure 2-25)

Copies of Service Contracts

2-13 Summing Up

To be knowledgeable, efficient, and professional, building managers and operators must have available adequate statistical data upon which to base their decisions. These facts will allow the manager/operator to

1. Market the product
2. Administer the operations
3. Operate efficiently
4. Plan and budget accurately
5. Save research time
6. Make decisions
7. Measure your efficiency
8. Achieve goals

They will also be able to

- manage the buildings more effectively
- research and recommend improvements
- make accurate long- and short-term plans
- make more efficient use of building and resource manpower
- research products, equipment, suppliers, and trades
- deal with an emergency
- control the purchase of equipment, tools, supplies, parts, and material inventory
- monitor all major expenditures
- plan new projects
- take over a building

Chapter 3

SECURITY, SAFETY, AND FIRE PROTECTION

3–1 Introduction

The safety and security of the occupants and operating staff of a building must be included when considering the responsibilities of real estate management. Reports of serious fires, bombings, hostage situations, crime, and structural failure only emphasize the awesome responsibility we undertake when we design, build, and operate a building.

When planning new projects or managing existing buildings, our actions should discourage crime, minimize loss or damage during a crisis, and institute measures that result in safe practices for the building's operating staff and occupants.

To safeguard against loss of life and property due to a fire, the National Building Code outlines a building's minimum fire safety regulations. These standards cover design and construction, materials used, electrical/mechanical systems, alarms, firefighting equipment, fire exits, and other equipment that affects the safety of the occupants.

Even though all possible safety features may be incorporated in the construction of a building to protect the occupants against fire hazards, the building is not safe unless the building's operating staff is trained to accept full responsibility for the maintenance of safe conditions and to enforce regulations established by management.

3–2 Security

The dictionary defines security as "The state or feeling of being free from fear, care, danger, etc.; safety or a sense of safety." Security has always been a major concern for building owners and managers, and the increase in incidents of theft, arson, hostage-taking, and bombing, make it more difficult to maintain every day.

Proper planning during the design and construction of a building will assure that a building will have a security system that will satisfy the needs of the occupants. When planning a new building, consideration should be given to the following:

—Location of the building

—The type of tenants

—The interior layout

—The entrances and exits

—The elevators

—The potential for theft, vandalism, bombings, and other problems

When choosing a security system, the following should be analyzed and considered:

—Degree of security required

—Areas requiring protection

—Type of communication system needed

—Budget limitations

—Training of operating personnel

Police are continually amazed to find that many apartment owners pay for high-security locks and, at the same time, issue master keys to anyone and everyone. These keys are often found lying in easily accessible desk drawers in leasing and sales offices.

CONTROLLING THE KEYS

Professional key making could be traced from the early iron monger to the present space age technician. The iron monger originated the early locks and what are now called bit keys. Yale introduced a pin tumbler key, which was copied from an idea used by the Egyptians for locking the gates around their cities.

As with every other profession, so-called "handymen" appear with an ability to do simple repairs connected with a craft, but who never master the technical aspect necessary to perform quality work. The pin tumbler key is accurately designed and yet the handyman key cutter can abuse these accuracies with a cheap key duplicating machine and blanks.

When these inaccurate keys are used, they cause undue wear to the pins and cylinder. Eventually further duplication of the key is impossible, and the cylinder must be replaced. Today, we have the means to measure and originate a key by simply knowing its dimensions—including spacing of the center of root depths.

KEY-CUTTING CODE MACHINE

The modern key-cutting code machine does not have any stops and gauges applied to it before making a key. It requires the printed information about the spacing of the cuts and their root depths to be supplied by the manufacturer. (See the Dominion Lock sample in Figure 3-1.) This information, along with the Bitting List (Figure 3-2), allows a locksmith to originate any key with an accuracy of less than .002, using the key-cutting code machine.

THE BITTING LIST

A bitting list is a detailed listing of a building's master key system showing the root depth of cut for each key. When keying a building, the manufacturer prepares a bitting list showing a series of bitting numbers and their root depths. A typical bitting list would be similar to the list illustrated in Figure 3-2.

HOW THE SYSTEM WORKS

1. The cylinder numbers shown on the list (Figure 3-2) are stamped on each cylinder.
2. For security reasons, the numbered cylinders are not installed in numerical sequence in a building.
3. Each building is supplied with a master key. The use of a grand master key, which would allow a person to open all the locks in several buildings, is *not* recommended. During construction of a new building it may be necessary to make several master keys. These keys should be numbered and signed for when issued. After the structure is built these master keys must be returned and destroyed. *Master keys for building operating staff must be kept to a minimum.*
4. When ordering the hardware for a new building, six extra cylinders with keys should be ordered. These are substituted when a problem develops, or when a tenant vacates.
5. New tenants should sign for their keys on the incoming inspection form.
6. Extra keys would be kept in a suitable key case. These would only be keys for vacant units and would be tagged with the unit number.
7. When issuing a work or purchase order for repairs to a faulty cylinder, or to replace lost keys, the cylinder number and the name of the manufacturer should be shown on the work or purchase order. The

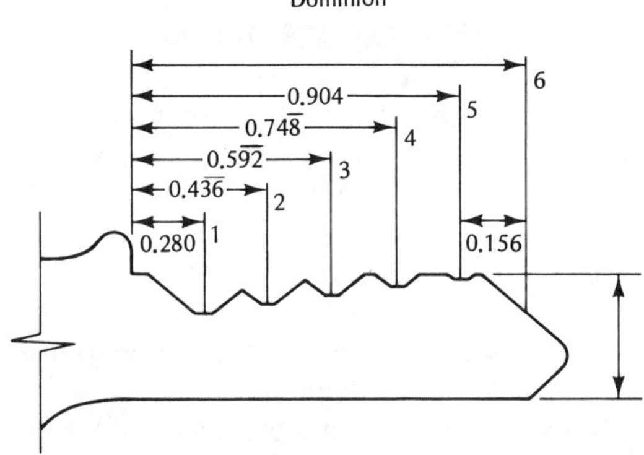

Bitting numbers	Root depth	Bitting drop
0	.325	0.015
1	.310	
2	.295	use
3	.280	cutter
4	.265	number
5	.250	JMC-2
6	.235	
7	.220	
8		
9		
0		

FIGURE 3-1 Spacing of the cuts and root depths. (Courtesy of Jensen Lockcraft, Inc.)

CYLINDER NO.	COLUMN 1	CYLINDER NO.	COLUMN 2	CYLINDER NO.	COLUMN 3
1	10400	5	10420	9	10440
2	10404	6	10424	10	10444
3	10406	7	10426	11	10446
4	10408	8	10428	12	10448

FIGURE 3-2 The bitting list. A bitting list could be defined as a detailed listing of a building's master key system showing the root depth of cut for each key.

person with the bitting list would then set the key-cutting machine using the appropriate code numbers. Let us say that the cylinder was code number 7 and that the manufacturer was Dominion Lock. The bitting list shows the code for number 7 as 10426 (Figure 3-2). The cutting machine would be set as follows (Figure 3-1): .310 for number 1; .325 for zero; .265 for number 4; .295 for number 2; and .235 for number 6. The machine would then cut an exact duplicate key for cylinder number 7. Without this system you may inadvertently duplicate another key or even the master key.

SECURITY AND THE BUILDING HARDWARE

Planning for the security of a building starts with the decision about the type and quality of the building hardware.

According to statistics provided by the International Association of Chiefs of Police, more than 50 percent of residential burglars gain entrance by forcing inadequate or unlocked front or rear door locks. The Association recommends that doors be equipped with dead bolt or interlocking-type locks. Both are invisible from the outside and are locked by turning a thumb turn on the inside.

Door frames should be tight and their hinges should be hidden. If the door has a window, a double cylinder lock that requires a key to lock from either the inside or the outside is recommended. Statistics show that 25 percent of all intruders gain entrance by breaking the glass, and reaching inside to release the thumb turn on the door lock. The double lock will overcome this problem.

It should be stressed that with this type of lock, there must always be a key handy so that the doors can be unlocked in case of a fire. The doors can only be locked (or unlocked) from either inside or outside by using a key.

COMMON SERVICE AREAS

It is recommended that common service areas be keyed with a different keyway and not included in the master key system. This will eliminate the problem of people inadvertently using their unit keys in the common areas.

It is not uncommon for someone to insert the wrong key and find that the door will not unlock. Many keys are broken off in the keyway when they try to force the lock to open. Restricting the keyway to the service keys also eases the wear on the tumblers, thus reducing the number of service calls.

CONCLUSIONS

Without a system of key-cutting, key, and hardware control, the cost of maintenance and replacement will increase considerably. Use of several different locksmiths could result in the unnecessary replacement of cylinders. If these replacement cylinders are made with cylinders manufactured by a different company, or the codes are ignored, it may eventually lead to a re-keying of the building. To minimize expenses, and to maintain security and control, a quality system must be purchased originally and properly maintained throughout a building's life cycle.

OTHER SECURITY SYSTEMS

It may be necessary to use a pass system when tight security is necessary. Some operations require badges to be worn at all times. Passes may have laminated photos, magnetically-encoded information on them, or they may be used as an insertion device to open doors, control elevators, etc. Keeping the exterior properly illuminated and using a television camera and monitor are methods commonly used to improve security in many buildings.

Security Service

Many companies specialize in the installation of detection devices that are triggered in various ways. These signals can be used to

1. Alert police to investigate and call the owner.
2. Alert the security company who would alert the police and call the owner.
3. Alert the owner.
4. Trigger an audible alarm or light up the area, and frighten the intruder.

Guards and Doormen

Many buildings use security guards or doormen to provide security at the entrance and to patrol the building and the grounds. Unfortunately, these are often low paying jobs and they attract a less than qualified person.

Electronic Equipment

There are many electronic devices that can be purchased or leased. The level of security needed would determine which system—sound, movement, broken circuit, visual, or light beam activated—should be acquired.

Management today has many options available to assure that a building is adequately secured. Probably a combination of several methods will do the job and keep the costs reasonable.

3-3 Safety

LIFTING AND CARRYING

Lifting depends to a great extent on the skillful use of the right muscles, and not on sheer strength. The experienced person crouches as close to the load as possible with the legs bent at about a 90 degree angle at the knees; the back should be as straight as possible. To lift the object, the legs should be straightened, at the same time swinging the back to a vertical position.

The National Safety Council suggests that men should life no more than 75 pounds or half their own weight, whichever is less. Women should lift no more than 35 pounds or one-third of their own weight.

Several other pointers are worthy of note.

1. Grip with the whole palm of the hand.
2. Lift by easy stages.
3. Keep the feet 8 to 12 inches apart for balance.
4. Do not twist the body while lifting or carrying.
5. Carry with arms close to the sides and fully extended.
6. Lower the load by bending the legs with back and arms straight.

SAFETY RULES FOR WINDOW CLEANERS

Authorities in accident prevention recommend that no one under eighteen or over fifty years of age be permitted to do window cleaning at heights.

No outside window work of any kind should be done when weather conditions—snow, ice, high winds—are likely to constitute a hazard. Smoking should not be allowed. Acid solutions should never be used, because they may be hazardous to the individual, his clothing, and to surrounding building materials. Proper ladders or scaffolds are essential, and the use of stacked boxes or other unstable supports should be discouraged.

While any action that might break the glass should be avoided, in the event of breakage all broken pieces on ledges and the area below the window should be immediately and carefully collected and packaged for the garbage. This applies particularly to splinters of glass that may be hidden in grass or dirt.

SAFETY RULES FOR GARBAGE COMPACTORS

1. Keep access door closed when compactor is in operation and locked when not in use.
2. Report any hazard or malfunction of the compactor to the immediate supervisor as soon as noted.
3. Do not bypass any electrical switches or safety limit switches.
4. Lock all compactor equipment panels and operating controls when not in use.
5. Keep arms and body clear of all moving parts of the compactor.
6. Call for help at first sign of any smoke or fire.

HOW TO USE A LADDER SAFELY

Every employee should be familiar with the basic guidelines for the safe use of ladders. They should not be used for any other purpose than that for which they were designed.

1. Examine all ladders before they are used. Ladders requiring repairs should be tagged and marked: *"Dangerous—Do Not Use."*
2. Use only ladders equipped with safety feet or sharp spurs. Where the ladders appear insecure, lash the top to a fixed support. This is particularly advisable with long ladders or where there is a

possibility of the ladder slipping, shifting position, or being bumped. When necessary, secure the ladder to the building.

3. Set the ladder on a secure footing. Put a board under the spikes if it is being used on a metal floor plate, cement floor, or other smooth surface. Keep all tools, equipment, or other debris away from the base of the ladder. Ladders should not be placed on boxes, barrels, or other unstable bases.
4. Place the base of the ladder one-fourth of its length from the wall to obtain a safe working angle. There should be at least 6 clear inches behind each rung.
5. Open a step ladder fully before mounting. Make sure that all movable parts operate freely. It should extend 3 feet above the upper level of a wall or landing. Never use a ladder in a space used as a hoistway.
6. Face the ladder squarely when going up or down. Sliding down ladders is dangerous.
7. Keep both hands free for climbing up and down ladders and keep hands away from electrical wires or other sources of power, especially when using aluminum ladders. Small articles should be carried in the pockets or on a belt. Larger articles may be lifted or lowered from elevated positions by a hand line.
8. Lock or bolt the door when it is necessary to place a ladder over a doorway.
9. Barricade the area, or position someone in front of the ladder when it must be placed in an aisle or in a location where it could be struck by a person or other object.
10. Fasten a board across the top of the ladder, secured by screws, when it is to be placed against a window sash. The board should be of such length to span the opening and rest on each side of the window frame.
11. Securely lash or fasten ladders when they are to be used on a roof.
12. Keep ladders clean and free from dirt or paint which may conceal defects. All surfaces of rails and rungs should be kept free of grease, oil, or other materials which could contribute to a hazardous condition.

VENTILATION AND AIR CONDITIONING DUCTS

Periodic cleaning of air duct systems and attention to repair operations are very important. Failure to observe these points has caused many fires in air conditioning systems.

Inspections to determine the amount of dust and waste materials in both discharge and return ducts should be made at least twice each year or until the appropriate frequency of inspections is determined for each installation. Cleaning should be done as soon as an inspection indicates that it is necessary.

At the same time, cooling and heating coils should be cleaned, if required. This may mean scraping, brushing, or using other mechanical means to loosen any material missed by a vacuum cleaner.

Along with duct inspection, the outside fresh air screens should be examined. Check for accumulations of combustible material near the intake and conditions in surrounding buildings that might allow smoke or fire to be drawn into the ducts. Check the operation of any safety dampers designed to protect openings against exposure to fire. When combustible materials are removed, arrangements should be made to prevent their accumulation in the future.

Filters should be kept free of excess dust and combustible material. It is good practice to renew or clean filters when resistance to air flow has risen to five times its original resistance or when it has reached 0.5 inch water gauge, whichever is greater. In many installations a warning light or buzzer alerts personnel to change filters.

Disposable filters must not be cleaned and reused. Care must be taken when using liquid adhesives in liquid adhesive-type filter reservoirs. An adhesive with a low flash point would be considered a serious hazard.

Fire doors and fire dampers should be checked once a year to make sure that hinges and other moving parts are in good operating condition. When making repairs inside ducts or plenum chambers, or near air intakes, care should be taken in the use of welding and grinding devices. Sparks result in many fires.

FAN SAFETY

Fans are air-moving devices manufactured in a wide range of sizes and types. They become a potential danger to life or property when improperly used or installed. Installation should always be performed by experienced and trained personnel, and electrical connections must be made by qualified electricians.

All fans have moving parts that require guarding in the same way as other moving machinery. Where a fan is accessible to the general public, maximum safety guards must be used, even at the cost of some performance. Fans located less than 7 feet above the floor usually require special attention to comply with local regulations.

Fans used in warm air, ventilating, or air conditioning systems may be driven directly from the motor shaft or through a belt drive. In every case, where a rotating part such as a shaft or belt is exposed, a suitable guard must be securely mounted.

Fans present an additional hazard in their ability to draw in and blow out loose materials. Solid objects can be discharged as dangerous projectiles, or loose material may be blown into the eyes of anyone in the vicinity.

Intakes to ductwork, even at a distance from the fan, should never be used without protective screening. Access doors should not be opened when the fan is running. When the fan is started for the first time, a preliminary check should be made to assure that there is nothing in the ductwork.

When excessive vibration occurs, a fan should be shut down immediately and checked. Otherwise it may vibrate until it destroys itself. Shattered blades may break through the guards, creating a further hazard.

ELEVATOR EMERGENCY

Professional building owners and managers should always buy a full maintenance contract from a reputable elevator manufacturer. In the event of trouble call for service immediately. Do not attempt to release passengers trapped in a stalled elevator. Only in the case of extreme emergency such as a fire would one attempt to force the doors.

While awaiting the arrival of the serviceman:

—Locate the floor where the elevator is stopped.

—Determine if anyone is in the cab.

—Reassure the persons trapped that help is on the way and that there is no danger.

Passengers often drop small objects such as car keys or pocketbooks into the elevator pits. To retrieve small objects, call the service company and request the help of a service mechanic.

BOILER EMERGENCIES

Many boiler accidents can be avoided if the safety features of the equipment function as they are designed. The building operator should be familiar enough with the boiler and heating system to know that the protective devices are operable. He also should be familiar with the routine operation of steam and hot water heating boilers, and know what action to take should an abnormal condition occur, such as the loss of water level in the gauge glass.

For safety reasons it is strongly advisable that more than one person have the knowledge to operate the heating system in each building. They should know how and where to shut off the fuel entering the building. They should post the manufacturer's rules for routine and emergency operation applicable to the installation.

Boiler rooms must be provided with exit doors which open outward. All exits should be marked and well lit. All doors should be easily opened and no debris should be placed on either side of them.

Good lighting encourages good housekeeping. To check gauge glasses, pressure gauges, safety valves, and other fittings, good lighting is necessary. Cardboard or wooden packing boxes, old stoves and refrigerators, old pipes or water hoses, and other discarded material should not impede access to the boiler, its controls, or switches.

Equipment rooms should be clean and tidy. All equipment should be painted and color coded.

POTENTIALLY DANGEROUS HOUSEHOLD PRODUCTS

All potentially dangerous household products—bleaches, cleansers, floor polishers, and the like—need warning signs. Unfortunately, these products usually contain chemical ingredients that can be dangerous.

Since February 29, 1972, the container of a hazardous household product must provide information to consumers. It tells them

—The hazard in symbols and words.

—The name of the hazardous chemical in the product.

—What to be aware of.

—The first aid treatment required.

The phone numbers and addresses of a doctor, the nearest poison control center, and the fire department should be kept near the phone.

Do you have products on hand now that are hazardous? If so, label them according to Figure 3-3. Do not store these products in a place where children can reach them.

Have the container with you when you phone the poison control center or the doctor, and take the container with you, if you go to the hospital.

TIPS FOR OCCUPANTS

—Follow the rules of the building.

—Keep storage and locker room areas clean and tidy. Never store flammable liquids or materials in these areas.

—Never use matches or candles when a locker or storage area is dark.

—Discourage careless smoking—use large safety ashtrays and only dispose of ashes when they are cold.

—Trash is fuel for a fire—*Throw it out!*

FIGURE 3-3 Hazard symbols.

—Never force cartons, coat hangers, bundles of paper, or other bulky items into garbage chutes where they may cause a blockage.

—Never put burning materials (cigarettes, ashes) into garbage chutes. The chutes *do not* feed an incinerator!

—Never dispose of flammable liquids or aerosol cans in the garbage chute.

—Never use a barbecue on a balcony.

—Avoid all unsafe cooking practices.

- *Never* go out and leave cooking food on or in the stove. Double check appliances when leaving a unit.
- Always make sure the stove is *off* when not in use.
- Do *not* overheat cooking oils.

—Familiarize yourself with the building exits, the location of fire alarm stations, fire extinguishers, and smoke detectors.

ELECTRICITY CAN KILL!

In order to understand the dangers of electricity, let's look first at what it can do to the human body.

The severity of electric shock depends on the amount of current (amperes) flowing through a victim. (Current flow is determined by applied voltage and resistance of flow path.) Other factors which contribute to damage caused by electricity are parts of the body involved, duration of current flow, and—in the case of alternating current—frequency of the current.

Skin surface provides resistance to current flow. Callous or dry skin offers fairly high resistance. Resistance drops off sharply, however, when the skin is moist. Once the current passes the skin barrier, it flows more steadily through blood and body tissues.

Alternating current tends to contract a victim's muscles, often preventing him from letting go. Voltages as low as 25 or 30 volts have caused this muscle contraction. Although the initial current flow at this voltage might not be fatal, it would be sufficient to burn the skin which would in turn eliminate skin resistance. Thus, the duration of electric contact plays an important role in determining effects of electrical shock.

PRECAUTIONS AGAINST ELECTRICAL HAZARDS

1. Avoid touching energized or "hot" wires. Observe a safe minimum distance.
2. Treat all electrical conductors as being alive until proved to be dead by actual testing.
3. Treat insulated conductors as if they are bare conductors since their insulation may be faulty.
4. Use only electrical cords which are in good condition. Cords with frayed or cracked insulation should be destroyed. Roll up and store cords carefully, keeping them dry and free from kinks and twists.
5. Use polarized plugs and properly installed grounded wiring. A professional electrician should do the installation. It is cheap life and fire insurance.

6. Portable power tools should be equipped with three wire cords and attached only to properly grounded outlets by a three-pronged plug.
7. Electrical equipment should not be used in damp or wet places. Cords (such as those of electric shavers) should not dangle in water or lie on wet surfaces. Do not use electric space heaters, radios, or appliances in bathrooms, laundry rooms, or near kitchen sinks.
8. All permanently installed appliances should be properly grounded. This is especially important in the case of washing machines, dryers, electric ironing machines, and other equipment that may be used in the dampness of a laundry room.
9. The installation, use, and maintenance of any electric wiring or equipment, whether fixed or portable, must comply with the provisions of local ordinances. Overheating of such equipment and short circuits in improperly installed or maintained equipment are two major causes of fires.
10. Temporary wiring should be *only temporary* and must be replaced with adequate wiring installed by an electrician.
11. Avoid "octopus" plugs (too many extension cords plugged into an electrical outlet). Do not overload wall outlets.
12. Look for electrical equipment that does not work right or smells unusual. Strange odors from applicances or lights can be the first sign of fire.
13. Keep heat-producing devices (electric baseboard heaters) away from flammable materials.
14. Do not overload circuits by using multi-outlet devices.
15. Do not use extension cords to supply fixed or permanent equipment. Ap-

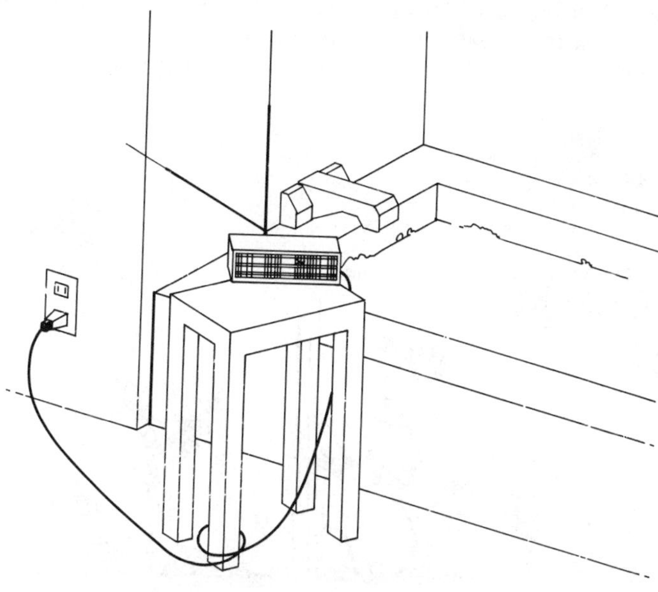

FIGURE 3-4 Electrical hazards.

pliances should be either permanently connected to or plugged directly into convenience receptacles.

16. Do not replace blown fuses with fuses of a higher rating or use any other means to restore power. *Should the fuse continue to blow, call an electrician.*

EFFECTS OF ELECTRICAL SHOCK

Injury or death from electric shock may result from the following effects of current on the body:

1. Contraction of chest muscles to a degree that causes suffocation from prolonged exposure.
2. Temporary paralysis of the nerve centers controlling respiration, which often continues long after the victim is removed from the circuit.
3. Ventricular fibrillation. Circulation ceases and death results when vital organs are starved of oxygen. The heart, when in a fibrillating state, apparently cannot recover spontaneously.
4. Suspension of heart action by muscular contraction. The heart sometimes resumes normal rhythm when the victim is freed from the circuit.
5. Hemorrhage and destruction of body tissues, resulting from heat due to heavy current flow.

The longer current flows through the body, the more serious the result. If the victim is to be revived, only very short exposure can be tolerated. In the majority of electrical accidents, current flows from hand to hand or hands to feet. Such a path involves both heart and lungs, and the results are likely to be serious.

RESCUING AN ELECTRIC SHOCK VICTIM

Switch off the current if possible and time permits. If the switch cannot be located immediately and the supply is through a flexible cord or cable, the current may be shut off by removing the plug or even breaking the cable or wrenching it free. *Never attempt to shut*

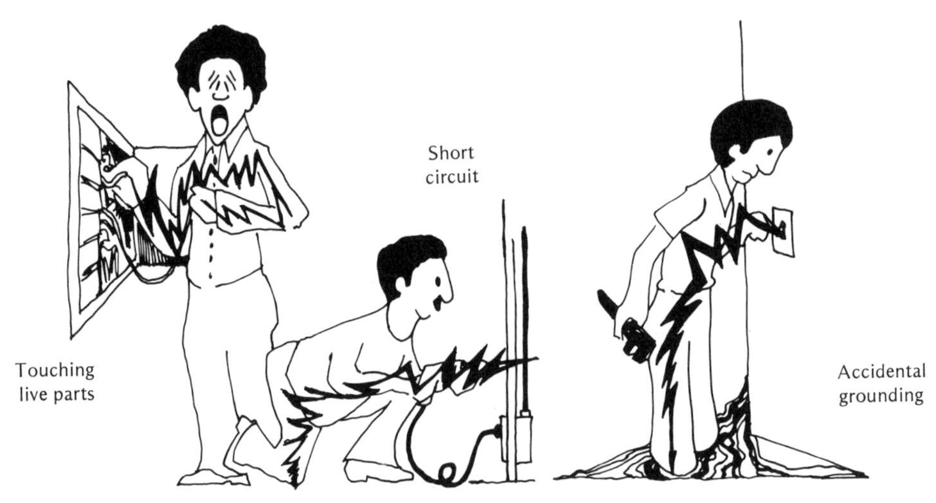

FIGURE 3-5 The major causes of electrical shock.

off current by cutting the cord with knife or scissors.

If the current cannot be shut off, the greatest care is necessary in removing the victim. Household rubber gloves, water hose (rubber or plastic—be sure there is no water in them), a dry unpainted stick, or a clean dry rope can be used to free the victim.

After the victim has been removed from contact with the circuit, quickly check his breathing. If he is not breathing and appears to be unconscious

1. Begin artificial respiration immediately—every second counts.
2. Send for a doctor.
3. Continue artificial respiration without interruption until patient begins to breathe or until a doctor pronounces him dead.
4. When patient begins to breathe on his own, treat him for shock.
   (a) Reassure the victim once he regains consciousness.
   (b) Turn the victim on his back with head to one side.
   (c) Loosen clothing about the neck, chest, and waist.
   (d) Keep patient warm.
   (e) If he complains of thirst, he may be given sips of water, tea, coffee, or other liquids—but not alcohol.
   (f) Do not apply heat.
5. Treat burns.
   (a) Avoid handling the affected area more than necessary.
   (b) Do not apply lotions of any kind.
   (c) Do not remove burned clothing or break blisters.
   (d) Cover the area, including any burned clothing, with a prepared dry sterile dressing if possible.
   (e) Bandage firmly except when blisters are present or suspected, in which case bandage loosely.
   (f) Immobilize the affected area by suitable means.
6. Transfer victim to hospital.

ARTIFICIAL RESPIRATION

Various methods of artificial respiration are practiced, but the most popular ones are the Holger-Nielson method and the mouth-to-mouth method. Every building operator should be familiar with one of these methods.

The Holger-Nielson method (also known as the "back-pressure arm lift" method) was the method most widely used in the past because it was easily taught and required the least exertion on the part of the operator. However, the oral, or "mouth-to-mouth," method has gained popularity rapidly in recent years.

The Holger-Nielson Method

The back-pressure arm lift method of resuscitation should be known by everyone. A few minutes of practice will master the technique, which may save a life. This method is shown in Figure 3-6.

Quick action is imperative; start resuscitation at once. Even though many minutes have passed, the victim may still be alive.

Position of Victim Lay the victim on stomach. Bend elbows, put one hand upon the other, the head resting with cheek on hands. Make sure nose and mouth are free of obstructions, draw tongue forward if necessary.

Position of the Operator Place one knee with the inner side in line with the victim's cheek, six to twelve inches from the top of the head. Place the other foot with the heel in line with the victim's elbow. Place the hands on the victim's back with the heel of the hands on the lower part of the shoulder

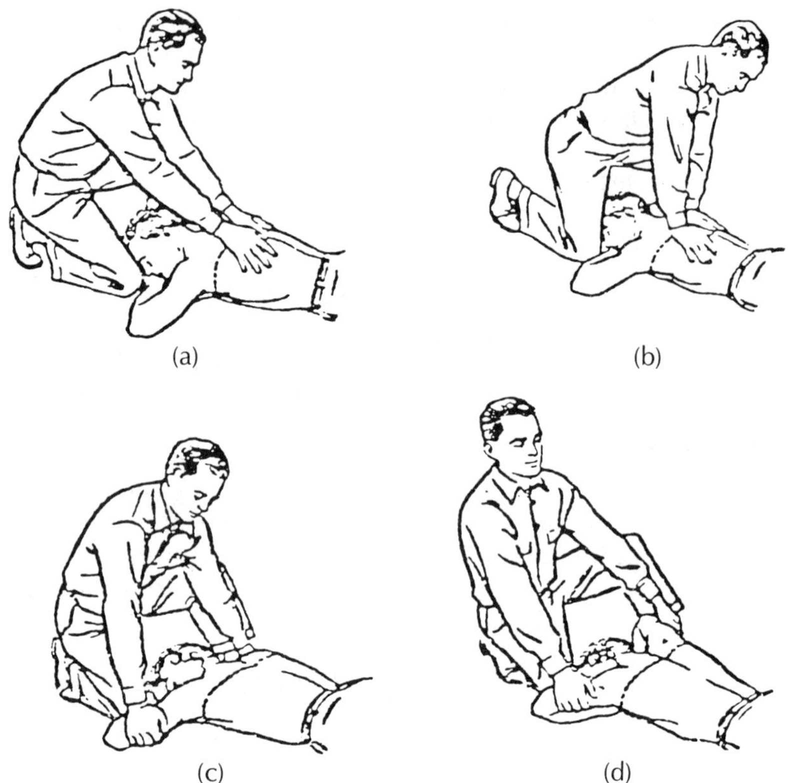

FIGURE 3-6 The Holger-Nielson method. Movement 1: (a) place hands; (b) apply pressure. Movement 2: (c) release pressure and grasp elbows; (d) lift elbows, lower elbows. Repeat about 12 times per minute.

blades, the thumbs alongside the spine, and the fingers pointing to victim's feet. The fingers may also be spread downward and outward, with the tips of the thumbs just touching (Figure 3-6A).

Movement 1 Keeping the arms straight, rock gently forward until the arms are vertical or almost vertical, using no special force, counting "one, two." This pressure causes expiration (Figure 3-6B).

Movement 2 Now rock back, counting "three," and slide hands past the victim's shoulders until they can grip the upper arms near the elbows (Figure 3-6C). Raise and pull on the arms until tension is felt, counting "four, five." Take care not to raise the chest off the ground (Figure 3-6D). This movement causes inspiration. The operator's arms should remain straight for the whole period. Counting "six," gently lower the victim's arms to the ground, and replace hands in original position. Repeat cycle ten to twelve times a minute. Continue without interruption until natural breathing is restored or until a doctor instructs otherwise.

When breathing is restored, keep patient quiet; do not let him walk. Keep him warm and move him on a stretcher. Should breathing stop after being restored, use artificial respiration again. Send for the nearest doctor as soon as the accident is discovered.

Be careful not to apply too much pressure. The amount should be just enough to lightly compress the chest. The smaller the victim, the less pressure that is required. The following pressures are sufficient for the average victim:

—24-30 pounds for an adult.

—12-24 pounds for children and slender women.

— 2-4 pounds for infants.

If the victim sustained chest injuries, do only the arm raising and lowering procedure at the rate of twelve times per minute. If the arms are injured, place them at the side of the body, and do the complete procedure, but insert your hands under the victim's shoulders and raise them for inspiration. If the arms and chest are both injured, do arm raising and lowering by inserting your hands under the victim's shoulders only.

The Mouth-to-Mouth Method

This method of resuscitation is illustrated in Figure 3-7. Posters suitable for wall mounting are available from your Worker's Compensation Board.

The rapid rise in popularity of the mouth-to-mouth resuscitation method can be attributed to its effectiveness, relative ease of application, and the fact that it does the least harm to an injured victim.

Mouth-to-mouth resuscitation for infants and small children follows the same general technique shown in Figure 3-7, but with a few important changes. The first step is to clear all foreign matter from the mouth. Figures 3-8 through 3-10 show in detail how mouth-to-mouth resuscitation is performed on infants.

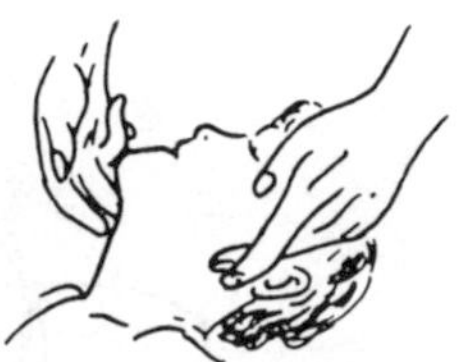

FIGURE 3-7 Mouth-to-mouth resuscitation for infants and small children. After placing the child on his back, use the fingers of both hands to lift the lower jaw so that it juts out.

FIGURE 3-8 Mouth-to-mouth resuscitation for infants and small children. Place your mouth over BOTH THE MOUTH AND THE NOSE of the child in order to form a leak-proof seal, and breathe with shallow puffs of air at the rate of about 20 per minute.

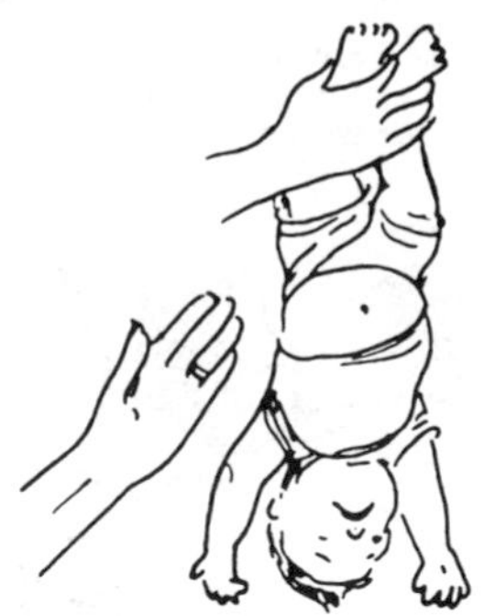

FIGURE 3-9 Mouth-to-mouth resuscitation for infants and small children. When resistance to the blowing efforts is encountered, recheck the position of the jaw. If the air passages are still blocked, the child should be suspended momentarily by the ankles or inverted over one arm and given a few sharp pats between the shoulder blades to dislodge obstructing matter.

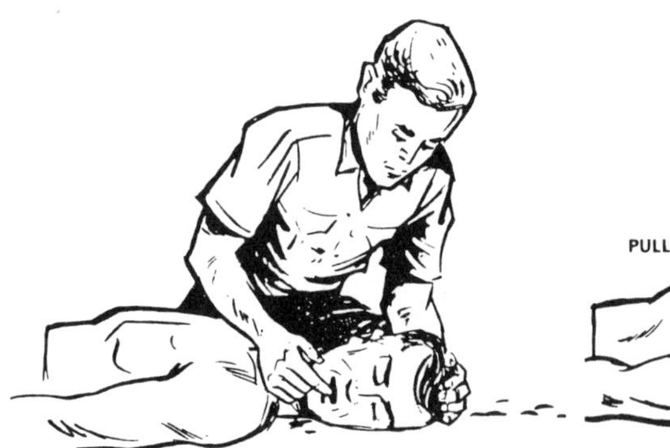

A. Place victim on his back. Turn his head to the side, wipe out his mouth quickly. Use fingers to get rid of any foreign matter.

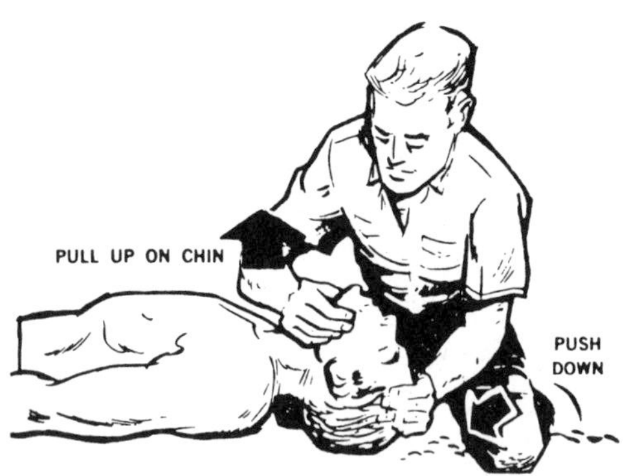

B. Push head down and back with one hand. Pull chin up and out with the other.

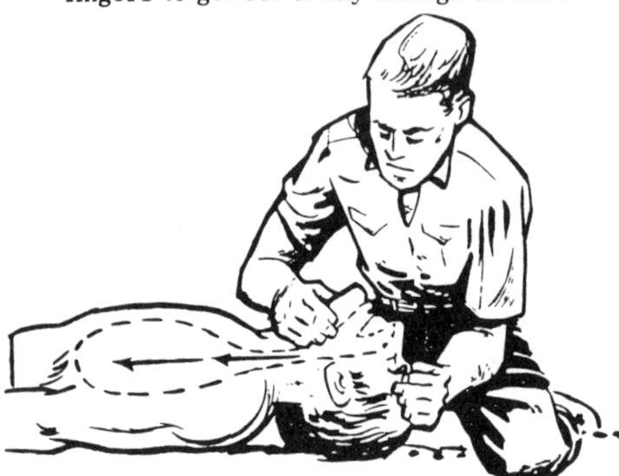

C. This is how air passages look after Step B. The head and throat are now in correct position for rescue breathing.

D. Place mouth tightly over victim's mouth and pinch nostrils closed to prevent air leakage.

E. Breathe into victim's mouth until his chest rises.

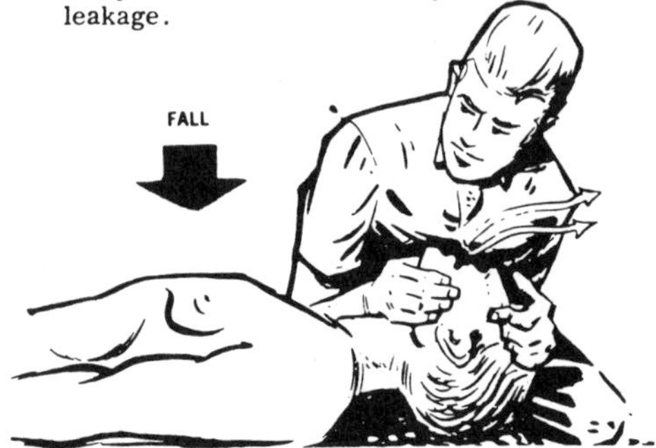

F. Remove mouth from victim's to allow breath to be exhaled. Count 3 and repeat.

FIGURE 3-10 Mouth-to-mouth resuscitation. Repeat about 12 times per minute.

3–4 Fire Protection

FIRE SAFETY IN HIGH-RISE BUILDINGS

Buildings in all large cities are built to standards set by their local codes. Developers, designers, builders, and operators must be familiar with these codes. Managers are, at times, required to relocate walls, doors, windows, and other building structures. Care should be taken to ensure that these changes do not violate the local building codes. Materials should be non-combustible wherever possible.

High-rise buildings are required to have their own standpipe system. The system is usually supplied from the building's fire pump and/or connected to a municipal water system. All systems provide for fire department connections at street level of the building. These connectors are called "siamese" connections. Water can thus be pumped into a piping system that independently supplies hose lines on all floors, and especially on the floor where the fire is located. The hoses are located so that they are no farther than 75 feet from any occupied space.

Fire pumps are generally electrically-driven centrifugal pumps, and they sometimes have a standby source of power in case there is a power failure. The fire pumps should be regularly inspected to assure that the valves, switch gear, motors, bearings, water seals, and other electrical/mechanical components are operable.

The National Building Code of Canada defines a high-rise building as

1. Every building used for assembly, business, personal services, mercantile, or industrial purposes that is more than
   a) 120 feet in height, measured between floor level of top story and grade;
   b) 12 stories in building height;
   c) 60 feet in height where the total population of the building from all floors served by the exit stairs exceeds 300 persons per unit of exit width of such stairway.
2. Every building used for institutional or residential purposes that is more than
   a) 6 stories in height;
   b) 60 feet in height measured between floor level of top story and grade.
3. Every building containing a floor area above the third story designed for patients confined to bed.

Fire safety should be one of the major concerns of operators in high-rise buildings. Even though these buildings are constructed in compliance with very strict building codes in regard to design, construction, and materials, they cannot be considered to be "fireproof" in the true sense of the word.

The basic materials of construction—steel and concrete—will retard the spreading of fire but, unfortunately, other materials used in the construction, such as foam wall insulation, insulated cables, ceiling tiles, and partitions, are all combustible to some degree, with some of them producing dense, toxic smoke during combustion. In addition, the building contents—wall-to-wall carpeting, drapes, furniture, plastics, equipment—will often burn with great ferocity.

EVACUATION

Evacuation of high-rise buildings presents special problems. Some buildings have a daily population of a small city.

Elevators should never be used during a fire. A fire will affect their modern heat-sensitive electronic floor call buttons, causing the elevator car to stop on the fire floor itself, thus exposing the occupants to the fire and smoke. Heavy smoke may also block the view of the photoelectric eye in the door and cause the door to stay open.

Evacuation through windows via ladders is only possible on the lower floors; fire department ladders do not reach any higher than the sixth or seventh floor.

That leaves the stairways for evacuation, provided they are not blocked by smoke. However, the large number of people in some buildings and the time it would take to move them all out of the building via the stairs make total evacuation of a building by stairs often impractical, if not impossible. For instance, it takes about half an hour to empty a 40-story building with only 40 persons per floor, moving down a 44-inch wide staircase, and providing nothing holds up the orderly flow of people. During this time a lot can happen in a building that is on fire. Evacuation also may interfere with the firefighting procedure. The firemen have to use the stairways when the elevators are out of operation.

It is generally agreed, and experience has proven, that it is often better for people to remain in the top half of a high-rise building when lower floors are on fire rathe than trying to get out of the building. Smoke control, of course, then becomes vitally important.

Awareness of all the conditions mentioned should make the building operating staff realize how vitally important it is to keep fire and smoke detection systems, alarm systems, and firefighting equipment in top working condition. *Enforcement of all the fire regulations is essential.* One door blocked open between a smoke-filled floor and the fire exit stairway will render the stairway useless, trapping the people on the upper floors. Proper education of the building occupants regarding fire safety regulations and what to do in case of fire is even more important in high-rise buildings than in smaller dwellings. This task falls squarely on the shoulders of the building manager and the operating personnel. Failure to provide this information could result in loss of life when an emergency arises.

The best protection possible is the existence of sprinkler systems in all buildings. These sprinklers snuff the fire out in the beginning stages or prevent it from spreading. Sprinkler systems are now required in basements, restaurants, licensed premises, and retail areas in high-rise buildings. In many newer buildings, fire and smoke detection systems are now used. Even though these systems are effective, they are only warning systems; too much time is often lost between detection of the fire, activation of the alarm, and the first attempt to put the fire out or to call the fire department.

SAFETY FEATURES

Prior to 1973, apartment buildings in Canada had the following built-in safety features:

1. Fire resistive construction.
2. Fire alarm system.
3. Interior fire escape stairways.
4. Interior water supplies for firefighting (standpipe).

High-rise buildings built after 1973 have the following features:

1. *An approved fire alarm system.* Activation of an alarm box on any floor should
   - —cause an alarm to sound at a central control facility;

—indicate on an annunciator panel at the central control facility the location of the alarm box activated;

—cause the alarm to be transmitted to the fire department.

2. *A two-way voice communication system.*
   This system shall consist of

   —handsets connecting each floor with the central control facility;

   —loudspeakers operated from the central control facility to all areas of the building.

3. *A central control facility.*
   This control facility shall be located on the street entrance floor and will be readily accessible to firefighters entering the building. It should include

   —the voice communication system;

   —an audible fire alarm warning device;

   —means to activate all fire alarm warning devices simultaneously throughout the building;

   —an annunciator panel.

4. *Control of elevators by keyed switches in an emergency.*
   This key-operated switch shall

   —allow the elevator to be operated independently from group operation control and without interference from floor call buttons;

   —render door protection devices inoperative;

   —cause the "door-close" button, when pressed, to reclose the doors immediately.

   —cause the "door-open" button to operate only under constant pressure on the button.

5. *Provision of a firefighters' elevator.*

6. *Sprinkler systems for certain essential areas.*

7. *Stricter requirements for smoke and flame spread limits on surfacing materials.*

8. *Means of smoke venting.*
   Each floor area shall be vented to the outdoors either by smoke shafts, windows, or the building exhaust system.

9. *Provision for the fire protection of electrical feeders.*
   Feeders for emergency equipment shall be installed in service spaces protected against exposure to fire.

10. *Provision of emergency power.*
    In buildings over 120 feet, emergency power shall be available to operate elevators, emergency lighting, and alarm and communication systems.

LOSS PREVENTION TIPS

A point-by-point summary of safe practice actions that increase loss prevention follows:

1. Provide and maintain in good operating condition portable fire extinguishers, pull stations, sprinkler heads, fire pump, smoke detectors, heat sensors, standby batteries, and the annunciator.

2. Do not block fire doors or leave them in an open position. These doors prevent rapid spreading of smoke and fire through the building. Locate fusible links for fire doors (these melt at certain temperatures and allow the door to close automatically) so that they will function properly in case of fire. Have spares on hand and do not paint them.

3. Wear eye, head, or face protection where there is a reasonable probability

of injury from equipment or from a dangerous chemical.

4. Make sure that guards are installed to protect against fan blades or V-belts. Do not wear loose clothing or ties near rotating equipment. Rings are also a hazard.

5. Keep all tools and equipment clean and in a safe operating condition. Ground all stationary electrically-powered equipment, tools, and devices located within reach of a person who can make contact with any grounded surface or object. Always use the right tools and equipment for a job.

6. Check with your insurer about storing flammable liquids. Paints and oils should be kept away from open flames and stored in metal-lined and ventilated locked closets. Use a Canadian Standards Association (CSA) or Underwriter's Laboratories (UL) certified container for gasoline (called a "jerry" can). These containers should not be filled within a building.

7. Practice good housekeeping habits in storage areas, work areas, and common areas. When stripping, waxing, or damp mopping, use the standard warning signs. Keep all floor surfaces clean, dry, and free of protruding nails, splinters, loose boards, holes, or projections.

   Do not use unsatisfactory cleaning materials or methods that leave floors slippery. Oils are not suitable for rubber tile. Oils become a fire hazard when allowed to soak into wood floors. Excessive use of ordinary wax for polishing wood, tile, and similar surfaces is not recommended because of the slippery nature of wax.

   Cleaners are available for removing oils and wax, but in no case should a volatile liquid such as gasoline be used. Prevention is the best cure, and concerned building operators should be trained to promptly clean up slippery materials spilled on floors.

8. Snow and ice on sidewalks and entrances is a hazard to occupants and visitors. Shovels, ice scrapers, or power-driven plows should be used to clear sidewalks as quickly as possible. Snow and ice should be piled on lawns and around trees, rather than pushed into streets or left to cover edges of the walk. A chemical ice remover, *used only on icy areas,* is preferable to sand for use around the entrance, as sand will be tracked into buildings. *Salt is corrosive.*

9. Keep halls and stairs clear of packing boxes and other materials. Access to emergency exits should not be obstructed by baby carriages, boxes, bicycles, or other objects. Staircases leading to exit doors should also be free of all obstructions; stairtreads must be in good condition and should not be slippery. Handrails should be firmly attached.

   Emergency exit doors allow direct exit from the building. These doors should be self-closing and swing open to the outside. They are equipped with special hardware, popularly known as "panic hardware," which locks the door and does not allow it to be opened from the outside. However, the door can easily be unlocked from the inside by exerting a light pressure on a pushrod, thus no key is needed.

   Emergency exit doors should NEVER be locked with a padlock or other locking device, or nailed shut. The door hardware should be kept in good operating condition.

10. Increase the safe use of halls, stairs, and equipment rooms by providing adequate lighting.

    All exit ways and exits should be identified by readily visible signs. The signs and access to exits should be lighted when artificial lighting is necessary for normal use. If emergency lighting is provided, it should be tested regularly. Make sure it will be available during an emergency. Battery-operated emergency lighting should be frequently checked to ensure that the batteries are fully charged.
11. Defective wiring causes many electrical fires. Wiring is affected by overloading, vibration, moisture, corrosion, heat, and cold. These conditions weaken insulation and can cause short circuits, arcing, and fires. Common causes of fires at circuit breakers are pitted contacts, loose parts, and loose connections. Only competent and well-trained electricians should be used for new installations or for troubleshooting electrical problems.
12. *Never hesitate to call the fire department.* Many major fires result from delayed alarms. Call the fire department when you see a wisp of smoke, when you smell a little smoke, or when you spot a small fire.
13. Plans of action for an actual fire should be developed. Actions taken by the building operating staff prior to the arrival of the fire department will greatly influence the outcome of a fire.
14. The operations staff should know
    —Who to call in case of an emergency: names and phone numbers.
    —Location and purpose of all shut-off valves, sprinkler lines, water, steam, fuel, or other flammables.
    —Location of switches that control power and lighting.
    —Evacuation of occupants is more important than fighting the fire.
    —The fire protection system and how it works.
    —The location of all electrical utility transformer vaults. These should be checked daily and any problems should be reported to the utility company immediately.

THE FIRE TRIANGLE

The danger of fire pervades all aspects of life. It is therefore necessary that everyone be aware of fire prevention. In high occupancy buildings, the precautions which must be taken to prevent fires take on added importance.

HOW DO FIRES START?

Understanding the chemical reaction of a fire helps to know what will extinguish a fire.

Ordinary fires result from the combination of fuel, oxygen, and heat. When a combustible substance is heated to its ignition temperature, it will burn as long as there is oxygen. Fuel, oxygen, and heat are the three ingredients necessary for a fire to start. This is illustrated in Figure 3-12. Remove any side of the triangle and the fire dies.

WHAT TO DO WHEN A FIRE IS DISCOVERED

—If the alarm has not been activated, sound the alarm.

—Phone the fire department.

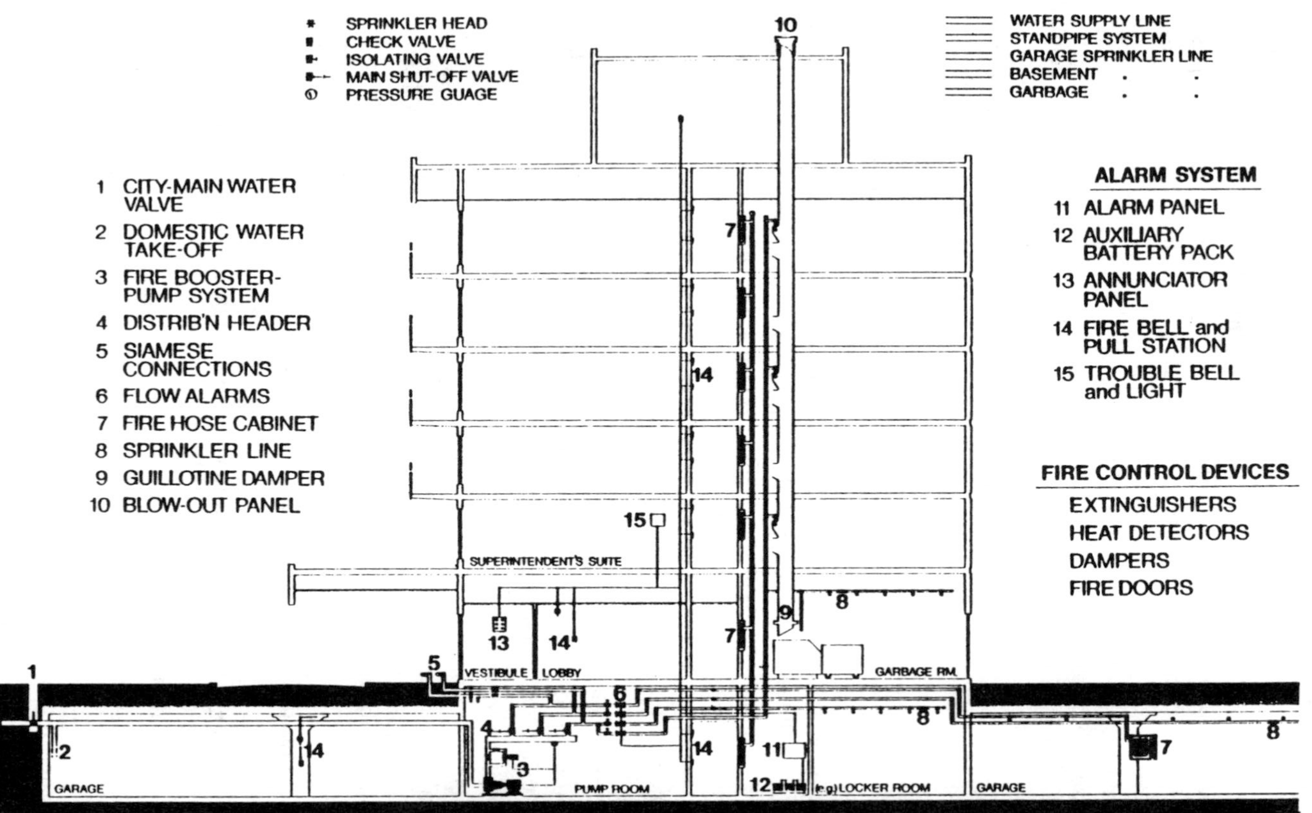

FIGURE 3-11 Typical apartment building fire control system. (Courtesy of The Cadillac Fairview Corporation, Limited.)

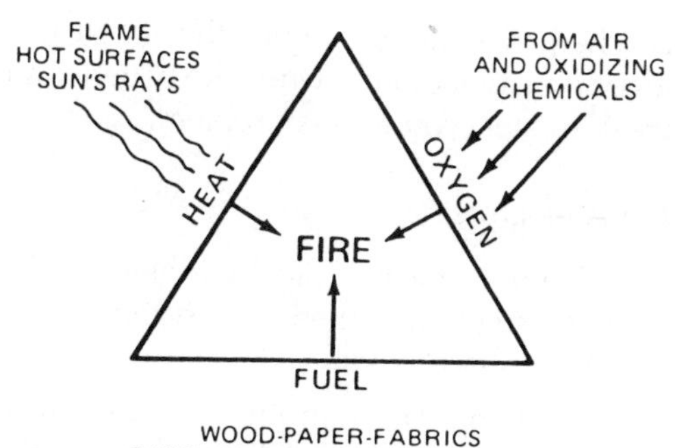

FIGURE 3-12 The fire triangle.

FIGURE 3-13 Manual alarm station.

—If the alarm has been activated, check the annunciator panel for the location of the fire.

—Make sure that someone is in the lobby to direct the fire department.

—Lock the elevators.

—Use the stairs to get to the floor where the alarm was sounded.

—If it is a small fire, use a fire extinguisher.

—If the fire is large, make sure that no one is in the room or unit, and close the door.

—Alert everyone on the floor.

—Lay out the fire hose to the unit.

THE FIRE ALARM

Manual Alarm System

It is essential that, as soon as a fire is detected in a building, the alarm is sounded to alert the occupants. Most buildings are equipped with the familiar manual alarm stations which are strategically located throughout the building. The alarm station (Figure 3-13) is basically an electric switch which energizes the alarm system when the lever is pulled down.

Alarm systems in many larger buildings, schools, and institutions, are tied in with the fire department's alarm center. When such an alarm system is energized, it automatically sounds a coded signal to the fire department indicating the need for assistance and, at the same time, identifies the building which originated the signal.

Many people believe that all alarms, when activated, automatically alert the fire department. This is not always the case, so it is a good practice to call the fire department immediately.

Early detection of a fire is vital if extensive building damage is to be prevented. A fire in its beginning stage is usually controllable, but once the fire is established flames may spread rapidly, and the danger to life and property become severe.

Unfortunately, even though a building may be equipped with numerous manual alarm stations, the alarm is often not sounded until the fire is well advanced.

SMOKE AND FIRE DETECTORS

Smoke Detectors

Many fires generate a lot of smoke before flames build up and begin to spread. Often the heat developed in the smoke stage of a fire is insufficient to actuate a fire detector of the heat-sensing type, and considerable time may be lost between the start of the fire and the time the alarm is activated. Meanwhile smoke may fill rooms and hallways making orderly evacuation of the building difficult or impossible. To reduce the time between the start of the fire and the actuating of the alarm systems, smoke detectors are often used in preference to fire detectors.

Smoke detectors are devices that sense the presence of smoke and actuate an alarm when the smoke density reaches a critical stage.

Ionization-Type Detector

This is a spot-type smoke detector that electronically responds to the presence of combustion particles in the air. When the amount of particles reaches a predetermined level (the detector should not react on light cigarette smoke), the detector triggers the alarm.

Sometimes the alarm will go off if you burn something on the stove or if you are broiling. Once you clear the smoke or stop broiling it will stop sounding.

If the unit is electrically wired, it is equipped with a built-in light which, when lit, shows that the unit is energized.

Fire and smoke detectors are very reliable devices provided they are periodically inspected and tested. Some detectors are battery-operated to make them independent from the regular power supply. These batteries should be checked at regular intervals. Discharged batteries render the alarm useless. Some units sound when the batteries are weak to alert you to this problem.

Fire Detectors

A fire detector is basically a heat-sensing device, usually mounted against the ceiling, which responds when

—the temperature in the area it is supervising reaches a predetermined level;

—the temperature in the area rises at an unusually fast rate.

The first type of detector, called a "fixed-temperature fire detector" (Figure 3-15), comes in various designs, but they all have a heat-sensitive element that reacts by actuating the alarm system when the temperature in the area reaches a set high limit. These detectors are usually non-adjustable.

The second type of detector, called a "rate-of-rise detector" (Figure 3-16), actuates the alarm when the temperature increase exceeds a stated number of degrees a minute. It usually can be adjusted to react more or less quickly depending on the application.

WHAT TO DO IF THERE IS A FIRE IN A UNIT

—Alert everyone in the unit.

—Call the fire department immediately.

—Occupants should leave the unit, close doors behind them. Try to leave the door unlocked if possible. Take along a wet towel.

—Sound the fire alarm in the corridor.

—Leave the floor via the stairway.

DO NOT RUN. NEVER USE THE ELEVATORS.

FIGURE 3-14 Ionization-type smoke detector. (Courtesy of Walter Kidde & Company of Canada, Limited.)

FIGURE 3-15 Fixed temperature fire detector. These fire detectors are fixed temperature models that will close a set of contacts when the air surrounding them equals or exceeds the thermal rating of the detector. When the air has cooled off, the detector will reset and the contacts will open. (Courtesy of Walter Kidde & Company of Canada, Limited.)

—Be prepared to encounter heavy smoke and heat. Cover nose and mouth with a wet towel.

—If exit route is unsafe, seek refuge in a neighbor's unit.

—*Do not panic*—WAIT TO BE RESCUED. In a fire-resistive building, occupants should remain in their units with doors closed.

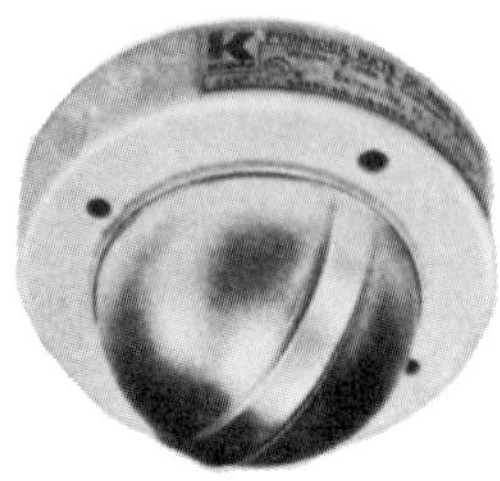

FIGURE 3-16 Rate-of-rise and fixed temperature elements. The heat detectors illustrated will automatically reset in both the rate-of-rise and fixed temperature elements. (Courtesy of Walter Kidde & Company of Canada, Limited.)

WHAT TO DO IF THERE IS A FIRE IN THE KITCHEN

If a pan on the stove catches fire

—Turn off the heat.

—Try to smother the flame by covering the fire completely with a pan cover. Care should be exercized to avoid burning yourself or your clothing.

—*Never try to carry a burning pan.*

If a fire starts in the oven

—Turn off the heat.

—Close the oven door to smother the flames.

—*Never put water on a grease fire!* It will splatter and spread the flames.

If the fire is anything but a *small* fire do not attempt to fight it.

WHAT TO DO IF YOU HEAR THE ALARM

Check the suite door with your hand:

—If it is warm or hot *you should not open the door*—the fire may be right outside your door.

—If the door is cool to the touch, you should open it and check the corridor for smoke.

—If the corridor is clear, you can either leave the floor using the stairway or stay in the unit.

If you decide to leave the floor, you should close the door of the unit. Remember to *never run and to never use the elevator.* You should take a wet towel with you to cover your nose and mouth if you encounter smoke.

WHAT DO DO IF THE CORRIDOR IS IMPASSABLE

—Remain in the unit.

—Keep the door closed—stuff all cracks and vent openings with wet towels or clothing.

—Stand on a balcony or near an open window.

—Signal position by waving.

—*Don't panic*—wait to be rescued. In a fire-resistive building, a person is safer in his unit with the door *closed* than he is attempting to escape through fire and smoke.

WHAT TO DO IF SMOKE AND HEAT BLOCK YOUR EXIT

—Stay calm.

—Where there is smoke, *crawl* close to a wall with your mouth and nose covered with a wet towel.

—Put closed doors between you and the smoke and heat. Seal off cracks around doors, and block all vents with wet towels or sheets.

—Find a room with an outside window. Open it at the top and bottom, if possible.

—Signal from the window; use the phone to tell the fire department where you are, even if they are already on the scene.

WAYS TO PUT OUT A FIRE

To put out a fire you must be familiar with the various classifications of fires.

CLASS A—Fires involving ordinary combustibles, such as wood, paper, and rubbish.

CLASS B—Fires over the surface of flammable mixtures: oil, paint, gasoline, thinners.

CLASS C—Fires in or near live electrical equipment.

CLASS D—Fires involving combustible metals, such as magnesium, zirconium, and sodium.

To stop a fire:

1. Knowledge of the fire triangle (Figure 3-12) is helpful, if one is to competently combat fires. In Class A fires, it would probably be impossible to remove the fuel

or oxygen so you must try to remove the heat. Water can be used to cool the fire. Portable water hand extinguishers and standpipes with fire hoses are available for this purpose.

2. Class B fires can sometimes be extinguished by removing the fuel. The simplest way to extinguish a natural gas fire or a fire in any flammable liquid that is *flowing from a pipe is to shut off the valve, thus cutting off the fuel supply.* When the liquid is in tanks or on a floor, the fire can be smothered, cutting off the oxygen supply. Carbon dioxide (CO_2) extinguishers dilute the oxygen that the fire needs. Dry chemical extinguishers interrupt the chemical action as well as smother the fire.

   WARNING: Never throw a stream of water on a Class B fire. You may splatter flaming liquids over a wide area, spreading the fire out of control. *Never use a water extinguisher on live electrical equipment. The electric charge may follow the water stream back to your body and you may be electrocuted instantly.*

3. Class C fires must be controlled with non-conducting material. Carbon dioxide (CO_2) extinguishers are supplied in all areas with electrical equipment. Dry chemical is non-conducting and can be used when necessary. *After the electric current has been cut off,* you can use water to put out the fire.

4. Class D fires require special firefighting techniques. This type of fire is common to industrial plants, where suitable equipment to control the fire is usually available.

FIRE EXTINGUISHER TYPES

Portable fire extinguishers, also called "first-aid" extinguishers, are the first line of defense against any fire.

Extinguishers and/or extinguisher locations should be marked to indicate the suitability of the extinguisher for a particular class of fire. The following recommendations for marking extinguishers are contained in the various local fire codes and standards.

Extinguishers suitable for Class A fires should be identified by a triangle containing the letter "A." Background color should be green.

Extinguishers suitable for Class B fires should be identified by a square containing the letter "B." Background color should be red.

Extinguishers suitable for Class C fires should be identified by a circle containing the letter "C." Background color should be blue.

Extinguishers suitable for more than one class of fire should be identified by multiple symbols.

Pressurizing Fire Extinguishers

Pressure is required to propel any extinguishing agent onto a fire. Major firefighting apparatus depend on motorized pressure pumps and on the pressure in water mains to apply water or water fog to a fire.

FIGURE 3-17 Fire extinguisher markings.

The advantage of "first aid" extinguishers is that each has its own built-in pressurizing system: the first aid equipment is not put out of order by failure of the municipal or building water supply.

There are several ways to pressurize portable fire extinguishers.

Stored Pressure In carbon dioxide extinguishers, for example, the liquid CO_2 is stored at a pressure of 850 pounds per square inch at room temperature. When the extinguisher is operated, the pressure forces out the liquid CO_2, which expands 450 times its stored volume to form a fire-smothering gas.

Some water extinguishers make use of a CO_2 cartridge for stored pressure. When the extinguisher is used, the cartridge is punctured, and the released gas forces out the water. Dry chemical extinguishers use CO_2 or nitrogen cartridges to propel fire-smothering powder.

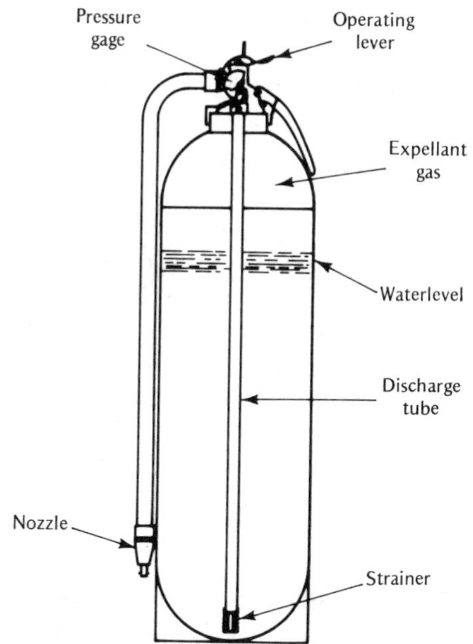

FIGURE 3-18 Stored pressure extinguisher.

Soda acid and foam extinguishers generate their own pressure when chemicals within the extinguisher are mixed to produce gas that expels the extinguishing agent, either water or foam. Both of these extinguishers have become obsolete and should be replaced by stored pressure, carbon dioxide, of dry chemical extinguishers.

Check that hose nozzles are not dented or plugged. To do this, remove the hose and blow air through it. Make sure that the pin is in place and that the extinguisher cannot accidently discharge.

In the stored pressure water extinguisher (Figure 3-18), the expellant gas and extinguishing agent are stored in a single chamber, and the discharge is controlled by a shut-off valve. A pressure gauge located at the top of the extinguisher gives a constant reading of the pressure in the cylinder. These units are capable of both continuous and intermittent operation.

To operate, pull the locking pin and squeeze the handle, directing the stream at the base of the flames, working from side to side or around the fire. This unit should not be inverted for operation.

The modern water extinguisher uses a cylinder of CO_2 to apply pressure to expel the water onto the fire. Advantages are that no annual recharge is necessary as in the soda-acid type, and there is no danger of corrosion from acid, which may destroy the usefulness of the unit. The extinguisher contains pure water. A cylinder of carbon dioxide is held in a cage in the neck of the extinguisher. When the unit is inverted, a pin pierces the seal of the carbon dioxide cartridge and permits the proper amount of gas to flow out and create enough pressure to expel the water.

The contents of the tank should be checked periodically and, although the water does not have to be changed, it should be kept up to the "full" mark. The carbon dioxide cartridge should be weighed annually. If the cartridge is one-half ounce or more below the weight stamped on it, the cartridge should be replaced.

The antifreeze extinguisher is simply a CO_2-powered water extinguisher with antifreeze crystals added to the water.

Carbon Dioxide (CO_2) Carbon dioxide extinguishers contain liquid carbon dioxide under a pressure of 800 to 900 pounds per square inch at normal room temperature. The extinguisher consists of a heavy steel cylinder, a quick release valve, a hose, and a funnel-shaped horn (Figure 3-19). The liquid carbon dioxide becomes a carbon dioxide gas when released from the nozzle. These extinguishers do not require protection from freezing, but *they should not be located where the ambient temperature is above 120°F.*

Carbon dioxide is essentially nonconductible and, therefore, is suitable for use on fires in live electrical equipment (Class C). Carbon dioxide is also effective on small Class B fires where the gas will exclude or dilute the oxygen, thereby smothering the flames. These extinguishers may also be used on small Class A fires, but must be followed up with water to cool deep burning embers.

Portable carbon dioxide extinguishers are available in sizes from 2½ to 20 pounds. The model number is the weight of the liquid carbon dioxide contents held in the cylinder at 850 pounds per square inch pressure at 70°F. The effective range is from 3 to 6 feet, and the duration of discharge is from fifteen to fifty seconds, depending on the size of the extinguisher.

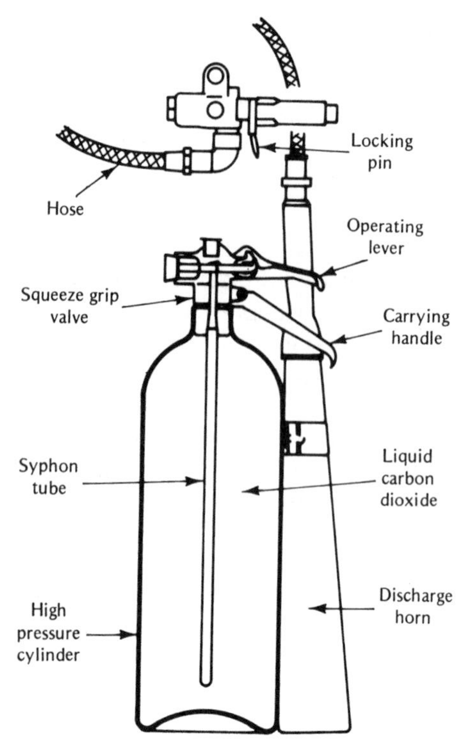

FIGURE 3-19 Carbon dioxide (CO_2) extinguisher.

The toxicity of carbon dioxide is practically negligible, but when used in unventilated rooms or a confined space, persons should take precautions to avoid breathing the gases or fumes. The carbon dioxide gas can dilute the oxygen supply below the necessary minimum to sustain life.

DO NOT grasp the discharge horn during operation; hold it by the insulated handle only. These extinguishers expel carbon dioxide gas and some snow at a temperature of −79°C (−110°F). Touching the horn may result in very serious burns.

These extinguishers can be operated intermittently by operating the valve, but do not depend on the valve for any appreciable time because it may leak.

Carbon dioxide extinguishers must be recharged immediately after use. Once the diaphragm seal has been broken, the valve alone cannot hold the pressure for more than a few hours or days. *This extinguisher must be shipped to an authorized dealer for recharge.* Before shipping, discharge all the remaining gas and inspect the complete extinguisher. *If the hose and horn are not damaged, do not ship them with the extinguisher.*

Dry Chemical Dry chemical extinguishers contain an extinguishing agent in dry powder form, plus components producing water repellency and free flow of the agent. The chemical powder inhibits the flame chain reaction of the fire. Chemicals used are sodium bicarbonate, potassium bicarbonate, and ammonium phosphate.

The powder is propelled by either carbon dioxide or nitrogen. There are two types of dry chemical portable extinguishers. Figure 3-21A shows the cartridge-operated type in which the expellant gas (carbon dioxide) is contained in a small cartridge until it is released into the extinguisher shell when the cartridge is punctured. This cartridge is either

(a)

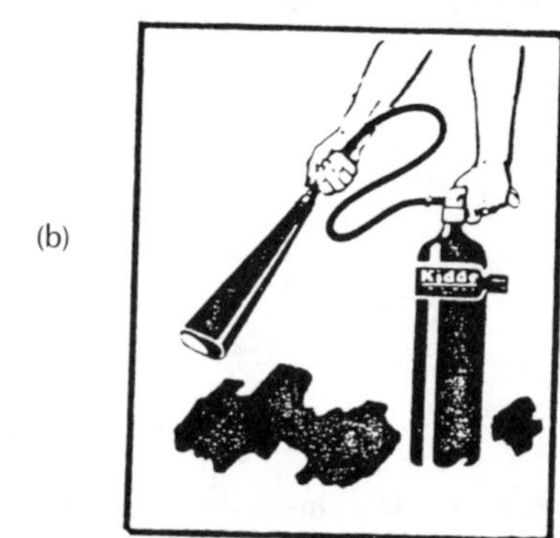
(b)

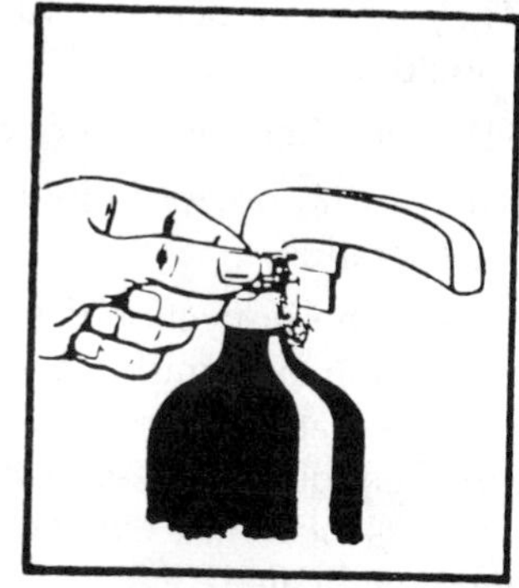
(c)

(d)

FIGURE 3-20 How to use a CO_2 extinguisher. (a) Lift from bracket carry to fire in right hand. (b) Pull locking pin; grasp insulated hose handle in left hand. (c) Point hose at base of fire. (d) Pull trigger (or on other types, squeeze grip or twist handle) to open valve. Direct the discharge at the base of the flames and progress forward with a side-to-side sweeping motion. (Courtesy of Walter Kidde & Company of Canada, Limited.)

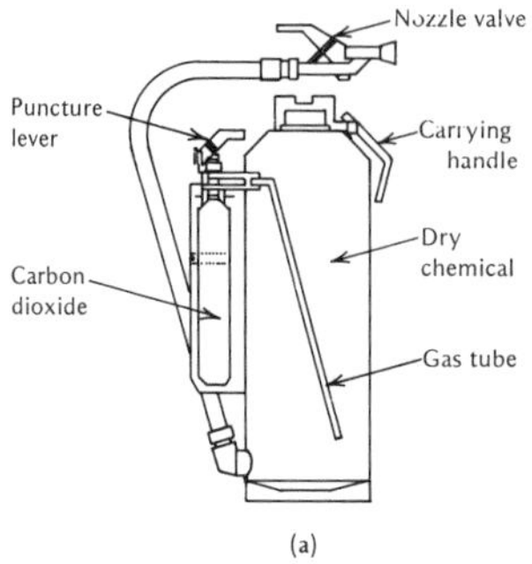

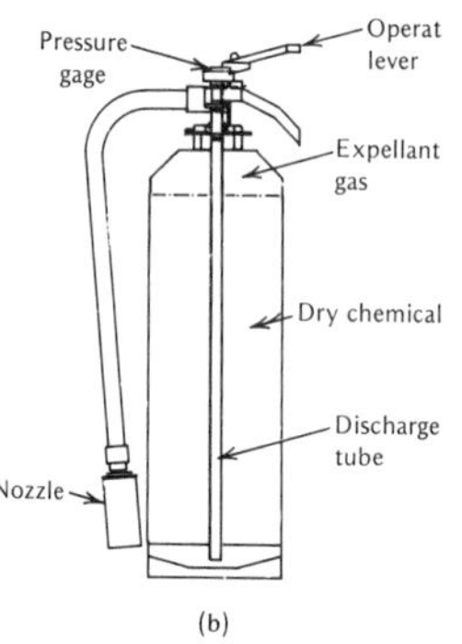

FIGURE 3-21 Dry chemical extinguishers.

mounted outside the shell, as shown, or it is contained within the shell. Figure 3-21B shows the stored pressure type in which expellant gas and dry chemical are stored together within the shell.

Dry chemical extinguishers are effective on Class B fires (oil, grease, paint, gasoline). They are also suitable for Class C fires because the powder is not a conductor of electricity. *These extinguishers can be used on small Class A fires, but must be followed up with water.*

Portable dry chemical extinguishers are available in sizes from 5 to 30 pounds. The weight of the unit is based on the amount of specially processed powder in the extinguisher. The effective range is 5 to 20 feet, and the time of discharge is ten to fifteen seconds, varying with the size, type, and manufacturer.

Dry chemical extinguishers do not require protection from freezing, but when exposed to outdoor temperatures, the carbon dioxide cartridge should be replaced with a nitrogen cartridge.

CARE OF PORTABLE FIRE EXTINGUISHERS

As mentioned previously, portable fire extinguishers are first aid equipment only. They have a limited quantity of extinguishing material and, therefore, must be properly used so that this material is not wasted. Fire extinguishers require regular, inspection and maintenance to ensure efficient and safe operation. Most extinguishers are pressurized and must be handled with care.

Portable fire extinguishers should be given a quick check every three months to give reasonable assurance that

1. They have not been activated, wire seals should be intact.
2. Hose and horn are free of obstructions.
3. There is no obvious physical damage or deterioration.

Record the inspection date on the tag attached to the extinguisher and initial it. Also make sure that there are no obstructions that will prevent quick access to the extinguisher and that its location is either clearly visible or properly indicated.

Extinguishers must be kept fully charged at all times and must be recharged immediately after use even though only partially discharged. Regular maintenance of an extin-

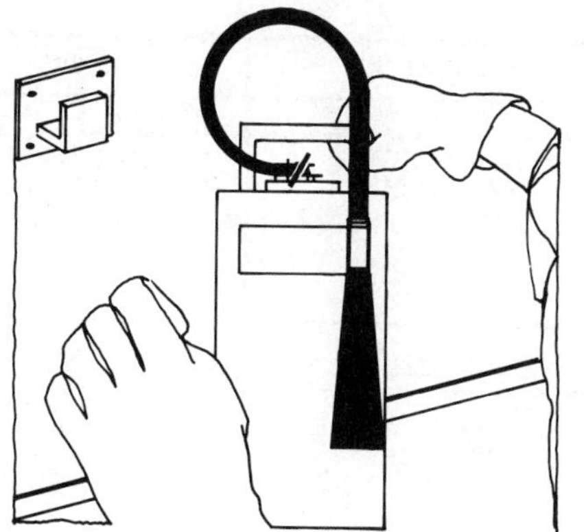

1. Remove from the carrying bracket.

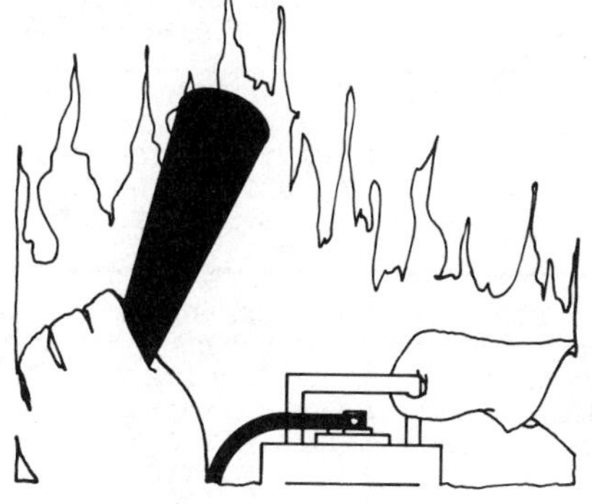

3. Point nozzle directly into the fire.

2. Pull locking pin; free nozzle with left hand.

4. Pull trigger and direct discharge at the base of the flames. Best results are obtained by attaching the near edge and progressing toward the back of the fire, moving the nozzle rapidly with a side-to-side sweeping motion.

FIGURE 3-22 How to use the dry chemical extinguisher.

DESCRIPTION	CARBON DIOXIDE CO_2	DRY CHEMICAL	WATER
CLASS A FIRES	NO	YES - BUT	YES-EXCELLENT
PAPER, WOOD, CLOTH EXCELSIOR, RUBBISH, ETC.	NOT RECOMMENDED FOR OCCUPIED AREAS. QUANTITY REQUIRED TO EXTINGUISH A CLASS A MATERIAL TOXIC.	SMALL SURFACE FIRES ONLY.	WATER SATURATES MATERIAL AND PREVENTS REKIND'
CLASS B FIRES	YES-EXCELLENT	YES-EXCELLENT	NO
BURNING LIQUIDS, GASOLINE, OILS, PAINTS, COOKING FATS, ETC.	CARBON DIOXIDE LEAVES NO RESIDUE DOES NOT EFFECT EQUIPMENT OR FOOD STUFFS.	CHEMICAL SMOTHERS FIRE	WATER WILL SPREAD FIRE, NOT PUT IT OUT.
CLASS C FIRES	YES - BUT	YES - EXCELLENT	NO
FIRES IN LIVE ELECTRICAL EQUIPMENT, (MOTORS, SWITCHES, APPLIANCES, ETC.)	CARBON DIOXIDE IS A NON CONDUCTOR LEAVES NO RESIDUE. DOES PRODUCE CONDENSATION WHICH COULD DAMAGE SOME EQUIPMENT.	CHEMICAL IS A NON CONDUCTOR SCREEN OF DRY CHEMICAL SHIELDS OPERATOR FROM HEAT.	WATER IS A CONDUCTOR AND SHOULD NOT BE USED ON LIVE ELECTRICAL EQUIPMENT.
RANGE OF STREAM	3 TO 6 FEET	10 TO 15 FEET	45 FEET
PRESSURE SOURCE	GAS COMPRESSED IN CYLINDER	GAS FROM PRESSURE CARTRIDGE OR INTERNAL PRESSURE STORED IN CYLINDER	STORED AIR PRESSURE
RATED CAPACITY (MOST COMMON)	2½-5-10-15-20 POUNDS (NET WEIGHT OF GAS)	5-10-20-30 POUNDS (NET WT. OF POWDER)	2½ GALLONS
RECHARGING	AFTER USE WEIGH SEMI-ANNUALLY TO DETECT LOSS FROM TAMPERING, ETC.	AFTER USE WEIGH CO_2 SEMI-ANNUALLY OR CHECK PRESSURE GAUGE.	CHECK PRESSURE SEMI-ANNUALLY
HYDROSTATIC TEST	ALUMINUM SHELL 12YRS. STEEL SHELL 15 YRS.	EVERY 12 YEARS	EVERY 5 YEARS
TESTS MUST ALSO BE CONDUCTED IMMEDIATELY AFTER ANY INDICATION OF A MECHANICAL MALFUCTION OR SIGNS OF SHELL CORROSION.			

FIGURE 3-23 Extinguisher types and uses chart. Each class of fire calls for specialized action. Using the wrong extinguisher may do more harm than good.

guisher must be done at least once a year by an experienced maintenance mechanic. Maintenance includes a thorough examination, repair, recharging, or replacing when necessary.

Ensure that the hose elbow and orifices of the nozzle are not clogged, that threaded connections are tight, that the powder is in free-running condition, and that the cartridge has not lost weight due to leakage. (It should be weighed on an accurate scale.) If cartridge weight is 10 percent below the stamped weight on the hexagon head, it must be replaced. A stored pressure-type unit must be weighed to determine if it is fully charged with dry chemical and the gauge checked to determine if it is fully pressurized.

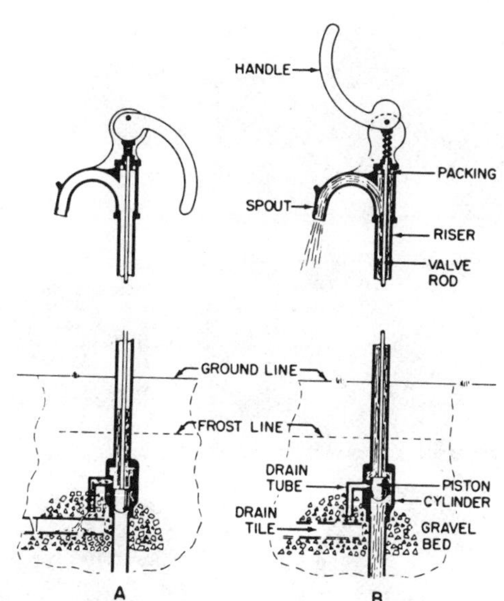

FIGURE 3-24 Frostproof hydrants. A frostproof hydrant: (a) closed; (b) opened. As soon as the hydrant is closed, water left in the riser drains out the drain tube as shown in (a). This prevents water from freezing in the hydrant in cold weather. (Courtesy of Reston Publishing Company.)

FROSTPROOF HYDRANTS

Frostproof hydrants are basically faucets, although they may differ somewhat in design from ordinary faucets. Two important features of a frostproof hydrant are (1) the valve is installed underground—below the frost line—to prevent freezing; and (2) the valve is designed to drain the water from the hydrant when the valve is closed. Figure 3–24 shows one type of frostproof hydrant. It works as follows: When the handle is raised, the piston rises, opening the valve. Water flows from the supply pipe into the cylinder, up through the riser, and out the spout. When the handle is pushed down, the piston goes down, closing the valve and stopping the flow of water. Water left in the hydrant flows out the drain tube into a small gravel-filled dry well or drain pit.

As with ordinary faucets, leakage will probably be the most common problem encountered with frostproof hydrants. Worn packing, gaskets, and washers can cause leakage. Disassemble the hydrant as necessary to replace or repair these and other parts.

THE STANDPIPE

Standpipes consist of vertical pipes extending from the city water supply or fire pump on the lower floor to the top floor or roof. They are fitted with valved outlets at each floor for the attachment of fire hoses. At the bottom of the pipes, branch lines extend outside the walls, providing connections for the fire department pumper hoses (see Figure 3–25). These connectors must be visible at all times.

A standpipe and inside hose system provide a means of supplying water to fires on

FIGURE 3-25 Connections for the fire department pumper hoses. (Courtesy of Kent Fire Protection.)

any floor in a building. They are especially needed where sprinkler protection is not provided and in areas of building not readily accessible to hose lines from outside hydrants.

Standpipe systems are designed for two types of service:

1. Small hose streams (1½-inch hose), for use by building occupants.
2. Large hose streams (2½-inch hose), for use by the fire department.

Standpipes are often designed to supply both large and small size hoses.

According to the method of water supply, a standpipe system can be classified as a

(a) Wet system—the supply valve to the system is open permanently, thus system is under pressure at all times.

(b) Dry system—the standpipe is empty, and supply valve is closed until water is required. The supply valve is then opened either manually, by remote control, or automatically when the hose valve is opened.

In smaller buildings the wet standpipe system usually receives water directly from the city water supply. The dry system may be connected to the city supply and/or it may receive water from the fire department pumper via the outdoor connection.

In high-rise buildings the city supply would not be able to supply water to the upper floors or if it could, the pressure would be insufficient. In these buildings the standpipe system is usually zoned (approximately twelve floors to a zone) to limit the pressures at the hose outlet. Each standpipe zone is then supplied either by the water storage tank on the top floor of the zone (the water being fed by gravity), or the water is supplied by a fire pump placed below the level of the water storage tank of the zone below (the water being fed upwards into the system).

THE FIRE HOSE

A fire hose is usually an unlined tube of linen fabric. Hose nozzles have no shut-off valves.

Fire hoses should only be used to fight a fire and not for any other purpose. If a fire occurs in an area near a hose, the hose should be removed from its rack and laid out in the direction of the fire, ready for use only if the extinguisher fails to put out the fire. To start the flow of water, open the hand valve connected to the standpipe. Tenants or building staff should not activate the hose if it is over 1½ inches in diameter.

The hose should not be returned to the rack until it is thoroughly dried. To assure complete draining and drying it should be hung vertically in a well-ventilated area.

At least once a year the hose should be laid out and reracked in such a way that the folds are located in a different part of the hose.

When testing the standpipe valve, disconnect the hose, since it is important to keep the hose dry to avoid mildew and deterioration.

FIRE HOSE STATION

A fire hose station (Figure 3–26) is for the use of the building occupants. One end of the 1½-inch or 2½-inch hose is permanently attached to the valved standpipe outlet, the other end to the nozzle. Hose and nozzle are stored on a hose rack, and the whole assembly is often mounted in a cabinet with glass door. A fire extinguisher is usually stored in the cabinet with the hose.

FIGURE 3-26 A fire hose station. (Courtesy of Kent Fire Protection.)

AUTOMATIC SPRINKLERS

Automatic sprinkler systems have advantages that make them very effective in fire protection. They begin to put out a fire soon after the fire has started and while it is still easily extinguished. The sprinkler heads usually drop water directly onto the fire, including fires not readily visible from patrolled areas.

In buildings considered to have a rather high fire hazard, such as those with a predominantly wooden construction, each sprinkler nozzle may protect about 70 square feet of area, while in relatively "fireproof" buildings the sprinkler may cover as much as 196 square feet.

Principal sprinkler systems are (1) wet pipe, in which all pipes are continuously full of water, and (2) dry pipe, which is usually installed in unheated buildings and contains no water except during a fire.

When the sprinkler system is actuated, the building alarm system—often directly connected to the city fire alarm system—is also actuated.

One type of sprinkler head is the Quartz-bulb Type (Figure 3–27). The heat-sensitive bulb is transparent and contains a colored liquid. At about 58°C (136°F), the liquid bursts the bulb, releasing a spray of water. The water hits the deflector which distributes the water in a widespread pattern. The unit (A) stands vertically above exposed piping, while the pendent type (B) projects down below the ceiling from concealed pipe.

Another common type of sprinkler head is the Solder-link Type (Figure 3–28). A valve

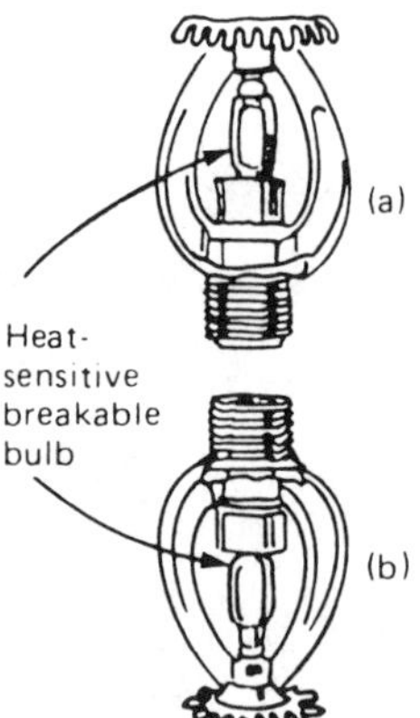

FIGURE 3-27 Automatic sprinkler, quartz-bulb type. (Courtesy of Kent Fire Protection.)

disc is held on its seat by two levers which are held in position by a solder-type link with a low melting point. The solder link melts when exposed to heat at a predetermined temperature, at which point the levers drop out, the valve opens, and the spray of water is released.

Sprinkler heads are rated on the basis of their operating temperature. The rating should be at least 25–35°F above the maximum ceiling temperature expected in order to keep a sufficient safety margin to prevent accidental release of water.

Sprinklers must be of approved makes and types and must not be altered in any way. They must not be used to support ornaments or signs. Experienced service people should regularly check sprinklers to make sure that they are in good condition, free from corrosion, unpainted, and not bent or otherwise damaged. It is advisable to keep an adequate supply of extra sprinklers on hand, together with a sprinkler wrench, in a cabinet provided for that purpose.

There is a standard color code for sprinklers, and replacement should be made only with a head of the same color as the defective head.

FIGURE 3-28 Automatic sprinkler, solder-link type. (Courtesy of Kent Fire Protection.)

Although infrequently, sprinkler systems do fail to control fires. The National Safety Council has compiled a list of some of the causes of failure in sprinkler systems (with suggestions for preventative measures in parentheses):

1. *Failure due to human errors by*
   a) Not keeping all supply valves open;
   b) Shutting the supply valves prematurely during a fire.
2. *Freezing of wet system sprinkler pipes.* (Heat the sprinkled area or convert to dry system.)
3. *Defective dry pipe valve, or slow operation of dry system because of its excessive size.* (Check valves at frequent intervals or subdivide system.)
4. *Foreign material obstructing the system.* (Flush out system and provide clear water at intake through use of filter screens.)
5. *Improper drainage because of faulty installation.* (Check pitch of pipes and eliminate low spots.)
6. *Sprinklers obstructed by stock piled too high, sprinklers isolated by temporary partitions or shelving, and sprinklers shielded from heat.* (Improve housekeeping and maintain at least 18 inches of clearance around sprinkler heads. Increased clear-

ance up to 36 inches should be provided over large, closely-packed piles of combustible cases, bales, cartons, or other such stock.)

7. *Corrosion of sprinklers.* (Use sprinklers specially designed for use in such locations.)
8. *Inadequate supply of water because of faulty design or poor maintenance.* (Check to make certain that water conditions have not changed since original installation.)
9. *Closed Sprinkler Valve.* When reviewing the reasons why sprinkler systems fail, it was found that supply valves are often closed. To control this problem the Canadian Underwriters' Association and the Factory Mutual System recommend that
   —All sprinker valves should be identified and tagged.
   —A closed sprinkler valve should be red tagged (see Figure 3–29) until it is opened again.
   —All valve closures should be logged using the Factory Mutual Form illustrated in Figure 3–30.

THE CLOSING OF THIS VALVE SHUTS OFF VITAL WATER SUPPLIES TO THE AUTOMATIC SPRINKLER SYSTEMS. A FIRE IN THE PROPERTY WHILE THIS VALVE IS CLOSED MAY GET OUT OF CONTROL AND NO AUTOMATIC ALARM WILL SOUND.

OPEN AS SOON AS POSSIBLE WHEN REPAIRS ARE COMPLETED.

NOTIFY YOUR INSURERS WHEN PROTECTION IS RESTORED.

VALVE CLOSED

FIRE PROTECTION IMPAIRED

IT IS EXTREMELY IMPORTANT THAT FIRE PROTECTION SERVICES BE RESTORED AS SOON AS POSSIBLE. EXTRA CARE SHOULD BE TAKEN UNTIL THE VALVE IS OPENED. WATCHMEN SHOULD BE INSTRUCTED AND MANUAL FIRE HOSES BE IN READINESS FOR ANY FIRE EMERGENCY.

cua canadian underwriters' association

FIGURE 3-29 **Sprinkler line valve closure tags.** (Courtesy of the Factory Mutual Insurance Company and the Canadian Underwriters' Association.)

*3-5 Life System Audit

Stairwells

(1) How many stair exits per average floor? ____
(2) Are the stair entrances clearly identified?
   (a) Signs ____________
   (b) Exit lights ________
   (c) Color code ________
(3) What type of emergency stairwell lighting?
   (a) Emergency power-generated __________
   (b) Battery-operated lights ______________
(4) What is the frequency of
   (a) Emergency power generator tests? ______
   (b) Service of emergency light batteries? ____

*Courtesy of Mr. Mel Willman—The Cadillac Fairview Corporation

RECORD OF VALVE CLOSURES

Factory Mutual System

LOCATION OF VALVE OR NO.	AREA CONTROLLED	TIME & DATE CLOSED	TURNS TO CLOSE	TIME & DATE OPENED	TURNS TO OPEN	LOCKED OPEN		DRAIN TEST		SIGNED BY
						YES	NO	STATIC	RESID.	

FIGURE 3-30 Record of valve closures. (Courtesy of the Factory Mutual Insurance Company.)

(5) What is the frequency of
- (a) Stairwell checks? ______
- (b) Lighting? ______
- (c) General Inspection? ______

(6) At what level do the stairwells exit?
- (a) Lobby ______
- (b) Outside ______
- (c) Other ______

(7) Are there alternate stair exits? Yes ____ No ____

(8) If there are alternate stair exits, are they clearly identified with floor level arrow markings? Yes ____ No ____

(9) Is the local fire department acquainted with the stair exits from the building? Yes ____ No ____

Emergency Communications—Public Address (P.A.) System

(1) Does an emergency P.A. communications system exist? Yes ____ No ____

(2) Is it connected to the emergency power system? Yes ____ No ____

(3) What is the location of the microphone? ______

______

(4) Is it equipped with
- (a) Floor selector switches? Yes ____ No ____
- (b) All call switches? Yes ____ No ____

(5) Is there a house or fireman's telephone system? Yes ____ No ____

(6) What is the location of the speakers on a typical floor? ______

______

(7) Are these speakers in the stairwells? Yes ____ No ____

(8) Are there announcements made in the event the fire alarm is activated? Yes ____ No ____

(9) Who makes the announcements? ______

______

(10) Is there a format of predetermined messages which may be announced? Yes ____ No ____

Elevators

(1) Total number of elevators ______

(2) How many elevators serve all floors? ______

(3) Are the elevators equipped with voice communication? ______

(4) What is the location of the receiver? ______

______

(5) Is the intercom connected to emergency power? Yes ____ No ____

(6) Are the elevators equipped with
- (a) Fireman's service? Yes ____ No ____
- (b) Dead man control? Yes ____ No ____

(7) Do the elevators return to ground level by
- (a) Activating fire alarm? Yes ____ No ____
- (b) Smoke detector? Yes ____ No ____

(8) How many elevators may be operated on emergency power service? ______

(9) Are operating checks made of
- (a) Fireman's service? Yes ____ No ____
- (b) Dead man control? Yes ____ No ____

(10) What are test frequencies? ______

(11) Who tests the operations?
- (a) Operating staff ______
- (b) Security Staff ______
- (c) Elevator Service Staff ______

Fire Alarm System

(1) Indicate type of alarm-indicating devices
Rate of Rise Heat Detectors ______
Manual Pull Stations ______
Sprinkler System Flow Alarm Switch ______
______
Smoke Detectors ______
Ionization Products of Combustion Detectors
______
Infrared Detectors ______
Alarm Contact on Restaurant Chemical Extinguishing Systems ______

(2) Is the fire alarm system electrically supervised for wiring faults? Yes ____ No ____

(3) Is the fire alarm system interconnected with the emergency power system? Yes ______ No ______

(4) Location of the alarm annuciating panels: ______
______

(5) What type of audible signal?
(a) Bells ______
(b) Horns ______
(c) P.A. System ______

(6) Does the activating of a fire alarm device
(a) Shut down the air handling system? Yes ____ No ____
(b) Release electromagnetic door releases? Yes ____ No ____
(c) Return elevators to ground level? Yes ____ No ____

(7) Is the alarm system
(a) Zoned? Yes ____ No ____
(b) Non-zoned? Yes ____ No ____

(8) Does the activating of a pull station indicate
(a) Alert Alarm? Yes ____ No ____
(b) Evacuation Alarm? Yes ____ No ____

NOTE: Alert Alarm—Intermittent ringing bells
Evacuation Alarm—Steady ringing bells

(9) What is the location of the fire alarm system reset? ______
______

(10) Is the fire alarm system
(a) Tested regularly? Yes ____ No ____
(b) Serviced regularly? Yes ____ No ____
(c) Name of service company ______
______

(11) Is the fire alarm system installed per existing local code? Yes ____ No ____

(12) List all operating personnel who are familiar with the operation of the fire alarm system:

Standpipe System—Sprinklers

(1) How many standpipes per floor? ______

(2) How many fire hose cabinets per floor? ______

(3) Are the fire hose cabinets equipped with extinguishers? Yes ____ No ____
(a) What types of extinguishers?
Water ______
Chemical ______
CO_2 ______

(4) What is the exterior location of the city fire pumper connection for the standpipe system?
______

(5) What is the frequency of inspection for
(a) Fire extinguishers? ______
(b) Hoses? ______

(6) Who performs the inspections?
Building Personnel ______
Contractor ______

(7) What areas of the building are sprinkled?
Below grade ______
Garage ______
Office space ______
Elevator shafts ______

(8) Does a water flow in the sprinkler system activate the fire alarm system? Yes ____ No ____

(9) Are the sprinkler systems
(a) Wet? ______
(b) Dry? ______
(c) Both? ______

Emergency Procedures

(1) Is there an emergency procedure plan established? Yes ____ No ____

(2) Does the operating staff have procedures to follow in the event of fire? Yes ____ No ____
Bomb threat? Yes ____ No ____

(3) Is there a program in effect to inform the tenants of procedures in the event of a fire? Yes ____ No ____

(4) Has an evacuation of the building been attempted? Yes ____ No ____

(5) If yes, how long did it take to evacuate? ______
______

(6) In the event of a bomb threat call, are there guidelines for the security staff or receptionist to use when talking to the caller? Yes ______ No ______

(7) Have the tenants been instructed in the organization of a floor warden system to assist in evacuation or other emergencies?
Yes ____ No ____

(8) Is there a small-scale floor plan, which indicates the fire exits, stairwells, fire hose cabinets, and fire alarm pull stations available for each floor? Yes ____ No ____

	ACCT. NOS.	SUB TOTALS	TOTAL
BUILDING HARDWARE	37		

ASHTRAYS AND WALL URNS	371	
CYLINDERS	372	
DOOR CLOSERS	373	
DOOR HANDLES	374	
KEYS	375	
LOCKSETS	376	
PADLOCKS	377	

FIRE PROTECTION SYSTEM	49	TOTAL	

ALARMS	491	
BATTERIES	492	
HOSES AND EXTINGUISHERS	493	
MOTORS AND PUMPS	494	
PIPING, VALVES & CONTROLS	495	
SPRINKLER SYSTEM	496	
TESTING	497	

SECURITY SERVICES	60		

ALARM DEVICES OR T.V.	601	
GUARD SERVICE	602	

FIGURE 3-31 Summary of budget expense schedules, repair and maintenance categories; security, safety, and fire protection.

3-6 How to Budget for the Necessary Funds

As with other services and electrical/mechanical systems, we must identify the expense classifications, establish the maintenance programs, have an adequate inventory of spare parts, and ensure that there is a proper allocation of funds for these purposes.

The budget expense schedules in Figure 3–31 detail the security, safety, and fire protection items that need funding. Inventory lists would supplement and help determine the amounts eventually entered as an expense total.

Chapter 4

HOUSEKEEPING SERVICES

4-1 An Overview

In this chapter we will study the ways to attack and control the enemy of good housekeeping—*dirt*. If all the dust and soil that is a part of the average city's air fell at once, in one year, it would bury us in up to 21 feet of dirt. Fortunately, it doesn't all fall at once, or we would need to use bulldozers instead of dust mops.

Complete removal of soil involves three basic steps:

—collection
—packaging
—disposal

A breakdown in any one of the three basic soil removal steps will cause incomplete cleaning.

If you think about the cleaning process in terms of soil removal, packaging, and disposal, troubleshooting becomes much easier. If you use a dirty mop or a vacuum that is overloaded with dirt or mechanically unsound, collection will be poor; it also follows that packaging will be incomplete and disposal will be nonexistent.

Cleanliness is the purpose for housekeeping and can be broken down into two classifications:

—Germicidal cleanliness, such as in kitchens, rest rooms, hospitals, and garbage areas. These areas must not only look clean, but must actually be free from soil and contamination.
—Cleanliness for the sake of appearance.

This chapter will deal mainly with preventive maintenance, problem solving, and techniques for professionally carrying out the housekeeping tasks.

In order to achieve above-average housekeeping productivity, we must ensure the organization of the following:

—personnel
—responsibilities
—tasks

—standards of cleanliness
—time (workload)
—task procedures (schedules)
—equipment

General housekeeping maintenance tasks can be organized into daily, periodic, and special task groupings. To organize and achieve the desired standard of cleanliness, the following must be considered:

—An appropriate program for the area serviced.
—The need to avoid overcleaning as well as undercleaning.
—Base standards on service performed, frequency of the service, work skills, and habits of occupants.

Good housekeeping is often the criterion in judging a university, school system, hospital, or apartment, or indeed any type of building used by the public. Dirty halls, odoriferous toilets, and a general state of untidiness are all negative influences.

4-2 Special Housekeeping Jobs

GERMICIDAL CLEANING

Very often housekeeping staff erroneously assume that a shiny floor implies a sanitary floor. In hospitals, the control of infectious diseases must be seriously considered, and sanitation must also ensure germ control.

In other buildings the concern is not as critical as in a hospital, but a basic understanding of the sanitation problem is necessary so that critical areas—such as saunas, showers, public washrooms, garbage areas, and swimming pools—can be properly maintained to reduce the possibility of bacterial contamination.

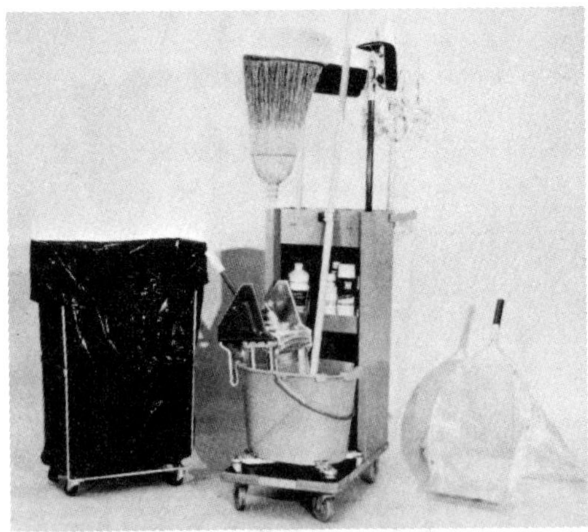

FIGURE 4-1 Typical housekeeper's cart. (Courtesy of Sanitary Products Company, Limited.)

The staff must understand why mops must be properly cleaned, the importance of not spreading dust when dry mopping, the importance of hand washing, and how to carry out their housekeeping tasks and reduce the possibility of contamination by bacteria, fungi, and viruses. Conditions suitable for the growth of these organisms are food, moisture, and proper temperature. If one or all of the conditions are removed by drying, cleaning, refrigeration, or high heat, growth will stop. In many applications this means of growth reduction cannot be controlled and chemical disinfection must be employed. In chemical disinfection, the requirement for moisture continues as a means of carrying chemical disinfection to the organism.

To clean and disinfect the areas requiring this special type of cleaning, we use a "quaternary ammonium chloride" compound. This material attacks the cell walls of the organisms, changing the permeability of the membrane and allowing the contents of the cell to seep out into the surrounding medium where they can be destroyed. This compound also combines with the cell enzymes to stop the manufacture of food for the cells.

EQUIPMENT REQUIRED

—Container of recommended germicidal cleanser
—Hose
—Hosemaster (or other similar degreasing gun)
—Sponge
—Recommended green abrasive hand pads
—Deck scrub brush
—White rubber wall squeegee (used in tiled areas which are difficult to reach)
—Floor squeegee
—Rinse cloths
—Rubber gloves (to be worn by all personnel)

GARBAGE COMPACTOR CONTAINERS

Before empty containers are attached to compactor they should be cleaned in the following manner:

FIGURE 4-2 "Hosemaster" degreasing gun. (Courtesy of Gilmour Manufacturing Company.)

1. Fill Hosemaster plastic bottle with full-strength germicidal cleanser.
2. Set Hosemaster degreasing gun spray at 2 ounces per gallon dilution.
3. Spray inside of container thoroughly, using hot water, if available.
4. If gross soil is adhering to inside of containers, agitate with a stiff brush.
5. Set spray to clear water and rinse out. It is absolutely necessary that you rinse with clear water when using a germicidal cleanser.

GARBAGE COMPACTOR ROOM

Daily, all inside and outside surfaces of the garbage compactor unit should be thoroughly sprayed with a Hosemaster degreasing gun set at 2 ounces per gallon solution of a germicidal cleanser, using hot water, if available. Agitate gross soil with a stiff bristle brush and hose clean with fresh water.

Note: Care should be taken not to spray the electrical panel. The floors, walls, and ceilings of the compactor room should be hosed with a Hosemaster, using hot water, if available. Always spray the walls from the floor up, so that the germicidal cleanser only runs where the wall is wet.

BASEMENT INCINERATOR ROOMS

After the incinerator room has been cleared of waste each day, use a Hosemaster degreasing gun set at 2 ounces per gallon solution of germicidal cleanser and spray the room. Agitate gross soil and rinse the room completely. Use hot water, if available.

CORRIDOR GARBAGE ROOMS

A solution of 4 ounces of germicidal cleanser per gallon of water should be kept on hand. Fill hand spray and cover all walls and floor with solution. Always spray from the bottom up, to avoid the solution running on the soiled wall and causing streaking. Also spray inside of chute opening. Wring out cloth in clean water and rinse all surfaces. This operation should be done on a twice-weekly basis.

GARBAGE CHUTES

Once a week a solution of 2 ounces of germicidal cleanser per gallon of water should be poured down the chute every nine floors, from the top down, attempting to contact the total inner surface of the chute. A 2-gallon pail is usually used for this purpose. Following this, the water source (hot, if available) to the flushing ring should be opened to flush down the chute.

WINDOW WASHING

Most management companies use a window washing contractor to wash the inaccessible windows. The building staff should keep the accessible windows clean, especially in public areas and lobbies. When cleaning an empty suite in an apartment building, the windows exposed to the balcony would naturally be cleaned.

INTERIOR GLASS CLEANING

Apply a little cleaner to the glass using a vertical spray motion; then use a cloth pad to spread it over the rest of the glass area. Rub the glass with the cloth pad (or paper towel) until the cleaner drys. Avoid using too much glass cleaner.

How to Clean a Window Using a Squeegee

Materials needed are

—Window Cleaner
—Buckets
—Cloth Pads
—Brushes
—Sponges
—Squeegee

First, use sponge and water to wash the glass. Use squeegee to remove water. There are two basic squeegee motions—side to side and top to bottom. Excess water will collect in the lower corner of the window. The blade of the squeegee should be wiped with a sponge or cloth pad after each stroke.

SHOWERS AND WASHROOMS

The proper cleaning of showers, washrooms, and toilet rooms is probably one of the most important aspects of building maintenance. These rooms receive more attention from the public than any other in the building. People will judge the remainder of the building by the cleanliness of these rooms.

Some toilets are designed and built in such a way that the use of a Hosemaster is impractical. If this is the case use a hand spray solution of 4 ounces per gallon instead of the Hosemaster.

1. Empty all waste and sanitary napkin receptacles.
2. Clean the floors thoroughly using dry mop if necessary.
3. Check and refill dispensers for toilet tissue and hand towels. Make sure each is functioning correctly.
4. Daily, thoroughly spray all walls and floor areas with a Hosemaster set at 2 ounces

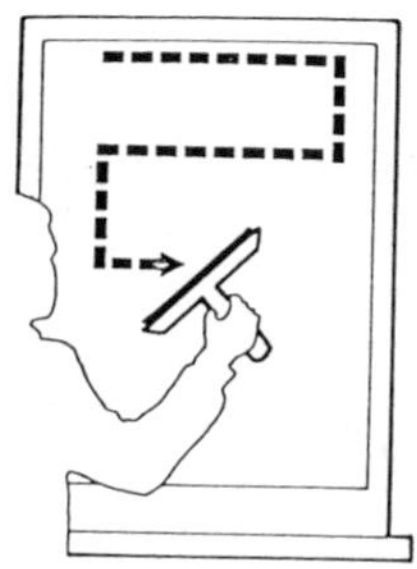

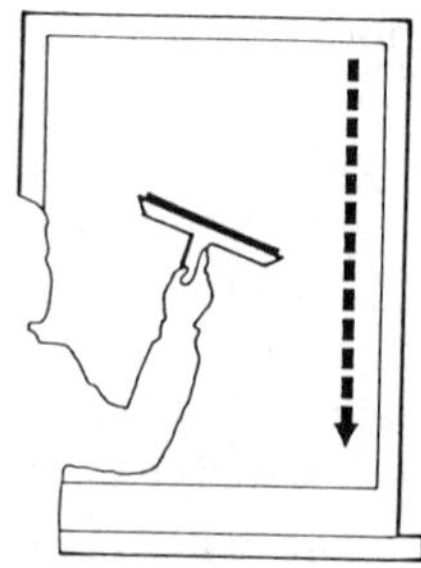

FIGURE 4-3 Efficient squeegee motions. Efficient squeegee motions make water run toward trailing edge and away from cleaned area.

per gallon of germicidal cleanser, using hot water. Agitate all surfaces with a sponge before rinsing off. It is suggested that once or twice a week you scrub with a green Scotch-Brite Hand Pad to prevent scum build-up. Hose down walls and floors with clean water, and use a squeegee to speed up drying.

5. Spot-clean walls, partitions, and doors. Check areas where dust and dirt are likely to collect.
6. Clean all mirrors and glass.
7. Clean all hardware and pipes, especially those under the sinks. Also clean the underside of sinks and tanks.
8. Clean top and bottom of toilet bowl with a sponge dipped in toilet bowl cleaner.

   CAUTION: When using toilet bowl cleaner, protect hands with rubber gloves. Avoid contact with eyes.

SAUNAS

Daily, spray the whole sauna room with a Hosemaster set at 2 ounces per gallon solution of germicidal cleanser and hot water. Let stand for about a minute. Agitate solution on seats with green Scotch-brite Hand Pads. Rinse down with clean water. The floor of the sauna should be scrubbed with a brush.

SMALL WASHROOMS

1. Empty waste receptables.
2. Damp mop floors.
3. Make sure that the toilet tissue and hand towel dispensers are filled and operating properly.
4. Clean outside of toilet tank and all wash basins and faucets with a cleaner suitable for these fixtures.
5. Clean the outside and inside of the toilet bowl with a bowl cleaner applicator dipped in toilet bowl cleaner.
6. Clean the mirror and glass.

LOCKER ROOMS

Damp mop floors with a solution of 2 ounces of germicidal cleanser and hot water. Rinse with clear water. If the area has a trapper mat, do not replace until the floor is thoroughly dry.

Damp wipe lockers with clear water twice a week. Check interior of lockers weekly for leftover clothing or other items. Wash interior of lockers, as required.

VENETIAN BLINDS

There are no quick and easy methods for cleaning venetian blinds. A chemically-treated dust cloth will do a good job for on-location cleaning.

If blinds are heavily soiled and require washing, this is done best by removing the blind, placing it across a narrow table with nails in it to prevent the blind from slipping, flattening out the slats, and scouring with a stiff brush and detergent, then wiping with a dry cloth. Scrub the tape as you proceed. If tapes are of the colored cloth-type, they may shrink and fade, so they should be stretched while still wet. White tapes that have become dingy can be bleached while still hanging, with a solution of sodium hypochlorite. Keep moving the blind up to another set of slats until the bottom of the blind is reached, then turn over and clean the other side. If the slats are greasy, they can be cleaned with a steel wool pad dipped in a detergent solution.

WALLS AND CEILINGS

To do this job properly, you should have on hand two pails and two sponges. One pail and sponge can be used for the cleaning solution, (hot water and a recommended all-purpose cleaner), and the other pail used for rinsing (with clear water).

GRAFFITI

The dictionary defines graffiti as a rude inscription or drawing found on rocks or walls. In our industry it is generally accepted that any defacing of the building is classed as graffiti.

Corridor wallpaper is often a victim of graffiti. The usual markings are the result of ball point ink, crayon, lipstick, magic marker, heel marks (around elevators), and pencil.

Most of this marking is removable without damage to the wallpaper, with Graffiti Mark and Stain Remover. Care must be taken with the remover as there is a tendency for vinyl wall covering to soften and become tacky. It is recommended, therefore, that the damaged or marked area be wet down with clean tap water before applying the Graffiti remover.

If the marked area is small and relatively easy to remove, the Graffiti remover may be applied directly, but in any event, the area should always be wiped afterwards with a wet cloth or sponge.

Always use a clean cloth in applying the Graffiti remover and a separate clean cloth for water application. Turn the cloths frequently or smudging could result. Trace the stain with the product and wipe softly; do not rub vigorously. Some marks will need a longer penetration time.

Remember, always retain a wet clean cloth for final wipe off and to stop action of the product.

Some marks, such as ball point ink, which have been present for a long period of time, may be impossible to remove. If regular inspections are made by the building staff, new marks will be easier to remove, since very little of the mark will have penetrated into or through the wall covering. Removal of all marks as soon as discovered will help minimize this problem.

SPOT CLEANING

In order to keep little cleaning jobs from becoming big ones, it is very important that you have a regular day-to-day routine of spot cleaning and dusting. Carry a spray gun with a mixture of 2 ounces per gallon all-purpose cleaner and water. Use this mixture to remove spots from walls, woodwork, and ceramic tiling and paneling. The solution can also be used to spray on a cleaning cloth to wipe off entrances to the apartments, elevator cabs, and control panels.

LAUNDRY ROOM

In any public area, a daily maintenance program is essential.

The machines themselves should be washed twice a day, if necessary, so that they are always clean. Use suitable materials to assist you with this chore. Special attention should be given to the upper tub cover, which catches spilled and caked detergent.

Floors should be cleaned daily. Walls, ceilings, and windows should also be cleaned as scheduled.

FLUORESCENT LIGHTS AND FIXTURES

For removal of dust, use either a vacuum cleaner with a brush-type attachment at the end of a wand, or wipe with a damp sponge, and dry with a clean cloth.

For removal of dirt adhering to the surface of polystyrene or plexiglass fixtures, wash with a sponge dipped in a solution of hot water and all-purpose cleaner.

From a preventive maintenance viewpoint, considerable time can be saved by organizing and combining a group relamping program with the fixture washing schedule.

DUSTING

Removal of dust from furniture is essential. Proper dusting involves removal of the dust, not brushing it from one location to the other.

Flat surfaces should be dusted daily. Vertical surfaces may be dusted weekly.

All dusting should be scheduled to assure that this activity is not neglected.

HOW TO CLEAN AN APARTMENT

As with any housekeeping chore, it is essential that you fully understand how to properly use the materials required to do the job.

1. Remove all leftover debris from the apartment and the balcony.
2. Remove all light fixtures and clean them. Replace all burned-out light bulbs. Wash light shades with all-purpose cleaner.
3. Soak stove fixtures in a mixture of warm water and stripper. Heat oven to 180°. Shut off oven. Spray oven with oven cleaner. Make sure oven has a broiler pan. *For safety, pull out black cartridge block from electric service panel before cleaning.* Check fuse panel on stove. Clean, if required.
4. Clean and wash out refrigerator; make sure there are two ice-cube trays and one butter dish in the refrigertor. Check that rubber gasket around door is clean. Do not use an electric kettle or any other type of heater to melt ice.
5. Clean ceiling vents in kitchen and bathroom and check that the vent is working. If not, call for service.
6. Wash all windows and windowsills inside and all balcony windows outside. Clean metal frame with a suitable cleaner.
7. Clean all venetian blinds.
8. Clean all kitchen cupboards inside and out, including drawers and bread board.
9. Complete cleaning of stove and oven. Clean under and beside the stove by pulling out the stove.
10. Complete cleaning of kitchen counter, including sink and taps.
11. Clean kitchen floor, being sure to remove all old wax with stripper and hot water. Wash or rinse with water. Using a lamb's wool pad, apply two coats of a resilient sealer, allowing twenty minutes for each coat to dry. Rinse lamb's wool pad in cool water and use to apply wax; let dry and apply a second coat. Be sure to clean behind refrigerator and stove.
12. Recaulk bathtub enclosure as required. *Do not caulk over dirty or old caulking.*

13. Wash tile in bathtub enclosure. Wash medicine cabinet and vanity cupboard, using an all-purpose cleaner and water. Clean black stains from grouting and caulking with a household bleach.
14. Clean mirror in bathroom with window cleaner.
15. Clean bathroom fixtures, tub, toilet basin, and taps with an all-purpose cleaner and a toilet bowl cleaner inside the toilet bowl.
16. Replace shower curtain rings as required.
17. Wash tile floor, making sure grout between tile is clean, using all-purpose cleaner and water or stripper and water where necessary.
18. Clean all light fixture covers, wall socket covers, telephone covers, and replace any that are missing.
19. Clean inside of all other cupboards, such as the linen closet, broom closet, and clothes closet, using all-purpose cleaner and water.
20. Clean hardwood floors with a liquid hardwood floor wax; shake well before using. Apply a thin coat of wax and let dry.
21. If suite entrance door is pre-coated, wash the door, then polish inside and out. If painted, clean with warm water.
22. Wash out milk box with all-purpose cleaner and warm water.
23. Polish hardwood floors using red or white buffing pads.
24. If clean, dust louvers in kitchen doors.
25. Report any porcelain chip problems to the management office.
26. Re-washer all taps; clean faucet screens; and replace kitchen swing spout "O" ring and washer seats if required. Remove and clean shower head.
27. Check operation of heating system.
28. Check operation of intercom system.
29. Apply yellow warning sticker (for cigarette and hot pot burns, scratches) to counter top and refrigerator.
30. Apply fire stickers inside cupboard door. (See Chapter 3—Safety, Security, and Fire Protection.)
31. Remove weatherstrip, if any, around apartment door. Install rubber bumpers to hold door firm and to allow free air flow.
32. Clean and wax threshold wood.
33. Be sure to dust top of threshold door.
34. Check door stops and hinge pins.
35. Check to see if kitchen globe socket is loose.

METAL CLEANING

There are several metals in general use today in building structures, equipment, and furniture. Many buildings use metal exclusively in doors, windows, frames, and elevators, and probably the most popular of these metals is aluminum.

Aluminum

Comes in mill, satin, or bright finish. Wash with a mild soap and warm water; rinse, then dry. If exceedingly dirty, first clean with a solvent cleaner, then use a mild abrasive cleaner on a damp cloth. Rinse well, then dry. Make sure that you use a product that will do a proper job.

Bronze

Wash with a neutral cleaner; if still dirty, use an alkaline cleaner with a corrosive inhibitor. This can be applied with a cloth, after which it should be thoroughly rinsed with clean hot water.

Stainless Steel

Routine cleaning can be done with soap and water. Always rinse and dry after washing. If deposits are still apparent, use stainless steel polishing powder, always rubbing with the grain or direction of the polishing lines. Never use ordinary steel wool or steel brushes, as particles left behind may cause rust.

Copper and Brass

Routine maintenance is the same as with bronze. Lacquered copper and brass require daily polishing. The polish should be applied by rubbing back and forth instead of in a circular motion. If copper or brass is very dirty, it can be cleaned with a solution of tri-sodium phosphate. Rinse well after cleaning.

4-3 Floors

AN OVERVIEW

As we gathered the information about floors and floor covering for this chapter, it became quite evident that the proper choice of floors initially is as important a decision as the choice of the proper structural and electrical/mechanical components that form part of any building.

While all the building components and mechanical equipment require the careful scrutiny and care of the building staff, the systematic maintenance of all types of floors also requires considerable knowledge and attention.

It is estimated that 50 percent of the maintenance and operations workload in a building is taken up by floor care. There have been complete books written about floor care. These books should be purchased and used to upgrade the skills of the building staff. We will only endeavor to cover the basic floor care procedures for each type of floor. It is not our intention to compete with other housekeeping texts.

Recent years have seen the development of a wide variety of new flooring materials, both hard and resilient, and various new grades of commercial carpeting. A wide range of sealers, cleaners, waxes, finishes, and equipment of all types are also now available for the maintenance of these flooring materials. You should be constantly testing and researching the products and materials available. The manufacturer's representative is usually trained to provide instruction for the building staff. Make full use of this service.

Floors and floor coverings are something that architects, designers, and builders are beginning to realize can have a lasting effect on the appearance and profitability of a building. We coordinate the decor around the floor, and we

—walk on it;
—ride on it;
—spill on it;
—stain it;
—dust mop it;
—sweep it;
—scrub it;
—seal and wax it;
—shampoo it;
—wear it out in some cases;
—replace it if it wears out or if the wrong floor is installed initially.

CHOOSING THE RIGHT FLOOR

In short, those charged with the responsibility for choosing, maintaining, and replacing floors and floor coverings must know what they are doing. Housekeeping tasks are much easier when designers choose the floor or floor covering for the specific job it is expected to perform.

Briefly, the following criteria should be used during the decisionmaking process:

1. Cost
2. Estimated life
3. Availability
4. Maintenance characteristics
5. Appearance and safety
6. Replacement

Cost

No project should be considered without evaluating costs of materials and installation, both from the standpoint of intial cost, life of the investment, estimated expense, and replacement cycle.

Estimated Life

Determine durability characteristics under expected traffic and maintenance conditions, with the expectation that both resilient floors and carpet will last longer than original estimates. A cost per square foot, or per square yard, is a good analysis to make when determining what type of material to use.

Availability

Is the product readily available? Is it likely to have a reasonable period of continuing availability in case replacement material is needed or expansion calls for the same product in the future? Is it available competitively so you can get a sound bid on both material and labor?

Maintenance Characteristics

What are you looking for in terms of maintenance problems, cost, and appearance levels, and how much can you afford to spend? Include provisions for floor protectors, walk-off mats, and recognize that more permanent floor covers may be required.

Appearance and Safety

Safety, especially from fire and vandalism, must be a major objective. Appearance is closely related to maintenance, but also involves an evaluation of what you are trying to achieve in use of various interior finishes.

Replacement

Desired appearance level and the maintenance program contribute to the length of the replacement cycle. Therefore, you must consider how soon, how often, and how important is the cleaning and replacement cycle?

BUYING FLOOR TREATMENT AND MAINTENANCE

Once you have purchased the right floor, you must complete the purchase by using the proper system of maintenance.This involves the equipment, the strippers, cleaners, sealers, and coatings that are all compatible with the choice of the floor. Choosing the right floor and the right equipment, materials, and custodians that will professionally maintain the floor will certainly pay big dividends.

SPECIFICATIONS

You should prepare specifications for the purchase of equipment and cleaning materials to suit your needs.

TERRAZZO FLOORS

The word terrazzo hints at its early history. Derived from the Italian terrace or terrassa it has come to mean "a form of mosaic flooring made by embedding small pieces of marble and granite in mortar and polishing."

Although exact construction methods may vary, generally a slush underbed of cement is first laid on the sub-floor. To this is added terrazzo topping, a combination of marble chips and Portland cement. Additional marble chips may be sprinkled into the surface. Next, the surface is troweled and rolled with heavy rollers.

After the topping has cured,the terrazzo is finished by grinding the surface with progressively finer grit stones until a smooth, lustrous surface is created.

Frequently the machine used to grind terrazzo is a heavy-duty rotary floor machine. The baseboards and inaccessible areas are ground with a heavy-duty flexible shaft equipped with a smaller grinding stone. Sometimes the cove is precast and finished elsewhere and installed on the job.

To achieve different color effects, the Portland cement may contain various mineral pigments. Incidentally, Portland cement is named for the Isle of Portland, a peninsula on the south coast of Great Britain. The most expensive grade of Portland cement is white. The greyer shades are less costly.

Cleaning Characteristics

Terrazzo, like other hard surfaces, is extremely easy to maintain if you know what you are doing. Probably more terrazzo has been cleaned to death than worn out. An eloquent case for terrazzo's durability is the existence of several terrazzo floors in the Mediterranean area known to be more than 3,000 years old. In Pompeii, once the hardened lava and ash were scraped off, one terrazzo floor appeared almost new.

You really need to know only three things to maintain terrazzo. One, keep it free of acids, alkali, and oils. Two, protect the floor, especially the grouting, with a penetrating-type seal finish. Three, use the correct detergents.

The National Terrazzo and Mosaic Association recommends that the detergent pH should be lower than 10.0. Read the liquid detergent label on the material you are using. It should read "No free alkali" or an equivalent statement. The NTMA specifically warns that soaps and scrubbing powders containing water-soluble inorganic or crystallizing salts should never be used on terrazzo, because they leave a film. Unless you have an analytical testing lab down the street, you'll have to rely on the manufacturer for this information.

Because rust is a tough stain to remove from terrazzo, avoid the use of steel wool. Invariably, small particles will break off and cause rust stains.

Oil is a real enemy of terrazzo. Once it penetrates, it is nearly impossible to remove; therefore, *non-oily mop dressings are essential.*

Recommended Care

DAILY—Dust mop and damp mop as needed.

PERIODIC—Seal and finish as needed. Use a penetrating-type terrazzo seal. Avoid seals which may turn yellow and discolor. Normal stripping and buffing procedures are suitable. Use of steel wool pads should be avoided because of possible rust stains.

CONCRETE FLOORS*

At one time, painting concrete floors was quite popular. However, once painted, the floor had to be periodically repainted to maintain a good appearance. Removing the old paint to do something else was a first class mess! But paint manufacturers claim they have made giant strides in the past few years. Concrete paints are now available in oil and latex base. For most applications, the latex base seems to be preferred today. In any case, new concrete should not be painted for eight to ten weeks after it is set. It must be etched if oil base paint is used. Paint may be applied by brushing, spraying, or rolling. Two coats are generally recommended.

Most chemical manufacturers sell concrete seals. Usually these are clear compounds that harden the cement and seal the pores. If heavy floor traffic is expected, the concrete should also be finished. This procedure is similar to maintenance on soft tile floors. On the other hand, unsealed concrete should never be finished. If less than complete protection is desired, use only a sealer.

It is still essential that the floor be absolutely clean prior to seal application. Use quantity required to raise sealer to surface level.

Recommended Care

CLEANING—To remove loose, dry surface soil from unsealed surface, use oil-free sweeping compound in conjunction with broom of tampico or light fiber bristles.

To remove loose, dry soil from sealed surface, sweep with a brush of nylon or horsehair bristles.

*Portions of this section are reprinted with permission from *Floor Maintenance Manual,* Trade Publishing Company, 1972.

BRICK FLOORS

Brick is a very common building material, although its use for interior floors is fairly recent. Brick flooring is generally used in the same areas as slate, marble, or terrazzo. Common brick is sometimes used for floors, although it is subject to soiling and darkening as a result of heavy-foot traffic. More commonly used today are "brick pavers," which have a denser, smoother surface, and which are more resistant to soiling than common brick. Brick floors are installed over concrete sub-floors, for support of the weight, and may be laid in a "sand cushion" for leveling the brick courses and to aid in avoiding breakup of the mortar joints between the brick. Maintenance is usually accomplished by sweeping with a soft hair broom to remove loose soil on and between the bricks, and by power vacuuming to remove more stubborn soil build-up. The floor may also be cleaned with common detergent soaps to remove top soiling; a power vacuum water pickup may be used to remove excess moisture and detergent. Brick floors are occasionally waxed with a non-buffable polymeric-type finish for protection and higher gloss, often desired in lobby areas.

MARBLE-SLATE-STONE FLOORS

Of the many types of stone used for floors, marble has in the past been the most common. The Greek Parthenon and other ancient buildings testify to stone's durability. Although few stone floors have ever worn out, many have had their attractive appearance marred by improper care.

The broad definition of marble is any limestone hard enough to take a polish. Pure marble is white. The finest grade is called statuary marble and its use was made famous by such great sculptors as Leonardo da Vinci and Michelangelo. The unique translucent appearance of statuary marble is created by light penetrating ½ to 1-½ inches into the marble and then being reflected back to the surface. Colored marbles are caused by the addition of certain other minerals and impurities in white marble.

Marble is limestone that has been changed by the action of high heat and intense pressure deep underground, which hardens the stone and creates an even grain throughout. This makes possible a highly polished surface and provides the close-grained material so favored by sculptors and architects.

Although marble is capable of taking a very high polish, most floor marble is honed. This is a lustrous non-glossy finish which tends to hide small scratches and other evidence of wear. Use of highly polished marble is limited to walls or other decorative surfaces not subject to severe abrasive wear.

A more porous marble is travertine. Composed of relatively recently formed limestone, travertine has the unique property of being comparatively soft when first quarried and then hardening on exposure to the atmosphere.

Occasionally, granite is used for floors. Granite is a hard crystalline rock which was once molten, but which slowly cooled and hardened deep under the earth. The slow cooling allowed the rock to form a finely-grained structure which, like marble, enables it to take a high polish. Granite is usually grey, although some granite produced in Finland is red.

Slate, probably best known for the old school house blackboards and pool table tops, is another flooring material. Like marble, slate is a metamorphic rock, produced by great heat and pressure under the earth from clay and shale. Slate is most frequently used in flagstone-type floors. It will not take a high polish and in its natural state is only available in dark blue-grey colors.

Hundreds of different types of stones have been used for floors. In general, most types of stone are quite durable, very hard, and have similar maintenance characteristics. Slab quartzite is becoming more popular.

Cleaning Characteristics

Stone floors do have some problems. The porous grout or cement between the stone pieces, such as in a flagstone floor, presents a different cleaning problem than the stone surface. The stone itself, although extremely durable, must be protected from staining-type spillage. In addition, certain high alkaline cleaners can cause damage. Harsh abrasive materials, such as the black stripping pads commonly used on tile floors, can scratch softer stone surfaces. *Test any abrasive material in an inconspicuous area before committing the entire stone floor to that particular type of maintenance.*

Acids represent the greatest danger to stone floors. Very strong acids can actually eat a hole in the stone or the grouting. Mild acids will etch and roughen a polished surface. Even weak acids, such as soft drinks or the citric acid in oranges, can cause a slight etching if allowed to dry.

Slate and several of the other softer stone floors have a tendency to "bloom" or dust under foot traffic. The solution is a proper seal, properly applied. In fact, all stone floors will benefit from sealing and finishing. This presents a smooth, relatively impervious surface which will resist staining spillage. It will also make dust mopping easier by decreasing drag on the dust mop. Sealing and finishing will also decrease the slip hazard when the stone floor is wet.

Obviously, oily sweeping compounds or oily dust mop dressings should be avoided.

See the text on ceramic tile for a discussion of the grout problem.

Many slate floors already installed were treated with a terrazzo-type sealer and this cannot be reversed. This creates a high sheen finish which is not desirable on this type of floor.

Recommended Care

DAILY—Dust mop and spot mop as needed.

PERIODIC—Seal and finish as needed. Use a recommended seal. Avoid seals which may turn yellow and discolor the stone. Normal stripping and buffing procedures are suitable. Avoid the use of steel wool pads, since broken off particles may cause rust stains.

CERAMIC TILE FLOORS*

Although ceramic tile originated more than 6,000 years ago when the Egyptians first used Nile mud to make fired tile, widespread use of floor ceramic tile did not occur until the early thirteenth century in Europe.

In recent years major advances have been made in the manufacture of unglazed mosaic tile. Now made on high-speed production machinery, mosaic tile is available in a wide variety of colors and shapes, including squares, hexagons, rectangles, and circles.

Quarry tile, a close cousin to mosaic, is most common in the brown shades; however, other colors are also available. The manufacturing processes are similar to unglazed tiles. Quarry tile is usually made in various sizes and shapes.

Most quarry and unglazed tile resists a wide variety of chemicals. Ceramic tile is virtually stainproof and is extremely durable. For this reason, ceramic tile is frequently used in high-spillage areas such as dining rooms, kitchens, rest rooms, operating rooms, and swimming pools.

Cleaning Characteristics

The major cleaning problem with ceramic floors is not the ceramic tile but, like marble and terrazzo, the grouting which holds the floor or wall tiles together. Most cement grouting is porous and can be damaged by acidic and alkaline substances. *The use of a penetrating terrazzo-type seal for grouting protection is advisable.* Sealing a ceramic floor that has lost its glaze due to wear or chemical action and which has thus become porous is also recommended. An epoxy grouting is suggested when a glazed quarry tile is installed.

Finishing is a "maybe" issue. If you have a severe black marking problem, adding a metal complex floor finish may reduce housekeeping costs. If the unglazed ceramic or quarry tile is difficult to dust mop, and sealing does not produce a smooth surface, finishing may help. Most people who seal ceramic or quarry tile floors are happy with the results. If a floor is sealed, it should be protected by a recommended finish.

The only daily cleaning needed by ceramic floors is dust mopping. Wet spillage may require a little damp mopping. If the floor becomes badly soiled, it can be scrubbed using almost any detergent and nylon abrasive pads. *Steel wool pads are not recommended since they may leave rust spots.*

Recommended Care

DAILY—Dust mop or damp mop as spillage and soil conditions dictate.

PERIODIC—Sealing recommended pri-

---

*Portions of this section are reprinted with permission from *Floor Maintenance Manual*, Trade Publishing Company, 1972, pp. 25, 35.

marily for group protection. Waxing is permissible, but generally is not needed. Scrubbing with detergents and abrasive pads will remove heavy soil concentration. *Avoid the use of steel wool pads. Acids may attack the grouting.*

HARDWOOD FLOORS

Hardwoods are divided into two separate types. Birch, beech, and maple are known as the close grain woods. Oak, the open grain wood, usually requires a wood filler prior to final finishing. The filler plugs the minute crevices and opens pores in oak. You can finish oak without filler, but the resulting surface will be dimpled, thereby collecting dirt more readily and increasing the dust mop drag. Oak and maple constitute the lion's share of wood floors installed each year. More common in recent years has been the use of parquet blocks, usually 12 inches by 12 inches or larger, for corridors, elevator lobbies, or decoration, especially in retail stores or shops. Some common types of parquet flooring are pre-finished to provide a high gloss; the square blocks are formed from wood strips, glued or mechanically fastened together. Blocks of parquet wood are often reinforced with epoxy resins for greater durability, dimensional stability, and unusually attractive appearance. The blocks are usually laid in mastic, since most commercial areas have a concrete sub-floor.

Sealers

Since water emulsions raise the grain in raw wood, it is essential to coat the floor first with two or three coats of floor sealer. There are three popular conventional floor sealers—phenolic, alkyd, and epoxy. The phenolic coatings transfer their amber color to the floor and darken as time passes. The alkyds are not as tough or abrasive-resistant as the phenolic or epoxy sealers.

In recent years another finish has appeared—polyurethane. Although urethane finishes are more expensive than conventional sealers, they wear about two-thirds longer, show less dirt pickup, never have to be waxed or polished, and need only a simple damp mopping to restore the original appearance. Water resistance of urethane is excellent. They are also resistant to vegetable oils, fatty acids, and soaps.

It is always advisable when refinishing a floor with urethane to lightly sand the floor. It does not adhere readily to other finishes and this could mean poor wear results.

All sealers, if left exposed to the air, will be adversely affected. Once a varnish has oxidized it cannot be redissolved. Conventional sealers may be thinned with naptha; the urethane should be thinned with thinners supplied by the urethane supplier.

Cleaning Characteristics*

Exact maintenance of wood depends in part on the type of finish. In general, it is wise to keep the floor clear of grit, sand, and other abrasive material with a daily dust mopping. *Oily dust mop dressings should be avoided since they may stain the floor.* Scuffs on most finishes can be removed by buffing with a nylon polishing pad or 00 steel wool. *Be sure to dust mop after buffing.*

The big problem with wood is staining. Once spillage such as Mercurochrome or ink has been allowed to soak into the wood, removal is difficult, if not impossible.

---

*Portions of this section are reprinted with permission from *Floor Maintenance Manual,* Trade Publishing Company, 1972, p. 25.

Waxing almost any finish will increase its durability and cleaning ease. However, water emulsion waxes should not be used. Instead, a solvent-type liquid or paste wax is preferred. Most manufacturers recommend application with a lamb's wool applicator or a soft cloth. Allow thirty to sixty minutes for drying and then buff. If you are using a combination cleaner and wax, allow at least six hours before buffing. The solvent must have time to evaporate. This wax should never be stripped in the usual soft tile sense of the word. *Water is an enemy of wood.* Instead, most wax manufacturers provide a solvent wood cleaner. *Do not use wood furniture polishes. They are much too slippery.*

Recommended Care

DAILY—Dust mop as needed with a non-oily dressing.

PERIODIC CARE—Wax and buff as needed. Recoat the floor finish and patch as the floor material and wear dictate.

4-4 Floor Care

PREVENTIVE MAINTENANCE

Preventive maintenance begins as soon as a new floor is laid. The on-site construction staff must understand how to prepare or protect a new floor so that problems such as damage to the floor and/or grouting are minimized. The major concerns are

—Protection of surface materials against damage due to incorrect choice of material.

—Protection against using improper maintenance techniques.

—Protection against the use of the wrong equipment, materials, and supplies.

CONSULTATION

When considering the choice of a new floor, or a proper maintenance program, it is wise to seek assistance before making a decision. Ask someone who is familiar with the day-to-day maintenance for the floor you are considering. Once the floor is installed, you will not be anxious to remove it.

SWEEPING

There are a number of tricks the professional knows that will make your job easier. Generally the only time hand sweeping is best is when the floor surface is too rough, too heavily loaded, or too wet for dust mopping. Dust mopping is much easier and faster.

The exact choice of fiber in the bristle is extremely important. For instance, horsehair, a fine bristle, does an excellent job with dust. Coarse bristles, such as bass or bassine, do a good job with heavier and larger types of soil. This is why some push brooms which will be used to sweep both large and small soil have horsehair on the outside with another stiffer fiber on the inside.

Although a push broom is usually used in large open areas, a good old-fashioned corn broom may be the easiest way to sweep rooms with many nooks and crannies.

Watch your broom handle. With your attention on the working end of the broom, it is easy to accidentally get the other end in trouble. Besides things on tables, watch out for overhead lights.

A well-maintained push broom or corn broom makes your job easier. Establishing a uniform sweeping rhythm will also make your job easier. Keep piles of dirt out of

FIGURE 4-4 Types of brushes and brooms. (Courtesy of Sanitary Products Company, Limited.)

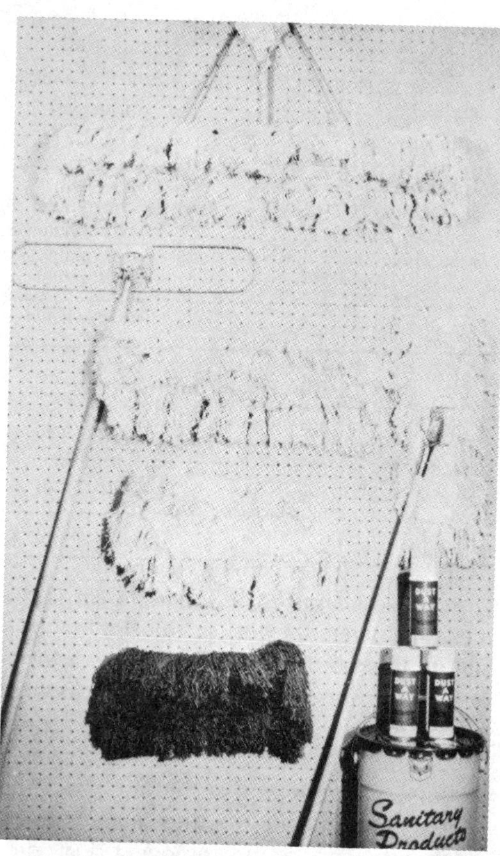

FIGURE 4-5 Types of dust mops. (Courtesy of Sanitary Products Company, Limited.)

trafficked aisles. Optimum sweeping is achieved by using the bristle tips and avoiding bristle "roll under."

It has been said that you can always tell a good worker by the way he sweeps the floor.

DUST MOPPING*

The first dust mops were made of cotton yarn, and were soon followed by synthetic saran models. The major advantage of the synthetics was their ability to mold dust as the result of static electricity created by the dust mopping procedure. Friction caused by the mop passing along the floor surface caused the dust to adhere to the fibers of the mop head. This largely eliminated the need for treating the mops.

Most of the dirt on your floor will be in one of two places—either on the floor finish or in the floor finish. If it is on the finish, you can remove it by dust mopping, spot mopping, damp mopping, wet mopping, or scrubbing. The accompanying chart shows the relationships and roughly how long each method will take.

*Portions of this section are reprinted with permission from *Floor Maintenance Manual*, Trade Publishing Company, 1972, p. 90.

Soil on Floor Finish

Method of Soil Removal	Normal Rate Range Per 1000 Sq. Ft.
Dust Mopping	3–10 minutes
Spot Mopping	6–15 minutes
Damp Mopping	15–20 minutes
Wet Mopping	30–40 minutes
Scrubbing	45–120 minutes

Soil in Floor Finish

Method of Soil Removal	Normal Rate Range Per 1000 Sq. Ft.
Stripping	150–200 minutes

Your best choice for soil removal is the method nearest the top of the list that will still do the job. In other words, it is a lot of needless, extra hard work to strip a floor if proper maintenance will restore its former appearance.

Floor dust mopping is the last job to be done in any area after routine cleaning. Dust mopping is effective in removing dust, dirt, and litter. If the litter is especially heavy (such as wood shavings), or if the floor is rough (such as unsealed concrete), it may be best to use a push broom.

Dust mopping is important because it helps prevent more serious floor defects, such as soil film and encrustations. If the floor is regularly dust mopped, the floor finish will actually last longer. Additionally, there is less dust on the furniture.

If you pay particular attention to the room's corners and edges, the center of the floor will almost seem to take care of itself.

Quality Requirements

When floor dust mopping is completed, the entire floor, including the corners, edges, and behind doors, should be free of dust, dirt, and litter. Floor dust mopping does not remove scuffs, black marks, or wet spillage.

When your dust mop gets dirty, wash it. This is no less often than when the dirt has reached almost to the backing. In most buildings, particularly hospitals, dust mops are changed more frequently.

When storing your dust mop do not set it on the floor. Instead, hang it up, or leave it on the cart.

Scrape up any chewing gum on the floor using either a putty knife or a razor blade holder.

As you dust mop the floor, you will make little piles of dirt in locations where they will be easy to pick up later. Do not pile dirt in doorways or traffic ways because, even late at night, thoughtless people have a tendency to track this dirt onto the clean floor. Do not move piles of dirt long distances, as they tend to dribble out around the edges of the dust mop.

Summary

Keep the same leading edge on the dust mop. This prevents soil drop-out. Do not allow piles of dirt to accumulate in traffic lanes or doorways. Change the mop head when it becomes heavily soiled or sooner if directed otherwise. Launder map heads as needed.

Try various patterns and strokes for your dust mop to accommodate existing conditions. There is no "best way" that covers all situations.

STRIPPING*

Stripping is the most laborious, and time consuming, of the maintenance methods

*Portions of this section are reprinted with permission from *Floor Maintenance Manual,* Trade Publishing Company, 1972, p. 105.

FIGURE 4-6 Dust mopping a corridor. Keep the mop head flat on the floor with strands spread evenly. Use a push stroke. Do not lift mop from the floor except for shaking.

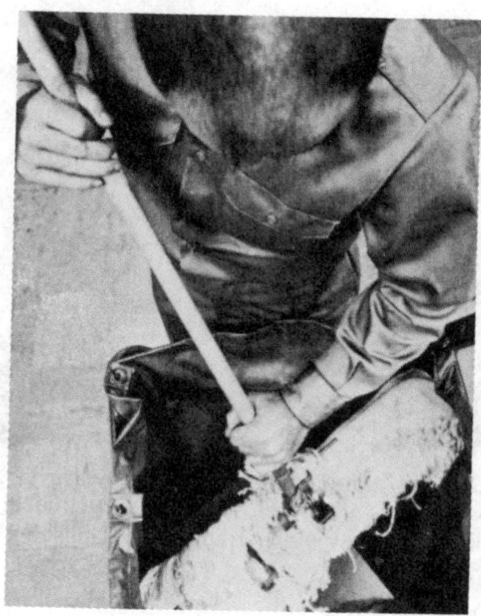

FIGURE 4-8 Cleaning the mop head. Dust mops should be kept clean. Do not dust mop (sweep) with a dirty or soiled mop-head. Periodically the dust mop should be shaken out in the cleaning cart bag. (Courtesy of the Trade Press Publishing Company.)

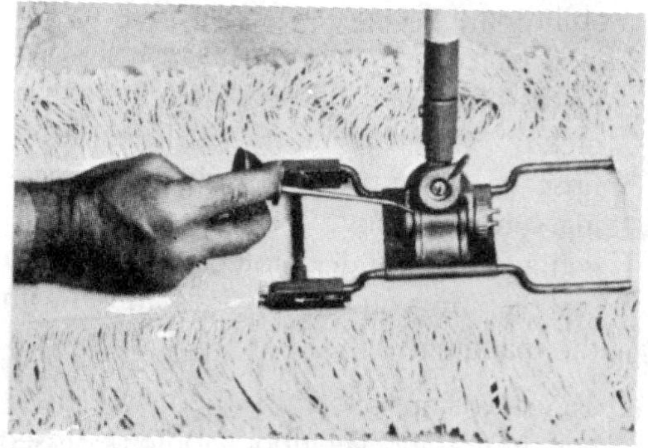

FIGURE 4-7 Maintain the swivel head. As with other moving parts, a periodic drop of oil is recommended. (Courtesy of the Trade Press Publishing Company.)

used on soft and hard floors. It should be a last resort action. Only when the floor no longer responds to mopping and re-finishing should it be stripped. Generally you should strip a floor when the finish is worn through and the seal is broken. The soil can now work its way under the finish, causing a discoloration and dull finish.

Do not confuse stripping with scrubbing. Scrubbing is an incomplete stripping process. It removes only the top few layers of floor finish. However, scrubbing and stripping are done in nearly the same way, the difference being in the choice of detergent and in the length of scrubbing. A strong stripper will strip a floor, whereas a weak detergent and less scrubbing will only remove the top few layers of floor finish. It is a delicate balance. Do not strip if a less laborious technique will restore floor appearance.

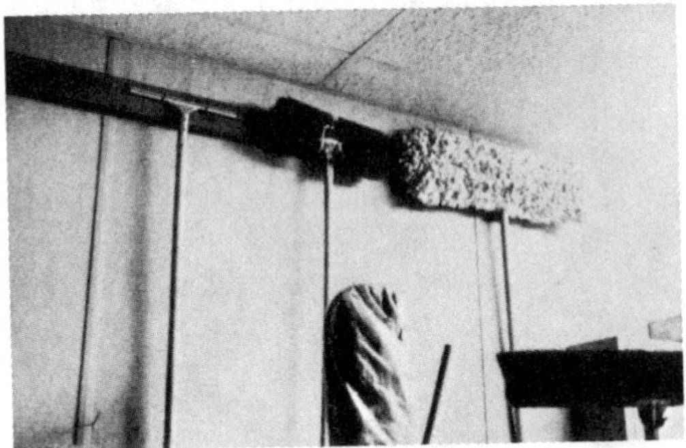

FIGURE 4-9 Storing the dust mop. Always hang up a mop when it is not being used. Allow air circulation on all sides. (Courtesy of the Trade Press Publishing Company.)

Requirements

When a floor is stripped, all of the finish is removed. A completely clean floor has a dull, lifeless appearance. It may even have a whitish cast. Build-up should be gone from the edges and corners. If the floor has a sealer coat, it may or may not be desirable to remove this coat. Stripping normally refers only to finish removal, but water emulsion surface seals can be stripped, too. Permanent solvent base penetrating sealer cannot be removed.

Materials Needed For Stripping

1-brown stripping pad
1-Mermaid stripping mop
1-Mermaid rinse mop
1-2 pail dolly and wringer
1-baseboard scrub brush
1-"Doodle Bug"
1-stainless steel sponge
1-wet/dry pick-up (if available)
1-floor machine and driving pad

Recommended stripper is used to remove old finish from the floor. *This is its sole purpose.*

Method

1. Sweep the floor.
2. Flood a small area at a time with the stripper and allow about five minutes for the stripper to work. Use hot water with 8 ounces per gallon of stripper.
3. Using the baseboard scrub brush or "Doodle Bug," clean around the baseboard and corners, and have your floor machine and brown stripping pad ready for use.
4. Start scrubbing one way with the machine, slowly, being careful not to splash the walls. After you have completed this area, go back over it in the opposite direction, crisscrossing the same area, to ensure against the possibility of missing a section of the floor. Be sure not to let the stripper dry before you are ready to pick it up. Otherwise, you will have to run your machine over it again. If the stripper is left to dry, it turns into a grey paste. Be careful not to get too far ahead of yourself. *Remember, it is better to do a small section at a time, and do it properly, than to attempt too large an area and have to go over it again.*
5. When you are sure that you have stripped the designated area to the best of your ability, the second step is to pick up the old finish. The same mop is used to pick up the old finish and put it into the pail of pick-up water. With the stripper mop, rinse and pick up all of the old finish, making sure to change the water when it is getting dirty and discolored. If you have a wet pick-up, you pick up the solution with the machine.
6. The next step is to rinse the area. *This is very important.* The floor should be rinsed with a rinsing mop and hot water. You must remove all the alkaline from the floor to neutralize the surface. Flood the area

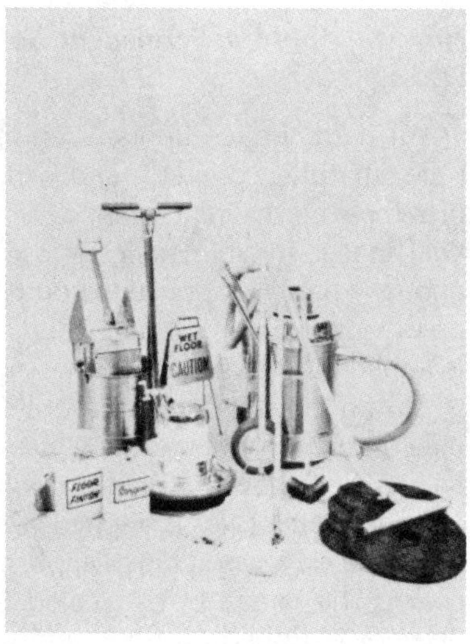

(a)

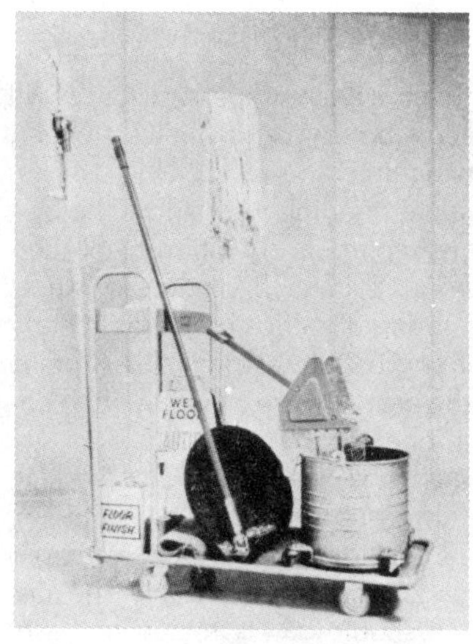

(b)

FIGURE 4-10 Tools required for floor stripping. (a) Tools required for floor stripping include floor machine and drive pad, wet pick up vacuum, buckets, wringer, stripping pads, "Wet Floor" signs, foot wiping carpet scrap, small bucket, sponge, utility brush, wax applicating equipment and baseboard tool. (b) A cart such as this will make your job easier and save wasted trips for forgotten items by acting as a mobile service closet. (Courtesy of the Trade Press Publishing Company.)

with clear hot water, pick up the water, and let dry. Check the floor by rubbing your hand over it to see if a grey film shows. If it shows, it means there is still dirty finish and alkaline on the floor. Remember, you started out to do a really good job of stripping—don't spoil it now by not rinsing properly. *Make sure everything is rinsed from the floor.*

Safety Precautions

Since floor stripping involves fair quantities of water on the floor, you should always put out "Wet Floor" signs to alert people to the slippery wet floor.

Floor stripping involves strong detergents and lots of water. Both can damage tile floors. Read the label on the stripper can and follow the recommended dilutions. Tiles may work loose if you leave water standing on the floor for too long a period. Usually fifteen to thirty minutes is acceptable, but leaving a tile floor wet with detergent during your lunch hour may cause problems.

FIGURE 4-11 "Wet floor" caution signs. (Courtesy of the Trade Press Publishing Company.)

Summary

A floor that has been properly stripped will not only look better, but will last longer, thereby saving time and labor. Only you, in your individual building, will know the best time for this important operation to be performed. Choose a time when you can expect the least amount of traffic—preferably early in the morning or late at night. Be sure to barricade the area you are working on to ensure that no one will slip.

Before applying the finish, hand clean corners and baseboards. When applying finish, stay at least one tile's width away from permanently placed objects. Only the last coat of finish should barely touch the baseboard.

SEALERS

Basically, there are two methods available to dress all surface materials:

1. Application of a permanent solvent base penetrating sealer on hard surfaces, such as terrazzo, slate, marble, concrete, and certain quarry tile floors.
2. Application of a water emulsion surface sealer on resilient vinyl asbestos or certain quarry tile floors. Caution: a permanent solvent sealer should *never* be used on a resilient vinyl asbestos floor.

Both sealers are designed to

—Protect original surface material from heat, acids, oils, alkalis, dyes.

—Maintain its structural stability and increase its longevity.

—Enhance its appearance—an ideal base when high luster is required.

How to Apply a Permanent Solvent Base Sealer

All hard surface floors, such as terrazzo, slate, marble, concrete, and certain quarry tiles must be sealed as soon as installed. It is vital that a suitable sealer is used and that enough coats are applied to completely build up the sealer to the surface. Then, a final coat is applied to the surface.

On an existing floor, the only areas that may require further sealing are the traffic areas. The final coat could possibly be worn.

Permanent sealer is applied with a lamb's wool pad on a wood block applicator, in thin coats. The area to be sealed should be properly stripped, rinsed, and completely dry.

First, test an area to determine if the sealer is necessary. If the test indicates a honeycomb or discoloring appearance, further sealing is unnecessary.

The sealer must be applied using a circular motion and not a straight line. Sealer should only be applied when you have plenty of time and will not be disturbed by people walking on the floor before it is properly dry.

Do a *small* area at a time.

After the sealer has been completely applied, destroy the lamb's wool pad—it cannot be used again.

Again, consultation with the supplier of your materials is advisable before commencing any sealing job.

Sealing Resilient Floor Tile

Materials Needed

1-Floor sealer applicator (for small areas)

1-Lamb's wool pad (for small areas)

1-Nylon mop (for large areas)

1-Pail and wringer (for large areas)

Resilient water emulsion surface floor sealer

Resilient floor water emulsion surface sealer is milky white in color. This sealer should be applied to a new or used floor. The floor must be properly stripped, rinsed, and dry before applying the sealer.

Usually, old floors will not require re-sealing unless the seal is broken, thus allowing soil to work its way under the sealer.

Resilient floor sealer is used for sealing vinyl asbestos tile floors. Drying time is about twenty minutes. Apply with a clean nylon mop. If you are doing a large area, use a clean pail and wringer. Put the nylon mop into the pail of sealer, wringing out the excess sealer from the mop, and apply a thin coat of sealer over the area. This sealer is not the same as the permanent sealer. When the first coat is dry, apply a second thin coat. If someone walks across the floor, you can go back and fix it before it drys. After the area has been completed, take the nylon mop or lamb's wool pad, and using cold water, rinse out all the sealer.

FLOOR FINISH APPLICATION

Materials Needed

1-Floor applicator (for small areas)

1-Lamb's wool pad (for small areas)

1-Pail and wringer (large areas)

1-Nylon mop (large areas)

Floor Finish

After the floor sealers are completely dry, apply a floor finish to protect the floor. On a small area, use a floor applicator and a lamb's wool pad. On a large area, use a nylon mop and a clean pail with a wringer. Do not mix the nylon floor finish mop with a stripper, damp, or rinse mop. This mop is like a paint brush to a master painter and should be kept meticulously clean. Rinse the mop in cold water after each and every time it has been used.

Estimate the amount of finish needed and pour into a clean bucket. One gallon should cover 1,000 to 1,500 square feet depending on the type of floor. If the area is small, leave the finish in the original container and pour directly on to the mop.

The floor should be dry and completely free of old wax, soil, and cleaning solution. Applying new wax over old wax and soil can cause unsightly build-up and discoloration of floors. If applied over dried cleaning solution, the wax may crawl, streak, turn yellow, or remain tacky.

The first coat of finish should be applied as close to the baseboard as possible, without splashing it. Use a one-way motion of the mop. After the finish has dried to the touch (roughly fifteen minutes), the second coat can be applied. This coat should be applied only within 12 inches of the baseboard. A third and fourth coat should be applied within twelve inches of the baseboard, also. An accumulation of finish at the edges of the floor only picks up dirt and discolors over a period of time. The purpose of the floor finish is to protect the traffic areas of the floor and give it a hard shine. *Do not over wax.* Four thin coats are better than one thick coat. Buffing the floors just after the finish has been applied is not recommended. *The finish should not be buffed for at least three days to allow it to cure properly.*

After the floor is finished, the only maintenance required is to sweep the floors with a saran dust mop and damp mop with clear cold water. All-purpose cleaner, added to water, can be used to pick up spillage or any heavy soil that may be tracked into the building. Use 1 or 2 ounces per gallon of water. Avoid damp mopping, even with an all-purpose cleaner, with anything other than *cold* water. Using hot water will soften the finish and absorb soil.

From time to time, the traffic areas on the floor should be examined. If damp mopping fails to bring out the shine, these areas should be "touched up" with one, or if necessary, two thin coats of floor finish in these traffic areas. Caution: The area to be waxed must be rinsed thoroughly with clear water before applying wax.

TREATMENT OF WAX BUILDUP

If terrazzo or tile floors become yellow, it does not always indicate that they are dirty. It could be an indication of over waxing. To correct this, two or three layers of floor finish should be removed from the floor. By using the floor machine, with a scrubbing pad and 2 to 4 ounces of all-purpose cleaner per gallon of *lukewarm* water, you can remove two to three layers of wax and bring the finish back to a neutral color. After rinsing the floor properly, a thin coat of floor finish should be applied.

FIGURE 4-12 Types of mop heads and handles. (Courtesy of Sanitary Products Company, Limited.)

FLOOR MOPPING*

Mopping removes soil by two methods. Encrusted soil is partly removed by the physical action of the mop and partly removed by the detergents.

Spot mopping means mopping only the dirty portion of the floor. This may be the traffic lanes or only spillage spots. Either a sponge mop or a string mop can be used.

Damp mopping means the entire floor is mopped just once with a damp mop.

Wet mopping means a detergent solution is laid on the floor; the solution is allowed to work. The area is worked with a mop or floor machine, which loosens the soil and makes it easier to remove. Next, the dirty solution is picked up, usually with a mop, but a wet vacuum cleaner may be faster. The entire process is repeated with clear rinse water.

Quality Requirements

If the floor has been damp mopped or wet mopped, it should be nearly free of dust, dirt,

*Portions of this section are reprinted with permission from *Floor Maintenance Manual*, Trade Publishing Company, 1972, pp. 101–102.

and water soluble soil. The floor should be almost free of black marks.

Safety Precautions

Mopping floors is no easy job. It can be potentially dangerous and destructive. Not everyone can do it well. For instance, if you leave water on the floor too long, the tiles may pop loose. If the detergent solution is too strong, tiles can crack and dry out. In bad cases, the floor may look like alligator hide.

In only a few minutes, an amateur slopping up baseboards can create hours of hard work for others.

"Wet Floor" signs should always be put out to warn passers-by. A wet floor is a slippery floor. If someone slips and falls, there may be expensive law suits.

Banging up furniture should be avoided.

How to Mop a Floor

Tools Needed

Mops—12 to 16 ounce for women
24 to 32 ounce for men

Buckets and wringers (Number depends on method)

Mop abrasive pad

Dust mop

Counter brush

Dust pan

Putty knife

Measuring cup

Detergent

Safety sign

First, mix the detergent solution to the proper strength. An 8-ounce plastic cup is handy for measuring detergent. *Don't guess. Don't count "glugs." A glug on a 1-gallon can be anything from 2 to 6 ounces, depending on how thick the detergent is.* Some mop buckets have embossed gallon marks, which makes measuring the water easier. Stir the mop solution with a mop, and go to the work area.

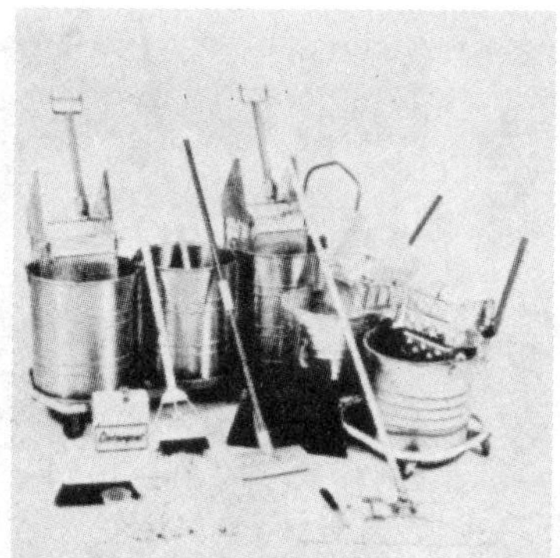

FIGURE 4-13 Tools needed for mopping a floor. (Courtesy of the Trade Press Publishing Company.)

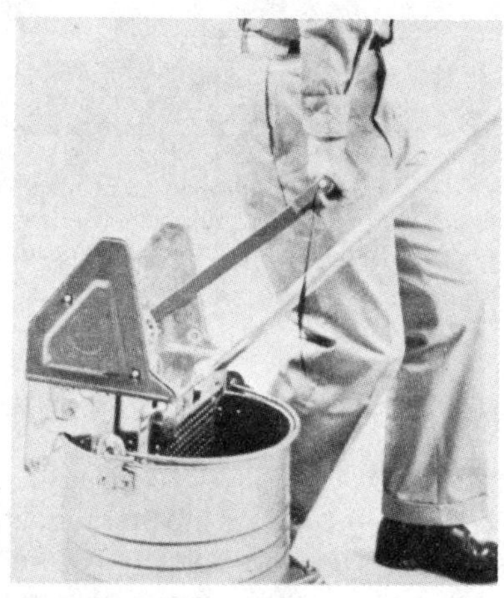

FIGURE 4-14 Wringing out the mop. When mopping, wring out the mop by leaning on the wringer. The easy way is to face away from the wringer while keeping your arm straight. (Courtesy of the Trade Press Publishing Company.)

FIGURE 4-15 The figure eight style of mopping. In open areas the figure eight style of mopping is used. Swing the mop from side-to-side in eight-to-ten foot strokes. (Courtesy of the Trade Press Publishing Company.)

FIGURE 4-16 The push-pull method of mopping. In furnished areas use the push-pull method of mopping. (Courtesy of the Trade Press Publishing Company.)

FIGURE 4-17 Mopping tip. You will save work if you dust mop the floor before you damp or wet mop it. Dust mopping removes loose dirt and litter. It will make your mopping solutions last longer and will be easier to do a better job. KEEP THE MOPS AWAY FROM THE WALLS.

Two-Bucket System of Mopping

This method is not quite as fast as the one-bucket system, but it does a better job. Detergent solution is in one bucket. The second bucket contains clear water and becomes the pick-up bucket. The detergent solution is put down on the floor and then picked up and put in the pick-up bucket. If you put it in the detergent bucket, you'll be putting dirty detergent solution on the next floor you mop.

Mops are always squeezed into the pick-up bucket. As the pick-up bucket becomes full, it is emptied. It is necessary to change your detergent solution less often; you merely use it up.

Once you have finished the mopping and picking up, rinse mop the entire area using a bucket containing clear rinse water. (Figure 4-18)

Summary

Local needs will dictate the exact method used to mop floors. In general, avoid letting water stand on the floors. Avoid the use of strong detergents; the amount of detergent must always be measured as directed by the manufacturer. Both can cause extensive floor damage. Avoid slopping up baseboards and furniture legs. Hold the mop with one hand while the other hand cups the end of the mop stick. Move the mop from side to side in rhythmical 8- to 10-foot sweeps. Never start a fresh mop next to a baseboard. Always mop next to baseboards with nearly dry mops. At the completion of the job, clean all equipment. *Mops should not be allowed to dry standing with their heads on the floor.*

FIGURE 4-18 Two bucket system of mopping. Detergent solution is in one bucket. The second bucket contains clear water and becomes the pick-up bucket. (Courtesy of the Trade Press Publishing Company.)

STAINS

Environment has a definite effect on the quality of an employee's work, as well as his reaction to his supervisor and the general public. The appearance of your floors, free from stains, will help to achieve this.

Stains should be treated as soon as possible, as they become more difficult to remove after they have dried. However, no one should attempt to remove stains unless he knows what the stain is and why a certain type of remover is being used. Only as a last resort should chemicals be used to remove stains. When removing stains with chemicals, directions should be carefully followed (i.e., if the procedure specifies treatment with a solvent prior to cleaning, it may be that if reversed, the alkali in the soap would set the stain and make it impossible to remove).

Stain removers (1) dissolve the substance that causes the stain; (2) absorb the stain; or (3) act as a bleaching agent. Thus, stain removers fall into three general classes:

1. Clear solvents which dissolve grease, chewing gum, lipstick.

2. Absorbents such as chalk, talcum powder, blotting paper, or cotton which absorb fresh grease or moist stains.
3. Bleaches such as household ammonia or lemon juice which discolor stains.

Realizing the importance of knowing the nature of the stain, the custodian should ask himself the following questions before trying to remove it:

1. Is it a water-base stain? . . . Use water to remove it.
2. Is the stain alcohol? . . . Use alcohol to remove it (i.e., removing a tincture of iodine stain).
3. Is the stain acid? . . . Use an alkali to neutralize it.
4. Is the stain alkali? . . . Use an acid to neutralize it.
5. Is the stain grease? . . . Use soap.
6. Does the stain contain albumin (milk or blood)? . . . Do not use a hot solution (it will cook the albumin).

For common stains in your building, prepare a chart listing the kind of remover to use on specific stains or specific surfaces. It is a constant challenge to produce effective results. Remember: Floors (any floors) that are deeply embedded with sand or soil deteriorate quickly and once they have started wearing, no amount of cleaning will bring them back. Proper and regular maintenance creates a pleasant environment.

The condition of your floors should and will add aesthetically, as well as economically, to your building. When we purchase our supplies, we should evaluate not only how far or how many square feet the product will cover, but most important, how long and how well it will serve us—before we consider price. More often than not, the "expensive" quality products will outserve and outlast inferior ones, so that, ultimately, you save not only on materials, but also your floors will be protected properly and will look their very best.

4–5 Carpet Care

AN OVERVIEW

To an industry accustomed to working with hard and soft types of solid floors, carpeting is a different experience. Location, color, construction, and fiber determine what kind of care a carpet requires. A wrong guess on any one of these factors can double or triple carpet cleaning costs. Like any other floor, cost depends entirely on what you do to the floor. Clean a floor with a toothbrush and it will cost a mint.

Because of soil tracks, carpet does not mix well with other floor surfaces. Use carpet in all areas of the building unless there is an overwhelming reason not to do so. Eliminate islands of tile and carpets. From a housekeeping standpoint, this eliminates the need to move water and floor machines over carpet to periodically maintain the hard floor surfaces.

Contrary to common belief, people seldom grind out cigarettes on carpets. This practice will be even less of a problem because of the "no-smoking" bylaws now being enacted in many areas.

Carpeting can make a significant contribution to both the overall image of a building and the productivity of an office. Carpet color is a major housekeeping factor and we should know the problems with various colors, other than compatability with the decor of the area being carpeted.

CARPET FABRICATION METHODS:

Carpets today are fabricated—combining the pile and backing into one integral fabric—by a variety of methods. They include:

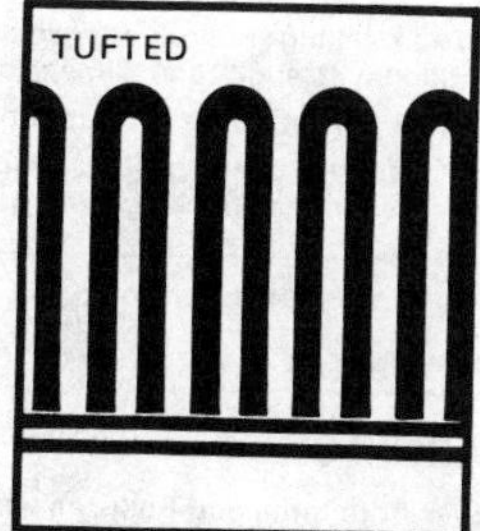

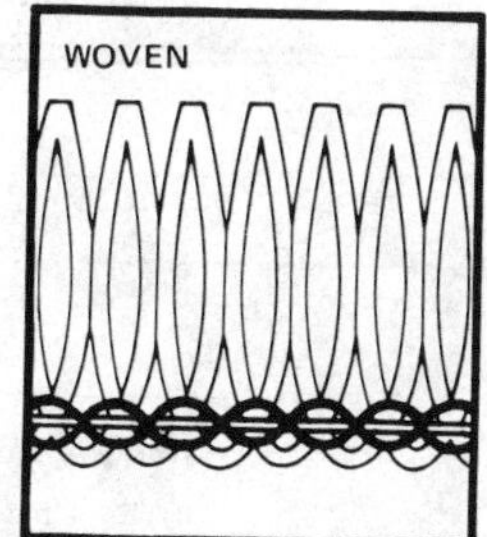

TUFTING—Stitching tufts of pile yarn into a pre-woven backing material with a tufting machine, which operates basically like a gigantic sewing machine. Utilizing hundreds of needles, plus electronic and other devices governing the needles for pattern effects, this method now accounts for more than 90% of carpets sold.

WEAVING—The traditional way of making carpet on a loom, interlacing the yarns forming the backing and the pile. The lengthwise yarns—chain, stuffer, and pile—are the warp. The yarns going across the carpet are the weft, or filling. Looms used for carpet weaving are the velvet, Axminster, and Wilton. Woven carpets continue to be important in contract installations where certain textures and intricate patterns are specified.

KNITTING—A method by which carpets are made on a specialized knitting machine using different sets of needles to loop together the pile, backing, and stitching yarns.

NEEDLEPUNCHING—A manufacturing method by which the fibers are punched or needled into a structural material and then compressed into a felt-like fabric. Used mainly in indoor-outdoor carpet types.

FLOCKING—A method of embedding very short fibers in a backing, usually done electrostatically, producing a cut pile surface with a velvety look.

FIGURE 4-19 Carpet fabrication. (Courtesy of Sanitary Products Company, Limited.)

Carpet Color

—Solid colors magnify the effects of dirt.

—Solid light and dark colors also easily show litter and soil.

—Carpets with patterns maintain good housekeeping appearance.

Carpet Fibers

Carpets are available in a wide variety of fibers. Wool is the oldest and probably most respected of carpet fibers. Due to cost, most commercial carpeting fibers are now synthetic. They are known by various trade names, but the generic names are acrylic, nylon, polyester, polypropylene (polyolefin), triacetate, viscose, and olefin. Nylons, along with polypropylenes, show top wear resistance.

Location of Dirt in Carpet

Carpet maintenance is basically a function of dirt location and its removal. When soil is on the top surface of the carpet, it is relatively

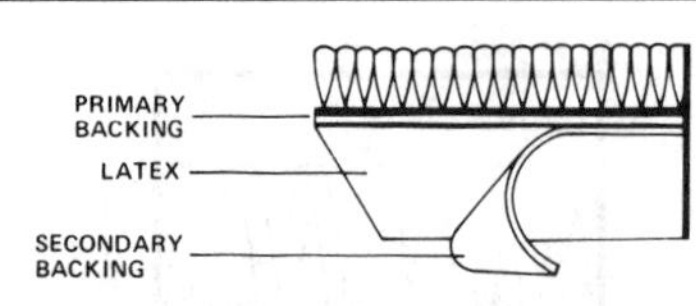

CARPET BACKING

The backing on the underside of a carpet secures the tufts and gives additional strength and dimensional stability to the floor covering.

Most carpets have a double backing:

1. Primary backing—that which the yarn is tufted into.
2. Secondary backing—the outer backing.

TYPES OF BACKING

JUTE—A natural fiber from India and Pakistan which, after woven, is used for backing to add strength, weight and stiffness.

POLYPROPYLENE—Synthetic thermoplastic resin, available in woven and non-woven constructions.

Jute has been the traditional carpet backing and still is the most widely used material for both primary and secondary backing. However, primary backings of man-made fibers have been developed recently and usage is growing rapidly, especially in indoor-outdoor qualities and in carpets tufted on fine gauge machines. Backings of man-made fibers are:
1. Non-allergenic. 2. Lightweight. 3. Resistant to mildew, dry rot and odor. 4. Plentiful supply. 5. Stable.

LATEX—(not an actual backing)—Milky fluid used as synthetic adhesive to seal tufts to the primary backing.

FOAM BACK—An added backing of foam rubber which is generally ⅛" to ¼" in thickness and serves as a self-cushion for the carpet.

HIGH DENSITY FOAM—Same as foam back, but utilizing a heavier than normal grade of rubber compound. High density foam back should contain no less than 38 oz. (1075gm) of weight per square yard (m) and a minimum thickness of ⅛" (.32cm).

FIGURE 4-20 Carpet backing. (Courtesy of Sanitary Products Company, Limited.)

easy to remove. In fact, sometimes picking up surface litter by hand, with a carpet sweeper, or with a lobby pan is the fastest and most effective way. Once the soil sinks beneath the surface of the carpet, it is in the pile. Dry soil in the pile slowly sinks toward the carpet backing, but as wet soil dries, it becomes encrusted around the carpet fibers.

*Walk-Off Carpets**

Stop the dirt at your door and you won't have to clean it off your floor. Floor mats catch dirt. They direct traffic. They protect floors. They help provide a psychological transition from one floor area to another.

The most important thing about floor mats is that they must be BIG. A small door mat is kicked aside. It is stepped over. Nobody uses it. Only door-to-door salesmen wipe their feet anymore. To be effective, door mats must be big enough to be walked on. The average person walks with a pace of about 30 inches. Small women may take short 24½-inch steps. Some tall men stride out at almost 3 feet. On the table below it would seem apparent that to get both feet on the mat at least once, the minimum mat should be about 70 inches long. To wipe off each foot twice requires a 136-inch long mat for normal unbroken pacing.

LENGTH OF PACE (TOTAL TRAVEL)

	Small Women	*Average*	*Tall Men*
First Step	24″–26″	28″–30″	32″–34″
Second Step	48″–52″	56″–60″	64″–68″
Third Step	68″–78″	84″–90″	96″–102″
Fourth Step	96″–104″	112″–120″	128″–136″

*Portions of this section are reprinted with permission from *Floor Maintenance Manual,* Trade Publishing Company, 1972, p. 49.

DEFINITIONS OF KEY CARPET TERMS

PILE (OR YARN) WEIGHT—Refers to the ounces (grams) of surface yarn per square yard of carpet. Considered with pile height and density factors, plus the type of fiber used, pile or face weight is a major index of quality.

PILE HEIGHT—The height of the yarn above the carpet backing expressed in thousandths of an inch (cm). In Wilton and velvet carpets, which are woven over wires, the term "wire height" may be used.

PITCH OR GAUGE—In woven goods, the number of pile ends or tufts across a 27" (68cm) width is the pitch. In tufted carpet, the term "gauge" is used. This denotes the widthwise spacing of a row of tufting needles.

STITCHES, ROWS, OR WIRES—These terms refer to the number of tufts along one inch (cm) of carpet length. "Wire" usually denotes a velvet or Wilton carpet.

TOTAL WEIGHT—Refers to the weight per square yard (p.sq.m) of the pile yarns, primary backing, secondary backing, and coatings.

CONSTRUCTION—Describes the method by which the carpet is fabricated.

FIGURE 4-21 Key carpet terms. (Courtesy of Sanitary Products Company, Limited.)

This data on length of pace is extremely accurate, because considerable research has been done on walking by industrial engineering groups, the U.S. Army, and many others. What is not known is the effect stepping on a mat has on a person's pace. It is a guess, and only a guess, that a person's stride reduces dramatically when he goes from one floor surface to another. For safety reasons, a person probably takes shorter paces until he is certain of the surface underfoot.

The second factor is mat location. Seldom is a mat located so a person can walk directly over it without opening a door. Stopping and starting to open the door again means reduced stride. If there is a double set of doors, perhaps even a 3-foot wide mat between the doors is sufficient to get both feet once. Any mat will help.

PADDING

Padding, the "underlay" or "cushion," adds comfort, quiet and insulation to the floor-covering. It also acts as a shock absorber and thus extends the life of the carpeting.

The three most widely used types of padding are the rubber type, urethane, and the natural type hair and fiber blends.

The natural paddings tend to be firmer than the "bouncy" rubber or urethane pads.

Your choice depends on whether you desire a cushiony effect or one that is more firm and solid. Natural paddings are made in a variety of weights based on ounces per square yard. Synthetic cushionings are made in a variety of thicknesses ranging from ⅛" to ½" (.32cm to 1.27cm).

FIGURE 4-22 Carpet under padding. (Courtesy of Sanitary Products Company, Limited.)

Minimum Lengths for Shoe Cleaning

Generally, to clean both feet once you meed a mat at least 5-feet long. To clean both feet twice, you need a mat about 10-feet long.

If mat size is restricted by a mat recess, it may be possible to fill the recess with plywood or other material and lay a proper size mat over it.

Wear Control

Carpeting in heavily traveled spots receives hard wear. For a better appearance and longer life for your floor covering, try to give these areas breathing spells. If possible, walk-off carpets should be turned around, so the carpet will wear more evenly.

Walk-Off Carpet Cleaning

The carpets should be removed to an area where they can be washed and scrubbed with a deck brush. Use a recommended detergent solution of one-part to four-parts water. Rinse the detergent out with clean water, using a wet and dry pick up. Draw out as much water as possible. Leave the rugs on the floor for eight hours to dry.

Basic Care and Maintenance of Carpet

Carpeting is really easy to maintain. A simple, regular care plan will help you maintain the beautiful appearance of your carpeting. To maintain the carpet's best appearance, follow this basic care plan, which applies to all carpets and rugs.

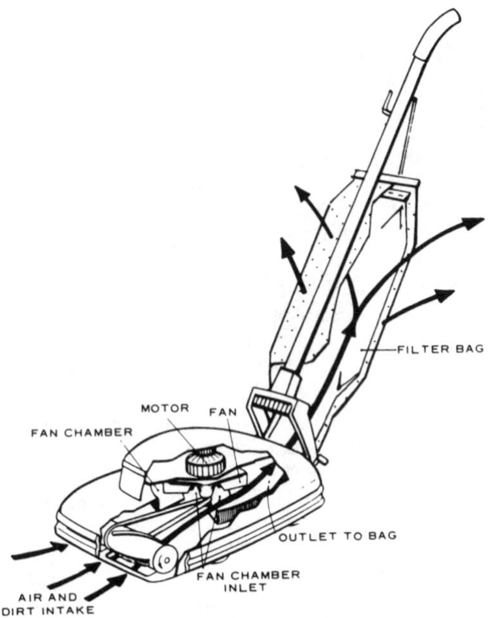

FIGURE 4-23 The upright carpet cleaner. A good upright carpet cleaner will remove three times as much dirt as a straight suction air cleaner. Frequent use of a good vacuum cleaner prolongs carpet cleanliness and appearance, and, in some cases, extends the period between wet cleaning. (Courtesy of American Institute of Maintenance.)

VACUUMING

Corridor Carpets

Corridor carpets should be vacuumed a minimum of twice a week. Regular vacuuming of carpets, using a heavy-duty vacuum, is essential.

Several points on proper vacuuming should be noted:

1. The vacuum must be kept in a good operating condition.
2. The proper adjustment to the head should be made to compensate for the various pile heights. It should be set to a height that gives slight resistance when the machine is moved in reverse.
3. When vacuuming, the operator should walk forward for the full length of the cord without straining the cord. The forward operation of the vacuum cleaner will pick up 40 percent of the dirt. This forward action is mainly a suction action.

   The operator then moves in reverse, covering the same area, and the brushes on the vacuum cleaner now do their job. This operation does the deep pile cleaning and accounts for 60 percent of the dirt.
4. In order to avoid overheating the motor and consequent motor burnouts, the cords must never exceed a maximum of 50 feet. *Never use an extension cord.*
5. A vacuum cleaner must never be stored with any dirt in the bag. The bag should never be more than half full.
6. Unscheduled vacuuming problems arise in corridors from time to time. This requires spot vacuuming and for this purpose the lighter upright machine should be used.

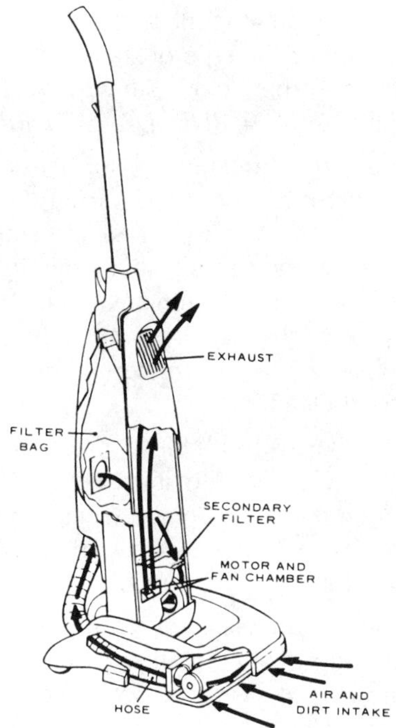

FIGURE 4-24 The heavy duty upright carpet cleaner. The pick-up needs of the original uprights used in the home now vary in size from 10 inches to 2 feet, and have twin motors (one for the brush and the other for pick-up). Many are now power driven and move the cleaner over the carpet with practically no effort on the user's part. (Courtesy of American Institute of Maintenance.)

SPOT AND STAIN REMOVAL

Almost every carpet or rug is the victim of spills from time to time. Most of these accidents are easily taken care of if you follow a few simple rules.

1. Prompt action is essential in order to clean the spill up before it sets. Ninety percent of all spills can be removed without staining the carpet if they are tackled at once with water and the blot-up method of stain removal. The blot-up method of removing spilled materials consists of absorbing the spill so nothing is left in the carpet. First, wet cloth with water. Any clean and absorbent cloth will act like a blotter if pressed firmly against the spilled material. In effect, you are transferring the stain from carpet to cloth.

   Proceed to use solvent if stain has *NOT* been blotted out. *DO NOT RUB*. Rubbing will only spread the stain. Instead, place solvent on a clean, dry cloth. Then apply cloth firmly to the stain. For surface stains, press down and hold. For deeper stains, place a weight on the cloth and allow some time for stain to be absorbed.
2. Keep cleaning materials on hand, ready for use.
3. Try to identify what caused the spot or stain and remove it by following directions carefully.

Most spills are made of materials that will dissolve in one of three solutions.

1. WATER SOLUBLE STAIN REMOVER
   —Sugars, starches, salts. Dissolve in water.
   —Oil will *NOT* dissolve in water.
2. DRY CLEANING FLUID
   —Oils, butter, fats. Dissolve in dry cleaning fluids (non-flammable), such as found in a "Spotting Kit."
3. DETERGENT SOLUTIONS
   —Many oily materials can be dissolved using a low-phosphate heavy-duty cleaner, one-part to four-parts water, which acts as a connector between the water and oil molecules.
   —Some materials are acidic or alkaline by nature. These spills should be neutralized to prevent possible damage to the carpet.
   —Acid stains, such as fruit juices, should be neutralized with a diluted ammonia solution. Mix a tablespoon of house-

hold ammonia with two-thirds cup of water.

—Alkali stains such as bleach, oven cleaner, and urine should be neutralized by a diluted vinegar solution. Mix one-third cup of vinegar with two-thirds cup of water.

Spot Removal Kit

Your spot removal kit should contain

1. Dry cleaning fluid (non-flammable), such as perchloroethylene.
2. Detergent solution—a low-phosphate heavy duty cleaner, one-part to four-parts water.
3. Acid solution—mix one-third cup of white vinegar with two-thirds cup of water.
4. Alkaline solution—add one tablespoon of ammonia to three-quarters cup of water.
5. Clean, white absorbent cloths, a sponge, and an eye dropper.

Next, pre-test your "spot removal kit" materials in an inconspicuous corner of the carpet to insure that the dry cleaning solvent will not cause any damage. Put a small amount of cleaning solvent on a cloth; press it firmly against the damp area while you count to ten. Check the cloth to insure that no carpet dye was transferred.

Now you are ready for any accidental spill. When it happens, determine what was spilled and consult the stain removal chart and directions to find out whether you use a dry cleaner or the detergent cleaner.

How to Remove Spills and Stains

1. Scrape or spoon up excess materials.
2. Blot up spill with clean, white absorbent cloth wetted with clean water.
3. Place a small amount of cleaning solvent, selected for the type of stain, on a clean, white absorbent cloth. Blot up excess material. *DO NOT RUB, DO NOT BRUSH.*
4. Repeat step three until no further progress is made. It is best to work from the outer edge toward the center of the stain. Be patient. Some stains take a while to come out. If a second cleaning material is necessary and the stain is not completely removed by the first material, then try the second cleaner.
5. After thorough blotting, place one-half inch of clean, white absorbent cloth over the damp area. Then add weight to insure firm contact to the material. Allow six hours for drying, if possible.

If you are unable to determine what was spilled, apply dry cleaner first and blot, repeating if effective. If not effective, use detergent solution and blot, repeating if effective.

GUM is easily removed by QUICK freezing it with dry ice or using "By-Gum" with an eye dropper. After it is frozen, simply scrape it off and remove any residue with dry cleaner solvent. Some stains will need special chemicals and procedures, such as those used by professional carpet cleaners.

4-6
Pest Problems

AN OVERVIEW

Insects are the most numerous form of animal life. There are nearly one million different species of insects and they inhabit nearly every niche of the environment. In-

DISSOLVE THESE WATER SOLUBLE SPILLS IN DETERGENT SOLUTION		DISSOLVE THESE OILY TYPE SPILLS WITH DRY CLEANING FLUID
Alcohol	Ice cream	Ball pen ink
Beer (V)	Ketchup	Butter
Bleach (V)	Milk	Cosmetics (except lipstick)
*Blood (AV)	Mustard	Crayon
*Chocolate	Permanent ink	Food stains
Carbon black	Soft drinks	Grease
Coffee	Soot	Gum
Crepe paper	Syrup	Household cement
Egg	Tea	Metal polish
Food colour	Urine	Oils
Fruit juice (A)	Vomit	Shoe polish
Gelatin	Water colours	Tar
*Grass	Wine (V)	
Gravy		

LEGEND

* These are combination materials that may need both dry cleaner and detergent to dissolve all the ingredients. Apply the solution recommended for the group it belongs to and repeat until there is no effect. Apply the other solution and repeat until stain is removed.

(A) Apply a small amount of the ammonia solution to neutralize the acidity of the stain.

(V) Apply a small amount of the vinegar solution to neutralize the alkalinity of the stain.

pH OF COMMON HOUSEHOLD PRODUCTS

ALKALINE	ACIDIC
pH 14 - caustic soda	pH 6 - milk
pH 13 - sodium metasilicate	pH 5 - boric acid
pH 12 - trisodium phosphate	pH 4 - Coca Cola
pH 11 - ammonia	pH 3 - wine and vinegar
pH 10 - Ivory soap	pH 2 - lemon juice
pH 9 - borax	pH 1 - phosphoric acid
pH 8 - eggs	pH 0 - hydrochloric acid

pH 7 - neutral

FIGURE 4-25 Stain removal chart.

sects possess a tremendous ability to survive, which results from their physical construction and their ability to reproduce.

Common insect pests in buildings are cockroaches, flies, ants, silverfish, centipedes, millipedes, clover mites, termites, and other wood-destroying organisms.

In addition to these pests, rats, mice, pigeons, sparrows, and starlings cause problems in buildings.

Pest management companies often say "Insects and rodents are never the problem. They are the results of other problems."

PEST CONTROL

Pest control is considerably more than the use of pesticides to kill insects and other pests. Good housekeeping practices and sanitation help prevent an outbreak of pest problems.

Pest control is divided into two phases:

1. Keeping an outbreak to a manageable level, called "clean-up" or "clean-out" by the professionals.
2. Using contracted or preventive services which, through regular chemical applications, forestall reinfestation.

PEST CONTROL SERVICES

We feel that this problem can best be controlled by using a professional pest management service. The following information will help you understand the service and how you can help monitor it.

Professional pest management is the science and business of protecting the health and comfort of man, domesticated animals, plants, plant products, buildings, and structures from insects, rodents, birds, weeds, wood-destroying fungi, and related pests.

In general, a pest control operator must

1. Be able to recognize a wide variety of animals, plants, and kinds of damage.
2. Have a respectable understanding of chemical pesticides and their safe use.
3. Be able to operate and repair a variety of sprayers and other equipment.
4. Have the ability to understand and work with people.
5. Be a businessman.

In order to evaluate effectively pest control services, spend some time with the pest control operators as they carry out their preventive control programs. It is important to understand the types of pest control services, some common pest problems, and the safe use of pesticides.

COMMON HOUSEHOLD PESTS

Flies

All flies go through a four-stage life cycle: egg, larva, pupa, and adult. The presence of fruit and house flies are positive evidence of unsanitary conditions.

There are many kinds of flies: bottle flies, flesh flies, fruit flies, moth flies, and cluster flies. Any one of them could be called a house fly.

Larva cluster flies are parasites on earthworms. The adult fly invades the homes in great numbers during the fall where they are found in windows and attics, attempting to stay warm over the winter.

Preventive control involves keeping garbage cans clean, regular garbage removal, removal of animal wastes, proper covering of privies, disposal of dead animals, use of screening. Both fruit flies and house flies reproduce quickly, the entire egg to adult cycle taking only a few days.

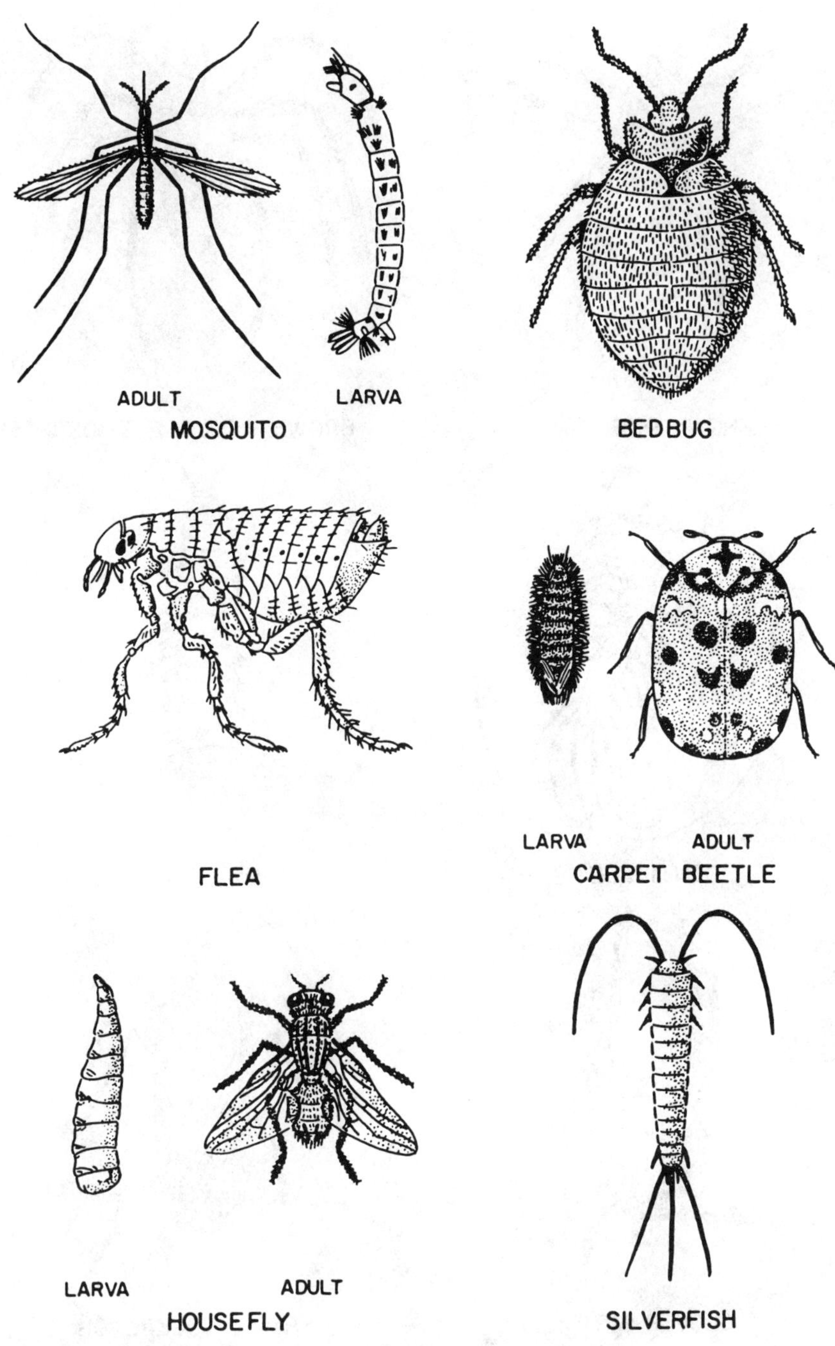

FIGURE 4-26 Common household pests. (Courtesy of Prentice-Hall, Inc.)

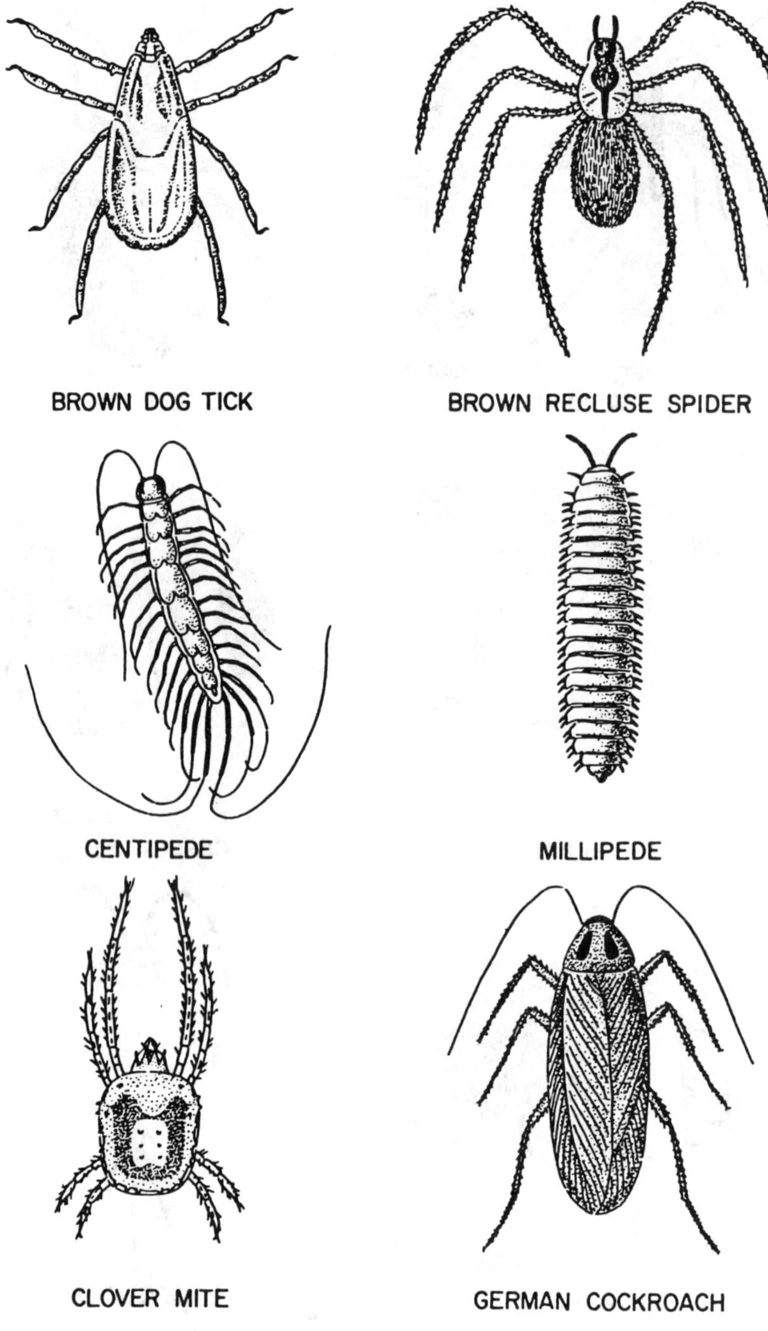

FIGURE 4-27 Common household pests. (Courtesy of Prentice-Hall, Inc.)

Cockroaches

The cockroach passes through a three-stage life cycle: egg, nymph, adult. The eggs are carried by the female in a capsule during part or all of the incubation period, depending on the species. The eggs hatch into nymphs which closely resemble the adult, except that they are wingless. The nymphs grow by shedding their skin and, finally, transform into adults.

The American cockroach is brown, while the oriental roach is black. These insects live in basement areas, around sumps, incinerators, and garbage compactors. They prefer dark, moist underground utility tunnels. They will infest upper floors of buildings by migrating along pipe chases, and will emerge from behind escutcheon plates. These insects will live more than one year, and the period from egg to adult takes approximately one year.

The German roach is light brown and is found around food. This roach, under favorable conditions, will pass from egg to adult in thirty or sixty days. Because of its reproductive potential and its common occurrence in food service areas, this will probably be the most important insect you will have to control (Figure 4-27).

Ants

Ants are the most prolific of insects. They are social insects living in colonies with a caste system including queen, male reproductives, soldiers, and workers. Most ants live in the soil although some species, such as the pharaoh ant (a very small black ant) and the carpenter ant, (a very large black ant), will live in buildings. Ants go through a four-stage life cycle: egg, larva, pupa, adult. In the spring large numbers of specially-produced winged males and females swarm from the nest in a nuptial flight. In this manner the species disseminates itself in the environment. These swarming ants are often mistaken for termites.

Silverfish

Silverfish and firebrats are very primitive insects. These insects are carrot-shaped. Silverfish are silvery in color and firebrats have a black mottled appearance. Silverfish often infest desks, closets, and bathrooms. They also infest heating tunnels in building complexes. Firebrats live in a specific temperature range (90°F plus), whereas silverfish infest areas in the 60-80°F temperature range. These insects feed on starch and microscopic molds. While they are harmless, their presence is disturbing.

Centipedes

Centipedes, millipedes, and sowbugs are not true insects, but are related to insects. These are the familiar hundred-legged, thousand-legged, and pill bugs. These organisms are primarily outdoor arthropods living in leaf mold, under rocks and sticks, and in similar areas. They may habitate in crawl spaces and basement areas of buildings.

Stored Product Pests

Food products stored in paper containers or opened containers that are not resealed tightly are susceptible to infestation. Flour, rice, corn meal, macaroni, and similar cereal or farinaceous products quickly become infested by pests. The most common insects are the confused flour beetle, saw-tooth grain beetle, cigarette beetle, and Mediterranean flour moth.

If the storerooms are not well cleaned, the area is apt to become infested by beetles referred to as dermestids including the larder beetle. All of these insects go through the

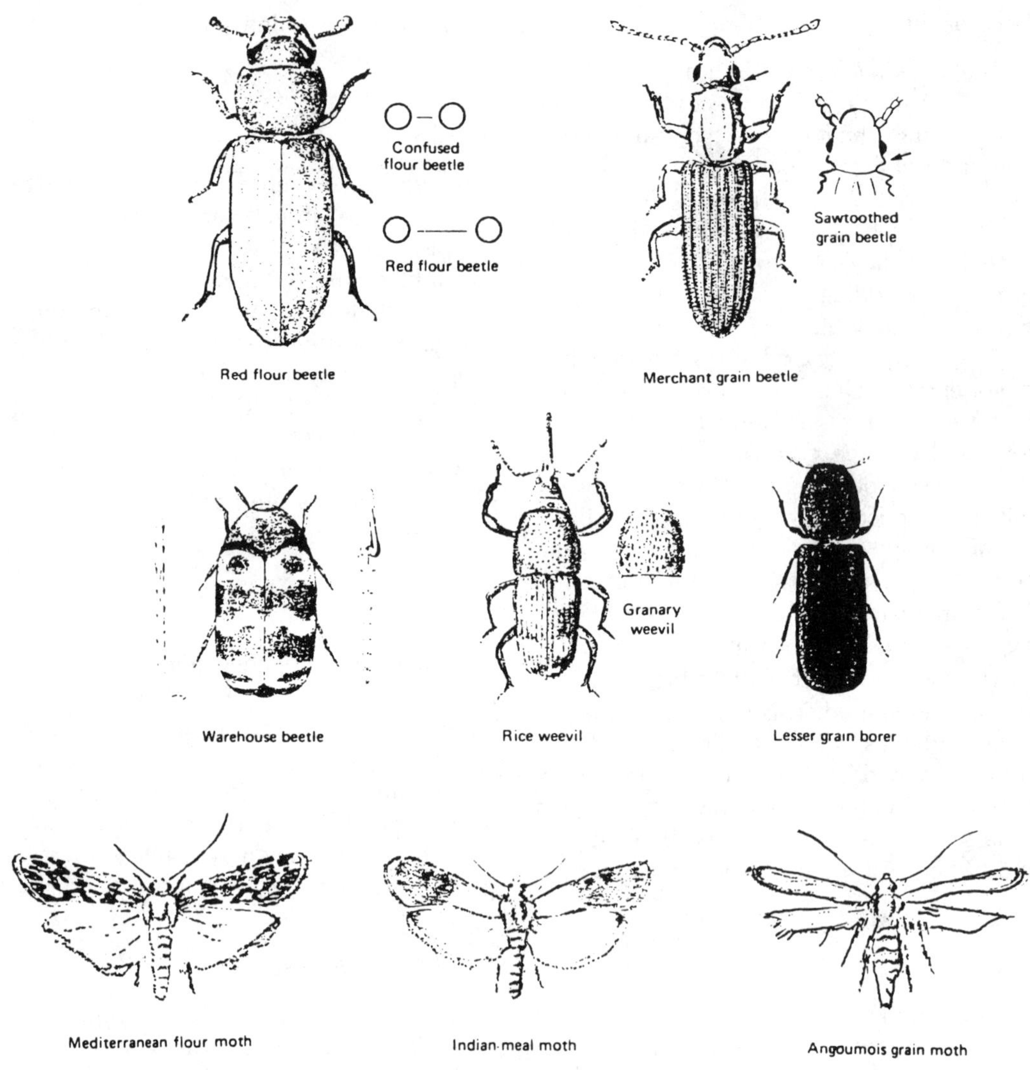

FIGURE 4-28 Stored product pests.

same four-stage life cycle mentioned before: egg, larva, pupa, adult. Generally, the life cycles are short (60, 90, or 120 days) for the transition from egg to adult. The adults themselves may live from six months to one year.

Generally, tenants hesitate to report a pest problem when it is first noticed. When they do report it, the problem is usually critical.

All the kitchen cupboards must be cleared completely and treated by the pest control operator. All flour, sugar, and other loose grain products must be thrown away to ensure elimination of the pest.

Clover Mites

Clover mites are another relative of the insects. The landscaping around buildings creates ideal conditions for the development of large populations of this pinhead-size mite. In the spring and at other times during the year, large numbers of these mites can be seen crawling up building walls, on window sills, and entering buildings. While they are harmless, their presence is disturbing to personnel, and they leave unsightly red stains when they are squashed.

OTHER PEST PROBLEMS

Birds

Pigeons, sparrows, and starlings are also pests. Bird droppings deface buildings and statues. They serve as a reservoir for bacteria and mold, causing lung infections. The bird nests are always infested with mites and other ectoparasites of birds. These combined factors make these birds a major nuisance and a health hazard. The control of birds is a new field, which usually requires the expertise of a reliable bird control firm.

Wood Destroying Pests

Termites, carpenter ants, and various wood-boring beetles pose a threat to the integrity of a building structure. Termites are very primitive insects and are more or less cosmopolitan in distribution. There are several different types of termites—dry wood termites and others. Each of these species has somewhat different biological requirements and each has its own particular point of attack. Termites feed only on cellulose-containing materials, so large modern buildings are not structurally endangered as a result of infestation. However, subterranean termites, for example, can feed on form boards left in place during construction and live in the soil in these form boards. Subsequently, the worker termites may find their way into the building through hairline cracks and crevices in the poured concrete. Then, during the spring, the adults may swarm into the building itself, a spectacular and annoying occurrence as tens of thousands of these insects suddenly appear in a public area.

There are a number of wood-boring beetles that one is likely to encounter—shot-hole borers, powder post beetles, and old house borers, to name a few. In cases of severe infestation, these beetles can present a structural hazard. For the most part, their presence is an annoyance resulting from the formation of sawdust and the continuous appearance of holes, large and small, in surfaces of infested wood. These beetles tend to be very long-lived. The four-stage life cycle may require two or three years and the adults may live five or more years.

Rodents

Rats and mice can be a severe problem to the property owner or manager. These pests can damage electrical wiring, causing short circuits and fires. Rats are aggressive when cornered and will attack and bite. Rats damage food and property estimated at one billion dollars per year. They transmit diseases such as bubonic plague, murine typhus, salmonellosis, rat-bite fever, rickettsial pox and leptospirosis.

There are *two* common species of rats (roof rat and Norway rat) that have many common names. Roof rats are slightly smaller than Norway rats. They are expert climbers and are often in higher portions of buildings. The Norway rat is much more common. This rat prefers to live in burrows, but can also survive in conditions favored by the roof rat.

Rat nests are well protected. They are built of any soft material. They may be found in burrows, tangles of tree limbs, trash, dumps, and piles of rubbish. In buildings, they live in wall voids, underneath floors, and in undisturbed rubbish and/or stored material.

The Norway rat is large with a strong body averaging one pound or more. The Norway rat prefers food with high carbohydrate and protein content, and will feed on nearly anything including fruit, vegetables, meat, and sugar. They will live for six to twelve months and are sexually mature in two to three months. The female produces an average of four to seven litters per year and eight to twelve young per litter. The survival rate depends on food supply, weather, disease, condition of the females, and competition. Rats eat about one ounce of food per day and require a source of water.

Mice are a problem for the same reasons as rats. They damage large amounts of food and property and spread disease. Mice are primarily nibblers and consume only about one-tenth ounce of food per day. They may not require water since they are able to obtain it through the food they eat. Mice live about one year. The female produce approximately thirty to thirty-five young per year, averaging six to eight litters.

A SUMMARY OF THE PEST PROBLEMS

The prevention of most maintenance problems is simpler than the correction of a problem. Pest control efforts should begin with the prevention of infestation. Preventing infestation is accomplished in several ways:

1. *Exclusion*—The pest-proofing of a building (physically) before trimming in to deny entrance to pests is of first importance. Doors and windows should be tightly fitted; all points of entry for utilities and other services should be sealed; screens and other mechanical barriers should be used. This is a function of the building maintenance and repair crew.
2. *Elimination of harborage*—All insects, rodents, and birds live and survive in an area because the environment provides the food and shelter they require. Denying food and shelter compels the pest to live somewhere else. The elimination of harborages and breeding areas requires the prompt disposal of all debris and trash. Elimination of weeds and other undesirable plant growth adjacent to a building and maintaining all storage areas in a neat and orderly manner is important. This includes maintaining an 18-inch clear perimeter area around storage spaces and palletizing storage to keep it off the floor. A proper effort is necessary to maintain a high level of cleanliness and good housekeeping. The use of pesticides is also necessary to prevent and control infestation.

The control of pests in buildings is a relatively simple matter and is an important aspect of housekeeping and sanitation.

Most rodent infestations can be controlled by the use of relatively safe anticoagulant baits and rat or mouse traps. These efforts should be combined with rodent-proofing and improved housekeeping.

Insect infestations may be controlled by the proper application of surface and/or space sprays.

Infestations of crawling insects can be controlled by the application of space sprays or fogging insecticides. These treatments should be supplemented with applications of surface sprays to the surfaces that the flying insects roost on and with attention to breeding areas of the flying insects.

A serious pest control problem should be brought to the owner or manager's attention immediately. The supervision of a serious pest problem by an expert will result in a high level of control.

It is hoped that the information provided in this chapter will help you to recognize pest problems, alert you to the urgency of treatment, and above all, understand the importance of good housekeeping.

4-7 How to Budget for the Housekeeping Services Funds

In this chapter we have endeavored to give you information that would make you aware of most of the housekeeping challenges and how to meet them. To assure achievement of the standards you set, you must also establish controls to eliminate problems with output, performance, and the use of equipment and materials. The budget expense schedules that follow are used for this purpose.

THE BACK-UP DOCUMENTS

As a back-up to these schedules, you will need the following:

1. Copies of specifications for all activities.
2. Copies of contracts if you use a contractor.
3. The square footages of all areas being serviced.
4. Room finish schedules and interior design drawings. If they are not available, they should be developed. This will help you plan for the future.
5. Schedules of housekeeping duties for building operations staff.
6. Inventory lists for all equipment and materials required to do the job.
7. And last, but not least, inspection reports on present conditions.

(Samples of most of this information can be found in Chapter 5—Groundskeeping Services.)

As this information is reviewed, you add the costs to each activity and develop a budget that will give you the funds needed to complete the planned housekeeping program. Items such as new or replacement equipment (and this could include replacements of floor coverings, both hard and soft), are not included in these papers because they are usually considered a capitalized expense. As such they would be included in those expense schedules.

THE EXPENSE CATEGORIES

Organizing the information into the expense categories shown has many obvious advantages. Organizing your thinking and the thinking of the operating staff is probably the most important feature of this system. The other big benefit is that the details developed allow you to organize the maintenance activities (such as carpet and wall cleaning), and detail the inventory needs (such as tools, uniforms, garbage bags, and cleaning materials). Bulk purchases of services and materials can pay big benefits when there are several buildings in the management portfolio. Single building owners can combine their needs through their trade associations.

	ACCT. NOS.	SUB TOTALS	TOTAL
CARPETING	25		
CLEANING	251		
REPAIRS AND PATCHING	252		
WALK OFF	253		
CLEANING SUPPLIES	26	TOTAL	
EQUIPMENT	261		
MATERIALS	262		
PAPER PRODUCTS	263		
OUTSIDE CLEANING SERVICE	27	TOTAL	
BUILDING	271		
GARAGE	272		
INTERIOR DECORATING	28	TOTAL	
DRAPES AND BLINDS	281		
LOBBY	282		
PAINTING & PAPERING	283		
WALL WASHING	284		

FIGURE 4-29 Summary of budget expense schedules, repair and maintenance categories; housekeeping services.

	ACCT. NOS.	SUB TOTALS	TOTAL
PEST CONTROL	29		
CONTRACT	291		
EXTRAS TO CONTRACT	292		
SIGNAGE	30	TOTAL	
CHANGES OR UPDATE	301		
DIRECTORY BOARDS	302		
WASTE DISPOSAL	31	TOTAL	
BIN PICK UP & REPAIR	311		
CHUTES	312		
COMPACTOR	313		
INCINERATOR (BURNER-FUEL-REPAIR)	314		
PLASTIC BAGS	315		
WINDOW CLEANING	32	TOTAL	
CONTRACT	321		

FIGURE 4-30 Summary of budget expense schedules, repair and maintenance categories; housekeeping services.

4-8 Housekeeping Services Terminology

Abrasive Cleaners Any cleaning products that are manufactured with granular materials.

Acidity The level of acid strength in a product.

Acrylic A manufactured carpet fiber of synthetic polymer composed of at least 85 percent by weight of acrylonitrile units. Also used in the manufacture of floor finish products. Certain types of polymers are known as "acrylics."

Asphalt tile A mixture of synthetic (man-made) fibers, lime rock, mineral fillers, and coloring. Asphalt binds the mixture together.

Axminster A loom-woven carpeting having each tuft of yarn individually inserted into the pile; generally cut-pile with even-level height.

Bacteria One-celled microscopic plants that may be harmless and useful, or dangerous and deadly.

Bactericidal Ability to kill bacteria, characteristic of germicidal cleansers.

Biodegradable Term used primarily for detergents, meaning that the detergent can be broken down by the normal bacteria found in the ground, in streams, and in waterways.

Broadloom Carpet woven wider than 27 and 36 inches. Widths may be 6, 9, 12, 15, or 18 feet.

Buffability The property by which scratches and other deformations can be removed by rubbing with some pre-chosen tool.

Cleaning-Disinfectant A chemical mixture of disinfectant and detergent which, when used as directed by the manufacturer, will clean surfaces and kill microorganisms simultaneously.

Conductive Flooring A floor designed to carry off built-up static electricity, reducing the possibility of explosion in hospitals, operating rooms, power storage, and loading plants. Spark-proof flooring is available in linoleum, vinyl, and troweled-on floors.

Curing The total period of time for complete setting of floor polishes. This can mean from twenty-four to forty-eight hours for total care.

Deodorant A product for destroying or eliminating offensive odors. Does not necessarily indicate disinfecting or germ-destroying properties.

Dilution The reduction of a concentration of one product by the addition of a carrier. Commonly refers to either water or a solvent.

Disinfection A chemical agent that will free a surface from the disease-bearing microorganisms ordinarily on inanimate objects; however, a disinfectant usually does not destroy bacteria spores or virus.

Etch To pit a surface by applying a suitable chemical solution. Usually refers to the use of acid on concrete surfaces to increase surface area and thereby improve adhesion by subsequent seal coatings.

Flash Point The temperature at which sufficient vapors of a potentially flammable product have accumulated in the atmosphere to present a fire or explosion hazard.

Fungicide A fungicide kills all types of fungi such as molds.

Germicide Anything that destroys bacteria; applies especially to chemical agents that kill disease germs, but not necessarily spores.

Gloss Defined as shine or sheen.

Grouting A concrete binder used to install ceramic tile.

"Heeling" A method of exerting pressure on a floor machine to remove rubber heel marks or heavily-soiled areas.

Hypochlorite A powerful disinfectant containing chlorine.

Jute A natural fiber from India and Pakistan that is woven and used for backing on carpets to add strength, weight, and stiffness.

Microorganisms Plants or animals visible only with aid of a microscope.

Neutral A chemical state that is neither acid nor alkaline; 7 on the pH scale.

Nylon A manufactured fiber used for carpeting (Polypropylene).

Olefin A manufactured fiber used for carpeting.

Oxalic Acid Commonly used for certain types of stain removal when normal detergents are unsuccessful.

Phenol-coefficient The gauge of a product's germ-killing power, compared to pure carbolic acid. A product with a phenol-coefficient of 2 is approximately forty times as effective as carbonic acid, and therefore can be diluted with forty parts of water.

Phenols Normally used in reference to one of the leading ingredients in detergent-sanitizers as floor cleaners for germicidal maintenance programs.

Pile Density The number of yarn tufts per square inch. Better wear and increased resistance to crushing are obtained with greater pile density.

Polymers A "Polymer" or "Co-Polymer" is a clear synthetic plastic material, particularly acrylics, vinyls, and polyethylenes, chemically emulsified into a water base. Applied to surfaces, it forms a transparent plastic film.

Poultice A combination of a powder and a liquid into a "pastelike" form and applied to a surface to remove soil and stains.

Resilient Flooring Softer floor surfaces capable of withstanding shock without permanent deformation or rupture.

Sealing To fill tiny holes in a floor surface.

Slurry A temporary suspension of insoluble solid or immiscible liquids in a carrier base. Usually referring to the stable suspension of dirt in a cleaner long enough for adequate rinsing. May also refer to the thick grey, soapy mixture created when stripping a floor.

Solvent Cleaners Are used widely both for general degreasing and a number of specific purposes, such as cleaning floors and driveways stained by lubricants.

Spores Bodies formed by some types of bacteria during their growth cycles which have a tough coating which resists sterilization.

Spray Buffing An intermediate floor finish program procedure that removes black scuff marks while improving or maintaining the gloss of the floor finish.

Sterilization Means the 100 percent killing of all living cells on or in a surface or space.

Stripping Removal of floor polishes and waxes by scrubbing with a detergent prior to re-applying a floor primer or polish.

Toxic Any substance that has the capacity to cause bodily injury through ingestion, inhalation, or absorption through the skin.

Use-Dilution The proper measurement of chemical and diluent as specified by the manufacturer to achieve the most efficient results.

Viscosity The property of a substance which indicates its thickness and thinness.

Wetting The ability of a solution to disperse or spread over an oily or otherwise water-repellent surface.

Yarn The basic raw material for textile use that can be fabricated into a carpet. Tufted, woven, and knitted carpets are made from yarn; flocked and needle-punched carpets are made of fiber.

Yellowing A discoloration of floor finish or wax due to oxidation or excessive sunlight.

4-9 Summing Up

Edwin P. Feldman, P. Eng., introduced his housekeeping handbook by offering these startling statistics, "four billion is spent every year in the United States for housekeeping and sanitation. (In Canada, it is estimated that about $500 million is spent.) This undertaking involves the efforts of 500,000 housekeeping workers. At least a fourth of the effort is wasted. This enormous waste is recoverable—not in some theoretical sense, but practically. Housekeeping, in a sense, has been swept under management's rug."

Studies of a building's repair and maintenance expenditures show that the cost for housekeeping is not one of a building's major expenses. However, spending the money wisely is as important as it is with high cost items.

It is important to realize that the cleaning dollar is broken down as follows: 90-95 percent for labor; 5-10 percent for material and equipment. Quality is essential for both factors.

Because labor is the major cost factor, the secret to success is to develop productive "knowledge workers." Management must be able to establish fair workloads that are organized into schedules of duties for the operations staff. These task responsibilities should be detailed in writing. In this way, the staff will know what it is responsible for and how the tasks interrelate. These schedules need not be cast in stone. The staff should be encouraged to suggest ways to improve its actions or timetables.

In any case, it is essential that persons performing any given task understand in detail:

—what they intend to accomplish;

—how to perform the task;

—the standard of cleanliness expected;

—the frequency;

—the equipment and supplies needed to do the job, and how they are used;

—safety practices and other considerations.

To ensure that the work is completed satisfactorily requires close supervision and regular inspections. Suitable training programs are essential. If the staff is experiencing difficulties in carrying out any part of its responsibilities, it should be encouraged to ask for assistance immediately.

Carrying out housekeeping tasks by the building operations staff, in a professional manner, is the only way that we can assure that money spent on housekeeping will be wisely used. A clean, attractive, well-maintained building gives the tenants, employees, and visitors to the building a feeling of confidence and security. Above all, the image of a company or an institution is considerably enhanced by a pleasing exterior or interior appearance of a building.

Chapter 5

GROUNDSKEEPING SERVICES

5–1 Planning

DESIGN PLANNING

First impressions are often the most important. When a prospective buyer is considering a real estate investment, or when tenants are considering a move, the exterior appearance, or the "curb appeal," of the property could be the initial reason they are considering buying or moving in. Conversely, poorly-maintained grounds could be one of the reasons that tenants move out. This is usually the first evidence of a deterioration of management maintenance standards.

Municipal governments have been demanding more and more open space around high-rise buildings, even in the core of the city. This means that more consideration must be given to these open spaces.

In order for you to get the best return on your investment, you must make good use of the total landscape area. To do this, you need the input of marketing and landscape maintenance specialists, as well as the landscape architect at the planning stage of a new building, to assure the best results.

Consideration should be given to driveways, entrances, drainage conditions, existing trees, direction of prevailing winds, underground utility services, recreation facilities, direction of the sun, watering facilities, parking, the view from the street, the view from above, and, of course, the initial cost and the cost to maintain. It is important to decide the areas where you intend to plant annuals, perennials, trees, and shrubbery.

DAY-TO-DAY MAINTENANCE

If initial planning fails to take into account the day-to-day maintenance needs, costly headaches may result. The lawn will have to be mowed, watered, and fed. Hedges may need additional trimming every other week. Shrubs and trees will need pruning, watering, and spraying. Trees that looked fine when planted may overgrow an area when they mature.

Some specimens may die and need replacement. Sidewalks may be difficult to clear and have poor drainage. Icing up of these areas, in the winter, necessitates the use of salt. This action deteriorates the concrete and kills vegetation. Sidewalks in the wrong place or that are not wide enough may encourage people to take short cuts and to walk on the edge of the grass, necessitating seeding or re-sodding every year.

"DOING THE RIGHT THING RIGHT"

If maintenance is not kept in mind when the original plans are drawn up, the owner may initially be paying for unnecessary expensive features. Sometimes, elaborate landscape features are costly to maintain. In fact, poor planning could lead to deterioration despite high maintenance costs. Initial low-cost landscape plans can also lead to high-cost maintenance. A properly planned landscape could prove to be relatively inexpensive to maintain. The secret is to "do the right thing right" during the planning, installation, and maintenance stages.

IN-HOUSE OR OUTSIDE SERVICE?

Regardless of what kind of landscape plan is installed, owners are faced with the decision about whether to use an in-house gardener or a competent landscape maintenance service to maintain the grounds. The secret to making the right decision is knowing what you want and being able to hire, direct, and control the people responsible for the building's "curb appeal."

To explain what we mean when we refer to knowledge and control, we have included enough information in this chapter so that you can develop a contract and specifications for your groundskeeping and snow removal services. Every geographic area would need to develop specifications to meet the needs of the area being serviced. Specifications for indoor landscaping would be developed to satisfy the needs of the installation. The specifications must form part of the contract to avoid misunderstandings about what is expected.

DEVELOPING A WORKLOAD

There are two main reasons why developing a groundskeeping workload is more difficult than developing a housekeeping or mechanical services workload:

1. The spring, summer, fall, and winter seasons cause workloads to change.
2. Workloads must be divided into regular maintenance, and/or new repair, planting, and possibly snow removal.

For organizational purposes, it is necessary to divide the workload into monthly cycles and to subdivide those cycles into weekly/daily schedules. When rainy days make outside work impossible, the daily schedule is advanced a day or substituted for another day's activities until the lost days are made up.

Work Classifications

Clean-up	pick up litter (daily) thorough clean-up (spring, fall) driveways, parking lots (as required) garbage disposal areas (as required) raking lawns leaves provide winter protection (fall)
Repairs and Maintenance	tree stake ropes fence boards painted surfaces broken branches sidewalks, parking lots, and playgrounds sod and soil tools and equipment
Ordering	supplies flowers, bulbs, other plants
Cultivation	flower beds and edges (spring, summer, fall) planters, pots tree circles
Seeding	lawns (August-September or February-March)
Planting	summer flowers (end of May) trees, shrubs, hedges bulbs (fall)
Watering	as necessary—deep water (November)
Mowing Lawns	cut 1½" to 2½" (weekly)
Fertilizing	lawns (spring, fall) flowers and other plants (summer)
Spraying	broad leaf weeds (March-April-August-September-October) insects and diseases (April to September)

As with other aspects of managing building operations, the interior and exterior landscaping requires the same kind of planning and organizing. Developing a workload is the first step in the planning exercise. To do this you require an as-built plot plan (see Chapter Two—Figure 2-3) of the exterior, along with details about interior landscaping, if it is a part of the building's design.

The areas to be maintained would dictate the equipment required to do the job. A knowledgeable groundskeeper would know what is required to do a complete, competent, and productive job.

CONTINUITY OF CARE

By applying time frames to the workload, you could decide whether to use a contractor or in-house staff. Unless the workload provides a full week's work, you would probably hire a contractor. The material that follows will not make you a gardening expert; there are many available for this purpose. It should, however, make you aware of the importance of the exterior and interior landscaping.

In summary, the information that follows involves:

- —Changes in design to eliminate problems such as repairing or replacing fencing and walks.
- —Cleaning up litter—sweeping sidewalks and outside parking areas.
- —Inspections—recommending annual and perennial planting.
- —Mowing, edging, sodding, seeding, fertilizing, spraying lawns.
- —Planting, digging, cultivating flower beds.
- —Spraying and pruning trees and shrubs.
- —Watering and maintaining the system.
- —Opening, closing, and maintaining fountains.
- —Using and maintaining all equipment, tools, and supplies.

5-2 Soils, Chemicals, and Fertilizers

SOIL ANALYSIS

The goal of all gardeners is to have good growth soil, as this is the basis for gardening success. Soils vary from loamy sand to clay. Clay soils present more problems for gardeners than any other item. Careful attention to the soil and the selection of plants to suit the soil condition is a prerequisite for success.

In order to plant trees or shrubs in clay soil, you would need to remove 50 percent of the soil, and mix in 15 percent composted manure, 15 percent sand, and 20 percent fresh top soil before replacing the soil.

An analysis of soil conditions would show the following:

	Sand	*Silt*	*Clay*
Loamy Sand	85%	10%	5%
Sandy Loam	65%	25%	10%
Loam	45%	40%	15%
Silt Loam	20%	60%	20%
Silty Clay Loam	15%	55%	30%
Clay Loam	28%	37%	35%
Clay	25%	30%	45%

Most evergreens, trees, and shrubs can be quite easily and successfully grown in sandy soils. Sand merely needs added humus to help it retain moisture and nutrients. Add 33 percent peat moss and 15 percent composted manure. If there is a humus deficiency, add organic fertilizers, manures, compost, leaf mold, sawdust, ground bark, or peat moss.

To assure gardening success, one must actually analyze the soil condition and properly prepare the area to suit the material being planted.

It is important that you are aware of any extreme condition in the soil. An acidic condition of 3.6 and an alkaline condition of 10.3 would be considered an extreme pH range for most mineral soils.

To find out exactly where your soil measures on the pH scale, you can use a soil testing kit, or send a sample of soil to a testing laboratory for analysis (Figure 5-1).

THE pH SCALE

Dig up trowel-size samples from the top 6 inches of soil from widely scattered spots. Mix thoroughly with the trowel (don't use your hands), and let the mixture dry in the air before placing in a container.

If the soil test indicates an acidic level below 5.5, add ground dolmite limestone (not hydrated lime) at the rate of 50 to 75 pounds per 1,000 square feet. Apply on dry soil with a spreader.

If the soil test indicates alkalinity of over 8.4, add gypsum, organic fertilizers, manures, compost, leaf mold, sawdust, ground bark, or peat moss. This humus has the advantage of practically limitless application. Spread as much as you wish on top of the soil, about 35 to 50 pounds per 1,000 square feet is usually sufficient, and spade it in.

WEED CONTROL

As with other problems encountered in project management, you should always find the cause of a problem before attempting a cure. Thin and weedy lawns usually result from poor maintenance, including such things as mowing too short, a soil that is too low in fertility, or lack of water. In some cases it may be wise to re-sod or re-seed and create

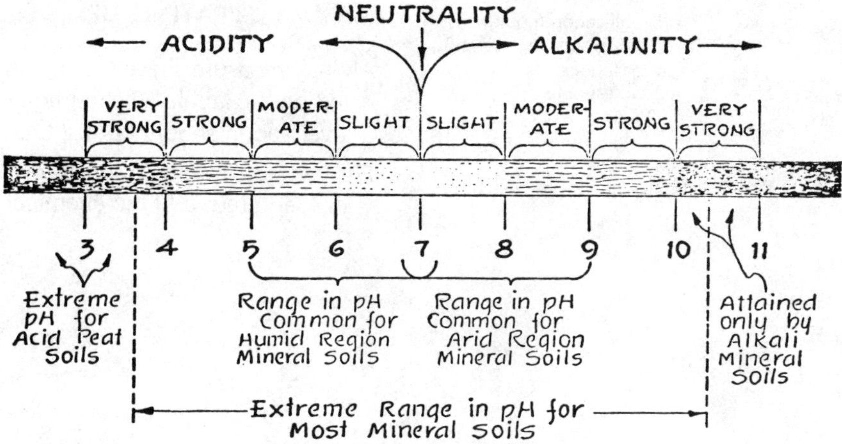

FIGURE 5-1 **The pH scale.** A measure of the hydrogen ion concentration (activity) of a sample of earth.

a new lawn, rather than trying to save the old one.

Weeds in the lawn probably cause more concern to the average gardener than any other condition. There was a time when lawn weeding meant crawling around on hands and knees pulling, digging, and prying out the weeds. Today, there are a number of weed-killing chemicals that will kill most weeds without doing any material damage to the grass.

If a lawn is well cared for, fertilized, and enriched with humus, the grass will grow so vigorously that a thick sod will form, practically killing most of the weeds by smothering.

There are three kinds of devices for applying a selective weed killer evenly over the entire lawn:

1. Hose-end applicators
2. Pressure spray tanks
3. Dry-fertilizer spreader

Knowing the chemical is the best guide on how to use it. The more effective chemicals are absorbed by the leaves and attack the stems and roots, thus killing the weed forever. It is important to use the right chemical for the right job, at the right time, with the right amount applied in the right way, under the right conditions.

CHEMICAL CONTROL

2,4-D and 2,4,5-TP are the best known of the herbicides. They kill broad-leafed plants by speeding growth so that the plants literally grow themselves to death. The chemicals are most effective at a temperature of 70°F and are ineffective below 50°F.

There are new selective weed killers that kill clover, chickweed, yellow oxalis, plantain, and knotweed.

The chemicals used for spraying weeds and insects are very dangerous and it is advisable to obtain a license. In some areas, a license is mandatory. Where it is not, follow precisely the instructions on the label or hire a professional. Quantities should not exceed the amounts recommended. The following table of equivalents will help you.

3 teaspoons	= 1 tablespoon (liquid)
1 ounce	= 28.35 grams (dry weight)
	= 6 teaspoons
	= 2 tablespoons
16 fluid ounces	= 1 pint
1 quart	= 32 fluid ounces
1 gallon	= 4 quarts
1 pound	= 16 ounces (dry weight)

SPRAYING TIPS

1. Always measure the exact amount indicated on the label. Whether liquid or dry, a level spoon should be just that.
2. Fill the tank to one-fourth the volume of water required; add the chemical; fill the

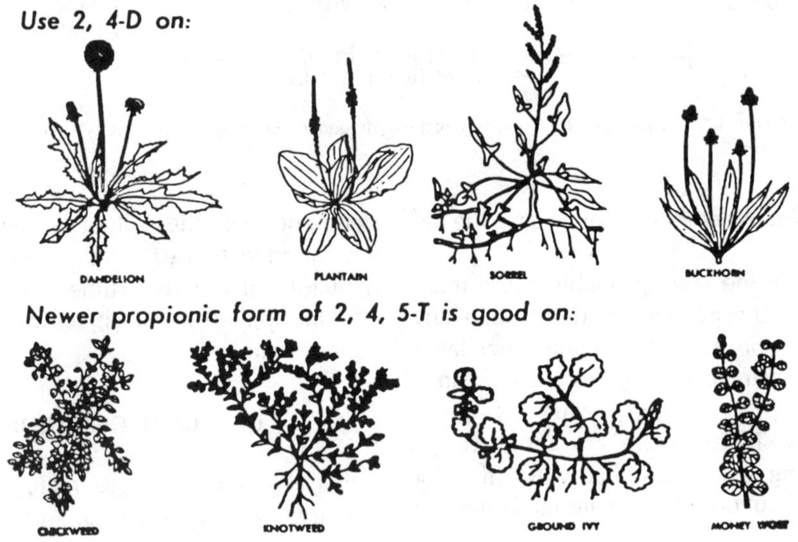

Everybody's pest:

FIGURE 5-2 The right chemical for the right job. (Courtesy of Prentice-Hall, Inc.)

tank. Never put the chemical in the tank while it is dry, because some chemicals will attack the walls of the tank, at full strength.

3. Spray the first shot onto a paved area. Insufficient agitation sometimes causes the first shot to have a stronger concentration of chemical.
4. *If it is too windy, don't spray*! Always spray against the wind so that the spray is blown to the ground (see Figure 5-3). Adjust to a fine spray.
5. Care should be taken not to overlap areas being sprayed because such areas receive a double application.
6. Spray at a regular walking rate, and walk forward.
7. If the nozzle clogs, clean out the orifice on a paved area.

THE WRONG WAY

SPRAY

WIND

THE RIGHT WAY

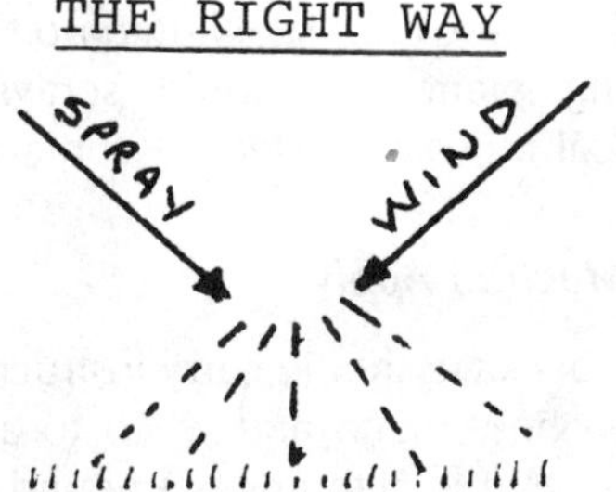

FIGURE 5-3 Spraying tip. Always spray against the wind.

8. If the temperature is over 85°F or under 50°F, *don't spray*.
9. Spray not less than six hours before an expected rain. Do not water for twelve hours after spraying.

SAFETY TIPS

1. Never store chemicals near food.
2. Never leave an empty or full container unattended.
3. Never spray and eat at the same time.
4. Destroy, burn, or hide empty chemical containers.
5. After spraying, wash your hands and face before eating or drinking.
6. If the spray has drifted, wash off the contaminated areas with a hose.
7. Always wash out the container with detergent after it has been used.
8. Once a sprayer has been used for killing weeds, only use it for this purpose.

CONTROL OF INSECTS AND PESTS

Shade trees, shrubs, and flowering plants are often attacked by insects and mites. Recognition of these pests is essential if we expect to develop prevention and control programs. Aphids and plant lice suck sap; mites rasp leaves, causing discoloration, reduced vigor, and leaf-drop; caterpillars and grubs of various types defoliate; scale insects encrust branches and twigs and suck the sap; borers of many kinds enter bark and wood, weakening and killing; diverse gall-making pests cause malformations of leaves, fruits, and branches. Certain root-feeding insects and mites transmit fungal and viral diseases of ornamental plantings.

Local county agricultural representatives can help by giving you information about insects and pests in your area. Entomological specialists at a local university will also help you identify pest problems and provide control recommendations. It is essential that regular inspections are conducted to uncover problems early. Proper timing for spray application is essential if you expect to control pest problems.

FERTILIZERS

All plants obtain carbon dioxide from air and mineral nutrients from the soil which are absorbed in solution by the root hairs. This food is used to produce new tissues and to maintain existing tissue.

The three plant food elements most needed in the garden are nitrogen, phosphorus, and potash. When you see grass beginning to turn yellow or pale green, chances are that an application of almost any lawn fertilizer will get it growing fast and green again. Grass has a continual need for nitrogen. Nature does a poor job of supplying that nutrient in quantities that are adequate to keep grass plants growing thick, green, and dense.

When deciding about the fertilizer you may require, the objective is to add the nitrogen at the time the grass plants need it. In the 10-6-4 formula on a fertilizer label number, the first number is the percentage of nitrogen, the second is the percentage of phosphorus, and the third the percentage of potassium. In most areas, grass grows actively for too many months to be satisfied by a once-a-year feeding. A spring and fall feeding is recommended.

Glossary of Fertilizer Terms

Nitrate or Nitrogenous A form of nitrogen available to the plant as is, regardless of temperature.

Ammoniacal or Ammonic Available to plants when converted by bacteria to nitrates.

Organic Describes sludge, cottonseed meal, and any others that must be broken down by bacteria.

Urea A synthetic organic that water and the enzyme urease change immediately to inorganic ammonia.

Urea-Form or Urea Formaldehyde A nitrogen fertilizer that has been specially compounded for slow release.

HINTS Read the manufacturer's recommendations for the fertilizer needed in your area. Contact your soil conservationist or county agricultural agent. Lime only acid soils.

Commercial Fertilizers

Granular These can be divided into three groups:

1. A general purpose fertilizer, high in phosphates for flowers, trees, and shrubs.
2. Lawn fertilizer, high in nitrogen.
3. Single-action fertilizers, such as ammonium sulphate, ammonium nitrate, and super phosphate.

Liquid These consist of liquid iron, used for greening plants, or liquid sprays whose chemical ratios are listed on containers.

How Much to Apply

The package should carry instructions that tell you how much and when to apply the fertilizer. A rule of thumb is 1 pound of actual

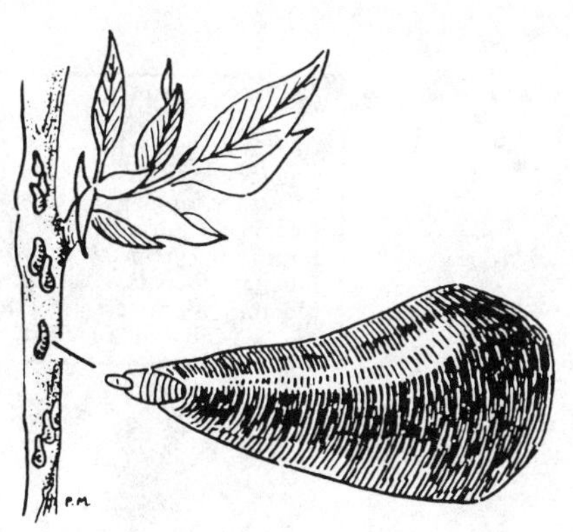

SCALE INSECTS FEED BY SUCKING JUICES FROM PLANT STEMS.

MAPLE BLADDER GALLS ARE CAUSED BY GALL-PRODUCING MITES.

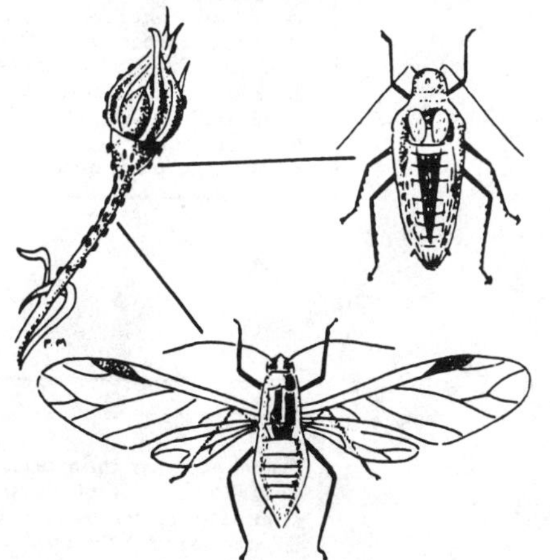

Both winged and wingless forms are shown. APHIDS SUCK PLANT JUICES.

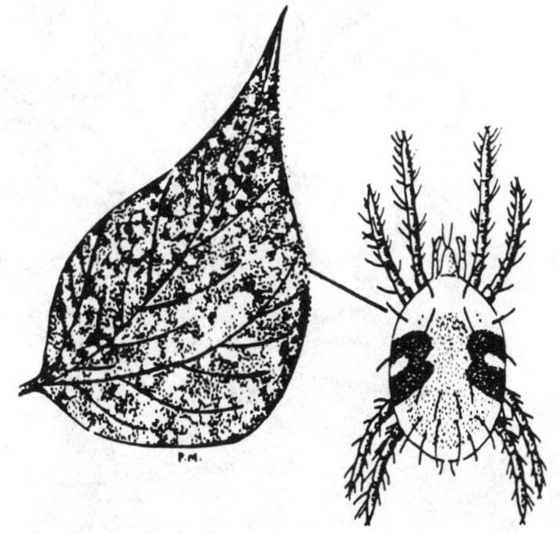

SPIDER MITES DAMAGE PLANTS BY RASPING TISSUE AND SUCKING JUICES.

FIGURE 5-4 Common garden pests. (Courtesy of Prentice-Hall, Inc.)

nitrogen per 1,000 square feet per month during the months when the grass is growing.

If we have a 100-pound bag of 10-10-10 fertilizer, it contains 10 percent nitrogen, 10 percent phosphorus, and 10 percent potassium. To figure in pounds, take the percentage and multiply by the weight of the bag: A 50-pound bag of 10-6-4 fertilizer contains 5 pounds of nitrogen, 3 pounds of phosphorus, and 2 pounds of potassium, or enough to feed 1,000 sq. ft. for five months.

Application Tips

Only a few dry fertilizers can be applied and forgotten. Most require a soaking in to

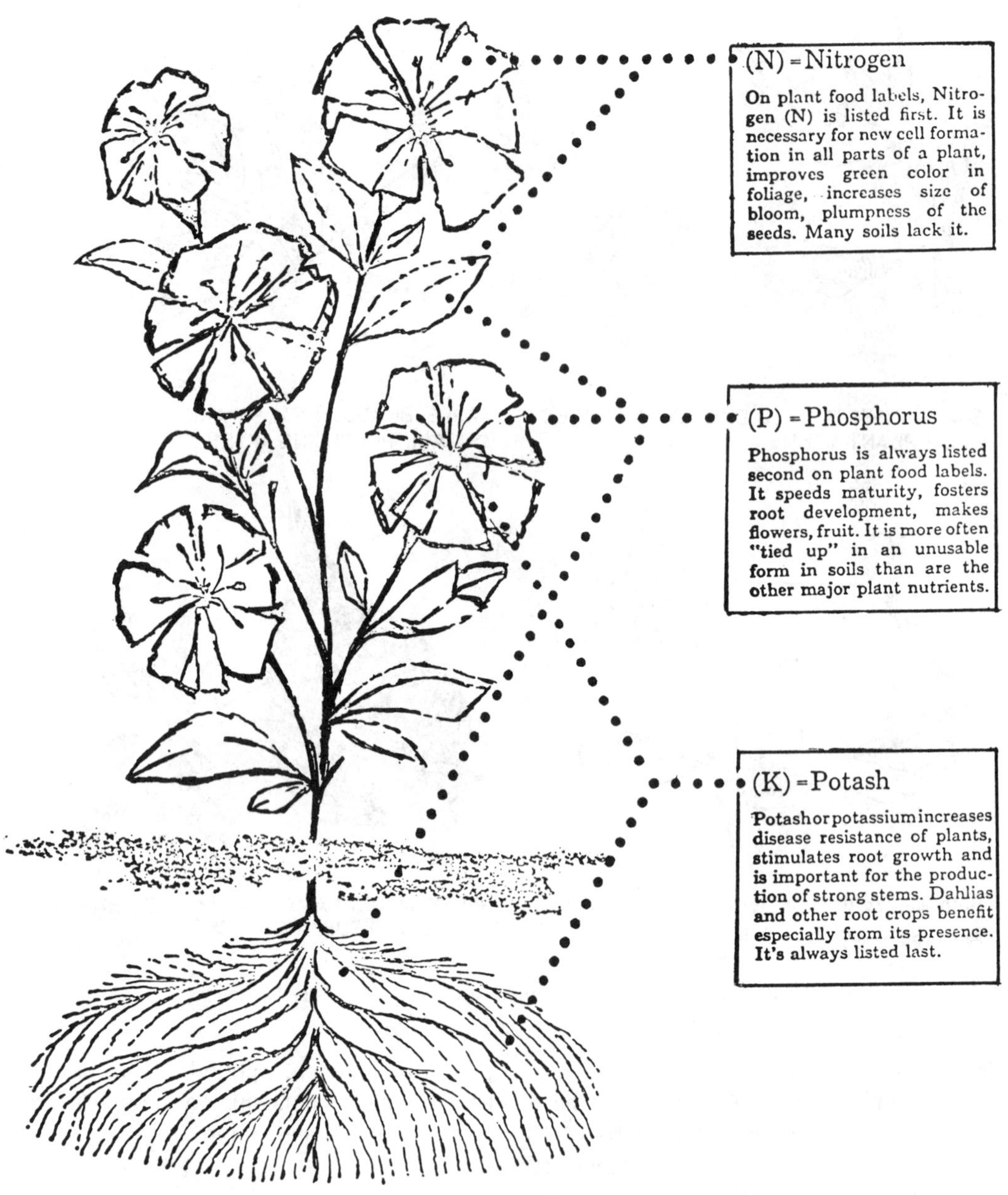

FIGURE 5-5 Understanding fertilizer formulas. (Courtesy of Mike Kelly, *Visual Concepts.*)

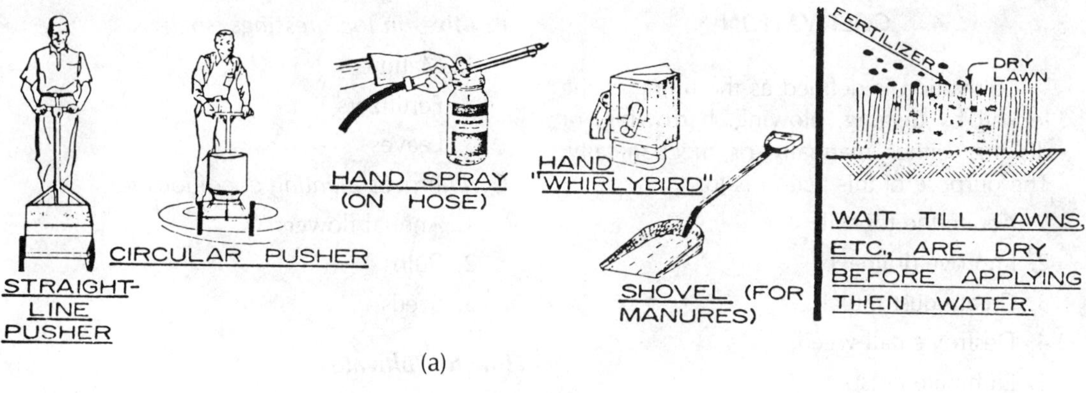

(a)

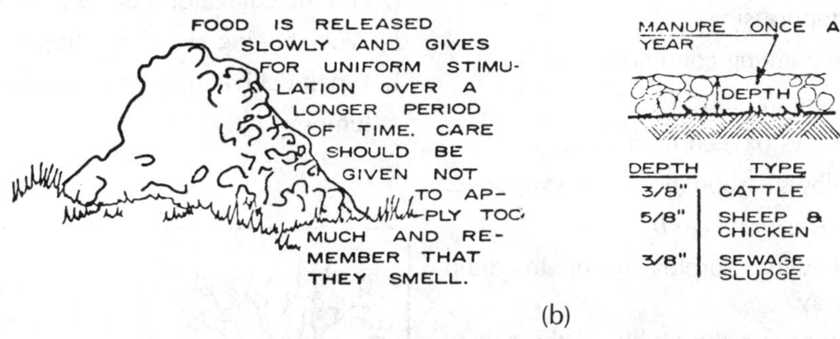

(b)

FIGURE 5-6 When and how to apply fertilizer. (a) Manures (use dry only); (b) Applicators.

get the feeding action started and to prevent burning of the blades of grass.

Keep fertilizer 6 inches from plant stems. Metal hopper spreaders must be washed and dried when the job is done to avoid caking of fertilizer and rusting of the metal.

When using a hopper spreader, start by doing two strips each way at the border. This gives you room to shut off the spreader when you turn the corners. You will burn the grass if you stop or turn with the hopper open.

Fertilizing Trees, Shrubs, and Hedges

Trees and shrubs need low analysis phosphorus fertilizer, such as 5-10-5 or 6-10-4. To determine the amount needed:

1. Measure the diameter of the tree 12 inches from the ground.
2. Use 1 pound for each inch of diameter.
3. Measure the height of shrubs.
4. Add fertilizer according to shrub height and diameter:

   4 feet or less—1–1½ pounds;
   4–6 feet—2–2½ pounds;
   6 feet or more—3 pounds.

The best way to fertilize a tree is to use a root feeder or punch 3-centimeter holes, 20 centimeters deep, and 50 centimeters apart beyond the spread of the branches. Each hole is back filled with peat or sand. Fertilize early spring and in late fall.

Fertilize evergreens, deciduous shrubs, and hedges in early spring using fertilizer recommended for these plants.

CULTIVATION

Cultivation is defined as the tilling of the topsoil by digging, plowing, harrowing, or disking, either manually or mechanically. The purpose of this action is to

1. Aerate the topsoil.
2. Improve drainage.
3. Create dust mulch.
4. Destroy small weeds.
5. Eliminate crust.
6. Mix in topdressing.
7. Improve planting condition.
   A. *Aerating the topsoil*
      1. Allows oxygen to enter.
      2. Allows carbon dioxide to evaporate.
   B. *Improves drainage by*
      1. Allowing surplus water to drain away.
      2. Improving the ability of the soil to retain water.
      3. Improving deeper water movement.
      4. Improving the availability of nutrients.
   C. *Creates dust mulch, which helps*
      1. Reflect the heat.
      2. Retain moisture.
      3. Keep weed seeds from germinating.
   D. *Destroys small weeds by*
      1. Burying them.
      2. By cutting the roots.
      3. Exposing them to the elements.
   E. *Eliminates crusting, which*
      1. Separates close-lying soil particles.
      2. Removes intense heat absorption.
      3. Removes puddling.
      4. Removes shrinking (cracking) of soils.
   F. *Mixes in top dressings, such as*
      1. Manure
      2. Fertilizers
      3. Leaves
   G. *Improves planting conditions for*
      1. Annual flowers
      2. Bulbs
      3. Seeds

How to Cultivate

1. Pull the cultivator, but keep the soil level.
2. When hoeing, use short chopping strokes.
3. When cultivating with a fork, break down lumps.

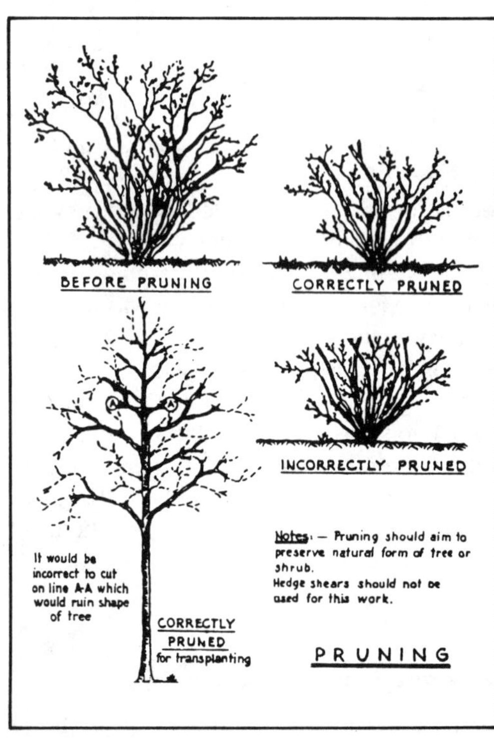

FIGURE 5-7 Good pruning practices. Bad pruning can ruin trees and hedges. (Courtesy of Prentice-Hall, Inc.)

4. Spade the ground in early spring or late fall.
5. When rototilling, stay away from tree roots; cultivate at a depth of not more than 2½ inches.
6. Smooth the beds with a garden rake.

When to Cultivate

After the ground has been watered or after a heavy rain, allow the soil to dry moderately before cultivating. Cultivating very wet soil will create a lumping condition. In the spring, cultivate every two weeks, during the summer cultivate every three weeks. Wait for two weeks after planting annuals—do not disturb the roots.

5-3 Pruning Trees, Shrubs, and Hedges

AN OVERVIEW

A good gardening maintenance program includes a program of trimming and pruning. Depending on the shrub, one to three trimmings may be required each growing season. There are many misconceptions about how and when to prune. Bad pruning can ruin trees and hedges—don't prune unless you know how. Trees should be thinned, shaped, and the dead wood removed by a tree specialist.

GOOD PRUNING PRACTICES

1. Use tools that are sharp and that make a clean cut.
2. Start to shape trees at planting time.
3. Diseased, dead, or broken branches should be removed when first noticed. Be sure the branch is dead and not dormant.
4. Leave no stubs or ragged cuts.
5. If two branches are rubbing, prune the weaker branch.
6. Always cut back to another branch or bud. If the end of the branch is dead, cut beyond and close to a bud.

WHEN TO PRUNE

In winter, while they are dormant, prune deciduous trees, and shrubs that need thinning or shaping.

In early spring, before growth starts, prune young wood of rose-of-sharon and peegee hydrangea back to two eyes; snowberry and hills-of-snow hydrangea close to the ground; french hydrangea, only enough to remove splindling shoots; buddleia, enough to remove dead wood and shape the plant; climbing roses by removing dead and two-year old wood; hybrid tea and hybrid perpetual roses by removing winter-killed wood and weak growth.

In spring, after flowering, prune forsythia, deutzia, weigela, beauty bush, mockorange, and lilac, by removing old wood from base; flowering almond by thinning out old wood.

In summer, after flowering, prune rambler roses, by cutting off spent flower heads and removing wood of two-years growth.

Anytime of the year, you can prune previously overlooked dead, diseased, or weak stems or branches.

DECIDUOUS SHRUBS

Most deciduous shrubs should not be pruned to form round globes, but should have a few branches removed to the ground in order to rejuvenate them. In early spring,

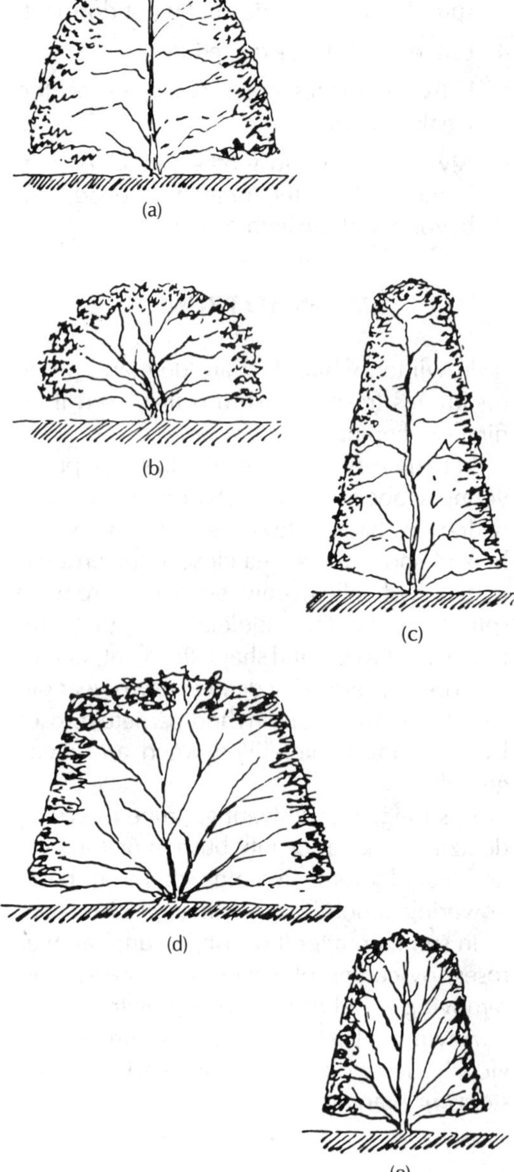

FIGURE 5-8 Good forms of hedge pruning. (a) Hemlock, White Pine, Japanese Yew; (b) Mugo Pine, Japanese Barberry; (c) Beech and Hornbeam; (d) Spreading form of Japanese Yew; (e) Privet, best form.

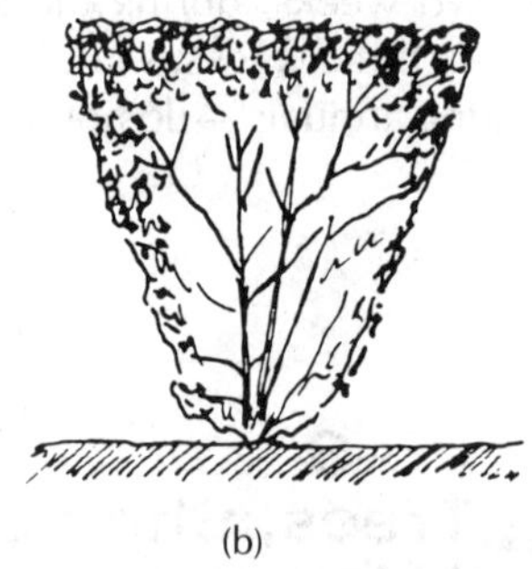

FIGURE 5-9 Hedge forms which are not satisfactory. (a) Privet, fair form, but it easily becomes the next type with sparse lower branches; (b) Privet, poor form, because the lower branches, deprived of light, become sparse.

prune only the later flowering shrubs that bloom on new wood. Prune early flowering shrubs such as lilac and forsythia immediately after they have finished flowering. Be sure to remove all "spent" flower heads from lilacs.

Evergreens may be pruned in April before growth commences or in July after new growth has matured. A light annual pruning is usually needed to keep plants in bounds.

It may be necessary to bind shrubs in the late fall to prevent them from becoming broken or misshapen by snow and ice during the winter.

5-4 Lawn Care

AN OVERVIEW

Lawns that are neat, trim, and green convey the image of a clean, well-kept building. To achieve this goal requires a proper initial landscape design and continuing upkeep and care.

Different grasses require different upkeep. Most of us have different ideas about what a well-groomed lawn should look like. There are many different models of lawn mowers and edgers, with different cut widths and different horsepowers. The workload of the project will dictate the equipment you require.

If you use a reel mower without a basket, mow in a counter-clockwise direction if your mower throws to the left, clockwise if it throws to the right, so that the mower will deposit part of its clippings on the uncut grass. On the next parallel trip, the mower will chop up some of the previous run's clippings. Finely cut clippings sift down into grass better than long pieces.

A reel mower is a precision instrument; as with all tools and equipment it must be kept in top condition. Does it sound right? A clanking could mean that a blade is out of alignment; adjust it immediately. Does it need oil? Is it cutting evenly? If it leaves rough spots or if tough blades of grass pass through unscathed, the blades are probably dull or out of alignment. If the blades revolve too rapidly, they are probably not set close enough to the cutting bar.

Grass should never be allowed to grow more than 3 inches high. It should be mowed at lease once a week and not lower than 1½ inches. Mowing is best done in the morning or evening, when the grass is more tender. Avoid mowing wet grass, as it will mash under mower wheels, stick to the blades, and slide under the mower.

5-5 Watering

AN OVERVIEW

Whenever you see a lawn that is green and lush during the summer months, you will find an efficient watering system. The system may be controlled manually by a knowledgeable gardener or it may be automatically programmed. Regardless of the system, it must be based on the following criteria if it is to be successful:

1. Rate of water penetration
2. Water capacity of the soil
3. Depth of topsoil
4. Depth of grass roots
5. Rate of water loss by evaporation and transpiration
6. Lawns need more water than plant materials

WATER PENETRATION

In a sandy soil, water will disappear immediately. With heavy clay soils, water penetrates so slowly that the average sprinkler will put out water faster than the soil will take it, and the water will run off onto driveways, flower beds, or the street.

HOW OFTEN TO WATER

Most gardeners recommend that it is wise to stretch the interval between watering to as many days as the lawn can take. Some gar-

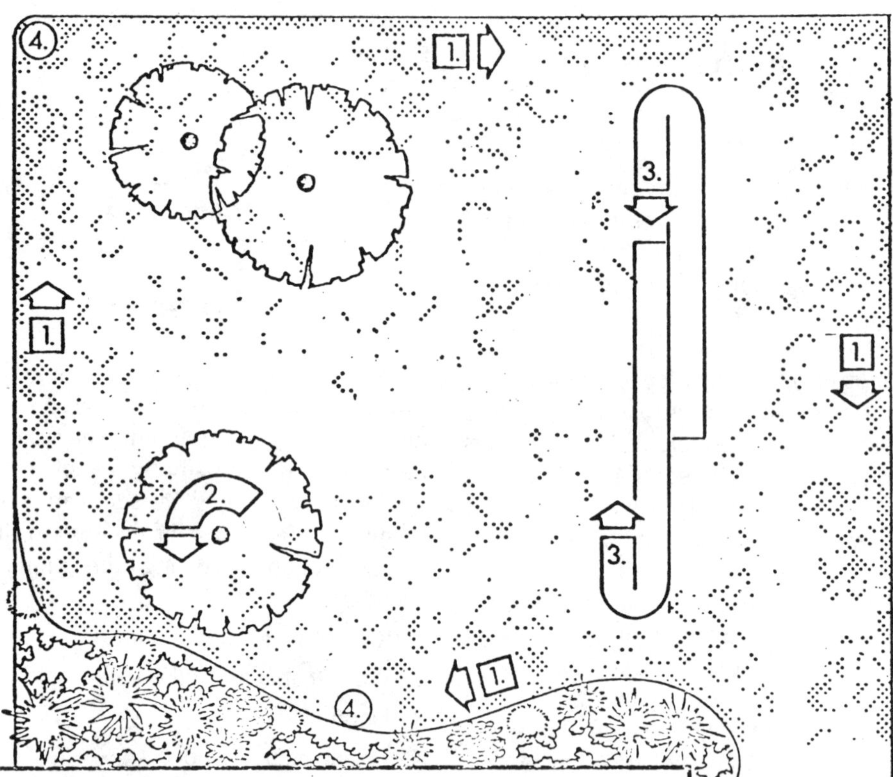

FIGURE 5-10 How to trim a lawn. 1. Cut three swaths around the perimeter, allowing the grass clippings to blow back on the lawn. 2. Cut around trees, planting areas, and other obstacles within the lawn area. 3. Cut in an alternating up and down direction. Change the pattern each week. For hard to get at areas, use a hand mower or clippers. 4. Finally, neatly edge and trim all sidewalks, driveways, planting areas, building edges, etc. (Courtesy of Mike Kelly, *Visual Concepts*.)

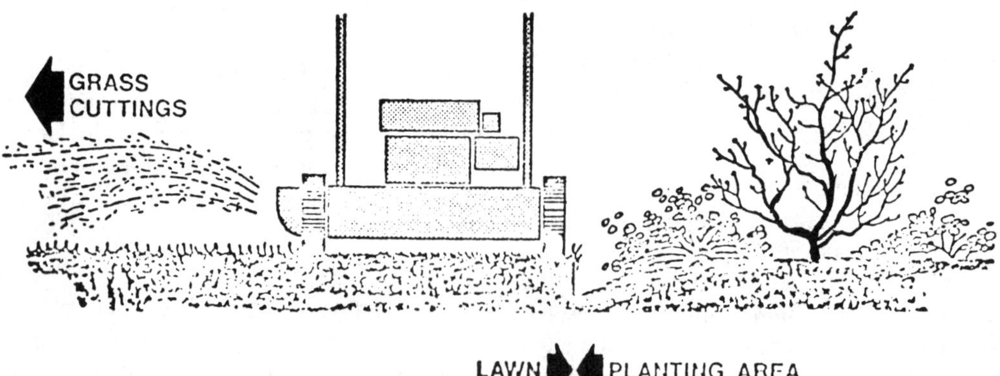

FIGURE 5-11 Blow the grass clippings back on the lawn. (Courtesy of Mike Kelly, *Visual Concepts*.)

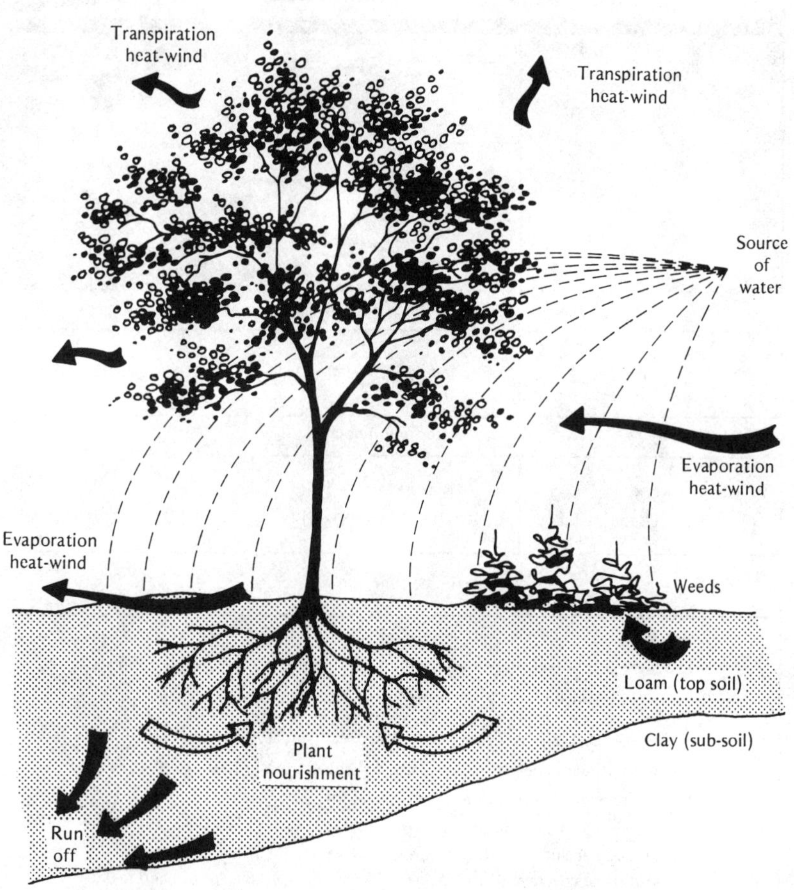

FIGURE 5-12 Loss of water. (Courtesy of Mike Kelly, *Visual Concepts.*)

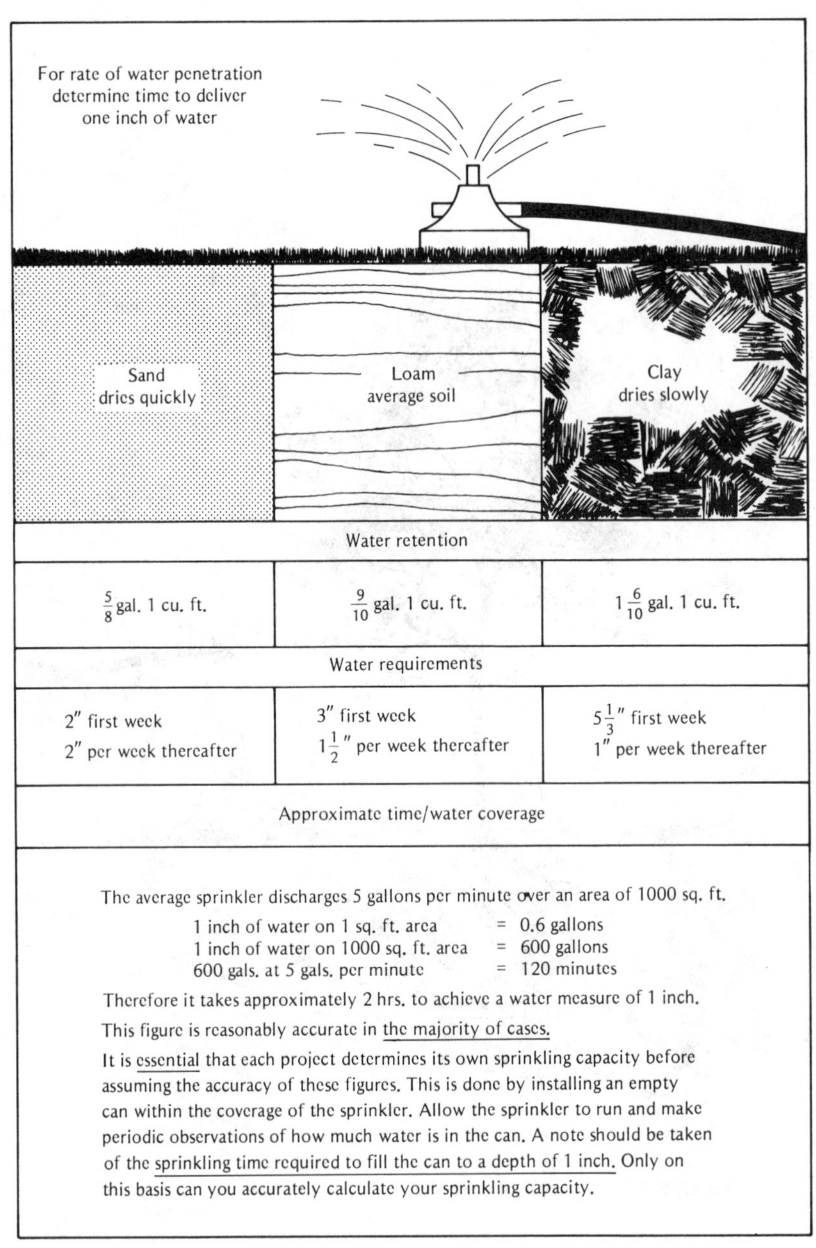

FIGURE 5-13 How much to water. (Courtesy of Mike Kelly, *Visual Concepts.*)

deners also say that an alternate wetting and partial drying out of the soil encourages healthier plant growth and deep rooting. As water is drawn from the soil by grass roots, more air enters and a better environment for growth is created.

Other gardeners maintain a partial drying out makes the grass suffer during hot weather. They give their lawns a light sprinkling every afternoon and evening. This system does not supply enough water to meet the grass plants' needs. Deep watering once or twice a week is safer than a light, frequent watering.

DEVELOP A WETTING PATTERN

By knowng the wetting pattern that the sprinkler makes, you can figure out the best possible spots on your lawn to run the sprinkler in order to get even penetration. In some instances, it may be wise to supplement one sprinkler system with another to make a compatible pattern. Flower beds may need hand watering while the grass area needs soaking. You should try to minimize the wetting of sidewalks, driveways, and buildings when watering the lawn.

FIGURE 5-14 Sprinkler heads used in irrigation systems. (a) Pop-up heads; (b) Pop-up with impulse head; (c) General purpose sprinklers. (Courtesy of Melnor Industries.)

TAG NO.	DESCRIPTION	MODEL NO. OR SIZE	COMMENTS
1.	EDGER - POWER	1½ to 3½ hp	Gasoline driven-more powerful than electric-wear goggles and gloves
2.	EDGER-SHEARS-POWER	16 to 30"	Keep cord free to avoid cutting it
3.	MOWER - HAND	16"	Set at 1½" for most hardy grass
4.	MOWER - POWER - REEL	2 to 4 hp	Does the neatest job. Does a poor job when grass is too high.
5.	MOWER - POWER -ROTARY	1 3/4-4 hp	Handle with respect-throws rocks etc.
6.	PRUNER - POLE	10 to 14 ft.	Metal handle-hazardous near electric wire
7.	ROLLER - HAND	110 to 300lb.	To increase weight to 400 lbs. add water. Drain before lifting - storing
8.	SPREADER-ROLLER TYPE		Close hopper while turning- don't let runs overlap
9.	SPREADER-HOPPER TYPE	24 to 25"	
10.	SWEEPER - HAND		Much faster than hand raking
11.	SPRAYER - POWER (for incecticides)	15 to 30 gal	Hire an arborist for big trees
12.	SPRAYER - HAND	1½ to 3 gal.	If used for insecticides or weed killer-keep for this purpose only
13.	TRACTOR	4 to 10 hp	
15.	WHEELBARROW	4 to 5 cu.ft	

FIGURE 5-15 Typical gardening equipment list. Account numbers 23-24.

5-6 Equipment, Plants, Tools, and Inventory

BULBS, CORMS, AND TUBERS

Bulbs are underground buds, encased in fleshy, scale-like leaves, where plant food is stored to carry the plant over to the next growing season. A variety of other plants have food storage structures, such as corms (gladioli), tubers (dahlias), rhizomes (iris), but the true bulb is distinguished by the presence of scales.

For Spring Cheer

One of the most miraculous acts in gardening is to tuck firm brown bulbs beneath the soil in the fall, let winter obliterate their hiding places, and then to awake some fine spring morning to find the garden gleaming with color.

DESCRIPTION	PART NO./SIZE	ON HAND	YRLY. USAGE	QTY. REQ'D.	COST	TOTAL COST
SOIL TEST KIT						
SOIL TEST REFILLS	6 OZ.					
TREE WRAP	4" x 35 FEET					
TREE WOUND DRESSING	1 QT.					
TREE STAKES	8 FEET					
"T" BARS	7 FEET					
#16 GALVANIZED WIRE	10 POUNDS					
FIRST AID KITS						
GREASE	TUBES					
OIL	QUARTS					
GLOVES - WINTER						
GLOVES - SUMMER						
TWINE						
GASOLENE CANS	1 - 2 - 5 GAL.					
MEASURING CUPS						
					TOTAL COSTS	

FIGURE 5-16 Accessories inventory list. Account number—331.

DESCRIPTION	PART NO./SIZE	ON HAND	YRLY. USAGE	QTY. REQ'D	COST	TOTAL COST
PATIO SLABS	60 x 75 cm.					
ROCKERY STONE	TON					
PEBBLES (3 TON MIN.)	TON					
BRICK SAND	TON					
PLANTERS						
GARBAGE CONTAINERS						
RAILWAY TIES	8 FEET					
FENCES						
HANGING BASKETS						

FIGURE 5-17 Landscape architectural components inventory list. Account number—332.

DESCRIPTION	HEIGHT	NO.REQ'D	COST	TOTAL COST
BIRCH - WHITE	HEIGHT 50 to 75 ft. SPREAD 40 to 50 ft.			
AMERICAN ELM	HEIGHT 80 to 100 ft SPREAD 70 to 80 ft			
LINDEN	HEIGHT 70 to 90 ft. SPREAD 50 to 60 ft.			
MAGNOLIA	HEIGHT 70 to 90 ft. SPREAD 60 to 70 ft.			

FIGURE 5-18 Trees and shrubs; requirements for new or replacement trees and shrubs. (Use local nursery catalogues to list the items required.) (This is merely an example of a list. An inventory listing would need to suit the requirements for your property and area.)

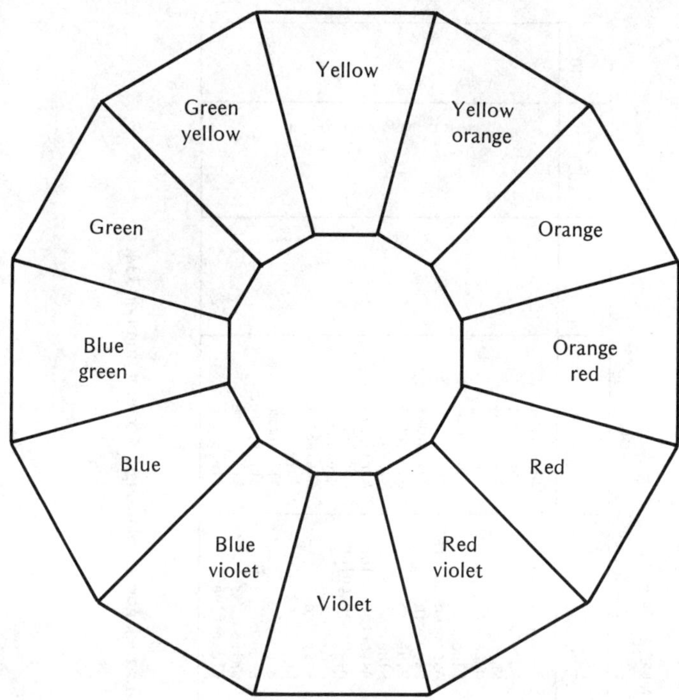

FIGURE 5-19 Keep color coordination in mind when planting. The primary colors are red, yellow, and blue. Oranges are the warm colors; blues are the cool colors; and complementary colors face each other across the wheel.

In an area where you are willing to let the grass remain uncut until the leaves of bulbs have disappeared, there is nothing more pleasant than naturalized crocuses and daffodils.

Bulbs placed in front of shrubbery are also delightful. Some bulbs fit well in a special border; smaller ones belong in the rock garden.

Tulips and crocuses can be planted just before the ground freezes, and daffodils can be planted whenever they are available from August through October. The smaller flowering bulbs—squills, snowdrops, snowflakes, glories-of-the-snow, grape hyacinths—are rewarding in the spring if planted in mid-autumn. Grape hyacinth foliage appears in the fall.

The secret of planting bulbs is to set them firmly in the bottom of a hole that measures three times the height of the bulb itself. Fill the hole with soil, press it down firmly, and level off the top. Spring will bring the miracle of bloom.

ACCOUNT NUMBER 334

VARIETY	COMMON NAME	HEIGHT IN INCHES	DOMINANT COLOR	BLOOMING TIME	REQ'D.	COST	TOTAL
Alyssum	Basket of Gold	10"	Golden yellow	April-May			
Anemone	Pasque Flower	12"	Purple	April-May			
Arabia Alpena	Rock Cross	12"	White	April-May			
Armeria	Thrift or Sea Pinks	10"	Hues of pink	June			
Aster Alpinus	Alpine Aster	8"	Blue	May-June			
Dianthus	Cushion Pink	8"	Assorted colors	May			
Heuchera	Coral Bells	15"	Deep pink	All summer			
Lavendual	Sweet Lavender	10"	Blue	June-July			
Myesatis	Forget-me-not	6"	Blue	May-June			
Phlox	Creeping Phlox	3"	Assorted colors	April-May			
Primula	Primrose	12"	Assorted colors	April-May			
Sedum Acre	Golden Mass	4"	Yellow	May-June			
Sedum Spectabilis	Stonecrop	10"	Rosy red	Aug.-Sept.			
Sedum Stonoleferum	Trailing Mass	6"	Brilliant pink	July			
Stokesia	Stoke's Aster	12"	Blue	All summer			
Veronica	Dwarf Speedwell	10"	Blue	All summer			
Viole	White Wonder	6"	White	All summer			
Violet	Frogroot Violet	4"	Clear blue	May			

FIGURE 5-20 Plant materials; perennials for rock garden plantings. Account number 334.

ACCOUNT NUMBER 334

VARIETY	COMMON NAME	HEIGHT IN INCHES	DOMINANT COLOR	BLOOMING TIME	REQ'D	COST	TOTAL
Aster	Michaelmas Daisy	48"-60"	Assorted colors	Sept.-Oct.			
Campanula	Canterbury Bell	24"	Assorted colors	June			
Carnations	----	18"	Assorted colors	July-Aug.			
Chrysanthemum	Cutting mums	30"	Assorted colors	Sept.-Oct.			
Columbine	----	24"	Assorted colors	May-June			
Coreopsis	Tickseed	24"	Yellow	All summer			
Delphinium	Belladonna	36"	Shades of blue	All summer			
Delphinium	Giant Hybrids	36"	Assorted colors	All summer			
Digtalis	Foxglove	36"	Assorted colors	June			
Gaillardia	----	24"	Assorted colors	All summer			
Gypsophila	Baby's Breath	30"	White, pink	July-Aug.			
Hibiscus	Giant Mallow	60"	Assorted colors	August			
Hollyhock	----	72"	Assorted colors	July			
Iris Germanica	German Iris	30"	Assorted colors	May			
Lathyrus	Perennial Sweet Pea	Climbing	Assorted colors	July-Aug.			
Papaver	Oriental Poppy	36"	Scarlet	May-June			
Physalis	Chinese Lantern	24"	Coral red	September			
Platycodon	Balloon Flower	24"	Blue, pink, white	July-Sept.			
Pyrethrum	Painted Daisy	24"	Assorted colors	May-June			
Phlox	----	36"	Assorted colors	July-Sept.			
Rudbeckia	Cane Flower	36"	Light blue	July-Sept.			
Shasta Daisy	Alaska Daisy	24"	White	All summer			
Tritoma	Red Hot Poker	36"	Orange, white, yellow	July-Sept.			
Anthemis	----	30"	Yellow & gold	All summer			
Australis Baptisio	False Indigo	36"	Lovely blue	May-June			
Catananche	Cupid's Dart	24"	Violet blue	July to frost			
Eupatorium	Mist Flower	24"	Dark blue	Sept. to frost			
Monarda	----	36"	Assorted colors	June-July			
Dictamnus	Gas Plant	30"	Rose, white	June-Aug.			

FIGURE 5-21 Plant materials; perennials for background planting. Account number 334.

ACCOUNT NUMBER 334

VARIETY	COMMON NAME	HEIGHT IN INCHES	DOMINANT COLOR	BLOOMING TIME	REQ'D	COST	TOTAL
Aconitum	Monkshood	48"-60"	Blue	Aug.-Sept.			
Ajuga	Bugle Plant	12"	Blue	May-June			
Hasta	Plaintain Lily	36"	White, blue	July-Aug.			
Myesetis	Forget-Me-Not	12"	Blue	May-Oct.			
Polemonium	Jakob's Ladder	12"	Blue	May-June			
Pulmonaria	Lungwort	12"	Blue, pink	April-May			
Violet	Wood Violet	5"	Blue	May			
Trolius	Globe Flower	18"	Orange-yellow	May-Sept.			
Lily of the Valley		8"	White	May			

FIGURE 5-22 Plant materials; perennials for shaded areas plantings. Account number 334.

ACCOUNT NUMBER 334

VARIETY	COMMON NAME	HEIGHT IN INCHES	DOMINANT COLOR	BLOOMING TIME	REQ'D	COST	TOTAL
Aster	Michaelmas Daisy	15"-24"	Assorted colors	May-Oct.			
Liatris	Gay Feather	36"-60"	White, purple	July-Sept.			
Linum	Blue Flax	24"	Blue	May-Sept.			
Papayer	Oriental Poppy	36"	Scarlet	May-June			
Pyrethrum	Painted Daisy	24"	Assorted colors	May-June			
Tritomo	Red Hot Poker	36"	Orange spikes	July-Sept.			
Sedum	Stonecrop	10"	Rosy red	Aug.-Sept.			
Carnation		18"	Assorted colors	July-Aug.			
Dianthus	Hardy Pinks	18"	Assorted colors	All summer			
Coreopsis	Tickseed	24"	Yellow	All summer			
Iris Koemfers	Jap Iris	24"	Assorted colors	June-July			
Phynalis	Chinese Lantern	24"	Coral red	September			
Shasta Daisy	Alaskan Daisy	24"	White	All summer			
Dianthus Barbatus	Sweet William	18"	Assorted colors	June-July			
Epiredum	Barrenwort	9"	Red, white	May-June			

FIGURE 5-23 Plant materials; perennials for border plantings. Account number 334.

ACCOUNT NUMBER 334

VARIETY	COMMON NAME	HEIGHT IN INCHES	DOMINANT COLOR	BLOOMING TIME	REQ'D	COST	TOTAL
Aster Noude	New England Aster	48"	Purple, pink	Aug.-Sept.			
Hibiscus	Mallow	60"	White, pink, red	July-Aug.			
Lobelia	Cardinal Flower	36"	Red	July-Aug.			
Myesotis	Forget-Me-Not	16"	Blue	May-Oct.			
Physostegra	False Dragonhead	18"	Pink, red	Aug.-Sept.			
Primula	Primrose	12"	Assorted colors	April-June			
Trollius	Globe Flower	18"	Orange-yellow	May-Sept.			
Violet	Wood Violet	5"	Blue	May			
Anemone Japanica	Windflower	12"	Assorted colors	Aug. to frost			

FIGURE 5-24 Plant materials; perennials for wet locations. Account number 334.

ACCOUNT NUMBER 334

NAME	SUN OR SHADE	HEIGHT IN INCHES	COLOR	BLOOMING TIME	USES	# IN A FLAT	# OF FLATS	COST	TOTAL
*Ageratum	Sun	4"-5"	Blue	Summer & fall	Border & graves				
Arabis (Rock Cress)	Sun	6"	Pure white	April & May	Rockery, borders				
Sweet Alyssum	Sun	2-1/2"	Blue, white	All summer	Rockery, borders				
*Asters	Sun	2"-3"	Assorted	August to frost	Background				
Double Balsam (Lady Slipper)	Shade	15"	Assorted	All summer	Rockery, borders				
Blue Lace Flower	Sun	24"	Sky blue	July to frost	Background				
Calendula	Sun	24"	Orange shades	June to frost	Background				
Cornflower (Bachelor's Button)	Partial shade	24"	Assorted	Summer to frost	Background				
Candytuft	Sun	18"	Rose, red, pink, white	Summer to frost	Border, rockery				
Cockscomb	Sun	30"	Red shades	All summer	Background				
Clarkia	Partial shade	24"	Assorted	July to October	Background				
Cosmos	Sun	48"	Assorted	July to frost	Background				
Dahlia	Sun	18"	Assorted	July to frost	Background				
Dianthus (Pink)	Sun	12"	Assorted	July to frost	Bed or border				
*Dusty Miller	Sun	6"	Silvery foliage	----	Border or grave				
Euphorbia (Snow-on-the-Mountain)	Sun	24"	Green foliage	----	Border				
Forget-Me-Not	Partial shade	8"-10"	Blue	April	Border, rockery				
Four-O-Clock	Sun	30"	Red, yellow, white	Summer	Bushy plant for backgrounds				
*Impatience	Partial shade	6"	Red shades	Summer & fall	Border, edging				
Strawflowers	Sun	30"	Assorted	All summer	Background				
Kochia (Burning Bush, Mexican Fire Bush)	Sun	30"	Green foliage turns to red	----	Rows or borders				
*Lantana	Partial shade	8"	Assorted	Summer to frost	Border or mass display				
Marigolds	Sun	6"-36"	Assorted	All summer	Border or edging				
*Pansies	Partial shade	6"-8"	Assorted	May-June	Border or edging				
*Petunia	Sun	8"-24"	Assorted	Spring to frost	Border, mass planting				
Portulaca	Sun	3"	Assorted	Summer	Rockery, edgings				
*Salvia--Dwarf	Sun	6"-10"	Scarlet	All summer	Border, mass plant				
*Salvia--Tall	Sun	18"-30"	Scarlet	July to frost	Border, mass plant				
*Snapdragons	Sun	30"	Assorted	Summer & fall	Background				
Verbena	Sun	6"-8"	Assorted	Summer & fall	Bed or border				
Zinnias	Sun	36"-45"	Assorted	Summer to frost	Background				

*Best produced from small plants

All other varieties may be planted from seed.

FIGURE 5-25 Plant materials; annual flower plantings. Account number 334. (Use local nursery catalogues to prepare lists.)

DESCRIPTION	PART NO./SIZE	ON HAND	YRLY. USAGE	QTY. REQ'D	COST	TOTAL COST
SANDY LOAM (SHREDDED)	1 CUBIC YARD					
TOPSOIL (SHREDDED)	1 CUBIC YARD					
TRIPLE MIX	1 CUBIC YARD					
MUSHROOM COMPOST	1 CUBIC YARD					
LIME	25 kg					
FERTILIZERS	15/20/25 kg					
ISOTOX	1 GALLON					
CYGON 2E	500 ml.					
DIAZINON	500 ml.					
SLUG KILLER PELLETS	500 ml.					
CHLORDANE (SPRAY OR DUST)	500 ml./1 kg.					
CRABGRASS KILLER	1 GALLON					
2-4-D ESTEMINE	1 GALLON					
KILLEX	1 OR 5 GALLON					
WEED PREVENTER	25 lbs.					

FIGURE 5-26 Soils, fertilizers, and chemicals inventory list. Account number 335.

DESCRIPTION	PART NO./SIZE	ON HAND	YRLY. USAGE	QTY. REQ'D	COST	TOTAL COST
SALT	20 kg					
SAND	Ton					
CALCIUM PELLETS	50 lbs.					
SALT/SAND/CALCIUM MIX	TON					
CALCIUM FLAKES	100 lbs.					
ICE SCRAPER						
SNOW PUSHER						
SNOW SCOOP						
WINTER GLOVES						
WINTER MITTS						
SNOW FENCE	50 feet					
"T" BARS FOR SNOW FENCE	7 feet					

FIGURE 5-27 Inventory and equipment list (winter condition control). Account numbers 343, 344.

DESCRIPTION	PART NO./SIZE	ON HAND	YRLY. USAGE	QTY. REQ'D	COST	TOTAL COST
GARDEN HOSE	50' x 3/4"					
GARDEN HOSE	50'x 1/2"					
SOAKER HOSE	50 ft.					
HOSE COUPLINGS						
WASHERS						
WATERING CAN-PLASTIC	2 GAL.					
WATERING CAN	1 1/2 GAL.					
WATERING CAN	7 QT.					
HOSE NOZZLE						
PAIL - PLASTIC						
PAIL - GALVANIZED						
EXTENSION HANDLE	4 FT.					
SPRINKLERS-OSCILATING						
SPRINKLERS PULSATING WITH SPIKE						
SHUT-OFF VALVE-ONE WAY AND TWO-WAY						

UNDERGROUND SPRINKLER SYSTEM

SPRINKLER HEADS	1"-½"-3/4"					
KEYS	1"- ½" - 3/4"					
ADAPTER ELBOWS	1" - ½" - 3/4"					
COUPLINGS BRASS	3/4"					
COUPLINGS RE-USABLE	1/2"					
MIST SPRAY NOZZLES						
SHRUB NOZZLES						
STATIONARY HEADS						
COUPLER KEYS						
					TOTAL COSTS	

FIGURE 5-28 Watering equipment inventory list. Account number 337.

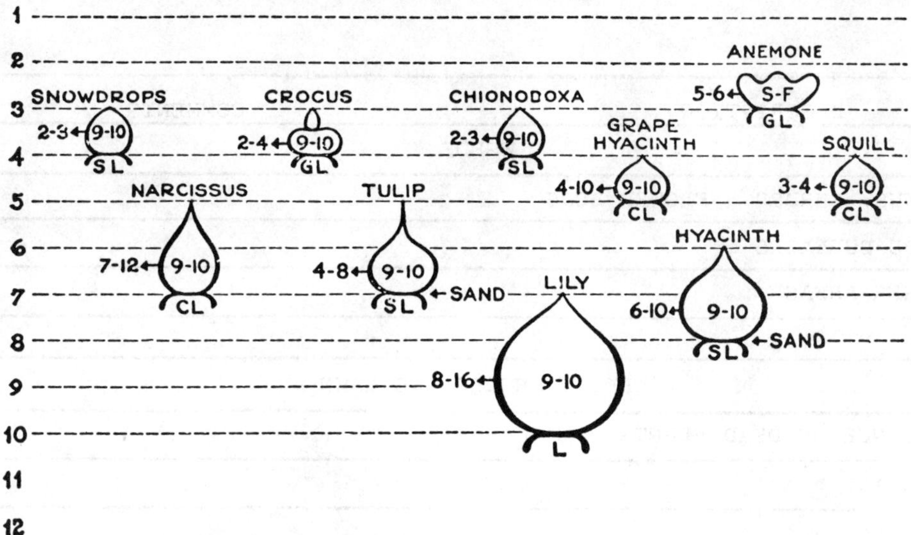

FIGURE 5-29 Plant materials; bulbs, corms and tubers. Depth and distances for planting bulbs. Figures in the left column show the depth for planting; those beside the bulbs show the proper distances apart. Figures within each bulb tell the month to plant. The letters indicate the ideal soil for the bottom of the hole. CL stands for clay loam; SL, sandy loam, GL, gravelly loam, and L, loam.

5-7 Grounds Maintenance Inspection Check List

There are several reasons why a grounds maintenance check list is a good idea. First, it is quite easy to become accustomed to the general appearance of the grounds and accept it as being adequate. Second, by detailing the grounds, we realize the complexity of the responsibilities involved and that it is quite easy to gradually allow the property to deteriorate. Third, someone is being paid to do the job right. When conducting a thorough inspection of an area, you should understand that it would be abnormal to find everything perfect. It is the little things that count, and unless the original standards are maintained, a property will slowly deteriorate. Inspections help pick up the little things that are so easily missed and they also are the only way to provide input for the budgets.

5-8 Preparing a Groundskeeping Budget

We have all heard the expression, "Beauty is in the eyes of the beholder." This is true, in every aspect of building design and maintenance, including ground maintenance. If you ask a person what impressed him about the

DESCRIPTION	COMMENTS
WEEDS	
LAWNS, SHRUBS & FLOWER BEDS	
HARD SURFACES	
OTHER AREAS	
TREES, SHRUBS AND LAWNS	
ABSENCE OF DEAD PLANTS	
PRUNING	
EDGING	
OTHER CONDITIONS	
PHYSICAL FEATURES	
SIGNS & LIGHT POSTS	
SIGNAGE	
POSTS, CHAINS & OTHER BARRIERS	
FENCES	
TRASH CONTAINERS	
OUTDOOR FURNITURE	
TRASH & PAPER	
EROSION CONTROL	
ROADS & OTHER HARD SURFACES	

FIGURE 5-30 Grounds inspection report. Conduct inspections during the growing season. Carry a set of material and inventory lists with you during the inspection so you can make decisions about next year's planting and at the same time prepare your lists.

	ACCT. NOS.	SUB TOTALS	TOTAL
GARDENING	33		

ACCESSORIES	331	
ARCHITECTURAL CHANGE	332	
CONTRACTOR	333	
PLANT MATERIALS	334	
SOILS, CHEMICALS & FERTILIZER	335	
TOOLS & EQUIPMENT	336	
WATERING	337	

SNOW REMOVAL	34	TOTAL	

CONTRACTOR	341	
FUEL & REPAIRS	342	
SALT & SAND	343	
TOOLS	344	

VEHICLE MAINTENANCE	35	TOTAL	

CAR ALLOWANCES	351	
FUEL	352	
INSURANCE	353	
MAINTENANCE	354	
TIRES	355	

FIGURE 5-31 **Summary of budget expense schedules, repair and maintenance categories; groundskeeping services.**

grounds, it would be the general apperance, and whether or not it was neat and trim. Therefore, it is important that routine maintenance chores are never neglected.

However, it was the initial design and installation that created the standards, and it is the planning and implementation of long-term goals that will assure that the appearance and standards are maintained. Building all of the needed activities into a zero-based budget will assure that the funds needed to achieve the goals are provided. Without this system, it is presumed that it is very expensive to "do the right things right," and funds would not be available or assigned for specific needs. Experience has shown that "negative motivation" downgrades the property and eventually costs more.

This budgeting system is a planning, control, and communications tool, and it includes inspections and review of previous expenditures, and because of the details that are illustrated in Figure 5-31, pinpoints every action and purchase.

In addition, it allows us to take advantage of every opportunity to save without allowing the landscaping to deteriorate.

Chapter 6

STRUCTURAL SERVICES

6–1 An Overview*

In 1974 the British government considered the problems of building maintenance serious enough to warrant a thorough investigation. It was estimated that one-third of the output of the construction and building industry in the British Isles was for the maintenance of buildings; the amount spent at that time was reported at five billion dollars per year.

Some of this money was for the redecoration and cleaning of buildings and some was for the replacement of materials that had a relatively short natural life when compared with the life of the building. It was estimated that one-fifth of the total cost of repairs was spent on the rectification of defects arising from errors in design or construction, many of which could have been avoided by correct detailing or better workmanship. If the cost due to loss of facilities is then added to the actual cost of repair, it becomes clear that the elimination of "avoidable" defects provides valuable financial benefits.

Prevention is better than cure, and we can reduce the frequency of defects by choosing appropriate materials, details, and methods.

*Portions of this chapter are reprinted with permission from Common Defects in Buildings, H. J. Eldridge, B.Sc. Crown Copyright, 1976.

Wherever possible, we will include in the descriptions of each defect that follows, a note on the preventative measures in new construction.

Paul Channon, M.P., The British Minister of Housing and Construction from 1972 to 1974, recognized the need for a full study of this problem and formed a "Committee on Building Maintenance."

This committee, in the course of its investigations for the British government, saw the need for a guide to aid the correct diagnosis of defects. The Property Services Agency of the Department of the Environment asked Henry Eldridge to write a book in response to the committee's recommendation. The author spent many years investigating failures in all kinds of buildings, both public and private.

Don Clark, the manager of Structural Services at the Cadillac Fairview Corporation in Toronto, Ontario, also spent many years investigating problems, diagnosing the causes, recommending remedial action, and supervising their satisfactory correction. Eldridge and Clark's findings, and the findings of the Committee on Building Maintenance, are identical, confirming the serious nature of the problems. That is the bad news.

The good news is that if we know the cause and effect, we also should know how to prevent the problems.

In this chapter, we hope to communicate sufficient information to enable you to recognize and correct structural problems as early as possible.

For those involved in design and construction, we hope to make you aware that proper design and careful attention to details during construction will help keep these costly problems to a minimum.

Defects occur in buildings for a variety of reasons. This is, perhaps, not surprising when one considers the wide range of materials and techniques used in the construction of buildings, differences in the conditions on building sites, and the varied occupational uses of the completed building. Small wonder that materials do not always perform in the manner intended or reach their full life expectancy.

A defect can be repaired satisfactorily only if its cause has been correctly diagnosed; experience has shown that errors are too often made. Sometimes this happens because it is not possible to obtain all the relevant information, but more often it is because the symptoms have not been fully investigated or the information has not been correctly interpreted. *It is not unknown for remedial work to be specified that had an effect opposite to what was, in fact, required.* Errors may be not only expensive and ineffective, but on occasions may actually aggravate the defect, making more extensive work necessary. It is far too easy to attribute every defect to "settlement" or "bad luck."

For example: You were called about a leak in the ceiling of a bedroom. There are a number of things you can immediately evaluate:

1. Is it a townhouse or an apartment building?
2. Is it a top floor?
3. Is it a suspended ceiling or plaster on slab?
4. If it is a suspended ceiling, what pipes could be running through it?
5. Is the water coming from a light fixture?
6. Are there stains in the ceiling plaster further away?
7. When was it first noticed?

8. Is it raining out?
9. Is it a cold day out?
10. Is there ice, snow, or water lying on the roof?

This type of questioning could go on and on. With a little knowledge of what to look for, the right questions to ask, and most important of all, the power of observation, you can save much time and frustration. This will not only make you look good in the eyes of the occupant, but it can make your job easier, quicker, and more satisfying.

With a better understanding of how a building is constructed and how its components fit together, your task in evaluating a situation will be easier.

Correct diagnosis depends on the collection and assembly of all the relevant information, a knowledge of the behavior of building materials and methods of construction, and a capacity for drawing the right conclusions from the evidence. It cannot be overemphasized that we should approach a problem with an open mind and put away any preconceived ideas. The contents of this chapter are, therefore, designed to direct attention to the basic starting point of diagnosis. This is particularly important in cases of cracking or dampness. Many defects have symptoms that are superficially similar, and it is important to know how to recognize those signs that will distinguish between them.

Much has been published about building defects, their causes, and cures, but, unfortunately, the information is scattered over a wide range of publications and is not easily accessible. Moreover, the published advice on remedial work often assumes that the cause of the failure is already known; in practice, although the symptoms will be apparent, the underlying factors may be obscure. If a wrong diagnosis is made, the treatment is unlikely to be successful and money will be wasted.

6-2 Principles of Diagnosis

The diagnosis of defects can be one of the most interesting aspects of building maintenance and of building construction in general, if it is approached in the right spirit. It can, in fact, be compared with crime detection: One begins with the symptoms of the defect as the first clues and proceeds to build up the evidence by careful investigation, before finally marshaling all the data to solve the mystery or diagnose the probable cause of the fault. The building detective requires a sound knowledge of both building construction and the chemistry of building materials and can, in truth, be considered an expert.

One of the challenges of defect diagnosis is the wide variety of circumstances and causes that confront the investigator. Nevertheless, the observance of certain procedures and the adoption of a systematic approach can greatly ease the detection process. We endeavor to give some guidance on these general requirements so that you might appreciate that we require a specialist in construction problems to assure proper diagnosis.

The first essential is to discard any preconceived ideas of the cause of the defect in question. *Never use the diagnosis as a means of confirming an opinion already formed, but start with an unbiased mind, ready to assess impartially all the data available.*

COLLECTION OF DATA

Everything that would appear to be relevant should be observed and recorded. However, sight is not the only sense that should be used in the investigation. Some defects have a characteristic smell, while with others, touch may reveal a looseness; no faculty should be ignored in the detection process.

As many data as possible should be collected. The amount of time available for doing this will vary with the circumstances, but if the information collected is incomplete, more time will be wasted later. Therefore, even when speed is vital, adequate time should be allowed for the collection of all the essential information. *Do not jump to conclusions; you may be wrong.*

Information may be obtained from a visual inspection of the defect and the surrounding area; site tests; laboratory examination of samples of materials; interrogation of and discussion with those concerned with the design, construction, maintenance, and occupation of the building; and from the drawings, specifications, and other documents relating to the building.

A close inspection of the affected area should be made and when access is not possible, a good pair of binoculars should be used. Detailed information concerning the upper parts of buildings can be obtained in this way, often with a considerable saving of time. Records of the data may be made by taking notes, by the use of a portable tape recorder, or by using a camera. *Photographs are especially worthwhile as they provide a permanent record, useful when an example is required of a particular defect for educational or feedback purposes, or when the collected information has to be passed on to another person to make the diagnosis.* Photographs are valuable as evidence in cases of dispute.

A small triple-lens magnifying glass is also extremely useful. It will help to establish whether a crack is new or old by revealing the amount of dirt and debris in the crack, or the presence of paint on its sides, a certain indication that the crack was present before the wall was last decorated. Mold growths, woodworm holes, and their accompanying debris are other items that can be more readily examined and identified by magnification.

ORAL INFORMATION

Much information can often be obtained from the people connected with the design, construction, and subsequent occupation of the building, especially regarding the history of the defect. This may only relate to the time when the person first saw the defect and not necessarily to when it actually occurred. All oral information should be recorded for later confirmation, if necessary. This applies particularly if the defect is likely to be the subject of a dispute, when the informant may be trying to protect his own interests. Secondhand information should be treated with reserve, and if it seems to be significant, every effort should be made to confirm it from other sources.

RECORDED INFORMATION

Efforts should be made to see the drawings of the building. These should reveal details of the construction, thus saving much of the exploratory work otherwise required to expose hidden detail. A distinction must be drawn, however, between "as designed" and "as built" drawings, for variations made during the course of construction are often not recorded. It is wise to develop a Building Profile Manual, as explained in chapter two, containing both details of construction and up-to-date records of alterations, additions, and maintenance carried out since the building was occupied. This information is helpful when establishing the history of the defect.

The specifications for the building are sometimes useful and may be vital if there is a question of liability involving design or construction.

Any reports on the defect which have already been produced should be obtained and studied since they may contain information and opinions that should be considered in the light of further evidence available.

6-3 Basic Building Construction

The first and foremost ingredients of any structure are the size and weight of the building, soil conditions, and shape or architectural design.

TYPES OF LOADS

There are a number of types of loads which will determine the size of the columns or supporting walls.

The loads or combination of loads must be transmitted to the foundation by the building frame and the various materials which act with the frame in the finished building. These loads are transmitted to the foundation by the structural components of the building.

The amount of weight the foundation walls will bear, and the soil conditions where the footings are to be poured, will determine the size and shape of the footings.

Before a building of any size is built, a company that specializes in soil stratigraphy

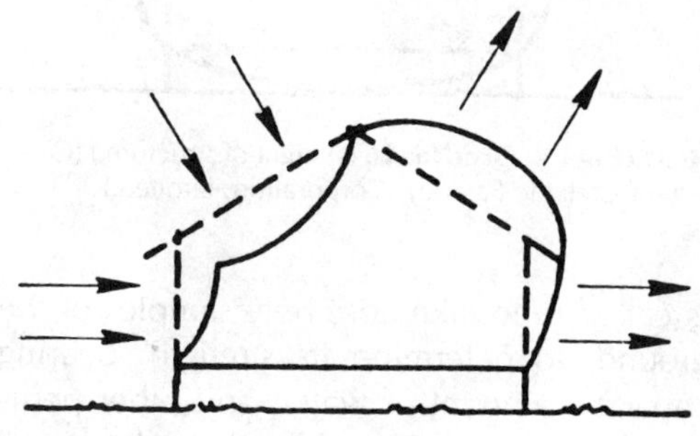

FIGURE 6-1 Wind loads. (Courtesy of Cadillac Fairview Corporation, Limited.)

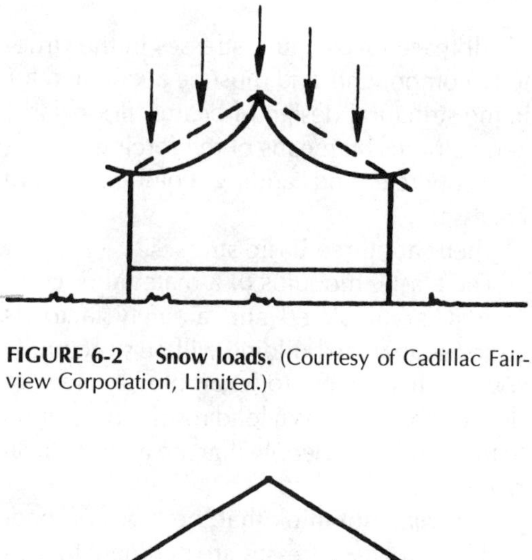

FIGURE 6-2 Snow loads. (Courtesy of Cadillac Fairview Corporation, Limited.)

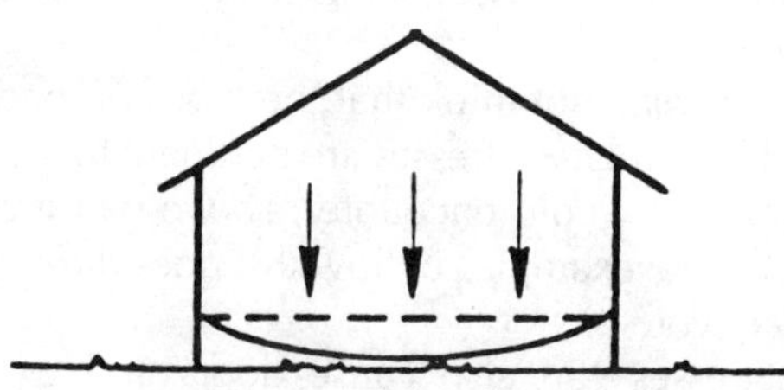

FIGURE 6-3 Live loads (People and furnishings—50 lbs. per sq. ft.). (Courtesy of Cadillac Fairview Corporation, Limited.)

FIGURE 6-4 Dead loads. (Weight of structure.) (Courtesy of Cadillac Fairview Corporation, Limited.)

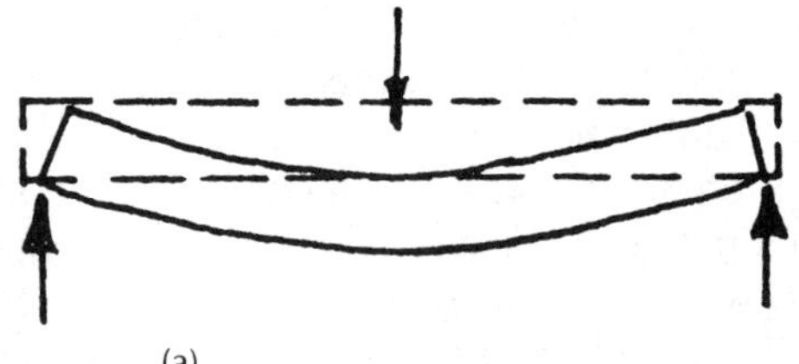

(a)

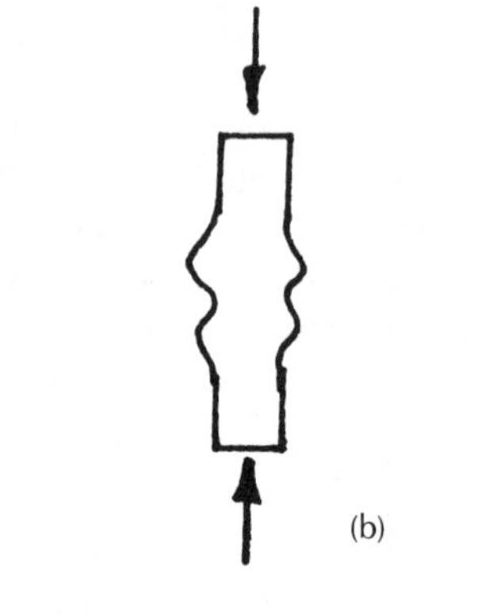

(b)

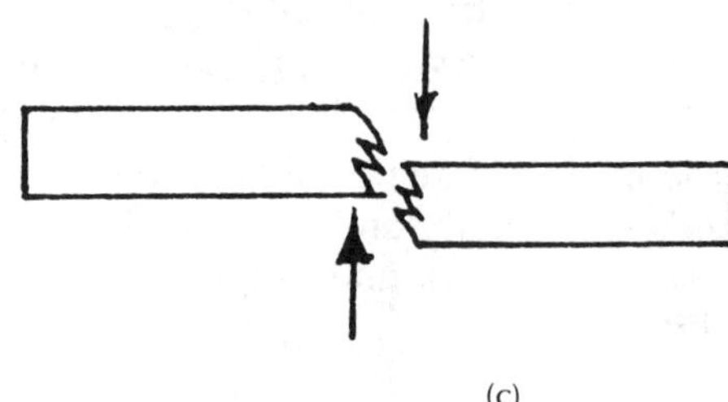

(c)

FIGURE 6-5 The three basic stresses. (a) Tension; (b) Compression; (c) Shear. (Courtesy of Cadillac Fairview Corporation, Limited.)

is called in to take bore hole samples of the ground, to determine its strength, bearing capacity, amount of water, and other pertinent information. These data help determine where to place the footings.

STRESSES

All these loads cause stresses in the structural components and must be accounted for in the structural design of beams, floor slabs, and columns by means of reinforcing steel in the concrete and adding columns where necessary.

There are three basic stresses.

The elastic modulus of a material or component is calculated and a safety factor is added so that the building will be structurally sound. This is why, for example, an elevator or assembly hall has a load restriction or limit to the number of people that are allowed in at one time.

You may not think that the types of loads and their related stresses are pertinent to anything you would encounter, so we will give you a few examples of how this does directly affect you.

Stresses can also cause doors and windows to jam if fitted too tightly during construction.

Another familiar problem due to loading stresses is a natural reaction known as "plastic creep," which can take up to three years to stop. This is the action of the flat slab, at the least supported point between columns, deflecting or sagging under tension, causing a number of things to happen: It can cause a void under a wall separating two apartments. This will allow noise and smell transfer. Sometimes, instead of a void, the block wall bearing on the slab will come down with the slab, causing settling cracks.

TYPES OF BUILDING CONSTRUCTION

There are two basic types of structure—bearing wall and slab construction.

Bearing Wall

This is an older form of construction and is not used in modern day high-rise buildings because it is normally limited to four to six floors.

- Refers to small buildings.
- Called bearing wall because weight of building is on exterior walls and main interior walls.
- Each floor holds the weight of the floor above.
- The higher the building, the larger or wider the bearing wall, e.g., the Empire State Building in New York City, whose ground floor is about 5 feet thick.
- Waste of space, time, and material.
- More difficult to put a new door or window into wall construction.
- Normal construction would be 4-inch brick, 1-inch space and ties, 8- to 12-inch concrete block walls.
- Most buildings of this type are slab on grade, which means the ground floor slab is on fill.
- This slab will sometimes sink if the ground is not properly tamped.
- Because brick and mortar are under pressure, little or no tuck pointing is needed.
- No slab edges to paint or spall.
- Floors above grade are generally steel joist bearing on exterior block wall, with a 2- to 3-inch concrete poured floor slab on ribbed steel decking, with some reinforcements running at right angles to ribs for added strength.
- Roof slab is similar to the floor slab, with the addition of one of the various types of roofing.

Slab Construction

Slab construction simply means that each floor is poured as a concrete slab, with reinforcing and the use of formwork that is later removed after the curing period. Concrete or reinforced columns or shear walls support these floors.

There are a number of types of slab construction:

1. One-way slab (spans one way).
2. Flat slab, for heavy loads (spans all ways).
3. Flat slab, for light use as in apartments.
4. Ribbed slab (spans all ways).
5. Waffle slab (spans all ways).
6. "T" slab (usually precast and prestressed).

The most commonly used slab for apartments is the flat slab for light use.

These slabs, which extend from outside edge to outside edge of the building, are supported on a series of structurally-located columns or shear walls. Other relevant facts about slab construction:

- A column can vary in size and location according to the load it carries; it runs from the underside of the basement slab, the entire height of the building.
- A shear wall is a steel reinforced wall generally 8 to 12 inches thick and can run the entire width of a building from sub grade to the underside of roof; it is strategically placed to bear the loading, also with the apartment layout in mind.
- Each floor slab bears directly on the supporting columns or walls and carries the weight of all loads of that particular floor only. This slab also carries the weight of

the curtain wall, precast concrete, or other panels that enclose the perimeter.

Each brick panel wall is subject only to its own weight and is not under any bearing load as in the case of a bearing wall construction.

Unless the mortar is a good mixture and its consistency is watched or supervised during the construction, the strength of the mortar can vary and, consequently, each floor or area being worked on by the bricklayer can react differently.

Too strong a mixture of cement will cause hairline shrinkage cracks in the mortar. This will allow water entry. Too little cement mixture will cause sandy mortar and again allow water entry. A proper mixture of sand, cement, and lime is essential in a good mortar mixture. This is one of the biggest downfalls of slab construction and costs many companies thousands of dollars every year to rectify. The problems, causes, and cures will be taken up later.

One other problem encountered with slab construction is plastic creep. This is a natural reaction of the concrete slab sagging or deflecting and can take years to reach its fullest extent.

6-4 Causes of Defects

Defects in buildings occur because the original design was inadequate, because the building was not constructed in accordance with the design or with accepted good prac-

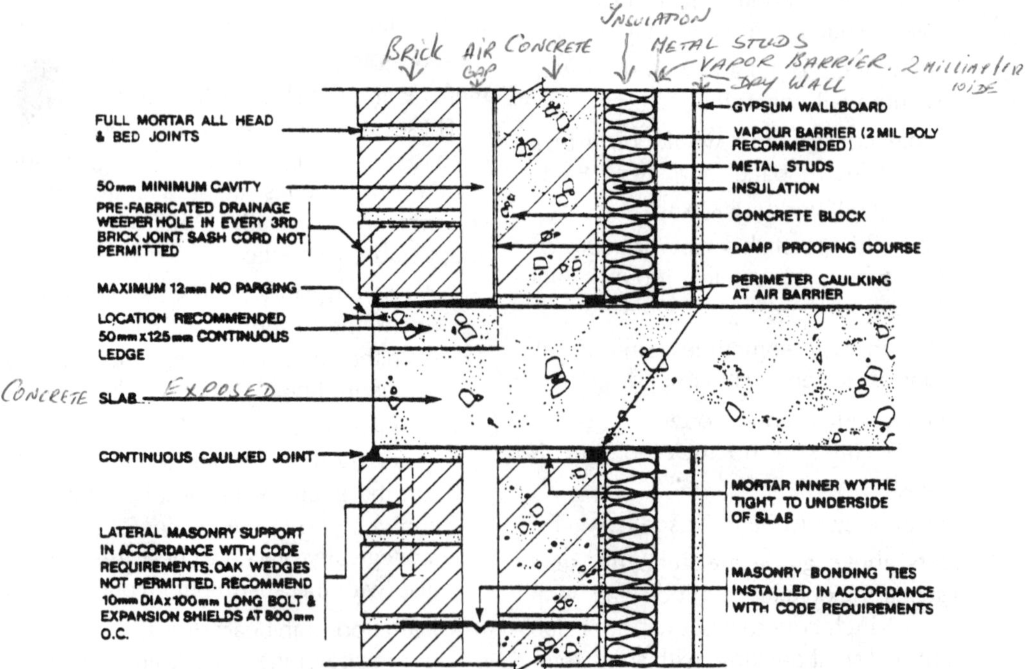

FIGURE 6-6 Exposed slab edge detail. (Courtesy of Cadillac Fairview Corporation, Limited.)

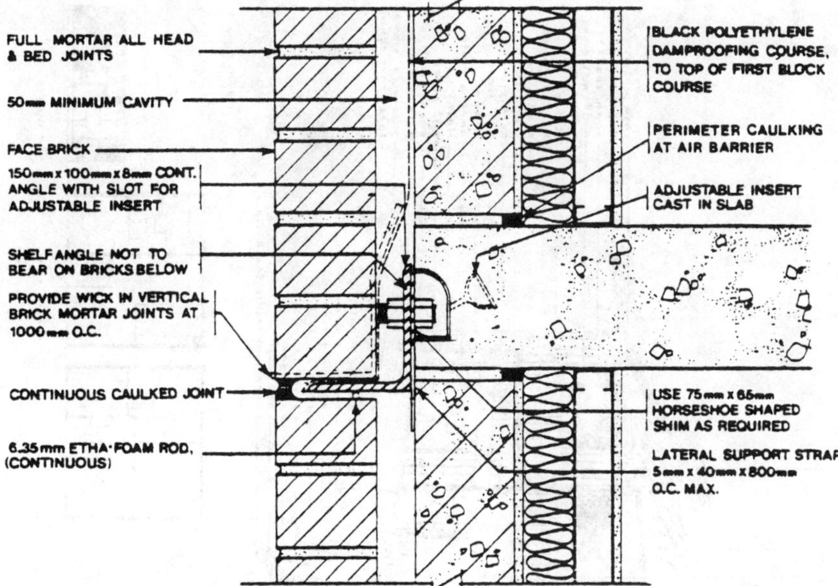

FIGURE 6-7 Shelf angle detail. Shelf angles carrying brick veneer walls above allow water to bypass the slab edge. The detailing of a dampproofing course onto the shelf angle, weepers, and caulking are all critical to the success of a shelf angle detail. Caution needs to be taken in anchoring and torquing all shelf angles. (Courtesy of Cadillac Fairview Corporation, Limited.)

tice, because the workmanship was below standard, or because the building has been subjected to forces and agents not allowed for in the design.

Basically, the majority of defects result from

(a) The application of forces, either externally or internally, greater than those that the building as a whole, or the components or materials of which it is made, can withstand.

(b) The effects of materials, whether in a gaseous, liquid, or solid state, including those that contribute to the external climatic conditions and those which result from the occupancy of the building.

(c) The effect of biological agents, e.g., fungi.

(d) Changes in temperature.

These factors may lead to

1. Changes in the composition or condition of the materials used in the construction of the building; such changes may render the materials more susceptible to applied forces, although they were adequate before the changes took place.
2. Changes in the construction, ranging from slight cracking, not affecting stability, to complete destruction.
3. Changes in shape, size, or weight.
4. Changes in appearance, including color.

Slight changes from the original condition may not be considered as defects, but this depends on the circumstances. Major changes will usually be considered as defects, but may not be if they do not affect the appearance.

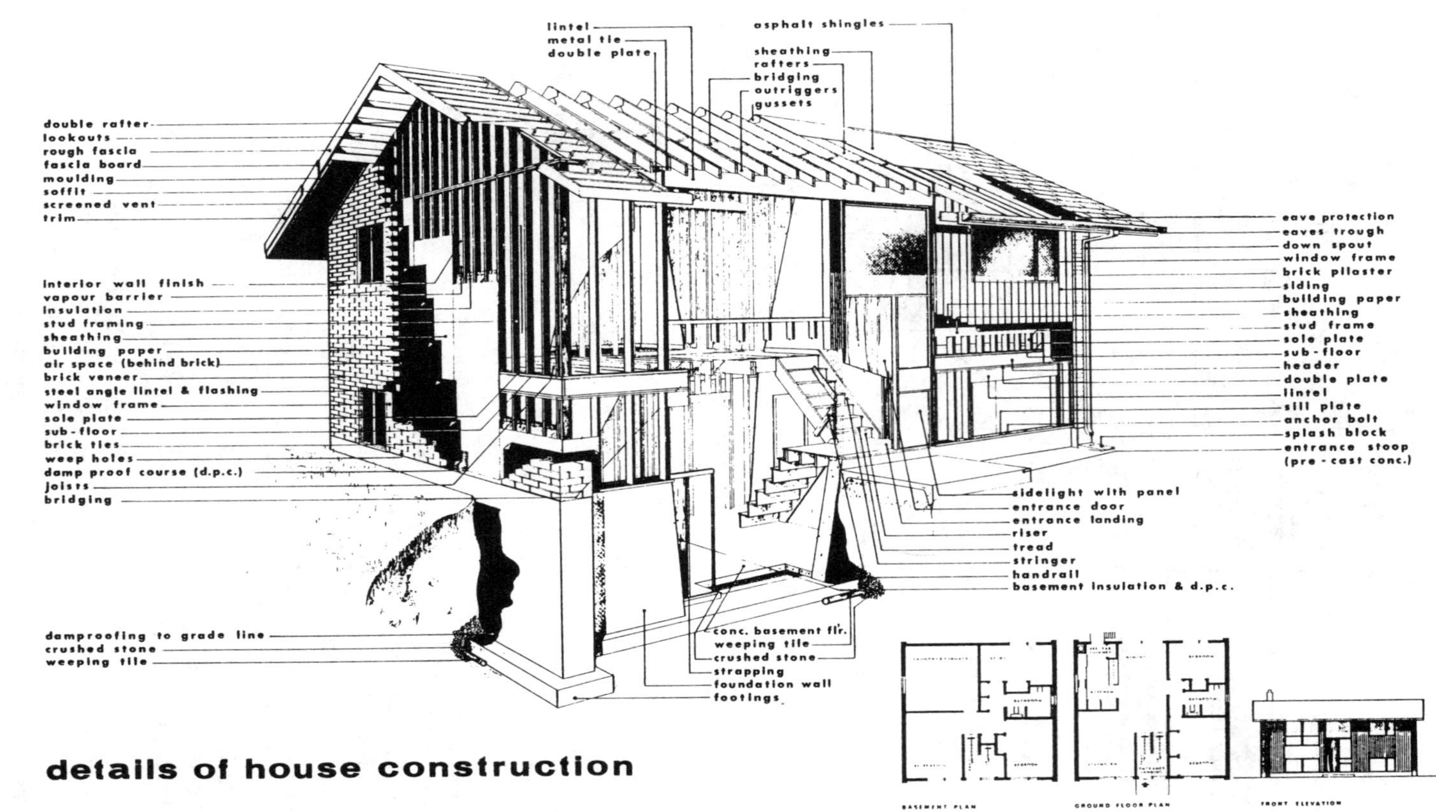

FIGURE 6-8 Details of house construction. (Courtesy of Central Mortgage and Housing Corporation.)

In general, changes in composition result from

- fire
- the effects of gases, liquids, and solids
- biological agents

Changes in the structure result from

- applied physical forces, including those from ground movements
- climatic conditions

Changes in shape, size, and weight result from

- effect of changes of temperature

Changes in appearance could result from

- wear
- effect of sunlight

From a more practical aspect, however, the majority of defects can be placed in one of three main groups. The boundaries are by no means clear-cut and there will often be overlapping. These groups are

1. Defects caused by dampness that is visible or, as in the case of dry rot, that provides the conditions for other agents to operate.
2. Defects caused by applied forces, generally leading to the appearance of cracks.
3. Defects caused by changes in size.

Some defects in the last group will have been caused by changes in moisture content and some of the cracking will likewise have its origin in dampness, e.g., moisture expansion of clay brickwork, but these facts may not be known to the person responsible for remedying the defect. We see only the result and will, therefore, look for guidance under the heading of what we see and not its cause, for this is often unknown at the time.

Far too often the defects occur because the designer has not appreciated that changes can take place in the construction or in the materials used and has, therefore, not provided sufficient safeguards in his design. Materials are blamed for defects when the fault lies in the choice of materials unsuitable for the conditions to which they will be subjected. It is also sometimes claimed that considerations of costs determined the choice of materials that have failed; but almost any materials can be used satisfactorily if their limitations are recognized and taken into account in the design. What is really needed is a better understanding of the inherent properties of materials. Designs would be improved if the concept of *"troubleshooting in advance"* was employed more often, and this would undoubtedly lead to a reduction in the numbers of defects that occur in buildings.

Poor workmanship, especially non-compliance with the instructions given in the specifications, is also responsible for the occurrence of defects. The lack of maintenance, or incorrect maintenance, often reduces the effective life of a material.

6-5 Change in Size

The size of most porous building materials increases with an increase in their water content and vice versa. Often the changes will not be noticeable, but many result in trivial defects, and some result in defects of appreciable magnitude. The decrease in size when wet materials dry out leads to shrinkage cracks, particularly noticeable in the early life of the building and often the subject of much argument.

The water content of some materials, especially timber, and to a lesser extent, cement products, alters with changes in the water content of the air, and are subject to almost continuous changes in size. Some changes are significant; many are not.

The absorption of water, even in the form of water vapor, may lead to a considerable permanent expansion from chemical changes. Some ceramic products, such as bricks and tiles, may expand and lead to cracking of the brickwork, and the attack of sulphates on concrete can be very extensive.

CHEMICAL ACTION

Water may provide the necessary conditions for other forms of chemical attack on building materials. An example is alkali attack on paint films. Paints are often applied to alkaline surfaces, but no defects will arise unless the surface is so damp that alkaline solutions are formed and brought into contact with the paint.

WEATHER

Defects in buildings and building materials are often said to be caused by the weather, especially when severe or unusual conditions have been experienced. However, careful diagnosis will demonstrate that faulty design, the wrong choice of materials, or faults on site are usually the root cause of the defect, with the weather only providing the appropriate conditions for the failure to occur. These conditions lead to the various physical and chemical changes described previously.

"Frost" is a good example of damage attributed to weather conditions. Cold weather should do no immediate harm to buildings properly designed and constructed with appropriate materials. Unprotected surfaces will be susceptible to sudden drops in temperature, and frost may affect other materials, particularly those mixed with water, if unprotected during construction; frost may also affect porous materials exposed over a long period of time.

The durability of materials may be reduced by exposure to weather, some by surface erosion and some by chemical changes, but this is usually a slow process and an early breakdown is more likely to be due to other factors.

BIOLOGICAL ACTION

Water, or water vapor, is required to provide the right conditions for the growth of fungi, such as dry and wet rot, molds, and algae. The amounts of water may be critical, but it should be assumed, if such growths are present, that the part of the building in which they occur is, or has been, damp.

6–6 Cracks

Cracks result from applied forces greater than those that the building or its components can withstand. These forces may have been applied externally, internally, or been built up in the materials of the building as a result of chemical changes. There may be a single force or a combination of forces, having a single cause or several causes.

Much of the cracking that occurs early in the life of a building is inevitable, since it is due to the internal forces built up in many materials when the water used in the construction process dried out. Such cracking is generally superficial, and if so, is easily repaired and will cause little trouble later on. Where it is more significant, the repair work may have to be repeated periodically, because subsequent dimensional changes of the materials due to thermal and moisture content variations are likely to be accommodated at the cracks, the opening and closing of which will adversely affect the stability of the materials used as fillers.

The structural significance of cracks tends to be exaggerated; this is a natural reaction of the owners or occupants of a building. Obviously, some cracks will be an indication of instability, but many others that look quite serious may have little or no effect on the stability, either because the building has a high factor of safety, or because the affected area does not contribute to the stability of the structure.

INVESTIGATION OF CRACKS

As a guide for the investigator, the following evidence should be detailed:

1. Direction—See Figure 6-10.
2. Extent—Note starting and finishing points.

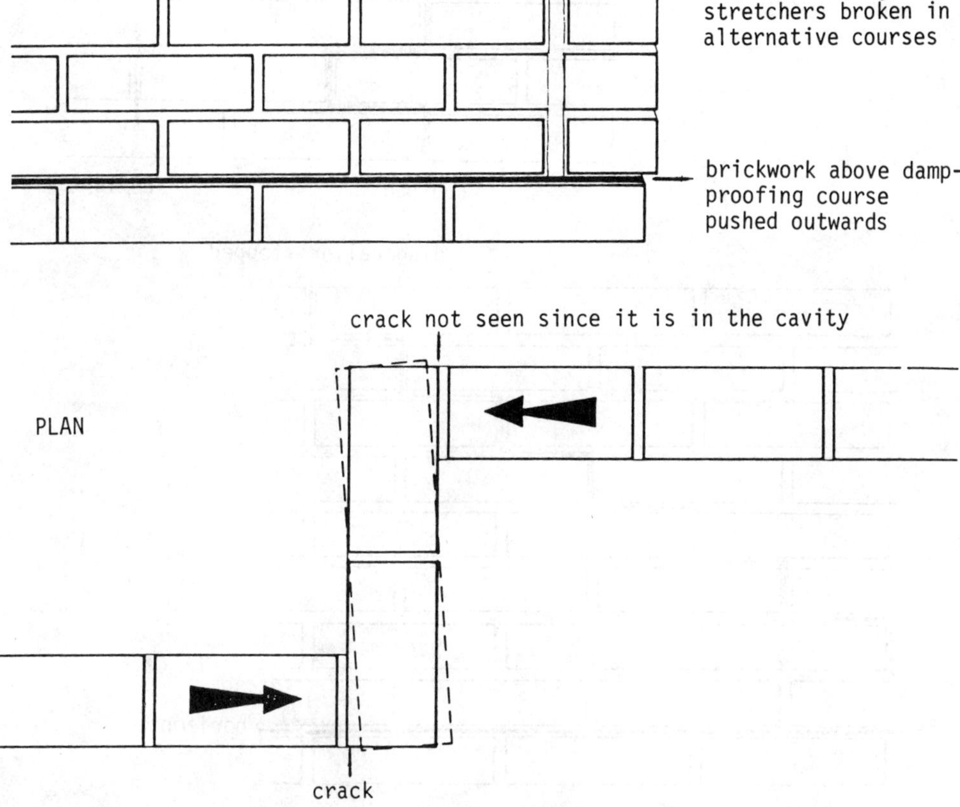

FIGURE 6-9 Forms of cracks in brick or blockwork. (Reproduced from *Common Defects in Buildings* with permission from the Controller of Her Majesty's Stationery Office, England.)

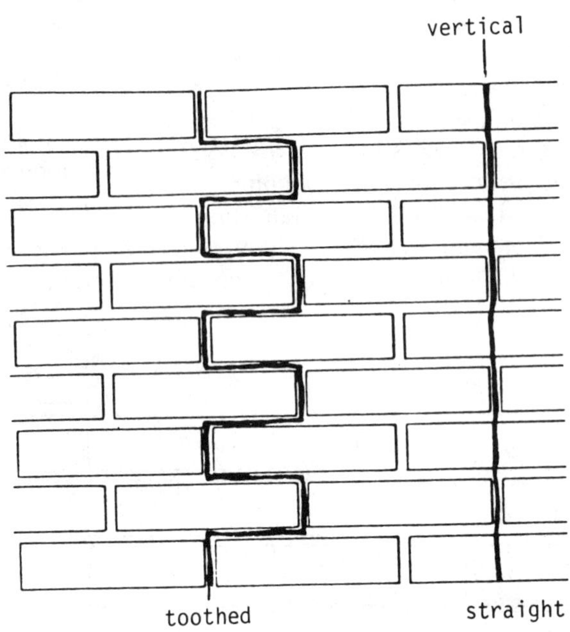

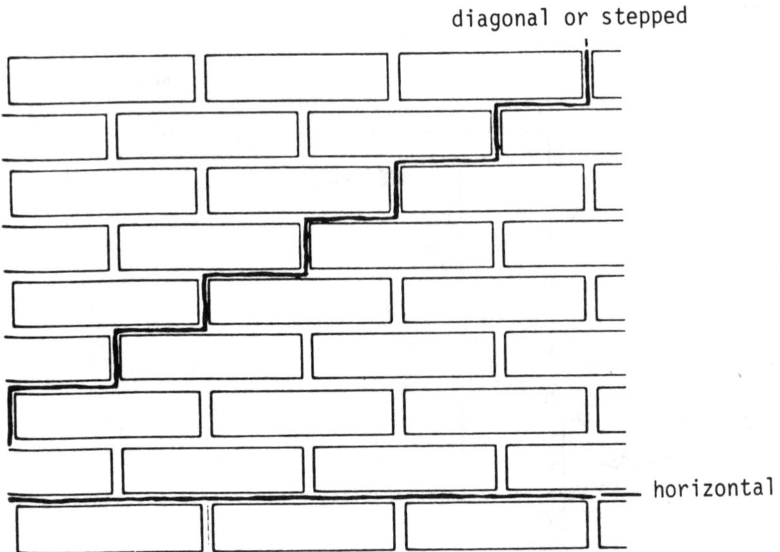

FIGURE 6-10 How to describe cracks. (Reproduced from *Common Defects in Buildings* with permission from the Controller of Her Majesty's Stationery Office, England.)

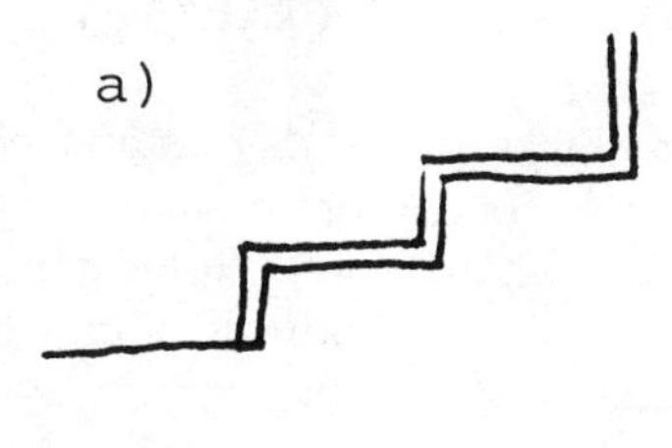

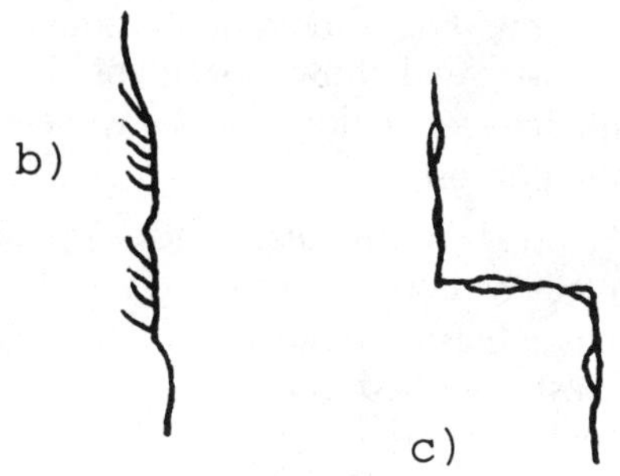

FIGURE 6-11 Cracks. (a) Settling cracks; (b) Shear cracks; (c) Shrinkage cracks. (Courtesy of Don Clark.)

3. Width—Note if there are any changes in width.
4. Depth—Use a piece of fine wire.
5. Alignment—Pass a fingertip across the crack.
6. Sharpness of edges.

Cracks occurring in plaster walls are caused by a movement, usually in the structural wall, and can be caused by one of three actions.

These cracks can sometimes move along the floors, up the entire height of a building, or can show up in the brick exterior. Each of the cracks should be handled differently, depending on its severity and reoccurrence. Use of an elastic material to bridge the crack will allow movement. As this material is difficult to use, it should only be applied by plasterers. An alternative would be to have a plasterer provide plaster stops. This method leaves a joint in the wall, but will resolve further cracking of the plaster.

Cracking generally has an adverse effect on appearance, though it is suprising how long cracks can go unnoticed; sometimes for several years. Statements made about the date of a crack's occurrence must be treated with considerable suspicion.

The extent to which a crack allows rain penetration will depend on various factors, such as the construction of the building and the degree of exposure. The part played by capillarity in the passage of water is much greater with fine cracks than with wide cracks where it may be nonexistent. Wide cracks may be susceptible to wind-driven rain, but this will depend largely on whether the construction will allow the passage of air. Cracking in the outer leaf of a properly-built cavity brick wall may not allow rain penetration into the interior of the building, but if there are wall ties, water may be transferred across the cavity to the inner leaf.

Cracks can result from any of the following causes, though it does not necessarily follow that cracking will inevitably occur:

1. Movement of the ground
2. Overloading
3. The effects of gases, liquids, and solids
4. The effect of change of temperature
5. Vibrations

6-7 Plaster Problems

Plaster problems and their repair are a constant irritation for building managers. It is important, therefore, to identify the problems and to provide suitable guidelines for repair.

It is not uncommon for someone to repair the same areas over and over again because they do not understand the problems or how to correct them.

PLASTER DETERIORATION

Plaster deterioration, or the crumbling and powdering effect, is caused strictly by the presence of moisture, either in the form of water or water vapor.

(a) Deteriorated plaster, caused by water, whether it be rain water leaks at windows, walls, or roofs, must be replastered after the leak is located and repaired.

(b) Deteriorated plaster, caused by water vapor in the form of condensation on a cold surface, would also require replastering. This cold surface can be located at a window, window frame, wall, or ceiling. Sometimes the problem shows up in the form of mold. The only effective remedy is to insulate and provide a vapor barrier. Many times this is not practical. If necessary, insulation and drywall can be glued, screwed, or nailed over the existing surface. Before this action is taken, proper assessment of the condition must be made.

If the problem is around metal window frames, make sure plaster is not in contact with the frame by providing plaster stops ("J" molding) around its perimeter. Prime new plaster and paint with two coats of alkyd semi-gloss to retard moisture attack. Insulation of the aluminum frame is possible, but costly. Some areas will simply have to be repaired as necessary.

PLASTER CRACKS

Plaster cracks occur due to movement. Plaster cracks occur on poured concrete, concrete block, and solid plaster partitions. To determine the type of wall, simply tap or sound the wall.

(a) Most cracks occur at the joint between two dissimilar materials. Plaster stops ("J" molding) should be introduced to separate and allow movement. Do not fill between molding or you will defeat the purpose.

(b) Stepped or irregular cracks on concrete or concrete block walls should have plaster removed to bare wire mesh installed across the crack, and replastered.

(c) Cracks occurring in solid plaster walls should have an expansion joint provided by installing plaster stops back to back.

POPPING PLASTER

There are a number of theories about why plaster pops at random. However, we do know that the delamination is taking place between the putty coat and the scratch coat. We also know that the problem is accelerated during hot, humid weather.

Over a poured concrete wall, strapping and drywall can be applied.

Over a concrete block wall, drywall can be nailed directly.

Both methods cover the problem and are followed by painting and decorating the repaired surfaces.

An alternative to both of these methods is to apply gypsum board, or metal lath and plaster, but this method is prohibitive due to cost.

SQUASH, HANDBALL, AND RACQUET BALL COURTS

The deterioration of the end plaster walls in recreation courts has led to research into the cure.

Because these walls are subject to premature failure, no white coat should be used. Instead a cement plaster should be used and finished with an epoxy paint and a fiberglass mesh coating.

WALL TILES

One of the most irritating and costly problems is the replacement of ceramic wall tiles in the tub and shower areas.

The cost for removing and replacing the tile is prohibitive. Much of this expense could be saved by specifying the proper wall base treatment and the adhesive. Inspection and supervision of each installation would also ensure that the standards are maintained.

During the life of the building, regular inspections would reveal problems that could be corrected early enough to avoid retiling. Using a straightened paper clip as a probe to test the grouting will detect water penetration behind the tiles. This condition must be corrected as soon as it is detected.

TUB GROUTING

It is essential that the tub and soap holder are properly caulked. The caulking may have to be cleaned with an algaecide or be replaced. Before recaulking, all dirt, soap, and grease must be removed. *Caulking should not be attempted by anyone not trained to do this job.*

Black marks sometimes show up on the caulking around the tub and showers without adequate ventilation. The presence of soap in the water hastens the growth.

A strong solution of chlorine laundry bleach and a little detergent, applied with a stiff brush, will remove the black stains, but they will keep coming back as long as the dampness continues. Wiping down the tub or shower wall after bathing will help keep this problem under control.

6-8 Dampness in Buildings

We will study the appearance of dampness inside a building, but not any of the consequential effects, which will vary greatly with the nature of the defect and the length of time it has been allowed to continue. The consequential effects are often serious, especially if repairs are delayed for long periods, and it cannot be emphasized too strongly that remedial work to eliminate dampness should be carried out at the earliest opportunity. Dampness is generally noticed only when it appears internally.

Dampness is one of the most difficult faults to trace and diagnose. There are innumerable ways in which water can be present in a building and several of these may occur in the same building at the same time and even be responsible for the same damp patch. The location of one source must not be used as an excuse for discontinuing the investigation into the source of water. Unfortunately, there are far too many instances where this has been the case, and the wet patch has quickly reappeared.

Most buildings are assembled from a variety of materials, many of which are water-absorbent. The sources of water are briefly discussed below under several broad headings.

The presence of excessive amounts of water in a building is almost certainly the cause of a greater proportion of defects than any other single cause or agent. The appearance of damp patches on the interior surfaces of a building is at the least a nuisance or an annoyance, but at its worst, the consequential damp conditions may affect the health of the occupants and cause much damage to the building materials. A summary of the effects of dampness on building materials is given below.

Water is often responsible for the redistribution of dirt on the face of a building, leading to streaking on the surfaces and other unsightly effects. It may also redistribute constituents of materials that in turn may produce defects. A particular example is the migration of soluble sulphates from bricks, either into other materials where they may cause damage, or simply to the face of the brick where they appear as unsightly efflorescence.

Dampness also causes changes in the performance of various materials. An important example of this is the effect dampness has on the "R" value of insulating materials. This alteration can in turn have repercussions both on the physical structure of the building and on the comfort of the occupants.

WATER PENETRATION

Water enters many buildings as a result of rainfall, either directly through defects in the roof or walls, or indirectly by absorption. It may then be transferred for some distance via cracks in the structure or finishes, or along hollow sections such as those used in curtain wall construction. A search should always be made for such paths, remembering that they may be some distance from the point where the dampness shows on the internal finishes.

A number of factors affect water penetration through masonry walls and each item must be assessed on its own merit. This report is broken down into cause and cure.

FIGURE 6-12 The migration of soluble sulphates from bricks. Unsightly efflorescence may appear on the face of the brick. (Reproduced from *Common Defects in Buildings* with permission from the Controller of Her Majesty's Stationery Office, England.)

CAUSES OF WATER PENETRATION

The *CAUSE* of rain or moisture penetration can be any one or combination of the following:

1. Faulty brickwork
2. Poor quality or wrong type of mortar
3. Poor quality or wrong type of caulking
4. Design and detailing problems
5. Quality of workmanship related to all of the above

It is important to repeat that a problem can only be corrected satisfactorily if its cause has been properly diagnosed. A wrong diagnosis sometimes happens because it is not always possible to obtain all the relevant information, or because the symptoms have not been fully investigated.

One of the challenges of defect diagnosis is the wide variety of circumstances and causes which can confront the investigator. Nevertheless, the observance of certain procedures and the adoption of a systematic approach can greatly facilitate the detection process.

The use of the rainwater infiltration or leakage form was designed to organize the investigation of this sort of problem. By answering the questions asked on the form, you will learn how to investigate the problem. By distributing the copies, you will be communicating your findings. Resolving and correcting the problems should follow before they become serious (Figure 6-14).

CURES FOR FAULTY BRICKWORK

It is generally accepted that two properties of bricks will affect a wall's resistance to moisture penetration:

1. The permeability of the brick to water.
2. Brick's ability to bond with mortar.

In the first case, water may pass through the brick in the wall and come out the other side (called initial rate of absorption).

POROUS BRICK

All bricks have a porous structure, the nature of which depends on the raw material, the method of formation, and the firing temperature during the manufacturing process.

The permeability of extruded (stiff-mud) bricks is not likely to be significant in the problem of moisture penetration of masonry, but the permeability of drypress and soft-mud bricks may be important.

If porous brick is the problem, the best solution is to either cover it with a siding or with shielding. An alternative would be to stucco or rebuild. Silicone treatment of walls has been used with limited success and would only be a temporary measure. Silicone is only mildly successful relating to porous bricks. Many times you will accelerate or create spalling brick because, in effect, you provide a vapor barrier on the outside surface, disallowing moisture to escape, causing spalling.

GLAZED BRICK

Full or partial glazed brick will eliminate, in part, the problem of rain absorption, but full glazed has the inherent problem of spalling (popping off). This can be resolved, as noted above for porous brick. Semi-glazed brick has been very successful.

FAULTY MORTAR

In other cases, certain properties of the brick and mortar may adversely affect the bonding between the brick-mortar interface, thus enabling water penetration. Taping un-

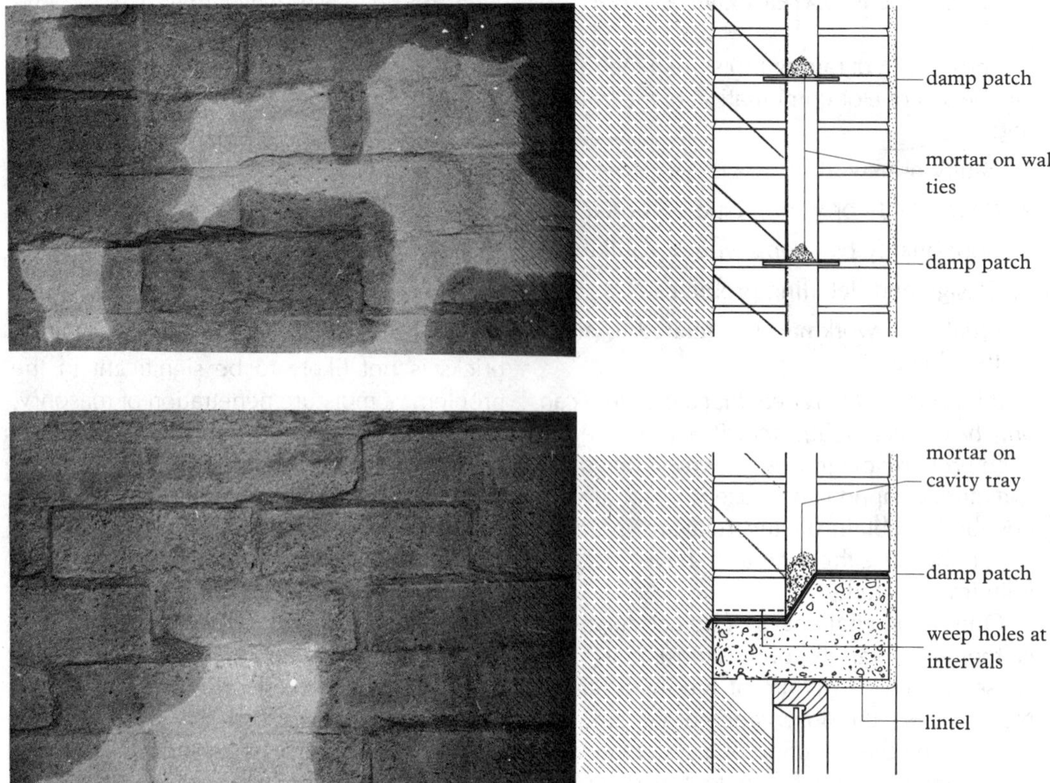

FIGURE 6-13 Transfer of water across the cavity of a cavity wall. Dampness on internal surface of external skin of cavity wall. (Reproduced from *Common Defects in Buildings* with permission from the Controller of Her Majesty's Stationery Office, England.)

glazed bricks and scrubbing a special mortar mix into the voids will correct this problem. More serious mortar problems can only be corrected by removal and pointing all mortar joints.

The only way to avoid repeating this problem during new construction is knowing the type of brick ordered, specifying the correct mortar, and having careful control by someone who knows and understands good practice.

Rather than getting involved with all the pros and cons of mortar types, the problems are simply stated as follows:

1. The bond between brick and mortar (which was discussed under "Brickwork").

2. The problem of soft, sandy mortar is usually caused by freezing prior to curing or the joint becoming saturated and frozen. The other possibility is a slop lime mortar mix having no structural capacity. If the problem is only on the surface, you may be able to use the grouting method. If the problem is deeper, you will need to solid point every joint at least ½ inch or to the depth of deterioration.

MAINTENANCE REQUEST
RAINWATER INFILTRATION OR
RAINWATER LEAKAGE

RWL **00004**

BUILDING	SUITE NO.	DATE
RESIDENT'S NAME	PHONE NO. RES:	BUS:
REQUEST:		

RESIDENT'S CONSENT

I WISH TO HAVE THIS REQUEST ATTENDED TO AND I HEREBY AUTHORIZE CADILLAC FAIRVIEW RESIDENTIAL MANAGEMENT TO ENTER MY APARTMENT SHOULD IT BE NECESSARY TO USE A SERVICE AGENCY OTHER THAN CADILLAC FAIRVIEW RESIDENTIAL MANAGEMENT OR SHOULD MORE THAN ONE VISIT BE REQUIRED FOR CORRECTION. I ALSO SIGNIFY MY CONSENT

REQUEST RECEIVED BY — RESIDENT'S SIGNATURE — DATE

CONDITION FOUND UPON INVESTIGATION

1. Which room is it leaking in?
2. Where is leak in the Room? Under window ☐ Above window ☐ At sides of window ☐ At floor level ☐ In corner of suite ☐ In clothes closet ☐ At ceiling ☐ On wall with no windows ☐ Is it an outside wall ☐ Inside wall ☐
3. Which direction is leaking area facing? East ☐ West ☐ North ☐ South ☐
4. Was there enough water to warrant using Wet vacuum ☐ Mop ☐ A cloth ☐
5. If leaking under radiator, did you check piping? Yes ☐ No ☐
6. Is this the first report of problems in this apartment? Yes ☐ No ☐
7. Does it happen each time it rains? Yes ☐ No ☐

INSPECTOR'S COMMENTS

INSPECTOR'S SIGNATURE

COMMENTS FROM STRUCTURAL DEPARTMENT

INSPECTOR'S SIGNATURE

ACTION INITIATED BY STRUCTURAL SERVICES

ACTION TAKEN	NUMBER	WHO TO CORRECT	DATE ISSUED
WORK ORDER			
PURCHASE ORDER			

FIGURE 6-14 Rainwater infiltration maintenance request. (Courtesy of Cadillac Fairview Corporation, Limited.)

3. Another problem with mortar is the tooling and buttering of joints, and is further explained under the heading "Workmanship."

The type of mortar recommended for non-loading bearing exterior walls is type-N mortar: one part cement, one part lime, six parts sand. The type of mortar recommended for load bearing walls is type S 2.1.8.

BOND BETWEEN BRICK AND MORTAR

More often than not, the problem of moisture penetration is due to the lack of bond between the brick and mortar.

Assessment of this problem can be made by removing a few bricks from the wall and taking special note of the bond. If the mortar is smooth on the interface between the brick and mortar, then a lack of bond exists that will allow water entry. This condition will eventually cause the deterioration of both brick and mortar.

TAPING AND GROUTING

The solution to this problem is tape grouting, or in the case of glazed brick, simple grouting. This is a method of literally scrubbing a special mortar mix into the voids. Unglazed brick needs to be taped before grouting. Another method might be to solid point all mortar joints, but this method is more expensive.

CAULKING COMPOUNDS

These are elastic materials that are used to caulk windows, doors, cracks, joints, and other areas of movement. They are also used to seal two different type of surfaces and provide for movement, such as steel to concrete, or glass to metal. Sealants are used more extensively on exterior weather-exposed surfaces than on the interior of buildings. The most commonly used today are the polysulfide base or silicone rubber base. Other types of caulking materials that are available are oil, urethane butyl rubber, and acrylic-based. The last two of the group are less expensive than the first type, but their use is limited and their life expectancy, in some cases, is short.

Some sealants can be poured and some are used with a gun. They come in a variety of components. Some are one-part (air-cured) and others have two parts, consisting of a base and an activator. They can be applied hot or cold. The surface preparation is the most important part of a good caulking installation and starts with cleaning and drying. The temperature of the surfaces that are to receive the caulking and the temperature during the setting period must be controlled to meet the manufacturer's specifications.

CURES FOR FAULTY CAULKING

One of the more serious problems with structures today is that great masses of brick, glass, and concrete are put together with little consideration given to

(a) Heat loss

(b) Air infiltration

(c) Water penetration

At the junction of all dissimilar materials, other reasons for caulking failure are:

1. Poor workmanship
2. Poor quality of the material
3. Wrong material specified
4. Poor joint design

Poor quality material will soon delaminate and break bond, allowing moisture to enter and heat to escape, as well as resulting in colder drafty windows and walls.

The right type of caulking should always be specified for a particular job. If water is evident, use a caulking that won't be affected. If there is a possibility that water is going to pond, use a polysulfide or urethane or any type that won't revert.

Make sure all joints are clean, dry, and free from oils or mortar droppings. Upper exposed slab edge joints should be mortared but not caulked, in the event moisture should have to escape. The lower slab edge joint should be mortared solid ⅜ inch maximum in size and caulked. Bricks should not protrude more than ½ inch from the face of the slab edge; frogs should never be exposed; quoins should never be used as stretchers; and all top coursing vertical joints should be covered with caulking. Poured concrete floor slab edges should never be pargeted. Pargeting has a tendency to break loose, allowing water entry, thus causing failure to both brick and caulking below.

Caulking between dissimilar materials is crucial and requires skill and an understanding of its end function. The proper design of the joint is as important as the type of caulking. Packing rods and window splines are to be used with care.

Poor workmanship in any of the above noted areas will cause failure sooner or later. *To ensure quality of workmanship, one inspection of each and every drop should be made.*

DESIGN AND DETAILING

Every good builder should go back to existing buildings and learn from past mistakes so as not to repeat the same problems. To assure a better chance of success, problem areas should be detailed when designing a new building. This is better than changing or making on-site decisions during construction.

QUALITY OF WORKMANSHIP

It goes without saying that professional bricklayers and caulkers, properly supervised, can save a lot of maintenance expenses. Poor workmanship is related to most structural problems. The expense is triple: once to build the first time, second, to remove, and third, to replace.

The success of masonry walls depends on the workmanship in bricklaying, the bricklayer's understanding of the type of brick, the workability of the mortar and the ability to bond to the brick, weather conditions, retempering of mortar and size or mortar joints, a solid filled joint, and the proper tooling.

Workmanship in the application of caulking will again determine the success or failure of a watertight structure.

CONCLUSION

In conclusion, workmanship, or the lack of it, is the major reason for most of the problems related to water penetration through masonry. Fancy designs and fancy details are not required to overcome many of the problems experienced. Good old-fashioned common sense and pride in workmanship will resolve many of the problems.

As you can see, the correction of these problems should only be attempted by experts. Quick action by the building staff or property manager can, by calling for help, keep the cost of repairs to a minimum. All problems should be documented by the structural services expert and passed back to the designer and builder to avoid repeating the problems in the future.

CONDENSATION

Let us start with water. Water is water—we drink it, we bathe in it, boil it, and get steam or moisture that disappears into the air. At this point it becomes "humidity" or moisture in the air. In apartment buildings, generally speaking, condensation problems can only be caused by conditions within the suite. Condensation begins to form on any cool surface, the same way it forms on a cold bottle when you take it out of the refrigerator.

Most people are confused about where the moisture comes from. Some think it is leaking in around the windows because that is where they see it first. Many people find it hard to accept that moisture originates within the house or apartment from such normal activities as washing, bathing, cooking—or even breathing.

RELATIVE HUMIDITY

Most people cannot understand the matter of RELATIVE HUMIDITY. The confusion starts at this point. Yet relative humidity is easy to understand if we remember just one fact—*WARM AIR CAN HOLD MORE MOISTURE THAN COLD AIR*.

There is naturally a point at which air cannot hold any more moisture (water vapor). At this point, the relative humidity is 100 percent. If air has one-half the moisture it can possibly hold, then we have 50 percent relative humidity, one-quarter, 25 percent, and so on, at a given temperature. Humidity readings are always related to temperature.

However, remember that *WARM AIR HOLDS MORE MOISTURE THAN COLD AIR*, and it's a lot more moisture, NOT just a few drops.

To give 100 percent relative humidity at 70°F, a certain volume of air (7,000 cubic feet in this case) can hold 16 pints of water. At 31°F, this same volume of air only holds 4 pints of water.

Although apartment buildings usually lack humidity, condensation on windows is a problem that occupants encounter from time to time. Most cases of window condensation can be controlled by the tenant if he understands why the problem exists.

The suggested levels of relative humidity in a home are between 20 percent and 35 percent.

Remember, the outside temperature will determine the amount of humidity allowed inside.

DEW POINT

The temperature at which vapor in the air turns to a liquid (condensation) is called the "dew point." This usually occurs on the windows and causes the watering, frosting, and icing of windows.

When the outside temperature is −7°C (19.4°F), condensation will begin to form on double-glazed windows if the humidity is as high as 40 percent. At −18°C (0°F), the indoor humidity should be no higher than 30 percent.

With single-glazed windows the humidity level must be even lower—no more than 15 percent when the outside temperature is −18°C (0.4°F).

Watch the windows—when they begin to steam up, you have all the humidity you need. Turn off humidifiers.

CAUSES OF CONDENSATION PROBLEMS

Basically, the cause of excessive humidity is lack of ventilation. The following are eight possible sources of condensation:

1. Room humidifier giving off too much moisture.
2. Fish tank or similar water-filled objects in the apartment evaporate into the air.
3. Drying clothes in the apartment.
4. Using a vaporizer or kettle—steam evaporates into the air.
5. An over-active humidifier or leaking air conditioning unit attached to the furnace in townhouses.
6. Inadequate ventilation.
7. Excessive use of shower or baths.
8. Evaporation of heating system leaks.

Causes of Inadequate Ventilation

1. Bathroom and kitchen exhaust fans not operating; grill plugged or obstructed.
2. Entrances to apartments are weather-stripped.
3. Ducts in townhouses closed or plugged.

How To Cure Condensation Problems

Ventilation replaces humid household air with relatively dry outside air. In the average home, the air needs to be changed completely once every two hours to control humidity.

As soon as condensation forms on the inside of a window, steps should be taken to control moisture source and/or increase ventilation. Some helpful hints are

1. Open window and air out apartment.
2. Check that exhaust fans in kitchen and bathroom are operating—a piece of tissue will be held to the grill if the fans are working properly.
3. Remove weatherstripping from around entrance doors, and make sure that the rubber bumper stops are in place.
4. Turn down humidifier or vaporizer, if present.
5. Keep apartment at proper temperature.

AIR/VAPOR BARRIERS

It has become more apparent in recent years that not enough attention is given to the design of air/vapor barriers, their installation, and primary function.

A good case-in-point is the termination of the wall vapor barrier with a flat roof vapor barrier. This detail does not allow for the overlapping of these barriers at the roof joists, thus causing condensation problems. The detail instructs the construction site staff to provide a vapor barrier, but the detail fails to show how this is to be accomplished. The information contained in Figure 6-15 should help overcome this problem.

Another typical problem is poor detailing and a lack of understanding related to the transfer of cold to inside areas, particularly in townhouses built of masonry and concrete.

The barrier, usually a polyethylene film, should be *continuous* and envelop a structure. Any splits, even a nail hole, will allow air to sneak through.

In townhouses where the roof structure is an exposed concrete slab edge with inside ceilings plastered directly on the underside of the slab, mold and mildew can grow along the cold ceiling perimeter and around protruding uninsulated bay windows if a vapor barrier problem exists.

These problems are not confined to townhouses. Other problem areas could be plastered shear walls that extend to the exterior; air leaks around window perimeters due to inadequate packing prior to windows being installed; uninsulated closets on exterior walls; and no insulation around such things as electric receptacles. Problems can occur in any type of structure.

All these problems, and many more, relate to understanding good basic design. Proper attention to detail and a knowledgeable con-

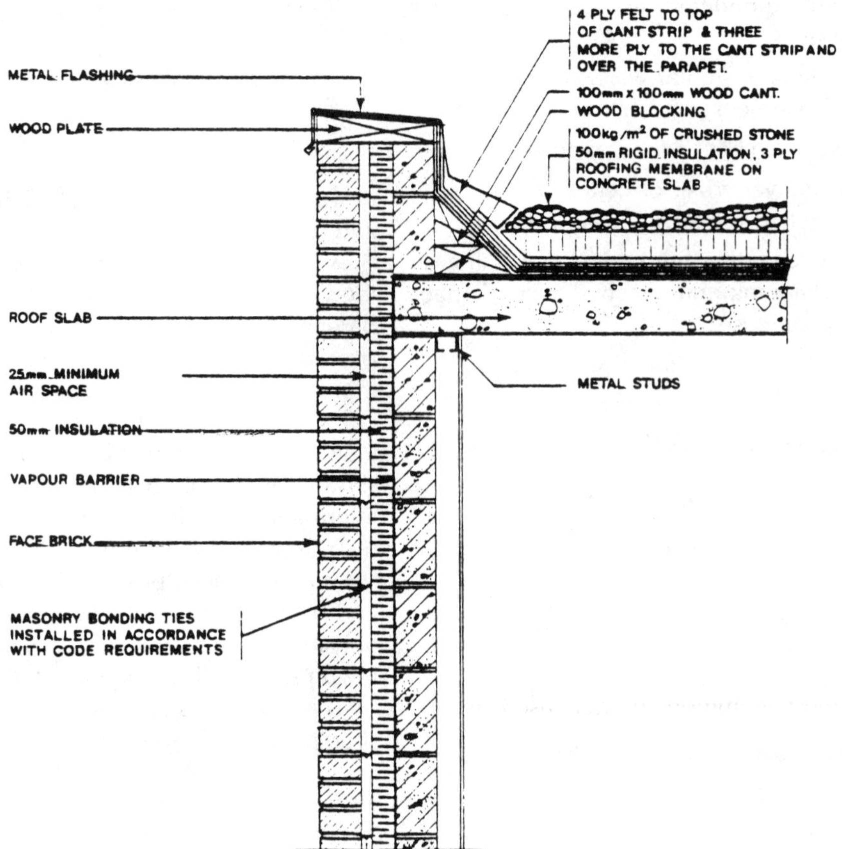

FIGURE 6-15 The air/vapor barrier. The purpose of the air/vapor barrier is to assure that whatever humidity there is in the structure does not make its way into the walls. (Courtesy of Cadillac Fairview Corporation, Limited.)

struction team will eliminate this problem at no extra cost. *Air/vapor barriers need to be drawn in, not just noted.*

The biggest single problem encountered in townhouses is inadequate vapor barriers and insulation. The problem is not one of a general design error or simple omissions from the drawing or job. The problem is a lack of understanding on the part of all parties involved about how to "tie in" all the various elements to make it work. Perhaps a full understanding of "dew point" would assist, or even overcome, to a large degree, the problems encountered.

The problem is, quite simply, the forming of condensation in cold areas such as above windows having steel lintels; the junction of walls to roofs, both flat and sloped; the roofs and floors of bay windows; the junction between walls and floors; and in the joist space between the inside ceiling and the roof above. As you can see, the problem encompasses both townhouses and high-rise buildings.

AVOIDING MOISTURE PROBLEMS

In order to avoid moisture problems, we must control humidity. This can be accomplished with proper use of an air/vapor barrier and proper ventilation.

An air/vapor barrier is installed to ensure that whatever humidity is in a structure does not make its way into the walls. This barrier is ideally a layer of some material that is impervious to the passage of water vapor and air. It should envelop the structure, keeping the moisture inside. Any split in the barrier will allow air to sneak through. *The purpose is to eliminate all air leaks, if possible.*

The most common barrier used is a 6-millimeter thick polyethylene film.

ATTIC VENTILATION

In the attic of a house there should be 1 square foot of unobstructed free ventilation openings for each 300 square feet of ceiling area. The openings should be located so as to allow good cross ventilation from end-to-end and top-to-bottom.

Because of very limited air space, ventilation becomes more difficult in houses with flat or gently-sloped roofs. Unless air leakage into the attic space is minimal, the area for ventilation openings in these types of structures must be doubled to 1 square foot for every 150 square feet of ceiling—when the building is insulated inside. If the structure is insulated outside the building shell, the space between the ceiling and roof should not be ventilated since it is now part of the heated interior.

6-9 Asphalt Paving Maintenance

Pavement maintenance is a major activity of every highway, street department, and building owner. Usually the maintenance man is called to "make every dollar do the work of two." This is not easy, but having someone that is knowledgeable inspect, decide on the repairs required, and supervise the completion of repairs to the damaged area will virtually assure that "every dollar will do the work of two."

Large differences in soil types, climate, traffic, and other factors make for a great variance in problems, even in small areas.

Yet, despite these differences, there are maintenance methods that can be used equally well to overcome the problems.

WHAT IS PAVEMENT MAINTENANCE?

"Pavement Maintenance" is not easy to define. Some call pavement improvement "Maintenance." Others include the work which keeps the pavement in its as-constructed condition.

The definition which seems to fit best is: Pavement maintenance is the routine work performed to keep a pavement, under normal conditions of traffic and normal forces of nature, as near as possible to its as-constructed condition.

WHY THE NEED FOR PAVEMENT MAINTENANCE?

All pavement requires maintenance because the stresses that produce minor defects are constantly working. The stresses include

1. Changes in temperature and moisture content
2. Traffic
3. Small movements in the underlying or adjacent earth

They are simply the end results of the process of wear, which begins when construction ends.

PREVENTIVE MAINTENANCE

The early detection and repair of minor defects is, without doubt, the most important work done by the person responsible for pavement maintenance. Cracks and other surface breaks, which in their first stages are almost unnoticeable, may develop into serious defects if not soon repaired. This may occur quickly in an underdesigned pavement under heavy traffic.

For this reason, regular inspections should be made by a qualified person, if you wish to ensure the best use of your pavement maintenance dollars.

An inspection made from a moving vehicle, even one which creeps, is usually not close enough to detect areas where distress may begin.

What To Look For

1. Small surface defects
3. Small signs of mud or water on the pavement

DRAINAGE MAINTENANCE

A good form of preventive maintenance is the seasonal inspection and cleaning of drainage systems. If drains are working properly, some of the major causes of pavement damage will be eliminated.

REPAIRS

Repairs should be made as quickly as possible after the defect is discovered. Often, weather conditions make temporary repairs necessary to prevent further damage until permanent repairs can be made.

Making repairs at the proper time involves the careful balancing of several factors and requires both experience and judgment. In all cases of pavement distress, it is best to determine the cause or causes of the problem before repairs are made.

By doing this, the repairs can be made that will not only correct the damage, but will also prevent or retard its happening again. Time and money spent for such repairs are well spent because *repairs done properly will not have to be made over and over.*

Successful pavement maintenance requires a knowledge of all paving materials and how to use them. The inspector and the people carrying out the repair must have this knowledge.

TIMING

Patching or resurfacing work should be done during warm (50°F - 10°C or more) and dry weather. When hot or warm mixtures are placed on cold surfaces, they may cool so fast that adequate compaction is difficult.

This does not mean that repairs cannot be made during cold or damp weather, but they require much greater care during such periods. A delay may result in allowing small surface breaks to progress into major failures.

PATCHING MIXTURES

High quality, hot mixed patching mixtures, although more costly than other patching materials, result in longer lasting patches. The major cost in patching lies in placing the patch, *not in the cost of the material.*

When proper equipment and procedures are used, the surface of the patch should be at the same grade as the surrounding pavement.

If hand tamping is used, however, the surface of the compacted patch should be slightly higher than the pavement. Traffic will compress the patch further (Figure 6-16).

CRACKING

Cracking takes many forms. Simple crack filling may be the right treatment in some cases. In others, complete removal of the affected area and the installation of drainage may be necessary.

To make proper repairs, the *first step is to determine the cause of cracking.*

The repair techniques for the correction of various forms of cracking discussed in this chapter are not necessarily the only correct ways to do the job. But they are proven techniques that should result in neat, long-lasting repairs.

Alligator Cracks

These are interconnected cracks forming a series of small blocks resembling alligator's skin or chicken wire.

Cause In most cases, alligator cracking is caused by excessive deflection of the surface over unstable subgrade or lower courses of the pavement. The unstable support usually is the result of saturated granular bases or subgrade. The affected areas, in most cases, are not large. Sometimes, however, they will cover entire sections of a pavement. When this happens, it is probably due to repeated loads that exceed the load-carrying capacity of the pavement.

Repair Since alligator cracking usually is the result of saturated bases or subgrades, correction should include removing the wet material and installing needed drainage. Asphalt plant-mixed material can then be used for the full depth for a strong patch. (This may be the least expensive repair because of the single operation with one material.) If the asphalt plant-mixed material is not available, new granular base material in layers not exceeding 6 inches each, are compacted in. The granular base should then be primed and patched.

6-10 Painting

INTRODUCTION

Painting is not often considered a particularly important aspect of project management. It has, however, been one of the major expenses and because of this, deserves more serious consideration.

It should be kept in mind that labor costs for applying paint account for 80 percent of this expense. Obviously, it is important that

FIGURE 6-16 Patching the asphalt. (Courtesy of the Asphalt Institute.)

the paints chosen are suited to the application. This is the purpose of the following specifications.

Proper coordination of colors, hiding power, and protection from deterioration are all important. Colors should not be disturbing or distracting. Equipment rooms, garages, and color coding are all painted for other than aesthetic purposes. Dirty equipment and equipment rooms allow the motors to suck in dust and grit and lead to costly repairs and down time for equipment.

The importance of keeping the equipment rooms bright and clean cannot be stressed too often. The best way to accomplish this is to paint and illuminate all equipment rooms and underground garages.

Using fluorescent lighting in these areas is a further advantage because the reflected light from the ceilings and walls and the low wattage will quickly pay for the cost of painting.

Color coding identifies all the equipment, especially shut-off valves, and makes for easy identification during emergencies.

The choice of paints should be determined by the following factors: color, washability, toughness, adhesion, aging, stability, resistance to abrasion, scrubbability, weathering, and corrosion resistance.

The following painting specifications provide a standard for both the contractor and the people having the work done.

Anything less, or different than written, is either substandard or beyond the bounds of these specifications and should not be acceptable.

PREPAINTING CONSIDERATIONS

Since nothing can be inflexible, a list of "Prepainting Considerations" is provided to stimulate questions and alleviate problems prior to having the work carried out. This should also eliminate any misunderstanding and the need for "extras" in the contract price.

Alternatives are given in some instances. The choice is to be made by the manager or those in charge, not by the contractor. Remember, the cost of the material is only 20 percent of the total painting cost. It follows that the quality of the material will not increase or lower the total cost. Using materials as specified will give you a job that will do what you want it to do. *A poor job will deteriorate quickly and the property will lose its appeal.*

INTERIOR PAINTING

- Does the apartment need painting?
- Does the apartment need partial painting?
- Is any plaster or other such repair required?

- Are window perimeters to be painted with semi-gloss alkyd to alleviate deterioration of plaster?
- Are common areas to be semi-gloss alkyd or flat?
- Are all walls to be painted with a washable flat alkyd or nonwashable flat latex?
- Are wall plates painted? (They shouldn't be.)
- Is floor trim natural finish or painted?
- If the floor trim is natural, does it need to be sanded and resealed?
- Are windows and frames wood, steel, aluminum, vinyl, or combination? (Painted window areas are always semi-gloss alkyd.)
- Are doors paint grade, slab, louvered, wood frame, steel frame, or aluminum? (Wood and steel areas are always semi-gloss alkyd.)
- Are radiator covers to be painted? (Always use semi-gloss alkyd.)
- Are closet doors, walls, or shelves to be painted? (Wood and steel areas in semi-gloss alkyd.)
- Are ceilings suspended acoustic, plaster, smooth, or stippled?
- Are kitcken cupboards paint grade or natural finish?
- Are cupboard interiors to be painted? (Everything in both kitchens and bathrooms should be semi-gloss alkyd.)
- Is there any wallpaper to be removed?
- Do any areas require more than one coat?

EXTERIOR PAINTING

- Are any repairs required?
- Is all exposed concrete to be painted? If concrete areas are flaking off, wire brushing will be necessary. (Consider canopies, roof areas, garage entrance and exits, balcony ceilings.)
- Are steel railings, handrails, pickets, dividers, or panels to be painted? (If rusting, wire brushing or grinding and spot priming may be necessary.)
- Are ground level light standards, steel grates, fences, stairwells, or playground and pool areas to be painted?
- Are exterior windows and doors paint grade? (Caulking should be checked on all paint grade exterior windows and doors prior to painting.)
- Are windows stormed? If so, storms will have to be removed to paint between.
- Consider townhouse entrance doors, frames, mail boxes, garbage rooms.
- Are there any galvanized metal roof flashings, eavestroughing, or downpipes to be painted? (If paint is peeling or flaking, all paint should be stripped off.)
- Are there any garages, garage door, and frames to be painted?
- Does roof fan housing require painting?

MISCELLANEOUS

- Do any motors or equipment require painting? (Painting of equipment and motors requires proper cleaning of grease and oil.)
- Do any equipment room floors or walls require painting? (Proper cleaning and

preparation of these areas is also important.)

6–11 Windows

It has been said that there are no permanent building materials. Because window and door frames are made of metal, we sometimes overlook the fact that they also need maintenance. This includes.

- re-sealing of all glazing
- new Schlagle (weatherstripping), new top and/or bottom glides or rollers on operating windows and doors
- cleaning or replacing bottom track

The objective is a watertight, draft-free window and door. As we attempt to conserve energy, this program becomes more and more important. It should be noted that the maintenance program could differ for some windows and doors.

PREVENTIVE MAINTENANCE

1. Check out all fixed and sliding window glazing for seal. This causes air infiltration, heat loss, and water entry. Remove and provide glazing tape if not previously done. Do not use a caulking sealant.

   If the glazing is already set in a glazing tape, check to make sure the bond is complete. This can only be done by removing the inside perimeter vinyl or aluminum stops (moldings).
2. Check, and if required, replace all deteriorated Schlagle (weatherstripping) on windows and doors. This includes inside and outside perimeters and the interlocks. *Taped-on Schlagle is not to be used as this type will pull off.* Poor weatherstripping will create loose fitting windows and doors.
3. Check fixed side of operating window and balcony door for defective Schlagle and/or seal. These two areas are usually a source of high air and water infiltration. Oversized Schlagle or caulking is usually required.
4. Check, and if required, replace rubber duster sweep at the top and base of sliding door and window interlock. This is a small sponge rubber block that plugs the gap on the bottom sill track and inhibits water and air entry.
5. Check out the weep holes on the outside of the aluminum frame for plugged drains. Some windows have two sets, one above the other, to drain the inside track and the outside track. Needless to say, this will disallow water to drain out, causing leaks inside.
6. Check and replace, if necessary, any defective removable window tracks. Some tracks are plastic and some are aluminum. The removable track is always under the inside sliding window. If found defective, it will cause the window to drop and it may leak or not slide easily.
7. The main reason tracks wear out is because the neoprene or nylon glides that are located on the bottom of the operating window are worn out, causing aluminum to wear against aluminum or plastic. New glides should be installed. Also check for nylon guides located at the top of some operating windows. These keep the window tight in the top track, eliminating rattling. Tracks should be cleaned and sprayed with a lubricating silicone.
8. Check rollers on balcony sliding doors and screens and on certain types of operating windows. Repair or replace as required.

WINDOW WASHING SPECIFICATIONS

A good building manager is constantly overseeing tradesmen working in his/her building. Many roof problems are caused by careless window washers. To help overcome these problems, we have developed specifications for window washers:

The outside cleaning only of those windows that are not accessible by reach; that is, all windows that are not encompassed by balconies are to be included.

All ground floor windows not encompassed by balconies and all lobby windows are to be included.

4″ × 4″ × 4′0″ long wooden pads, supplied by the property, to be used under the outrigger to protect the metal counterflashings at roof perimeters.

2′ square ½″ plywood supplied by the property, to be used under the opposite or weighted end to protect the roofing membrane.

Safety line tiebacks are to be made only to anchored eyebolts provided. If eyebolts (as in older buildings) are not provided, a safety line should be tied around the stairway or mechanical penthouse structure (Figure 6-31).

All outriggers, weights, pullies, ropes, and other equipment are to be used in a safe, professional manner as set out by the Construction Safety Association.

In buildings where holes are provided in the roof overhang for swing stage or bosun chair ropes, it is the responsibility of the contractor to remove the plugs and carefully replace them on completion of the work.

WINDOW LOCKS

The device illustrated will fit most side slide aluminum windows. These devices are to be fitted when requested by a tenant.

For those windows it will not fit, a simple-taping screw set into the vertical let of the aluminum window track will suffice. Please be sure to *NEVER* drill into the sill of any window as this will allow water to drain behind the wall onto the floor below.

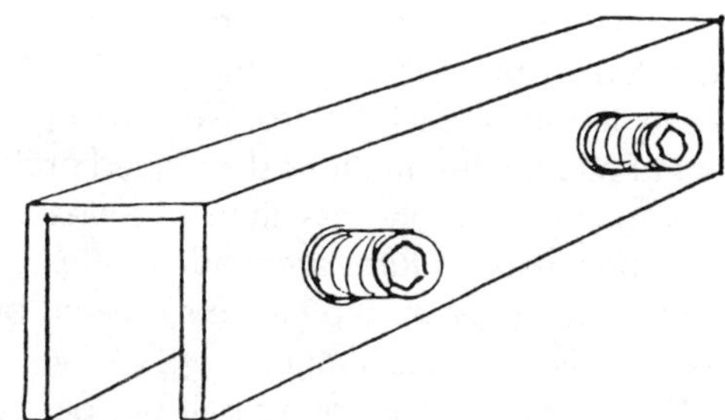

FIGURE 6-17 Window locks. (Courtesy of Cadillac Fairview Corporation, Limited.)

To all steel sash casement windows (winding), a screw can be placed in the base of the horizontal mullion (frame) where the winder arm operates, to restrict the opening to 4 inches.

6-12 Roofing*

AN OVERVIEW

Property owners in the United States have an almost totally avoidable $1.5 billion annual roofing expense. That is a realistic estimate of the cost of corrections and replacement installations necessitated by premature roofing failures on non-residental structures. This was reported in a roofing bulletin published by the Journal of Property Management, and was researched by Charles Cartee.

Cartee reported that "properly designed roofs installed in accordance with the tenets

*Portions reprinted with permission from "How to Care for A Built Up Roof" by G. E. Hann, Morgan-Grampion Publishing Company.

of good roofing practice can reasonably be expected to provide satisfactory service for twenty to thirty years. Yet from 10 to 15 percent of all new installations developed problems in considerably less than five years." Additional expenditures are made fruitless in an effort to cover up the cancers created by faulty design and installation.

The "built-up" roof of asphalt or coal tar pitch is one of the few major building components that is "manufactured" outside on the job site. A roof's life expectancy depends on the use of quality materials, assembled in the proper sequence, with good application techniques under proper climatic conditions. The life of a roof also depends on the prevention or early repair of damage caused by water penetration at edges, flashings, or around vents and piping. Regular inspections by building staff or structural resource specialists will result in early detection of problems. *Records should be kept of all inspections.*

The structural resource specialist should arrange for and supervise all roofing maintenance. Records of all work should be marked on a plan of the roof showing areas worked on, dates, type of work, and cost (see Figure 6-34). These records would be kept with your building profile information. Roofs are expensive today. Costs have escalated every year since 1960 and especially since 1973 when the price of oil escalated. It appears that this inflation factor will continue during the foreseeable future. As with all building components, quality in materials and workmanship are essential if we expect to overcome the high roofing costs. Inspections and preventive maintenance repairs will pay big dividends in the life cycle roof costs. Low-rise buildings, shopping centers, and industrial buildings that have a very large percentage of roof relative to the structure should be watched closely for any signs of deterioration.

This section will deal specifically with roofing, the theory of roofing, its make-up, and its various functions. We will also explain various problems, their causes and cures, to give you an awareness of roofing problems. It is not our intention to make you a roofing expert or to expect you to supervise work being done at your building. This is best left to the experts.

We do expect you to be aware of the potential problems so that you can recognize them and report a problem before it becomes serious. We also hope to explain the roofing preventive maintenance programs required.

Roofs need regular upkeep and care just like any other part of the building. But in many buildings, they get little, if any, attention—until they leak.

If you want to keep building maintenance costs down, do not wait for the roof to leak and cause water damage. That means you are too late—and you are in for some expensive remedies. Routine upkeep of a roof is always cheaper than more extensive emergency repair.

ROOF FUNCTION

Roof covering is probably the most important element in a building. It must protect the structure itself and provide for the comfort of the occupants while exposed to a wide variety of climatic conditions. Therefore, the function of a roof is to

- weatherproof
- waterproof
- insulate
- provide a walking surface for future service

A roof is exposed to many weather conditions from sub-zero temperature to extreme heating conditions. A roof surface can reach temperatures up to 190°F. Reflected radiation from adjacent surfaces, such as a glazed brick wall, can raise this temperature as high as 230°F. So the flexibility of the roofing components is one of the biggest considerations in a good roof. Thermal shock from 230°F to 60°/70°F less in one hour in a sudden summer storm can cause the mat to split.

The waterproofing of a roof system is entirely dependent on the type of bitumens used, their flexibility, durability, and in general, their ability to withstand adverse weather conditions, ultraviolet rays of the sun that oxidize the oils out of the bitumen, and the movement of water, ice, and snow.

Although roofing insulation is not directly exposed to weather conditions, it is exposed to the same thermal conditions. Insulation has to have the ability not to expand or contract; it has to have a high thermal value; it has to stand up to temperatures of hot bitumens applied during construction, which normally run around 190°F; and it needs to have a good compressive strength in order to handle traffic. One of the most important traits is that it cannot absorb moisture, whether it be in the form of water or condensation, or humidity.

Last, but not least, is the ability for the system to withstand traffic. This area is furthest from the minds of the designers, because a roof's function has always been only as a waterproofing. If a designer only realized the amount of work done off a roof, not only during construction, but afterwards, he would understand that a more durable roofing system should be developed. Such systems are available, but are presently about five times the cost of a conventional roof. The traffic problem during construction could be minimized if the roof was put on only after the various trades were finished, or if the concrete slab was waterproofed and the remainder finished only after all the trades had left the roof areas.

Unfortunately, the only true test of a roof is the test of time, and this can be very costly.

FLASHING AND COUNTER FLASHING DETAIL

Many buildings have outer walls or parapets that extend above the roof deck. If not properly constructed and joined to the roofing mat, they can be a prolific source of leaks.

The outer face of the parapet is usually an extension of the face masonry of the building. The inside face or back-up, however, may be made of common brick, building tile, concrete block, or even poured concrete. In between faces, if they do not meet, you may find loosely filled mortar and rubble, or hollow tile.

The most important part of a parapet in preventing water leaking is the coping, or counter flashing (Figure 6-18).

TYPES OF ROOFS

For simplicity, it may be stated that there are basically two types of roofs:

1. A flat built-up roof.
2. A sloped or shingled roof.

There are variations to these systems and the products used on each type of roof, but the roof types are still basically as stated.

1. A flat built-up roof which is the old conventional system (Figure 6-21).
2. A traffic deck or roof such as used for swimming pool decks, rooftop gardens, and sundecks.

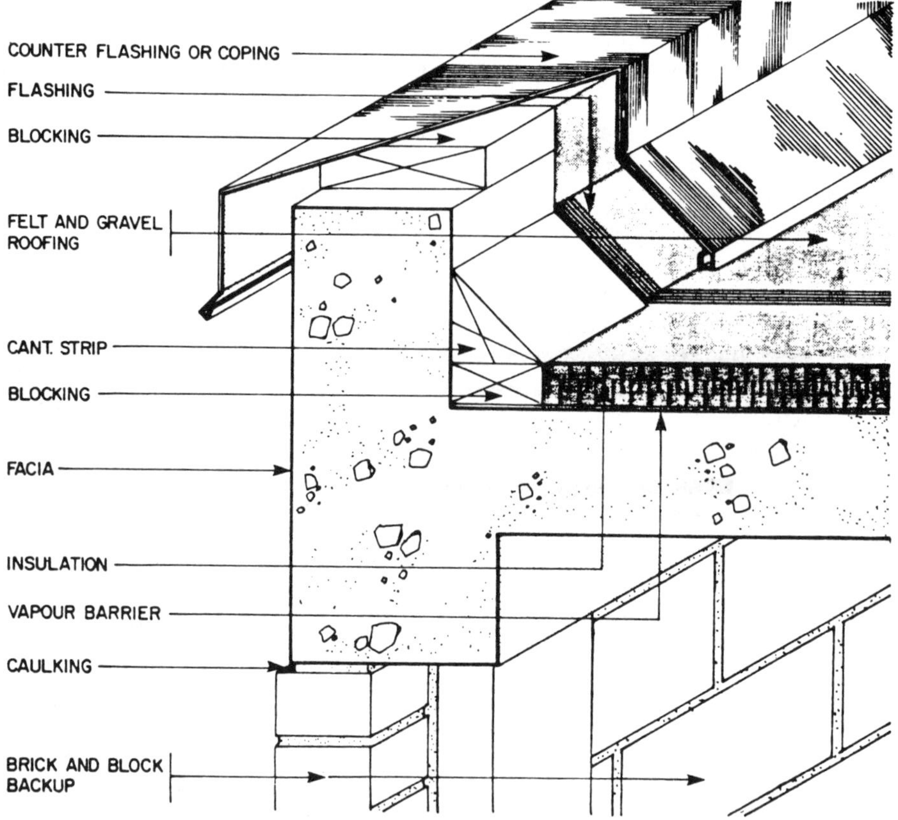

FIGURE 6-18 Flashing and counter flashing detail. (Courtesy of Cadillac Fairview Corporation, Limited.)

3. A similar (and fairly new) system called an upside down roof deck or an inverted roof membrane assembly (IRMA) developed by the Dow Chemical Company.

Flat Built-up Roof

The type of roof that is used on most of our buildings is the conventional flat built-up roof system, which consists mainly of

1. Vapor barrier
2. Insulation
3. Roofing felts
4. A flood coat of bitumen which is the waterproofing
5. The topping of gravel

The vapor barrier is one or two layers of 15 pound felts, hot mopped onto the concrete, then mopped again. The purpose of a vapor barrier is to prevent internal vapor from entering into the roof insulation. If the roof insulation becomes saturated externally, the vapor barrier will also help retard the water from entering through the roof deck.

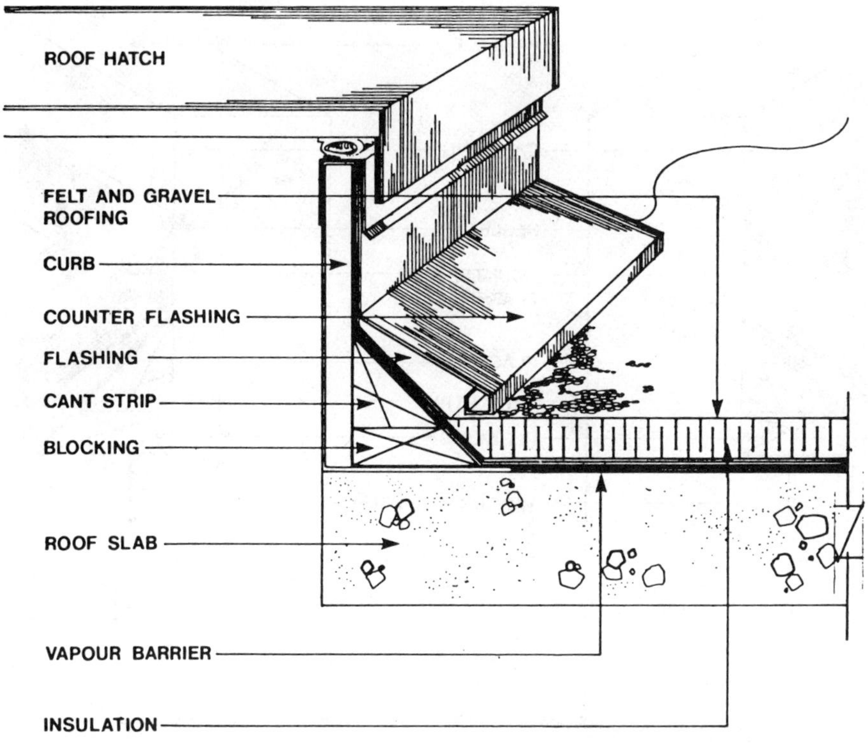

FIGURE 6-19 Roof hatch or skylight detail. (Courtesy of Cadillac Fairview Corporation, Limited.)

The purpose of insulation, of which there are many types of polystyrenes, polyurethanes, fiberglass, fiberboards, and mineral boards, is to retain the heat in the winter and to keep cool in the summer. If the insulation becomes saturated, as will fiberglass, fiberboard, and to a small extent, mineral board, it will lose its insulating value.

ROOFING FELTS

The roofing felts are a make-up of pulverized paper, made into a rolled sheet similar to tar paper. Years ago, these felts were made of partial rag content and had good strength and flexibility, but they now are very poor in quality. The weight value of the sheet is based on a one square foot area. The sheets are not waterproof, in fact they will absorb up to 85 percent of their weight in moisture. They are rolled into hot bitumen to give strength to the bitumen, which is the waterproofing. Normally there are four layers of 15-pound felts and a flood coat of bitumen over top.

There are two types of bitumens:

1. Tar or pitch
2. Asphalt

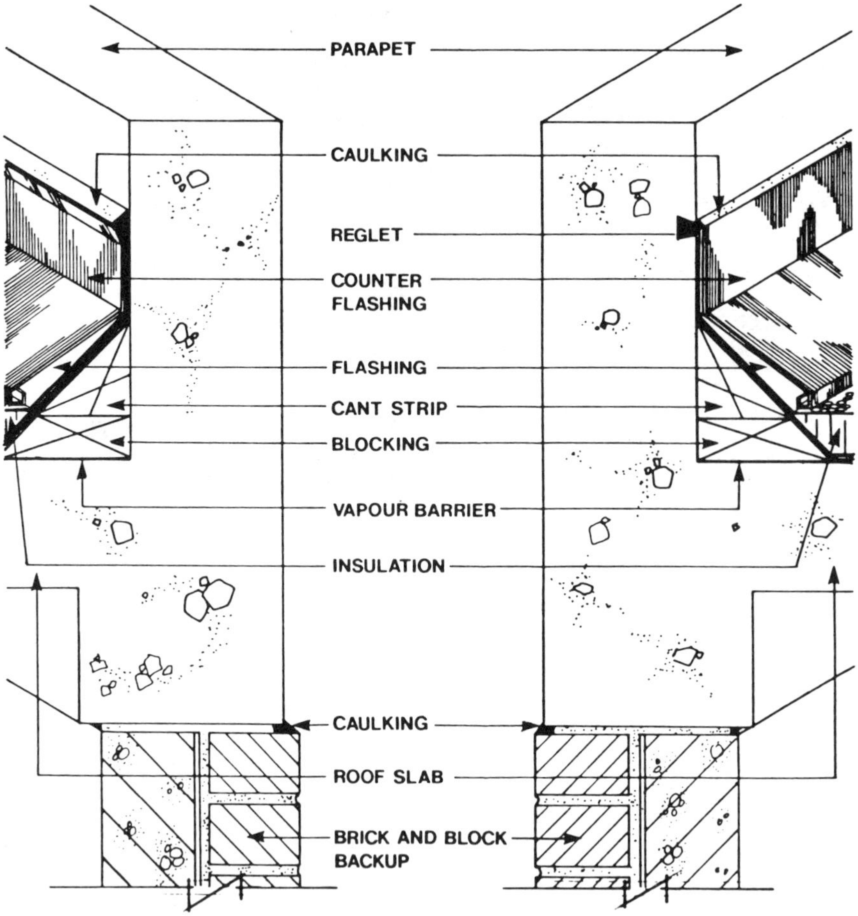

PARAPET
CAULKING
REGLET
COUNTER FLASHING
FLASHING
CANT STRIP
BLOCKING
VAPOUR BARRIER
INSULATION
CAULKING
ROOF SLAB
BRICK AND BLOCK BACKUP

FIGURE 6-20 Wall flashing detail. (Courtesy of Cadillac Fairview Corporation, Limited.)

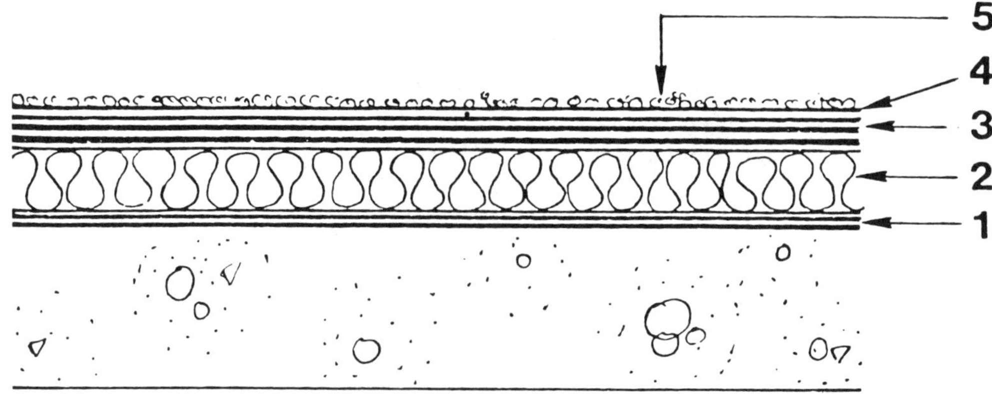

FIGURE 6-21 The flat built-up roof. (Courtesy of Cadillac Fairview Corporation, Limited.)

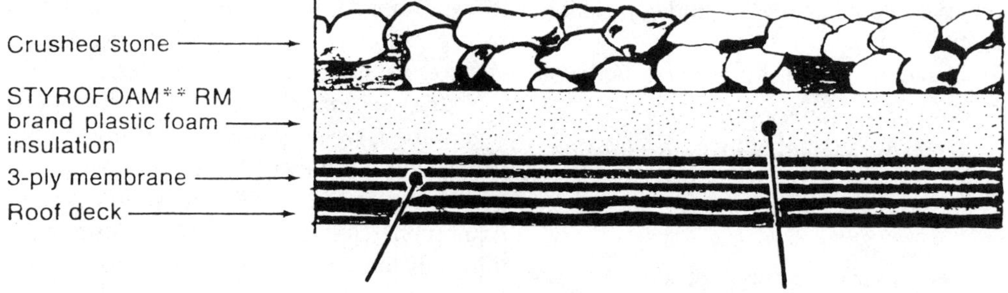

(a)

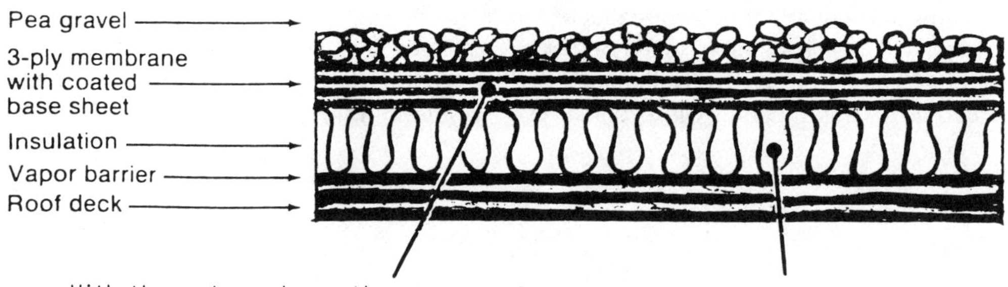

(b)

FIGURE 6-22 The advantages of an inverted roof. (a) Irma system; (b) Conventional built-up roof. (Courtesy of Dow Chemical Company.)

Most older buildings used the tar type, but because it is more available, asphalt is now being used. Tar is not as flexible as asphalt, but tar will stand up better under ponding water conditions.

The gravel on a roof serves two functions:

1. To hold down the roofing system.
2. To reflect the sunlight and protect the bitumen.

ROOF PROBLEMS

Wind blowing across a rooftop and up the side of a building creates a negative pressure and tends to lift. By using the gravel to reflect the sun, you create a cooler roof, but the drawback is if the roof mat is punctured, the gravel will cover the hole. Some roof systems now eliminate the gravel and aluminize the entire roof for greater reflectivity. It is easier to detect any holes or problems in the roof mat with this type of roof, but it can also be punctured easier. Bonding of this system is essential because wind lift becomes a factor.

You can tell if the insulation is saturated by the spongy effect you get by walking on a saturated area. This situation will eventually cause vapor pockets and ridging of the felts. Fiberglass has less compressive strength than other insulation and feels soft normally, so it is important to know the type of insulation before coming to any conclusions. *Report any spongy conditions immediately.*

Once the basic roof system has been determined, we must then decide how to finish off the perimeter of the building, at the penthouse walls, at soil stacks, and around equipment sitting on the roof. Also, such things as television aerials, pitch pockets for handrailings and swing stage eyelets, and numerous other objects must be considered.

These areas, unfortunately, are never given enough consideration in the initial design stage and are the biggest cause of failure to roofs. See Figures 6-18, 6-19, and 6-20 for details.

HOW MOISTURE ATTACKS ROOFS

1. Moisture infiltrates from above through
   - —open joints (copings, reglets, expansion joints)
   - —defective flashings (ruptures in membrane flashings, open seams in metal flashings)

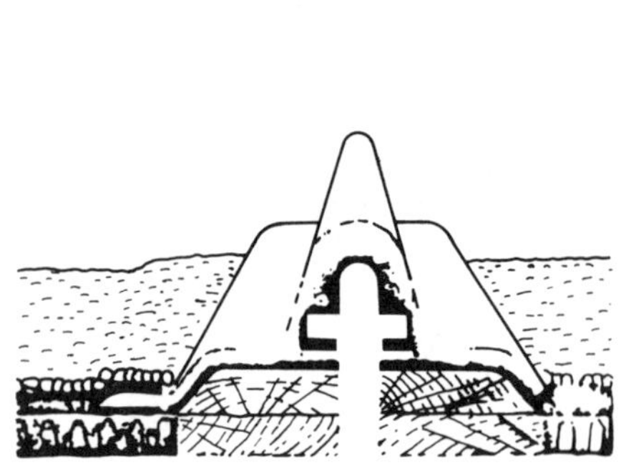

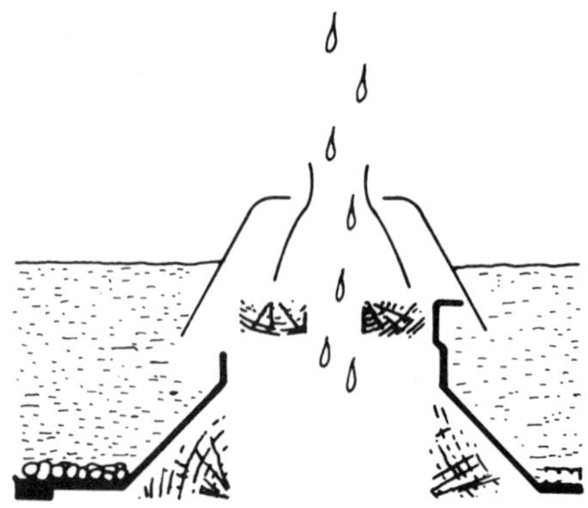

FIGURE 6-23 Leaking expansion joints.

—porous parapets
—faulty gravel stops and edgings
—porous copings
—breaks and blisters in roof mat

2. Vapor migration from below
—from manufacturing operations
—from high humidity conditions
—from occupants (vaporizing moisture estimated at 1/4 pound per hour per person)

LEAKING EXPANSION JOINTS

Expansion joints are required on large single-story buildings having vast roofs. Without them nature forms its own expansion joints by causing the roof mat to split. Eventually the roof will leak (Figure 6-23).

EXPOSED FELT EDGES

Quite often the wind and weather will play a big role in disturbing a roof. Bare, exposed felts, when attacked by the sun's rays, become dry and delaminated and act as a wick for water (Figure 6-24).

PRESSURE RIDGE SPLIT

A pressure ridge is a ridge or blister caused by vapor pressure from under the roofing felts and usually runs in a straight line pattern because the vapor will find the nearest means of escape, which is around the individual slabs. The ridge will eventually split, letting out the trapped vapor and letting in water. Insulation vents are sometimes installed to alleviate this pressure (Figure 6-25).

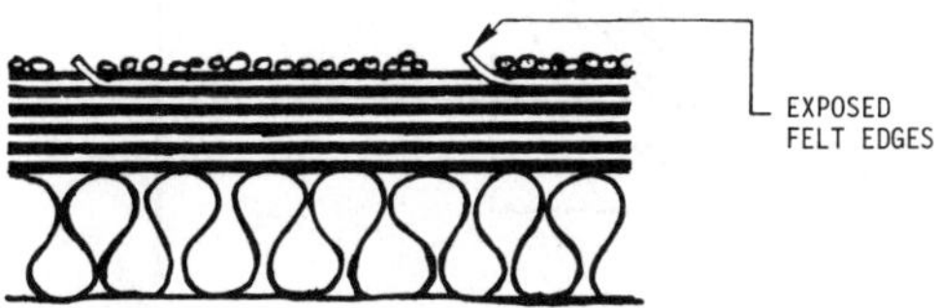

FIGURE 6-24 Exposed felt edges. (Courtesy of Cadillac Fairview Corporation, Limited.)

ROOF VENTILATORS

Roof ventilators are installed to help release this vapor pressure and dry out the insulation before the insulation loses its insulating value (Figure 6-26).

COUNTER FLASHINGS

Where metal counter flashings go up a wall and terminate, it is called either a reglet or an integral caulking flange. Both are sealed joints and if a split or separation occurs, water will enter the roof system.

Counter flashings around fan housing units are a source of possible trouble because of the suction created. All jointing should be caulked and watertight; tops should be convex to shed water; inspection doors should have a drip ledge cover; and any cable leading to or from the building should have a drip loop and a proper seal at point of entry (Figure 6-27).

ROOF HOPPERS

Roof hoppers or drains tend to be in a high spot, unfortunately, for the drain to run down a column or bearing wall without too much ceiling space; when the unsupported slab deflects, that area of the roof becomes low.

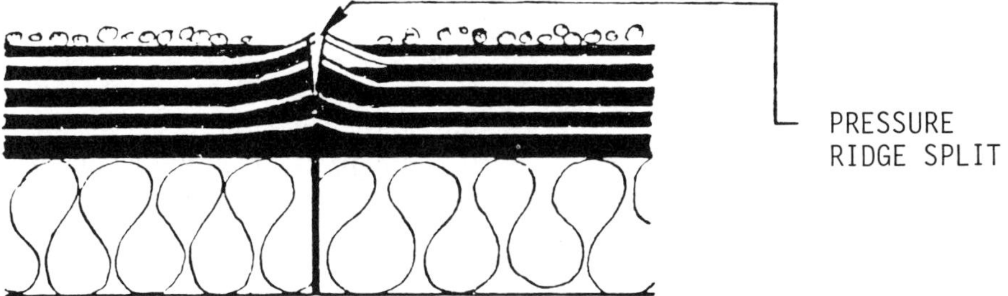

FIGURE 6-25 Pressure ridge split. Pressure in a blister caused by vapor can amount to 600 lbs. per square foot. (Courtesy of Cadillac Fairview Corporation, Limited.)

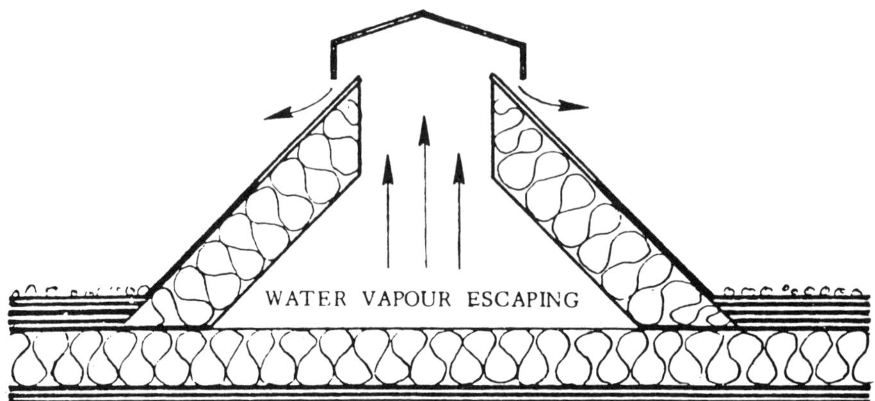

FIGURE 6-26 Roof ventilators. If a roof feels soft and spongy in areas, the condition should be investigated and corrected as soon as possible. (Courtesy of Cadillac Fairview Corporation, Limited.)

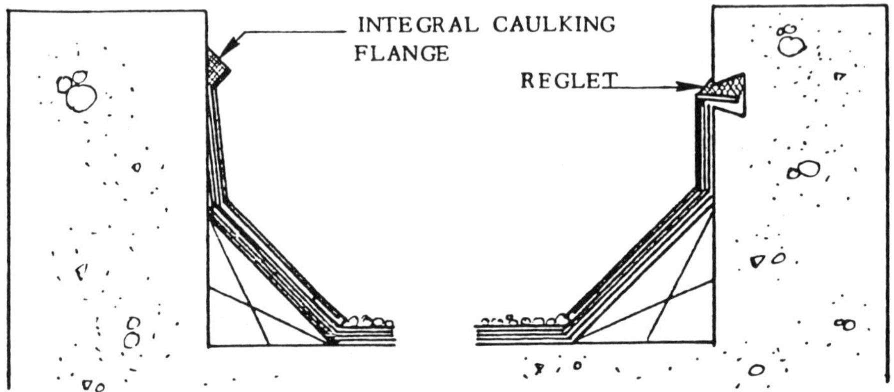

FIGURE 6-27 Counter flashings. Counter flashings are areas of possible trouble. (Courtesy of Cadillac Fairview Corporation, Limited.)

EXPOSED METAL VENT PIPES

Soil Stack Vent

Some buildings have lead flashings around soil stack vents through the roof that rupture and split very easily. If this is noticed, it should be reported so a stack jack (cover) can be placed over the joint (Figure 6-28).

Exhaust Vents

Bathroom and kitchen exhaust roof fans of the smaller variety, such as in townhouses and garden apartments, tend to sweat when the warm humid air being exhausted hits the dry cold outside air (winter). This causes vapor to form on the vent, which sometimes finds it way back into the room below (Figure 6-29).

CARELESS TRADESMEN

Any hard object, such as a concrete block or brick, broken glass, or even screws that are left on a roof during the very hot months, can easily puncture the roof felts. Therefore, if work is done on a roof or off the roof, equipment and rigging should be checked to make sure that a pad is provided that is sufficient to carry and distribute the load. The roof is not a traffic deck (Figure 6-30).

ELEMENTS THAT CAN RUIN A ROOF

Outside Interference

Roof mats are not designed for extra accessories such as signs and electric wires. Nor are they intended for regular foot traffic. Many agencies are not careful, when installing such services, to provide the extra precautions of flashing and mastic waterproofing. Sign supports or braces are spiked or bolted to any convenient spot on the roof, regardless of its structural relationship. Anchorage planks are spiked or lagged to the

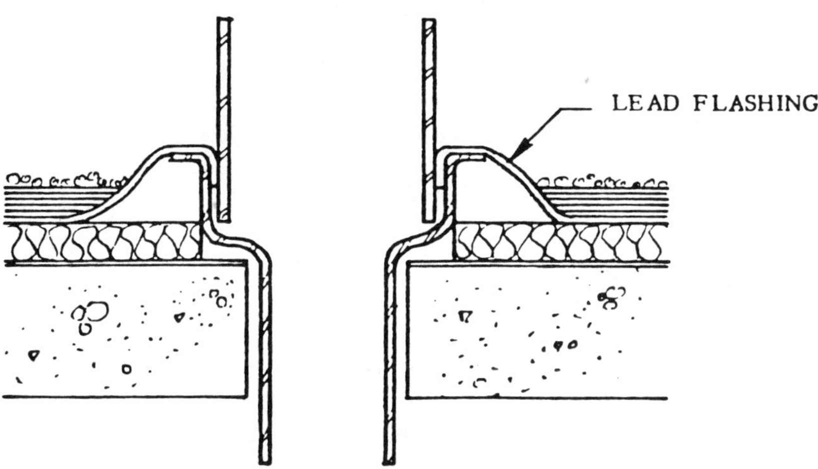

FIGURE 6-28 Soil stack vent. Lead flashings around soil stack vents split very easily. (Courtesy of Cadillac Fairview Corporation, Limited.)

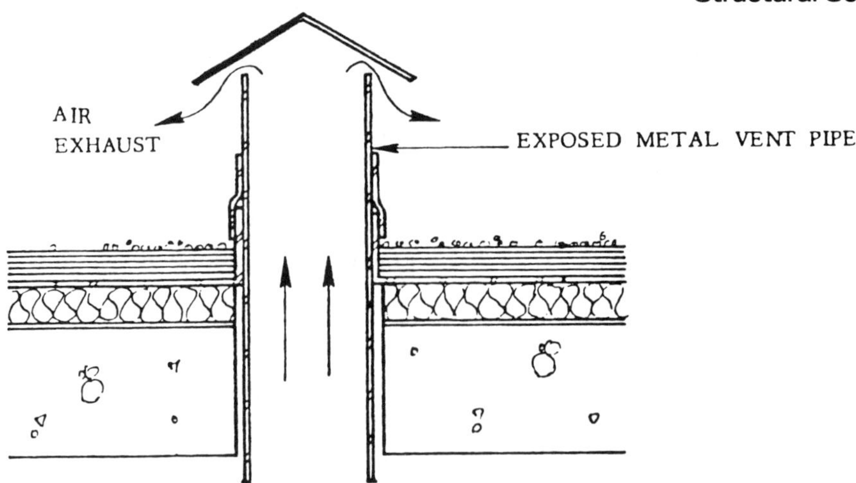

FIGURE 6-29 Exhaust metal vent pipe. Because of the unequal expansion of roof mat and metal, flashing splits and ruptures can occur along these areas. (Courtesy of Cadillac Fairview Corporation, Limited.)

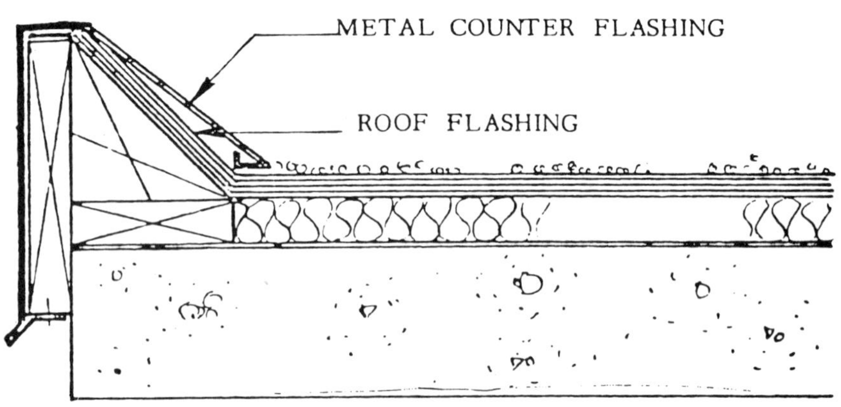

FIGURE 6-30 Careless Tradesmen. Careless window washers or tradesmen stepping on counter flashings can cause the metal to puncture or split the roof membrane. (Courtesy of Cadillac Fairview Corporation, Limited.)

deck, piercing both the mat and deck, and causing serious leakage.

Sun

Most roofs do not wear out—they dry out. Hot sunshine on a roof causes the volatile ingredients of tar or asphalt to evaporate. The asphalt oxidizes and becomes brittle. Slowly, the roof mat loses its elasticity—the surface coating becomes checked and flakes off, exposing the felt. What you have left is a dried-up roof felt that acts like dry paper—brittle,

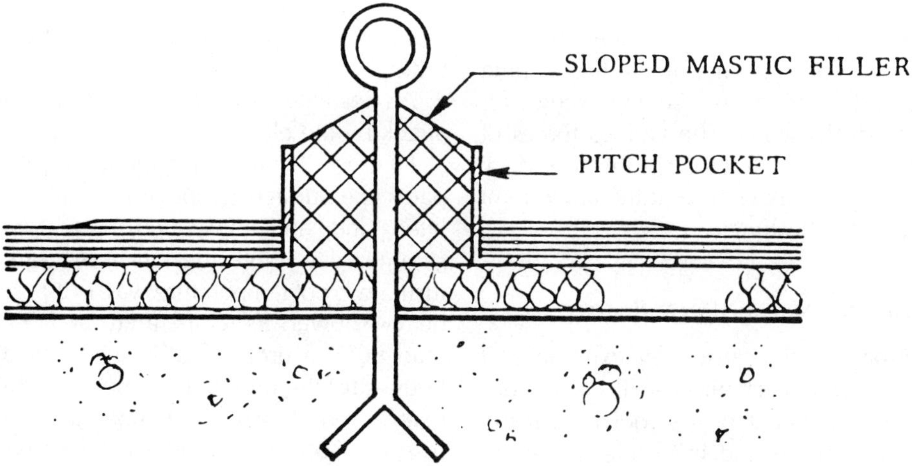

FIGURE 6-31 Pitch pockets. Pitch pockets are provided to seal various small objects, such as cables, stair legs, and railing pickets. If not properly topped up to shed water, they provide a direct entry for water into the roof insulation and into the building. (Courtesy of Cadillac Fairview Corporation, Limited.)

easily torn, and in the last stages, ready to absorb rather than repel moisture. It is susceptible to easy damage from wind, rain, and foot traffic. It also loses the elasticity to respond to temperature change stresses, and so it cracks.

Water

When water seeps into a dry roof, or steals through a crack, it causes a leak. But worse damage is yet to come with freezing weather, which turns the moisture into ice. Ice tears and heaves the roof, leaving it wide open.

Drainage

A good roof drains well, usually into gutters. It doesn't have any hollows that will hold stagnant water, which rots an asphalt mat. All low points have drains with properly sized downspouts. Valleys between monitors or saw-teeth are pitched to an outlet at either end, or to a center drain.

Wind

A strong wind takes advantage of any weakness in the roof mat or structure. It drives rain into defective joints in the mat or parapet, it tears at loose seams, and it sways roof structures.

Settlement

Settlement of roof or wall structures is not unusual. It will cause trouble wherever the horizontal and vertical surfaces meet. As walls settle, or as roof timbers dry and shrink, extra strains are exerted on flashings. Or the roof may settle below the level of the drain pipe. This will cause either a back-up of flood water, or a leak through the crack around the drain.

Temperature Changes

Expansion and contraction are at work all the time. Expansion strains in a new wood or concrete structure often cause the roof mat to tear. Seasonal changes in temperature expand and contract mortar in the coping joints, and provide an opening wedge for water to do its worst. The various forces of expansion and contraction in the roof deck and building walls wrestle at the angle joint and strain the flashings.

How Thermal Shock Affects Roofs

Thermal shock, caused by extreme and rapid temperature changes, will cause considerable movement of the roof mat. If the roof mat is brittle and inflexible, it cannot take such movement, and invariably, it will crack. This condition is more critical during the winter months because the bitumen is brittle.

An insulated roof is more vulnerable to attack by the elements.

Figure 6-32 illustrates this point. It compares the surface temperatures on an insulated and an uninsulated roof during a summer day. Note that at 11:30 a.m., the insulated roof temperature was 142°F. After a heavy shower, its temperature at 1:00 p.m. read 80°F, a drop of 62°F. In the next half hour, after the rain had stopped and the sun reappeared, the surface temperature quickly rose to 135°F. On an adjacent roof without insulation, during the same period, the maximum temperature change was only 15°F.

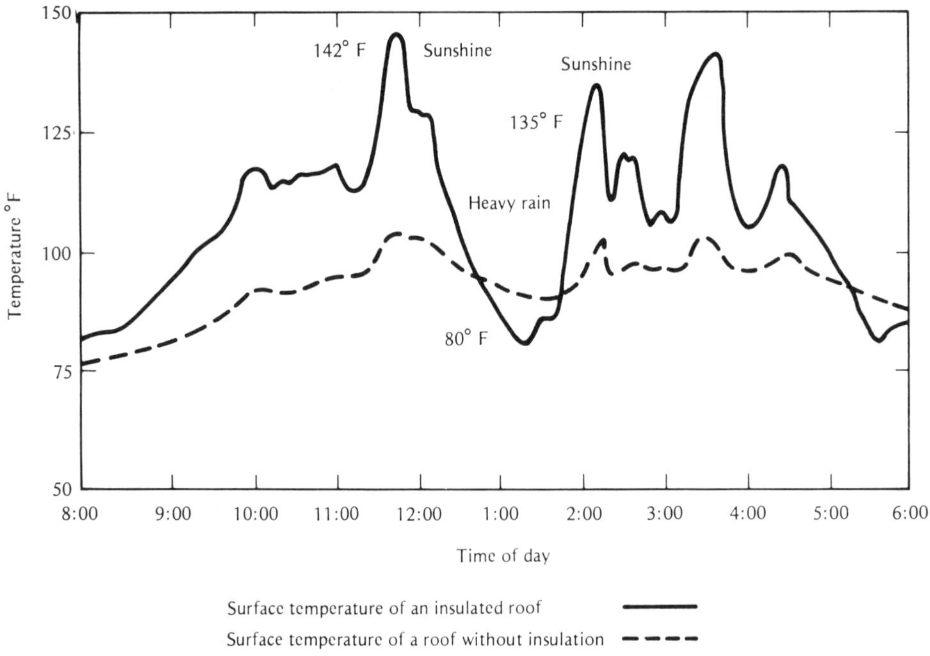

FIGURE 6-32 How thermal shock affects roofs. An insulated roof is more vulnerable to attack by the elements. (Courtesy of the Tremco Manufacturing Company.)

ROOF INSPECTIONS

Take frequent looks at your roof. Good care of a roof begins with regular inspection of the roof premises for signs of weakness or repair. The biggest step in holding down maintenance expenses is to catch roof troubles before they are born, or while they are still young.

You can expect any person to find the bad leaks, but it takes a qualified person to spot the small leaks. Your inspector has to know what to inspect and what to look for. Competent inspection includes many points—copings, parapets, flashings, skylights, ventilators, inside and outside walls, ceilings, and so on.

Semi-Annual Inspections

Inspect the roof every six months, preferably in the early fall to anticipate winter weather, and in the early spring to prepare for the hot summer sun.

Special inspections of the roof should be made after a violent rain or windstorm, after a nearby fire, or after "outside-interference" workmen have been on the roof.

How To Inspect

Is it better to inspect area by area, or item by item? For instance, is it better to inspect all copings, then all parapets, then all flashings, or do you inspect everything in one round of the roof walls?

The method is a matter of choice and convenience. Certainly it seems sensible to complete one roof at a time. The important thing is not to miss any parts of the roof.

Use a Checklist

The best way to make sure you do not overlook an important detail in roof inspection is to use a checklist. You can easily make up your own form, or you might get one from a contractor. Use a separate sheet for each roof.

A typical checklist shows all major roof items in the left column, such as copings, parapets, roof deck, roof covering, drains and gutters, skylights, and penthouses. Under

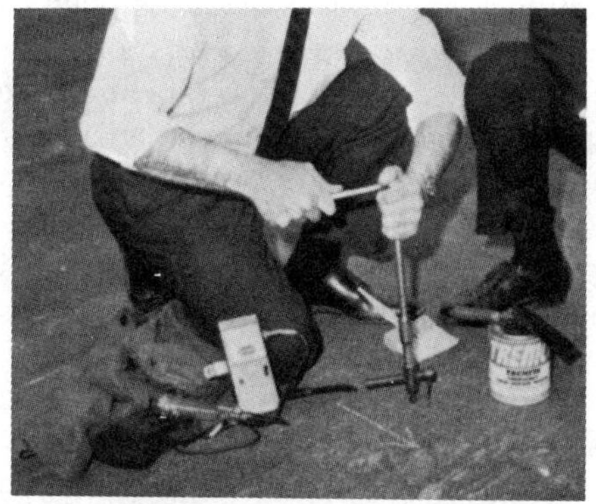

(a)

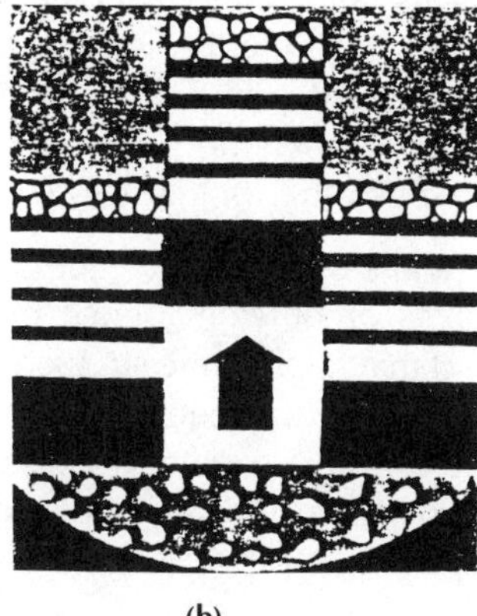

(b)

FIGURE 6-33 Roof inspections. (a) A moisture meter detects any trace of dampness within the roof system and guides strategic placement of vents to dry out wet insulation. (b) A core-analysis is taken to determine the true condition of the felts, insulation, vapor barrier, and roof deck, irrespective of the outward appearance of the roof. (Courtesy of the Tremco Manufacturing Company.)

each item is a subdivision of the point to be checked. For example, under roof covering you might list blisters, loose or torn seams, cracks, old patches, condition of mat. Across the top of the page are headings for vertical columns—condition OK, number of defects, repair at once, repair when convenient, check next inspection, special comments.

A good roof inspector will look at many things besides the roof mat for clues to actual leaks or those in the making. Obviously, the first thing to do is ask the building maintenance staff if there are any known leaks, or any complaints of leaks from employees. Such reports help pinpoint other symptoms later on. (See Figure 6-14, Rainwater Infiltration or Leakage Report.)

We have grouped the symptoms into convenient parts of the roof structure.

Exterior Walls of Building Look for settlement cracks or other evidence of building movement that might have strained the flashing or displaced drainage facilities. Efflorescence—the whitish, powdery excretion from mortar joints—may mean there are leaks in the coping or parapet above.

Interior Walls Stains or seepage indicate leaking walls or roof. Damp walls, chipped, or discolored paint are clues to roof leakage.

Underside of Roof Deck Look for any signs of deterioration from leakage above. If the deck is of wood, list rotted or warped boards for replacement. Make a note to check roof above any watermarked boards. Sometimes a wooden roof deck is weakened by excessive heat and humidity from processes below it.

If the deck is of concrete or gypsum slab, look for cracks and stains. Spots of rust might come from wet reinforcing rods. In a gypsum deck, leaking water usually causes spalling. In metal decks, rust spots mean trouble with condensation or leaks.

Topside Only a few defects are apparent in a topside inspection. A sharp indentation or break at right angles to the boards in a wood deck points to a sprung board. If the roof mat gives under you, the board may be rotted. But there are secondary clues. Cracks in roofing felt may be due to cracks in the roof deck. It is always a good idea to check the roof deck wherever you find leaks or holes in the roof mat.

Drainage Check for any changes in the original slope of the roof. Has any part of the deck sagged, to produce hollows for standing water?

In a wood deck, you can try to correct or restore the proper level by timber shoring. When this is not feasible, and the hollow is less than 4 inches, a good remedy is to fill the low area with asphalt mastic either above the old mat or under a new one. Always add a water repellent surface over it.

Deeper hollows can be repaired by a "saddle" or false roof that bridges the depression. This is covered by a new roof to match the built-up roof. Hollows in concrete roofs can be built up the same way. Sometimes you can clear the trouble by adding or relocating a drain.

Drainage System Make sure no rainwater accumulates on the roof during a rainfall. Slow-acting drains and gutters may cause a back-up of water above the parapet flashing. See that all drains are sound, flush to the roof, and clear of debris. If settlement or expansion has worked a drain spout above the roof level, re-install it.

Copings Coping troubles are mostly of two kinds: either the coping material loses its water repellency and absorbs moisture, or the mortar in the coping joint cracks. In either case, water drains down into the parapet, and where it will finally come out is hard to tell.

Often you can see the effects on the outside facing as you approach the building. More than likely, however, the leak will drain out of the inside facing because of poor masonry work. Once frost gets in, mortar and bricks may be pushed out of the wall by ice pressure.

Flashings Flashing flaws are among the most common causes of roof troubles. Too often flashing defects are overlooked when you inspect the roof for leaks. Look for loose flashings, or for torn or even missing sections.

Be sure to check all flashings for tightness of bond. A metal flashing may be in good condition, but may fail to do its job because of improper bond. This will allow water to seep between the edge of the mat and the base flashing, or between the counterflashing and the wall. Also, a flashing that is not turned up far enough may allow back-up water to stand against the wall and leak down to the roof deck.

Once water gets behind a flashing at the parapet angle, frost action follows. The flashing is loosened from its fastenings, thus opening the way to worse damage.

Metal flashings, unless made of copper or other fairly noncorrosive metal, are subject to rust. It pays to give metal flashings a good protective coating. They are poor protection once they get holes.

You can replace defective metal flashings with so-called membrane flashings at lower cost. There are several types to satisfy various conditions. The "sliding and overlapping" type is most commonly used. Sometimes the "accordian pleat" type is necessary, or the "regleted" type. All are equally effective when properly employed.

Roof Mat Roof mat troubles are not usually traceable to a single cause. When you spot the following symptoms, check carefully for the cause so you can make the right repairs.

Blisters Three main causes for blisters are

1. Misapplication has entrapped air.
2. Leaks have allowed moisture to form pockets between layers.
3. Volatile ingredients have given off gases that have formed pockets.

ROOF MAINTENANCE CONSIDERATIONS

1. Leave the roof alone. Your roof may be guaranteed, and its condition is the responsibility of those who laid it. So you decide to ignore the roof's deterioration, even at the risk of the building's wellbeing.
2. Rip it off. But would you go to the expense of buying a new roof if the present roof had value in it that can be repaired?
3. Cement a new covering to the old roof. This practice of putting on a "cap sheet" seldom proves satisfactory. You are expecting one or two new plies to do the job of a multiple-ply roof. You do not get a good bond—heavy winds may tear it. The moisture absorbed by the old dried-up roof may cause serious blisters in the new roof.
4. "Hot mop" the roof. Such treatment builds up the coating, but it does not resaturate the dry felt, and it prolongs the roof life very little. Very heavy hot applications check and crack readily.
5. Apply a resaturating agent. This may preserve the roof, but it is no cure for leaks. It works only if the roof is watertight and you use an agent that insures continued flexibility and water resistance.

6. Cover the entire roof with a flexible membrane embedded into the roof and coated with a roof preservative. Where there are still whole felts left on the old roof, but cracks and breaks occurring, this treatment may give the roof a new lease on life.

A good roof, properly maintained, will last the life of a building. The secret of trouble-free, low-cost maintenance lies in the regular resaturation of surface treatment of the roofing mat with a proper penetrant or coating while it is still sound and whole. And the early repair of cracks and breaks by the simple membrane treatment is economically sound and safe.

When breaking of felts is widespread, however, and deterioration is well advanced, we recommend you have the roof completely removed and a new roof built up from the base. Do not try to save such a roof by merely coating it with tar or asphalt. Unfortunately, many maintenance supervisors have been educated to believe nothing can go wrong with a roof that a few barrels of asphalt or tar, and maybe a cap sheet, will not cure.

Typical Roof Scale Drawing

A schematic drawing or plot plan of the roof can be a big help in making inspections.

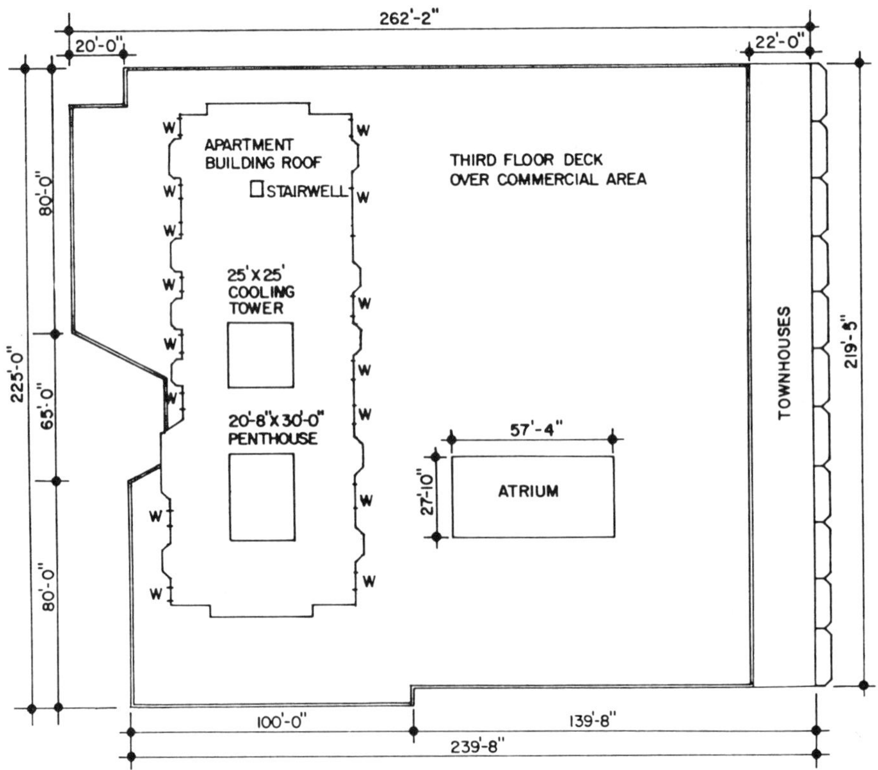

FIGURE 6-34 A typical roof scale drawing. A schematic drawing or plot plan of the roof can be a big help in making a roof inspection. (Courtesy of Cadillac Fairview Corporation, Limited.)

To be of value, show on this plan the location of each roof, and when installed. Also state who did the job, guarantee (if any), and approximate dimensions. Set up an inspection chart. After each inspection, enter brief notes on the condition of the roof and the general nature and cost of repairs. These data will prepare you for the next inspection, and guide you on future repairs and choice of new materials and methods to be used.

One helpful technique is to note any weak points on the roof that you feel do not need repair until after the next inspection, but that must be checked at that time.

Roof Survey and Maintenance Plan

1. Prepare a scale drawing of each roof area.
2. Detail age and history of each roof.
3. Make an inspection to determine present conditions.
4. Classify each roof as to type of construction.
5. Designate roofs that require corrective action and establish a sequence of priority.
6. Correct areas that require immediate attention.
7. Recommend a realistic budget for future repairs.
8. Set up a roof maintenance control ledger showing completed work, work in progress, and anticipated work.

SUMMARY

No book, however complete, will insure effective roof maintenance or repair. The skill, adaptability, and good judgment of the people on the job are important factors in doing a good job.

Technically, there should not be any mystery about how to obtain proper roof maintenance. It requires three simple procedures:

1. Regular inspection to catch defects early.
2. Determination of the best remedies.
3. Proper application of corrective measures.

6-13 Building Hardware

AN OVERVIEW

When decisions are being made about the choice of building hardware, they deserve more serious consideration than they usually receive. Many manufacturers make cheap products that provide good-looking alternatives to their quality product. It is, therefore, essential that we are knowledgeable enough about building hardware so that we purchase something that will do what we want it to do, without being faced with continuing failures and eventual replacement.

There are three main classifications for building hardware: doors, windows, and cupboards. Our main concern is with door hardware, including locks and keys, butts and hinges, door closers, panic hardware, and doorknobs. It is easy to see that all building hardware is put to considerable use. It is essential that we understand the purpose of each component, how to maintain and trouble-shoot, and when to call in the professional.

HINGES

Hinges come in various shapes and sizes for the different applications throughout a building. Because of the weight and size of various doors, it is absolutely essential that a proper hinge is chosen for each door.

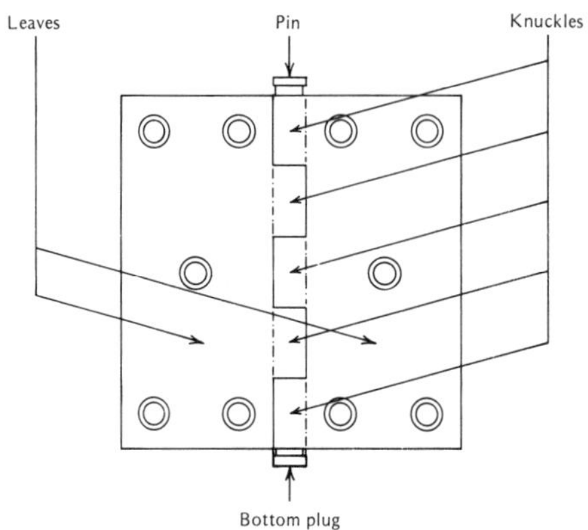

FIGURE 6-35 Standard hinge parts.

Standard Hinge Parts

The pin may be either removable or nonremovable. A pin may also be equipped with a bottom plug that is removable or nonremovable, or may not have a bottom plug at all. The important part of a hinge is the knuckles. A hinge may have three or five knuckles, depending on the size and weight of the door the hinges must handle. Usually a hinge has an odd number of knuckles. When hinges without ball bearings are used on heavy doors, they eventually wear between the knuckles. When this happens, the door drops, scrapes the floor, and will not latch properly.

You should be aware that all hinge screws should be snug, and hinge pins should be lubricated with a silicone spray.

Wherever possible, use three hinges to a door. It is good insurance. The great importance of the hinge side of the door is too often overlooked. A door that is not hinged properly is bound to affect the lock side of the door adversely and result in hardware trouble.

"Butts," really a contraction of the term "butt hinges," refer to those types of hinges butted (mortised) into both the door and the frame.

To specify hinges properly, there are a number of important factors to bear in mind:

(a) Type of metal required
(b) Finish desired
(c) Size needed because of door thickness and throw
(d) Type of bearing
(e) Design of tip
(f) Loose or fast pin
(g) Necessary screws or bolts for attaching

Half Surface Hinges

Half surface hinges are those in which one leaf is mortised in and the other leaf is surface applied. Half mortise hinges are those in which one leaf is mortised in and the other, narrower leaf is surface applied. These hinges are commonly used on Kalamein doors.

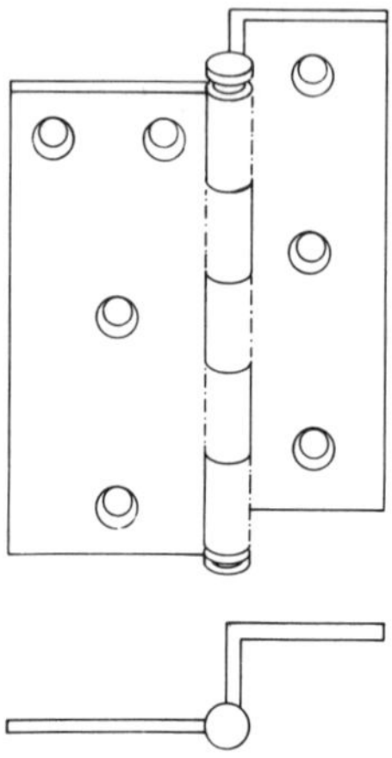

FIGURE 6-36 Half surface hinges.

Full Surface Hinges

Full surface hinges are those on which both leaves are surface applied.

THE HANDING OF DOORS

1. The hand of a door is always determined from the outside (Figure 6-39).
2. The outside of an exterior door is the street or entrance side.
3. The outside of an auditorium door is the corridor or hall side.
4. The outside of a room door is the corridor or hall side.
5. The outside of a closet door is the room, corridor, or hall side.
6. The outside of a single communicating door is the side from which the butts are invisible when the door is closed.
7. The outside of twin communicating doors is the space between the two doors.

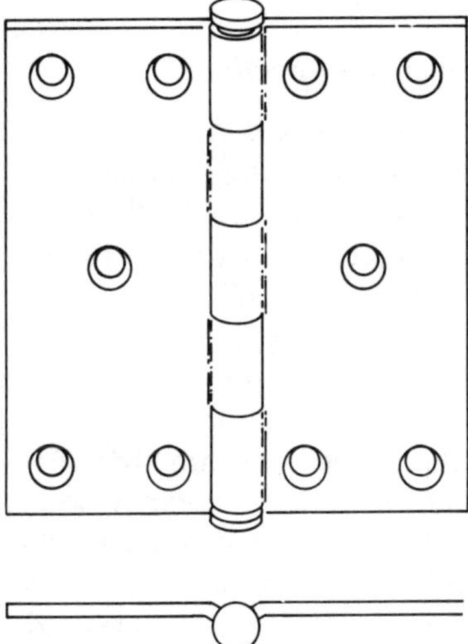

FIGURE 6-37 Full surface hinges.

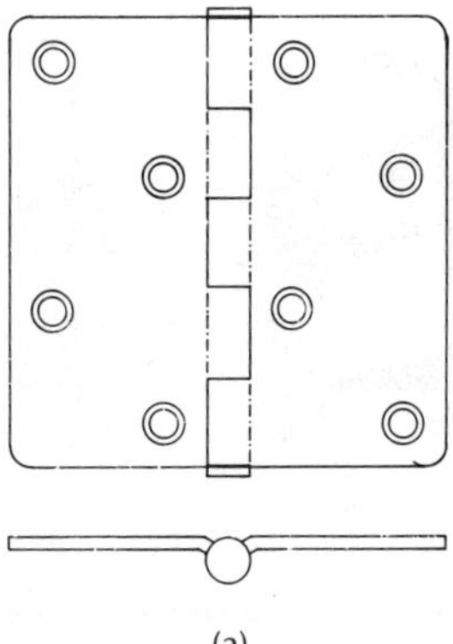

(a)

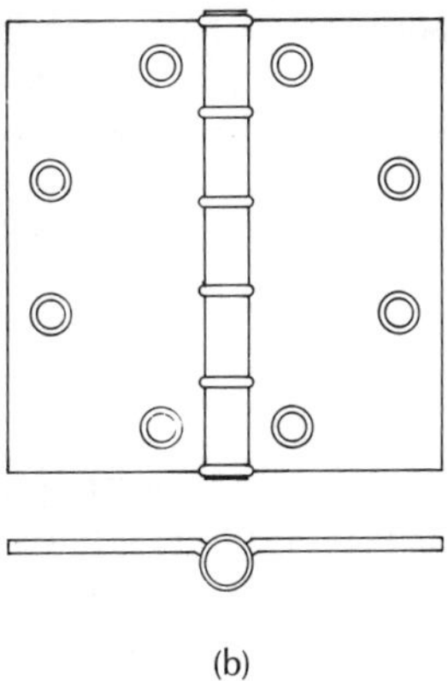

(b)

FIGURE 6-38 Mortise hinges. (a) Full mortise hinge, commonly used on hollow wood doors with wood trim. (b) Full mortise ballbearing hinge, commonly used on hollow metal doors with hollow metal frames.

BEVEL OF DOORS

A door is beveled when its edge is not at a right angle with the flat surface of the stile. The lock stile edge (leading edge) of a door may be furnished with a beveled edge in order to allow the door to fit more closely (Figure 6-40). The lock must have a beveled front to conform to the bevel of the door. The

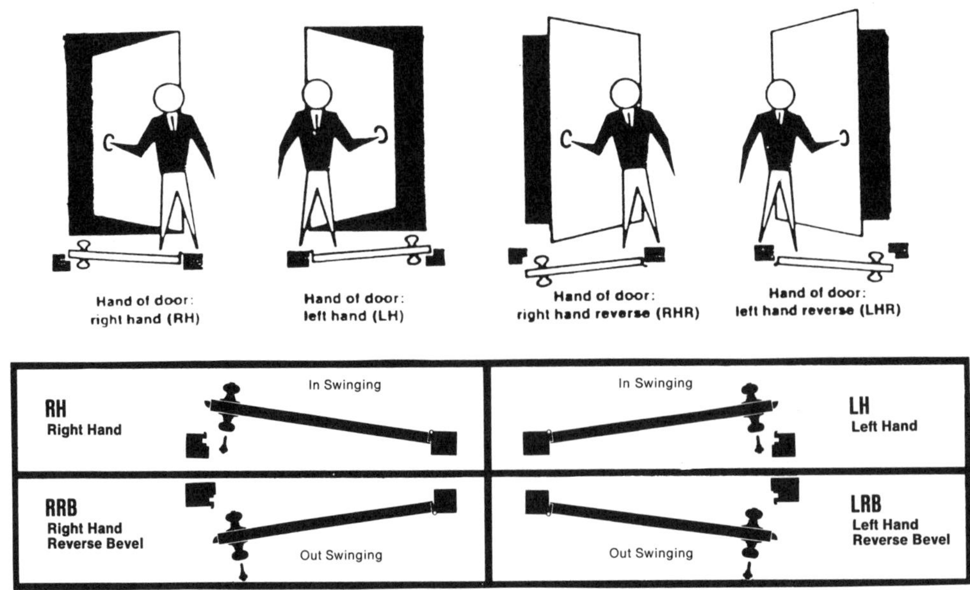

FIGURE 6-39 The handing of doors. (Courtesy of the Schlage Lock Company.)

bevel is determined by placing a square on the edge of the door; the difference in the measurement between the outside edge and the inside edge determines the bevel. The standard bevel is ⅛ inch on 2 inches.

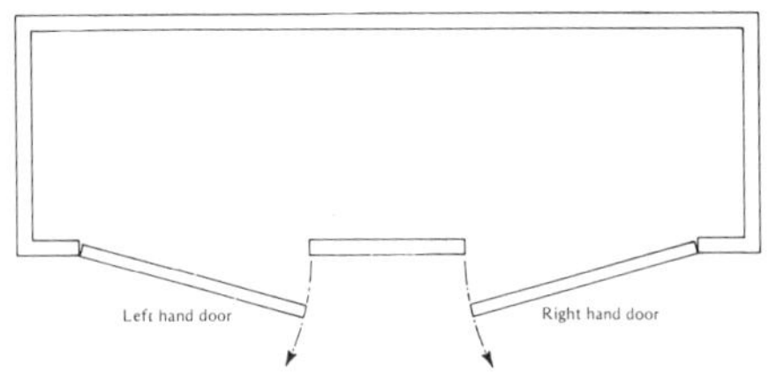

FIGURE 6-40 Hands of doors for refrigerators, cupboards, cabinets, and bookcases. The hand of a door is always determined from the outside.

DOOR CLOSERS

Maintenance Inspections

Periodic maintenance inspections will prolong the life of any door closer. During a maintenance inspection, all screws, bolts, and nuts should be carefully examined and tightened. This should include all bracket screws, arm bracket screws, and adjustable arm screws. If a closer is not operating efficiently, an examination of the door, frame, and other door hardware should be made. Many times a door hinge may be jammed.

All closers are stamped with the model number and the size on the shell. Be sure to state the specific model involved in any correspondence or conversation with service people.

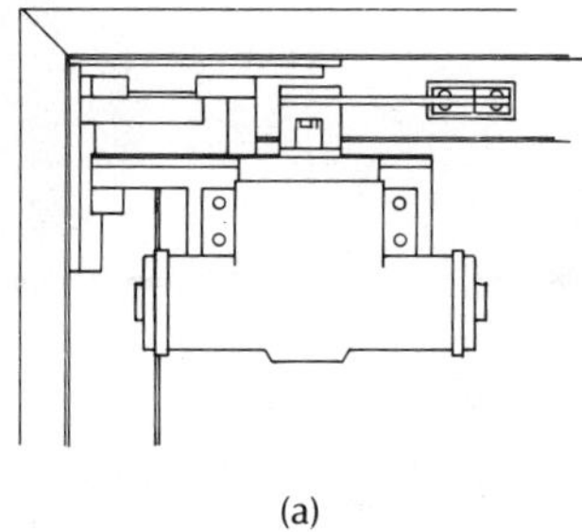

(a)

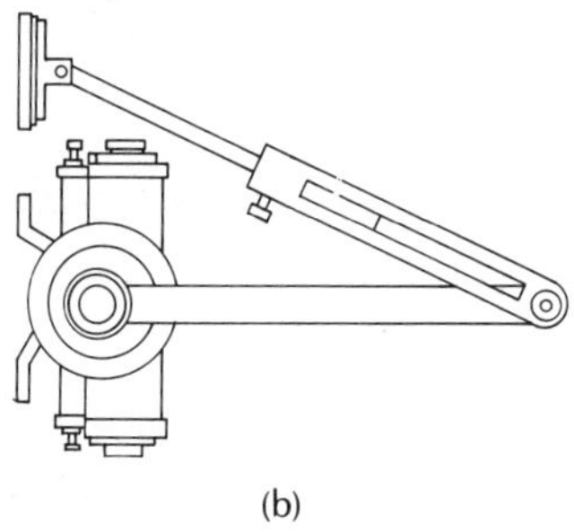

(b)

FIGURE 6-41 Door closers. (a) Front view; (b) Top view.

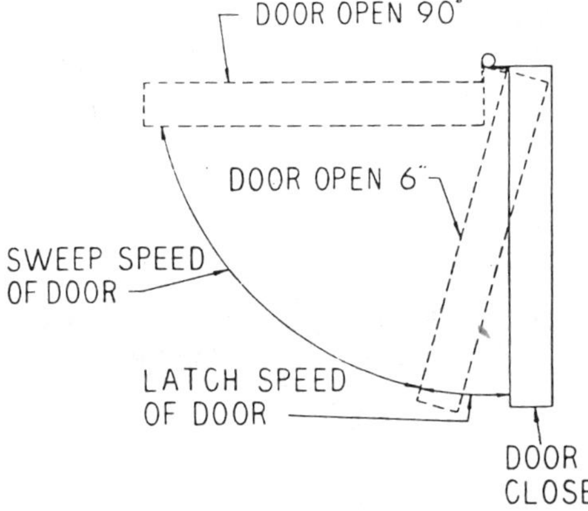

FIGURE 6-42 Door closer sequence.

Concealed Floor-Type Door Closer

This type of door closer is vulnerable to rain, snow, frost, and cleaning detergents. The initial cost, maintenance, and replacement cost are very high for this closer and its use is not recommended.

Door Closer Problems

1. Door closes too fast or too slow.
2. Door doesn't close smoothly.
3. Door doesn't close at all.
4. Door bangs against doorjamb.
5. Door slams on short opening or doesn't close properly.
6. Door opens with resistance.
7. Arm strikes top of door.

Door closers require minimal periodic mintenance to insure efficient operation and long life. An improperly adjusted or installed door closer shortens its useful life and places severe strain on the door, frame, and other hardware. All too often, a door closer is called upon to perform a function for which it was not intended, or is installed in a manner that prevents it from operating as it was designed.

A door closer is not designed to stop or limit the travel of a door. This function should

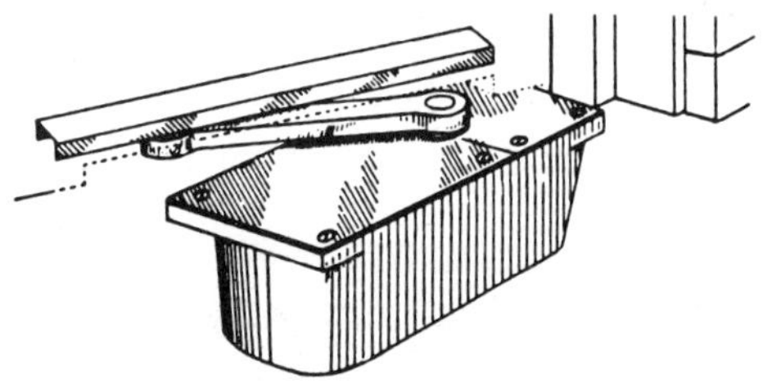

FIGURE 6-43 Concealed floor-type door closer. A single-acting checking floor hinge, with door hung on butt hinges.

be provided for by a unitized door control, a separate door holder, or a doorstop mounted on the floor or wall.

Common causes of unsatisfactory operation are improper arm installation and improper adjustment. Servicing of door closers should only be attempted by a professional. Being able to recognize a problem and calling for service before the door and the closer are damaged, is essential.

SECURITY

The building manager and the staff are the backbone of a good security system. They should control the keys and the door closers, and should be notified when tenants are away on holidays. Master keys must be closely controlled and should not be given to anyone.

The staff should be trained to replace cylinders and should replace them if a problem occurs or a tenant moves out. They should also ensure that all problems are corrected as soon as detected.

To further complicate problems, we are sometimes faced with obsolete locking systems in buildings. Qualified locksmiths can help you only as long as they have the parts available to repair and re-key existing buildings. Make sure that you establish a long-term plan of standardization and that the locksmith is involved in helping to decide a course of action.

Do not allow the building's security system to become too complicated or out of control.

KEYING OF LOCKS

The keying of locks for a large building (or group of buildings) may be arranged in any of three ways:

1. All locks differently keyed—each key is different and operates only one lock. The number of such locks in a series depends on the quality of the lock selected.
2. All locks keyed alike—that is, any key will open any lock in the series and can be furnished in any quantity.
3. Master keyed locks—all locks are differently keyed, but a pass or master key will operate any and all locks of the group or series.

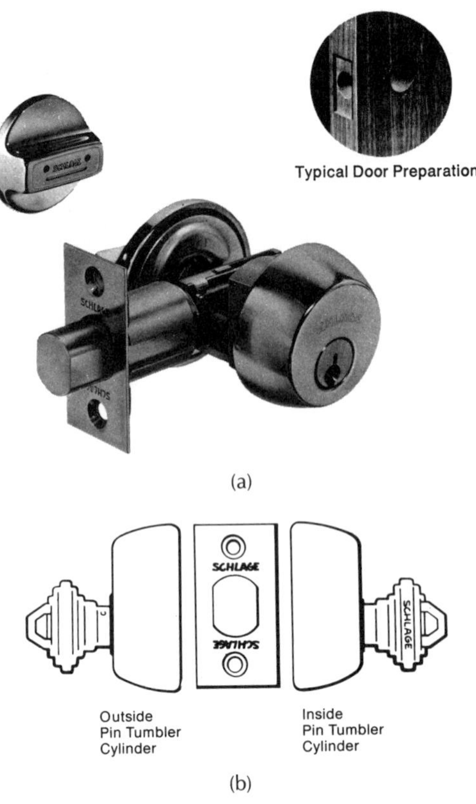

FIGURE 6-44 Tubular dead bolt. (a) With thumbturn night latch; (b) With double cylinder dead lock. (Courtesy of the Schlage Lock Company.)

Lock Functions

Though there are many lock functions available, we will only explain those commonly used.

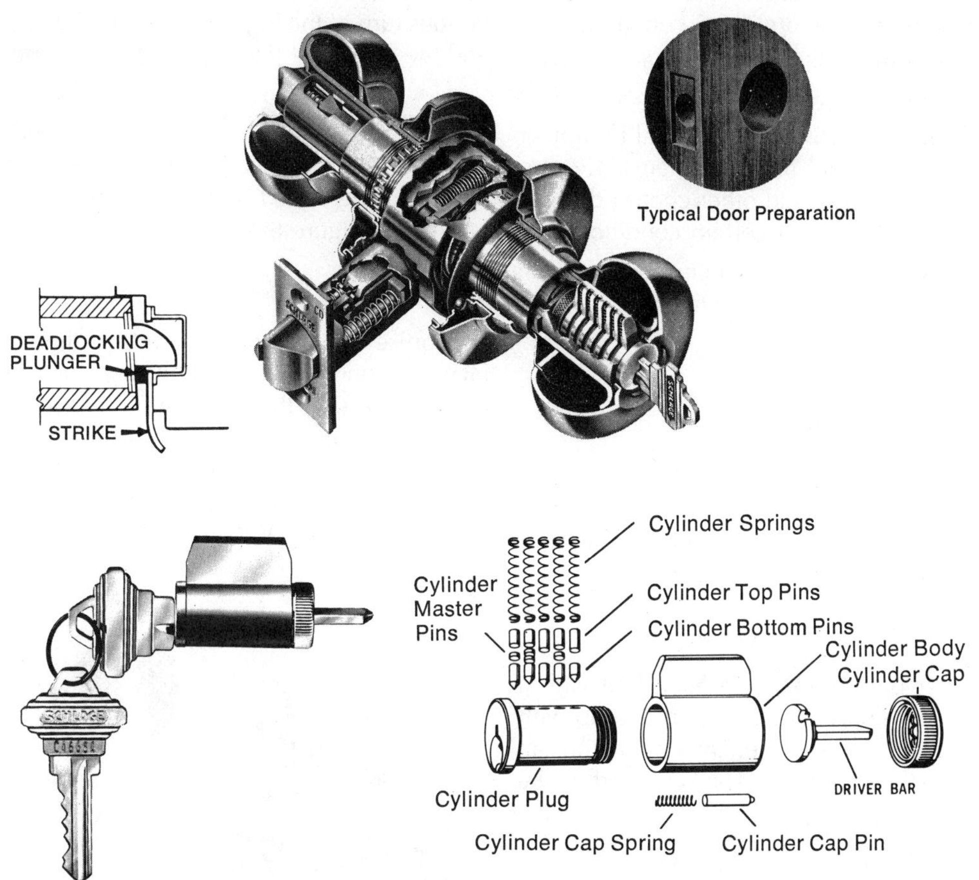

FIGURE 6-45 Tumbler key in knob set. (Courtesy of the Schlage Lock Company.)

Tubular Dead Bolt

Commonly used on tenant's suite entrance doors and the operating staff's lock-up areas.

This type of dead bolt provides higher security than the latch-type lock illustrated in Figure 6-45.

Tumbler Key in Knob Set

In tumbler locks, one or more flat tumblers must be moved to certain positions by a key before the key can engage and operate the bolts. These locks are generally used for interior doors of schools and for residences.

RESIDENTIAL ENTRANCE DOORS

Manufacturers have developed many products to meet the special and sometimes unique locking requirements for residential, institutional, and commercial buildings. To obtain satisfaction and maximum service from the locking devices, consideration should be given to the following factors:

1. Proper lock selection depends on the expected usage and climate conditions.
2. Proper installation by a qualified person using the proper installation tools.
3. Proper door control is essential to protect locks and other hardware items. The use of door closers and other control devices is necessary under certain conditions.
4. Proper maintenance includes following the recommendations of the manufacturer and always using the services of a qualified locksmith.

Lever Passage Latch

These handles are commonly used for any door that does not require locking. Rotating the lever handle on either side of the door retracts the latch bolt (Figure 6-46).

Grip Handle Entrance Locks

This type of lock has a latch bolt with a grip handle on the outside and a knob with stop button on the inside. The stop button can lock the thumb release. The key, used on the outside, can lock or unlock the door. Continuous turn of the key retracts both the latch and the dead bolt (Figure 6-47).

Lock and Security Cover

An additional dead bolt and security cover can be added to any door for added protection (Figure 6-48).

Mortise Rim Cylinders

Mortise rim cylinders mount on the surface with only mounting bolts and lock extensions passing through the door. Mortise lock devices are installed on the door with the lock itself fitting into a mortise cut into the door. Both of these devices are used for single door exits. Vertical rod devices are

FIGURE 6-46 Lever passage latch. Recommended for passage, closet, or any door that does not require locking. Both lever handles are always free. Rotating either lever will retract latchbolt. (Courtesy of the Schlage Lock Company.)

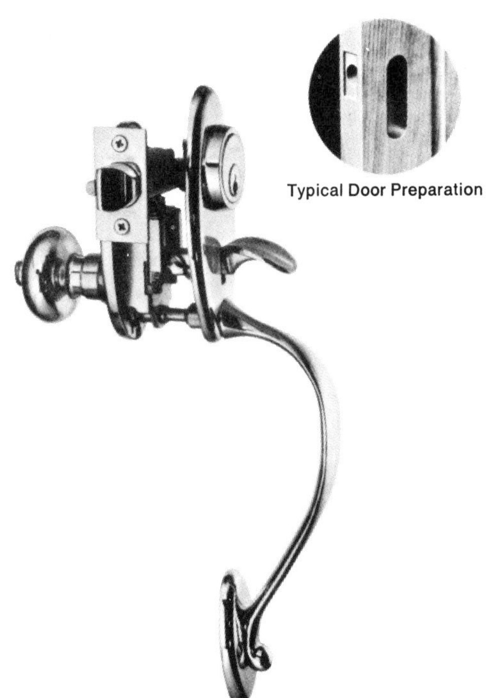

FIGURE 6-47 Grip handle entrance locks. (Courtesy of the Schlage Lock Company.)

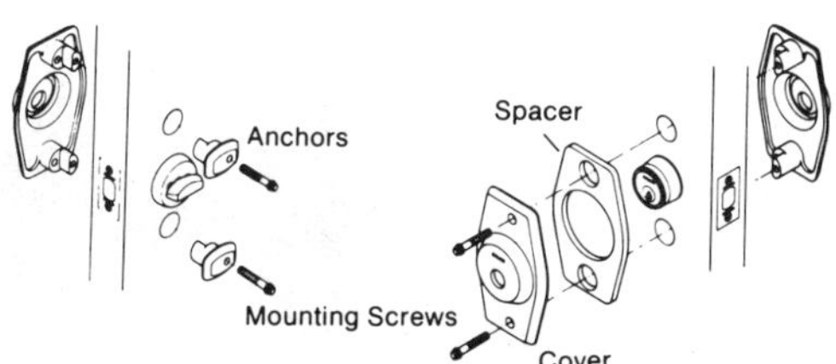

FIGURE 6-48 Lock and security cover. (Courtesy of the Schlage Lock Company.)

used when two doors are used on an exit (Figure 6-49).

Panic Exit Devices

Panic exit devices are used to provide a safe way out for any exit, yet provide security so unauthorized persons cannot enter. Such devices opeate merely by pressure against them. Many people have been killed or seriously injured by being trampled or suffocated while attempting to get out of an area in a panic situation. An emergency escape passage door should open with traffic flow (out) and have a latching device that would not require skill to open. Most panic exit devices may be dogged open, when security is not required, so traffic can move in either direction. As with locks, the only lubricant used on the mechanisms should be graphite. Most devices are made of bronze, stainless steel, or aluminum to be as decorative as possible, yet provide the proper safety and security (Figure 6-50).

BUILDING MANAGER'S RESPONSIBILITY

The manager should be aware of potential lock problems, regularly test common area locks, and know how to replace suite entrance cylinders.

For this purpose, a supply of cylinders and keys should always be on hand.

Suite entrance cylinders should be replaced for the following reasons:

1. They become defective—call for service when half of the spare cylinders are defective.
2. When a tenant moves out—switch cylinders.
3. If a tenant loses his keys—switch cylinders.

Lubricating Locks

Keep all locking devices suitably lubricated. All standard, well-constructed locks are made of brass and should *not* be lubricated with oil. The oil becomes sticky and keeps the tumblers from working properly. If oiled, it will be absolutely necessary, in a very short while, to remove all parts and clean thoroughly. The proper lubrication for a brass lock is graphite. Graphite is available in handy tubes or in liquid form with the trade name WD 40.

Checking Locks

If a key does not turn the lock freely and easily, the problem should be remedied, for a

FIGURE 6-49 Mortise cylinder long-throw front door lock. Mortise locks are difficult to install and may require special tools to cut the mortise in the door. (Courtesy of the Schlage Lock Company.)

key is not strong enough to be used as a pry or a lever. If the problem is not remedied, the key will eventually break in the lock, causing expense and inconvenience.

To properly check a lock

1. See that the key is pushed completely into the lock.
2. Try turning with thumb and forefinger. (Never use pliers.)
3. While turning with the right hand, lift up on the doorknob with the left hand. If this releases the pressure on the key, the metal plate on the doorjamb is too high and should be lowered, or the hinges are loose or worn. If lifting increases the pressure on the key, and pushing down on the doorknob releases the pressure, it is evident that the plate is too low and should be raised.

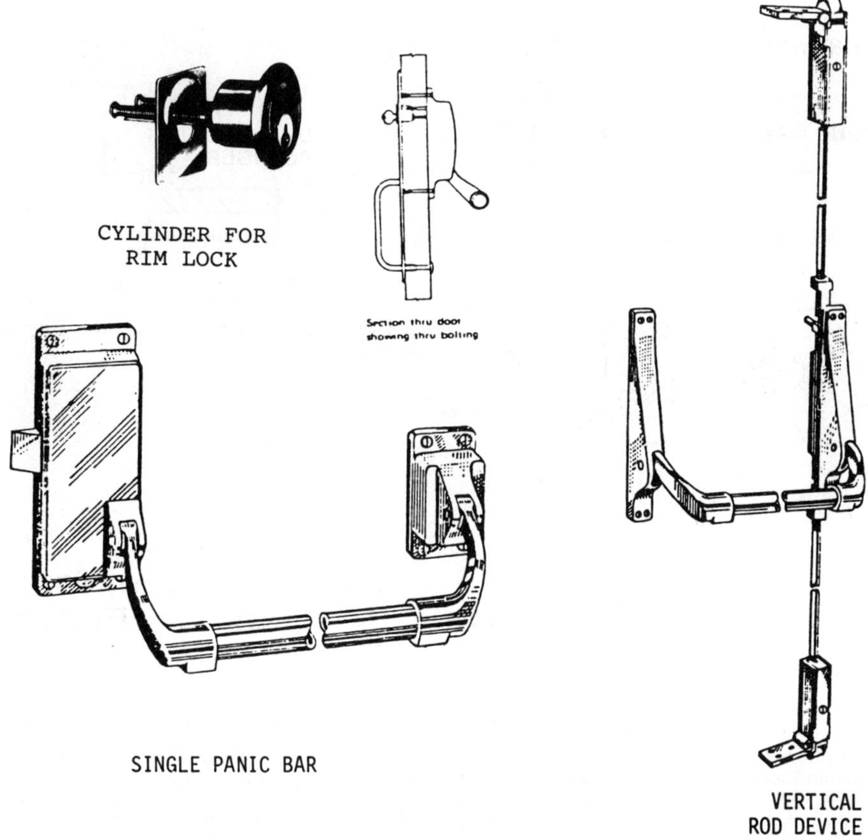

FIGURE 6-50 Panic exit devices. Cylinders for rim locks can be used with night latches, overhead garage door locks, sliding door locks, and exit bolts.

4. Push in on the doorknob. If this frees the key so that the bolt will turn freely, the plate is too close to the doorstop, which is the narrow strip of wood that the door slams against. This may be remedied either by moving the plate outward or moving the doorstop inward.

THE HAND OF A LOCK

Locks are factory assembled in knobs for right or left hand doors. When calling for service, the hand of the door must always be given. The cylinders should always be such that the keyway is proper. Some beveled

TO CHANGE LOCK HAND

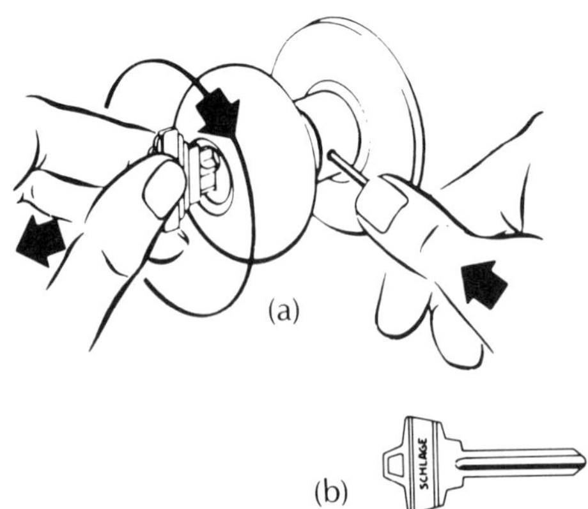

FIGURE 6-51 The hand of a lock. (a) Insert small nail or similar tool into hole in the outside hubcap. Exert pressure and at the same time insert key and turn slowly in clockwise direction until knob catch depresses; then pull off knob. Simply turn knob over and with key partly removed from cylinder, replace knob on spindle. Slide knob onto spindle up to knob catch. Turn key one-quarter turn in same direction as before, depress knob catch, and push knob into position. (b) Wafer key locks do not have to be changed for right or left hand doors; factory assembled with non-removable exterior knobs. (Courtesy of the Schlage Lock Company.)

fronts on certain locks are also specially made and are not reversible.

LOCKS EQUIPPED WITH DEADLOCKING PLUNGER

Locks are equipped with a deadlocking plunger on the latch bolt. Plunger stops against the strike, preventing the latch bolt from being forced when the door is closed.

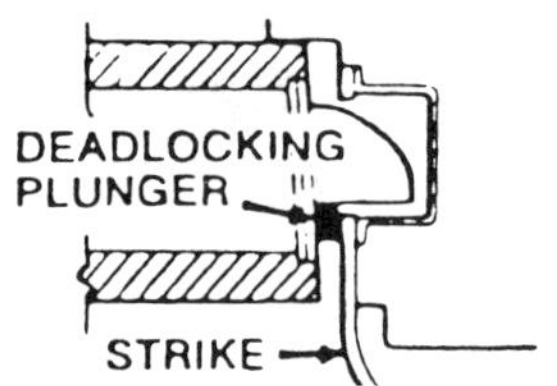

FIGURE 6-52 Deadlocking Plunger. (Courtesy of the Schlage Lock Company).

6–14 How to Budget for the Necessary Funds

Structural maintenance is usually done to preserve and/or improve the appearance of a building. Understanding the problems and knowing what to do about them should provide a better insight for owners and managers of buildings and help them to make intelligent decisions about spending money for structural maintenance.

Understanding and being realistic about planning, designing, building, and maintaining properties will pay off by eliminating avoidable problems wherever possible and will encourage the systematic allocation of funds for the ongoing maintenance of the buildings owned or managed.

Remember, there are no permanent building materials. When a structure is built, it is the beginning of its life span, not the end. Buildings are breathing, moving forms of inanimate life that require constant care—just like a human being.

In 1980, the National Association of College and University Business Officers reported that roughly $30 billion would be needed to catch up with the accumulated neglect of campus buildings.

About 70 percent of all college buildings in the United States were erected after 1950, more than one-third of them in an eight-year spurt after 1966, when federal funds flowed freely as administrators tried to accommodate the baby boom. By cutting corners with low-grade materials, designers often created buildings that aged prematurely and that were consuming energy in an inefficient and costly manner.

To add to the problem of poor design and inefficiency, regular maintenance was deferred as funds were used to pay for soaring energy bills and increasing costs of staff salaries.

It is a sad reality that we are training the future architects and engineers on these campuses. Unfortunately, they may not be learning the importance of quality design and construction or the benefits of preventive maintenance.

Perhaps some experiences in troubleshooting structural problems, awarding and supervising the repair contracts, and the managing of some of the estimated $30 billion in costs would alert everyone to the problem.

The need for training that would eliminate poor design, shoddy construction, and lack of preventive maintenance is clearly evident when one reads this horror story.

The costs involved for structural maintenance are usually high and, therefore, may be deferred in the hope they will disappear. Unfortunately, unless corrected as soon as detected, they only get worse. We hope that the material in this chapter will encourage a more realistic approach to maintaining the structure. We cannot emphasize enough the importance of regular inspections, the importance of recognizing a problem and having it corrected, and finally, the importance of allocating funds in the budgets for this work.

Budget expense schedules were developed to help you cover every structural item and are detailed in Figs. 6-53–6-55.

By detailing all the structural services items on these budget expense schedules, everyone is alerted to each component and what action is required to decide about funds for a specific maintenance activity.

Physical inspections are required of parts inventory, the facade, the building hardware, caulking, each occupied unit, the paint, floors, parking lots, sidewalks, roofs, walls, ceilings, and windows.

A separate budget expense schedule would be used for each building owned or managed. Funds would be allocated for every item of maintenance or purchase of parts. *Speculative funds should never be added to the budget.* However, an extra schedule could be used to make follow-up notes for future years.

	ACCOUNT NUMBERS	SUB TOTALS	TOTAL
BRICKWORK & STRUCTURAL CONCRETE	36		

CHIMNEYS	361	
GARAGES	362	
RETAINING WALLS	363	
SLAB EDGES	364	
TUCKPOINT, TAPE & GROUT	365	

BUILDING HARDWARE	37	TOTAL	

ASHTRAYS & WALL URNS	371	
CYLINDERS	372	
DOOR CLOSERS	373	
DOOR HANDLES	374	
KEYS	375	
LOCKSETS	376	
PADLOCKS	377	

CAULKING	38	TOTAL	

COLUMNS & SLAB EDGES	381	
DOORS, WINDOWS & BALCONIES	382	

FIGURE 6-53 Summary of budget expense schedules, repair and maintenance categories; structural services.

	ACCOUNT NUMBERS	SUB TOTALS	TOTAL
COUNTER TOPS & CUPBOARDS	39		

COUNTER TOPS	391	
CUPBOARDS	392	

DOORS	40	TOTAL	

BALCONY	401	
GARAGE	402	
OTHERS	403	

EXTERIOR PAINTING	41	TOTAL	

BALCONIES (PANELS, DIVIDERS & RAILINGS	411	
CONCRETE & MASONRY	412	
GALVANIZED METAL	413	
PRE-PAINTED METAL	414	
WINDOWS, DOORS & TRIM	415	

FLOORS	42	TOTAL	

TILES (CERAMIC - QUARRIE)	421	
TILES (HARDWOOD)	422	
TILES (VINYL)	423	

FIGURE 6-54 Summary of budget expense schedules, repair and maintenance categories; structural services.

	ACCOUNT NUMBERS	SUB TOTALS	TOTAL
PAVING (ASPHALT & CONCRETE)	43		

CURBS	431	
PAVING	432	
RAMPS	433	
SIDEWALKS & STEPS	434	

ROOFS	44	TOTAL	

EAVESTROUGHS & FLASHING	441	
PATCHING	442	
REPLACING	443	
SCRAPE & 3 PLY	444	

WALLS & CEILINGS	45		

CEILINGS (PLASTER & TILE)	451	
PATCHING (INC. PAINTING)	452	
TUB CAULKING	453	
WALL TILES (INC.GROUT,SOAP DISHES ETC)	454	

WINDOWS	46		

REGLAZING	461	
RESCREENING	462	
OTHER MAINTENANCE	463	

FIGURE 6-55 Summary of budget expense schedules, repair and maintenance categories; structural services.

Chapter 7

THE PLUMBING AND DRAINAGE SYSTEM

7–1 An Overview

WHAT IS PLUMBING?

The Latin word "Plumbum" means lead and the word "Plumber" originally referred to a worker of lead. The first pipe used to transfer water by the ancient Romans was made of lead. Lead pipe was also used until the end of the nineteenth century. Cast iron, galvanized iron, copper, and plastic have since taken its place.

Today, plumbing refers to the system of pipes that supplies the domestic water to the occupants of a building and carries the waste from the building.

The object of the system is to make water available where and when required in the building and to get rid of the water, and wastes, after it has served its purpose. In general, plumbing can be divided into three areas: the fresh water supply, the drainage system, and the fixtures and appliances.

WHY YOU SHOULD UNDERSTAND PLUMBING

The information in this chapter will help you in three ways:

1. To identify problems.
2. To understand the kind of plumbing repairs that the operational staff is expected to do.
3. To gain enough knowledge about the plumbing system so that you can communicate problems to the plumber.

Since a plumbing system requires service from time to time, shut-off valves are installed at strategic locations that allow problem areas to be isolated.

It is absolutely essential that project managers and operators become familiar with the complete plumbing and drainage system in their buildings. It is essential that they gather the correct name and sample of each plumbing part in the buildings being managed; have on hand the tools used to complete simple repairs; have schematic drawings of the plumbing and drains; and identify by tagging all pipes, pumps, and valves.

Valves should be tagged so that their functions are easily identified. Chained plastic holders containing color-coded cards identifying the functions is an ideal method.

Pipes should also be painted or color striped for identification. The following color codes are generally used:

Cold water—light blue
Hot water—royal blue

PIPING SYSTEMS

Water Supply System

In the water supply system, water flows under pressure to the desired locations. This pressure is either maintained by the municipality pressure or by a booster pump. Water lines used for this purpose are made of galvanized iron, copper, or plastic. Galvanized iron pipe has screw fittings; copper has flared or solder fittings. Soldered fittings and rigid copper pipe are most commonly used today. Several sets of valves may be employed so individual distribution lines may be shut off without affecting the whole system. A township main water valve must be installed outside the building to shut off the water supply to the building, when necessary.

Drainage Systems

In the drainage system, gravity causes the flow of wastes from the building and makes up the second system of pipes. Sewer lines handle liquid and solid waste and gases. Waste matter decomposes and generates methane gas, which is similar to the natural gas we use to heat our homes. To relieve any pressure, this system must be properly vented to the atmosphere and the inlets to the drains must be sealed to prevent gas from escaping into the building. Vents are extended through the roof, and traps are located near each point of entry (sinks, toilets, baths, floor drains). These drains must be cleaned on a regular basis, or they will block and cause suds back-up or an overflow of sewage.

Gas Piping System

Gas lines are made of black iron pipe with screw fittings. The size of the pipe must be adequate to supply gas to each appliance without the reduction of pressure.

A shut-off valve is installed near the meter. It is also mandatory to have a valve at each appliance. This allows one unit to be shut off for servicing without turning the gas off to all other units. All units are equipped with safety regulators. Lines should be capped if an appliance is removed and not replaced, even though a valve is installed at the appliance hookup. *Never use a match to test for leaks in gas lines!!!* If you suspect a gas leak, do not switch a light on in an equipment room. Call the gas company immediately.

INSPECTIONS

Periodic inspections of piping should be made where conditions could be considered severe. The corrosion of galvanized piping in buildings has become very serious in the past ten or fifteen years. The life of piping is shortened by vibration, chemicals, condensation, electrolysis, and by alteration of temperatures over short periods. (See Biological Fouling and Corrosion, Chapter One.)

INSULATION

Insulation of piping minimizes piping hazards resulting from condensation and excessive heat or cold. Of course, it will effect economies in heating and cooling the building. (See Chapter Twelve, Energy Management.)

7-2 Hot and Cold Water Distribution

The components of the fresh (potable) water distribution are shown on the drawing of a typical apartment building system (Figure 7-1). To give you an overview of the system we will identify each component as it is listed on the drawing.

IDENTIFYING THE SYSTEM'S MAIN COMPONENTS

Fire System Line

This illustrates that the city or municipality supplies the water used for the building's fire-fighting stations, as well as for the domestic water system in a building.

The water used for the "Fire Control System" by-passes the meter and is completely separated from the Distribution Water System. Sometimes, the fire control piping is a separate line.

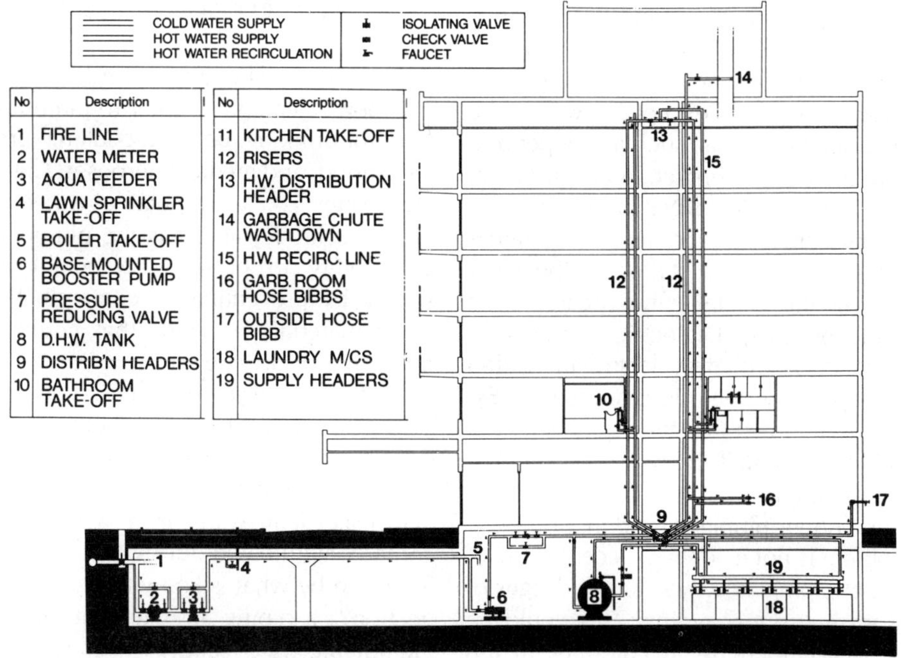

FIGURE 7-1 Hot and cold water distribution in a typical apartment building. (Courtesy of Cadillac Fairview Corporation, Limited.)

Water Meter

As this meter records the water consumption in the buildings, it is important to remind you about the waste caused by leaks, especially leaking taps and toilets. You should have a supply on hand of the proper-sized washers and seats, and all washers should be changed at least every two years. It is wise to keep a chart of the fixtures and schedule the replacements.

This action cuts down on complaints, and most important, conserves water and the energy required to heat it. Running hot water down the drain is a very costly and unnecessary expense.

Aqua Feeders

Corrosion of the galvanized water distribution piping is probably one of the most serious and costly problems faced by owners of buildings piped in this manner. The corrosion usually occurs in varying degrees along the entire length of pipe rather than at some particular point. An exception would be where dissimilar metals, such as copper and steel, are directly in contact. In this instance, electrolysis causes the pipes to deteriorate.

To retard this deterioration, a container that holds crystals was installed. As the water passes over the crystals, it is treated as it enters the building. Dielectric connections are used to control the electrolytic action when copper and steel pipes are joined. Experience has shown that the replacement of the corroded piping is the only way to eliminate the problem.

When copper piping is used in a building this problem is not evident. A recent study of samples of piping, however, showed signs of pitting in the copper piping. This could be caused by an increase in chlorides in the water. Local water should be tested periodically for signs of problem pollution if you expect to keep on top of potential problems.

Lawn Sprinklers

Maintaining lawns in a green healthy condition requires a moisture penetration of 3 inches to 5 inches on each application. Planters, shrub beds, and flowers also require watering to a different degree. The system should supplement the local rainfall pattern and should be controlled by the gardening staff. Plants require water for every physiological function, and if they dry out for even a short time, growth is severely stunted. These watering systems are a part of the water distribution and thus should be understood and kept in good repair. You should be aware that a leaking or broken underground line can cause your water bill to jump dramatically. Other damages, requiring costly repairs, can be caused by a severe leak that is not corrected.

POTABLE WATER SUPPLY

The cold and hot water distribution system transports clean, safe water to plumbing fixtures for drinking, bathing, cooking, processing of food, and medical purposes. Clean and safe water is called potable water in the plumbing trade, and it is the plumber's responsibility to protect the potable water supply by preventing its contamination by other materials or fluids that could cause poisoning or disease.

Waterborne diseases that can contaminate a water supply include cholera, typhoid fever, paratyphoid fever, amoebic dysentery, bacillary dysentery, hookworm, flukes, and diarrhea. Clean water in a system can become contaminated during use. Usually this is caused by what is known as a "cross connection": a piping arrangement that allows the potable water supply to be connected to a line or other source having contaminants. The cross connection usually occurs when pressure drops in the supply water line, and

STANDARDS FOR POTABLE WATER*

Physical Characteristics or Chemical Substance	*Concentration Scale or Parts per Million by Weight*
Color	20 (Platinum Cobalt Scale)
Turbidity	10 (Silica Scale)
Arsenic	0.05 ppm
Copper	3.0 ppm
Chloride	2.5 ppm
Chromium	0.05 ppm
Fluoride	1.5 ppm
Iron and Magnesium	0.05 ppm
Lead	1.5 ppm
Magnesium	0.3 ppm (combined)
Selenium	0.1 ppm
Sulphate	12.5 ppm
Zinc	0.05 ppm

*Standards of the United States Public Health Service for potable water in interstate traffic.

siphoning reverses the flow, causing the contaminents to enter the water supply (Figure 7-2).

PROBLEM AREAS

There is a danger of contamination where broken water and sewer lines can cross-connect. Other examples of potential problems are a rubber hose connected to a fresh water supply and left in a laundry sink, or connected to sprinkler heads below the surface of the lawn, which can siphon contaminants back into the potable water supply, if the supply pressure drops. Swimming pools are another potential source of a cross connection with the fresh water supply. Most local codes outlaw such connections unless backflow preventers are installed that stop reverse flow. Among other applications covered by backflow prevention are flush valves, hose bibs, fire protection systems, commercial ice makers, handheld personal showers, kitchen sink spray hoses, solar energy panels, water-connected coffee vending machines, domestic refrigerators, and the feed line to hot water boilers. (See Figure 7-2.)

THE WATER SUPPLY

Plumbing codes specify that buildings must have ample water supplied with sufficient pressure to operate in a safe and satisfactory manner. The purpose is to ensure that water will be provided to each plumbing fixture outlet according to its demand and pressure requirements. Thus, the potable water system is designed from the demand of the fixtures, and considers such factors as the pressure available in the municipal water main, the building height and friction losses, and a velocity limitation that prevents damage to the pipes.

THE PRESSURE REGULATING VALVE

The pressure at the street main is usually in the range of 45-60 lbf/in. (310-414 K^{P}a). If the pressure is higher, it must be regulated so as not to exceed 80 lbf/in. (552 K^{P}a), and preferably, it should be lower to provide pipes and fixtures some margin of safety from transient pressures and pressure shocks.

The pressure regulating valve (Figures 7-3 and 7-4) is installed on the house side of the water meter for the protection of the plumbing in the building. It regulates the water pressure to the requirements of the building.

THE BASE-MOUNTED BOOSTER PUMP

This pump (Figure 7-1, #6) is installed to provide sufficient pressure to raise the water to all floors of the building and to meet the demands of the occupants. Many use a "rule of thumb" of 4 pounds per floor plus 15 pounds. The volume is dependent on the diameter of the supply pipe. (See Chapter 11, Mechanical Services.)

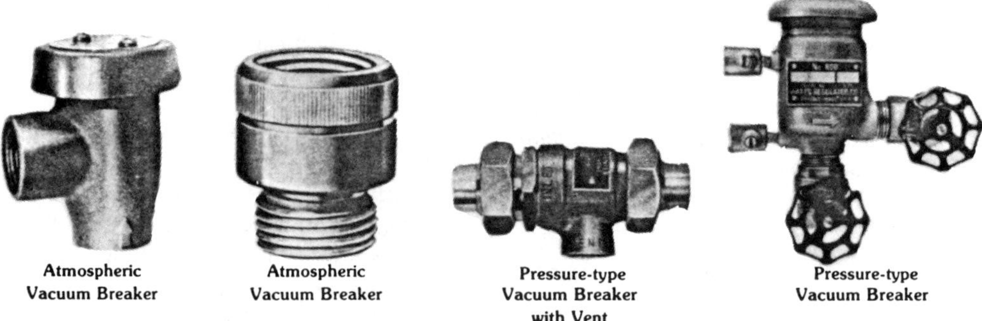

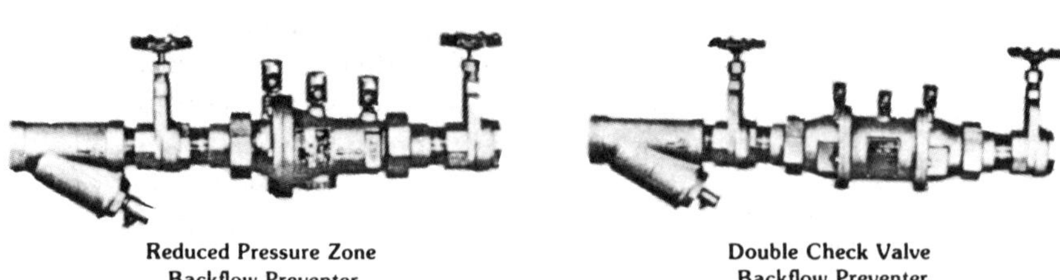

Backflow Preventers
(Watts Regulator Co.)

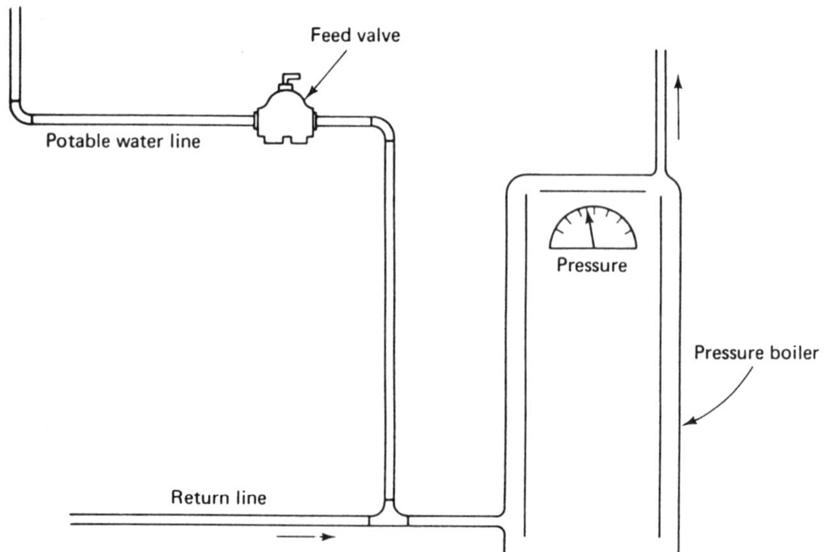

Direct connection to potable water supply allows back flow when the supply pressure is reduced below the boiler line pressure, permitting boiler water to flow into the potable water supply.

FIGURE 7-2 **Direct pressure cross connection.** (Courtesy of Reston Publishing Company.)

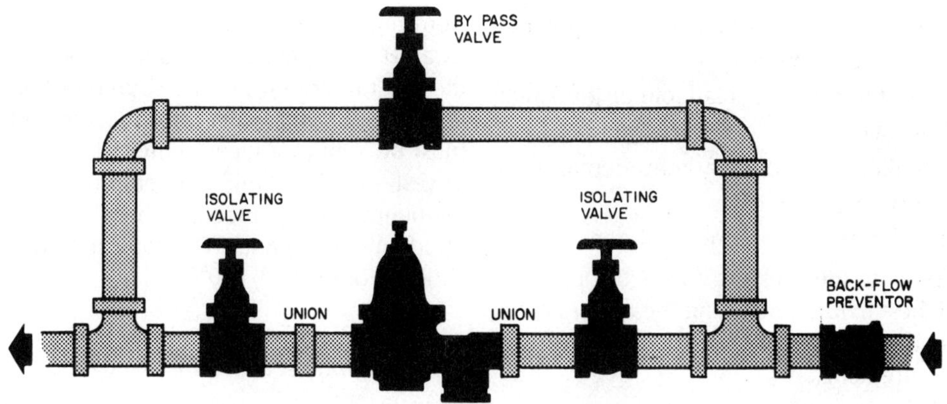

FIGURE 7-3 Pressure regulating valve piping arrangement. (Courtesy of Cadillac Fairview Corporation, Limited.)

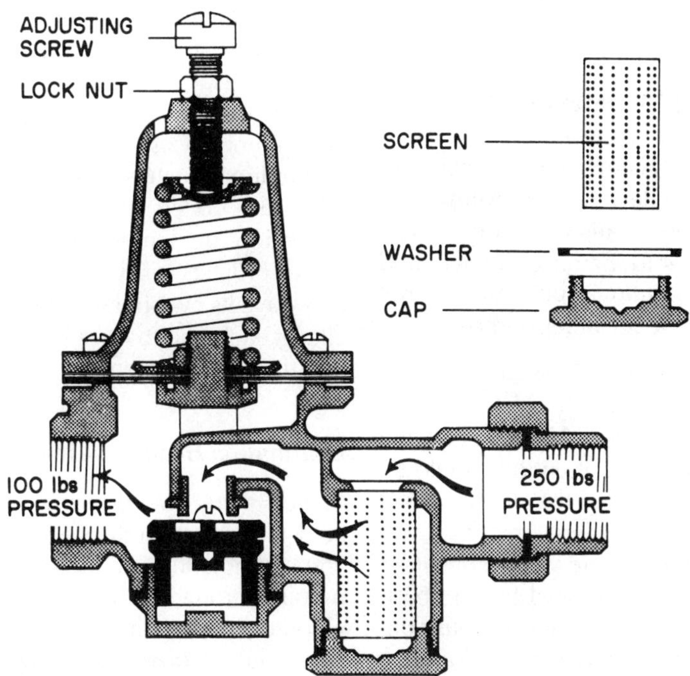

FIGURE 7-4 Cut-away of a pressure regulating valve. (Courtesy of Cadillac Fairview Corporation, Limited.)

When design engineers size the potable water supply, they must

1. Know the pressure available at the street water main.
2. Calculate the total system demand in supply fixture units.
3. Size the meter from the total demand.
4. Compute the pressure losses through the highest fixture, including the meter, static head to the fixture, and fixture pressure requirements.
5. Size the building supply pipe (coming out of the meter) from the total demand, available pressure, and pressure loss in the longest developed length (to the farthest fixture).
6. Size the principal branches for the hot and cold water, using the respective demands and minimum branch and supply pipe sizes.

HEATING THE DOMESTIC WATER

The plumbing system includes piping to and from a heating device, or a heating storage device that will satisfy the occupants' needs for hot water for bathing, kitchen, and laundry. In an institutional building, the hot water needs may be for other purposes.

Maximum Temperature

Because its use is dictated by the occupant and not by the weather, attention should be directed to the heating of the domestic hot water relative to any energy management program. Heating domestic water consumes 20 percent of the energy used by an apartment building and thus warrants serious consideration. The fuel used to heat the domestic hot water should be deducted from the fuel used to heat the building when monitoring an energy management program. Heat losses from uninsulated piping can cause as much as a 40°F temperature drop from the tank to the most remote user. The source of heating the domestic hot water and the storage tank must be kept in a clean, efficient state if the lowest possible tank temperature is to be maintained while meeting the needs of the building's occupants. The tank temperature should not exceed 120°F.

Direct or Indirect Systems

The geographic location of a building should be considered when deciding about the most economical way to heat and store the domestic hot water, and whether to use a direct or indirect heater. In cooler climates the indirect heater (Figure 7-5) is usually installed because the building heating boilers are used for most months of the year. In a warm climate it might make sense to use a direct heater for this purpose, or perhaps use solar panels.

Because of the higher energy costs, it is not uncommon to use a combination of direct and indirect heaters. Direct heaters are used when the boilers are off or when they are needed to supplement the building's load. In some projects each individual apartment may have its own hot water heating unit. This allows each unit to have its own utility meter and to pay for the energy used.

Distribution Headers—Take Offs and Risers

If you study the drawing of the hot and cold water distribution system (Figure 7-1), you will note that a building has many pipes running throughout its walls. These pipes are all potential problems, and broken pipes can cause serious flooding throughout the building. Fortunately, plumbing emergencies do not happen often, but when they do occur, they can cause havoc in a building.

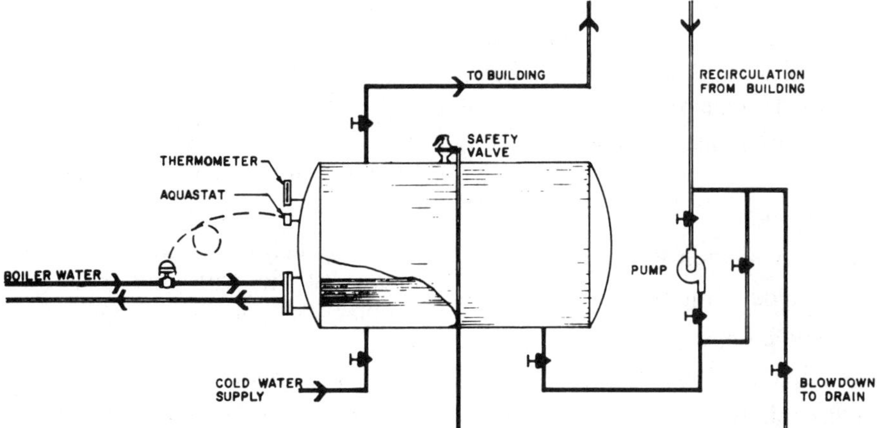

FIGURE 7-5 Heating and storing domestic hot water by using boiler water and a heat exchanger. To maintain a constant temperature of water and insure instant hot water in each apartment, the water is recirculated back to the tank and re-heated, if required. This tank is thermostatically controlled. To maintain the flow of water in the piping and remove loose scale from the piping, we have fitted a pipe which by-passes the circulation pump. Regularly, as often as necessary, the valve below the by-pass should be shut and all water flushed through the blow-down pipe to a drain. Shut down the recirculation pump while doing this. As soon as the blow-down is clear, the blow-down valve is shut and the valve to the system is opened. Start the recirculation pump. (Courtesy of Cadillac Fairview Corporation, Limited.)

It is imperative that we familiarize ourselves with the system, and that we have a piping plan which helps us locate all shut-off and recirculation valves quickly. Remember, when isolating a section of domestic hot water piping—shut both the supply and recirculation valves (Chapter Two, Figure 2-12). Tagging and charting will overcome this problem, and a copy of the plan should be included in the building profile.

GARBAGE ROOM STORAGE AND WASHDOWN

All garbage chutes must be washed down regularly. Most buildings have a washdown ring at the top of the chute. The procedure for washing them down is covered in Chapter Four. Hot water should also be available to wash down garbage rooms.

7-3 Plumbing Maintenance

AN OVERVIEW

Through the years, plumbing fixtures have gone through many stages of design. The key to plumbing repair is simple: replace each part with its exact duplicate. Learning the parts is more than half the task of repair. Take apart the fixtures and use the manufacturer's parts list to identify the components.

PLUMBING TOOLS FOR BUILDING OPERATORS

If we expect a building operator to carry out some plumbing maintenance, it is imperative that they have the proper tools and the proper sized parts, and that they are taught how to use them. The following tools are required for a building operator to carry out plumbing maintenance.

- Faucet seat wrench or Allen wrench to fit
- Socket wrench
- Plumber's wide adjusting pliers
- Long-needled point pliers
- Force-type plunger
- Closet Auger or "Snake"
- 8" adjustable wrench
- Faucet handle puller

IDENTIFYING THE PLUMBING FIXTURE PARTS

Making many common plumbing repairs isn't nearly as difficult as most people imagine. All it requires is reassembling a part by reversing the original process of removal. Take note of the parts as they are removed.

Wherever possible we will illustrate the positions of each part so that you can reassemble them by following the illustrations.

The size codings for "O" rings and washers (Figures 7-8, 7-9, and 7-12) will help you determine the size used in the building.

You simply place the "O" ring or washer over the matching illustration. By reading the size opposite the figure numbers, you can determine the outside dimension (O.D.), the inside dimension (I.D.), and the wall thickness.

This information should then be listed on the plumbing stock list (Figures 2-18, 2-19 and 2-20). Plumbing fixtures can be broken down into five classifications.

1. Kitchen Sink
2. Bathroom Basin
3. Tub and Shower Assembly
4. Water Closets
5. Urinal

All fixtures have

1. Handles (Figure 7-16)
2. Faucets and Center Sets (Figures 7-7)
3. Accessories (Figure 2-20)

Under each of the above categories, you should list the parts and their identifying manufacturer's number. (Figures 2-18, 2-19, and 2-20.)

To help control your parts inventory, so that you do not overstock any parts, we will show the maximum stock required *for every 50 suites in a building*. These figures will be shown in a column on the right side of the name of the parts. The re-order frequency will depend on how fast the parts are used.

A Typical Faucet

The cutaway illustration of a typical compression faucet (Figure 7-7) is almost self-explanatory. There are various styles of compression faucets and although the exterior appearance may vary, the principle of operation is basically the same.

Turning the faucet handle causes the threaded stem to be raised and lowered. At the base of this stem is a rubber washer. When the handle is turned to the "ON" position, the washer is lifted from the faucet seat, allowing water to flow freely through the faucet body and out through the spout. When the handle is returned to the "OFF" position, the stem is lowered, causing the washer to fit tightly against the seat and creating a water-tight seal.

A Leaking Faucet

The cause of a leaking faucet can be quickly traced to any of three common defects, all of which can be easily repaired by the building operating staff.

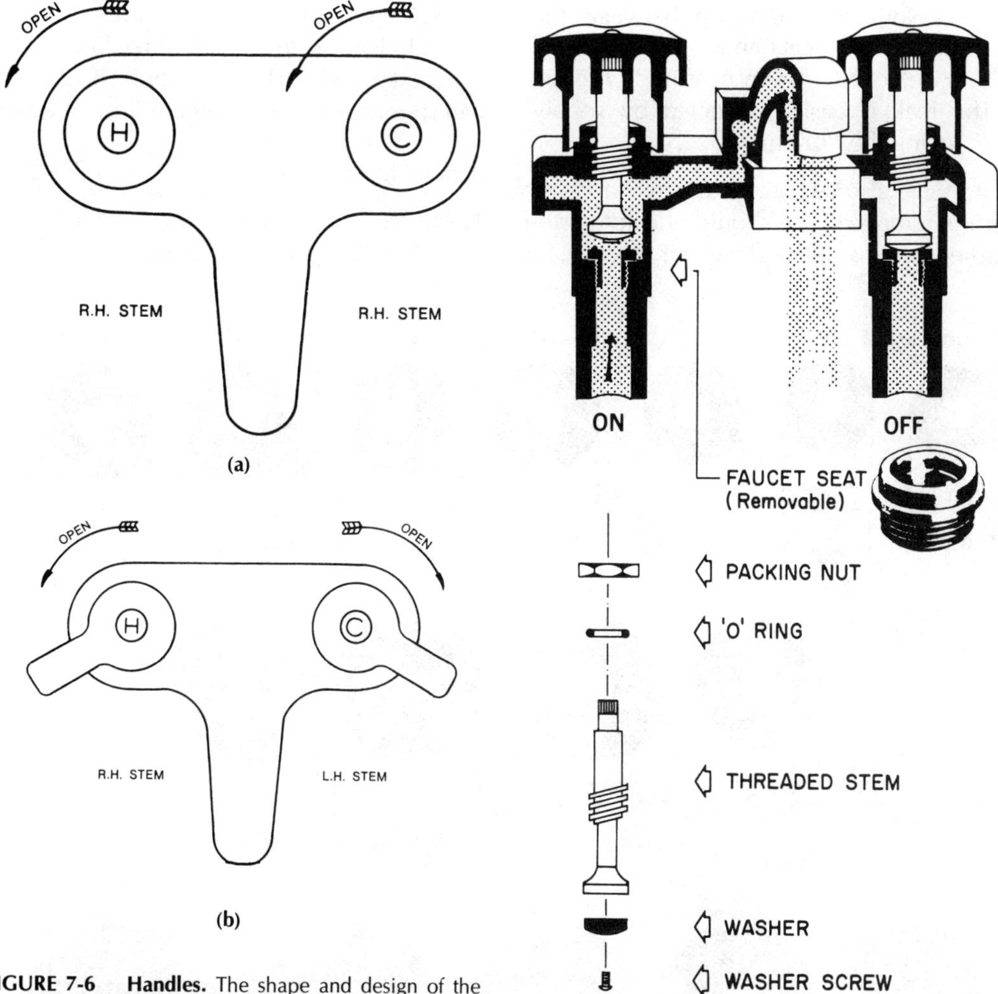

FIGURE 7-6 Handles. The shape and design of the handles not only give you the clue to the identity of the manufacturer, but also whether you require a different stem for the hot and cold faucets. Although most handles are round or fluted and use a right hand stem, a lever handle uses a right hand and a left hand stem. (a) Round or fluted handles (compression or self-closing type); (b) Lever handles (compression or self-closing type).

FIGURE 7-7 A typical faucet. (Courtesy of Cadillac Fairview Corporation, Limited.)

1. The most common cause of leaking is due to a worn washer. A worn out washer cannot maintain a watertight seal and should be immediately replaced.
2. If a leak persists after changing the washer, the fault is in the faucet seat. When the flat surface of the seat (against which the washer compresses) becomes rough, it will be impossible to prevent recurring leaks by merely installing new washers. Such roughness is caused by corrosion or by abrasion due to sand and rust particles becoming embedded in the washer. If the seat is removable, it is easily changed.

3. Leaks sometimes develop between the stem and the faucet handle. This is caused by a defective or even missing "O" ring. The leak is easily corrected by simply changing the "O" ring.

It should also be noted that when the valve stem is removed, one should check that the washer screw is still in place. It is possible for the valve screw to work itself loose and become lodged in the small water line within the faucet body. This condition, if ignored, will restrict or even cut off the flow of water.

Replacing the Washer

1. Shut off the water at the shut-off valve nearest the particular faucet.

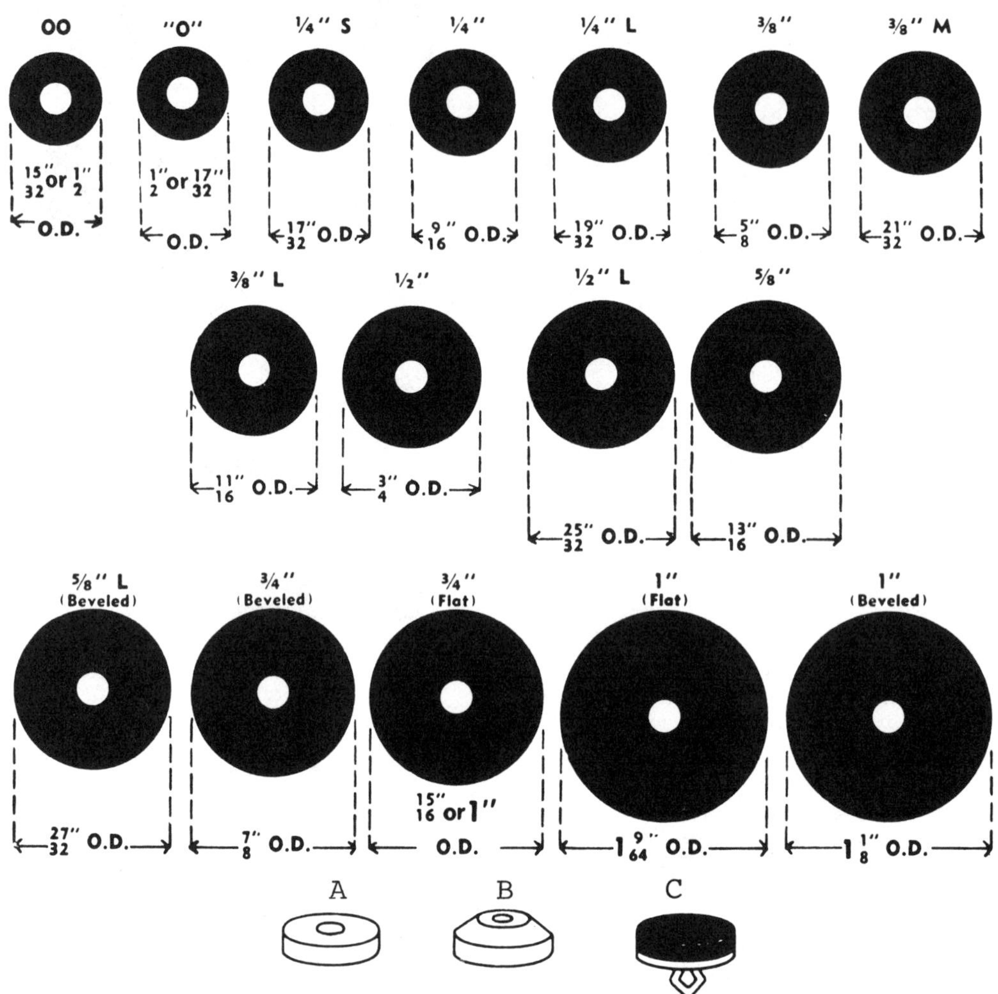

FIGURE 7-8 Washer sizing chart. If the rim around the bottom of the faucet stem is in good shape, you can use a type A washer, or a type B washer. If the stem is worn away, use a type C washer.

2. Disassemble the faucet handle, packing nut, packing, and spindle, in that order. You may have to set the handle back on the spindle and use it to unscrew and remove the spindle.
3. Remove the screw and the washer from the spindle. Clean out the cup and insert a new washer of the proper size.
4. Examine the seat of the faucet body. If it is nicked or rough, reface it with a seat dressing tool. If refacing fails, unscrew the faucet seat with an Allen wrench and replace it with another seat that is the same size.
5. Reassemble the faucet.

Replacing the Packing or "O" Ring

If a faucet leaks around the spindle when opened, new packing is required. To replace the packing, remove the handle, packing nut,

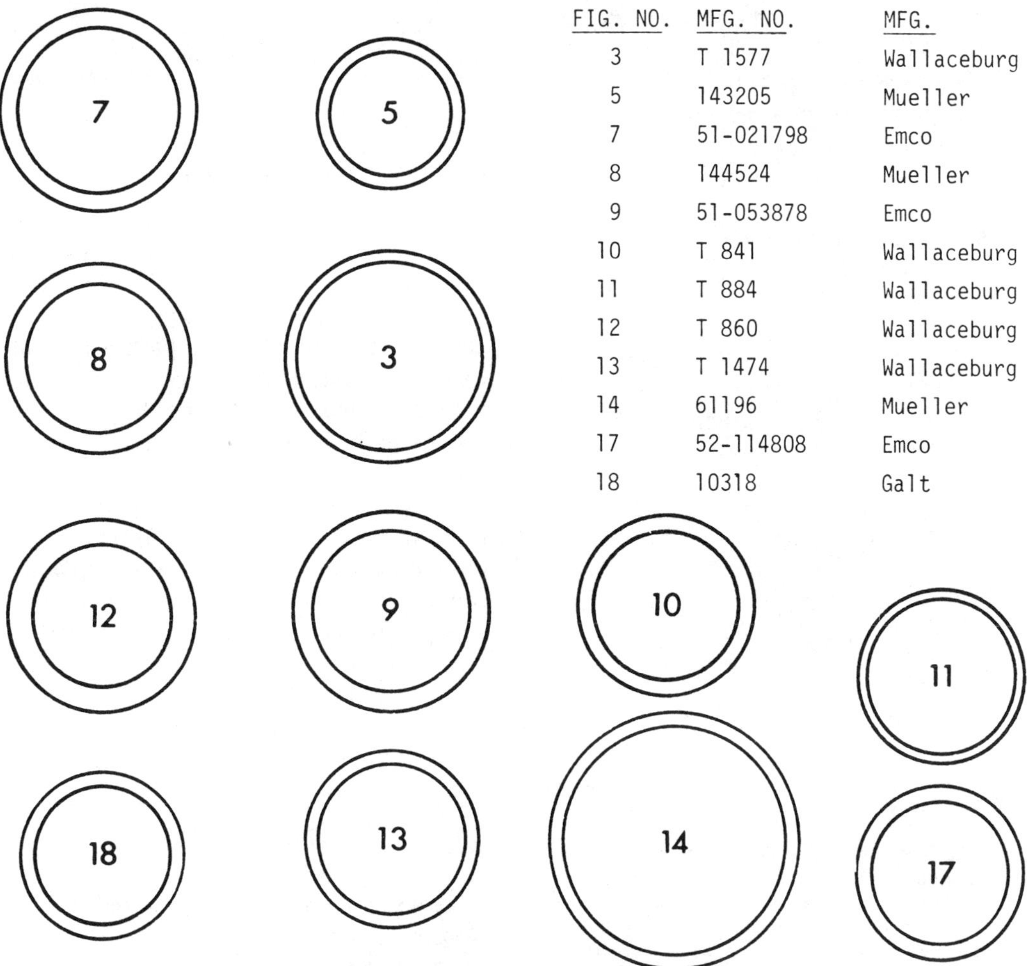

FIG. NO.	MFG. NO.	MFG.
3	T 1577	Wallaceburg
5	143205	Mueller
7	51-021798	Emco
8	144524	Mueller
9	51-053878	Emco
10	T 841	Wallaceburg
11	T 884	Wallaceburg
12	T 860	Wallaceburg
13	T 1474	Wallaceburg
14	61196	Mueller
17	52-114808	Emco
18	10318	Galt

FIGURE 7-9 Washer sizing chart, plastic or fiber.

and old packing, and install a new packing washer. Modern faucets often use an "O" ring instead of packing (Figure 7-12).

Replacing Faucets

After extended use and several repairs, some valves will no longer shut off tightly and must be replaced. When replacement is necessary, it may be advisable to upgrade the quality with equipment having better flow characteristics and longer-life design and materials. In some cases, ball valves deliver more water than globe valves. Some globe valves deliver more flow than others for identical pipe sizes. Y-pattern globe valves, in straight runs of pipe, have better flow characteristics than straight valve stops (see Chapter 11).

Tub and Shower Assembly

To replace shower and tub controls (Figure 7-13), shut off the water supply, open the control, and remove the handle, escutcheon plate, and faucet. Follow the same procedure as you would with other faucets (see Figure 7-7).

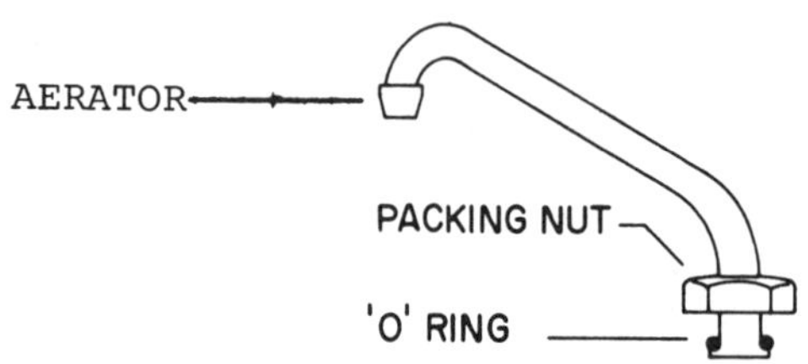

FIGURE 7-10 Kitchen swing spout. A leaking kitchen swing spout is not an uncommon occurrence and one that is easily remedied. Leaking is caused by a defective O ring seal beneath the packing nut, caused by one of the following: 1. The O ring is worn and should be replaced. 2. The O ring is missing. 3. The O ring is too small and should be replaced by an oversized O ring.

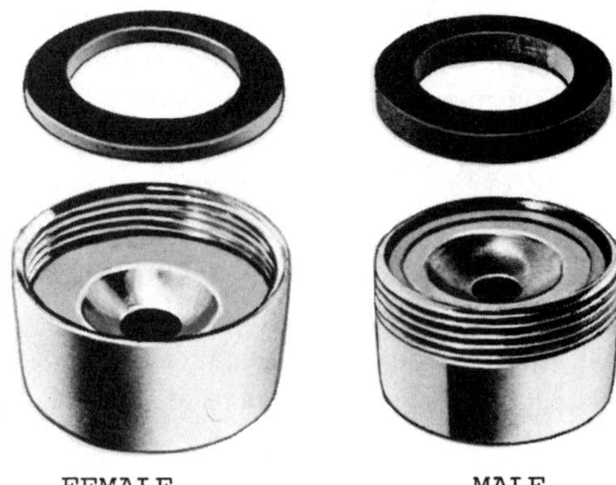

FIGURE 7-11 Aerators. Aerators stop the water from splashing and all spouts should be equipped with one. When servicing a fixture, check and clean the aerator.

Identifying the Faucets and Their Parts

Every plumbing fixture contains parts that were assembled in positions shown in each illustration in this chapter. To identify the manufacturer, note the design of the handle (see Figure 7-16). Obtain a parts list or catalogue from the manufacturer. Disassemble a typical kitchen and bathroom fixture and lay out the parts in sequence of disassembly. As you identify the parts, enter the manufacturer's part number opposite the appropriate part on the chart (Figure 2-18). Have spare parts on hand so that you are prepared to service the equipment. The folly of using cheap, irreplaceable equipment in a building, or of not using the same fixtures during a building's life, is easily understood. Use the "Kiss" principle. (The "Kiss" principle is to "Keep it simple—stupid.")

LEAKING PIPES

Leaks in pipes are usually caused by corrosion or damage to the pipe. Pipe damage is caused by freezing, vibration, water hammer, or by someone bumping the pipe.

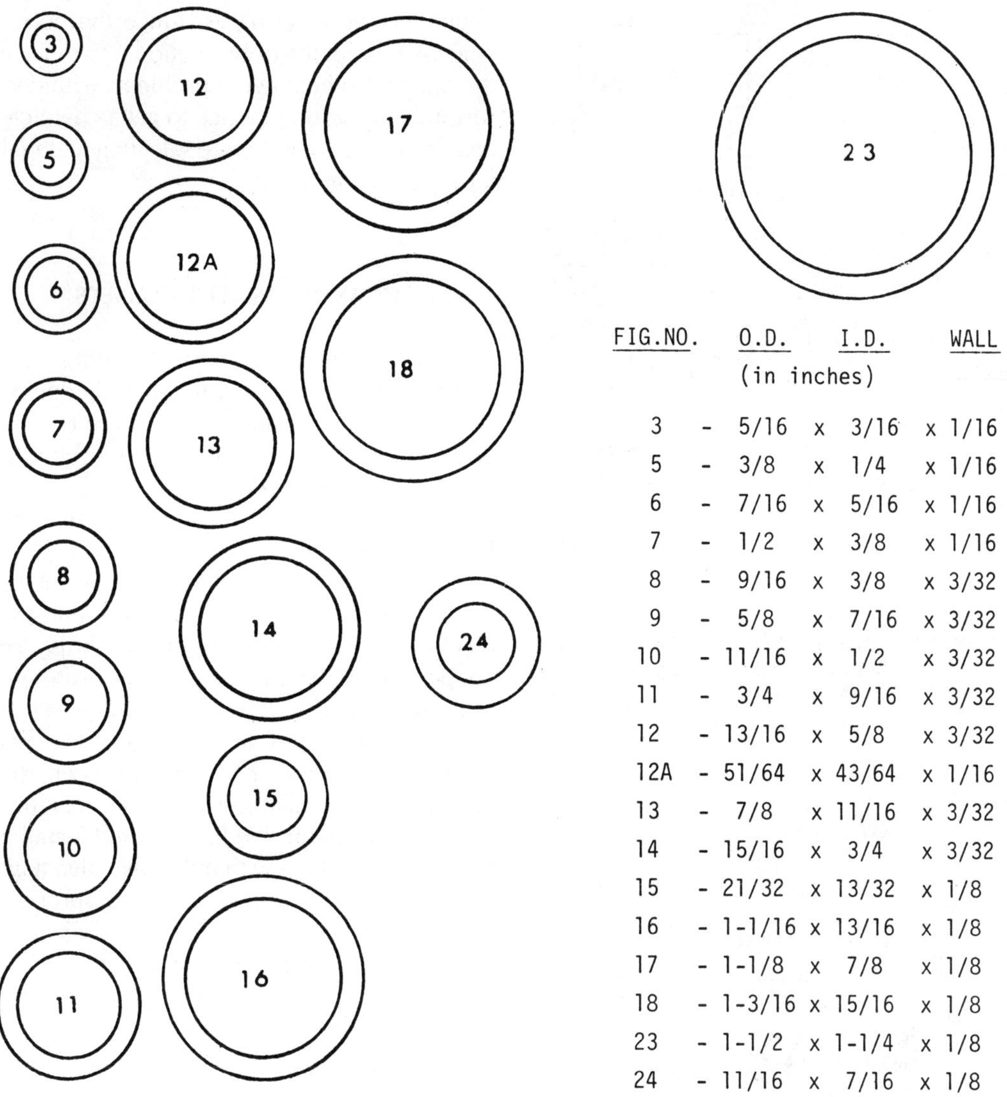

FIG.NO.	O.D.	I.D.	WALL
	(in inches)		
3	5/16	3/16	1/16
5	3/8	1/4	1/16
6	7/16	5/16	1/16
7	1/2	3/8	1/16
8	9/16	3/8	3/32
9	5/8	7/16	3/32
10	11/16	1/2	3/32
11	3/4	9/16	3/32
12	13/16	5/8	3/32
12A	51/64	43/64	1/16
13	7/8	11/16	3/32
14	15/16	3/4	3/32
15	21/32	13/32	1/8
16	1-1/16	13/16	1/8
17	1-1/8	7/8	1/8
18	1-3/16	15/16	1/8
23	1-1/2	1-1/4	1/8
24	11/16	7/16	1/8

FIGURE 7-12 O ring sizing chart.

CORROSION

Corrosion of piping is a serious problem (see Chapter One, Biological Fouling and Corrosion). Corrosion usually occurs, in varying degrees, along the entire length of pipe rather than at one particular point. However, corrosion sometimes shows up where the brass valve is joined with a galvanized pipe. Other exceptions would be where copper and steel are joined. Because the hot water is the electrolyte, dielectric connectors do not

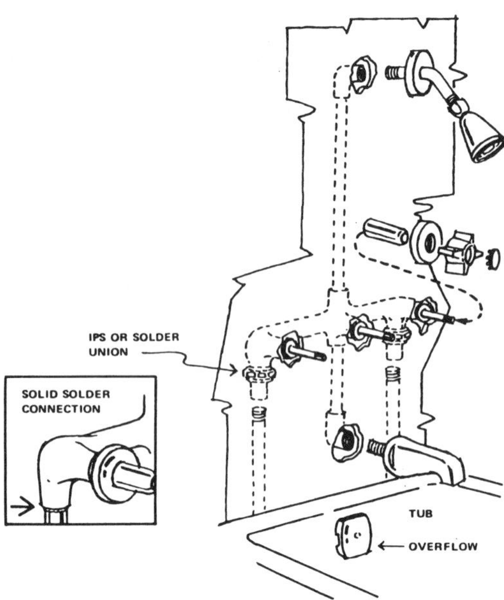

FIGURE 7-13 Tub and shower assembly. Shower fittings showing the water supply hookup. (Courtesy of Reston Publishing Company.)

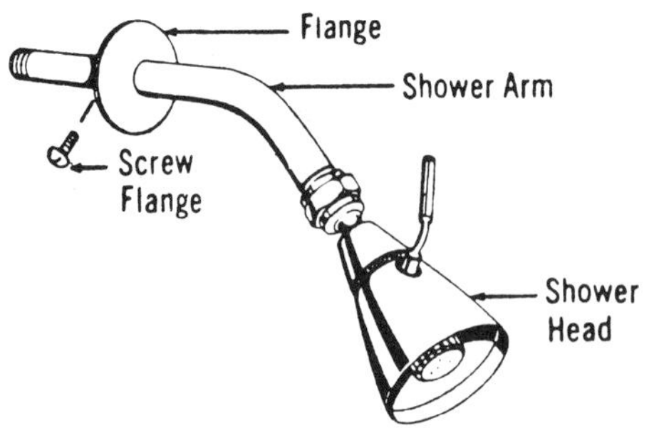

FIGURE 7-14 Shower heads. Problems with shower heads are usually solved by de-liming. It is wise to have spare heads for replacement purposes.

neutralize the electrolysis. Once the corrosion takes hold, the only solution is to replace the piping. To help avoid problems with corrosion, it is a good practice to get a chemical analysis of the water before selecting material for a plumbing system.

REPAIRING WATER CLOSETS

All water closet parts basically perform the same function. They vary in the design of the fixture and the flushing mechanism, but are enough alike that general repair instructions can be given for all designs.

Figure 7-18 shows a common type of flushing mechanism. Parts that usually require repair are the flush valve, the intake (float) valve, and the float. At one time the mechanisms were made out of brass or copper; today, we find many parts made out of plastic (Figure 7-23).

The rubber ball of the flush valve may get soft or out of shape and fail to seat properly. This causes the valve to leak. To correct, unscrew the ball from the lift wire and install a new one or replace with a flapper valve (Figure 7-20).

Replacing the Intake Valve Washer

A worn washer in the supply intake valve (Figure 7-22) will cause the valve to leak. To replace the washer

1. Shut off the water and drain the tank.
2. Unscrew the two thumbscrews that hold the levers and push out the levers.
3. Lift out the plunger, unscrew the cup on the bottom, and insert a new washer. The washer is made of material such as rubber or leather.

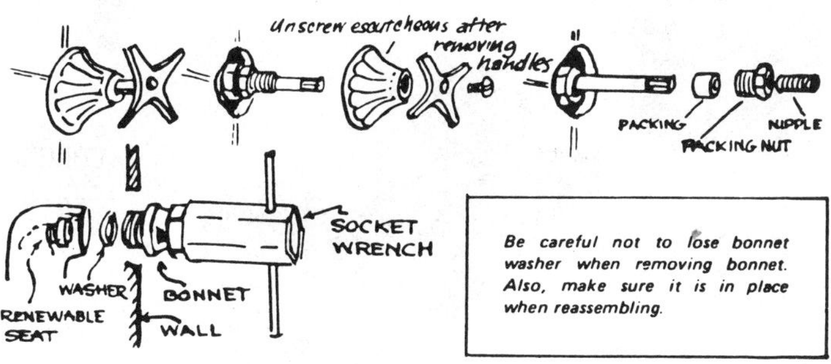

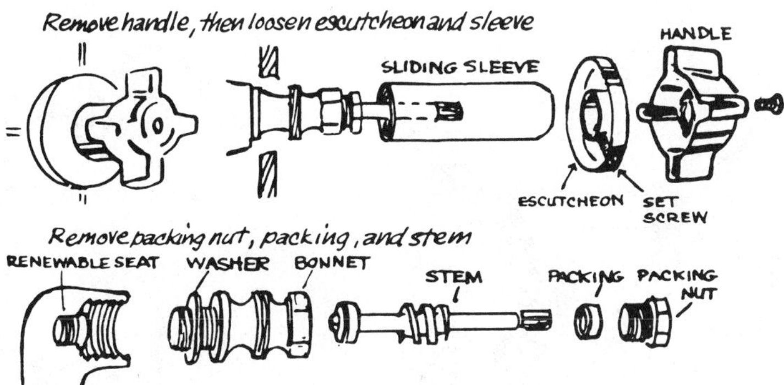

FIGURE 7-15 Removing a tub and shower faucet. (Courtesy of Reston Publishing Company.)

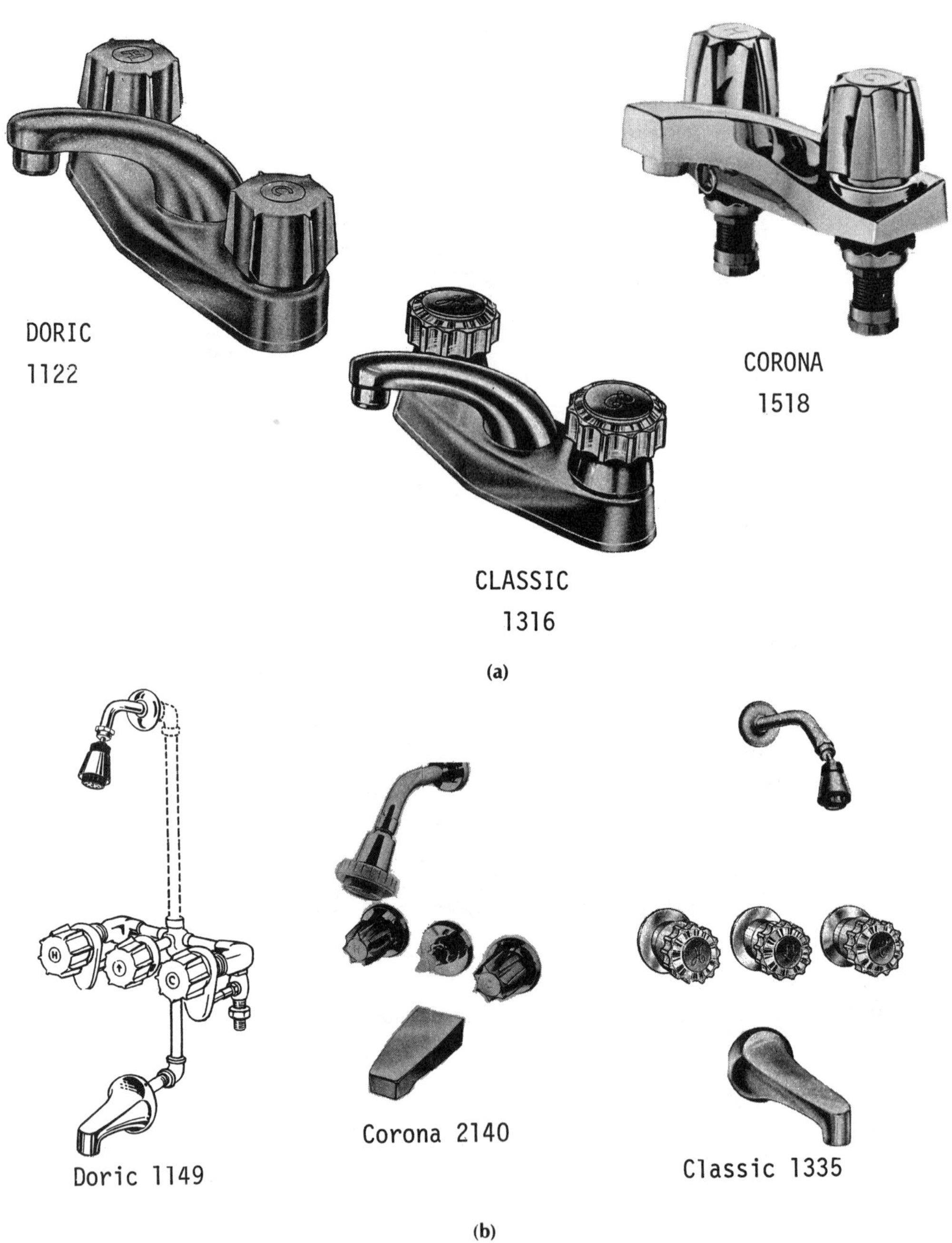

FIGURE 7-16 Identifying the faucets. (a) Emco handles; (b) Emco tub and shower handles. The make and model of the faucet parts can be identified by the shape of the handle. (Courtesy of Emco Limited.)

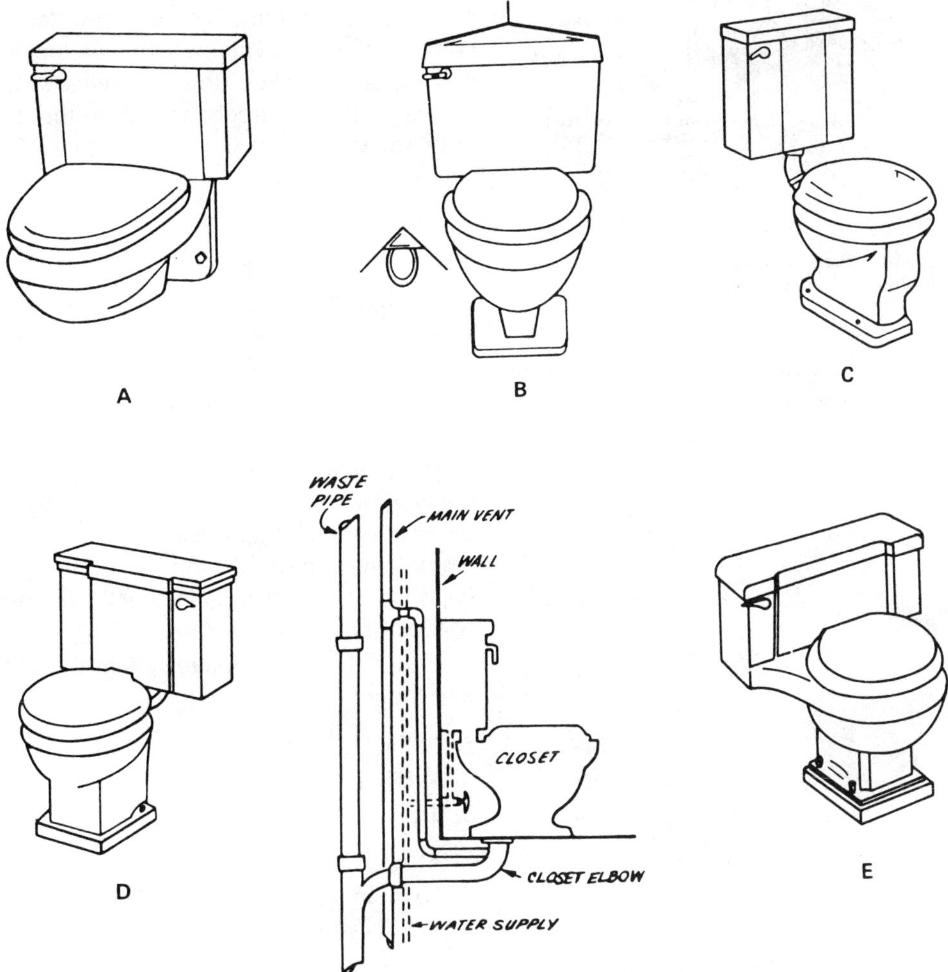

FIGURE 7-17 Toilet fixtures. Types of toilets: (a) Wall-hung—complete wall-hung toilets make it possible to clean the floor under the toilet. (b) Corner—The corner toilet is a space saver; note the triangular tank. (c) Two-piece with wall-hung tank. (d) Close-coupled tank and bowl—the tank, a separate unit, is attached to the bowl. (e) One-piece—One-piece toilets are neat in appearance and easy to clean, but are more expensive than two-piece models. (Courtesy of Reston Publishing Company.)

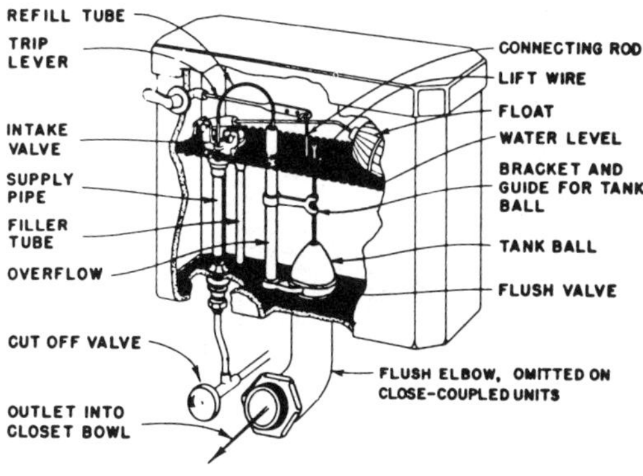

FIGURE 7-18 **Parts of a typical water closet.** (Courtesy of Reston Publishing Company.)

4. Examine the washer seat; if nicked or rough, it may need refacing. If the float-valve assembly is badly corroded, replace it.

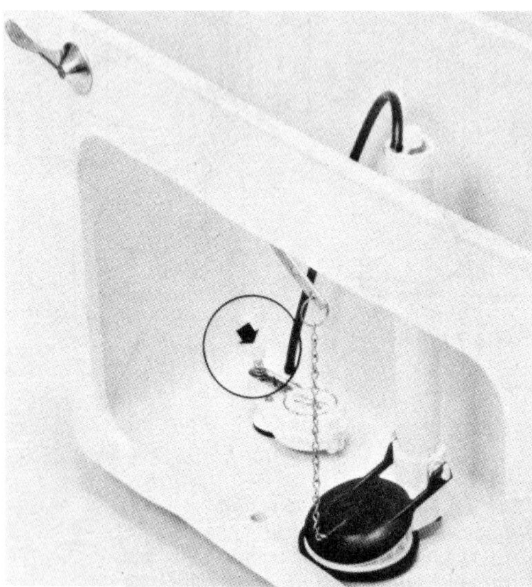

FIGURE 7-19 **The flapper valve.** This new type of flushing mechanism eliminates the ballcock. Water flow can be adjusted by turning the knob indicated by the arrow. (Courtesy of Reston Publishing Company.)

The Float Ball

The float ball may develop a leak and fail to rise to the proper position. (Correct water level is about 1 inch below the top of the overflow tube.) If the ball fails to rise, the intake valve will remain open and water will continue to flow. When working on the float ball, be careful to keep the rod aligned so that the ball will float freely and close the ballcock valve properly.

7-4 The Drainage System

AN OVERVIEW

The function of the drainage system is to safely move wastes, from a fixture to the sewer line, or to other means of disposal. The word "safely" must be emphasized since it is important to people's health that the drainage system functions correctly.

Generally, the drainage system is divided into the following:

1. The soil stack
2. Waste pipes
3. Traps
4. Vents

To help you understand the "Drainage System," Figure 7-24 shows a typical system.

IDENTIFYING THE SYSTEM'S MAIN COMPONENTS

Sanitary Sewer This shows that the main drain from the building is connected to the sanitary sewer beyond the property line for the building.

IF YOUR PRESENT UNIT LOOKS LIKE ONE OF THESE

TO INSURE PROPER SEATING, PRESS FLAPPER EVENLY DOWN ON VALVE SEAT BEFORE TIGHTENING COLLAR ON OVERFLOW TUBE.

1. FOR CONVENTIONAL BRASS VALVES

Remove old tank ball, wires and guide. Select right size collar for overflow tube. Slide collar to bottom of tube. Snap flapper arms onto collar. While pressing flapper evenly down on valve seat to adjust collar level tighten thumb screw securely. Attach chain to trip lever arm hole closest to handle allowing 1/2" of slack.

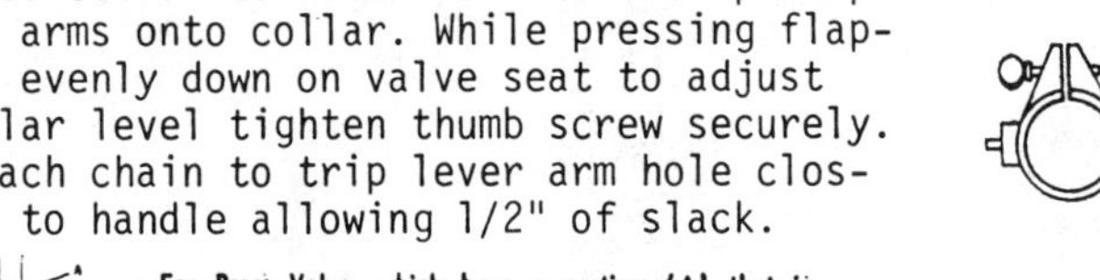

For Brass Valves which have a casting (A) that is on plane higher than the top of the valve seat (B) use the largest collar and tighten it around the casting (A) as shown.

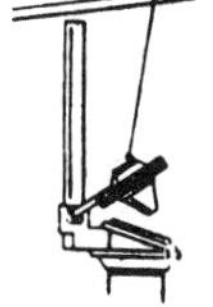

2. FOR PLASTIC VALVES WITH SOCKET HOLES

Remove old flapper and chain. Insert pivot pins in new flapper arms with pins facing inward. Spread arms and snap arms and pins into sockets that held old flapper. Attach chain to trip lever arm hole closest to handle allowing 1/2" of slack.

3. FOR PLASTIC VALVES WITH EARS

Remove old flapper and chain. Snap new flapper over ears. Attach chain to trip lever arm hole closest to handle allowing 1/2" of slack.

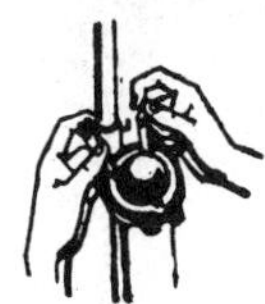

4. FOR CRANE BUILT-IN FLAPPER VALVES

Remove old flapper by unsnapping from base post. Take largest collar, spread open and slip wings over base post, one from each side; bring together, then tighten thumb screw securely at back. Snap new flapper over ears. Attach chain to trip lever arm hole closest to handle allowing 1/2" of slack.

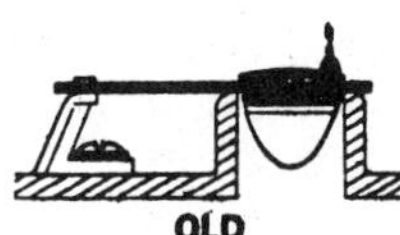

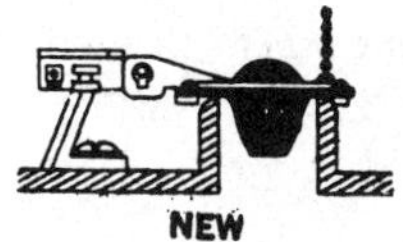

FIGURE 7-20 Installing the flapper valve. (Courtesy of the Crane Company.)

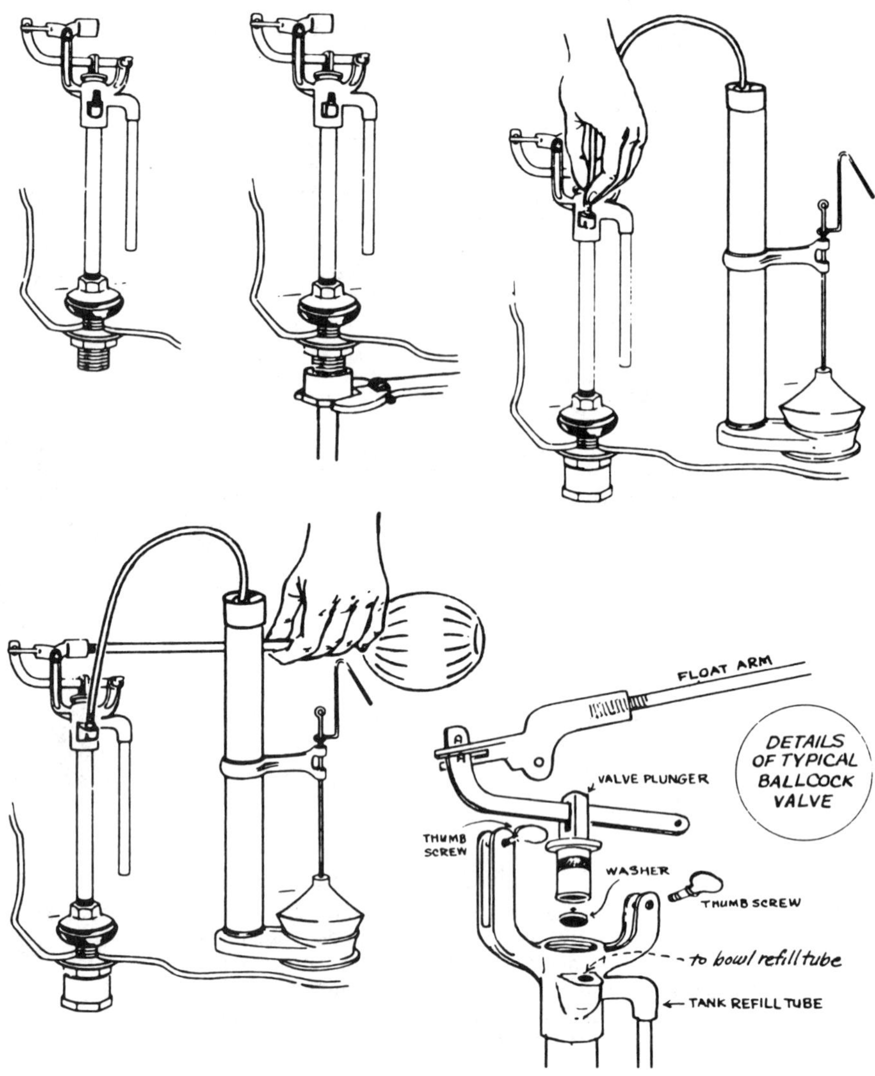

FIGURE 7-21 The water closet mechanism. These illustrations detail the actions involved in replacing the flushing mechanism. The parts of the ballcock valve are also shown. (Courtesy of Reston Publishing Company.)

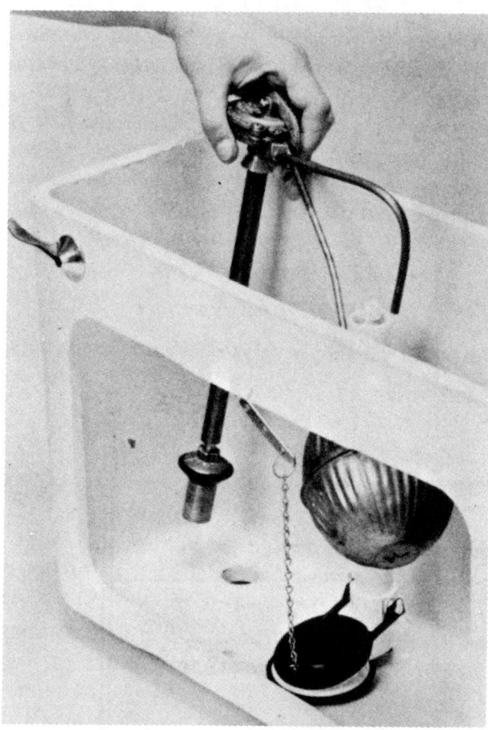

FIGURE 7-22 Removing the flushing mechanism. If necessary, the flushing mechanism can be easily removed by unscrewing it from the tank. (Courtesy of Reston Publishing Company.)

Vents

- Sanitary Sewer Vent
- Vent Stack
- Stack Vent

The vent is a pipe installed to equalize pressure between the fixture's trap and the waste pipe, and serves three purposes:

1. It permits water and waste to travel freely through the waste pipes.
2. It carries off dangerous sewer gases.
3. It prevents the back-up of wastes into a fixture located below another fixture that happens to be draining.

Generally, all vents are tied into the soil stack.

Building Trap The function of a trap is to provide a liquid seal between the fixture and the waste pipe. This seal prevents air from entering the waste pipe while liquid is flowing, and thus eliminates noise.

It also stops gas and unpleasant odors from entering the building or apartment from the sewer lines. Also note the traps installed under each fixture in the building.

Cleanouts If we expect the drainage system to function properly, it must be clear. Plugged drains can cause serious problems in any building. It is for this reason that the horizontal drains should be cleaned as often as required. The cleanouts should allow you to clean the lines both ways.

Main Stacks These are the main drains that run the height of the building and pick up all the waste from every plumbing fixture in the building. Unless the horizontal drains are kept clean, the main stacks will also eventually become plugged. This means that the wastes would not run out of the building and serious problems could result. These drains should be checked regularly and cleaned as often as necessary.

Auxiliary Stack Because of a problem with suds back-up in many buildings, the design engineers added an auxiliary stack that rises several floors in most buildings.

If suds are a problem, they are supposed to back up into this auxiliary stack. Some people believe that if the drains are cleaned regularly, the auxiliary stack may not be necessary. Funds for cleaning should be added into your expense schedules (Figure 7-41).

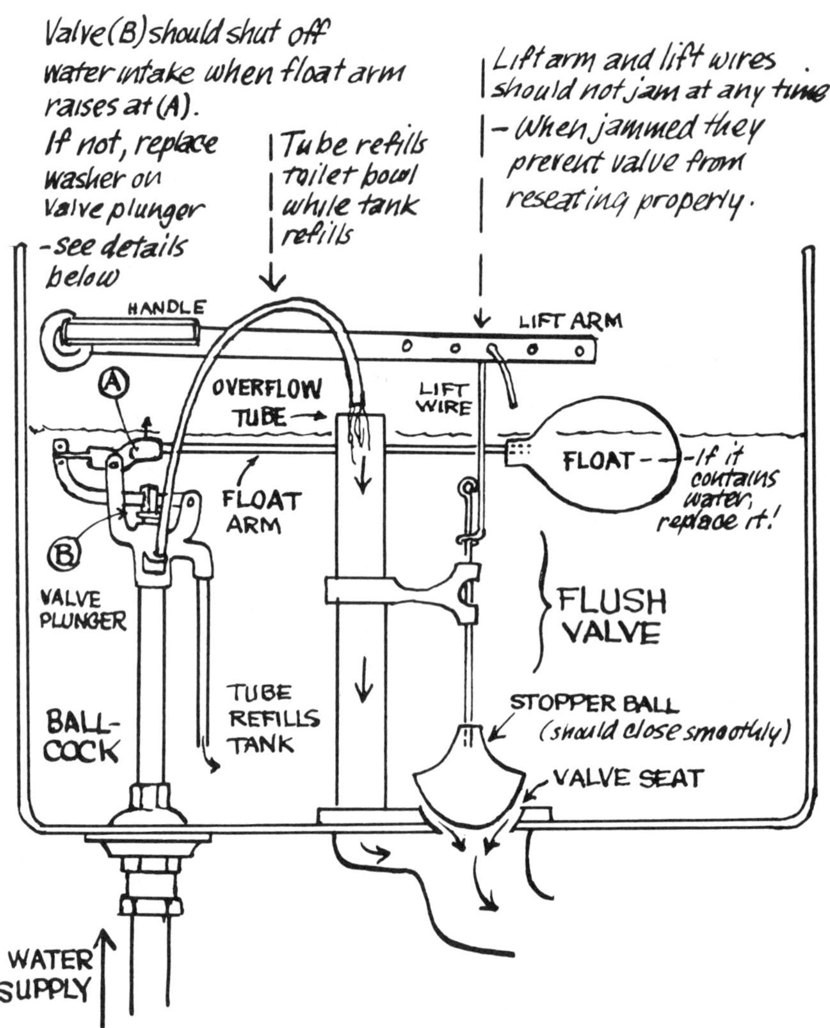

FIGURE 7-23 **Troubleshooting the toilet tank.** (Courtesy of Sterling Faucet Company.)

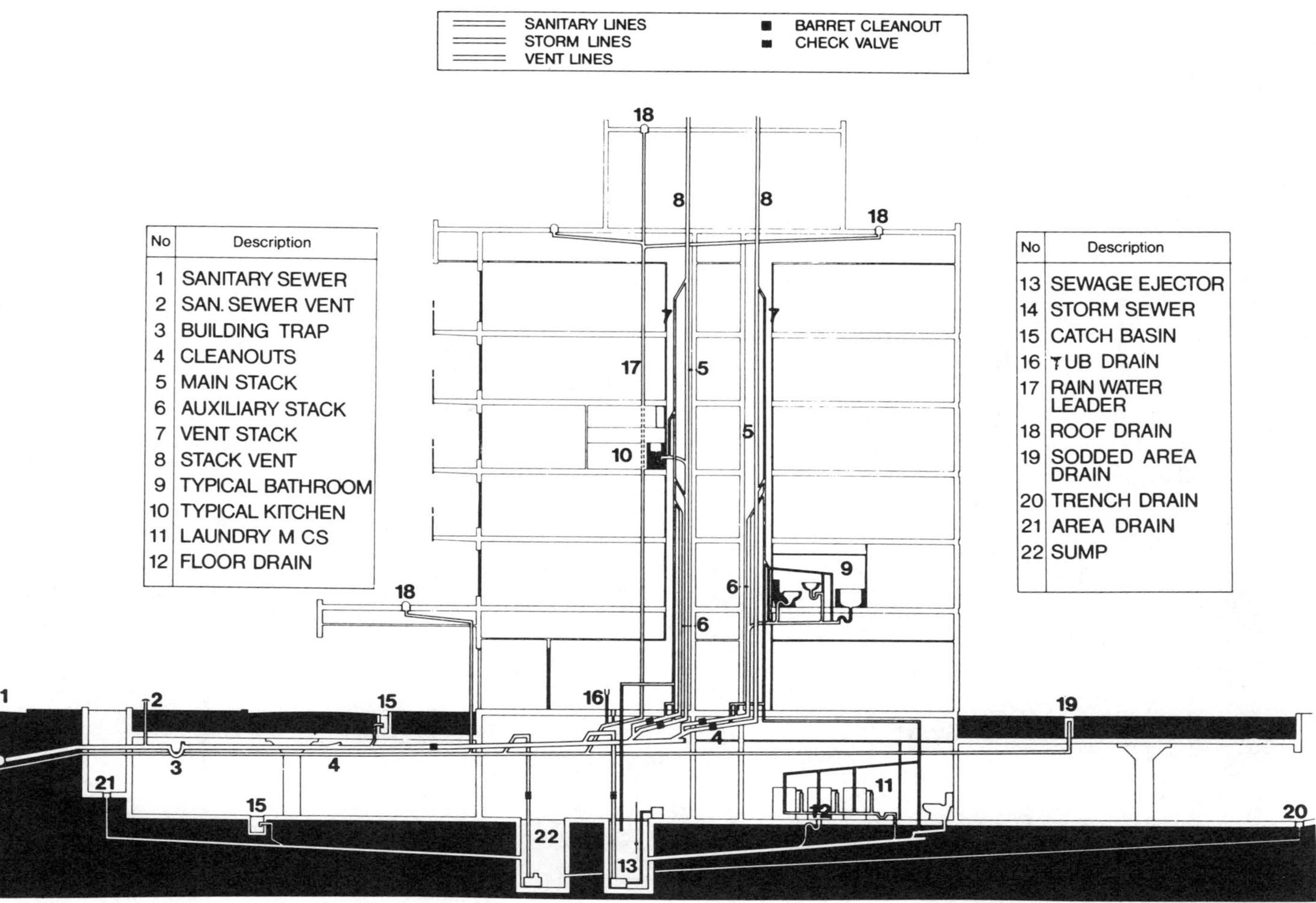

FIGURE 7-24 Typical drainage system in an apartment building. (Courtesy of Cadillac Fairview Corporation, Limited.)

Typical Bathroom This shows the drain detail for a typical bathroom and includes the venting of the toilet, sink, and bathtub.

Typical Kitchen This shows the drain and vent detail for the kitchen sink.

Laundry Machines This shows the drains, vents, and traps for the laundry room. Please note that because this room is lower than the main drain, the waste is gathered in a sump (22) and the sewage ejector pump (13) raises this to the main drain.

Floor Drains These are generally located in boiler rooms, locker rooms, and laundry rooms and also drain into a sump pit. Water should be added to these drains from time to time to maintain a water seal.

Storm Sewer The tub drain, catch basin, rainwater leader, roof drain, sodded area

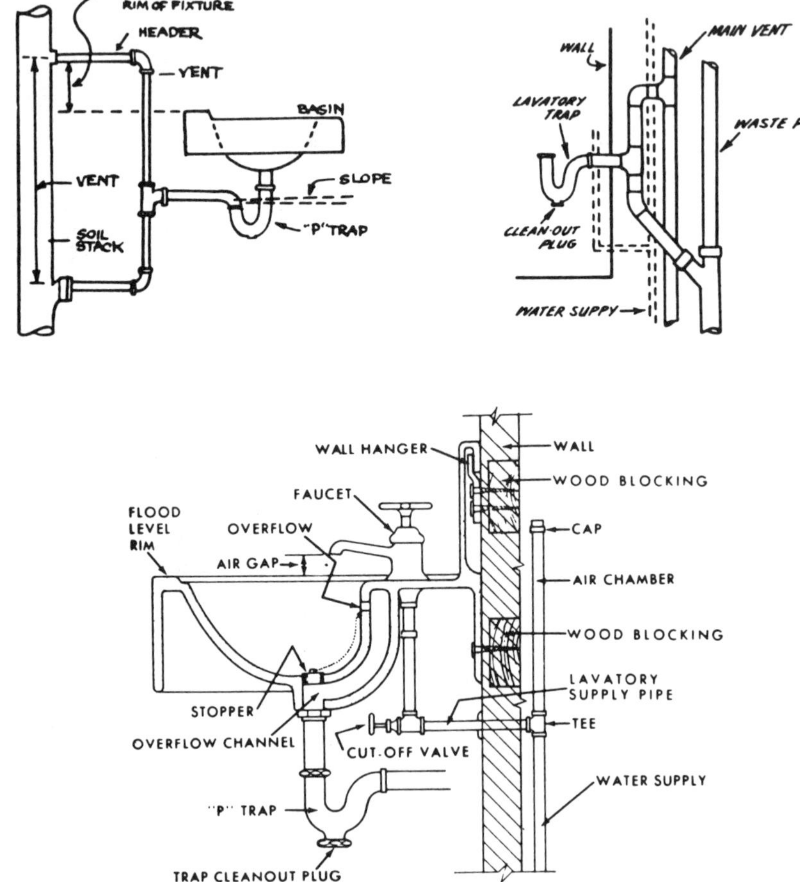

FIGURE 7-25 Tying the lavatories into the system. Every fixture is connected either to the main stack, or to smaller stacks that project through the roof. The entire system is open to the outside air. The stack itself serves a double purpose: the bottom section below the fixture is a waste line, and the portion above is a vent. (Courtesy of Reston Publishing Company.)

drain, trench drain, and area drains all run into the storm sewer.

All these drains must be kept clean in order to avoid flooding and funds must be included in the budget expense schedules for cleaning them. (Figure 7-41).

Sump This pit is scheduled for cleaning at least once a year along with the trench drains. The maintenance of the pumps and sewage ejector is also carried out at this time (see Chapter 11, Mechanical Services). The funds for this would also be included in the budget expense schedules (Figure 7-41).

CLEANING CLOGGED DRAINS

Drains may become clogged by objects being dropped into them or by the accumulation of hair, grease, dirt, or other matter. If the obstruction is in a fixture trap, usually the trap can be removed and cleared. If the obstruction is elsewhere in the pipe, professionals will need to clear the drain.

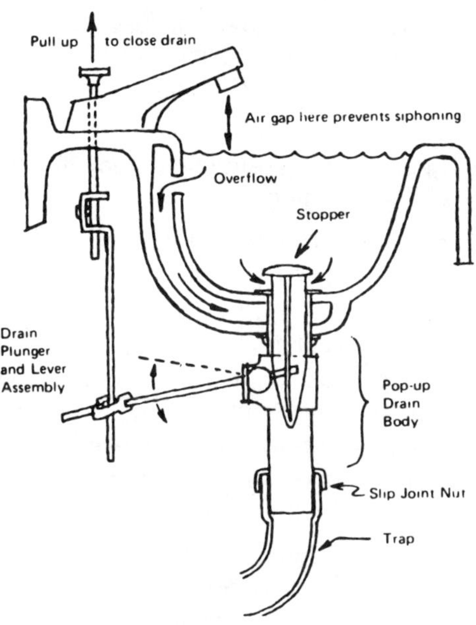

FIGURE 7-26 Operation of a pop-up drain. (Courtesy of Reston Publishing Company.)

CLOGGED TOILETS

Clogged toilets are one of the most common plumbing problems. Before calling the plumber, a plunger should be used in an attempt to clear the blockage. The cup of the plunger should be covered with water (fill the bowl almost to the brim) while doing this.

If the plunger fails, use a closet auger, which will usually open the drain. Start the auger into the bowl and crank clockwise until the obstruction is reached, then pull back, cranking in the same direction.

*Removing the Bowl**

1. Shut off the water.
2. Empty the tank and bowl by siphoning or sponging out the water.
3. Disconnect the water pipes to the tank.
4. Disconnect the tank from the bowl if the water closet is a two-piece unit.
5. Remove the seat and cover from the bowl.
6. Carefully pry loose the bolt covers and remove the bolts holding the bowl to the floor flange. Jar the bowl enough to break the seal at the bottom. Set the bowl upside down on something that will not chip or break it.

*Although we have included the step-by-step removal of the toilet bowl in the text, it is usually advisable to call the plumber when a problem cannot be solved with a plunger or a closet auger.

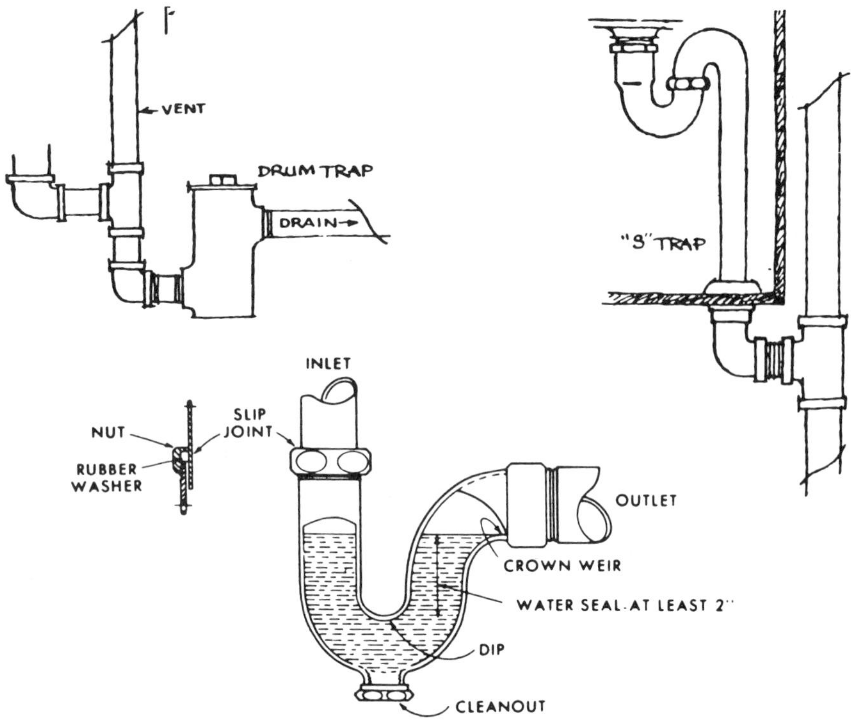

FIGURE 7-27 Three kinds of traps. As a safety measure against vermin and gases backing up all fixtures are equipped with traps directly under them. Toilets have built-in traps. The most common types are P and S traps. (Courtesy of Reston Publishing Company.)

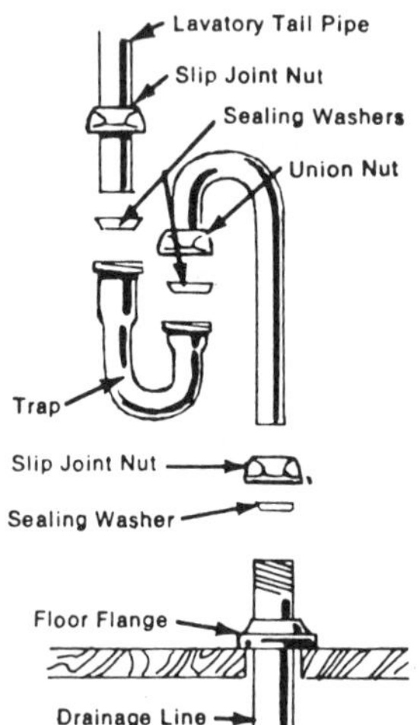

FIGURE 7-28 Servicing the drain line. (Courtesy of Reston Publishing Company.)

7. Remove the obstruction from the discharge opening.
8. Place a new wax seal around the bowl horn and press into place.
9. Set the bowl in place and press it down firmly. Install the bolts that hold it to the floor flange. Draw the bolts up snugly, but not too tightly, or the bowl may break. The bowl must be level; keep a level on it while drawing up the bolts. Replace the bolt covers.
10. Install the tank and connect the water pipes. It is advisable to replace all gaskets, after first cleaning the surfaces thoroughly.
11. Test for leaks by flushing a few times.
12. Install the seat and cover.

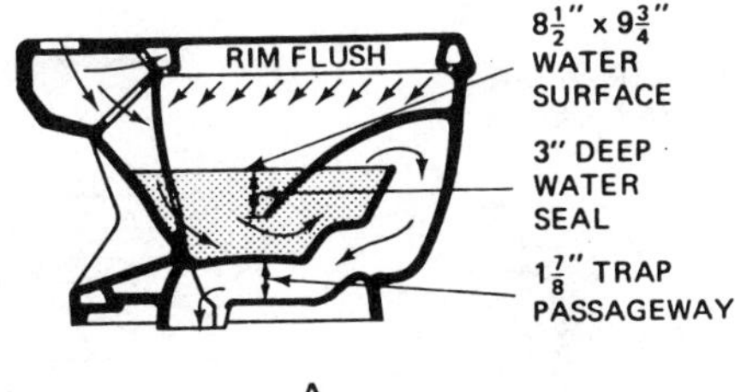

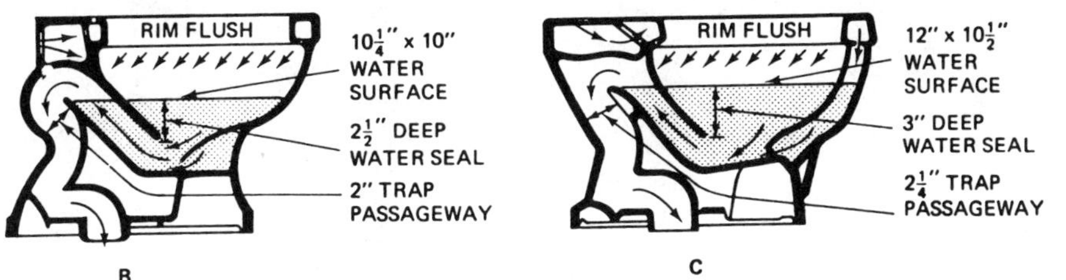

FIGURE 7-29 Water closet flush designs. Flushing actions of toilets: (a) washdown; (b) reverse trap; (c) siphon jet. (Courtesy of Reston Publishing Company.)

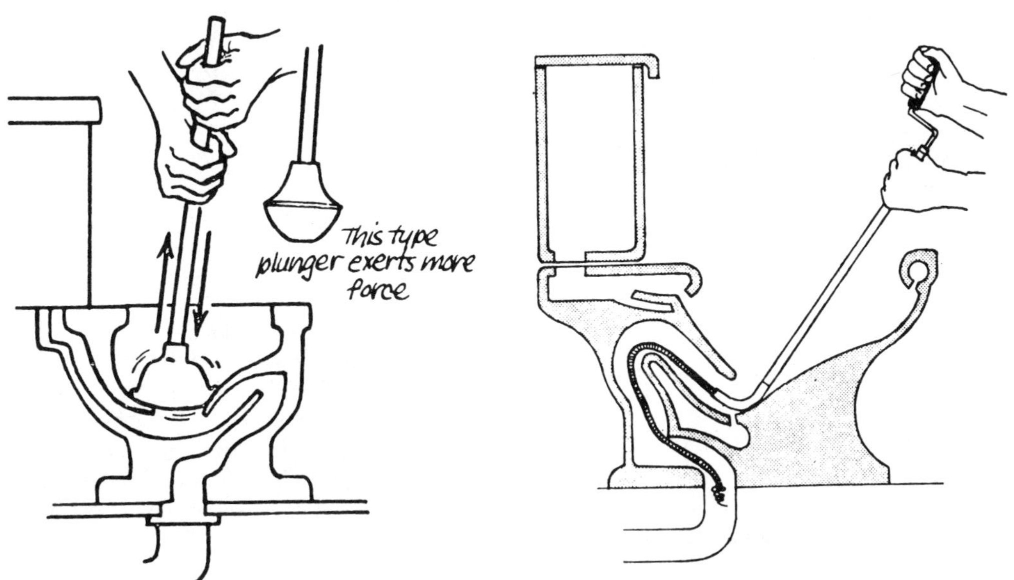

FIGURE 7-30 How to use the plunger. (Courtesy of Sterling Faucet Company.)

FIGURE 7-31 How to use the closet auger. (Courtesy of Sterling Faucet Company.)

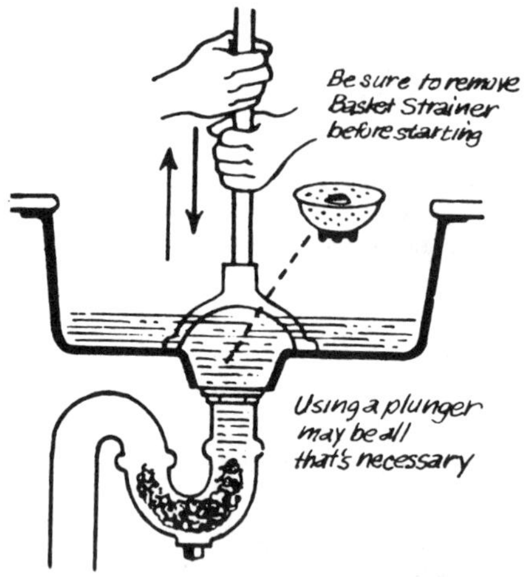

FIGURE 7-32 **Clearing a clogged basin: step 1.** (Courtesy of Sterling Faucet Company.)

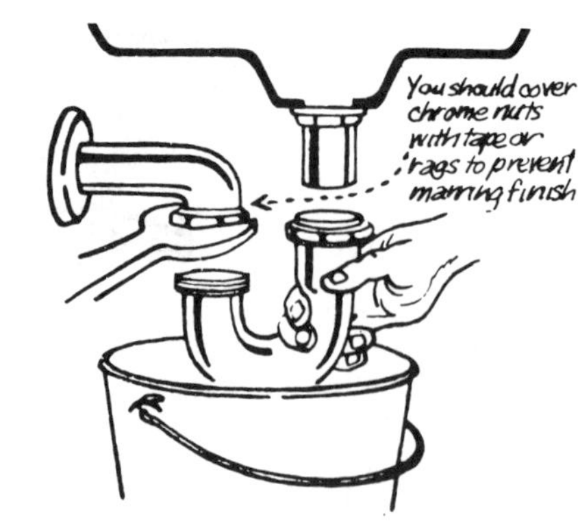

FIGURE 7-34 **Clearing a clogged basin: step 3.** (Courtesy of Sterling Faucet Company.)

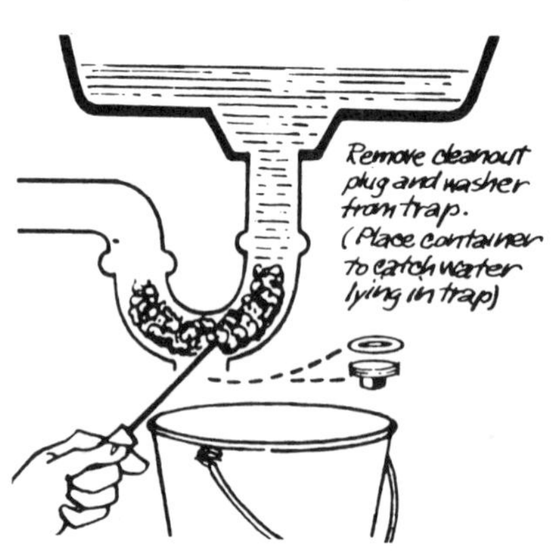

FIGURE 7-33 **Clearing a clogged basin: step 2.** (Courtesy of Sterling Faucet Company.)

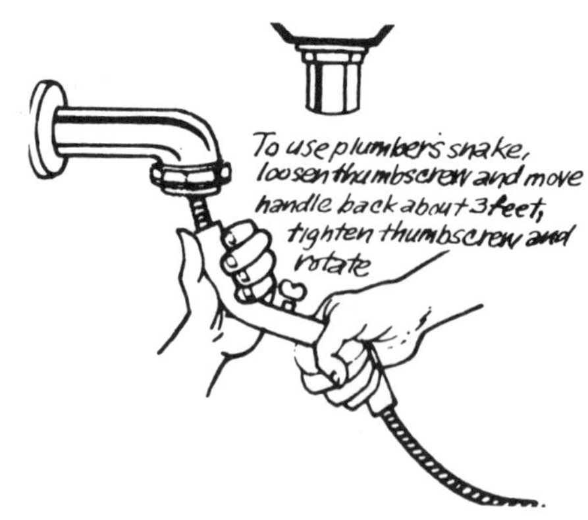

FIGURE 7-35 **Clearing a clogged basin: step 4.** (Courtesy of Sterling Faucet Company.)

CLOGGED BASIN AND SINK DRAINS

If the drain is not completely clogged, let hot water run for five to ten minutes; this may be all that is required. If the drain is completely clogged, use a suction cup plunger, making sure there is enough water in the sink to provide a seal. If the basin has an overflow, make sure to plug the opening before plunging (Figure 7-32). If the plunger does not clear the drain, remove the cleanout plug as shown in Figure 7-33. If there is no plug, remove the trap (Figure 7-34). If these actions are not successful, use an auger (Figure 7-35).

GREASE TRAPS

Grease traps are required in waste pipes from sinks and fixtures where greasy foods are prepared, and where dishes are washed that contained greasy foods. Grease traps are generally installed in restaurants, hotels, schools, laboratories, hospitals, and all institutional buildings.

These are installed in the waste pipe for the purpose of separating grease from the liquid retaining the grease. The construction of the trap permits sufficient cooling of the liquid to precipitate some grease from solution and to permit suspended grease to rise to the top of the trap where the grease is held.

STORM WATER DRAINAGE

Storm water systems convey precipitation from roofs, foundation walls, and areas adjacent to buildings to the storm sewer. In all cases, the storm water plumbing and sanitary plumbing are run separately inside the building. Outside the building, some systems have combined sanitary and drainage sewers. Most municipalities now have separate storm water sewers, and where they do, the two systems are not interconnected.

Storm water plumbing consists of the drain in the collection area, leaders, which usually run vertically and are called downspouts, and the storm drain itself, which is compar-

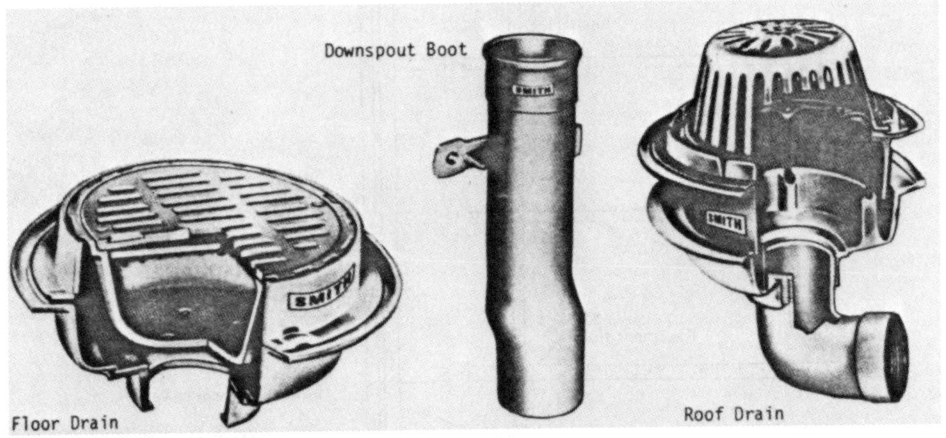

FIGURE 7-36 Drainage fittings. Roof gutters, storm drains, and leaders are sized from the projected area being drained and the maximum rate at which the rain is expected to fall. For most areas the sizing tables are calculated for a maximum rainfall of 4 in. per hour. The projected area equals the ground square footage the building occupies plus any roof overhang. It is independent of the pitch of the roof. Where the roof steps and is on two levels, it is customary also to add in 50 percent of the vertical wall connecting the two levels, although the validity of this calculation has been questioned. It is based upon the assumption that a driving rain will strike the wall portion and accumulate on the lower roof, but observations of accumulations along sidewalks adjoining large buildings that pose a similar circumstance do not bear this out. (Courtesy of Reston Publishing Company.)

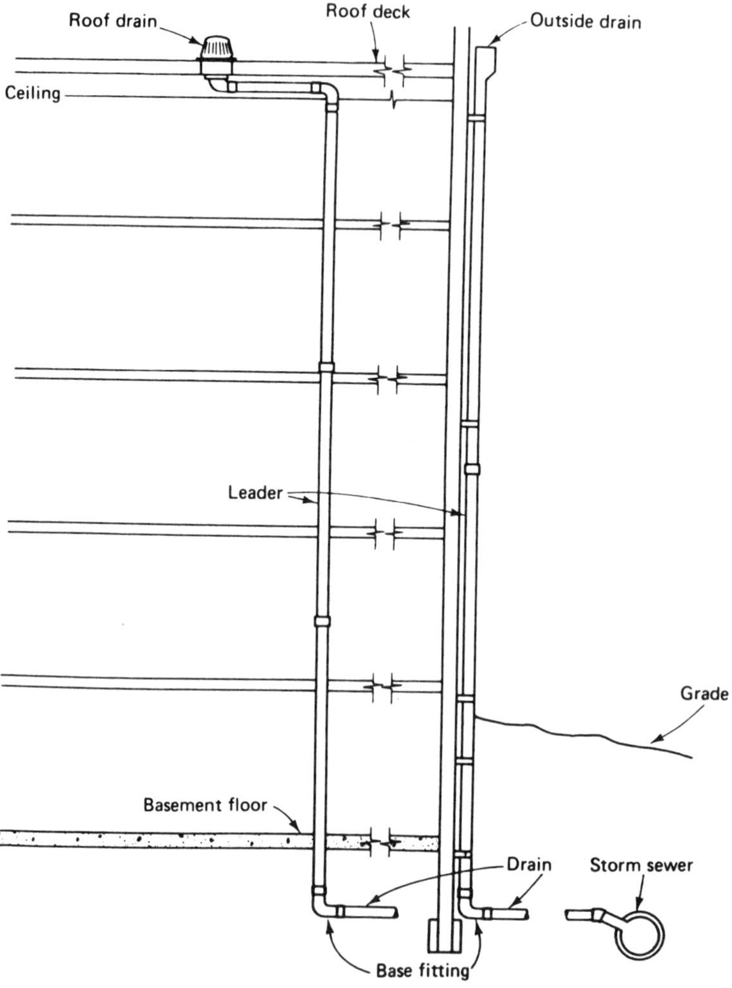

FIGURE 7-37 Inside and outside roof drain system. When the system is mounted to the outside of the building, the downspout is attached to the building and terminates at ground level in the storm water system. Above ground the outside leader can be pipe, sheet metal, or plastic, but below grade level either cast iron or other material that conforms to the code in the local jurisdiction must be used. (Courtesy of Reston Publishing Company.)

able to the horizontal building drain in sanitary systems.

7-5 The Swimming Pool

THE MAJOR COMPONENTS

1. The pool shell.
2. The functional equipment in and around the pool such as ladders, underwater lights, life rings, and diving boards.
3. The recirculation system for filtering, heating where installed, and chemical treatment of pool water.
4. The maintenance equipment for removing dirt and debris from pool surface, walls, and floors.

SAFETY EQUIPMENT

- Life rings and life hook(s).
- Lifeguard chair(s).
- Rope floats, cup anchors, and rope hooks for safety lines.
- Ground fault detectors for underground lights.

RECIRCULATION SYSTEM

The recirculation system includes all the pipes, fittings, and equipment necessary for filtering, heating, and chemically treating the pool water.

With pool water treatment, the same water recirculates continually, thus providing opportunity for the removal of suspended dirt, the destruction of organisms, and the maintenance of a comfortable temperature. Comfortable temperature means something different to everyone who swims. However, for health and chemical reasons, the water temperature should not exceed 78°F. At the same time, the water is subject to continual recontamination by leaves, seeds, algae, bacteria, hair, dead skin, lint, cosmetic oils, food, clay, sand, and silt.

The components of the recirculation system perform as follows:

The main drain is located at the deepest point of the pool on the end of the suction piping from the filter pump. It draws water from the bottom of the pool where dirt accumulates and permits complete drainage of the pool for maintenance purposes. It often incorporates a Hydro-Relief Valve for admitting ground water to an empty pool to prevent the shell from floating should the ground water rise above the bottom of the pool.

An automatic skimmer is mounted in the pool wall at water level and connects to a branch of the suction piping from the filter pump. *Its purpose is to promote surface flow across the pool*. Besides drawing in the water that requires most treatment because of exposure to sun, wind, and rain, it also removes floating dust and debris, leaves, and oil films before they can accumulate on floors and walls.

The inlet fitting returns the filtered water to the pool.

THE FILTRATION AND HEATING SYSTEM

THE FILTER

The filter removes insoluble, suspended matter from the recirculated water. As the dirt accumulates within the filter, the filter pump will not maintain the required rate of flow against the increased resistance. Conse-

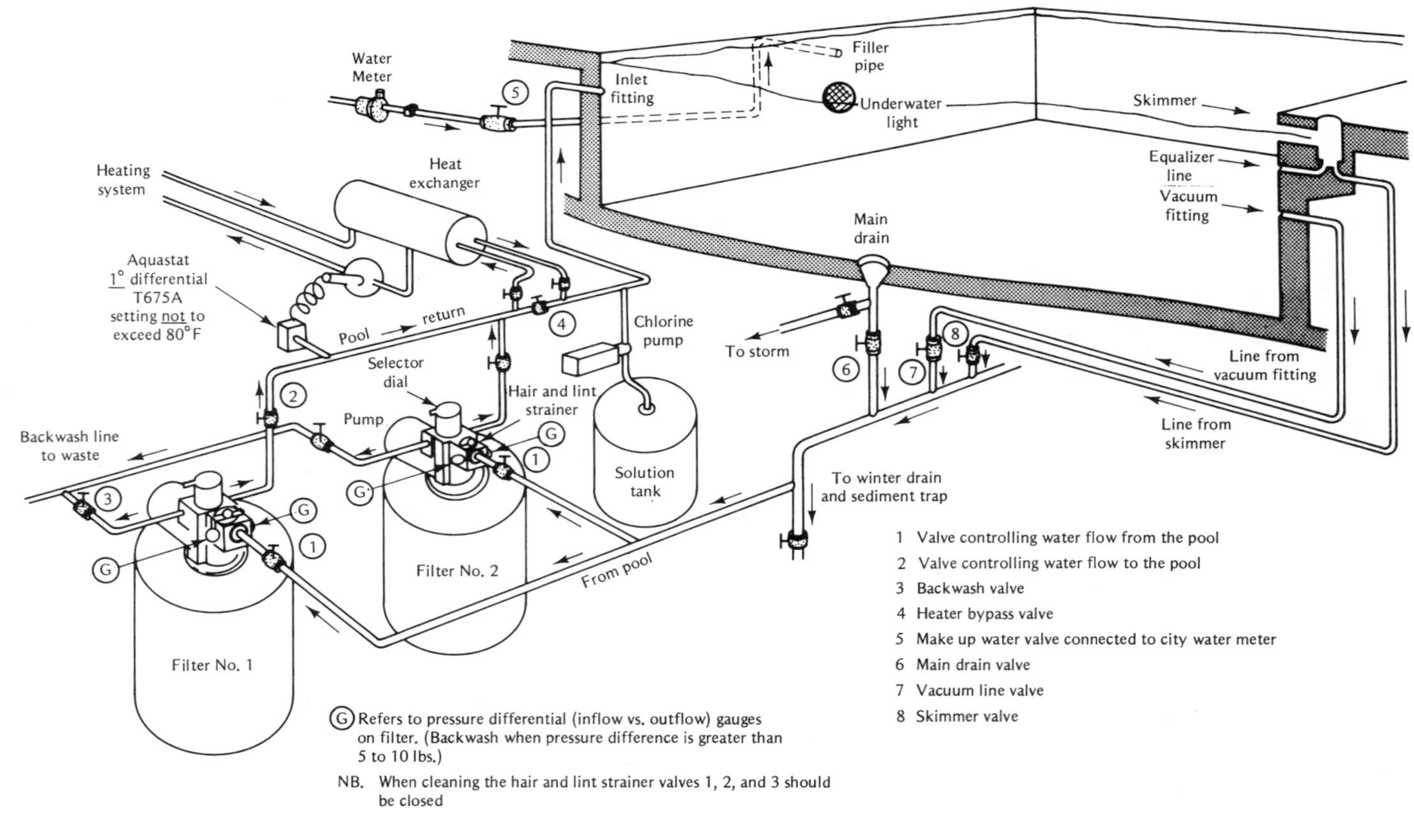

FIGURE 7-38 Typical swimming pool piping, filtering, and heating schematic.

quently, the filter requires regular cleaning or backwashing to maintain its efficiency.

FILTER PUMP

A self-priming pump, mounted at or above deck level, is capable of exhausting air from the suction system and raising water from the pool to establish and maintain operation. It can also operate the vacuum cleaner.

Most filter pumps have mechanical shaft seals, for which treated water provides an ideal application. A mechanical shaft seal requires neither attention nor adjustment; nor does it leak or overload the motor. When a seal fails, it must be replaced by a new one.

Some pumps incorporate a check valve in front of the hair and lint strainer.

Where the pump is above pool water level, the check valve prevents water draining from the suction pipe when the hair and lint strainer is opened. In addition to the valve in the suction line, the use of a gate valve in the pool return line is necessary to prevent the hair and lint strainer from emptying because of siphon action through the filter. This use of valves ensures a quick return to service because the system remains full of water so that repriming is unnecessary.

Where the pump is below pool water level, a check valve is ineffective. Gate valves in the suction and pool return lines are essential to prevent a flood in the filter pit when the hair and lint strainer is opened.

POOL OPERATING INSTRUCTIONS

Water filtration is a mechanical process that removes suspended particles and keeps the water clear to ensure safety and to look inviting to the bathers.

This is a general outline designed for Jacuzzi filters; there will be variations in all operating procedures where Swimquip Rapid Sand Filters are installed and a completely different technique is required for Diatomaceous Earth Filters. These variations should be explained to the individuals assigned to these pools.

Report all mechanical malfunctioning immediately to management. Do not allow minor problems to deteriorate into major problems.

Check Daily

- All valves for leaks.
- All bolts on filter unit for snug fit.
- Variations in the sounds of the electric motors.
- Water level in the pool—is it losing any water?
- Is the filter keeping the water sufficiently clear?
- Ground fault detector.
- Where a heater is installed, check its operation. Know whether it is manually controlled or whether it is automatically covered by a thermostat.

Operation of Equipment

The operating procedures should be carried out DAILY after the pool is vacuumed each morning. When the pool is heavily used during the day, the filters will have to be backwashed several times, and again in the evening.

Cleaning the Hair and Lint Strainer

Hair and lint strainers are provided in the skimmer(s) and at the inlet of the filter pump. They catch hair and large particles that would otherwise accumulate inside the system and clog pump, piping, or filter. *Emptying the hair and lint strainers is part of the daily mainte-*

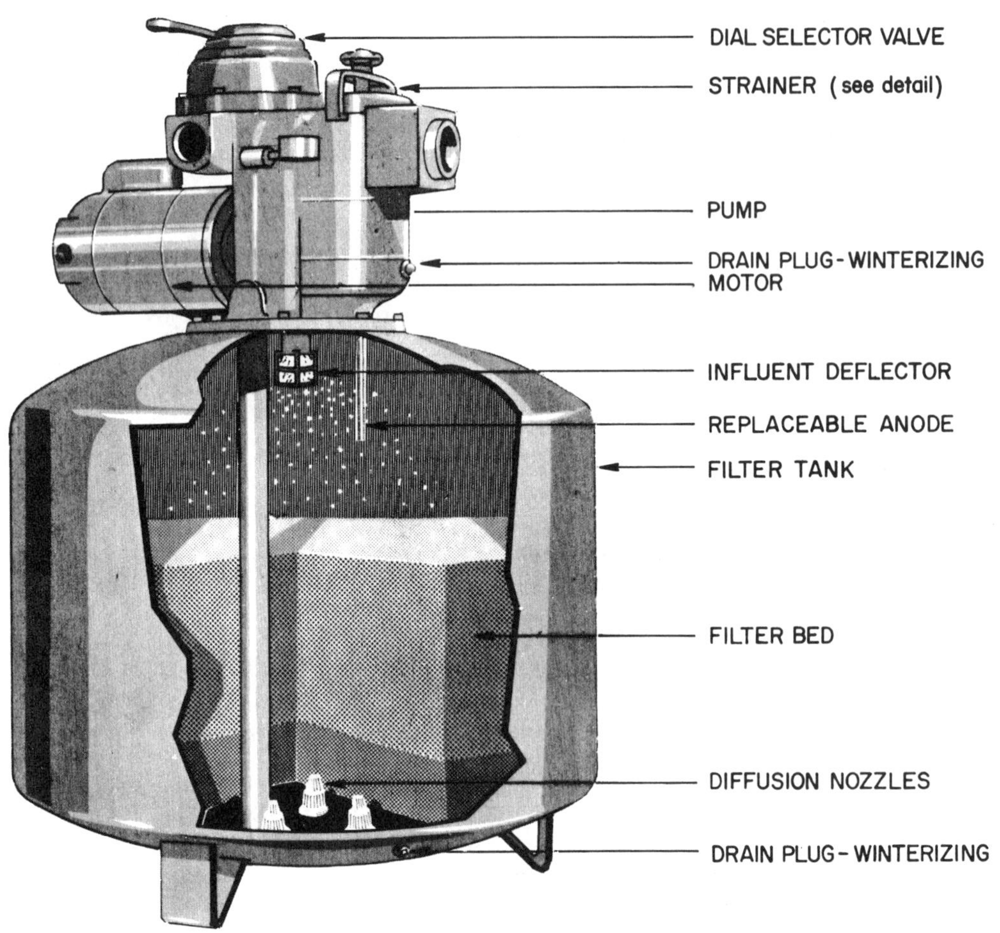

FIGURE 7-39 Cutaway of a swimming pool filter. The filter removes insoluble, suspended matter from the recirculated water. As the dirt accumulates within the filter, the filter pump will not maintain the required rate of flow against the increased resistance. Consequently the filter requires regular cleaning or backwashing to maintain its efficiency. (Courtesy of Jacuzzi Canada, Limited.)

nance to keep the recirculation system working at top efficiency (Figure 7-40).

When the unit is turned off for the backwash operation, the strainer should be cleaned before the backwashing begins. To clean:

- Turn off filter motor.
- Turn selector valve to OFF.
- Close all input and return valves.
- Remove cover from hair and lint strainer.
- Replace strainer basket and lids.
- Reset valves and commence backwash procedures.

Vacuuming the Pool

- Vacuuming must be done slowly and evenly whether dirt is visible or not.
- Light sediment is generally vacuumed with dial valve in the FILTER position. Clean strainer basket and check pressure gauges to see if backwashing is required after vacuuming.
- Depending on pool equipment, vacuum is attached to vacuum outlet or to one of the skimmers.
- Fill hose with water, inserting in pool. If using skimmer, close all other skimmers except the one you are using, including bottom drain.

Where a permanent vacuum line is installed for maintenance purposes, the vacuum line is connected to the suction system of the filter pump. The vacuum fitting is mounted on the pool wall below water level and is normally kept plugged except when the hose of the vacuum cleaner is connected to it by means of a hose-to-wall adapter. When vacuuming, be sure to close all skimmer valves.

FIGURE 7-40 The hair and lint strainer. (Courtesy of Mike Kelly, *Visual Concepts.*)

7-6 Budgeting for the Necessary Funds

BUDGET EXPENSE SCHEDULES

In order to budget the funds required to maintain the plumbing and drainage system, and the pool, we have developed thirteen main classifications. To back these up, you must develop equipment and parts summaries, decide on preventive maintenance activities, and, if warranted, include plans to upgrade the system.

	ACCT. NOS.	SUB TOTALS	TOTAL
PLUMBING & DRAINAGE SYSTEM	54		
DOMESTIC HOT WATER TANKS	541		
DRAIN CLEANING & REPAIRS	542		
MOTORS & PUMPS	543		
PIPING, VALVES & CONTROLS	544		
PLUMBING FIXTURES & PARTS	545		
WATER HEATERS	546		
POOL OPERATIONS	55		
CHEMICALS & ACCESSORIES	551		
CONTRACTORS	552		
ELECTRICAL	553		
HOUSEKEEPING SUPPLIES	554		
OPENING & CLOSING	555		
PLUMBING (FILTERS & PIPING)	556		
REPAIRS (DECK/FENCE/CABANA/PAINT, ETC.)	557		

FIGURE 7-41 Summary of budget expense schedules, repair and maintenance categories; mechanical services.

7-7 Glossary of Plumbing Terms

Air Chambers A vertical length of pipe with a cap at the top, extending from the distribution pipe at the point of entering a fixture; used to reduce hammering caused by a valve or faucet being suddenly shut off.

Back-siphonage The flow of water into a water supply system from any source other than its regular source. Also called backflow.

Backflow Preventer A device or means to prevent backflow.

Back Water Valve A device installed in a drain pipe or pipe to prevent backflow.

Barometric Loop A loop of pipe rising approximately 35 feet, at its topmost point, above the highest fixture it supplies.

Boiler Blow-off An outlet on a boiler to permit emptying or discharge of sediment.

Branch Any part of the piping system other than a riser, main, or stack.

Branch Vent A vent pipe connecting from a branch of the drainage system to a vent stack.

Building Drain That part of the lowest piping of a drainage system that receives the discharge from soil, waste, and other drainage pipes inside the walls of the building and conveys it to the building sewer beginning 3 feet outside the building wall.

Building Drain—Combined A building drain that conveys both sewage and storm water or other drainage.

Building Drain—Sanitary A building drain that conveys sewage only.

Building Drain—Storm A building drain that conveys storm water or drainage but no sewage.

Cleanout Plugs These are threaded plugs (as found in traps) to provide an opening for service purposes.

Collar A sleeve in back of a flange.

Continuous Waste Waste from two or more fixtures connected to a single trap.

Domestic Sewage The waterborne wastes derived from ordinary living processes.

Downspout A downspout is the rainleader from the roof to the building storm drain, combined building sewer, or other means of disposal, and is located outside of the building.

Drain Any sewer or other pipe or conduit that carries waste water or waterborne wastes in a building drainage system.

Drainage System Includes all the piping, within public or private premises, that conveys rainwater or other liquid wastes to a point of disposal. It does not include the mains of a public sewer system or private or public sewage-treatment or disposal plant.

Dry Vent A vent that does not carry water or waterborne wastes.

Fittings Parts of a pipe line other than straight pipe or valves, such as couplings, elbows, tees, unions, and increasers.

Fixture A receptacle attached to a plumbing system other than a trap in which water or wastes may be collected or retained for discharge into the plumbing system.

Fixture Branch The supply pipe between the fixture and the water distributing pipe.

Fixture Drain The drain from the trap of a fixture to a junction of the drain with any other drain.

Flow Pressure The pressure in the water supply pipe near the faucet or water outlet while the faucet is wide open or flowing.

Flush Valve A device located at the bottom of a tank for flushing water closets and similar fixtures.

Flushometer Valve A device that discharges a predetermined quantity of water to fixtures for flushing purposes and is closed by direct water pressure.

Grade The fall (slope) of a line of pipe in reference to a horizontal plane. In drainage, it is usually expressed in the fall in a fraction of an inch per foot length of pipe.

Group Vent A branch vent that works for two or more traps.

Horizontal Branch Drain A drain branch pipe extending laterally from a soil or waste stack or building drain, with or without vertical sections or branches, which receives the discharge from one or more fixture drains and conducts it to the soil or waste stack or the building drain.

Horizontal Pipe Any pipe or fitting that makes an angle of less than 45° with the horizontal.

Hot Water Hot water supplied to plumbing fixtures. The source of heat and storage of the water should be such that the temperature can be kept as low as possible and yet provide for the needs of the occupants. The temperature should not exceed 120°F.

Increaser A coupling with one end larger than the other. More specifically, a pipe fitting to join the end of a small coupling with inside connection to the end of a larger pipe with an outside connection.

Leader An exterior vertical drainage pipe for conveying storm water from roof or gutter drains.

Local Vent A pipe or shaft serving to convey foul air from a plumbing fixture or a room to the outer air.

Main The principal artery to which branches may be connected.

Main Vent The principal artery of the venting system to which vent branches may be connected.

Offset A combination of elbows or bends that brings one section of the pipe out of line but into a line parallel with the other section.

Plug A pipe fitting used for closing the opening in another fitting.

Potable Water Water free from impurities in amounts sufficient to cause disease or harmful physiological effects and conforming to the regulations of the public health authority having jurisdiction.

Recirculation Main The pipe used to return the unused domestic hot water to the storage tank.

Risers Water supply pipes that extend vertically one full story or more to convey water to branches or a group of fixtures.

Sanitary Sewer A sewer which carries sewage and excludes storm, surface, and ground water.

Sewage Ejectors A device for lifting sewage by entraining it in a high velocity jet of steam, air, or water.

Sewage Pump A permanently installed mechanical device other than an ejector for removing sewage or liquid waste from a sump.

Side Vent A vent connection to the drain pipe through a 45° Y fitting.

Siphonage Suction created by the flow of liquids in pipes.

Soil Pipe A pipe that carries liquid wastes and excrement.

Soil Stack A vertical soil pipe carrying liquid wastes and excrement.

Stack A general term used for any vertical line of soil, waste, or vent piping.

Stack Vent A stack vent is the extension of a soil or waste stack above the highest horizontal drain connected to the stack.

Sump A tank or pit that receives sewage or liquid wastes; located below the normal grade of the gravity system and which must be emptied by mechanical means.

Supports Devices for supporting and securing pipe, fixtures, and equipment.

Tempered Water Water at a temperature of not less than 90°F and not more than 105°F.

Trap A fitting that prevents the passage of air, gas, and vermin through a pipe without adversely affecting the flow of sewage and waste water.

Trap Seal The maximum vertical depth of liquid that a trap will retain, measured between the crown weir and the top of the dip of the trap.

Vacuum Any pressure less than that exerted by the atmosphere.

Vent A pipe or opening used for circulating air in a plumbing system and for reducing the pressure on trap seals.

Chapter 8

THE HEATING SYSTEM

8–1 An Overview

Over a period of several centuries, buildings have evolved from simple shelters providing the minimum requirements of safety and isolation from a sometimes hostile external environment into complex systems intended to satisfy many physiological and psychological needs. This evolution has assured the building occupants greater comfort and a more productive working environment. However, these improvements have not come without significant costs.

One cannot envision a successful building operation without a proper heating and ventilation system. That is why the information in this chapter is so important.

More than one-third of our energy is consumed in residential and commercial buildings; unfortunately, much of this consumption is unnecessary. Recent studies have demonstrated that with proper design, operation, and maintenance of commercial, residential, and institutional buildings, safe, healthful, and comfortable environments can be provided at levels much lower than the present energy consumption.

When designing new buildings or seeking energy savings in existing buildings, we must be able to calculate or determine the building's heating and cooling loads and be able to determine the energy required by the heating, ventilating, and air conditioning systems to meet these loads during occupied periods. The final challenge is to bring the actual consumption into line with what is required, thus keeping the building's occupants comfortable.

Whenever a hot water system is designed, all of the components (boiler, water temperature controls, pumps, circuits, valves, radiators, convectors) must work together to achieve the design intent. This harmony of operations results in longer system life, better system control, and savings in one of our most treasured resources—fuel.

In short, the information in this chapter should help the project management team provide comfort and safety for the occupants while operating the equipment efficiently.

8-2
What Is Comfort?

Comfort can be defined as any condition that, when changed, will make a person uncomfortable. Though this sounds paradoxical, it simply means that a person is not aware of the air conditioning systems when he is comfortable.

Comfort means different conditions to different people. It means being able to carry on any desired activity inside any room without being too cold or too hot. Most people don't care what combination of factors cause them to be comfortable as long as they feel comfortable.

If a person is uncomfortably warm, then the temperature or humidity (or both) is too high. In a first-class air conditioning system, one is not conscious of the temperature or the humidity, nor is there any disturbance because of equipment noise or air movement.

Air conditioning is the simultaneous control of temperature, humidity, air movement, and quality of the air to be maintained. Proper air conditioning can maintain any atmospheric condition regardless of variations in outdoor weather.

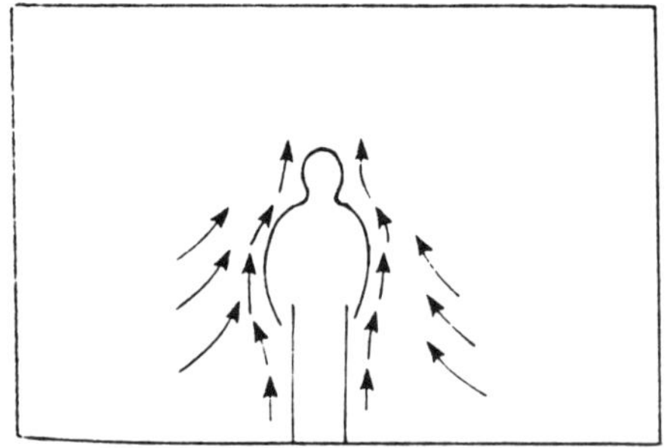

FIGURE 8-1 Convection. Cool air increases the rate of heat loss by convection while warm air slows the rate. (Courtesy of Reston Publishing Company.)

TRANSFER OF BODY HEAT

Since we are concerned with making people comfortable, we should study how heat is transferred from the human body. It should be understood that body heat is transferred to the surrounding air and surfaces by three natural processes: convection, radiation, and evaporation.

CONVECTION

During the process of heat transfer by convection, the body gives off heat to the surrounding cooler air. As the air warms, it moves in an upward direction. As the warm air moves upward, cooler air is pulled in behind it; this cycle repeats itself as the process of convection continues. It should be noted that cool air increases the rate of heat loss by convection while warm air slows the rate.

RADIATION

During the process of heat transfer by radiation, the body also gives off heat to the cool surface. Radiation differs from convection in one respect:

No air movement is required to transfer the heat. In the process of radiation, heat rays transfer the heat from the heat source, just as the sun's rays heat any surface they touch. The only difference is that in this case, people are the heat source.

EVAPORATION

During the process of heat transfer by evaporation, moisture is given off through the pores of the skin, it evaporates, removing heat from the body. Thus the evaporation of moisture from a warm surface removes heat and cools it.

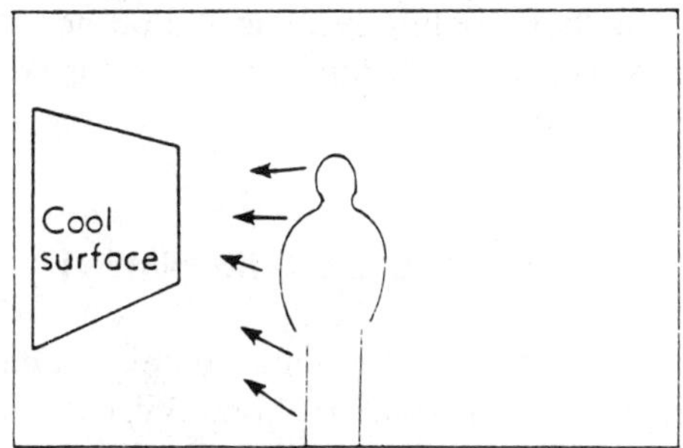

FIGURE 8-2 Radiation. Heat flows from a hot surface to a cold surface. (Courtesy of Reston Publishing Company.)

The rate of air motion affects the transfer of body heat by convection and evaporation. In the summer increased air motion increases the evaporation rate of heat from the body to help keep it cool. This is why buildings without air conditioners use fans to increase the movement of the air on hot days. In the winter a slower rate of air motion is desired, or the occupants will feel cool due to evaporative heat loss. But even in the winter it is desirable to have a flow of air to prevent the air from becoming stagnant.

The humidity (moisture content) of the air affects the rate of evaporative heat loss from the body. A high humidity (often occurring in the summer) will cause the surrounding air to absorb less heat from the body, making the occupant feel warmer. A low humidity (often occurring in the winter) allows the air to absorb greater quantities of body heat, making the occupant feel cooler. Resolution of a design problem may be to lower the summer humidity and increase the winter humidity.

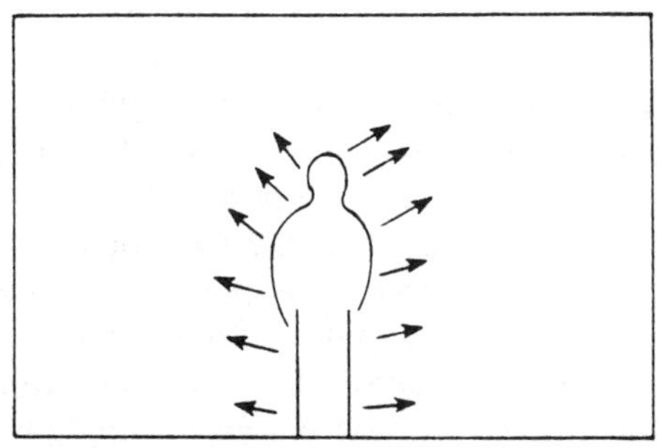

FIGURE 8-3 Evaporation. Moisture evaporates from a warm surface. (Courtesy of Reston Publishing Company.)

Temperatures of surrounding surfaces affect the radiant heat loss from the body, and surface temperatures in a room may vary widely. As an example, windows and exterior walls will probably be cooler in the winter than interior walls and the furniture. The inside temperatures of the floors and ceilings will depend on the air temperature on the other side. Comfort can be increased (in the winter) by directing the flow of warm air over these colder surfaces. This is why most heating elements (registers, baseboard heaters) are located under a window.

AIR TEMPERATURE AND BODY HEAT

The room air temperature affects the rate of convection and evaporative body heat losses. Since the room temperature will be below the body temperature of 98.6°F, there will be convective heat loss from the body. Generally, the body feels most comfortable in a temperature range of 72° to 78°F in the winter and 72° to 76°F in the summer. Of course, the range of comfortable temperatures varies with each individual and is affected by the person's clothing and activity.

SPACE CONDITIONS AFFECTING COMFORT

The conditions within a space (room) that affect the comfort of the occupant (because they affect the rate of heat loss from the body) are

1. Room air temperature (also called dry-bulb temperature).

2. Humidity or moisture content of the room.
3. Surface temperatures of surrounding surfaces in the room (also called mean radiant temperature, or MRT).
4. Rate of air motion.

The occupant will feel comfortable when each of these factors is within a certain range.

Also, no matter how much heat is introduced into a space, it is very difficult for the occupant to feel comfortable if he is sitting next to a very cold surface such as a window. The combination of the body heat loss on the side of the body nearest the window and the cold air coming through any cracks around the window makes this a difficult situation. An example: The temperature in a person's office was turned up to 76°F and he still felt uncomfortable. By rearranging the office so that there was an interior wall at his back instead of a window, he felt comfortable at 72°F. *Encourage people to move away from cold surfaces in the winter.*

COMFORT AND INDOOR-OUTDOOR TEMPERATURES

In the summer, comfort is also greatly affected by the relationship of indoor-outdoor temperatures. This is especially true in spaces that people occupy for short periods of time. When a person is in his residence or office for a long period of time, he becomes accustomed to a 75°F temperature and is comfortable. But when a person is in a space for short durations, generally up to one hour, he is most comfortable if there is only a 10° to 15°F difference between the outside and the inside temperatures. If it is 95°F outside, it should be about 80°F inside stores and shops for a person to feel comfortable. The common practice in stores, shops, and grocery markets, of setting their cooling systems at a 68° to 70°F inside temperature does not make for comfortable conditions.

COMFORTABLE ENVIRONMENT

People feel comfortable within certain ranges of air temperature, humidity, temperatures of surrounding surfaces, and air motion.

Experiments were made by The American Society of Heating, Refrigerating and Air Conditioning Engineers (ASHRAE) to determine the ranges of these variable conditions. The results were tabulated and made into the "comfort chart" shown in Figure 8-4.

In those areas where people will be basically inactive, such as in classrooms and hospital rooms, higher temperatures will be required than in those spaces where people will be active.

Generally, studies show that there is a definite link between humidity and air temperature when both air movement and surface temperatures remain constant. This air temperature to humidity relationship shows that in order to produce comfort, the humidity should decrease as the temperature increases. This means that in the winter it would be most economical to provide comfort with lower air temperature and higher humidity.

Women generally prefer higher temperatures than men. Similarly, older people prefer higher temperatures, as do people who live in southern climates. Of course, whether a person will be comfortable or not also depends on the type of clothing the individual wears and how active he is. A person wearing a sweater while cleaning the house will need a lower temperature than someone with a short-sleeved shirt on who is watching television.

8-3
What Is Heat?

The sense of touch tells a person whether objects are hot or cold. But it is misleading in telling just how hot or cold they are. The sense of touch is influenced more by the rapidity with which objects conduct heat away from the fingers than by the actual temperature of the objects themselves. Thus iron feels colder than wood at the same temperature because heat is conducted away from the fingers more quickly by iron than by wood.

FIGURE 8-5 **Heat is energy.** (Courtesy of The Trane Company.)

SCHOOLS	
Classrooms	72-74
Assembly rooms	68-72
Gymnasiums	55-65
Toilets and baths	70
Wardrobe & locker rooms	65-68
Kitchens	66
Dining & lunch rooms	65-70
Playrooms	60-65
Natatoriums	75

HOTELS	
Bedrooms and baths	75
Dining rooms	72
Kitchens and laundries	66
Ballrooms	65-68
Toilets and service rooms	68

HOSPITALS	
Private rooms	72-74
Private rooms (surgical)	70-80
Operating rooms	70-95
Wards	72-74
Kitchens & laundries	66
Toilets	68
Bathrooms	70-80

LIVING & WORKING	
Homes	73-75
Stores	65-68
Offices	72

THEATRES	
Seating space	68-72
Lounge rooms	72
Toilets	68

FIGURE 8-4 **Comfort chart (in degrees Fahrenheit).** Inside winter dry-bulb temperatures.

Heat always travels from a higher temperature to a lower temperature until "thermal equilibrium" is reached. "Thermal equilibrium" is the point at which the body being measured and its surroundings are at the same temperature.

Every object contains heat energy in both quantity and intensity. The intensity of heat within an object or substance is commonly measured by its temperature—fahrenheit or celsius.

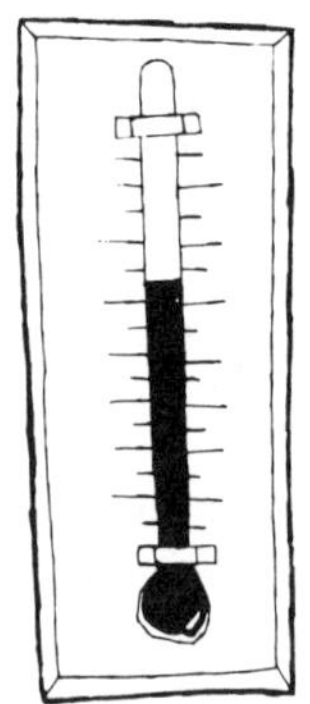

FIGURE 8-6 **Intensity of heat.** (Courtesy of The Trane Company.)

TEMPERATURE CONVERSION

With the metric system now being adopted on a wider scale, it is important to understand the relationship between fahrenheit and centigrade (celsius) readings.

Since 100 celsius degrees is equivalent to 212 fahrenheit degrees, the celsius degree is larger than the fahrenheit degree and poses a bit of a mathematical problem when we try to convert fahrenheit to celsius or vice versa.

From Celsius to Fahrenheit

(C × 1.8) + 32
Example: 100°C to F°
100 × 1.8 + 32
180 + 32 = 212°F

From Fahrenheit to Celsius

(F − 32) ÷ 1.8
Example: 212°F to C°
212° − 32 = 180°
180° ÷ 1.8 = 100°C

8-4 Forms of Energy Used to Heat a Building

The most common sources of building heat are the sun, electricity, gas, oil, and coal. The decision on which of the fuels to use is based on availability and cost of operation.

ELECTRICITY

Electricity is used as a fuel for a variety of heating systems, including baseboard radiant heat and electric coils in the ceiling and/or walls. In addition, there are electric furnaces for forced hot air systems, and electricity is used with heat pumps both to operate the system and to provide supplemental electric resistance heat for the system. Electricity has as an advantage its simplicity. It requires no

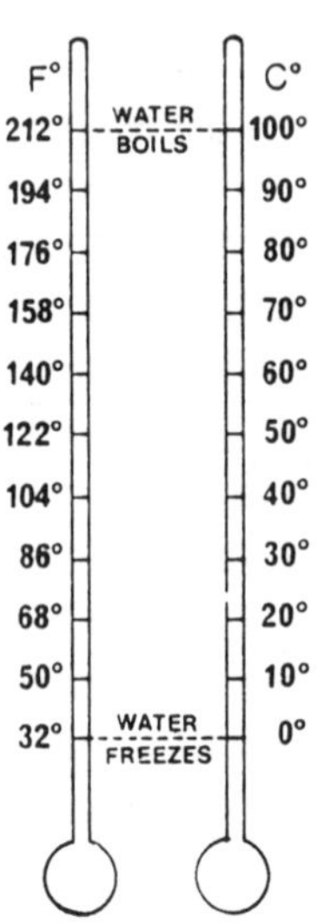

FIGURE 8-7 **Temperature conversion.**

chimney to remove toxic gases, and when baseboard strips and ceiling and wall coils are used, the system has individual room controls, providing a high degree of flexibility and comfort. Electric systems cost significantly less to install than other systems (including electric furnaces for forced hot air), and all electric systems (except heat pumps) require less upkeep and maintenance than systems using the other fuels.

COAL

Coal is rarely used for residential heating in new construction, and its use in industrial and commercial construction fluctuates.

The primary advantage of coal is that it is available, and there are ample supplies so that a shortage seems unlikely at this time. Generally, its cost is competitive with those of other fuels. Its disadvantages lie in the amount of space required for storage and the fact that it does not burn as completely as oil or gas, thus producing more pollution. Government regulations for clean air have also limited the use of some more polluting coals for industrial purposes.

OIL

Oil is one of the most popular fuels, and it is used extensively in the northeastern United States. The primary reason for oil's popularity has been its availability and historic low cost. It does require delivery by trucks to storage tanks located in or near the building, and the heating unit will generally require more maintenance than a gas heating unit. The selection of oil as a heating fuel has diminished somewhat since the oil embargo in the early 1970s. In addition, the cost of oil has risen dramatically since that time. Costs of other fuels have also risen, but the fear of not having oil if another embargo is imposed is one of the most important concerns.

Oil is available in various weights with various heating values and at different costs. Generally, the lower the number, the more refined the oil is and the higher the cost. Number 2 oil is commonly used in residences, while numbers 4, 5, and 6 are commonly used in commercial and industrial projects.

GAS

Gas, also a popular heating fuel, is used to heat the water in hot water systems and the air in forced air systems. Gas fuels available include natural gas, which is piped to the residence or building, and propane gas, which is delivered in pressurized cylinders in trucks and tanks and stored in tanks at or near the building. Since natural gas is available as needed, with no storage or individual delivery required, it is considered simpler to use. However, it is not available in many areas, and the more suburban the area, the less likely it is that natural gas will be available. The designer must first determine if natural gas is available.

SOLAR HEATING

The recent awareness that the supply of fossil fuels—oil, gas, and coal—is not unlimited, together with the sharp rise in the cost of these fuels, has stimulated research into the use of solar energy for heating and cooling of buildings.

The sun provides the earth with a tremendous amount of free, nonpolluting energy. It is estimated that the sun can supply 30,000 times the daily energy used in the world today. Various methods of collecting the sun's energy are now being studied; the method promising the best results uses solar collectors. This method has been successfully used to heat domestic water, swimming pools, and more recently, for heating and cooling of smaller buildings.

Although the initial cost of solar energy systems for heating and cooling is considerably higher than that of conventional systems, the time may not be far off when the general use of solar systems becomes economically justified. For this reason, a short description of the basic concept of solar heating is included.

Solar Collector

The solar collector is the essential piece of equipment that converts solar radiant energy to another useful energy form, most commonly heat. A typical flat-plate collector consists of an open insulated casing containing a plate with a black solar energy-absorbing surface. The heat absorbed is conducted to fluid either circulated through tubes or trickled across the plate's surface. Glass covers that are transparent to the short-wave solar radiation, but opaque to the long-wave radiation from the absorbing surface, close the box. The glass covers allow the solar radiation to enter the collector, but prevent it from escaping by re-radiation. Under favorable conditions, the flatplate collector can raise the temperature of the fluid up to 95°C.

Solar energy can be used to

1. Heat hot water for use in the building.
2. Provide heating for the building.
3. Provide cooling for the building.
4. Provide heating and cooling for the building.
5. Provide heating and hot water for the building.
6. Provide heating, cooling, and hot water for the building.

THE HEAT PUMP

The term "heat pump," as applied to a year-round air conditioning system, indicates a system in which refrigeration equipment is used, not only to remove heat from a space and to discharge it outdoors during warm weather, but also to heat the same space during colder weather by picking up heat from the outdoors and discharging it indoors.

In principle, the construction of the heat pump is similar to a refrigeration system used for air conditioning purposes, and its operation during the cooling cycle is identical. However, by the addition of certain modifications, the functions of the indoor and outdoor heat exchangers can be reversed during cooler weather. The outdoor coil (the condenser during the cooler cycle) is used as the evaporator to extract heat from the outdoor air, even though the temperature may be quite low, while the indoor coil (the evaporator during the cooler cycle) becomes the condenser, thus discharging this heat to the indoor space.

The basic modifications required to change an air conditioning system with compressor-type refrigeration into a heat pump are

(a) The addition of a reversing valve, which changes the flow direction of the gaseous and liquid refrigerant.

(b) A second liquid refrigerant expansion valve mounted near the outdoor coil.

(c) Two checkvalves, each mounted in parallel to an expansion valve.

A schematic diagram of the operation of a wall or window-mounted packaged heat pump is shown in Figure 8-8. The operation of this unit is as follows:

During the cooling cycle (a), the unit operates similarly to an air conditioning unit. The liquid refrigerant is supplied by expansion valve A to the indoor coil A. Check valve A is closed. In this coil the refrigerant absorbs heat from the warm space air circulated through the coil by the indoor fan, causing the refrigerant to evaporate. This vapor is drawn via the reversing valve into the compressor. The compressor discharges the hot compressed vapor via the reversing valve to the outdoor coil B, where the vapor gives up its heat to the circulating outdoor air and returns to its liquid state. This liquid then flows via check valve B and the reversing valve to expansion valve A to complete the cycle.

The heat pump described, employing fin-tube heat exchangers, is classified as an air-to-air pump. This type is most common for smaller capacities up to 25 tons as used for residences and small commercial buildings, although it is used for larger capacities as well.

To overcome the drop in COP (coefficient of performance) at lower outside temperatures, other types of heat pumps have been developed that obtain their heat from a natural source other than air and that use this source also as a heat sink (the substance for the absorption of the rejected heat during

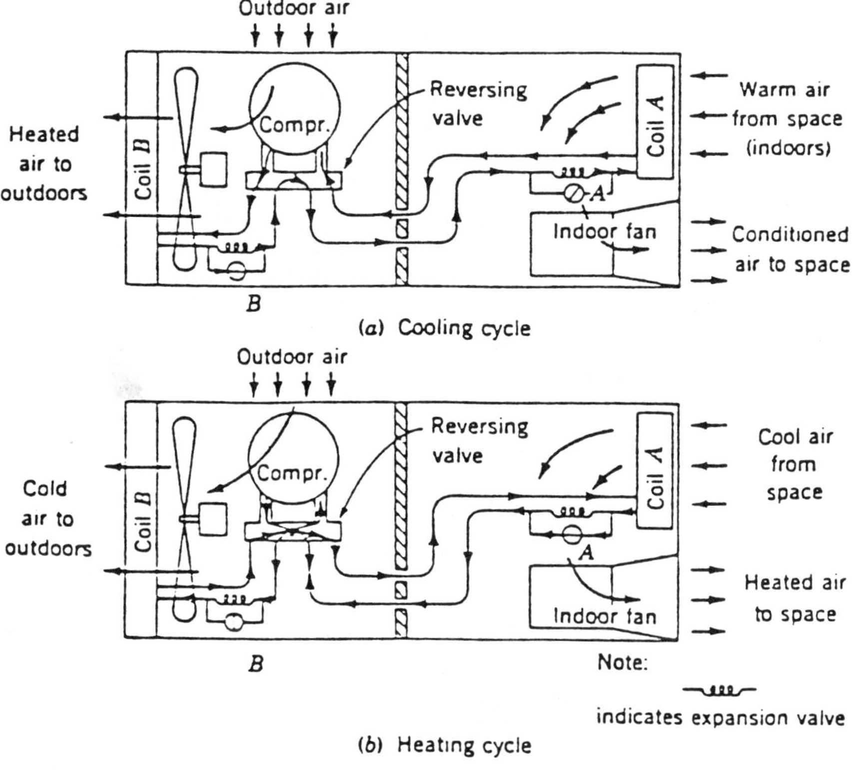

FIGURE 8-8 How the heat pump works. Schematic diagram showing the operations of a packaged heat pump.

summer operation). A short description of some of these methods follows.

Ground-To-Air Heat Pump

This method is sometimes used for small capacity units. The outside coil is buried in the ground below the frost line. Since the temperature of the ground at that depth remains well above freezing, even during very cold weather, the heat-absorbing capacity and thus the COP remain fairly steady, provided the heat transfer ability of the soil is sufficient.

Water-To-Air Heat Pump

When used for small capacity units, the outside coil is submerged and rests on the bottom of a well, river, or lake. Since the temperature of the water seldom drops below 4°C, even when ice is formed on the surface, the water will serve as a reliable and steady source of heat during the heating cycle.

The water-to-air method is quite common for large capacity heat pumps; however, instead of submerging the outside coil in a lake or river, the water is circulated around or through the tubes of a shell-and-tube heat exchanger inside the building and heat is then extracted by the evaporating refrigerant on the other side of the tubes during the heating cycle. The exchanger serves as a water-cooled condenser during the cooling cycle.

The unit is economical to operate when the heat pump alone is producing the heat.

At a 60°F outside temperature, the unit will provide 41,000 Btuh for heating. As the temperature goes down to 40°F, the unit will supply 32,000 Btuh, and yet more heat is required inside the space at 40°F than at 60°F. When it gets cold—20°F—outside, the unit will provide 21,000 Btuh. It is obvious that as the temperature goes down, so does the ability of the heat pump to produce heat. Thus, the heat pump is more efficient in warmer areas.

Heating Capacities

Typical 3-ton (36,000 Btuh) heat pump. Cooling capacity, 62° outside wet bulb, 85° air temperature entering evaporator.

Outside air temperature db°F	*Cooling Btuh*	*Watts*	**EER*
85	36,000	5,250	6.85
95	34,000	5,400	6.30
105	32,000	5,750	5.56

3-ton heat pump, heating capacity

Outside air temperature db°F	*Heating Btuh*	*Watts*	**COP*
60	41,000	5,300	2.46
50	38,000	5,100	2.37
45	35,000	4,900	2.37
40	32,000	4,700	2.17
30	26,000	4,300	1.92
20	21,000	3,900	1.71
10	15,000	3,500	1.36
0	10,000	3,100	1.02

4-ton heat pump, heating capacity

Outside air temperature db°F	*Heating Btuh*	*Watts*
60	52,000	5,900
40	41,000	5,300
20	28,000	4,800
0	20,000	4,300

2-ton heat pump, heating capacity

Outside air temperature db°F	*Heating Btuh*	*Watts*
60	31,000	3,850
40	22,000	3,300
20	14,000	2,700
0	8,200	2,200

*Energy efficiency ratio (EER)
*Coefficient of performance (COP)

8-5 Boiler-Burner Efficiency

It is important that the boiler operator and the people he reports to understand the process of combustion. If combustion is not carried out properly, the fuel will not be completely burned and less heat per pound of fuel will be produced, resulting in higher fuel bills. In addition, if combustion is not carried out in a proper manner, there will be a danger of explosion; smoke will be created contributing to air pollution; and soot will form, fouling up the heating surfaces, which also adds to the fuel costs and aids corrosion of these surfaces. Replacing boiler tubes and tube sheets is very expensive.

In order to help you understand the process of combustion, we have organized the information into two main areas of concern:

1. Combustion efficiency.
2. Boiler operating efficiency.

THEORY OF COMBUSTION

Combustion is the chemical reaction of the oxygen in the air with natural gas or other fuels, which produces heat by flaming. The production of this heat is the purpose of the combustion.

In order for the fuel to burn completely in the furnace, the following conditions must be fulfilled:

1. Enough air must be supplied to the furnace in order to provide sufficient oxygen to combine with all the combustible elements of the fuel.
2. The air and the fuel must be thoroughly mixed together so that each particle of fuel can come in contact with the necessary air. This thorough mixing of fuel and air is known as turbulence.
3. The temperature in the furnace must be high enough to ignite the fuel as it enters.
4. The furnace must be large enough to allow sufficient time for the combustion to be completed.

CHEMICAL TERMS AND SYMBOLS

A fuel is made up of various elements such as carbon, hydrogen, and sulphur. An element is a substance which cannot be broken down into any other substance. Each element is made up of atoms that combine together to form molecules of the element.

The atoms of one element may combine with atoms of another element to form a compound, e.g., carbon dioxide is formed when one atom of carbon combines with two atoms of oxygen. This combination is symbolized as CO_2.

Element and Compound Symbols

Element/Compound	Symbol
Carbon	C
Hydrogen	H_2
Sulphur	S
Carbon Monoxide	CO
Oxygen	O_2
Nitrogen	N_2
Carbon Dioxide	CO_2
Sulphur Dioxide	SO_2
Water Vapor	H_2O
Methane	CH_4
Ethane	C_2H_6
Butane	C_3H_8
Propane	C_4H_{10}

CONTROLLED COMBUSTION

In simple terms, combustion means "burning," but the process actually involves the oxidation of carbon in a gas. Natural gas will not burn unless it is mixed with oxygen,

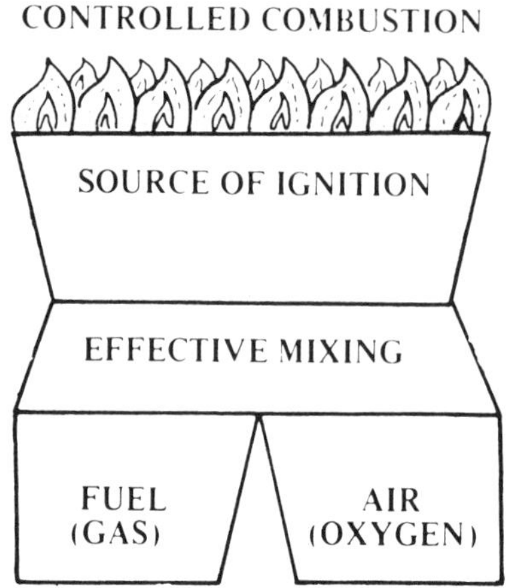

FIGURE 8-9 Combustion. Combustion takes place when a mixture of gas and air is ignited by a flame or a spark. (Courtesy of the Canadian Gas Association.)

which is about 20 percent of the air we breathe.

One molecule of methane requires two molecules of oxygen to produce one molecule of carbon dioxide with two molecules of water vapor. Similarly, 1 cubic foot of methane burns with 2 cubic feet of oxygen to produce 1 cubic foot of carbon dioxide and 2 cubic feet of water vapor.

However, the 2 cubic feet of oxygen is accompanied by 8 cubic feet of nitrogen (N_2) in the air, which is unchanged in the combustion process.

INCOMPLETE COMBUSTION*

When 1,000 cubic feet of natural gas is burned (without excess air), the water vapor would be about 10 gallons if allowed to condense. This fact illustrates the need to keep products of combustion above the dew point temperature in a venting system.

So far, the explanation of gas combustion has been based on the assumption that all of the carbon is burned completely to carbon dioxide. The products of "complete" combustion are harmless to the ecology.

If the carbon in a fuel does not burn with sufficient oxygen, a dangerous gas called carbon monoxide (CO) is produced. Most people are familiar with this hazard from automobile exhaust, particularly in a closed garage.

When methane burns with sufficient oxygen (O_2) for complete combustion, the products of combustion consist of carbon dioxide (CO_2) and water vapor (H_2O).

The chemical reaction for this combustion process is illustrated in the following formula:

$$CH_4 + 2O_2 = CO_2 + H_2O$$

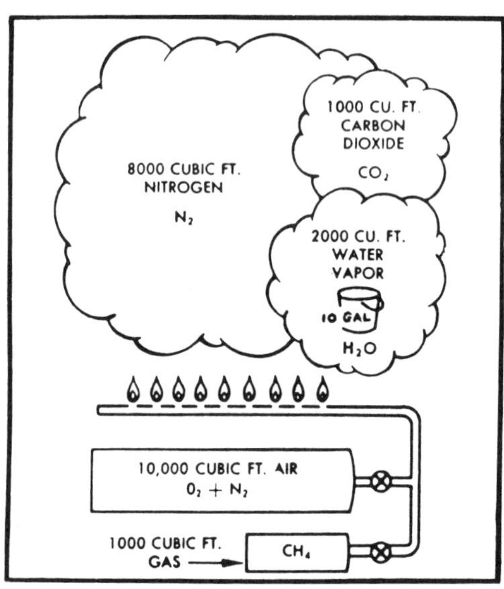

FIGURE 8-10 The chemistry of combustion. Volumes of each component are shown. (Courtesy of the Canadian Gas Association.)

*Reprinted with permission from the "Gas Appliance Installation Manual," Canadian Gas Association.

THEORETICAL AIR REQUIREMENT

The correct supply of air to the burners is really a continuous flow of air from outdoors to the boiler room, to the boiler, and changed to combustion products before leaving via the chimney back to the outdoors. This air is composed of 20 percent oxygen and 80 percent nitrogen. Two parts of oxygen are required for combustion and thus we use ten parts of air of which two parts are oxygen and eight parts are nitrogen. Therefore:

10 air = 2 oxygen + 8 nitrogen

or

1 cubic foot of natural gas requires 10 cubic feet of air (Actually 1 cubic foot of natural gas requires 9.1 to 10.6 cubic feet of air.)

COMBUSTION EFFICIENCY

It is important to emphasize that adequate openings must be provided to allow sufficient outside air to enter the boiler room. This helps ensure satisfactory combustion of the fuel. These openings must be in addition to doors and windows, which are usually kept shut in cold weather.

The oxygen required for complete combustion must be obtained from the air supplied to the furnace. The amount of air required to supply just enough oxygen for complete combustion is called the theoretical air. In actual practice, however, it is necessary to supply more than this theoretical amount of air in order to make sure that all particles of fuel come in contact with

Boilers with Atmospheric Burners	
Theoretical requirement	10 cu.ft. of air per cu.ft. of gas
plus	
50% excess air needed to meet the Gas Association limits for carbon monoxide in the flue gases	5 cu.ft.
plus	
permanent opening of draft hood	15 cu.ft.
Total air required	30 cu.ft. of air per cu.ft. of gas
Boilers with Barometric Dampers	
Theoretical requirement	10 cu.ft. of air per cu. ft. of gas
plus	
20% excess air for efficiency	2 cu.ft.
plus	
for barometric damper on the basis of approximate size of opening	3 cu.ft.
	15 cu.ft. of air per cu.ft. of gas
Boilers Connected to the Chimney	
Theoretical requirement	10 cu.ft. of air per cu.ft. of gas
plus	
20% excess air for CO_2 operation as a safety margin	2 cu.ft.
Total air required	12 cu.ft. of air per cu.ft. of gas

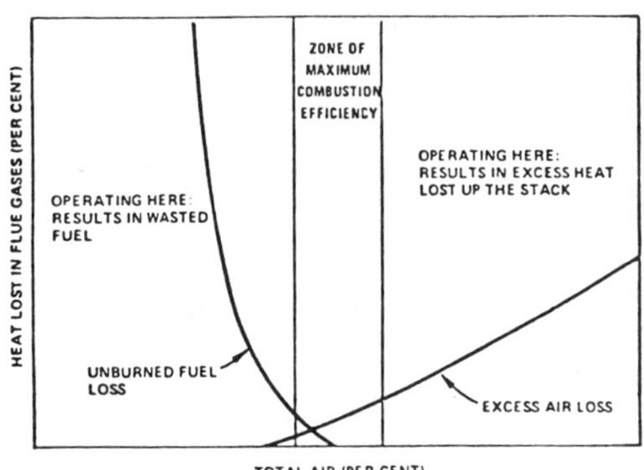

FIGURE 8-11 Effect of combustion air on boiler performance.

oxygen. The amount of air in excess of the theoretical air is called excess air and is usually expressed as a percentage of the theoretical air.

The amount of air required depends on the type of boiler used.

There is a relationship between the air required and the efficiency of the boiler. Decisions about the type of equipment purchased can be made when we understand combustion and its relationship to boiler efficiency. Replacing inefficient equipment and the losses incurred due to inefficiencies can amount to as much as ten times the imagined savings when a building is built. *Get all the facts before deciding.*

Perfect combustion is achieved when minimum excess air is desired to develop maximum efficiency—while still avoiding incomplete combustion. Boilers requiring 12 cubic feet of air for each cubic foot of gas are two and one-half times as efficient as the boilers requiring 30 cubic feet of air.

The following relationships affect combustion efficiency, and being aware of them helps us understand that adjustments should only be made by skilled professionals.

1. As excess air decreases, the percentage of CO_2 increases and stack loss decreases.
2. As stack loss decreases, combustion efficiency increases.
3. As excess air decreases and the percentage of CO_2 increases, combustion efficiency increases.
4. As the percentage of CO_2 increases, volume of flue gases decreases. The draft can then move the lesser quantity faster, speeding up the rate of heat transfer to the boiler heating surfaces. The exit flue gas temperature, therefore, decreases and combustion efficiency increases.

Maximum combustion efficiency will maximize boiler efficiency. Boiler efficiency is the percentage of gross Btu input that is converted to heat in the steam (or hot water in the case of a hot water boiler). Boiler efficiency is lower than combustion efficiency for a given system. A boiler efficiency range of 75-82 percent is considered good.

FLUE GAS ANALYSIS

"Flue gases" is another term for "products of combustion," and the flue gases present depend on the proportion of gas and air in the combustion mixture.

Theoretical perfect combustion is burning fuel with exactly the right proportion of gas and air. The flue gases are essentially water vapor, (H_2O), carbon dioxide, (CO_2), and nitrogen (N).

Perfect combustion is achieved when minimum excess air is desired to develop maximum efficiency—while still avoiding incomplete combustion.

Incomplete combustion results from an inadequate amount of air for the quantity of gas provided. When this happens, the flue gases contain increasing amounts of carbon monoxide and hydrogen, resulting in less water vapor and carbon dioxide.

Flue gases are usually analyzed for carbon dioxide (CO_2), oxygen (O_2), and carbon monoxide (CO). Various instruments are used to determine the presence of these gases.

HOW TO CALCULATE COMBUSTION EFFICIENCY

Proper proportioning and mixing, determined by flue gas analysis, will lead to maximum *combustion efficiency*. Combustion efficiency is the percentage of gross Btu input less the stack loss that is used to produce useful Btu output.

To calculate combustion efficiency, stack loss, or the sum of the sensible heat loss and the latent heat loss in the flue gas, must be determined.

Sensible heat loss is the amount of heat carried away by the dry flue gases. Latent heat loss is the amount of heat carried away in the flue gases because the water vapor in the flue gases does not condense back to the liquid state. Stack loss (sensible heat loss plus latent heat loss) is calculated by multiplying the volume of each flue gas by its heat content.

MEASURING COMBUSTION EFFICIENCY

The service mechanic carries a test kit with four pieces of equipment, which measure the smoke number, flue gas temperature, carbon dioxide concentration in flue gases, and furnace draft. Each of these factors affects the safety and efficiency of the furnace after the annual or semi-annual servicing.

Today, measuring burner efficiency is often achieved by using modern electronic equipment. It is important to realize that adjusting for efficiency cannot be achieved by guesswork.

The Bacharach Smoke Meter

The Bacharach Smoke Meter measures the amount of soot generated by the flame. The probe, attached to a hand-operated pump, is inserted through a small ¼-inch hole in the exhaust breeching between the furnace and barometric damper. A small volume of combustion products is withdrawn by ten small strokes and passed through a filter paper. The blackness of the stain on the paper is compared with a standard chart and reported as the smoke number on a scale of 0 to 9.

The Flue Gas Temperature Indicator

The flue gas temperature indicator is a dial thermometer, much like a meat thermometer, and operates over a temperature range of 200 to 1000°F (95 to 535°C). It is inserted into the

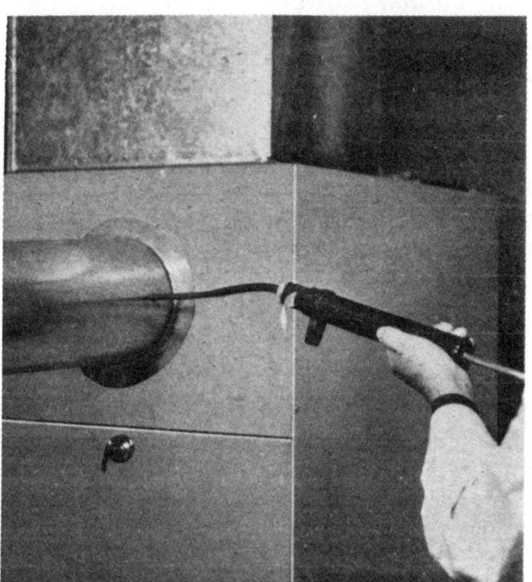

FIGURE 8-12 Taking a smoke spot sample using the Bacharach Smoke Meter. (Courtesy of the Department of Energy, Mines, and Resources, Canada.)

FIGURE 8-13 Taking the flue gas temperature reading. (Courtesy of the Department of Energy, Mines, and Resources, Canada.

FIGURE 8-14 The service mechanic taking a sample of the flue gases to measure carbon dioxide. (Courtesy of the Department of Energy, Mines, and Resources, Canada.)

flue gases through the same ¼-inch hole used for smoke measurements. The temperature is taken after the burner and circulating fan have veen running for ten minutes.

The Carbon Dioxide Analyzer

The carbon dioxide analyzer measures the amount of carbon dioxide in the flue gases. Carbon dioxide is a gas produced during combustion. Low readings indicate inefficient combustion. The same ¼-inch hole is used to withdraw a gas sample from the breeching. (Figure 8-14.)

The Draft Gauge

The draft gauge measures the draft or air buoyancy at the furnace exit after five minutes of furnace operation, using the same ¼-inch sampling hole. The draft requirement of the furnace is spelled out in the manufacturer's manual. Generally, an increased draft will lead to excessive heat loss up the chimney; a decreased draft will lead to soot formation in the furnace.

FIGURE 8-15 Draft gauge. Use of a draft gauge to adjust the draft to normal limits is required in gas conversion burner applications as well as field built-up units.

BOILER ROOM EFFICIENCY TEST REPORT

ADDRESS ____________________ TIME ______ DATE ____________

BOILER:

TYPE __________________________

STEAM or HW ____________________

MAKE & MODEL ___________________

BURNER:

GAS/OIL or BOTH ____________ MAKE & MODEL ________________

GAS PRESSURE (MANIFOLD) ______________________________W.G.

RATED INPUT _______________________ CFH/GPM

OPERATING INPUT ___________________ CFH/GPM

FLUE GAS ANALYSIS - O_2 ____________ %

FLUE GAS TEMPERATURE ____________ °FC

CO^2 ____________ % PPM

EFFICIENCY ______ %

FLAME SIGNAL ______________ V.DC/Microamps

CONTROL SETTINGS:

OPTG. AQUASTAT ____________ °F/C

HIGH LIMIT AQUASTAT ____________ °F/C

HEADER TEMPERATURE ____________ °F/C

RETURN TEMPERATURE ____________ °F/C

OPTG. PRESSURETROL ____________ PSI

HIGH LIMIT PRESSURETROL __________ PSI

AMBIENT TEMPERATURE ____________ °F/C

OUTDOOR TEMPERATURE ____________ °F/C

REMARKS: ____

____

PREPARED BY: ____

FIGURE 8-16 Boiler efficiency test report.

8-6
The Burner

BURNER START-UP

(Before starting, always make sure that the water level is normal.) When turning on a burner or when a boiler automatically starts, the following things occur:

1. Purge—air alone is introduced to clear the boiler of any combustible gases.
2. Pilot—the establishment of a stable pilot flame.
3. Ignition—usually about fifteen seconds after gas or oil is first introduced into the air stream and comes in contact with the pilot.
4. Established Flame—the fire scanner makes sure the flame is stable, at which point the ignition pilot is cut off.

BURNER SHUTDOWN

If the boiler will be shut down for extended periods, turn the switch to "off."

WHY NATURAL GAS?

Over the years we have developed several alternatives to wood and coal as a source of heat. Oil, natural gas, and electricity are now widely used. There are several reasons why natural gas is often preferred:

1. No ash is produced when gas is burned.
2. Little extra handling equipment required.
3. Easier to control.
4. Easily mixed with air.
5. Gas is clean.
6. Storage space not required.

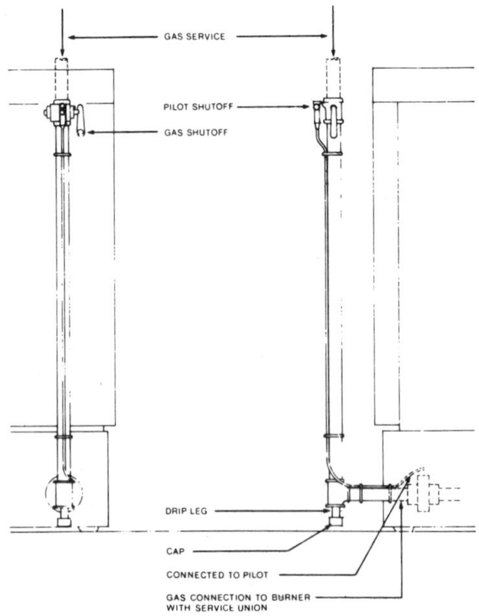

FIGURE 8-17 The shut-off valves. The gas supply line to the unit is run directly from the gas meter. A manual shut-off valve is installed outside the boiler room near the entrance in accordance with the gas code. A drip leg is provided in the gas line. This trap will prevent moisture and sediment from passing through the gas controls. *DO NOT TEST GAS PIPING WITH AN OPEN FLAME.*

OIL BURNERS

Many buildings have dual fuel burners and are capable of burning oil or gas. Most use No. 2 light industrial oil for standby fuel because this oil requires no preheating.

When burning oil, it must be broken up into a fine spray (atomization) before it can be properly burned. This is necessary in order for the combustion air to mix well with the oil to ensure efficiency.

When burning oil, extra handling equipment is required such as storage tanks, strainers, oil pumps, extra piping, and pressure relief valves. Despite this, dual firing burners are used for two main reasons:

1. A preferred interruptive rate.
2. The advantage of being able to alternate fuels during an energy shortage.

Something To Remember

When we use oil as a standby fuel, it is wise to keep the storage tanks full. Partially-filled tanks form condensation on the inner walls. Over a period of time, the walls of the tank will corrode. Also, empty fuel tanks are often the reason for lack of heat.

Light Oil Burners

Before oil can be properly burned, it must be broken up into a fine spray or vapor. This breaking up of the oil is called atomization, and it is necessary in order for the combustion air to mix well with the oil. It should be noted that heavy oils must be heated to approximately 200°F before they can be atomized, while light oils do not require this heating.

There are three types of oil burners:

1. Air and steam atomizing burners (low pressure).
2. Mechanical or pressure atomizing burners (high pressure).
3. Centrifugal or rotary cup burners.

Air Atomizing Oil Burner

The oil is supplied under pressure to the burner tip through the center tube, while the air flows through the outer tube. In the swirler, the oil is forced through a number of small holes into the path of the air, which atomizes the oil. The air-oil mixture then leaves the burner through the tip, which is designed to force the mixture into a cone-shaped, swirling pattern so it will mix easily with the secondary air supplied around the burner. This type of burner is usually used when burning No. 5 and No. 6 oil, preheated to 185-200°F.

Air atomizing burners require a compressed air supply. Usually, a small rotary air compressor is mounted on or near the front of the boiler and is then driven either directly by a small electric motor or with a V-belt by the motor driving a fan supplying the secondary air to the furnace.

Mechanical or Pressure Atomizing Burner

A pressure atomizing burner is usually comprised of the following components, as shown in Figure 8-20.

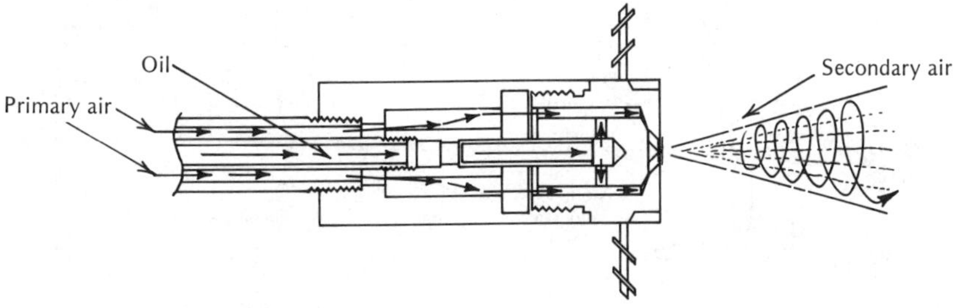

FIGURE 8-18 Air Atomizing Oil Burner. The air atomizing burner is commonly used on large packaged boilers.

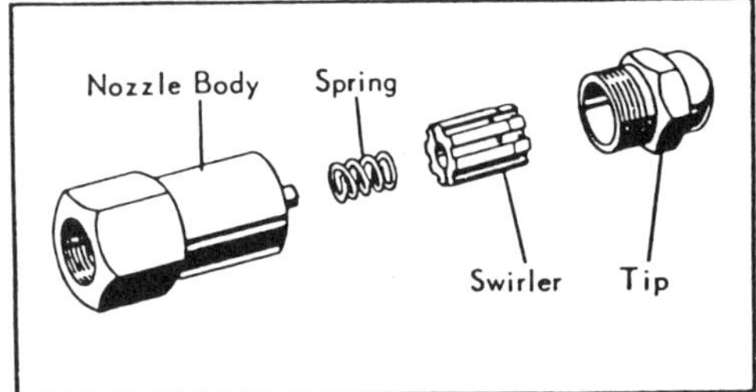

FIGURE 8-19 **Burner nozzle parts.**

COMPONENTS:

Blast tube, blower housing, motor, fuel pump, blower wheel, pedestal or flange mount, end cone or choke ring, high voltage ignition transformer, ignition electrodes, electrode mount, nozzle pipe, delayed oil valve (some models), nozzle, air diffuser, ignition wires or bars, pump drive couplings, nozzle adapter, and air volume controller.

Rotary Cup Oil Burner

The rotary cup oil burner is often used for larger-sized packaged boilers. In this type, the oil is pumped to the inside of a cup which is being rotated at about 3,500 rpm by an electric motor. Centrifugal force causes the oil to be thrown off the cup's rim in a fine spray. Primary air is forced in a whirling motion by a fan into the path of the oil spray. Additional secondary air needed for combustion is supplied to the oil spray as it leaves the burner.

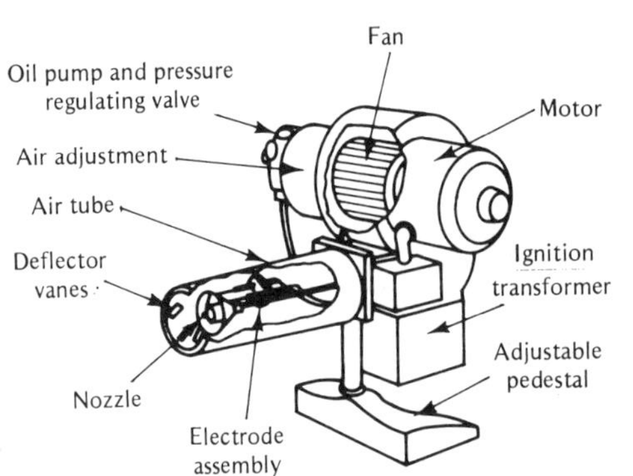

FIGURE 8-20 **Mechanical or pressure atomizing oil burner.** In this type of burner, the oil is fed under pressure, 80-100 psig., to the burner nozzle.

Fuel Oil Pumps

With the exception of some small domestic boilers and furnaces that use a gravity-fed type pot burner, all oil-fired boilers require a fuel oil pump to transfer oil from the storage tank to the burner and to build up sufficient oil pressure in the burner nozzle in order to achieve proper atomization. Rotary pumps, such as the gear pump or the internal crescent pump, are the most common type of pumps used for this purpose.

The oil pump forces the oil through a tube inside the hollow shaft to the spray opening inside the rotary cup. The oil pump draws the oil from the supply line, through a strainer, and then discharges it in the line to the burner at a pressure from 80 to 100 psig (per square inch gauge).

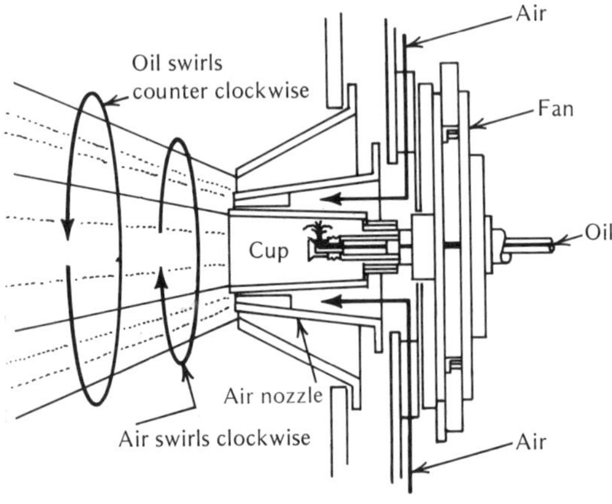

FIGURE 8-21 **Rotary cup oil burner.** The rotary cup oil burners are designed to burn No. 5 and No. 6 industrial fuel oils. Units are also available for use with No. 1 and No. 2 light domestic oils.

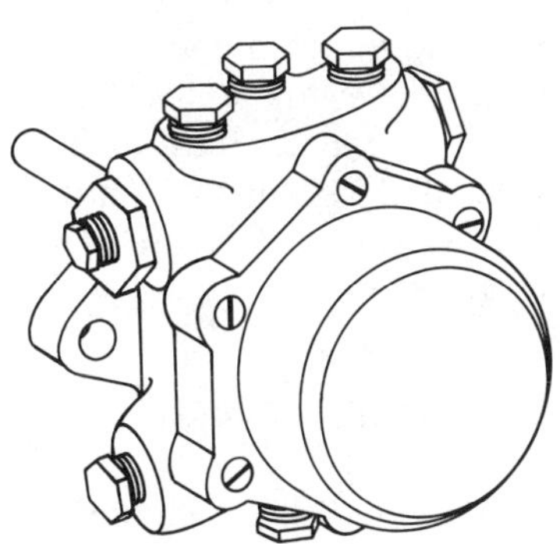

Webster pump model #2R

FIGURE 8-22 Fuel oil pump.

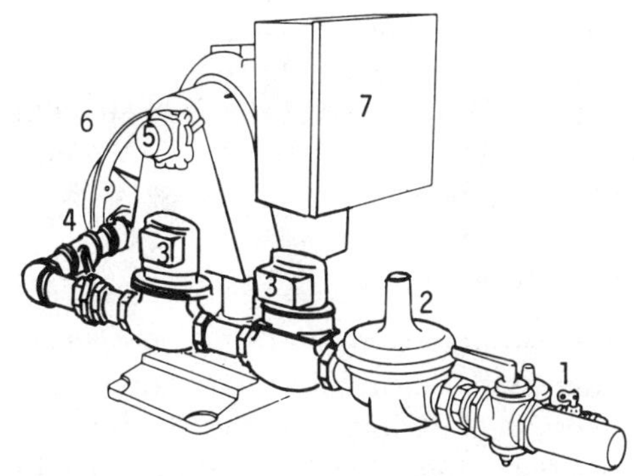

FIGURE 8-23 Main parts of a forced draft gas burner. 1. Gas shut-off valve; 2. Gas pressure regulator; 3. Safety shut-off; 4. Modulating valve; 5. Burner motor; 6. Burner; 7. Control panel box.

ASSURING COMBUSTION EFFICIENCY

To assure combustion efficiency, you require the services of a skilled, reputable burner mechanic. The fuel burning equipment must be kept in first class condition. The information included in this chapter will help you understand what you need and also help you monitor the efficiency.

OVERHAUL AND ADJUSTMENT

The burner service should include a complete overhaul before the boilers are shut down. This should be followed by an adjustment when the heat is turned on and a further inspection and adjustment during the heating season. Readings taken during these inspections should be recorded on the Boiler Room Efficiency Test Report (Figure 8-16).

SWITCHING TO OIL

In situations where a dual-fired gas/oil burner is used, the serviceman should be called to switch over the system. He will assure that the oil burner nozzle assemblies, oil strainers, and oil pumps are operating properly.

GAS BURNERS

Because gas is already in an atomized condition, further atomization at the burner is not necessary. Therefore, the main function of the gas burner is to provide for complete and turbulent mixing of the gas and combustion air.

Gas burners used for heating boilers differ mainly in the way air and fuel mix. They can be divided into two general classes:

1. The pre-mix burner. Part of the combustion air required is mixed with the gas inside the burner before the gas leaves the burner head.
2. The after-mix burner. All air required for combustion is mixed with the gas after it leaves the burner.

Atmospheric Burner

A very popular pre-mix type burner is the atmospheric burner. It has wide application in domestic appliances such as gas stoves, hot water heaters, and heating furnaces. They have recently been used extensively in commercial heating boilers as a cheap alternative to packaged boilers.

Ribbon-Type Burner

The gas-air mixture leaves the burner head through ports formed by herringbone-type, stainless steel ribbons that give the burner a quiet operation. Another feature of this burner is the fast light-off when the burner is started. It is suitable for use with various kinds of gases.

Mechanical Forced Draft Burner

Mechanical draft is draft that is produced by a fan or blower, which when used for a heating boiler, is usually driven by an electric motor creating the forced draft necessary to efficiently burn the fuel.

As we have stated previously, the correct amount of air required for combustion must be supplied to the furnace. In addition, the products of combustion (the combustion of flue gases) must be removed from the furnace and passed over the boiler heating surfaces on their way to the chimney.

To satisfy these requirements, a continuous flow of air and gas must be established through the boiler setting. To produce this flow, a pressure difference is required which is called "draft."

DRAFT CONTROL

The draft produced by a chimney of a certain height may vary considerably depending on changing conditions. Some of the conditions that affect the draft are

1. Temperature change within the furnace.
2. Temperature change outside the boiler.
3. Barometric pressure changes.
4. Air turbulence.

Draft Control for Forced Draft Burners

The fan or blower supplying the combustion air is nearly always driven by a constant speed electric motor. The capacity of the fan is large enough to supply all the required air at maximum boiler load. When the boiler is

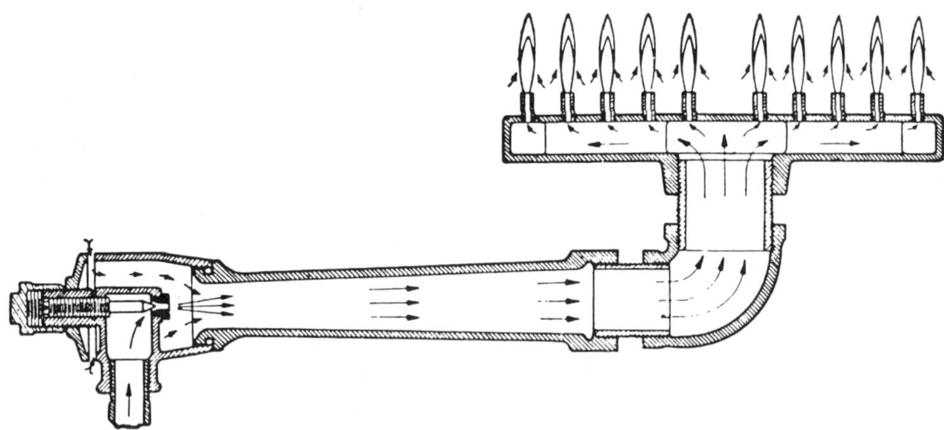

FIGURE 8-24 Atmospheric burner. Rectangular burner heads are most common for use in heating boilers. The gas-air mixture issues through multiple rows of small nozzles.

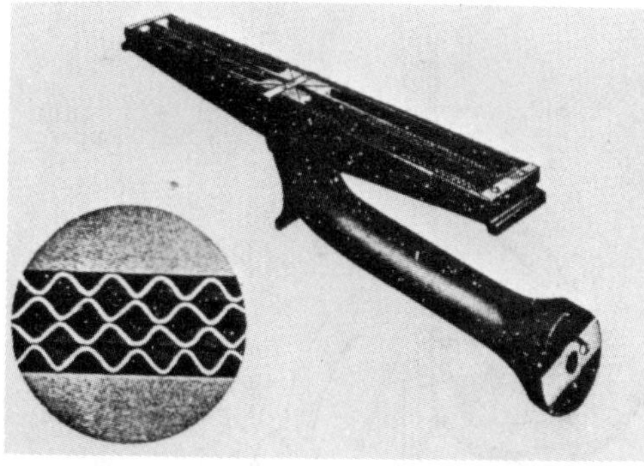

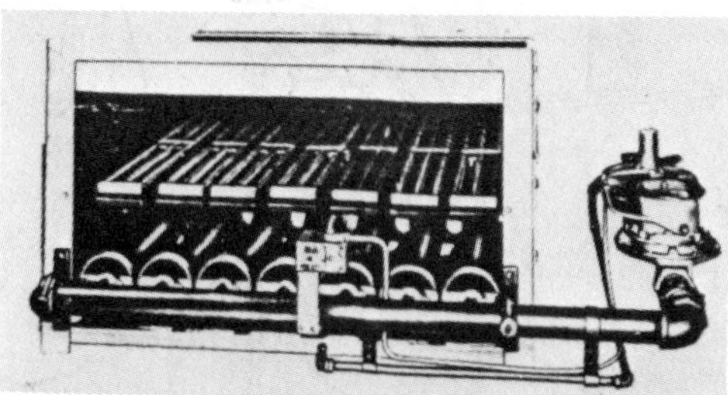

FIGURE 8-25 **Ribbon type burner.** A number of ribbon type burners can be mounted side-by-side in the base of a heater. All the burners are then connected to a common gas supply manifold.

equipped with a modulating control and motor that regulates the fuel supply in order to maintain constant steam pressure or water temperature at varying boiler loads, the air supply must also be regulated in direct proportion to the fuel supplied.

Draft Measurement

The pressure differential or draft required for heating boilers is usually quite small. It is measured in inches of water. This unit of measurement is equal to the pressure exerted by a column of water 1 inch in height; the abbreviation "in. wg." (inches of water gauge) is used to indicate the pressure. To convert inches of water gauge to pounds per square inch the factor 0.036 is used.

1 in. wg. = 0.036 psi

BURNER MAINTENANCE

1. Pull burner out and clean the diffuser.
2. Clean pilot tube.
3. Run a cloth through the scanner tube to keep the tube clean.
4. Wipe off motor damper so that it moves freely.
5. Keep all set screws tight.

Electrical Control Maintenance

1. Motor starters must be free of dust and dirt.
2. Starter contacts are silver faced and should never be filed. When silver has worn away, they must be replaced.
3. Thermal relay heaters, when tripped, should be allowed to cool for at least sixty seconds before the relay can be reset. If overloads trip out repeatedly when motor current is normal, call for service.

Fireye Programming Sequential Control

1. Keep free of dust and dirt.
2. Never file contacts—if contacts are dirty or slightly oxidized, clean by drawing a piece of hard finished paper between the contacts while holding them closed.
3. Check flame failure device once a week if boiler is in constant operation.

Burner Lubrication

The burner motor is equipped with a prelubricated, sealed bearing at the shaft extension end, and a standard ball bearing with provisions for extended lubrication at the

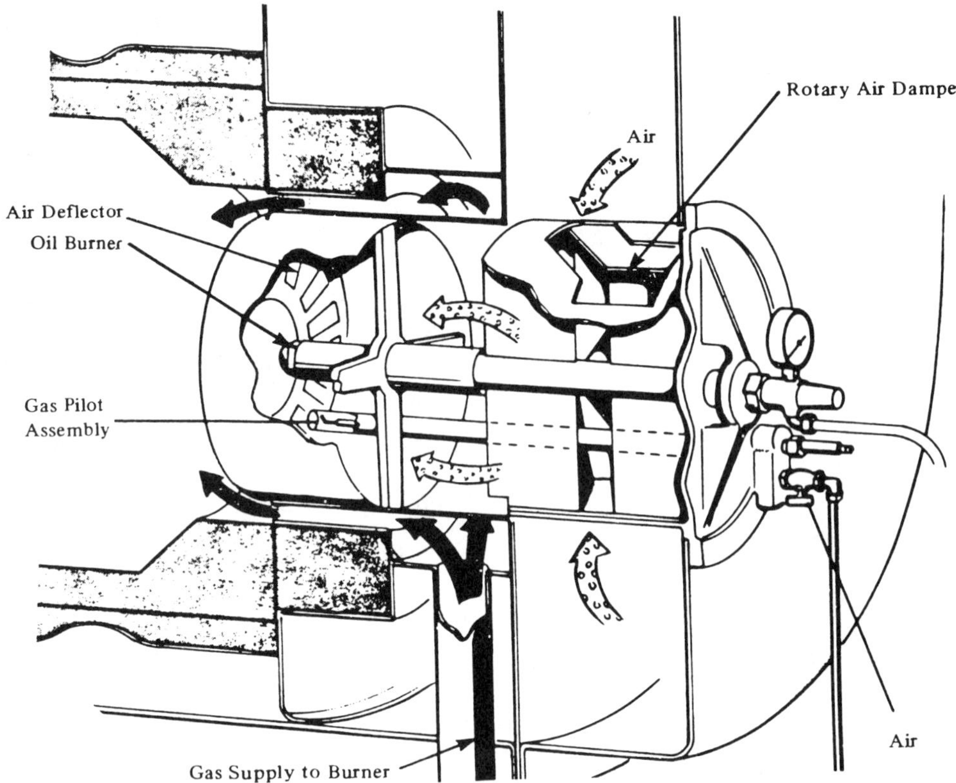

FIGURE 8-26 Ring type forced draft gas/oil burner. This type of burner is known as an after-mix or out-side mixing type, as the gas and air mix together after they leave the burner.

front end. Sealed bearing should be checked every three years. The front bearing should be lubricated once a year. Remove both ends of the filler and drain plugs and add approximately 1 or 2 ounces of grease. Replace the fill plug with a Zerk fitting and then add grease with a pressure gun. The bearing chamber should be kept less than one-third full to prevent overheating.

BURNER MALFUNCTION

Electrical Problem

Burner Motor Does Not Start

1. Check fuses at main and secondary switches.
2. Push red reset button.

Burner Motor Starts—Burner Does Not Fire

1. Make sure that electric eye on burner scanner is clean.
2. Check flame failure resets—push red button.
3. Check all belts for slippage or break.

If Burning Oil, Check

1. Oil level in storage tank.
2. Fuel oil transfer pump—should be operating.
3. Oil valves to the burner—should be open.

If Burning Gas, Check

1. The selector switch—should be turned to "gas."

Call for Service

If you have checked out the burner problem and are still unable to correct, call the burner service company. Give them all the details.

Service Record Label

Be sure that all service is recorded on the label whether done by yourself or the service company.

8-7 The Boiler

The boiler heats the water for circulation through the system. It may be rectangular or square (occasionally even round) and made of steel or cast iron. A boiler is rated by the amount of heat it can produce in an hour. The maximum amount of heat the system can put out is limited first by the size of the boiler selected. Boiler efficiency increases when the boiler runs for long periods of time, so the unit selected should not be oversized or it will run intermittently and be less efficient. Hot water boilers may use oil, gas, propane gas, coal, or electricity as fuel. Oil and gas boilers are most commonly used in residences.

BOILER CLASSIFICATION

Boilers consisting of a shell containing straight tubes through which the hot gases travel from the fire to the stack are classified as "firetube" boilers. The water in the shell surrounds the tubes and the heat from the hot gases inside the tubes passes through the tube walls to the water.

Another boiler design features one or more small diameter shells, called boiler drums, with a large number of tubes connected between the drums. Water circulates from the drum through the tubes back to the drum. The heat from the fire and hot gases comes in contact with the outside of the tubes. This type is known as the "watertube" boiler. Watertube boilers are used mainly in industry and in large capacity, high-pressure heating plants. They are not commonly used in low-pressure heating plants, although a simplified type of watertube boiler, known as the "tubular" boiler, is quite often used in residential hot water heating systems.

QUALITIES NEEDED FOR A GOOD BOILER

1. Should be simple, safe, and efficient.
2. Fuel burning efficiency should be 75 to 82 percent.
3. All parts of the heating surface exposed to fire or hot gases must be covered by water.
4. The circulation of water must be unrestricted and steady.
5. All parts of the boiler and fittings must be readily accessible for inspection, cleaning, repair, and operation.
6. To ensure the utmost possible transfer of heat from the hot gases in the furnace to the water in the boiler, the heating surface should be adequate.
7. So that the gases will be completely burned before passing to the stack, there should be ample combustion space in the furnace.

ADVANTAGES OF A PACKAGED BOILER

1. The chief advantage of a packaged boiler is that it can be mass produced. This reduces production costs and makes the initial cost lower than a boiler of the same capacity that is assembled at the site. Also, better workmanship can be expected as the boiler is assembled by more experienced and qualified personnel.
2. Packaged boilers require a much smaller floor space and building volume or height.
3. The boiler can be put to use in a shorter length of time after shipment, as it can be leveled quickly and requires only a reinforced flat concrete floor slab as a foundation. The additional erection of steam, water, and fuel piping is all that is necessary.
4. Most packaged boilers are easily accessible for cleaning, inspection, and repair due to hinged doors at the front and rear. These doors can be opened by removing a few bolts, thus making inspection or repair easier and more convenient.

Most packaged firetube boilers manufactured today are basically modified Scotch boilers. The original Scotch boiler was a large diameter boiler with an internal furnace, a reversing chamber surrounded by water (wet back), and a second pass consisting of a number of firetubes.

THE FIRE BOX BOILER

BOILER RATING

Boiler manufacturers list both gross and net Btuh ratings of the boiler. The gross Btuh is the heat input to the boiler by the fuel, and the net Btuh is the usable heat output that is available for use in the hot water system.

CIRCULATING PUMP

The hot water is circulated from the boiler through the pipes and back to the boiler by a pump. The pump provides fast distribution of hot water through the system, thus delivering heat as quickly as possible. The circulating pump size is based on the delivery of water required, in gallons per minute, and the amount of friction head allowed. Circulating pumps are not used on gravity systems.

THE FIRETUBE BOILER

The term "tube" is usually applied to those of a diameter of up to about 6 inches. Any tube over this diameter is called a flue. This long fire travel results in minimum draft loss, low flue temperature, and high boiler efficiency, resulting in lower fuel costs.

The tubes in a firetube boiler are attached at each end of the boiler to circular sheets with openings into which the firetubes are expanded and beaded at each end. The outer curved boiler shell holds these tube sheets in place.

Direct stays are secured at both the front and the back tube sheets, preventing warping of these sheets. This is the best and most direct form of stay for supporting parallel flat surfaces that are a considerable distance apart.

The fire- and water-tube boilers are also provided with manholes, handholes, and washout plugs so that the boiler can be inspected and cleaned as necessary.

Both of these boilers use the tubes to spread or increase the heating surfaces of the boiler above what you might achieve in a plain boiler with a heater under it.

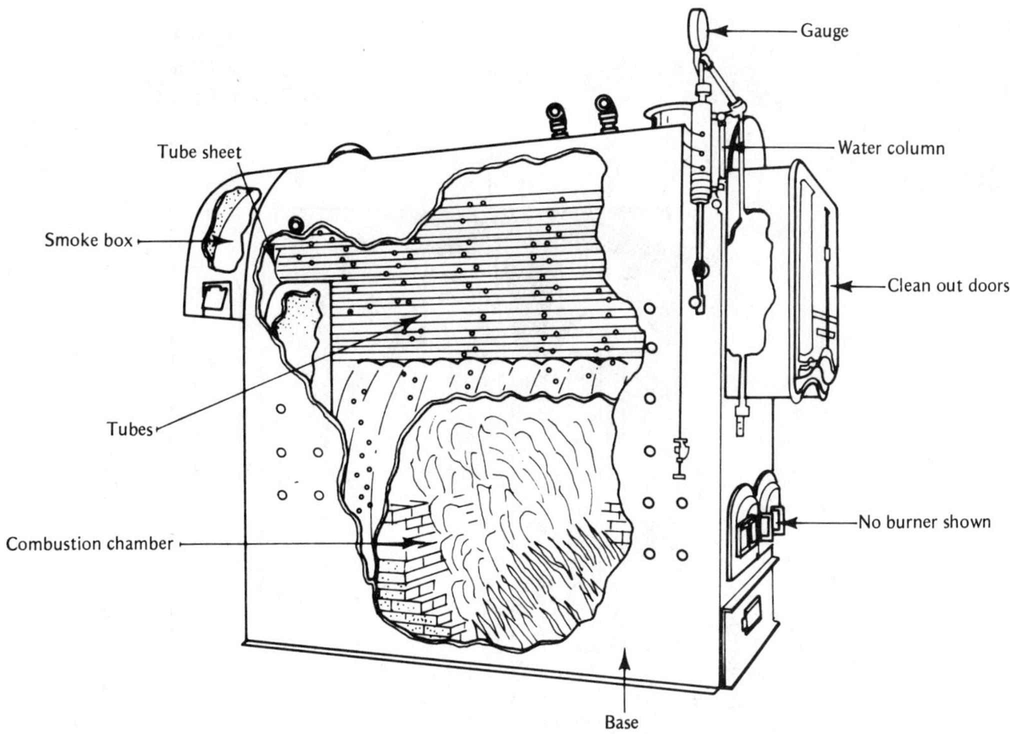

FIGURE 8-27 The fire box boiler.

BOILER GAS-FLOW PATTERNS

The diagrams in Figure 8-29 show the basic gas-flow patterns used today. All use an internal furnace or firebox as a first pass, then route the gases into various tube layouts.

Like the basic Scotch type, the 2-pass construction needs no baffles at rear tube sheet. It can be dryback or wetback design.

For longer gas travel, flow is turned again. The rear chamber or dryback 3-pass units have a refractory baffle to reverse gas; in wetback units, the submerged rear chamber effects the reversal.

To further increase length of the gas path, direction may be reversed again, constituting the 4-pass design.

PRESSURE REGULATING VALVE

This valve is located on the city water supply line to the boiler heating system and is generally found in the boiler room.

The function of a water pressure reducing valve (PRV) is to reduce high-pressure cold city water from the booster pumps to the desired lower pressure of the boiler and heating system. (Fig. 8-30.)

Once the system is filled, there is very little make-up water used and the valve will only

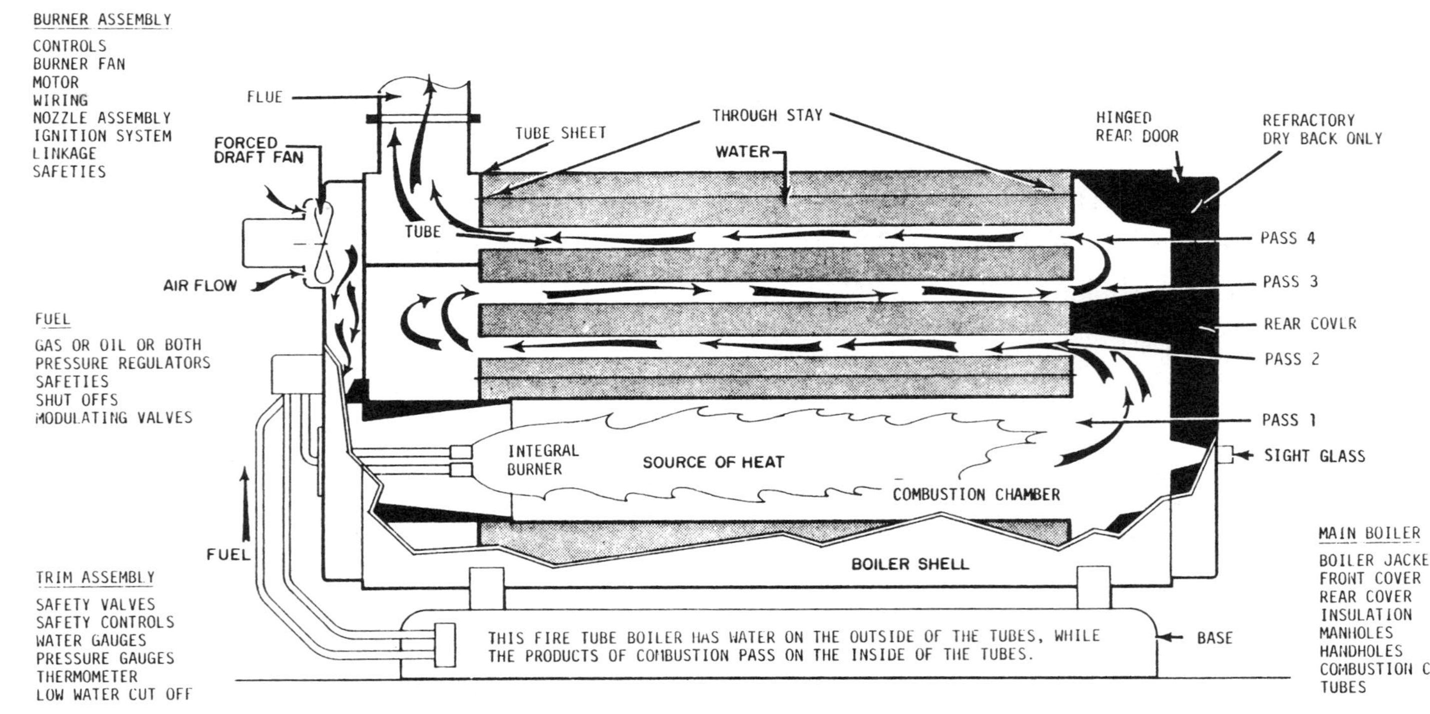

FIGURE 8-28 **Cleaver-Brooks 4 pass design hot water boiler.** (Courtesy of Cleaver-Brooks.)

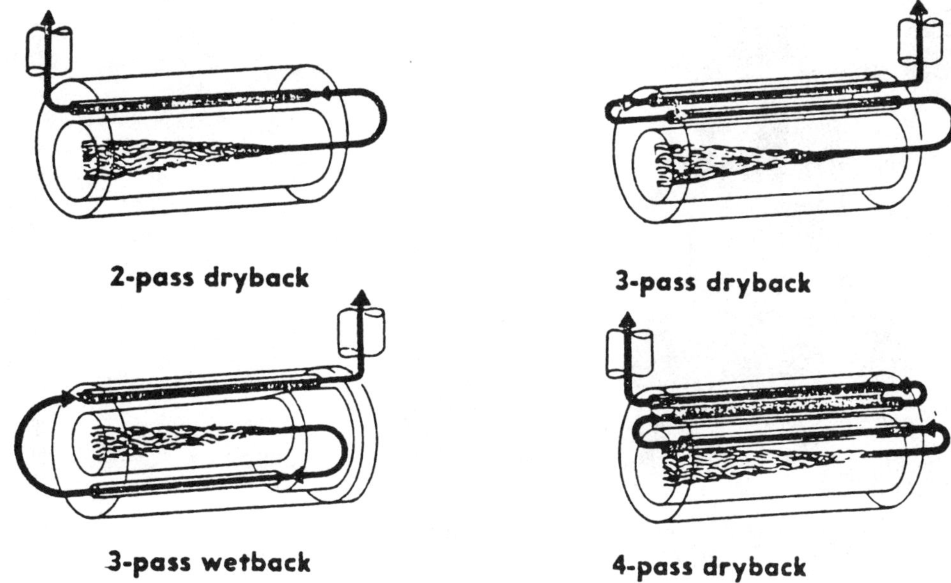

FIGURE 8-29 Boiler gas-flow patterns.

operate with a drop in pressure in the system below desired set pressure. Cold piping on the downstream side of the PRV is a sign that water is flowing and is usually an indication that the system is leaking to atmosphere.

WATER RELIEF SAFETY VALVE

When the pressure in the system exceeds 30 pounds per square inch, a spring-loaded valve opens, allowing some of the water to bleed out of the system and the pressure to drop. The valve should be located where the discharge will not cause any damage.

Operation of this valve would indicate the following:

1. Flooded cushion tank
2. Defective pressure regulating valve
3. Open regulating valve by-pass

LOW WATER CUT-OFF

The low water cut-off is a float-operated switch. Contact is made when the boiler water level is normal. In the case of a leak, the water level drops, opening the contacts and shutting off the burner. Some have to be manually re-set, others re-cycle and automatically re-set.

BOILER TUBE FAILURE

The failure of boiler tubes is a serious and costly problem, and considerable research has been undertaken to determine the cause and how to control the problem. These failures seem to be more prevalent in packaged firetube hot water boilers. Studies have determined that these failures are caused by the following conditions:

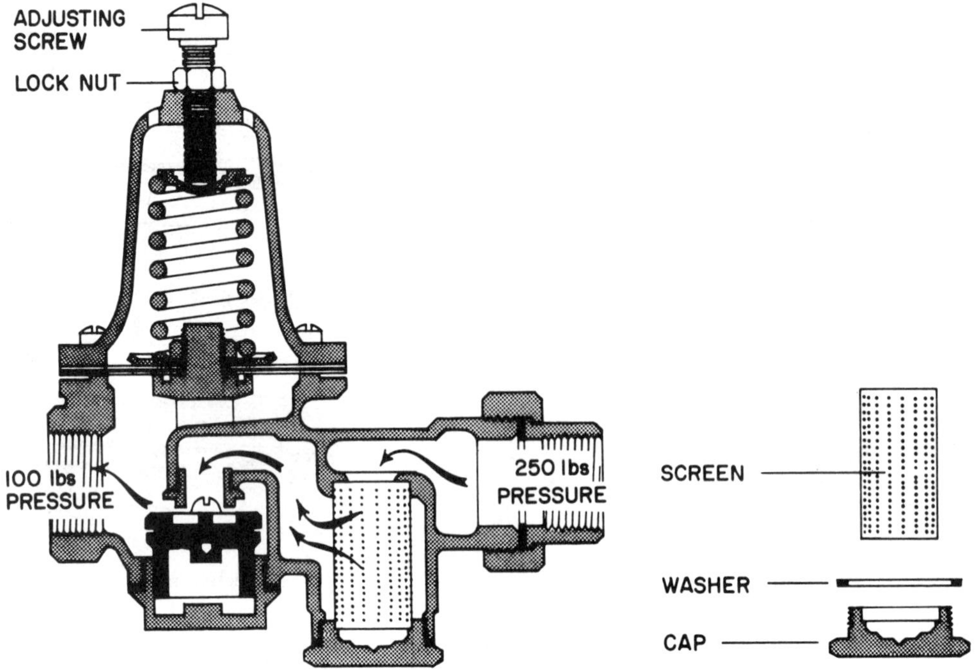

FIGURE 8-30 The pressure regulating valve. When the pressure in the system drops below 12 psi, this valve opens, allowing more water into the system; then the check valve automatically closes as the pressure increases. This maintains a minimum water level in the system. (Courtesy of Cadillac Fairview Corporation, Limited.)

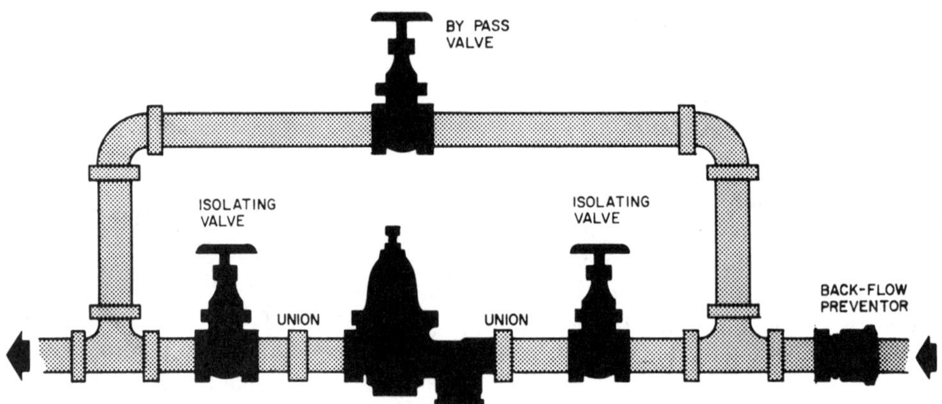

FIGURE 8-31 The by-pass valve. There are two functions for the by-pass valve assembly: (a) By by-passing the pressure regulating valve, we can speed up the filling of the system. (b) The system can be maintained manually while the pressure regulating valve is being serviced. (Courtesy of Cadillac Fairview Corporation, Limited.)

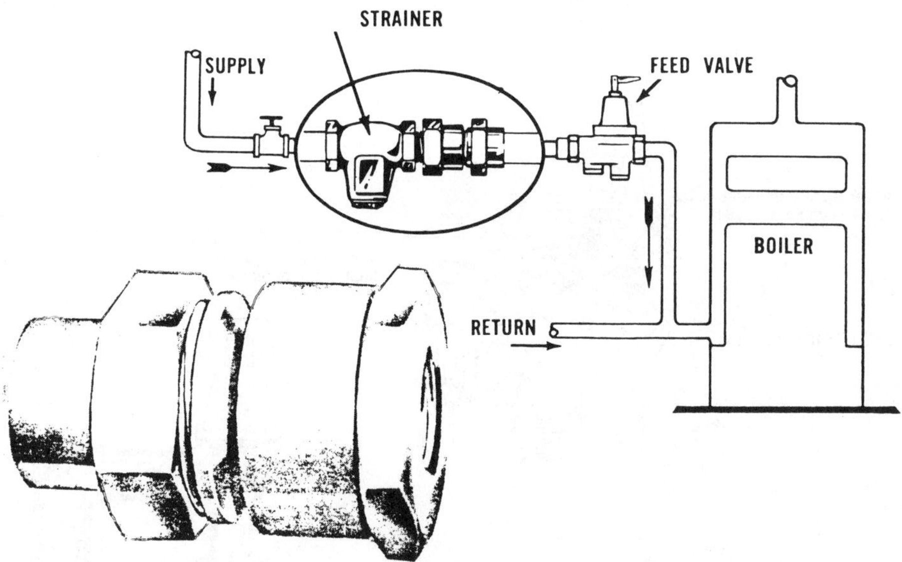

FIGURE 8-32 The boiler feed water system. Direct connection to the potable water supply allows back flow when the supply pressure is reduced below the boiler line pressure, permitting boiler water to flow into the potable water supply. A back flow preventer is installed to prevent this problem. (Courtesy of Watts Regulator Company.)

1. Overheating
2. Chemical attack from the water or fireside
3. Stress corrosion or thinning down from the fireside

Overheating

Studies being done presently indicate overheating is connected with the flow of the water through the boiler. The theory is that by reducing the flow, we will greatly reduce the problem of overheating.

Overheating could also be caused by deposits on the waterside that prevent adequate cooling of the tube metal, or by creating unusually hot zones on the tubes. Two of the common deposits found on boiler tubes and tube sheets are hard scale and sludge. This can be controlled by proper water treatment. The corrosion problem is the result of galvanic action due to dissimilar electrodes in an electrolyte. In most cases, it is a result of the steel pipe distribution system and copper convectors coming in contact with an electrolyte (the water in the heating system).

These galvanic couples are also present at nonferrous valve bodies and in heat exchangers and boiler tubes where copper tubes are expanded into ferrous tube sheets. The farther apart the dissimilar metals are located in the electromotive series, the more aggressive is the corrosion. During our investigation of the problems, we have measured up to 750 millivolts in experimental cells having steel and copper electrodes, and using heating system water on an electrolyte. The end result of these reactions is an accumulation of finely-divided iron oxide that is magnetic, abrasive, and, in combination with calcium scale, forms a very hard and

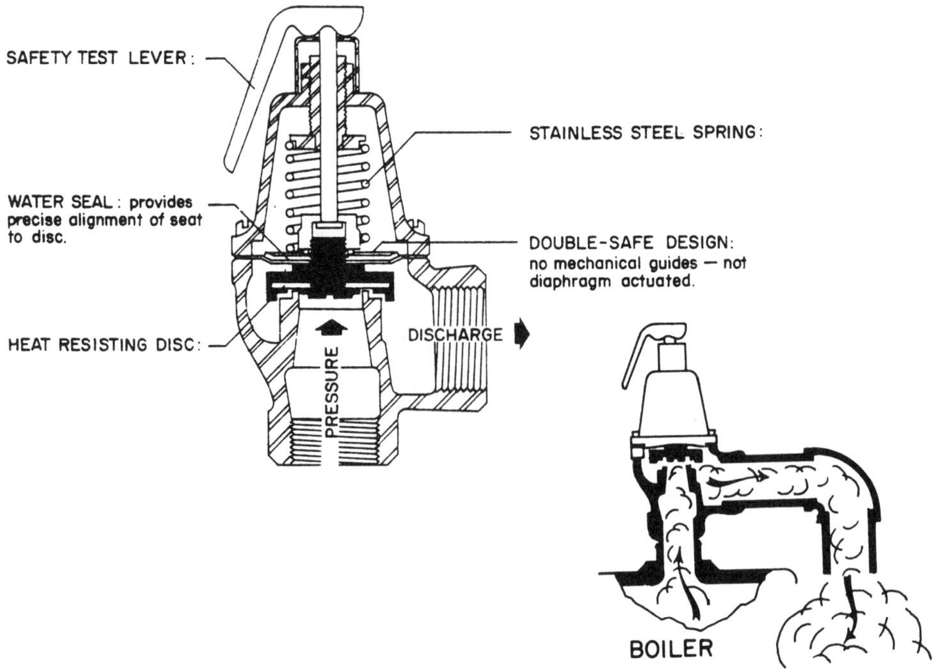

FIGURE 8-33 The water relief safety valve. Since the maximum emergency is created when steam forms in a hot water heating boiler, relief of steam pressure is essential for adequate pressure protection. The relief valve, acting as a steam safety valve, discharges steam at a faster rate than the boiler can generate it, thus restoring the system pressure to a safe level. (Courtesy of Cadillac Fairview Corporation, Limited.)

almost impervious coating on the water side of the heating surfaces.

Chemical Corrosion

The iron oxide found in heating systems is the result of the disintegration of the system's steel pipe. Proper water treatment chemical breaks down the calcium in the scale, dissolves all the metallic oxides, and establishes a mono-molecular insulating layer on the clean substrate metal. It is this insulating layer that inhibits current flow in the galvanic couples, thus arresting corrosion and stabilizing the problem. (See Chapter 1.)

There are basically two conditions that cause tube failures by chemically attacking the tubes of a hot water boiler:

1. *Acid*—Can be minimized by operating the boilers at the proper temperature and pH level.
2. *Oxygen*—This problem is created by a leak in the system. Fresh make-up water introduces fresh oxygen as the leak allows the chemically-treated water to run away.

Stress Corrosion

Regular fireside inspections, preventive maintenance, cleaning, and minor repairs can keep this problem under control. Efficient operating practices also ensure that the tubes will last for their expected life span of twenty years.

LOW-PRESSURE WATERTUBE BOILERS

Advantages

1. Compact; considerably smaller and lighter than firetube boiler of equal capacity.
2. No special foundation required.
3. Very short warm-up period required.
4. Bent or coil tube design avoids thermal stress and distortion.
5. Rapid response to fluctuating loads.
6. Comes as packaged unit, completely equipped with firing equipment, automatic controls, and safety devices.
7. Safer than firetube boiler in case of tube failure since boiler contains very little water and no disastrous explosion could occur.
8. Maintenance cost low, has a minimum of refractory.
9. Can be used in single or multiple unit installation. Each unit can be put into, or taken out of, service automatically when load varies, thus insuring maximum efficiency.

A watertube boiler has water passing through the inside of the tubes, while the products of combustion are on the outside of the tubes. These tubes are used to spread or increase the heating surface of the boiler above what you might achieve in a plain boiler with a heater under it.

There are no tube sheets in a watertube boiler; instead, the tubes are supported by upper and lower headers.

With this exception, all other components of a firetube boiler—gas train, control panels, safeties, shell, tubes, gauges—also apply to a watertube boiler.

BOILER MAINTENANCE INSPECTIONS

Daily log readings could indicate boiler operation problems. The operator should be able to correct most of them.

Any problems identified by an * require the services of a specialist who should be called for service.

Problem	*Probable Cause*
Pressure increases	- Cushion tank isolating valve closed. - Cushion tank water level too high. - Pressure regulating valve stuck open.* - Pressure regulating valve bypass valve open. - Defective pressure gauge.*
Pressure decreases	- Boiler tubes leaking.* - Leaks in heating system.* - Defective pressure gauge.*
Pressure increases and decreases with increase and decrease of boiler water temperature	- Cushion tank water logged.
Supply temperature does not recover	- Burner does not reach high fire.* - Tubes are fouled with soot.* - Fresh air intake is plugged. - Broken linkage on combustion air and/or gas valve.* - Defective temperature gauge.*
Return temperature extremely low	- Boiler isolating supply or return valve closed. - Defective temperature gauge.*
Stack temperature too low	- Burner stays on low fire.* - Stack thermometer defective.* - Tubes are fouled with soot.* - Fresh air intakes are plugged.* - Stack thermometer defective.*

IMPORTANT

Do not operate more heating boilers than are necessary to maintain building design

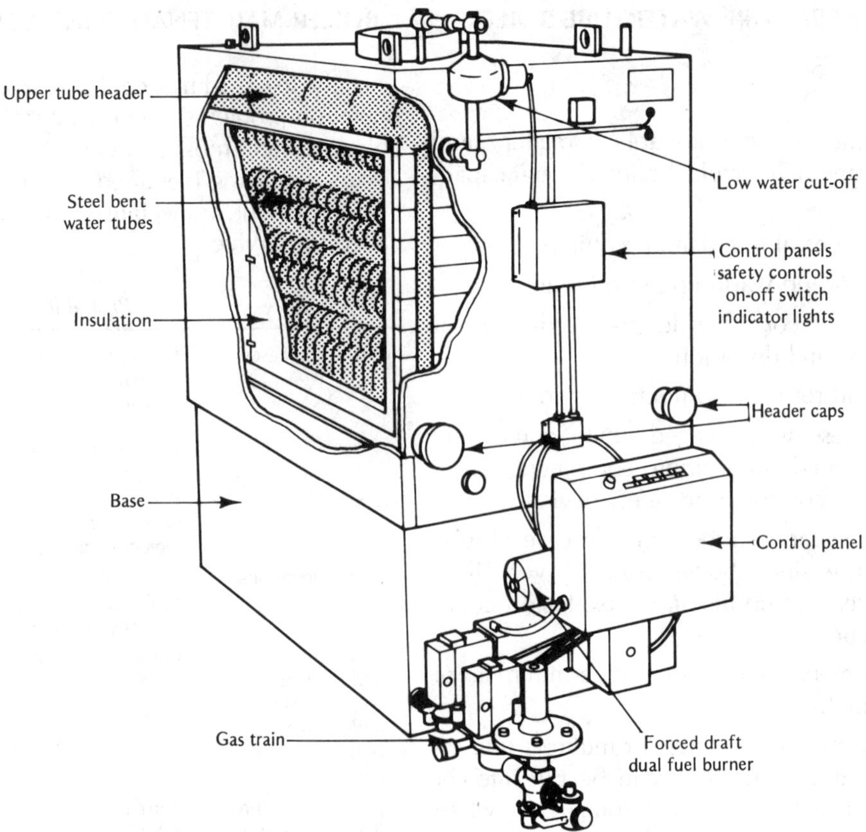

FIGURE 8-34 The low pressure watertube boiler. (Courtesy of the Bryant Corporation.)

temperature. If you require 200°F blend water and one boiler can maintain this temperature, *then only use one boiler*.

On the average, there are only a minimal number of days a year when 100 percent of boiler capacity is required. Thus, a two boiler building would only require the second boiler on the coldest days.

LEAKS

The heating system should be checked daily for leaks—any loss of water should be investigated and corrected. The loss of treated water is not only expensive, but the addition of fresh water to replace that lost by leakage contributes to scaling in the boilers and galvanic corrosion in the piping system due to the calcium introduced in the make-up water.

8-8 Heat Distribution

The selection of a heating system and the possible inclusion of air conditioning will depend on local climate conditions, degree of comfort desired, budgets, and fuel costs. An increasing number of owners want a system that incorporates total year-round air conditioning. Some type of heating unit must be used to efficiently distribute the heat from the source of heat to the room being heated. These heating units are classified as either a radiant or convector type, depending on the way the heat is being transferred.

It should be noted that heat is transferred or transmitted from one substance to another by three basic processes—*convection, conduction,* and *radiation*.

THE AIR-WATER SYSTEM

Radiant heating units expose the heat transfer surface so that the heat is transferred by radiation to the surrounding objects and by natural convection to the surrounding air.

Convection heating units enclose the heat transfer surface in a cabinet or other enclosure.

Convection units transfer heat by all three methods. Heat flows by conduction from the tubes to the slightly cooler fins. From the fins, it continues to flow by conduction to the cooler surrounding air. The air, as it warms up, expands. Expanded, the air becomes less dense so it rises, carrying the heat away from the fins by convection. Heat also radiates from the warm cabinet to cooler objects in the room. Incidently, radiation does not heat the air between objects, but only the objects themselves.

Both air and water are used to transport heat. Only enough air is circulated to provide ventilation, humidity control, and cooling that is needed for comfort during the heating season, or heating during the cooling season. The main heating and cooling load is handled by water.

The advantages to this system are less energy used to transport heat, less energy wasted to achieve temperature and humidity control, and less space needed for ducts.

THE ALL AIR SYSTEM

In forced air systems, the air is heated or cooled in a central unit and then delivered to the room through supply ducts. Air is returned to the central unit for treatment. Treatment could include heating, cooling, or humidifying. Once treated, the air is then recirculated through the rooms. It is interesting to note that we must circulate 375 cubic feet of air to transport the heat that 1 cubic foot of water will carry. Ducts take up valuable space, and if they are kept small, more power is needed to drive the fans. To satisfy the

FIGURE 8-35 Typical air-water convection units. (Courtesy of Mark-Hot.)

requirements of the space being air conditioned without wasting energy or sacrificing comfort, skilled technicians must design the systems.

The merits of the all air system are low initial cost, ease of maintenance, and good control over temperature and humidity. However, energy consumption is high when loads are variable.

FIGURE 8-36 Typical fan-coil unit. (Courtesy of Mark-Hot.)

THE ALL WATER SYSTEM

The simplest type of central heating and cooling system has fan-coil units in the rooms and only water is circulated throughout the building. Ventilation air is provided by fresh air intake in the wall of the space or just by infiltration.

Temperature is controlled by varying the water temperature in the coil and/or by changing the fan speed and thereby changing the air velocity over the coil.

Another variant of the all water system uses heat pump units in place of fan-coil units in rooms. Warm water is circulated through all the units in a building. Heat pumps in spaces that require heating take heat from the water loop while other heat pumps take heat from spaces that need cooling and reject the heat into the water. These systems have very low energy consumption and use electrical energy.

The Vertical Riser Monoflow Heating System

This type of monoflow system has a vertical supply riser from the boiler to the distribution supply main located in the ceiling of the top floor. Each line of convectors is served by a special tee called a monoflow tee. The water then returns to the same pipe that it is taken from. Each riser terminates at the return main in the basement and is returned to the boiler through this main. (Fig. 8-38.)

Heating Zone Pump Inspections

Problem	*Probable Cause*
Pressure differential too high	- Pump suction valve partially closed. - Valve blend temperature too high, and overheating suites, causing suite valves to close.* - Defective pressure gauges.*
Valve blend temperature too high	- Mixing valve controls set too low.* - Mixing valve controls defective.* - Mixing valve, by-pass valve open or partially open.
Valve blend temperature too low	- Mixing valve controls set too low.* - Mixing valve actuator defective.* - Blend temperature isolating valve closed or partially closed. - Pump pressure differential by-pass valve open. - Boiler temperature too low.
Return temperature to mixing valve more than 20°F below blend temperature	- Pump off. - Pump spring coupling broken.* - Return valve to mixing valve closed or partially closed.

Any problems identified by a * require the services of a specialist.

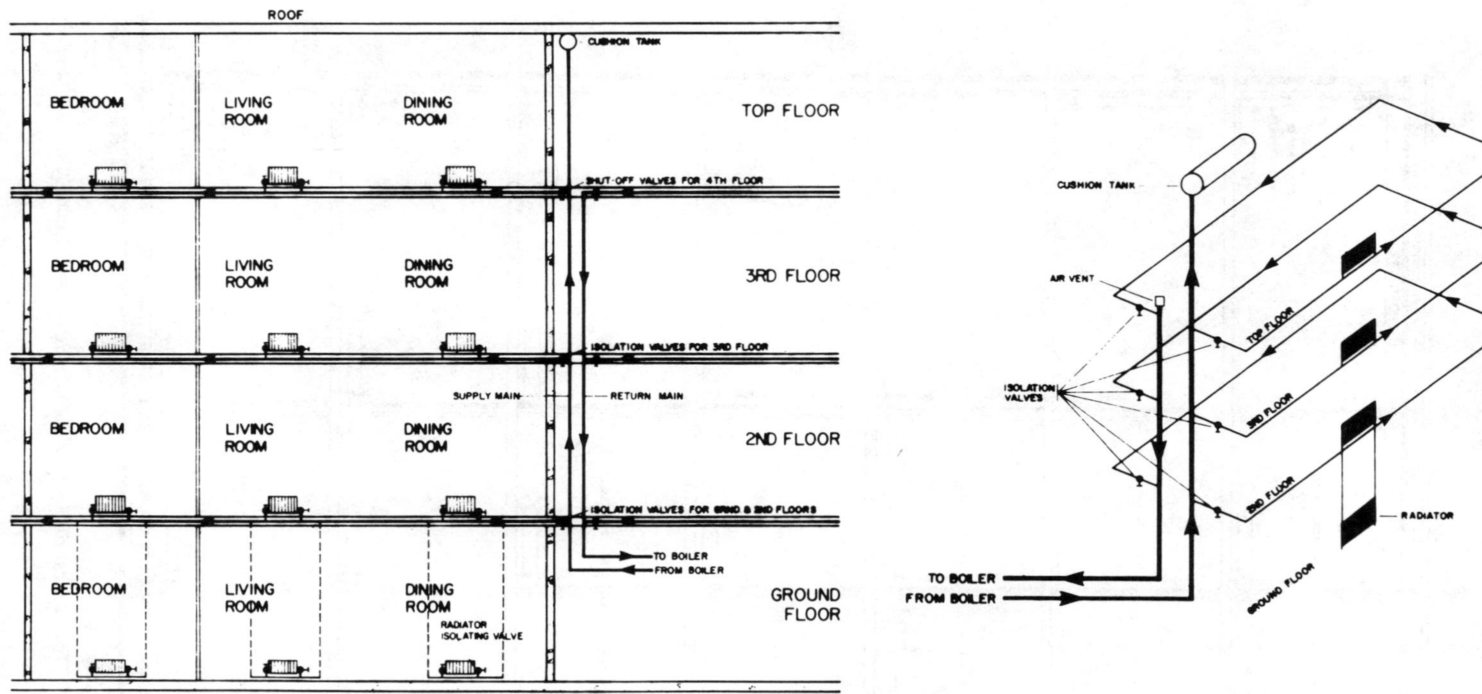

FIGURE 8-37 Loop monoflow system. This type of system has a supply and return main, which run from the boiler to the top floor of the building. The water flow is taken from the supply main, on the underside of the floor that it is serving, through the monoflow loop, and back to the return main. The flow through each convector or radiator from this loop is controlled by a special tee called a monoflow tee. The loop on the underside of the second floor also feeds down to the first floor, in buildings where there is no basement. This system is rarely used in the construction of low rise buildings today. (Courtesy of Cadillac Fairview Corporation, Limited.)

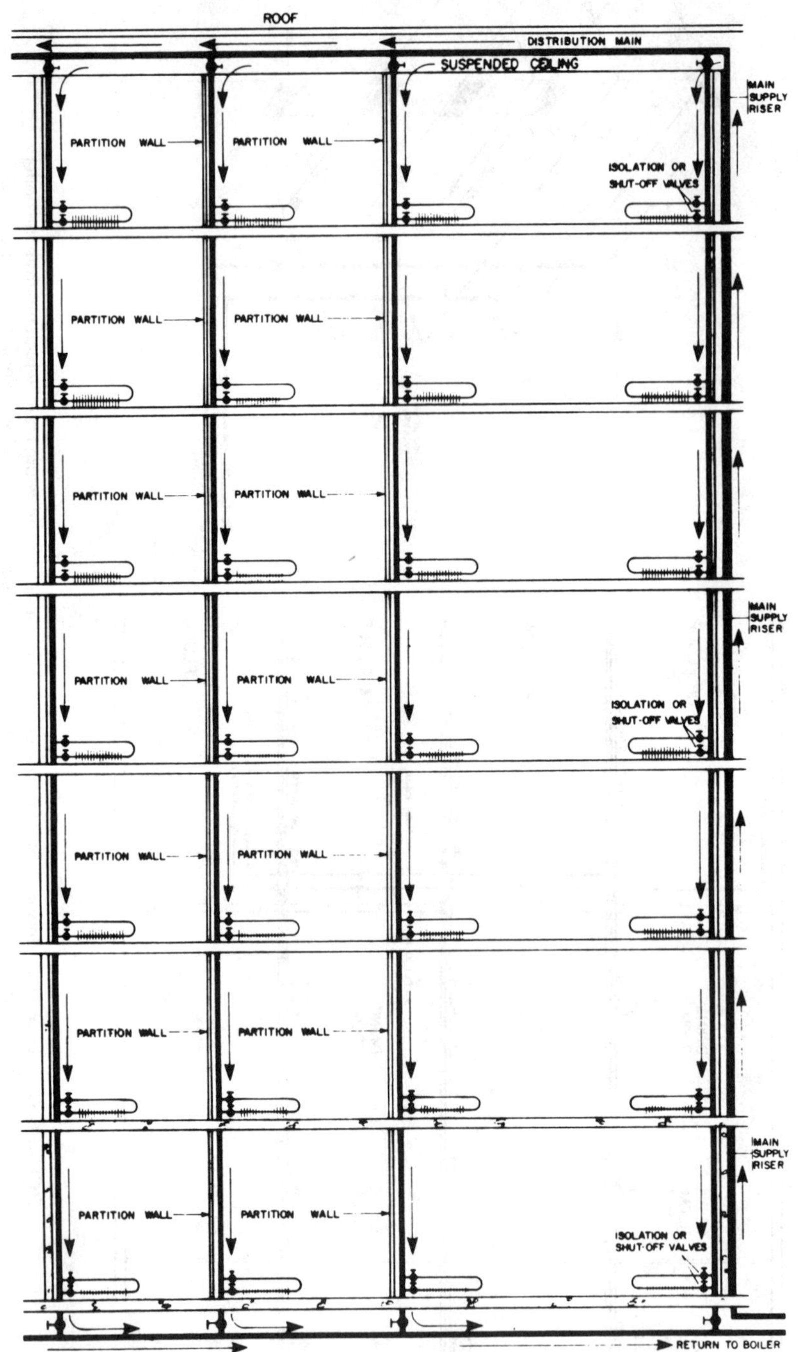

FIGURE 8-38 The vertical riser monoflow heating system. (Courtesy of Cadillac Fairview Corporation, Limited.)

The Two Pipe Heating System

This system has a supply main on the top floor, from which the water is distributed to the supply risers, then to the convectors in each suite, and back to a return riser. The water then goes to a return main and is returned to the boiler through this main.

WHEN TO SHUT DOWN HEATING PUMPS

Between seasons, spring and fall, building *heating pumps are to be shut down when the outdoor temperature rises above 15°C or approximately 60°F.*

GARAGE HEATING

Check the garage heating daily and insure that residents are not altering the thermostat settings. *It is not necessary to raise the garage temperature above 5°C (approximately 42°F),* and generally there is enough radiation from the garage piping system to prevent freezing, except at garage doorways.

RAMP HEATING

Garage ramps should be turned on as the weather dictates and *should be operated no higher than 50°C (approximately 120°F).* To prevent cracking of the concrete, the heat should not be turned off until the end of the heating season.

TEMPERATURE CONTROL

All hot water heating systems vary water temperature to radiators to match or offset the building's heat losses.

Some older systems vary the boiler temperature via indoor and outdoor sensors, and the whole system temperature, including the boiler, rises and falls to suit outdoor conditions.

More modern systems operate the boilers at a constant temperature for peak operating efficiency and vary the system water temperature through indoor-outdoor sensors and mixing valves to suit outdoor conditions.

Since only about 3 percent of the heating season requires full boiler capacity, multi-boiler systems have been installed in some buildings. This allows peak operating efficiency of the fuel burning equipment with additional boilers cutting in or out automatically as outdoor conditions demand. A further refinement is a sequence controller that allows any boiler to be the lead boiler and thus equalizes the wear on the equipment.

The system may also be zoned so that the temperature of the water to the zone in the sunlight or upper zone is cooler than the zone in the shade or lower area.

This system can be controlled in the following ways:

1. Electric
2. Electronic
3. Pneumatic (air operated)

Pneumatic Control System

A control system is a grouping of instruments or devices that regulate or control a variable and maintain it at a predetermined value. The variable may be temperature, humidity, or pressure.

A pneumatic control system consists of four essential parts:

1. Air compressor, filter, and reducing station.
2. Air piping and distribution system.
3. Controllers (thermostats, humidistats, pressure regulators).

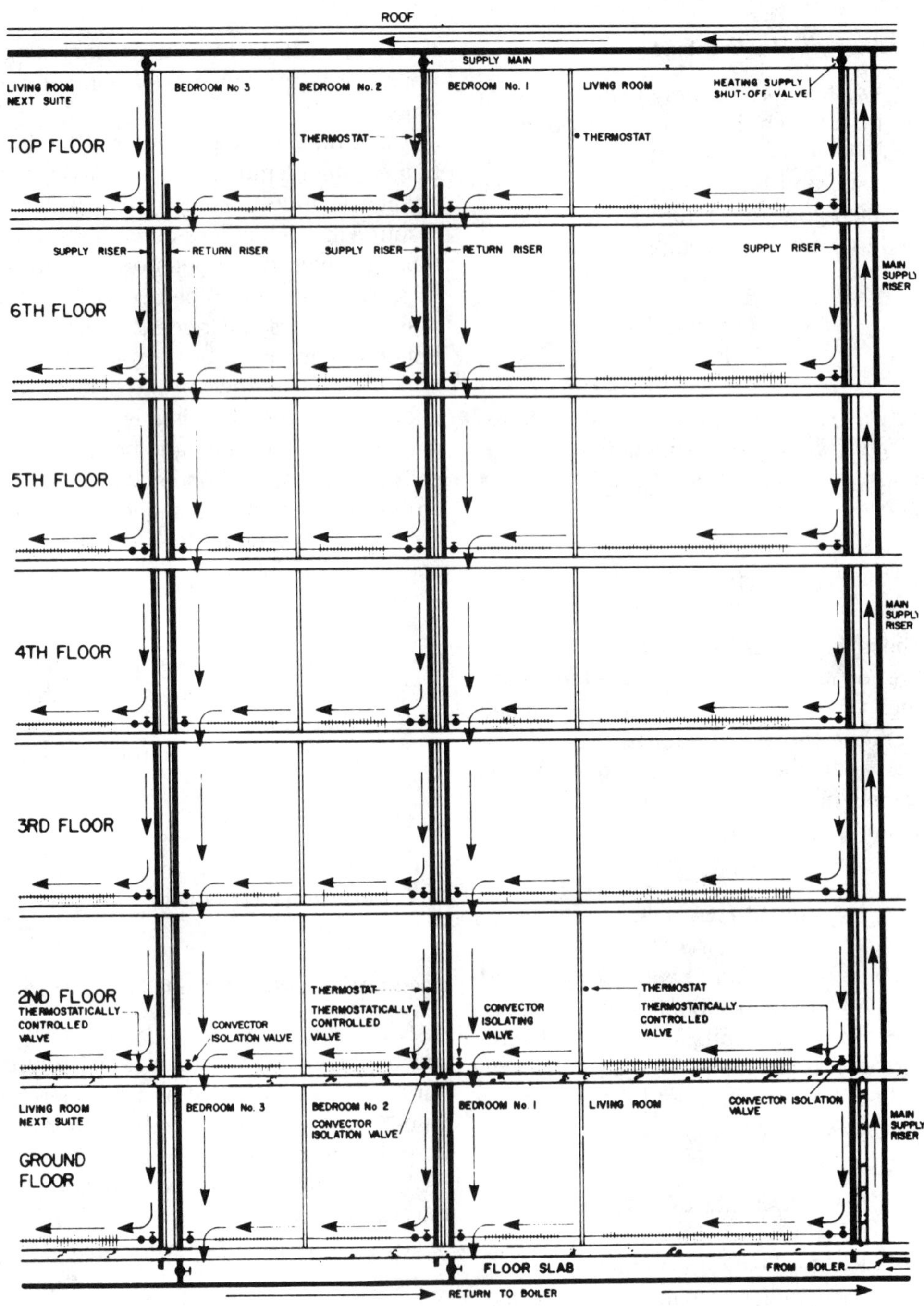

FIGURE 8-39 The two-pipe heating system. (Courtesy of Cadillac Fairview Corporation, Limited.)

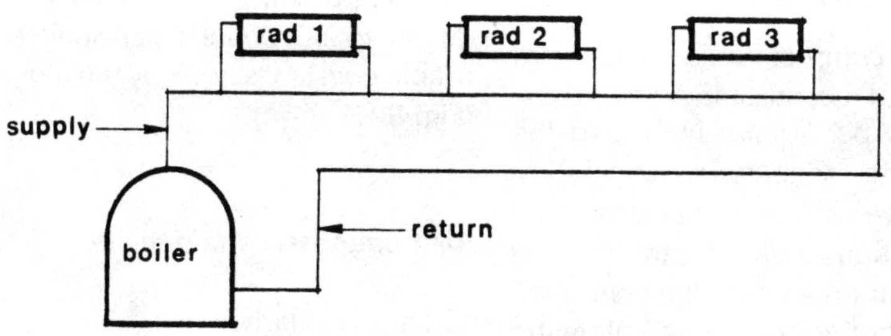

One pipe or monoflo system

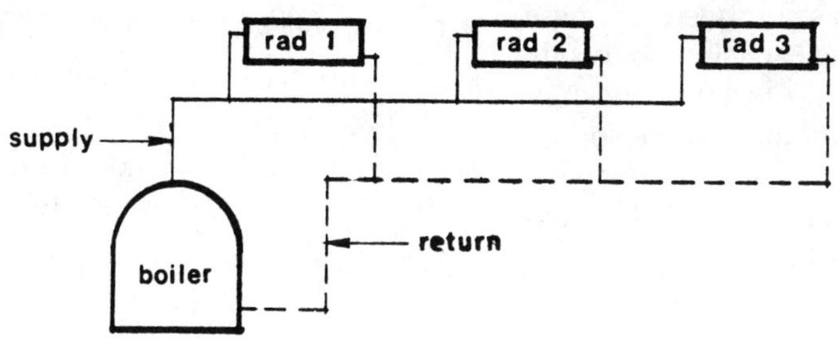

Two pipe direct return system

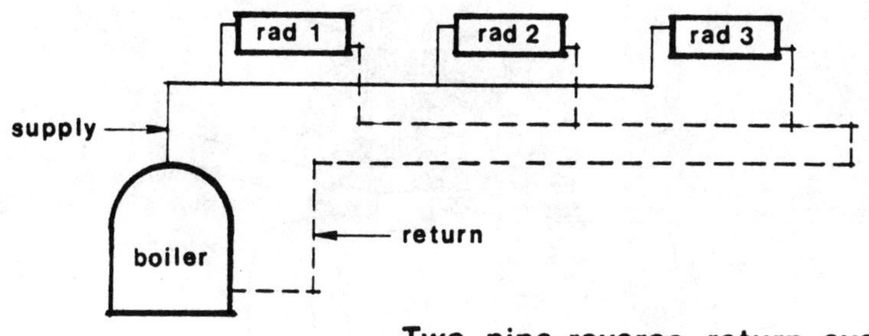

Two pipe reverse return system

FIGURE 8-40 Piping system schematics. (Courtesy of Cadillac Fairview Corporation, Limited.)

4. Controlled devices (valves, damper operators).

Typical Pneumatic Control System

Air from the compressor is supplied to each controller at a constant pressure, usually 15 pounds per square inch, and the controller in turn is connected by air pressure piping to the valve or damper operator it actuates. The function of the controller is to apply a varying air pressure to the controlled device. The controller acts as an automatic pressure reducing valve, regulating the air pressure to the controlled device in accordance with the controlled variable.

The air compressors furnished for these systems vary in size and capacity and usually operate in a range of 70 to 80 pounds per square inch. The size of the compressor depends on the size of the control system and the number of control units that must be supplied with air. (Fig. 8-42.)

All air compressors are equipped with a filter and reducing valve assembly. The filter will remove any moisture or impurities that may be present in the air. Air pressure is reduced to 80 pounds per square inch to a usable constant supply by the reducing valve. (Fig. 8-41.)

Air Compressor Maintenance

1. Dust regularly.
2. Air intake filter of washable type should be cleaned as necessary.
3. If belt driven, check belt tension, frays, cracks, pulley.
4. Check to make sure all holding bolts are tight.
5. Air intake filter of non-washable type should be changed as required.
6. Check cut-in and cut-out positions.

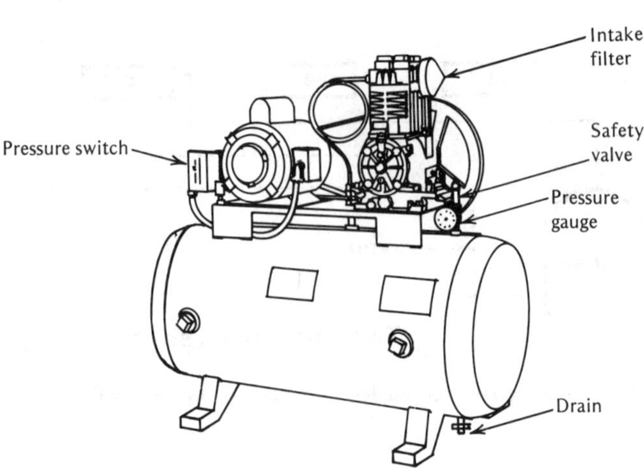

FIGURE 8-41 Horizontal tank air compressor.

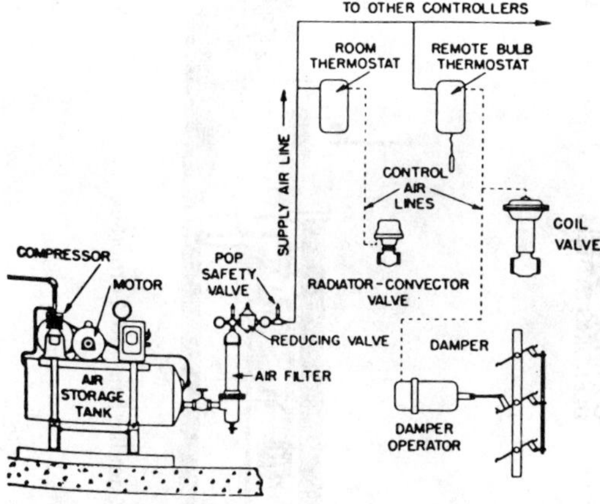

FIGURE 8-42 Typical pneumatic control system.

ELECTRIC (ON-OFF) BOILER OPERATION

The electric indoor-outdoor control, known as outdoor reset, ties into the on-off control circuit on the boiler and "cuts out" the burner whenever the water temperature going to the heating system gets to the set point. In effect, this prevents the addition of heat to the boiler water and monitors the boiler water temperature to the system requirements.

Similarily, it turns the unit on when the water temperature to the system falls below the differential setting on the controls.

The "high limit control" on the boiler is a safety device and shuts off the burner if the "on-off" control fails.

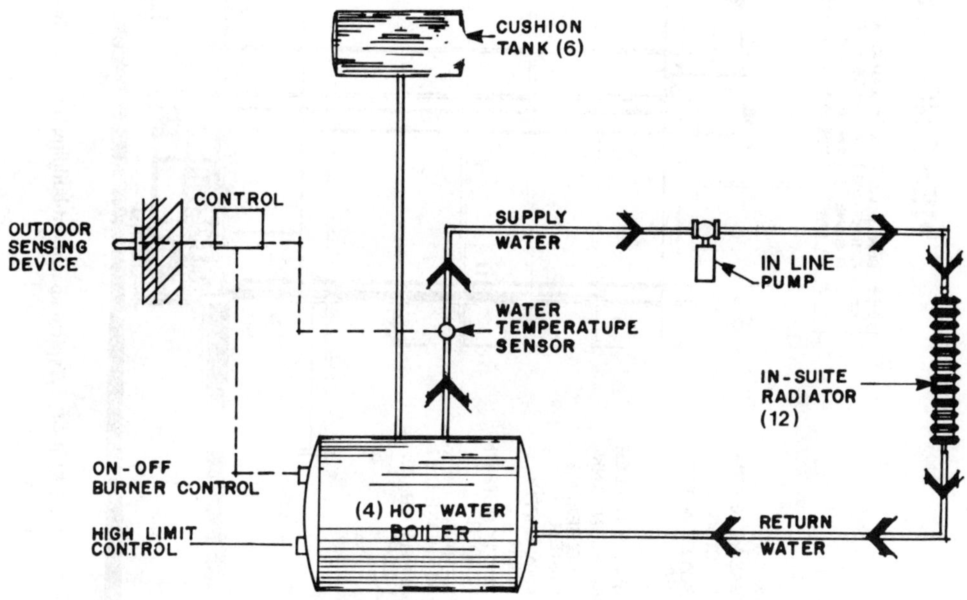

FIGURE 8-43 Electric (on-off) boiler operation. (Courtesy of Cadillac Fairview Corporation, Limited.)

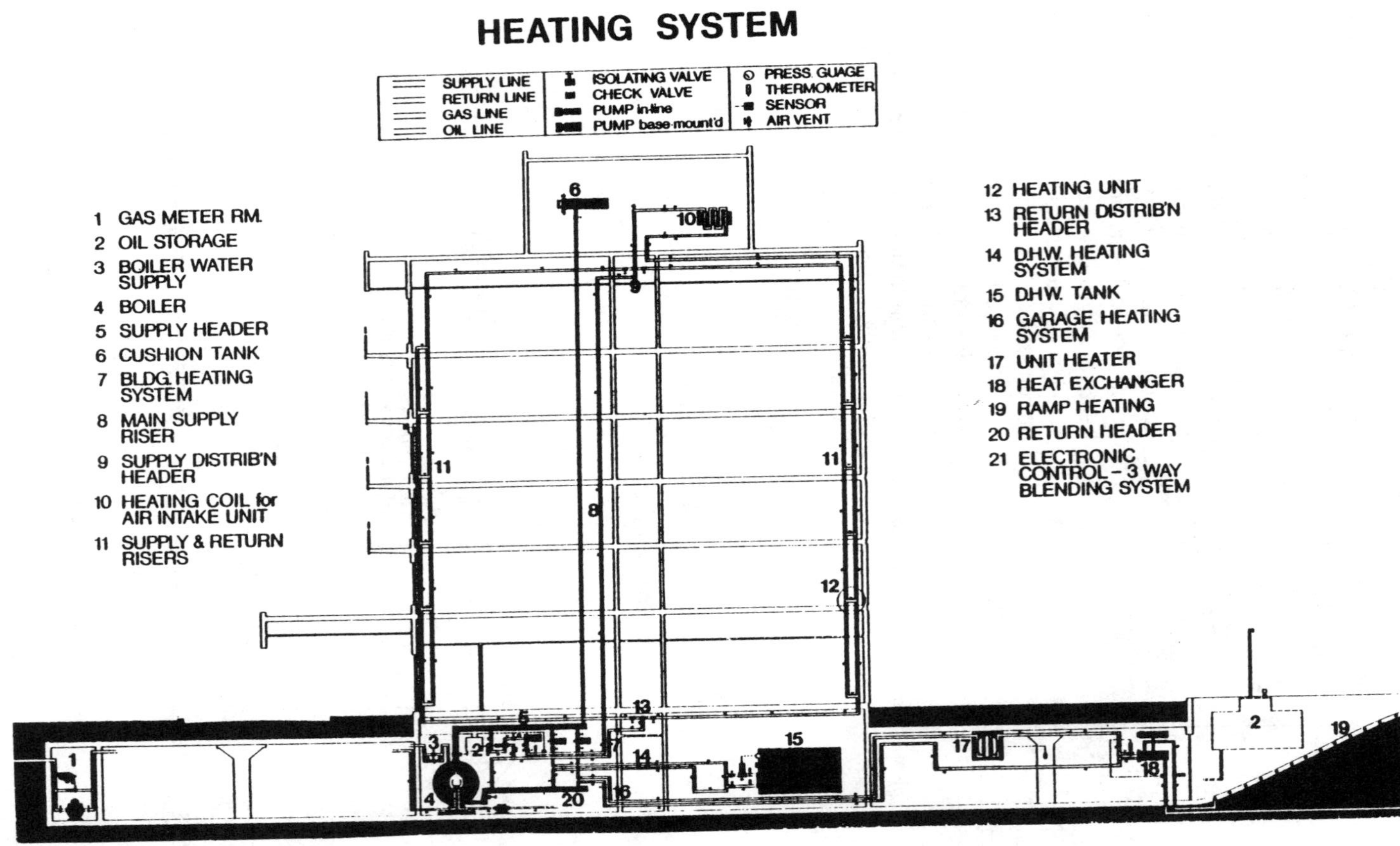

FIGURE 8-44 **Typical apartment building hot water heating system.** (Courtesy of Cadillac Fairview Corporation, Limited.)

CONTROLLING A THREE-WAY BLENDING VALVE

This is the most common application of an indoor-outdoor sensing system, known as outdoor reset, for varying the water temperature, and it is used in many buildings.

The master control transmits a signal to the operator or controller of the three-way mixing valve, which has two inlets and one outlet. (Fig. 8-46.)

The valve operator or controller then positions or repositions the valve stem, which changes the proportion of the hotter and cooler water entering each of the two inlets. The result is a change in the water temperature leaving the outlet and going to the system. (Fig. 8-45.)

In this sytem the boiler operates at a fixed boiler water temperature (average 200°F) and the mixing valves control the water temperature to the system by proportionately blending 200°F water from the boiler with return water from the system. This is called the *blend* water temperature.

Troubleshooting Blending Valves

1. Check the power supply and fuses.
2. Check the position of the valve stem to make certain it moves when the motor operates.
3. Make sure the packing is not leaking. Excessive leaking will wear out the valve stem, making repacking difficult.
4. If the valves are air operated, air pressure closes the valve and spring pressure opens the valve. Check the air pressure.
5. If the problem cannot be corrected, open the by-pass and call for service by a qualified mechanic.

The success or failure of an energy conservation effort depends on the blending valves operating efficiently.

THE HEAT EXCHANGER

A heat exchanger could be described as a method of transferring heat from one liquid to another without mixing the liquids.

Different forms of heat exchangers are used for the following purposes in an apartment building:

1. Heating glycol in garage ramps.
2. Heating corridor air supply.
3. Heating domestic hot water.

Figure 8-47 illustrates systems that are exposed to the elements, such as garage ramps and corridor air heaters.

There are two circulating pumps. One circulates the boiler water, the other, the glycol. The temperature of the boiler water is controlled by an aquastat in the glycol. *Ramp temperature should not exceed 120°F,* especially when plastic pipes are installed.

Once a year the servicemen should check the ramps for leaks and top up the glycol, if necessary.

Leaks can be detected by regularly checking the cushion tank sight glass. *Leaks must be repaired as soon as detected.*

Corridor air is controlled by a thermostat in the duct, which operates a three-way mixing valve set to maintain a corridor temperature of 68°F.

Typical Water-to-Water or Water-to-Glycol Heat Exchanger

In this system the glycol or water surrounds the tube bundle containing the hotter water from the boiler. Glycol is usually used to heat whenever there is a possibility of freezing. (Fig. 8-48.)

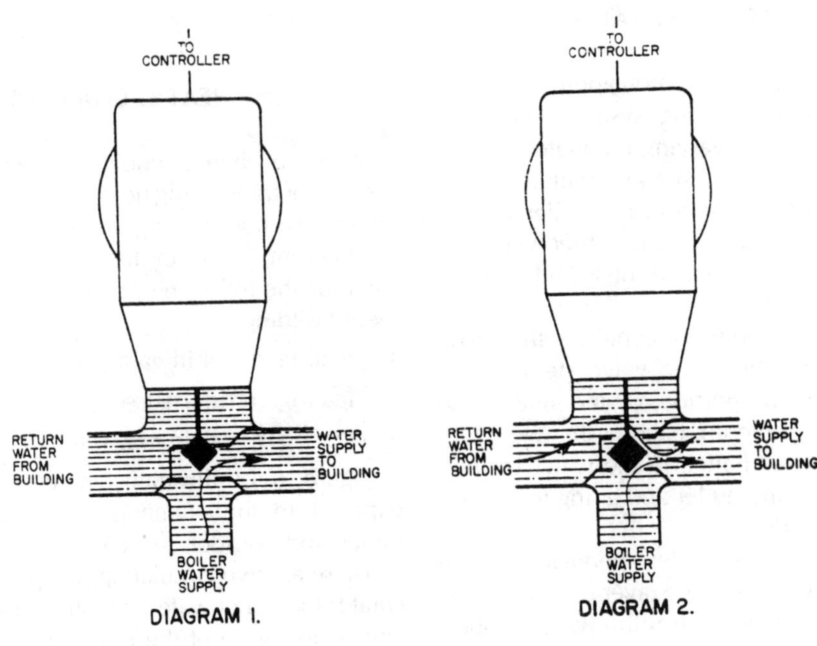

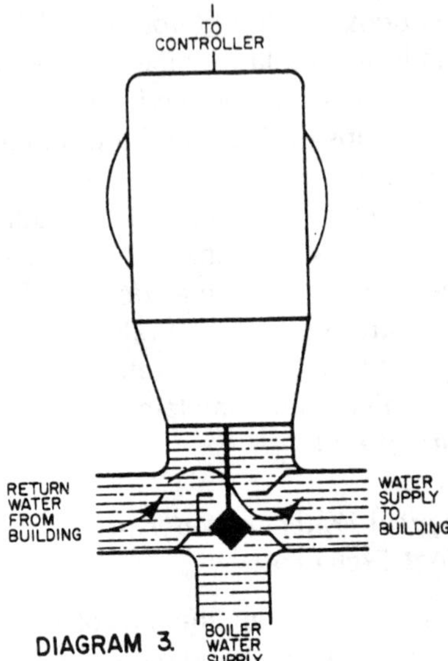

DIAGRAM '1' indicates the position of the valve when the controller calls for additional heat. The valve is now closed to the return water system and open to the boiler water supply.

DIAGRAM '2' indicates the position of the valve when the controller, which is connected to the outside sensor and the valve, calls for more or less heat. The valve is now in a position to use a blend of both return and boiler water.

DIAGRAM '3' indicates the position of the valve when the controller has been satisfied and no additional heat is required from the boiler. The valve is now closed to the boiler and only the return water is circulating through the system.

FIGURE 8-45 The three-way blending valve. (Courtesy of Cadillac Fairview Corporation, Limited.)

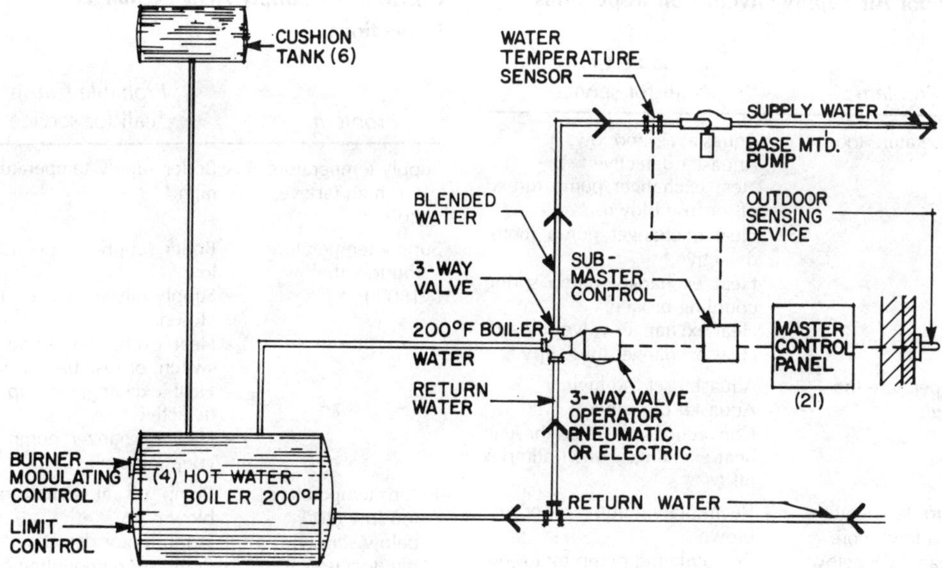

FIGURE 8-46 Typical three-way blending valve installation. (Courtesy of Cadillac Fairview Corporation, Limited.)

Ramp Glycol Heat Exchanger Inspections

Problem	*Probable Cause* *call for service
Supply temperature too high (above 200°F)	- Boiler supply temperature too high.*
Supply temperature too low (below 180°F)	- Boiler supply temperature too low.* - Supply valve to heat exchanger closed. - Heat exchanger pump off at switch, or fuse blown. - Heat exchanger pump motor defective.* - Heat exchanger pump spring coupling broken.*
Return temperature too low (20°F below supply temperature)	- Pump off at switch or fuse blown. - Pump motor defective.* - Pump spring coupling broken.
Supply temperature is higher than return temperature when pump is off	- Material convection through heat exchanger.*
Supply temperature is lower than return temperature when pump is off	- Reverse convection through heat exchanger.*

Ramp Glycol System Inspections

Problem	*Probable Cause* *call for service
Temperature too low	- Aquastat set too low. - Aquastat defective.* - Heat exchanger pump turned off or fuse blown. - Heat exchanger pump motor defective.* - Heat exchanger pump spring coupling broken.* - Heat exchanger valves closed. - Heat exchanger tube dirty.*
Temperature too high	- Aquastat set too high. - Aquastat defective.* - Convection of water through heat exchanger when pump is off.*
Return temperature too low (more than 15°F below tank temperature)	- Recirculating pump off or fuse blown. - Recirculating pump motor defective.* - Recirculating pump spring coupling broken.* - Recirculating pump isolating valves closed. - Recirculating pipes plugged.*

Corridor Air Supply Glycol Coil Inspections

Problem	*Probable Cause* *call for service
Temperature too low	- Aquastat set too low. - Aquastat defective.* - Heat exchanger pump turned off or fuse blown. - Heat exchanger pump motor defective.* - Heat exchanger pump spring coupling broken.* - Heat exchanger valves closed. - Heat exchanger tube dirty.*
Temperature too high	- Aquastat set too high. - Aquastat defective.* - Convection of water through heat exchanger when pump is off.*
Return temperature too low (more than 15°F below tank temperature)	- Recirculating pump off or fuse blown. - Recirculating pump motor defective.* - Recirculating pump spring coupling broken.* - Recirculating pump isolating valves closed. - Recirculating pipes plugged.*

Corridor Air Supply Heat Exchanger Inspections

Problem	*Probable Cause* *call for service
Supply temperature too high (above 200°F)	- Boiler supply temperature too high.*
Supply temperature too low (below 180°F)	- Boiler supply temperature too low.* - Supply valve to heat exchanger closed. - Heat exchanger pump off at switch, or fuse blown. - Heat exchanger pump motor defective.* - Heat exchanger pump spring coupling broken.*
Return temperature too low (20°F below supply temperature)	- Pump off at switch or fuse blown. - Pump motor defective.* - Pump spring coupling broken.*
Supply temperature is higher than return temperature when pump is off	- Material convection through heat exchanger.*
Supply temperature is lower than return temperature when pump is off	- Reverse convection through heat exchanger.*

Storage Tank Heat Exchanger Inspections

Problem	*Probable Cause* *call for service
Supply temperature too high (above 200°F)	- Boiler supply temperature too high.*
Supply temperature too low (below 180°F)	- Boiler supply temperature too low.* - Supply valve to heat exchanger closed. - Heat exchanger pump off at switch, or fuse blown. - Heat exchanger pump motor defective.* - Heat exchanger pump spring coupling broken.*
Return temperature too low (20°F below supply temperature)	- Pump off at switch or fuse blown. - Pump motor defective.* - Pump spring coupling broken.*
Supply temperature is higher than return temperature when pump is off	- Material convection through heat exchanger.*
Supply temperature is lower than return temperature when pump is off	- Reverse convection through heat exchanger.*

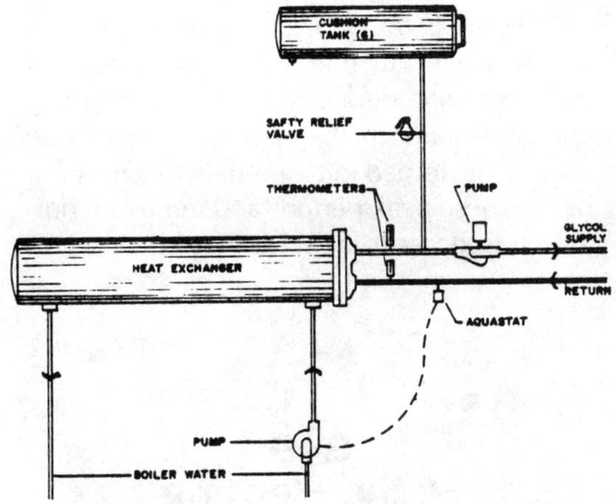

FIGURE 8-47 Typical water-to-water or water-to-glycol heat exchanger. (Courtesy of Cadillac Fairview Corporation, Limited.)

HEATING THE DOMESTIC WATER (AN "OCCUPANT SENSITIVE" ENERGY USER)

By piping part of the hot water from the building's heating system into a heating device, we can satisfy the occupant's needs for hot water for bathing (30 percent), kitchen (14 percent), and laundry (11 percent). This heating device may be a direct or indirect heater which may use oil, gas, electricity, or solar energy to function. (Figs. 8-48 and 8-49.)

Maximum Temperature

The maximum temperature of the water in the storage tank must never exceed 140°. A higher temperature would cause scaling and corrosion in the piping, as well as a serious corrosion problem in the whole system.

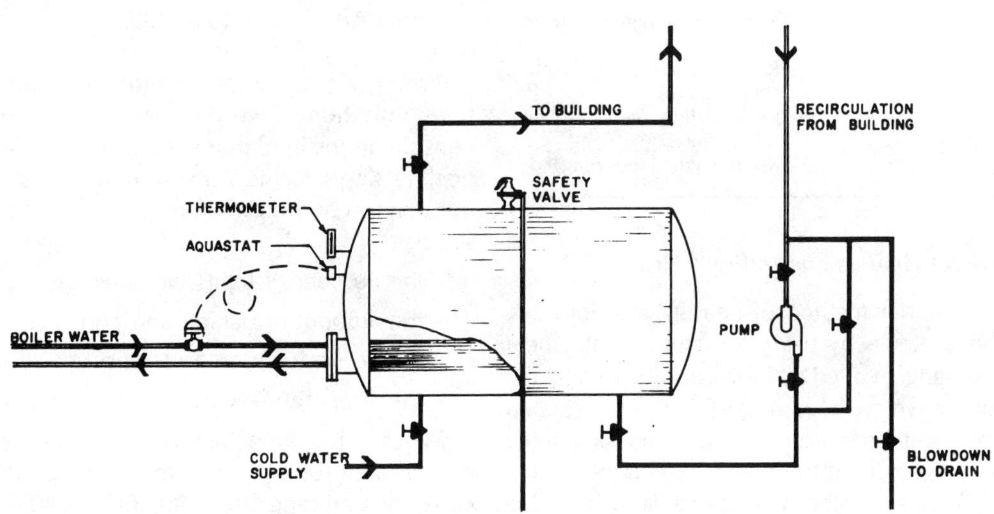

FIGURE 8-48 The "tube bundle" heat exchanger and storage tank. (Courtesy of Cadillac Fairview Corporation, Limited.)

DOMESTIC HOT WATER STORAGE TANK INSPECTIONS

Problem	*Probable Cause* *call for service
Temperature too low	- Pilot flame is out. - Aquastat set too low. - Aquastat defective.* - Heat exchanger pump turned off or fuse blown. - Heat exchanger pump motor defective.* - Heat exchanger pump spring coupling broken.* - Heat exchanger valves closed. - Heat exchanger tube dirty.* - Burner ports clogged. - Gas pressure too low.*
Temperature too high	- Aquastat set too high. - Aquastat defective or needs calibration.* - Convection of water through heat exchanger when pump is off.* - Main valve stuck open. - Dripping faucets. - Stacking effect.
Return temperature too low (more than 15°F below tank temperature)	- Recirculating pump off or fuse blown. - Recirculating pump motor defective.* - Recirculating pump spring coupling broken.* - Recirculating pump isolating valves closed. - Recirculating pipes plugged.*

Direct Heaters and Indirect Heaters

Another method of heating the domestic hot water is by using a water-to-water heat exchanger called a "tube bundle" to heat the water which is then stored in an insulated tank until required. The amount of energy needed to heat the water is dictated by the demands of the occupants and not the weather. (Fig. 8-49.)

Heat for this purpose is supplied by hot water pumped from the boiler and regulated by an immersion thermostat in the tank.

If we study the habits of the building's occupants, we will find that most of the hot water is required for one hour in the morning and two hours in the evening. The heaters should be turned on one-half to one hour before these peak periods and turned off during other times to achieve 35 percent to 40 percent savings in fuel.

8-9 Home Heating

THE FORCED AIR FURNACE (AN ALL AIR SYSTEM)

Forced air systems first gained popularity in the 1940s. New styles of residences, such as ranch bungalows, basementless, and split levels required changes in system design. There are three basic requirements for correct performance of forced air systems: accurate design, correct installation, and balancing.

When we consider comfortable conditions in a home, we are faced with many considerations in identical houses with identical heating systems. All sorts of things affect our comfort and the amount of fuel we consume:

- the number of lights we leave on
- the amount of baking and cooking
- the house location and exposure
- the temperature we keep our home at

When calculating the heating requirement for an eight-room house, the heating plant capacity may range from 80,000 to 140,000 Btu's per hour depending on the climate of the region. The most efficient heating plant is one that has just the right hourly Btu capacity and runs almost continuously. It provides an

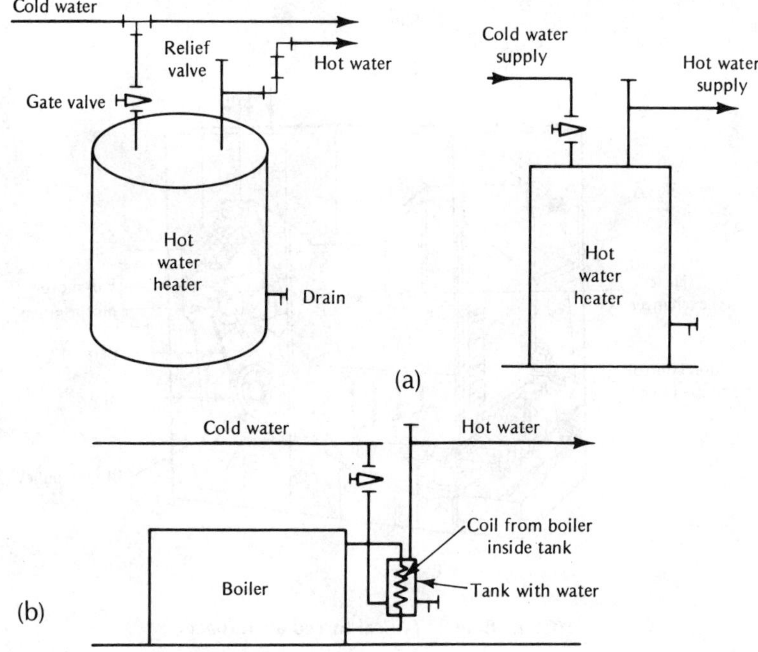

FIGURE 8-49 Methods of heating domestic water. (a) Direct heaters; (b) Indirect heaters—this method uses a heat exchanger coil to heat the water before it is distributed to the building. This type of heat exchanger is called a "side arm." (Courtesy of Reston Publishing Company.)

even flow of warmth to all parts of the system, and by not having to heat itself intermittently, saves fuel.

HOW A FORCED AIR FURNACE WORKS

In the furnace illustrated, circulating air enters at the bottom where a filter traps the dirt. The blower forces the air through a compartment called a heat exchanger, which contains metal passageways heated to a temperature of several hundred degrees by combustion gases rising inside. (Fig. 8-50.)

The passageway exteriors heat the circulating air as the blower forces it into the warm-air plenum of the network of ducts. A fan and limit control switches the blower off and on, and turns off the burner if circulating air temperature rises too high. The combustion gases, which do not mix with circulating air, escape through a stack to the chimney.

Winter air is unhealthfully dry because cold air retains less moisture than warm air does. The humidifier, when it rectifies that situation, enhances the heating system's efficiency because people feel more comfort-

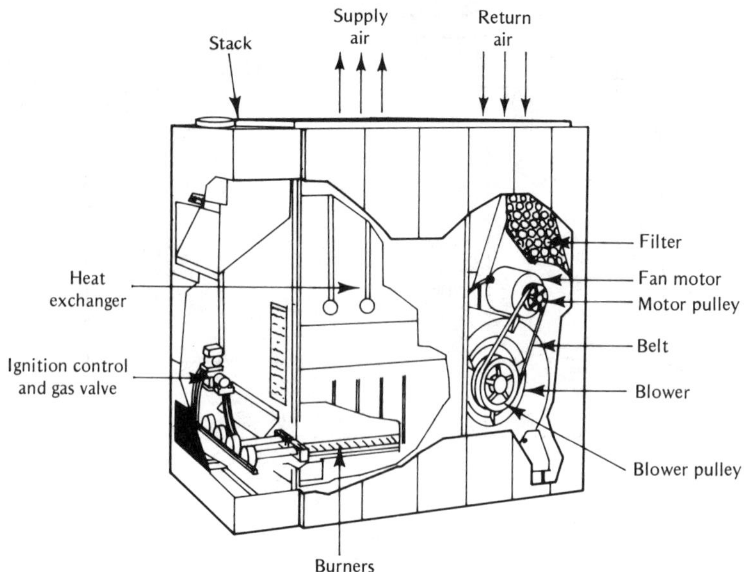

FIGURE 8-50 Typical forced air furnace.

able at lower temperatures in moist air than they do at higher temperatures in dry air.

WHY SYSTEMS NEED BALANCING

Air in the branch duct is produced by both the velocity and static pressure in the supply trunk duct. In some installations, a greater volume of air will be delivered through branches connected to the trunk duct close to the furnace unit than through the same size of branch connected to more remote sections of the trunk. This condition could cause inadequate air delivery to the more remote rooms and too much air delivery to rooms served by branches closer to the furnace. This factor, therefore, is an important consideration in the balancing process as applied to this type of air distribution system.

ELIMINATING DRAFTS

Depending on its velocity and temperature, the air flow could feel like a draft. In order to minimize this, the outlet air velocity must be low (about 200 feet/minute) and the outlet air temperature for high wall outlets no lower than 110°F and not lower than 115°F for low wall outlets. Usually air is delivered in a diffused fan pattern vertically upward over the areas of greatest heat loss, such as under windows. The air velocity should be at 400-500 feet per minute when the burner is operating. Ideally, the blower should be powered by a two-speed motor so that when the burner stops, the blower would operate at a lower speed. Such constant blower operation eliminates stratification and provides continuous air circulation.

THE FORCED AIR SYSTEM COMPONENTS

Most homes have central heat systems because these systems are more efficient and can be located in an out-of-the-way place, but still heat the entire home. The all air system combines the operation of several distinct units.

The Heat Producer

This may be an oil burner, a gas burner, or in some houses, an electric heater, a heat pump, or solar panels.

To light an oil burner, electric ignition is generally used. The main components of this ignition system are the transformer and two electrodes. In order to ignite the fuel-air mixture, a very hot spark is required between these electrodes. The transformer boosts the voltage from 120V to about 10,000V.

The Heat Exchanger

A heat exchanger is called a furnace if it heats air, or a boiler if it heats water or makes steam. The air, water, or steam go through passageways inside the exchanger that keep them separated from the combustion gases of the burner, which are expelled through a flue.

The Heat Distributor

Furnaces for forced air systems are available in various designs so that they may be located in the basement, crawl space, attic, or first floor of the building. In addition, each is usually classified in terms of the direction in which the air is delivered. The three basic types are upflow, counter flow, and horizontal, and there are several variations depending on the actual installation.

In a warm-air system, the air is drawn into the exchanger by a large fan (a blower) and sent through the ducts to warm-air registers. In a hot water system, water is forced through the exchanger by a pump (a circulator) and sent through pipes to convectors, a type of radiator. Steam rises under its own pressure from the exchanger, going through pipes to radiators. (Fig. 8-51.)

Humidifiers

Humidifiers are recommended for use in most heating systems. They provide extra comfort at a minimal cost, making them a good investment. The humidifier will fit right into the duct system as it is being installed.

The Ducts and Fittings

The ductwork is used to take the forced warm air from the furnace to the supply outlet and the cooler air from the return register back to the furnace.

The most commonly used materials for ducts are galvanized iron and aluminum. Both materials are relatively lightweight and easily shaped to whatever size duct is required, either round or rectangular. Minimum metal thicknesses required of these materials vary according to the size of the duct required, and they may have to be insulated.

A motor-driven fan is used to circulate filtered, heated air from a central heating unit through supply ducts to each of the rooms. As the hot air is delivered through the ducts and into the room through the supply outlet, cooler air from the space (room) is being returned through return grilles, into ducts and back through the central heating unit to be heated and sent back to the space. The ducts may be circular or rectangular, and their size depends on the amount of heated air which

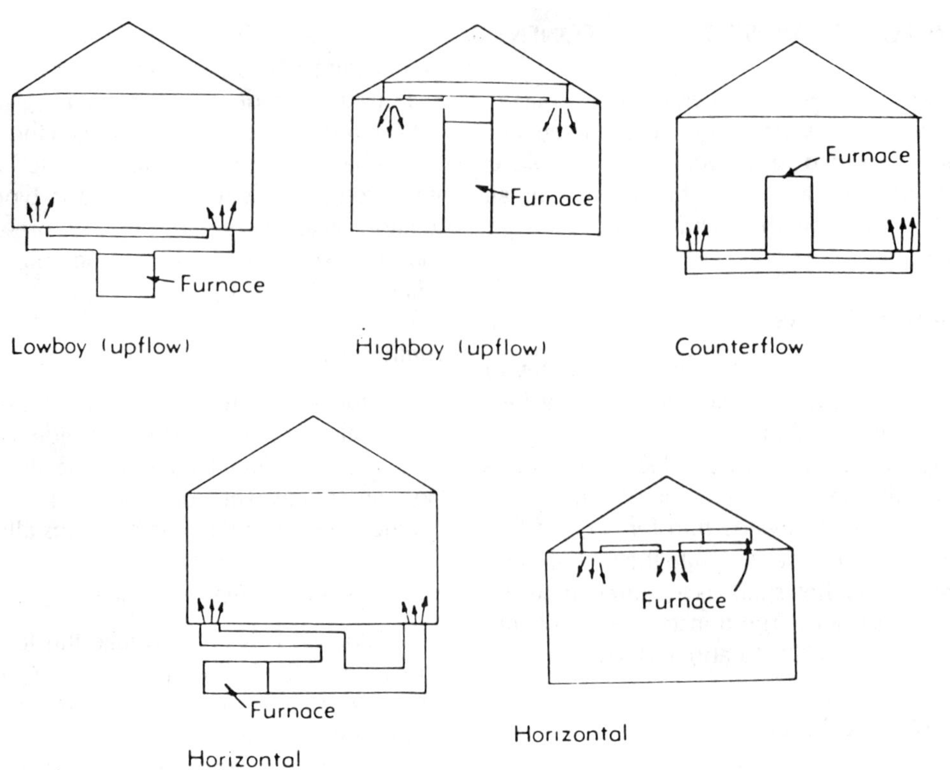

FIGURE 8-51 Forced air heat distribution systems and furnace locations. (Courtesy of Reston Publishing Company.)

must flow through them to maintain the desired temperature of the room. A variety of duct systems, or basic designs, may be used; several of the most common are shown in Figure 8-52.

Forced air heating systems are economical and generally easy to install. Filters are put in the system to reduce the amount of dust in the air. The furnace (heating unit) may be located wherever convenient in the building, including the basement, crawl space, attic, utility room, or garage, and in larger buildings it is sometimes located on the roof.

Temperature Controls

Most homes have one thermostat in the living area to turn the heating plant on and off. Buildings using hot water systems sense outside temperature and turn boilers on or off, or cause controllers to adjust zone valves that control the temperature of the water in the system. In-suite thermostats also control the flow of the hot water allowing for individual control in each of the occupied spaces. (Fig. 8-53.)

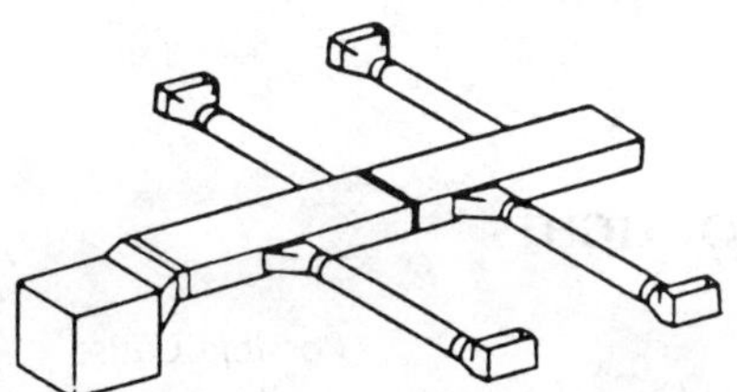

Extended plenum supply

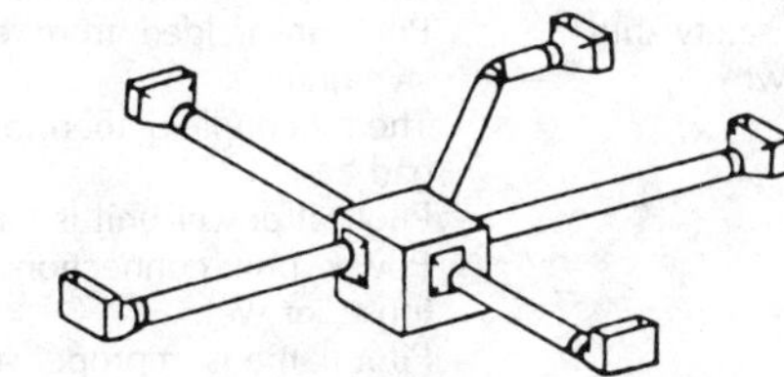

Individual supply system

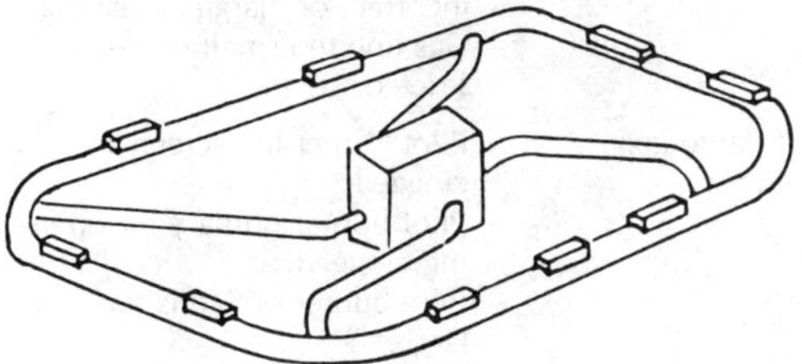

Perimeter-loop system

Typical heating duct systems

FIGURE 8-52 The ducting systems. (Courtesy of Reston Publishing Company.)

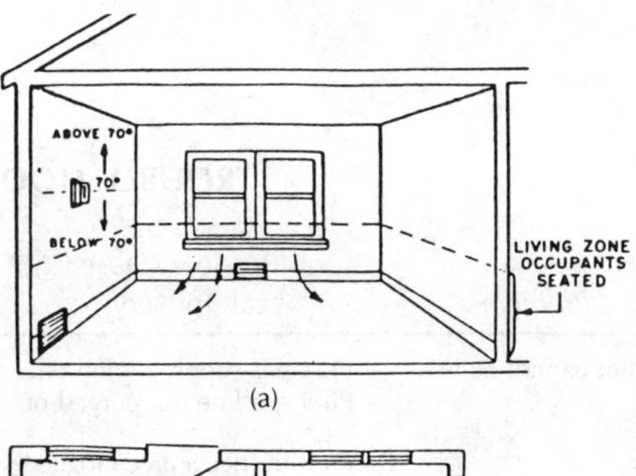

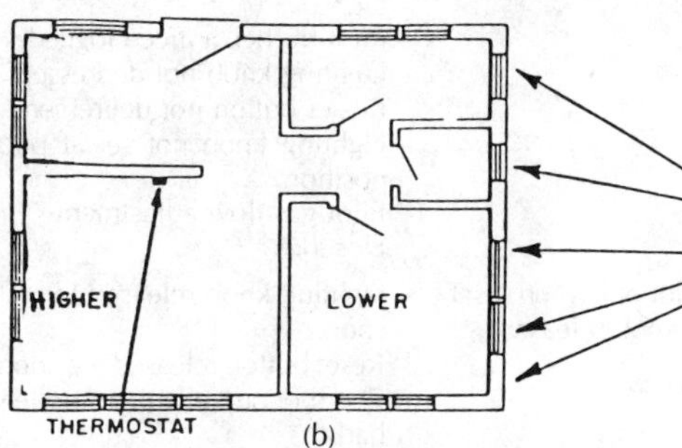

FIGURE 8-53 Temperature controls. (a) Room temperature distribution with the fan off; (b) Effect of wind on temperature distribution. (Courtesy of the Refrigeration Service Engineers Society.)

TROUBLESHOOTING BURNERS

Problem	*Possible Cause* *call for service
No heat	- Power not reaching burner.* - Pilot out.
Pilot does not light	- See troubleshooting pilot lights.
Pilot does not stay lit	- Pilot flame too large or too small and not heating thermocouple.

TROUBLESHOOTING FURNACE BLOWERS

Problem	*Possible Cause* *call for service
Noisy blower	- Moving parts need oil. - Belt worn. - Belt too tight or too loose. - Pulleys loose on shaft.* - Pulleys warped or bent.* - Blower running too fast. - Blower loose on shaft.* - Cable to motor rubbing against metal surface.
Insufficient air flow at warm-air registers	- Blower not running. - Belt too loose. - Blower loose on shaft.* - Blower running too slow.
Rushing noise or vibration in ducts	- Air velocity too high.
Dust on wall or ceiling near registers	- Access panel to blower compartment loose or open. - Blower compartment dirty.

TROUBLESHOOTING PILOT LIGHTS

Problem	*Possible Cause* *call for service
Pilot cannot be lit	- Pilot gas supply turned off. - Pilot gas line not purged of air.* - Pilot burner orifice clogged. - Lighting knob not depressed. - Re-set button not depressed. - Lighting knob not set at pilot position. - Pilot gas flow adjustment closed.
Pilot out when reset knob released	- Lighting knob released too soon. - Reset button released too soon. - Thermocouple or thermopile is bad.* - Pilotstat power unit is bad.* - Power unit connection dirty, loose, or wet. - Pilot flame not the right size. - Powerpile terminals shorted or loose.* - Pilot filter clogged.*
Pilot out	- Pilot burner orifice clogged. - Gas supply pressure too low.* - Pilot exposed to excessive draft. - Thermocouple or thermopile bad.* - Pilotstat power is bad.* - Power unit connection dirty, loose, or wet. - Pilot flame is improper size. - Powerpile terminals shorted or loose.* - Thermocouple cold junction too hot.* - Pilot burner lint screen clogged.* - Pilot unshielded from burner concussion. - Pilot filter clogged.*
Pilot burning, but on safety shut-down	- Gas supply pressure too low.* - Pilot unshielded from excessive draft. - Thermocouple or thermopile is bad.* - Pilotstat power unit is bad.* - Power unit connection dirty, loose, or wet.* - Pilot flame is improper size. - Powerpile terminals shorted or loose.* - Incorrect or marginal venting. - Gas line too small or restricted.*
Pilot flame lazy, yellow	- Pilot burner lint screen clogged.* - Pilot burner primary air opening clogged. - Pilot burner orifice is too large.* - Excessive ambient temperature. - Incorrect or marginal venting.
Pilot flame waving, blue	- Gas supply pressure too low.* - Pilot unshielded from combustion products.*
Pilot flame small, blue	- Pilot burner orifice clogged. - Pilot gas flow adjustment closed off. - Pilot burner orifice too small.* - Pilot filter clogged.
Pilot flame noisy, lifting, blowing	- Pilot gas pressure too high.*
Pilot flame hard, sharp	- Pilot burner orifice too small. - Typical of manufactured, butane air, and propane air.
Pilot turndown test result bad	- Pilot burner improperly located.*

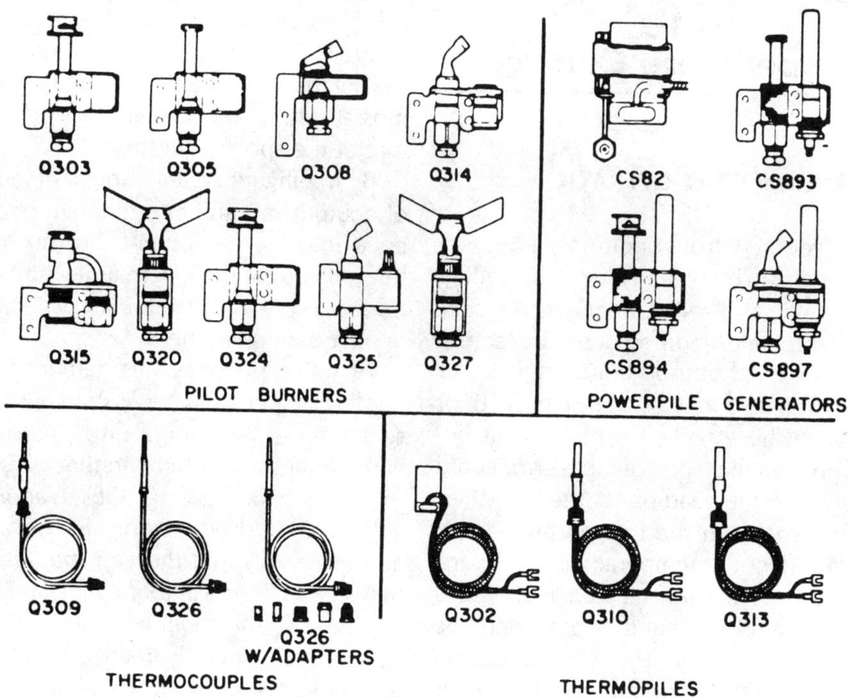

FIGURE 8-54 Troubleshooting pilot lights. Pilot burner flame should envelop ⅜ to ½ inch of Thermocouple or Thermopile tip.

TROUBLESHOOTING FORCED AIR FURNACES

Problem	*Possible Cause* *call for service	*Problem*	*Possible Cause* *call for service
No heat	- Power not reaching furnace. - Burner not functioning.* - Thermostat not functioning.*	Insufficient warm-air flow	- Blower not operating or too slow.*
Insufficient warm-air flow	- Air filter dirty. - Heat exchanger surface dirty.* - Air leaks in ducts. - Warm air registers dirty. - Damper on warm-air register closed. - Return-air grill blocked.	Large temperature difference between rooms	- Branch ducts improperly set. - Damper in branch duct or warm-air register closed.
		Dirt on walls or ceilings near registers	- Blower filter dirty. - Registers and grilles dirty. - Duct interiors have accumulation of dirt.

8-10 Temperature Control

THERMOSTAT OPERATION

Under good control conditions, a temperature difference between floor and ceiling may be as little as 3°–4°. Under average conditions, temperature differences are somewhere in the neighborhood of 5°, and under adverse conditions may be as much as 10° or more. Once these facts are realized, it becomes apparent that considerable error could be involved if the reading of the one thermometer located on the thermostat was assumed to reflect the temperature in all parts of the room. A thermostat can maintain a given temperature only at the spot where the thermostat is located. The accuracy with which it maintains temperature at this spot is entirely dependent on its degree of sensitivity. If other thermometers were suspended at various points in a room, they would also indicate relatively constant temperatures at those points. However, those temperatures may be higher or lower than the temperatures shown on the thermometer on the thermostat. This is not due to any fault of the thermostat itself, but is a result of the above named factors of air circulation, building construction, and outdoor temperatures.

Those factors must be considered when trying to straighten out a complaint on lack of comfort. Check the temperatures at various places in the house, particularly at the location of easy chairs and writing desks. It may be found that such points are 2° to 4° lower or higher in temperature than the thermometer reading on the thermostat. It is entirely possible that the thermostat may be indicating a 75° temperature, whereas the temperature at these spots of inactivity could be as low as 70°. This would indicate the reason for discomfort. To correct the condition in such a case, it may be necessary to increase the thermostat setting to obtain the desired temperature at the spot in question.

By intelligent engineering, a manufacturer of equipment can build the item of convenience into his equipment, but no manufacturer of equipment can manufacture comfort. *Comfort is the result of the proper application of adequate equipment.*

Actual experience has demonstrated that hardly one person in ten is comfortable when seated for any length of time in a space that is maintained at a temperature of 70° either for heating or cooling. *Observation of the actual thermostat setting in hundreds of homes reveals that the vast majority are set between 72° and 75° for heating and between 75° and 80° for cooling.*

It is not generally realized that different temperatures exist at the floor level, the breathing line, and the ceiling. (Figure 8-52.) The difference between these temperatures at different levels depends on building construction, air circulation, and the difference between indoor and outdoor temperatures. The floor temperatures descrease with a drop in outdoor temperatures, but the ceiling temperatures increase. This, of course, refers to differences in temperature where heating only is involved.

People may object to the procedure outlined because of the expense involved, their theory being that they cannot afford to operate on the basis of 75°. In that case, it will be necessary to use the figures you have obtained showing that the average room temperature is not the 75° that the thermostat thermometer indicates, but really the average of the figures determined by other thermometers placed in key positions. Raising the thermostat setting to 76°–77° results in a room temperature that is very near the actual 75°.

TROUBLESHOOTING THERMOSTATS

Problem	Possible Cause *call for service
Thermostat doesn't cycle often enough	- Thermostat not exposed to circulating air. - Heating plant too small or underfired.* - Thermostat heater set too high.* - Thermostat does not have heater.* - Thermostat contacts are dirty.
Room temperature swings excessively	- Thermostat not exposed to circulating air. - Thermostat heater set too high.* - Heating plant too large or input excessive.* - Thermostat does not have a heater.*
Thermostat jumpered; system won't work	- Thermostat not at fault. - Limit control set too low.* - Low voltage control circuit open.* - Low voltage transformer burned out.* - Main valve operator is bad.* - Bad terminal connection.*
Room temperature overshoots thermostat setting	- Thermostat mounted on a cold wall.* - Thermostat wiring hole not plugged. - Thermostat exposed to cold drafts. - Thermostat not exposed to circulating air. - Thermostat not mounted level.*
Room temperature overshoots thermostat setting	- Thermostat not properly calibrated.* - Thermostat heater set too high. - Heating plant too large or excessive input.* - Thermostat does not have a heater.*
Room temperature does not reach setting	- Thermostat not mounted level.* - Thermostat not properly calibrated.* - Heating plant too small or underfired.* - Limit control set abnormally low.* - Thermostat exposed to direct sun rays.* - Thermostat affected by heat from a fireplace, lamp, TV or appliances, stove or oven, register, or radiator. - Thermostat mounted on a warm wall.* - Thermostat contacts dirty. - Bad terminal connection.* - Clogged filter in a forced air furnace.
Thermostat seems out of calibration	- Thermostat not mounted level.* - Thermostat not properly calibrated.* - Bad terminal connections.* - Clogged filter in a forced air furnace.
Thermostat cycles too often	- Thermostat heater set too low.

IN-SUITE THERMOSTAT

The simplest type of central heating has a radiator or convector in the occupied space and only heated water is circulated throughout the building. Ventilation air is ducted in and exhausted out of the structure.

Temperature is thermostatically controlled; motorized valves are designed to give individual room temperature or zone control. The sunny side of the building may be separated or zoned from the north or shady side. These are controlled by the outside sensors that should provide heating when the "degree day balance" for the building is not maintained. (Fig. 8-55.)

In a house this balance could be 18°C or 68°F; in an apartment building this point could be 15°C or 65°F. In an office building or shopping center, this point could be 0°C or 32°F.

The sensors and controllers must be adjusted to achieve the heating and cooling required. Temperature is controlled by varying water temperature in the piping.

TROUBLESHOOTING MOTORIZED VALVES

Servicing Flair Electric Radiator Valve

1. The person investigating the problem should complete a Heating Maintenance Report. (Figure 8-60)
2. Remove the motor—leave the wires connected. Turn the thermostat up and down to determine whether the motor responds.
3. To indicate that power is present at the motor, short circuit the screw terminals on the transformer. A spark indicates that power is present. (Fig. 8-56.)
4. Using the proper tool, check to see if the stem rotates. If you are unable to turn the stem, leave the motor off and call for service immediately.

   If the stem is finally freed, but not moving freely, turn to the open position, leave the motor off, and call for service.
5. If the stem rotates freely and the motor does not operate, replace the motor.
6. The building operator should tag all replaced parts with the date and apartment number, and give the defective part to the manager along with the completed Heating Maintenance Report.

   NOTE: Never replace a complete valve body. This must be done by a qualified mechanic.

Periodic Maintenance

Inspect the valve annually for smooth operation and packing leakage. Repack only if required. Clean packing and re-lubricate as necessary to retain free movement of the stem. Clean the top and insert assembly and the exposed portion of the stem with a cleaner recommended by Honeywell. *Do not allow solvent to touch diaphragm as it will cause deterioration*. (Fig. 8-58.)

1. The person investigating the problem should complete the Heating Maintenance Report. (Figure 8-60)
2. Turn up the thermostat and listen for escaping air at the thermostat. This indicates that the thermostat is operating the valve. If you do not hear the escape of air, insert a thin piece of cardboard between the orifice to ensure the removal of dust and dirt.
3. If the valve is operating, the pipes to the radiator should heat up. If the opposite end is cold, it means that the valve is not opening. *CALL FOR SERVICE IMMEDIATELY*.
4. If the valve is stuck open, the apartment will be overheated. This is the way the valves are supposed to fail. *CALL FOR SERVICE*.
5. If the building operator calls for service and any parts are replaced, he should obtain the faulty parts. Tag them with the suite number and give the parts to the manager along with the completed Heating Maintenance Report.

Servicing Erie Electric Radiator Valve

1. The person investigating the problem should complete the Heating Maintenance Report. (Figure 8-60)

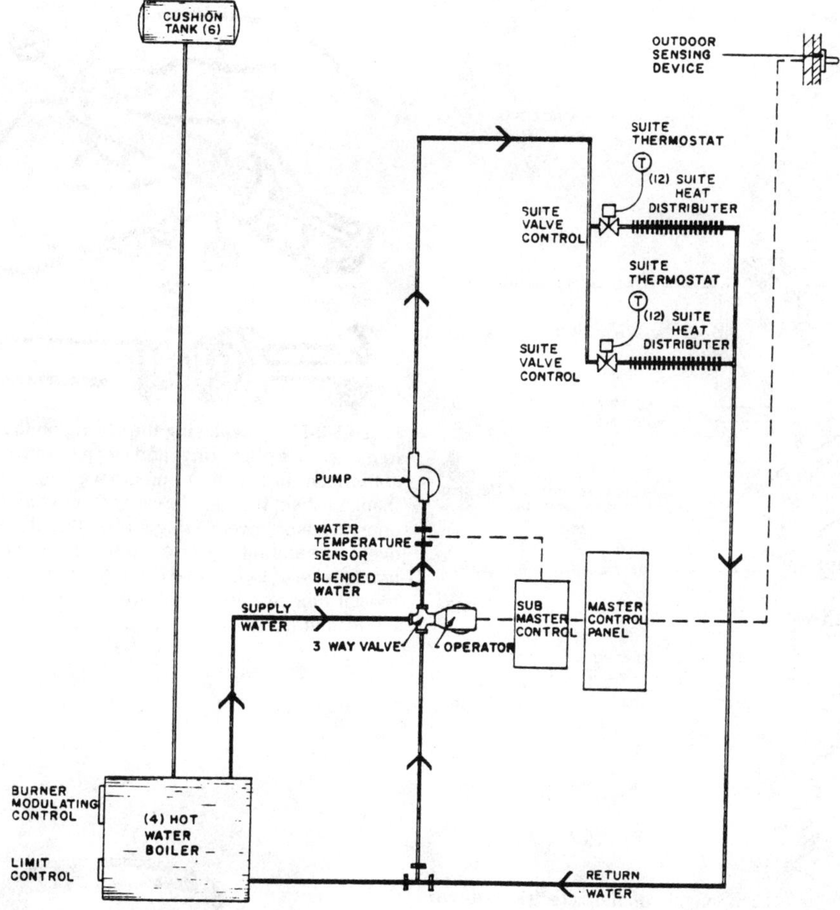

FIGURE 8-55 Controlling individual room temperature. (Courtesy of Cadillac Fairview Corporation, Limited.)

2. Turn the thermostat up or down and watch to see if the motor is operating.
3. If the motor does not operate, call for service.
4. If he calls for service and any parts are replaced, he should obtain the faulty parts. Tag with the suite number and give the defective part to the manager along with the complete Heating Maintenance Report.

8-11 The Operator's Responsibility

AN OVERVIEW

The boilers used in heating systems are designed with many automatic features. The responsibility of the operator is to oversee the

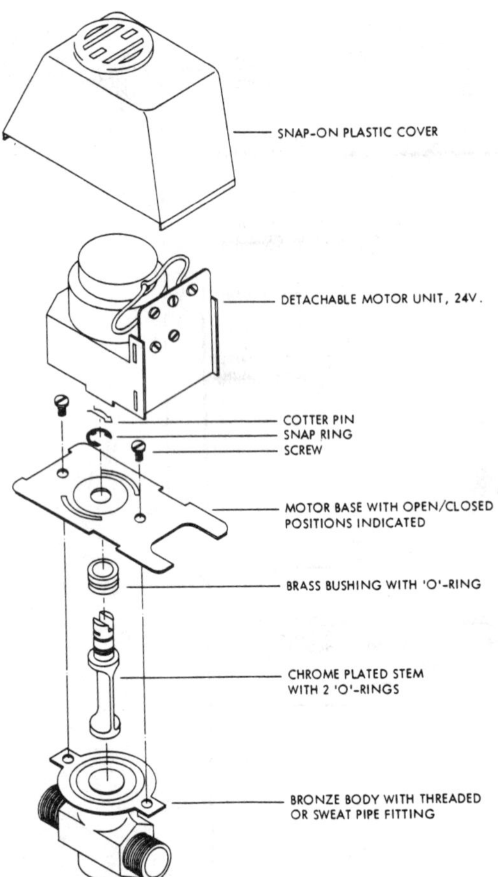

FIGURE 8-56 Components of flair electric radiator valve. (Courtesy of Flair Hydronics.)

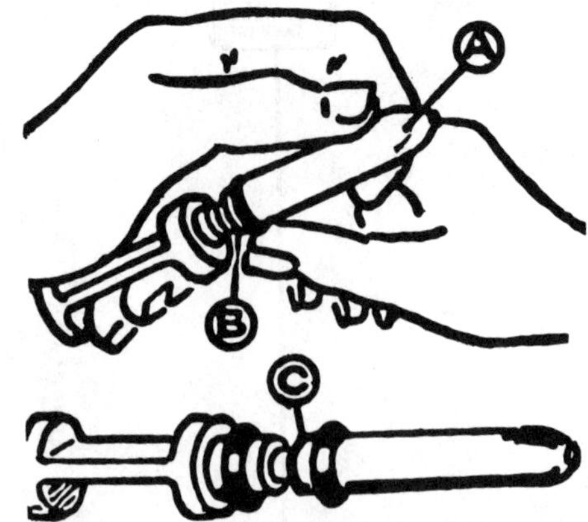

FIGURE 8-57 Replacing the O-ring on the flair valve stem. Remove old O-rings and clean O-ring grooves. Do not scratch surface of O-ring groove. Slip cone (A) over shank of stem, bringing lower edge of cone in line with upper edge of lower O-ring groove (B). Slip new O-ring over cone and into groove. Raise edge of cone to position at edge of top groove (C) and repeat process. Apply special lubricant in capsule on O-rings for permanent lubrication. (Courtesy of Flair Hydronics.)

general operation of the equipment and to ensure that the controls are functioning properly.

The boilers are equipped with operating and safety controls that will function for long periods of time. Do not assume that normal operation will continue indefinitely. *MALFUNCTION OF CONTROLS LEADS TO UNECONOMICAL OPERATION AND BOILER DAMAGE.*

Basically, the operator's responsibilities are as follows:

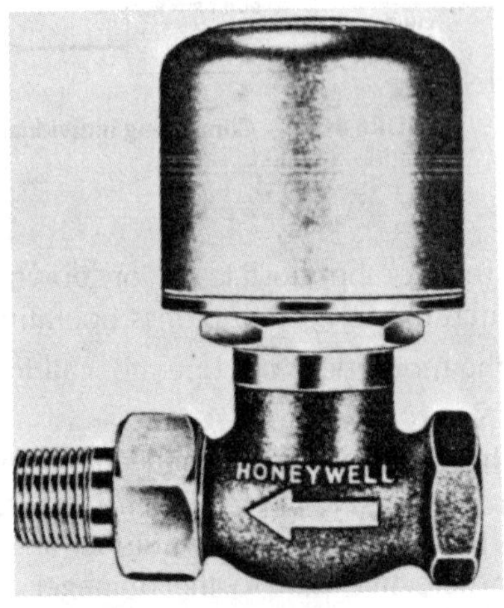

FIGURE 8-58 The Honeywell pneumatic radiator valve. (Courtesy of Honeywell.)

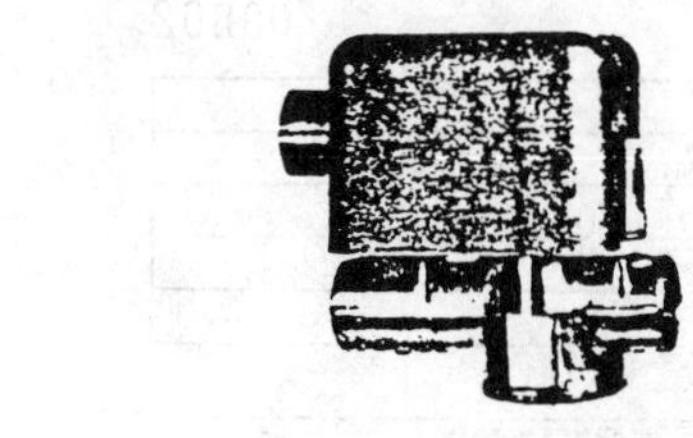

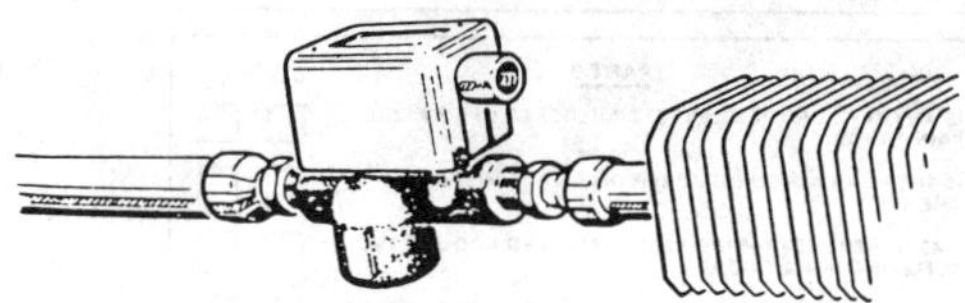

FIGURE 8-59 The Erie electric radiator valve. (Courtesy of Erie Valve.)

1. To inspect the boiler room and its equipment on a regular basis and to conduct "look, listen, and touch" inspections. *This monitors the system on a daily basis and indicates a malfunction virtually as it occurs.*

   In all buildings, the combustion controls should be adjusted professionally by your service contractor, who uses flue gas analyzing equipment to provide optimum fuel to air mixture, which restores economical operation. The service contractor should adjust the controls and burners to match the building heat loss, rather than the boiler capacity. *A building operator does not, under any circumstances, tamper with these controls.*
2. To accurately record the operating data on boiler logs and to immediately report unusual readings, leaks, or abnormal operation to the manager. All readings should be made on a daily basis.

   To maintain an efficient and economic operation, logging and recordkeeping is essential. It is most important that the outdoor temperature and the blended water temperature are recorded at the same time.

   Whenever the superintendent or engineer cannot be present, arrangements should be made for someone else to complete the log. The state of the heating plant operation, and any deviation from normal, are usually evident from a perusal of the logs and from the graphs showing the operation of the three-way blending valves. (See Chapter 12.)

   Three-way blending valve outdoor reset controls that have been calibrated do not require any further adjustment. *In case of a problem, call immediately for service. Do not tamper with them.*
3. To keep equipment rooms clean, as dust and dirt are the prime source of problems in motors and controls.
4. To keep all moving parts lubricated properly.
5. To attend personally to all heating complaints and record the data on the Heating Maintenance Request. Copies of these forms should be attached to the boiler log. (Figure 8-60)

8-12 Handling Heating Complaints

Daily equipment inspections will eliminate most, if not all, heating problems.

1. Always complete a Heating Maintenance Report. (Figure 8-60)
2. Try to establish whether the problem is related to an individual apartment or to the whole building. Check your own apartment for a clue. Questioning the ten-

MAINTENANCE REQUEST

—HEATING—

00802

BUILDING	SUITE #	DATE
RESIDENT'S NAME	PHONE # RES:	BUS:

REQUEST:

REQUEST RECEIVED BY

RESIDENT'S CONSENT

I WISH TO HAVE THIS REQUEST ATTENDED TO AND I HEREBY AUTHORIZE CADILLAC FAIRVIEW RESIDENTIAL MANAGEMENT TO ENTER MY APARTMENT. SHOULD IT BE NECESSARY TO USE A SERVICE AGENCY OTHER THAN CADILLAC FAIRVIEW RESIDENTIAL MANAGEMENT OR SHOULD MORE THAN ONE VISIT BE REQUIRED FOR CORRECTION I ALSO SIGNIFY MY CONSENT

RESIDENT'S SIGNATURE DATE

INSTRUCTIONS:
1: NUMEROUS CALLS MAY INDICATE THAT THE PROBLEM IS IN THE BOILER ROOM. COMPLETE SECTION B AND LIST SUITE NUMBERS IN THE COMMENTS SECTION.
2. IF PROBLEM IS IN THE SUITE VALVE COMPLETE SECTION A PART 1 AND IF PROBLEM IS STILL-UNCORRECTED COMPLETE PART 2.

A. CONDITIONS IN SUITE

PART 1

	YES	NO
1. ARE THE CONVECTOR ISOLATING VALVES OPEN FULLY?	☐	☐
2. IS THE SUITE VALVE FREE TO TURN?	☐	☐
3. DOES THE SUITE VALVE OPERATE ON DEMAND FROM THE THERMOSTAT?	☐	☐

4. THE RESIDENT'S THERMOMETER READING IS ____ °F
5. THE SETTING ON THE THERMOSTAT IS ____ °F
6. THE THERMOMETER READING ON THE THERMOSTAT IS ____ °F
7. THE DRY BULB READING IN THE SLING PSYCHROMETER IS

LIVINGROOM	BEDROOM	BEDROOM	
°F	°F	°F	°F

PART 2

	YES	NO
8. IS ANY PART OF THE CONVECTOR BLOCKED OFF BY FOIL, PAINT, ETC.?	☐	☐
9. IS THERE AN AIR CONDITIONER OR SLEEVE INSTALLED IN THE SUITE?	☐	☐
10. HAS WEATHER STRIPPING BEEN INSTALLED AROUND THE SUITE ENTRANCE DOOR?	☐	☐
11. ARE THE EXHAUST VENTS IN THE KITCHEN AND BATHROOMS OPERATING PROPERLY?	☐	☐
12. IS THERE A HUMIDIFIER IN USE IN THE SUITE?	☐	☐
13. IS THERE ANY HEAT GENERATING DEVICE NEAR THE THERMOSTAT (LAMP, T.V., ETC.)?	☐	☐
14. ARE THERE ANY NOTICEABLE COLD AIR DRAFTS FROM BALCONY DOORS OR WINDOWS?	☐	☐
15. ARE THE OPENINGS IN THE CONVECTOR COVERS CLEAR OF ALL WINDOW DRAPES?	☐	☐
16. ARE THE CONVECTOR FINS FREE OF DUST AND CARPET LINT?	☐	☐

B. CONDITIONS IN HEATING SYSTEM

1. BOILER PRESSURE	PSI
2. BOILER SUPPLY TEMPERATURE	°F
3. BOILER RETURN TEMPERATURE	°F
4. BLEND WATER TEMPERATURE	°F
5. BUILDING RETURN TEMPERATURE	°F
6. OUTDOOR TEMPERATURE	°F

COMMENTS:

INSPECTOR'S SIGNATURE

C. MANAGEMENT OFFICE

P.M. – INDICATE BY CHECK DOCUMENTS REQUIRED.

✓		SUPPLIER	DATE ISSUED
	WORK ORDER #		
	PURCHASE ORDER #		

WORK TO BE DONE

WHITE – MANAGEMENT OFFICE YELLOW – WITH BOILER LOG TO ENGINEERING SERVICES BLUE – SUPERINTENDENT

FIGURE 8-60 The heating maintenance request. (Courtesy of Cadillac Fairview Corporation, Limited.)

ant when he reports the problem could also provide a clue.

3. If you suspect a general heating problem, visit the boiler room first.
4. Check boiler temperature and pressure.
5. Check if all valves are open and pumps operating.
6. Check blend water temperature and relate this to the outdoor temperature. Check your heating graph to see if properly blended water is being delivered.
7. Check the burner to be sure it is operating. If not, follow the drill outlined on page 348 under "Burner Malfunction."
8. If the problem is corrected in the boiler room, call the tenant, explain what you have done, and ask him to call you if the problem does not correct itself.

9. If you establish that this is an individual suite problem, visit the apartment and follow the procedure outlined on the Heating Maintenance Report. (Figure 8-60)

THE CUSHION TANK

Because all hot water heating systems are closed, we utilize a cushion tank to maintain a stabilized system pressure. (Figure 8-61)

The term "cushion" means that there is a sufficient amount of air in the tank. This air cushion allows for the expansion and contraction of the system water without changing the system pressure. This expansion and contraction takes place when the system water increases and decreases its temperature. Air from the cushion tank cannot enter the system as long as the proper amount of water is in the tank.

The water level in the cushion tank may vary from one building to another. Once the proper water level is established, it should not vary. The water level will stabilize between one-third and two-thirds full in the tank.

Conditions Affecting Water Level

The loss of air or water from the cushion tank will affect the water level in the tank. When the tank loses its air cushion, it fills with water.

Reasons Why a Cushion Tank Becomes Waterlogged

1. There are major air leaks in the upper or air section of the tank, at the sight glass, or around piping connections.
2. The pressure regulating valve has failed in the open position, causing over pressurizing of the heating system, thus forcing air out through small leaks that would not normally be a problem.
3. The by-pass valve (figure 8-31) around the pressure regulating valve has been inadvertently left in the open position, causing over pressurizing of the system with the same result as mentioned in No. 2.

Problems Caused by a Waterlogged Cushion Tank

This condition would cause:

- the safety relief valve to activate, resulting in the loss of system water.
- leaks in pipe joints, valve packing glands, and flanges in the system.
- boiler tubes to weep, necessitating a boiler shutdown until the tubes are repaired.

Inspections

Regular inspections would indicate a slow but steady increase in the cushion tank water level, or a slow, but again steady increase of the system pressure. If a slight increase in either the water level or pressure occurs, do not be alarmed, as this could happen during the heating season, usually after a mild spell followed by a sharp drop in outdoor temperatures. This slight increase should not continue, however.

It is important to check the water level and system pressure daily, and to record conditions on daily logs. More frequent ad hoc checks are advisable whenever you are in the boiler room or cushion tank area.

Re-Establishing the Cushion

When a loss of air occurs and the cushion tank is waterlogged, the following actions are required to re-establish the cushion in the tank:

1. Turn off the boiler burner(s) that the cushion tank serves; do not isolate the boiler.
2. Turn off the water supply valve to the cushion tank.

3. Connect a hose to the drain valve that is located between the system supply valve and the cushion tank. *Do NOT open the air venting at this time as the pressure in the tank will force the water out at a faster rate.*
4. When there is a noticeable decrease in the water pressure, open the air venting valve at the top of the tank to allow air in and the water out.
5. When the water is completely drained from the cushion tank, close the air venting valve and drain valve, and disconnect the hose.
6. Slowly open the supply valve to the tank until it is in the full open position, and wait until the tank is filled with water to its normal level.
7. Start up the boiler burner(s) and return system to normal operating temperature and pressure.
8. After the system has returned to the normal operating temperature and pressure, check the water level on the cushion tank sight glass. If the water level is lower than the normal operating level, open the air venting valve and release air until the water is at its normal level, then close the valve tightly.
9. Check the city water make-up line (Figure 8-31) to the boilers; this line will be cold as the pressure regulating valve would have opened to replace some of the water drained from the cushion tank. Check the pressure regulating by-pass valve to make sure it is closed. The make-up line to the system will soon return to room temperature if both the pressure regulating valve and the by-pass valve are closing properly.

Loss of Water in the Cushion Tank

The water level in a cushion tank can be lost in two ways:

1. Through a small leak at the pressure relief valve, through the boiler tubes, or through other piping in the system. When any of these conditions exist, the pressure regulating valve will not open even after a small but steady decrease in the system pressure is observed. To temporarily correct this problem, open the pressure regulating by-pass valve (Figure 8-31) to bring the system back to the normal operating pressure. Once the pressure is normalized, close the by-pass valve and call for service.
2. Through a sudden rupture of the boiler tubes or the tube sheets. When this occurs, isolate the boiler and start the second boiler. Call for service. If there is only one boiler in the building, call for service immediately.

Correcting a Water Level Problem

1. Locate and repair the leaks in the system
2. Repair or replace a malfunctioning pressure regulating valve. (Figure 8-31)
3. Return system to normal operation by bringing the water temperature in the system up to a minimum of 180°F.
4. If the cushion tank water is still below its normal level, open air vents at the top of the tank and bleed off air until the water level is normal. Close the valve when the tank reaches a normal operating level.

8–13 How To Budget For The Necessary Funds

Maintenance programs, to be successful, must be carefully planned so that they encompass all of the activities required to main-

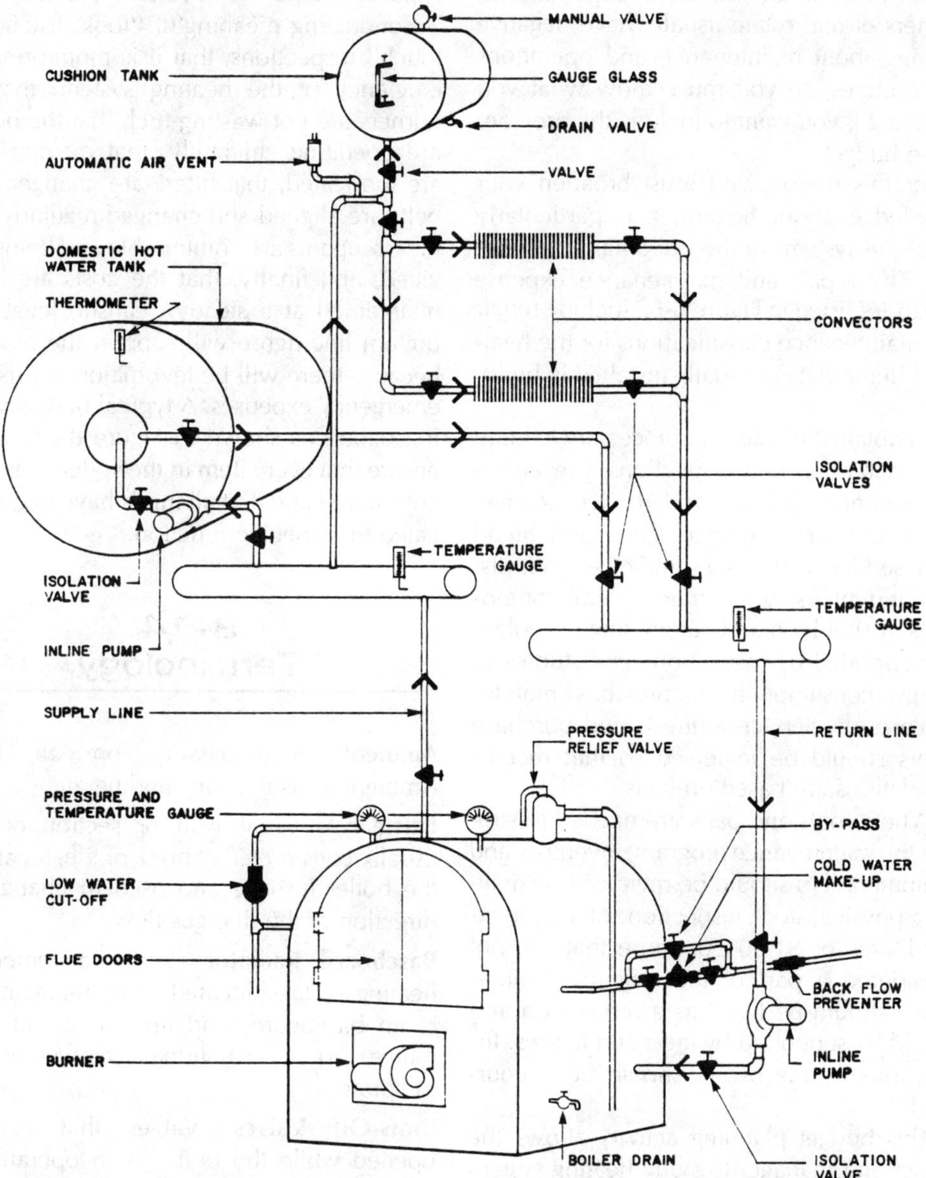

FIGURE 8-61 Heating system schematic. (Courtesy of Cadillac Fairview Corporation, Limited.)

tain the heating system at its highest level of efficiency without needless expenditures. Owners of real estate usually have negative feelings about maintenance and operations expenditures, so you must know what you are doing if you want to include the program in the budget.

For this reason, you must broaden your knowledge about heating and particularly about the systems in the buildings you manage. The repair and maintenance expense categories listed in Figure 8-62 include repair and maintenance classifications for the heating systems that are usually installed in buildings.

To obtain the funds, it is necessary to build the program around inspections, preventive maintenance, burner and boiler service, pump and motor service, zone and blend valve service, thermostats and other controls, fans and filters, and other system components. It should include upgrading or replacing supported by inspections and studies of energy consumption or previous maintenance costs. Service requests and purchase orders should be reviewed so that recommendations are based on facts.

Where tools and parts are needed to support the maintenance program, inventory and equipment lists should be reviewed by making a physical stock inspection. All major expenditures of $1,000 or more that are not considered a part of the ongoing maintenance should be listed as a renovation and should be supported by facts and figures. Inspections by the owner should be encouraged.

This budget planning activity allows the owner and manager to study heating system expenditures in advance. If properly prepared and presented, the owner should confidently authorize expenditures of $1,000 for preventive maintenance without approval.

The owner should be aware that every activity detailed on the repair and maintenance expense category is necessary—that the staff is conducting meaningful "look, listen, and touch" inspections, that it is monitoring the efficiency of the heating system, that the burners are not wasting fuel, that the boilers are operating efficiently, that moving parts are lubricated, that filters are changed, that belts are aligned and changed regularly, that the occupants are comfortable and being serviced, and finally, that the costs are being maintained at a steady, realistic level. The bottom line figure will support the program because there will be few major surprises or emergency expenses. A typical budget working paper, as shown in Figure 8-61, would ensure that every item in the system has been considered and that all funds have been allocated to a specific function.

8-14 Terminology

Ambient Encompassing on all sides. Ambient air is the surrounding air.

Baffle A partial wall or section of wall usually constructed of brick or tile, located in the boiler furnace and used to change the direction of the flue gas flow.

Baseboard Radiator An arrangement of heating surface located at or replacing the room baseboard, and applied as an alternative to conventional convectors or radiators.

Blow-Off Valves Valves that can be opened while the boiler is in operation in order to blow out sludge and sediment from the boiler. The boiler may also be drained if necessary by means of these valves.

Boiler A closed vessel in which fuel is burned to generate steam or hot water.

THE HEATING SYSTEM	ACCOUNT NUMBERS 53	SUB TOTALS	TOTAL
BOILERS, HEATERS, OR FURNACES	531		
BURNERS	532		
FAN COIL OR UNIT HEATERS	533		
FILTERS	534		
HUMIDIFIERS	535		
INCREMENTAL UNITS	536		
MOTORS & PUMPS	537		
PIPING, VALVES & CONTROLS	538		
WATER TREATMENT	539		

FIGURE 8-62 Summary of budget expense schedules, repair and maintenance categories; mechanical services.

Boiler-Burner Unit Boiler designed especially for gas or oil and sold integrally with the burner.

Boiler Heating Surface That part of the interior surface of a boiler subjected to heat on the one side and transmitting the heat to water (or steam or other fluid) within the boiler.

Boiler Horsepower The equivalent evaporation of 34.5 pounds of water per hour and at 212°F. Equal to a heat output of 970.3 × 34.5 or 33,475 Btu's per hour.

British Thermal Unit (Btu) The unit of energy or heat required to raise the temperature of one pound of water from 39°F to 40°F or from 60°F to 61°F under standard pressure, or 1/180 of the heat to raise one pound from 32°F to 212°F.

By-Pass An alternative path, in a duct or pipe, for a fluid to flow from one point to another, with the direction determined by the opening or closing of valves or dampers in the main line as well as in the by-pass.

Coefficient of Performance (COP) In the heat pump, the ratio of effect produced to electrical input.

Check Valve This is a valve that allows flow in one direction only. It will close automatically in the event of any reverse flow.

Combustion Chamber That part of the boiler furnace where fuel gases are mixed with air and burned. The terms "combustion chamber," "furnace," and "firebox" are often used interchangeably.

Combustion Gas Pass Used in connection with the number of times the combustion gases travel the length of the boiler. For example, in a two-pass boiler the combustion gases make two sweeps or "passes" through the boiler.

Combustion Gases The hot gaseous products from the fire. These are often referred to as "flue gases."

Condensate When the steam from the boiler is used in a heating system, in a process, or by an engine or a turbine, it will give up its heat and then condense to water, which can then be returned to the boiler. This water is known as condensate.

Conduction The transmission of heat from one part of a body to another part of the same body, or from one body to another body in contact with it, without appreciable displacement of the particles of the body.

Convection The transfer of heat from one point to another within a fluid by mixing one portion of the fluid with another.

Convector An arrangement of heat transfer surface contained in an enclosure with openings at top and bottom, thus heating air by convection.

Degree Day The product of one day and the number of degrees the daily mean temperature is below 65°F or 18°C. On a day when the mean temperature is 40°F, there are 25 degree days. The degree-day unit is used in eliminating the weather variable in determining heating load efficiency and in predicting fuel consumption.

Design Temperature The temperature that an apparatus or system is designed to (1) maintain or (2) operate against under most extreme conditions. The former is the inside design temperature, the latter is the outside design temperature.

Dew-Point Temperature The temperature at which a given mixture of air and water vapor is saturated.

Direct-Fire Heater A fuel burning device in which the heat from the fuel is transferred through metal to air, which is then introduced to the space to be heated.

Draft Fans These are mechanically-driven fans used to either blow air into the furnace via the windbox or to draw the combustion gases from the boiler and discharge them to the stack.

Drum The shell together with the heads form a drum. The terms "shell" and "drum" are often used interchangeably.

Dry-Bulb Temperature The temperature measured by a conventional thermometer.

Efficiency Ratio of output to input.

Feedwater This is the water that is fed to the boiler to replace the boiler water that has been converted to steam and drawn off from the boiler.

Finned Tube Extended surface in the form of fins on tubes or pipe.

Fittings These are devices that are fitted to the boiler and that make it easier and safer to operate.

Flash Point The temperature of oil where the vapor will ignite, but where there is not sufficient vapor to allow combustion to continue.

Furnace Either the combustion space in a fuel burning device or a direct fired air heater. In the latter case, not to be confused with a boiler.

Gauge Glass A fitting, which consists of a strong glass tube, used to show the level of water in the boiler.

Gauge Pressure Pressure within a vessel measured from atmospheric pressure as a base.

Grate Area The surface on which the fuel rests while it is being burned. This only applies to solid fuels such as coal, as a boiler using oil or gas fuels would not require a grate.

Handhole This is an opening into the shell, much smaller than the manhole, and is used for cleaning and inspection purposes. It is closed off by means of a bolted cover.

Head The heads are the steel plates that close off the ends of the shell. They are also referred to as "end plates," and if the shell contains tubes that are held in position by the heads, then the term "tube sheets" is also used for the heads.

Heating Medium A fluid used for conveying heat from a heat source to heat dissipating devices, including air, water, and steam.

Heat Pump A mechanical refrigeration system used for air cooling in the summer, and which, when the evaporator and condenser effects are reversed, absorbs heat from the outside air or (water) in winter and raises it to a higher potential so that it can also be used for winter heating.

Heating Surface The heating surface of a boiler consists of all parts of the boiler through which the heat is transferred from the burning fuel to the water. It includes all parts of the boiler plates and tubes that have water on one side and that are swept by fire or hot gases from the fire on the other.

High-Pressure Steam Boiler A steam boiler that operates at pressures above 15 psig.

Hot Water Boiler A boiler used to raise the temperature and pressure of the water it contains.

Humidity Usually water vapor mixed with dry air.

Hydrostatic Test On a boiler, the closing of all openings and pumping water into the boiler at a pressure (such as 50 percent) greater than the normal operating pressure. The purpose is to locate leaks or to prove that there are no leaks.

Hygrometer A device for measuring moisture in the air.

Infiltration Leaking inward. In heat transmission, applies to air entering the space through cracks around windows, doors, etc.

Infrared Radiant energy of a wave frequency inferior to visible red light, which, when it falls on a body, causes its temperature to rise. Commonly called radiant heat.

Insulation Thermal insulation is a material used (a) for walls and roofs of buildings or (b) for covering pipes, ducts, vessels, to effect a reduction of heat to a relatively large degree.

Limit Switch A control to limit some function. Examples are pressure limit switches that shut off the fuel burner when the steam pressure reaches a predetermined point, and temperature limit switches for hot water and warm air.

Lowest Permissible Water Level The lowest water level at which the boiler can be operated without damaging or overheating any part of the boiler.

Low-Pressure Hot Water Heating Boiler A boiler that operates at a pressure not exceeding 160 psig and or temperatures not exceeding 250°F.

Low-Pressure Steam Boiler A steam boiler that operates at pressures not above 15 psig.

Low Water Cutoff A safety device that will cut off the boiler burner if the water level in the boiler becomes dangerously low.

Manhole An opening through which a man may enter the shell. When the boiler is in operation, it is closed off by means of a bolted door.

Make-Up Water Water supplied to replenish that lost by leaks, evaporation, etc.

Mbh One thousand Btu's per hour.

Mercury Switch A glass tube employing mercury to establish electrical contact between circuits when the tube is tilted so that the mercury bridges the gap between contacts.

Modulating Adjusting control by increments.

Orifice Opening. Commonly used to apply to discs placed in pipe lines or radiator valves to reduce the fluid flow to the desired amount.

Perfect Combustion Fuel burning when all combustibles are consumed with no excess air so that only the theoretical amount of oxygen is used.

Pneumatic Operated by air pressure, as in pneumatic controls.

Psychrometer A device for measuring the humidity in the air and employing a wet-bulb and a dry-bulb thermometer.

Recirculated Air Air returned from a space to be heated, conditioned, or cleaned, then redistributed to the space.

Return Air Air returning to a heater or conditioner from heated or conditioned space.

Safety Valve A fitting that prevents the pressure within the boiler from exceeding safe limits. It will open and release steam from the boiler when the pressure reaches a set point.

Sensible Heat That heat which when added or subtracted results in a change of temperature.

Setting The brickwork surrounding the furnace in some boilers.

Shell Consists of one or more steel plates rolled into cylindrical form and welded together. The ends are closed by means of end plates or heads.

Soot Blower An apparatus that uses steam to blow away soot, dust, and other material from the boiler tubes.

Square Foot of Radiator The amount of heating surface in the form of radiators, convectors, unit heaters, or other devices that will emit 240 Btu's per hour.

Stack The stack or chimney is the vertical passageway that discharges the flue gases to the atmosphere some distance above the boiler.

Stack Effect The impulse of a heated gas to rise in vertical passage, as in a chimney, a small enclosure, or a building.

Standard Air Air at 70°F and 29.921 inches of mercury and weighing 0.07488 pounds per cubic foot.

Steam Water in gaseous or vapor form.

Steam Boiler A boiler used for the generation of steam. The boiler is only partially filled with water.

Steam Gauge A fitting that indicates the pressure of the steam within the boiler.

Steam Space Any steam boiler in operation is only partially filled with water, because a certain amount of space is required within the boiler for the storage of steam. This space above the water level is called the steam space of the boiler.

Therm One hundred thousand Btu's.

Thermacouple Two dissimilar metals joined together produce an electromotive force, which varies with the temperature.

Uptake Also referred to as the flue vent or outlet, it is the connection between the boiler and the stack.

Venturi A contraction in a pipe line or duct to accelerate the fluid and to lower its static pressure.

Viscosity Resistance to flow.

Water Column A chamber that is connected to the boiler and to which the gauge glass is attached.

Waterleg A water-filled section that surrounds the firebox in some boilers.

Water Line The height of the normal water level in a boiler.

Water Space The parts of a boiler that contain the water from which the steam is generated.

Wet-Bulb Temperature The temperature of the air measured by a wet-bulb thermometer and which is lower than the dry-bulb temperature in inverse proportion to the humidity.

Windbox The ductwork or chamber surrounding the burners on the outside of the boiler into which the air for the burners is introduced.

Zoning The division of a building or group of buildings into separately controlled spaces where different conditions can be simultaneously maintained.

Chapter 9

AIR CONDITIONING SYSTEMS

9-1 An Overview

WHAT IS AIR CONDITIONING?

Air conditioning is a process for treating air that simultaneously controls its temperature, humidity, cleanliness, and distribution to meet the requirements of the conditioned space.

Originally, air conditioning was confined to winter comfort; that is, to heating the home to a comfortable temperature in the winter by means of an open fireplace or a stove. Since then, the use of steam, hot water, electricity, and forced air furnaces has considerably improved the comfort level of the home during the winter. We can remove dust from the air and control the moisture and the temperature. The development of air conditioning allows us to enjoy a comfortable environment during the cold winter and the hot, humid summer.

A complete air conditioning system includes a means of refrigeration, one or more heat transfer units, air filters, a means of air distribution, an arrangement for piping the refrigerant and heating medium, and controls to regulate the proper capacity of these components.

COMFORT AND EFFECTIVE TEMPERATURE

There is no rigid rule as to the best atmospheric conditions for making people feel comfortable. Under the same conditions of temperature and humidity, a healthy young person may be slightly warm, while an elderly person may feel too cool. An individual who steps into a conditioned store from the blazing heat of the street experiences a welcome sense of relief, while the active clerk who has been in the store for several hours may find the conditions too warm for perfect comfort. Waitresses in a restaurant may feel somewhat warm, while the patrons seated at the tables find the atmosphere comfortable, or perhaps slightly cool.

The comfort of an individual is affected by many variables, such as health, age, sex, activity, clothing, food, and degree of acclimation, all of which play a part in determining the elusive "best comfort conditions" for any particular person. Hard and fast rules that apply to all conditions and to all people cannot be given; the best that can be done is to approximate those conditions under which a majority of the occupants of a room will feel comfortable.

Effective temperature is not an actual temperature because it cannot be measured by a thermometer. It is an experimentally determined index of the various combinations of dry- and wet-bulb temperatures under which most people will feel equally cool or warm. It is not an index of comfort.

Systems designed to achieve a temperature of 76°F (24.4°C) with a 50 percent relative humidity in the summer and a 40 percent relative humidity in the winter would be comfortable for many people.

HEAT TRANSFER

Heat is a form of energy. Every object contains heat and heat energy. If all heat is removed from an object, the temperature of the object will fall to absolute zero. Theoretically, this is minus 459.6° F.

Every object contains heat energy in both quantity and intensity (Figure 9-1). The intensity of heat within an object is commonly measured by its temperature. However, the quantity of heat in an object is altogether different. Quantity is not the same as intensity. A gallon of water may contain more heat than a quart of water, yet the temperature of the quart of water may be higher because its heat energy is more concentrated or intense.

THE BRITISH THERMAL UNIT (Btu)

The British Thermal Unit is used as a quantity measure of heat. A Btu is the amount of heat that must be added to 1 pound of water to raise the temperature of that pound of water 1 degree fahrenheit.

To define Btu in refrigeration terms, a Btu is the amount of heat that must be removed from 1 pound of water to lower the temperature of the water 1 degree fahrenheit (Figure 9.2).

Heat Cannot Be Destroyed

Heat can be transferred to other substances, such as air or water, but cannot be destroyed. In order to produce refrigeration,

FIGURE 9-1 **Heat transfer.** (Courtesy of The Trane Company.)

FIGURE 9-2 The British thermal unit. (Courtesy of The Trane Company.)

FIGURE 9-3 Heat cannot be destroyed. (Courtesy of The Trane Company.)

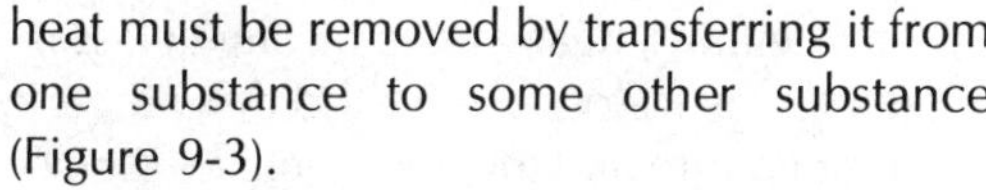

heat must be removed by transferring it from one substance to some other substance (Figure 9-3).

Btus per Hour

To designate rate of flow, the term Btus per hour is used. This term indicates the amount of heat that flows from one substance to another in one hour.

ONE TON OF REFRIGERATION

Cooling is measured in Btus per hour or in tons of refrigeration. This measurement is based on the heat necessary to melt 1 ton of ice in one 24-hour period. When 1 pound of 32°F ice melts, it absorbs 144 Btus. When one ton of 32°F ice melts, it absorbs 2,000 times as many Btus or 288,000. One ton of refrigeration = 288,000 Btus divided by 24 hours = 12,000 Btus per hour.

Frequently, people interchange the term ton and horsepower; they are not the same. Oddly enough in an air conditioning system, each ton of refrigeration requires approximately a one horsepower electric motor to drive the compressor; three tons, three horsepower; and so forth.

MEASURING THE PROPERTY OF AIR

Sensible heat is energy that results in a temperature change of a substance. This change is sensed or felt. The dry-bulb temperature, measured in degrees, is an indication of sensible heat.

Latent heat is simply the energy involved in a change of state, such as changing from a solid to a liquid, or from a liquid to a vapor. It cannot be sensed or felt. Dew point temperature, measured in degrees, is an indication of latent heat. (Fig. 9.4.)

The quantity of moisture in the air is measured as relative humidity. This is the amount of moisture in the air as compared with the amount the air would hold if fully saturated.

The motion of air is measured in cubic feet per minute. At 77°F, 13.5 cubic feet of air weighs 1 pound. The intensity of air is measured in feet per minute velocity. Intensity is sometimes measured in the number of air changes per hour.

The impurities of air are measured by the number of dust particles in 1 cubic foot of air. The bacteria count in air is measured by the colonies of bacteria in a cubic foot of air.

Smoke intensity is measured by the average size of particles in terms of a micron

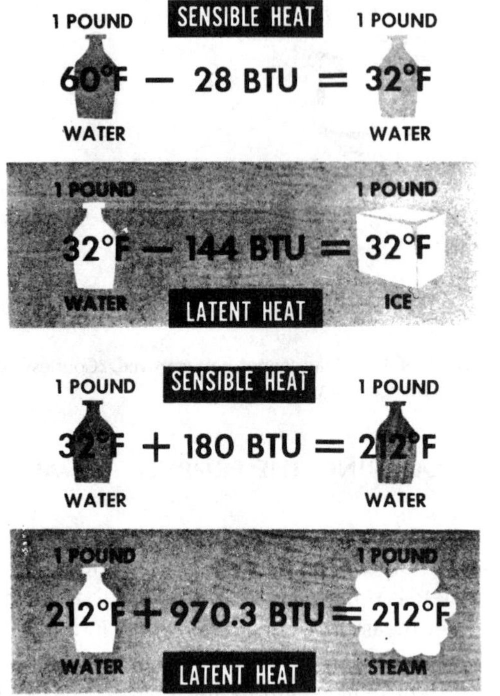

FIGURE 9-4 Measuring the property of air. (Courtesy of The Trane Company.)

(1,000 of a millimeter). Odors can only be detected by actual sense of smell, not by measurement.

AIR CONDITIONING LOADS*

When determining air conditioning loads, the heat gained from six major sources must be included. (Fig. 9.5.)

1. *Heat gained through walls, floor, and ceiling.*
   The heat gained due to transmission is the amount of heat that flows into the conditioned space from surrounding spaces. Normally, the air conditioned space is lower in temperature than the space surrounding it, hence, heat flows into the conditioned area through walls, partitions, floor, and ceiling. To maintain the lower temperature inside the conditioned area, the air conditioning equipment must have sufficient capacity to absorb all the heat from this source.

   There is an additional heat flow from sun-exposed walls or roof due to the heat given off by the sun's rays (solar radiation).
2. *Heat gained through glass.*
   As in heat gained through walls, floors, and ceilings, heat gained through glass includes heat flow due to the difference in temperature and the additional heat given up by the sun's rays. The amount of heat flow due to temperature difference varies with the type of glass used. The amount of heat gained due to the sun varies with the type of protection used, such as awnings, venetian blinds, and shades.
3. *Heat gained due to occupants.*
   Normally the human body dissipates heat at the rate of approximately 330 Btus per hour while at rest. This amount may vary, depending on the type of activity. It is customary to use 400 Btus per hour per person for the occupant load on the usual air conditioning installation. For unusual activity, such as dancing, the amount of heat dissipated may be approximately double that for normal activity.
4. *Heat gained due to lights.*
   The electrical energy used in lighting is dissipated in the form of heat. This heat must be considered in obtaining the total Btu load, at 3.412 Btus per hour watt consumed.
5. *Heat gained due to appliances.*
   Heat gained from appliances, shower baths, and baking is often encountered in

---

*Reprinted with permission of John H. Spence, Refrigeration Service Engineers Society, Des Plains, Illinois.

homes. Heat gained from grilles, toasters, coffee urns, and other heat-generating appliances in restaurants, as well as hair dryers and permanent wave machines in beauty parlors, are important sources of heat gain. The heat from each appliance must be included in obtaining the total Btu load, at the rate of 3.412 Btus per hour per watt.

For estimating approximate heat gain from electric motors in conditioned spaces, use the factor 3.41 Btus per watt. This is accurate for practical use.

6. *Heat gained due to ventilation.*

It is necessary to introduce some outside air to the conditioned space in air conditioning installations in order to eliminate objectionable odors. This outside air (called ventilation) must be cooled from outside to room conditions, and the Btu load included in the total load. The Btu load for ventilation is a very important factor in air conditioning.

Where it is not practical to introduce outside air for ventilation purposes, it is necessary to add heat gained due to natural infiltration of air.

Natural ventilation is one of the great variables in air conditioning heat gain loads. These variables include such factors as types of building construction (brick, concrete block, stone, or wood frame), whether or not wood frame buildings have an outside vapor seal, weather stripping around windows and doors, and the size of family. A home occupied by a man and a woman would not require the opening and closing of doors as often as one where there are several small children. (See Fig. 12-5).

In Figure 9-5, the arrows indicate various sources of heat gain.

Wind velocities must be considered, as wind creates temperature differences due to increased outside pressure against structures, even though the structure may be well built, properly sealed, and well insulated. (See Fig. 9-6.)

FIGURE 9-5 Sources of heat gain. (Courtesy of the Refrigeration Service Engineers Society.)

9-2 Humidity*

CONTROL OF HUMIDITY

Since humidity is such an important factor in summer comfort air conditioning, control of humidity in the atmosphere is accomplished by dehumidification or by humidification, depending on the amount of moisture in the air.

The means of reducing the humidity (dehumidification) are simple. To remove moisture from the air, it is only required to pass the air over a coil, the temperature of which is sufficiently below the dew point to precipitate the proper amount of moisture from the air. Since the dew-point of 80° dry

*Reprinted with permission of John H. Spence, Refrigeration Service Engineers Society, Des Plains, Illinois.

bulb and 50 percent relative humidity (67° wet bulb) is 60°, and the air temperature leaving the coil is usually around 50° to 65°, it is easily seen that a 40° to 45° coil will be somewhere near the correct temperature to do the dehumidification. The coil temperature, of course, depends on the amount and condition of the air passing over the coil and the first design conditions to be met. It is sometimes necessary to reheat the air off the cooling coil to bring it within comfort conditions. This can be accomplished with heating coils or by mixing with air by-passed around the coil.

Air humidification is effected by the vaporization of water, and always requires heat from some source.

Furthermore, humidification is used more often in connection with heating than cooling of air, although occasionally humidification is used in summer air conditioning.

9-3 Air Requirements*

QUANTITY OF FRESH AIR REQUIRED

In some areas, laws have been enacted requiring 30 cubic feet of fresh air per minute, per person, but more recently, with adequate filters available, this amount is usually reduced to the following:

- –10 cfm per person seated and not smoking.
- –15 cfm per person seated and light smoking.
- –20 cfm per person seated or slightly active and heavy smoking.
- –20 to 30 cfm per person dancing, smoking heavily, or where odors are a problem.

In office buildings where the sensible heat load is high, and few people are concentrated, enough fresh air should be brought into the cooled space to pressurize the inside. The pressure forces the cooled and used air to pass out through the cracks around doors and other openings rather than have warm, dust-laden, outside air leak in.

However, specifications regarding ventilation and infiltration of air into an air conditioned space depends on many factors, such as the type of building construction, the type and design of the building, the tightness of windows and doors, and the location of the air conditioned space within a given structure.

As a rule-of-thumb, 100 percent of the cubicle contents of the air in a room should be changed per hour. As an example, assume a room to be 40 feet × 10 feet × 10 feet, having ten people at rest and no smoking. Using the minimum recommended amount of fresh air per minute of 10 cfm times ten people, times sixty minutes, the result is 6,000 cubic feet per hour. To provide sufficient outside air to prevent infiltration (one air change per hour), it would require only 4,000 cubic feet per hour (this is found by taking the cubic content of the room, 40 × 10 × 10). In any case, the greatest figure should be used.

AIR PURITY

If air conditioning requires fresh air to be brought into a room, it must be done systematically to counteract or dilute the effects of respiration, moisture, odors, and carbon di-

*Reprinted with permission of John H. Spence, Refrigeration Service Engineers Society, Des Plains, Illinois.

oxide. In some areas filters should be employed, especially in manufacturing centers, to remove as much of the dust, fly ash, soot, smoke, and pollen as possible from the fresh or outside air. When involved in problems of air purification, it is suggested that guidance be sought from manufacturers of air filters, or reputable engineers qualified in air purification.

9-4 Air Pressure Problems

PRESSURE PROBLEMS CAUSED BY WIND

In general, pressures are positive on the windward side of a building and negative on the leeward side. Pressures on the remaining sides are either negative or positive depending on wind direction.

Pressures are generally negative over flat or low-pitched roofs, but may be positive on the windward and negative on the leeward side of high-pitched roofs.

Pressure in a building resulting from wind action will depend on the resistance of cracks and openings and their location with respect to wind direction.

It is difficult to predict wind velocities, because of the relationship between recorded statistics and what to expect at the site, for the following reasons:

- –Velocity varies with the height of the building.
- –Boundary layer roughness.
- –The relationship between vertical velocity gradient and pressure.
- –In general, velocity of wind action on the surface of a building is so complex that it inhibits any rational representation.

HOW A BUILDING AFFECTS WIND FLOW

The effects of wind flow against buildings in wind tunnels have been studied. The studies indicate that buildings deflect the winds upwards, downward, and laterally. As winds are deflected downward, they transport their higher velocities down from the upper levels, resulting in a localized great quantity of wind at the surface where the winds are two to three times as strong as the mean wind speed. These effects are amplified by streets lined with tall buildings.

STACK EFFECT

When the inside temperature in a building or room is different from the outside temperature, a difference in air density results. This creates a difference in pressure in the building, causing the air to rise. This condition is called stack effect.

In winter the inside temperature is higher, causing negative inside pressure and infiltration at low levels and positive inside pressure and outflow (exfiltration) at high levels. The reverse occurs when the inside temperature is lower than the outside temperature.

In each building there is a neutral pressure (zone) plane where pressures are equal.

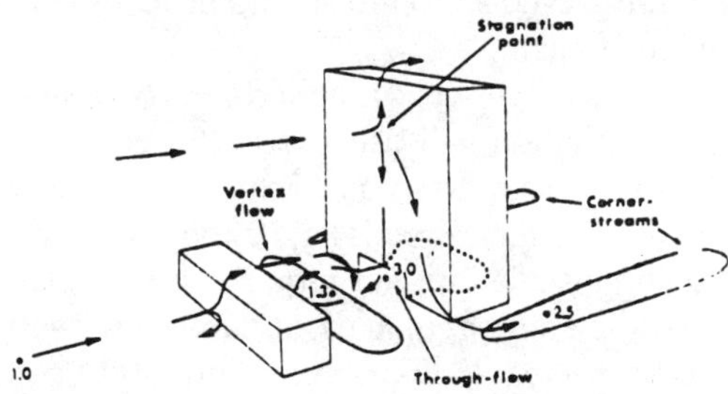

FIGURE 9-6 How a building affects wind flow.

–At any other level the pressure difference depends on the *distance* from the neutral zone and the difference between *densities* of inside and outside air.

–When air flow occurs, the pressure distribution is affected by resistance to the flow between floors and the exterior shell.

–In most buildings the internal vertical resistance is small, because of shafts (elevator).

Buildings with a mechanical exhaust have a higher neutral zone, which increases infiltration. Buildings that are pressurized have a lower neutral zone, which increases exfiltration. When the total air exchange is increased, the energy load increases.

9-5 The Ventilation System

AN OVERVIEW

Accurate and satisfactory air conditioning, involving field installed systems, requires adequate air distribution and circulation. This can only be accomplished by proper-sized ducts, as well as inlet openings for conditioned air, and correct outlet openings for returning used air to the apparatus to be conditioned again.

The average well-designed air conditioning installation will use about 25 percent to 33⅓ percent of fresh air of the total amount circulated. For example, a 10-ton air conditioning installation will require about 4,000 cfm total air circulated, of which at least 1,000 cfm would be fresh air and 3,000 cfm recirculated.

The ventilation system in a building is an integral part of the air handling systems. Exhaust fans remove air from rest rooms, kitchens, hoods, and many other odor generating rooms, while other air handling units bring in a fresh supply of air to take its place.

Air that is exhausted to the outdoors must be replaced by fresh air from air supply units or by infiltration through the cracks of doors, windows, or other apertures. Obviously, exhaust fans that are oversized (and many are because of previous code requirements), cause too much outside air to enter the building, with the resultant loss of valuable energy.

It must be emphasized that when the exhaust outlet on the roof of a building removes undesirable air, this air contains heat. Until recently this heated air was never considered as an expense or loss or that it was depleting our energy sources.

Today, reclaiming this heat is rapidly becoming an important way of saving energy. The average apartment suite requires about 17,600 Btuh of heat. Without a means of recovering this heat, about 9,300 Btuh are eventually exhausted from the building and wasted. (Figs. 12-32 to 12-34.)

INFILTRATION AND VENTILATION

Infiltration is the air that leaks through cracks and other openings around windows and doors and through walls, ceilings, roofs, and floors of all buildings. The magnitude of the infiltration depends on the type of construction, workmanship, and general structural condition of the building.

The rate of air flow into or out of a building due to infiltration, exfiltration, or natural ventilation depends on

–The amount of pressure difference between the inside and outside air.

–The wind.

–The difference in air density—stack effect.

–The mechanical supply and exhaust system.

–The resistances to air flow offered by openings or cracks in the building components.

Wind and stack effect raises the neutral zone on the windward side of a building and causes increased infiltration. On the leeward side the neutral zone is lowered, causing increased exfiltration. It should be noted that it is possible to have exfiltration on the windward side at the top of the building.

METHODS OF AIR DISTRIBUTION

Whenever a central fan or unit is used for air conditioning, some method must be used to convey the conditioned air from the conditioning unit to the space to be conditioned. The air could be treated to lower its dry-bulb temperature below the room temperature for cooling, or raised above the room temperature for heating. The method most commonly used is sheet metal duct work, although other materials, such as "transite," compressed fiberglass, plastics, and fabrics, have been used with success.

DUCTING AIR

Sheet metal ducts are referred to as low velocity or high velocity ducts and sometimes are erroneously referred to as low pressure and high pressure ducts. The terms low and high velocity are purely relative. In a low velocity duct arrangement, the velocities do not exceed 2,000 feet per minute; whereas in a high velocity duct arrangement, the velocities may go from 4,000 to 8,000 fpm and are characterized by relatively small leakproof round ducts.

Round ducts are usually used with high air velocities because (1) a thinner gauge of metal can be used, (2) reinforcing braces are not required, (3) they create less turbulence, and (4) they are usually less costly.

Rectangular duct work is usually used with low velocity designs because it is more flexible and saves space.

Suppose a duct must handle 5,000 cfm at a velocity of 1,400 feet per minute. This will require a duct 26 inches in diameter. The equivalent rectangular duct would be 18 inches by 30 inches. Thus, if the duct were run in a furred ceiling space, the saving in height would be 26−18, or 8 inches.

As the experienced serviceman knows, improper piping will often times cause all kinds of trouble in a refrigeration system. The same is true of the duct work of an air conditioning, a warm air heating, or a ventilating system. The best possible equipment will often fall short of its job requirements due to a poorly designed or an improperly constructed and installed system.

The basic elements of a simple forced circulation warm air system consist of a furnace or heat exchange unit, a centrifugal fan, a temperature-sensing device controlling the operation of the furnace and fan, suitable air filters, and a duct system.

The air is filtered, heated, and distributed to the various areas of the building. The engineer designs the system on the basis of the delivery of fixed quantities of air (cfm) to specific points in the building. If the distribution system (duct work) is not properly sized and balanced, the flow of air will not be as calculated and the system will not function properly.

THE FUNCTION OF A DUCT SYSTEM*

A duct is a tube, or pipe, that carries air between two points. Strictly speaking, in air conditioning terms, a duct system is the arrangement of ducts between the air conditioning equipment and the rooms to be cooled, not including such items as filters, casing, and cooling coil. However, we shall include in our use of the term "duct system" every item in the air passage network that offers resistance to air flow. From the standpoint of the fan, it makes no difference whether a resistance is caused by filters or by the use of a small duct; the effect on the fan will be the same. Resistance tends to restrict the flow of air through the entire system.

A window conditioner, or room cooler (Figure 9-7), is essentially a device with a minimum duct system, since the only items that offer resistance to air flow are built into the cabinet that contains the evaporator, the fan, and the air openings. In this minimum duct system, the air going into the cooler and the air discharged from it are handled without benefit of any ducts. Hence, in this type of cooler it is not convenient to remove air from another room or to deliver cool air to another space. In fact, the cooling effect is localized in the room in which the cooler is located.

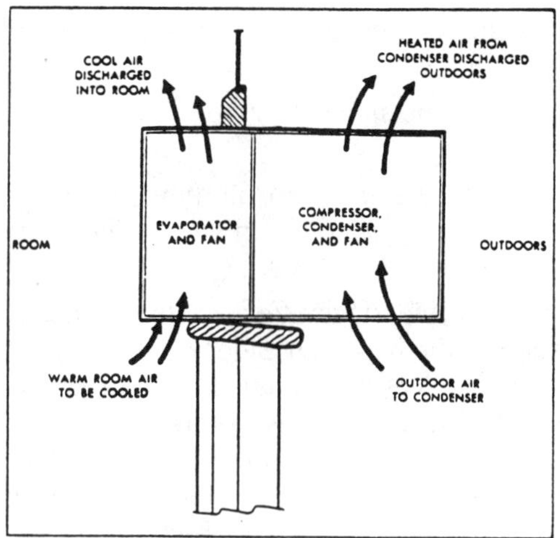

FIGURE 9-7 The window room cooler. Since air to and from the cooler is handled without external ducts, this unit cools a room with a minimum duct system. (Courtesy of the Refrigeration Service Engineers Society.)

THE ESSENTIAL PARTS

In contrast to the minimum duct system, let us examine one form of central air conditioning that is in common use: a warm-air furnace to which a cooling coil has been added. A diagram of the essential parts is shown in Figure 9-8, and the major parts of the duct system are labeled by capital letters, as follows:

Return Intake. The return intake is an opening through which air is removed from a room and sent to the cooling unit. In order to conceal the hole in the wall, a metal grille that contains a number of openings is installed. A return intake can be located at any of a number of positions in a room.

1. At the ceiling.
2. At the high sidewall.
3. At the baseboard, just above the floor line.
4. In the floor.

One return grille may serve more than one room. For example, a central return in a hallway may serve several rooms that open into the hallway. In practice, a relatively small

*Reprinted with the permission of the International Education Department, Refrigeration Service Engineers Society, Des Plains, Illinois.

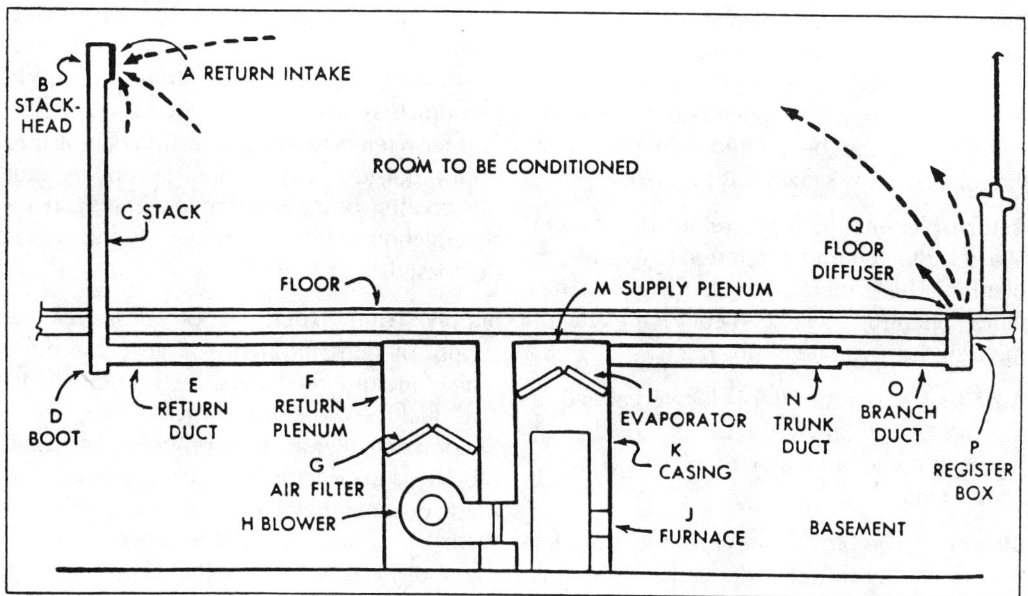

FIGURE 9-8 Air passage in a duct system. The lettered parts offer resistance to air flow. (Courtesy of the Refrigeration Service Engineers Society.)

number of return grilles are used in a house, and these are located in hallways and in out-of-the-way places.

The location of return intakes in a room or in a house is relatively unimportant. Contrary to what many laymen think, it is not possible to greatly alter the paths of air currents in a room by sucking air out of the room through a hole. The most important return-intake features, as far as size and location are concerned, are that openings be ample in size and that air not be unduly restricted in its flow.

Stackhead. The return grille is fitted into a metal box, which is referred to as a stackhead since it is attached to the top of the metal stack that carries the air down to the lower level.

Stack. The stack is a rectangular metal duct that fits into a studding space. Since the usual studding space is 14⅜ inch wide and 3⅝ inch deep, the depth of the stack is commonly 3¼ inch.

On the return-air side of a cooling system, through which air at room temperature is handled, the stack and stackhead are frequently omitted and the studding space is used as a duct passageway. Obviously, cost is greatly reduced by the omission of the metal duct. There is no objection to this practice as long as the wall through which the air is carried is not an exposed wall.

Boot. The boot is a connection or fitting that joins the stack to the horizontal duct at the lower level.

Return Duct. The return duct is a return passage for air. This duct can be made of galvanized iron, aluminum, or any fire-resistant material. The space between wooden floor joists can be utilized if the bottom of the joist space is sealed with a metal sheet.

Return Plenum. All the return ducts meet at a common chamber, referred to as a return plenum. This is merely a sheet metal box into which openings have been cut for the attachment of the separate return ducts.

Air Filter. The air filter is located ahead of the fan to sift dust particles out of the air before it comes in contact with the working equipment.

Blower. The blower provides the force for moving the air through the duct system. It is usually a centrifugal or squirrel-cage fan.

Furnace. The furnace is a heat exchanger of steel or cast iron in which fuel is burned and over which air is circulated in winter for heating. It serves no purpose in summer cooling.

Casing. The casing is a housing around the furnace. It consists of a rectangular sheet metal enclosure insulated on the inside so that heat will not be transmitted to the basement air outside the casing.

Evaporator. Many different arrangements of evaporator and furnace are available. The arrangement shown is a common one in which the evaporator is located above the furnace. The compressor and condenser (neither is shown) can be located either in some other part of the basement or outdoors. The resistance of the evaporator to the flow of air is large.

Supply Plenum. The plenum is a large box to which ducts are attached. It serves as a mixing chamber so that cool air leaving the evaporator has a chance to be mixed thoroughly before being sent out to the different ducts. In some installations the supply plenum may show a tendency to "sweat." This term refers to a condensation of moisture on the outside, which often disappears after the cooling process has been going on for several hours and the indoor humidity has decreased.

Supply Trunk Duct. Cool air leaves the supply plenum through a large trunk duct, which in turn feeds smaller branch ducts. This duct resembles the trunk of a tree, which becomes smaller as more branches are taken off. The trunk duct is usually rectangular and made of sheet metal. On the supply side of a warm-air furnace system the spaces between the floor joists and the wall studdings cannot be used alone as ducts. Fire protection codes prohibit the use of these combustible spaces as air passages, unless metal ducts are installed in them.

Branch Ducts. These smaller ducts supply cool air to the rooms. As many as a dozen branch ducts can take off from a single trunk duct in a small residential installation. The branch ducts can be round, square, or rectangular in cross section.

Register Box. This is the container in which the register is placed. If a register is located in a wall, it is placed in a stackhead.

Floor Diffuser. The cool-air opening into a room is covered by a device called a register, or diffuser. The register serves to control the velocity, the flow rate, and the direction of the air stream. A register is more than a pretty decoration to conceal a hole in a floor or wall. The resistance offered by a register to the flow of air can be substantial, particularly if the air is deflected from its normal path.

Room Air. Cooled air flows through the

rooms of the house and reaches the return intake without any appreciable resistance. This is because the air velocity is exceedingly low, approximately 50 fpm or less.

9-6 Air Distribution*

AN OVERVIEW

Since the 1940s, when forced air systems first started to gain popularity, there have been several significant changes in system design. Suitable design data and installation techniques have been developed by the industry at each stage in the evolution of new styles of residences, such as ranch bungalows, basementless, and split level houses. It should be noted, however, that there are three basic requirements for correct performance of air conditioning systems: accurate design, correct installation, and final balancing. Current methods of system design do not provide an automatically balanced system. No matter how well a system may be designed and installed it must be balanced after it is installed. While suitable design and installation information is available, there is a need for a method of system balancing that is consistent with system design practice and that can be carried out on the job in a short time.

Although we will use a residential air conditioning system to explain the many factors inherent in the operation of an air conditioning system, the same basic principles apply to larger installations.

Because the matter of heating is covered in Chapter 8, "Heating Systems," it will not be duplicated here. In this chapter, we will help you to understand the distribution of conditioned air, to recognize problems, and to know what to do about them.

AIR DISTRIBUTION SYSTEMS IN HOMES

There are two different types of air distribution systems used in homes. Each system has different physical, operational, and design characteristics. These are

(a) Graduated or Trunk Duct System

(b) Extended Plenum Perimeter System

The graduated or trunk system is commonly used for industrial and commercial duct installations, and has also been utilized in residential jobs. The main feature of this arrangement is that the system has the characteristics of a tree trunk; broad at the base and gradually getting smaller as branches sprout. The system, when properly designed and installed, provides good control of the separate air streams and uses a minimum of sheet metal.

The trunk ducts and branch ducts shown in Figure 9-9 are rectangular ducts; the usual duct depth is 8 inches. The branch ducts could be round ducts, however, in which case different fittings at the branch take-off points would be required.

This system was common before the 1950s, but it is rarely used today.

THE EXTENDED-PLENUM DUCT SYSTEM

This is the system commonly used today. Homes with the extended-plenum duct sys-

*Portions of this text reprinted in part with the permission of Mr. T.A. Clark, The Heating, Refrigerating and Air Conditioning Institute of Canada.

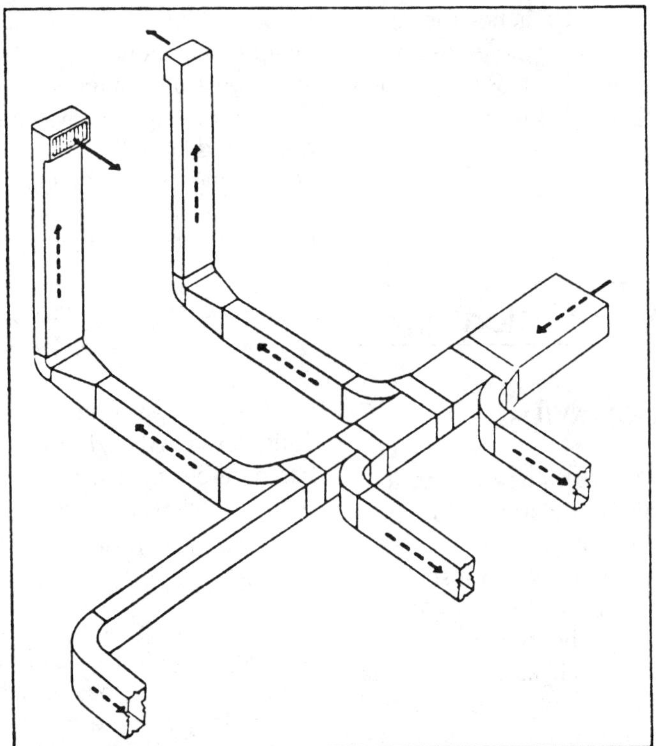

FIGURE 9-9 The graduated or trunk system. (Courtesy of the American Gas Association.)

tem are heated and cooled by a forced air unit using oil, gas, or electrical energy in the winter, and cooled by a refrigeration unit in the summer.

The main feature of the extended plenum is that the trunk duct does not vary in size even after branches have been taken off, but remains constant in the cross-sectional area.

Registers can be located in a ceiling and supply ducts can be overhead in an attic. This is a common arrangement well suited to a home being provided with a cooling system that is separate from the existing heating system, as in the case of a hot water radiator system.

Registers can also be located along inside walls at the baseboard, in the floor, or at a high wall location. Inside wall location of registers is common in homes built prior to 1950, since inside wall locations were preferred to exposed wall locations at that time. The duct system can be the individual duct type or the trunk duct type, depending on the size of the house and the location of the furnace. Because the extended plenum trunk duct is not reduced in size after each branch take-off, the air velocity in the trunk does not contribute to air flow in all branches uniformly along the length of the duct. On the contrary, the trunk velocity tends to promote an excess of air flow through branches connected at the remote end of the duct and to reduce the air flow to branches connected progressively closer to the unit.

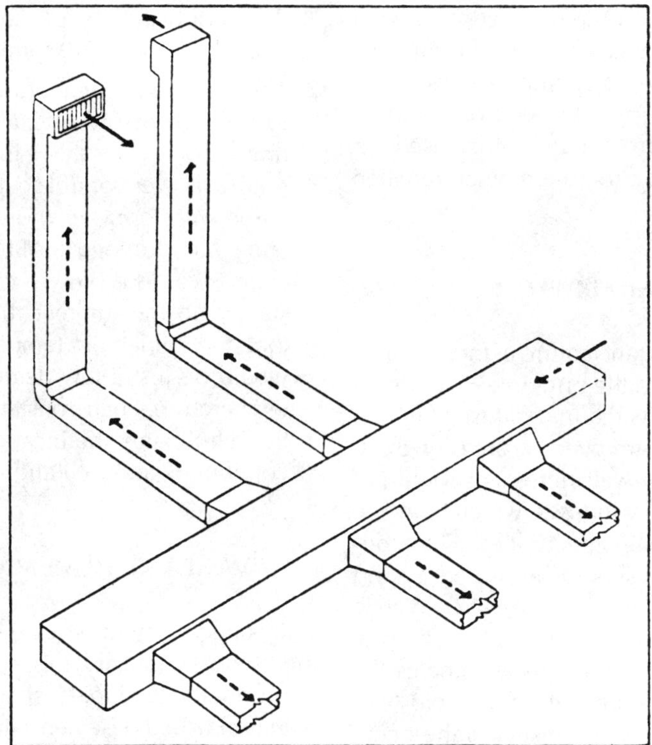

FIGURE 9-10 The extended-plenum duct system. (Courtesy of the American Gas Association.)

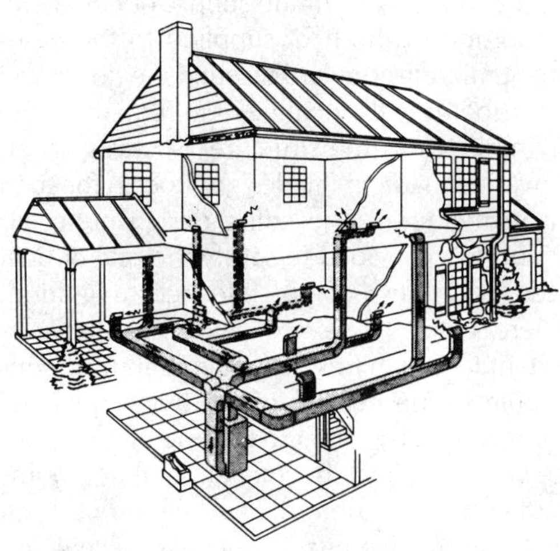

FIGURE 9-11 Supply air ducts.

In most installations it will be found that a greater volume of air will be delivered through branches connected to the extended plenum at the remote end of the unit than through the same size of branch connected to the trunk closer to the unit. This condition can cause inadequate air delivery to rooms served by branches near the unit and excessive air delivery to rooms served by the more remote branches. This operating characteristic is exactly the opposite of the graduated duct type of system. It is a very important factor in the balancing process for both types of systems. Because of this condition, it is essential that the supply plenum pressure for which the system was designed be established by the balancing process so that all branches will deliver the required volume of air. It is also necessary to start the air flow adjustments in the balancing process at the outlets connected near the end of the trunk ducts remote from the unit. Increased air delivery will raise a room temperature when heating.

ROOM AIR FLOW

The most important feature of the warm air perimeter system is the principle of air delivery. The air is delivered in a diffused fan pattern vertically upward over the areas of greatest heat loss. Low wall diffusers should not be used beneath windows which may be covered with full length drapes. Floor diffusers in this case should be placed a short distance from the wall (Figure 9-12) so as to discharge air on the room side of the drapes.

This method of air supply eliminates the formation of down drafts from the cold window and door areas and insulates the occupants from such cold surface. Another important advantage in this type of air delivery is the fact that the vertical air flow is not likely to impinge on the occupants.

This aspect provides two very important operational features which, if properly employed, can contribute materially to indoor comfort:

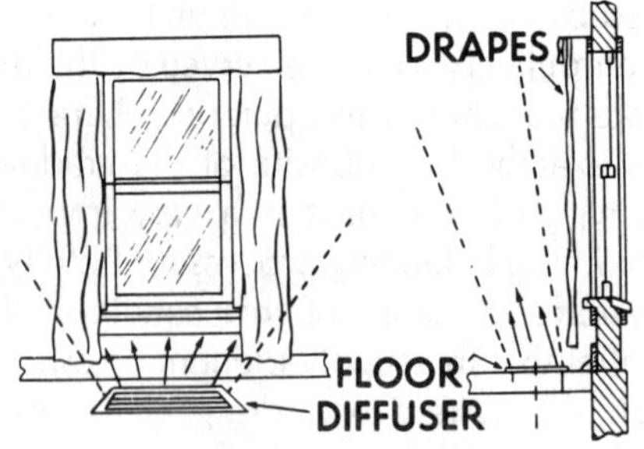

FIGURE 9-12 Location of floor diffusers.

1. The supply outlet air velocity may be relatively high (400-500 fpm).
2. The outlet air temperature does not have to be high in order to avoid creation of drafts. This means that it is not necessary to set the blower control so that the air circulation will stop when the outlet air temperature has dropped to 115°F or 100°F or even 80°F. The blower can operate constantly on the summer manual switch so that the outlet air temperature at times would be just a few degrees above room temperature. Such constant blower operation eliminates stratification and provides continuous air circulation.

VAGRANT HEAT MIGRATION

It is necessary to provide heat in or below the floors to ensure the comfort of warm floors in the occupied space. Even homes with unfinished basements are provided with sufficient warm air supply outlets to heat the basement. Some heat is also supplied to the basement by the heat losses from the casing of the unit and from the supply duct system. A portion of the heat supplied to the basement migrates upward through the floors and contributes to the heating requirements of the living areas of the structure. There is no allowance made in the design process for such heat migration. The entire design outlet air volume is provided to satisfy the rate of heat loss, regardless of possible heat migration. There seems to be no way to calculate the extent to which this heat migration may contribute to the heating of the living quarters. Rooms directly over the heating unit may receive more heat by migration than rooms farther from the unit. Also, some rooms, such as those over an attached garage, receive no heat by migration. Such rooms are entirely dependent on the supply of warm air in accordance with the design. Since heat migration is not allowed for in the design of the system, it is one of the factors that should be considered and allowed for in the balancing of the system after installation.

AIR DISTRIBUTION IN HIGH-RISE BUILDINGS

The air handling systems generally follow the same configuration, using a sheet metal enclosure with a fan to move air and using various arrangements of hot or cold coils to condition the air. All sorts of filter systems are used to trap the dirt particles in the air. These filtering units are an integral part of all air handling systems.

Considerable energy is used by these systems since they are almost always connected to the outdoors as a source of fresh air. The air dust causes plugged filters, which are one of the hazards of an energy conservation program.

Air handling systems have three basic designs:

1. *Built-up Units*—generally over 50,000 cfm in capacity.
2. *Factory Assembled Units*—from 2,000 cfm to 50,000 cfm.
3. *Smaller Units (Fan Coil Units)*—from 200 cfm to 1,200 cfm.

AIR SUPPLY SYSTEMS

Supply air to a room would be simple if there was only one room on the supply air system; however, there are usually many rooms on a system, each with a different requirement and each with a different personality. Some rooms receive sunshine while others are in the shade; some rooms have heat gain equipment installed in them and others have none; and some rooms have lots of people and lights, others have none. If all rooms on an air handling system receive the same temperature air, they will end up at different and sometimes undesirable temperatures; for this reason, all sorts of supply air systems were invented. An explanation of these systems will help us understand.

DOUBLE OR DUAL DUCT SYSTEM

Up until now we have explained the system as a single supply and return duct. There is also the possibility of using two supply ducts and one return duct. This would be similar to the three-pipe water system, in that one duct supplies warm air and one supplies cold air with the return duct carrying the mixture of the two back to the fan. This is called a double duct or dual duct arrangement.

When the air reaches its terminal point, that is, when it is introduced into the conditioned space, the velocity must be low enough to avoid creating drafts or noise. If low velocity duct work is used, it is only a matter of choosing the right diffuser or grille. However, with high velocity air, it is necessary to slow the air down, and in many cases, to reduce the pressure. This is done by using an attenuator box. From this box, low velocity ducts are run to the diffusers, or in some cases, a diffuser is mounted on the attenuator box (see Figures 9-13 and 9-14).

Dual duct was invented using the room thermostat to control the hot and cold air supply and thus give a blended temperature to satisfy the requirements of the occupants of the space being supplied.

There are two reasons why this system wastes energy:

1. It requires a lot of air pressure.

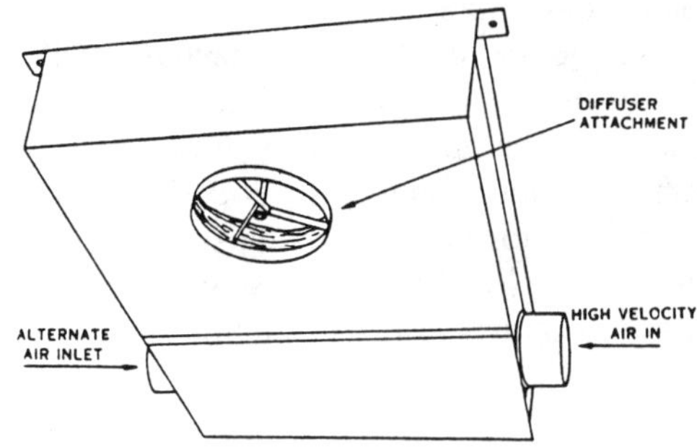

FIGURE 9-13 Attenuator box with diffuser attachment. (Courtesy of Tuttle & Bailey Company.)

2. While creating a comfortable temperature, it first cools the air and then heats it.

DUAL DUCT SYSTEM

Dual duct arrangements can be designed for either high or low velocities. In either case, a mixing arrangement must be used at each outlet or at each zone. These mixing boxes are equipped with a warm and cold air damper. The control is arranged so that some cold and some warm air are mixed and discharged through a diffuser or into the zone duct work.

TYPICAL VENTILATION SYSTEM

To help you understand the ventilating system, a cutaway drawing of a building is provided (Figure 9-16), which allows you to see the complete system at a glance. The main components of the system are numbered and will be explained separately. The most important areas will be enlarged and illustrated.

Corridor Air Supply

As explained previously the volume of air handled by a fan is the number of cubic feet of air per minute (cfm) at the fan outlet.

Some buildings have air that is filtered and heated before it is distributed by ducts into each corridor. Some large buildings have more than one unit.

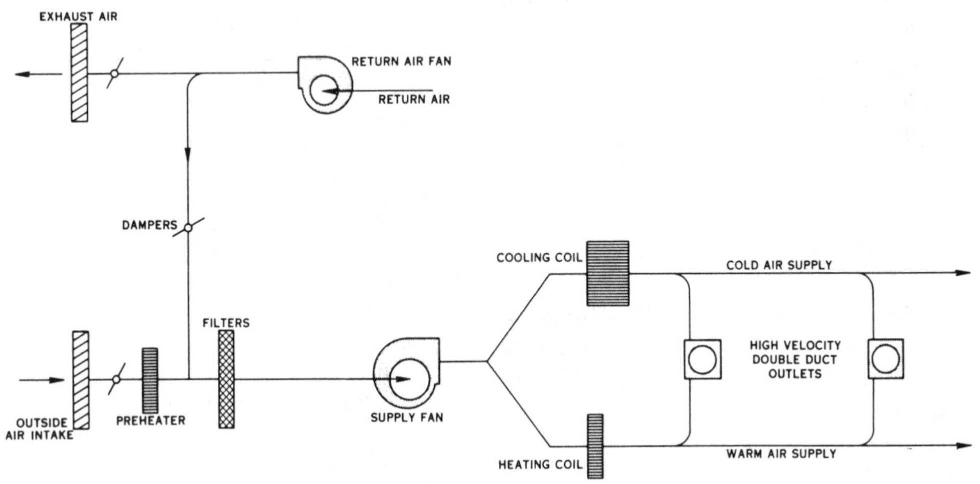

FIGURE 9-14 Double-duct, one-fan system. (Courtesy of The Trane Company.)

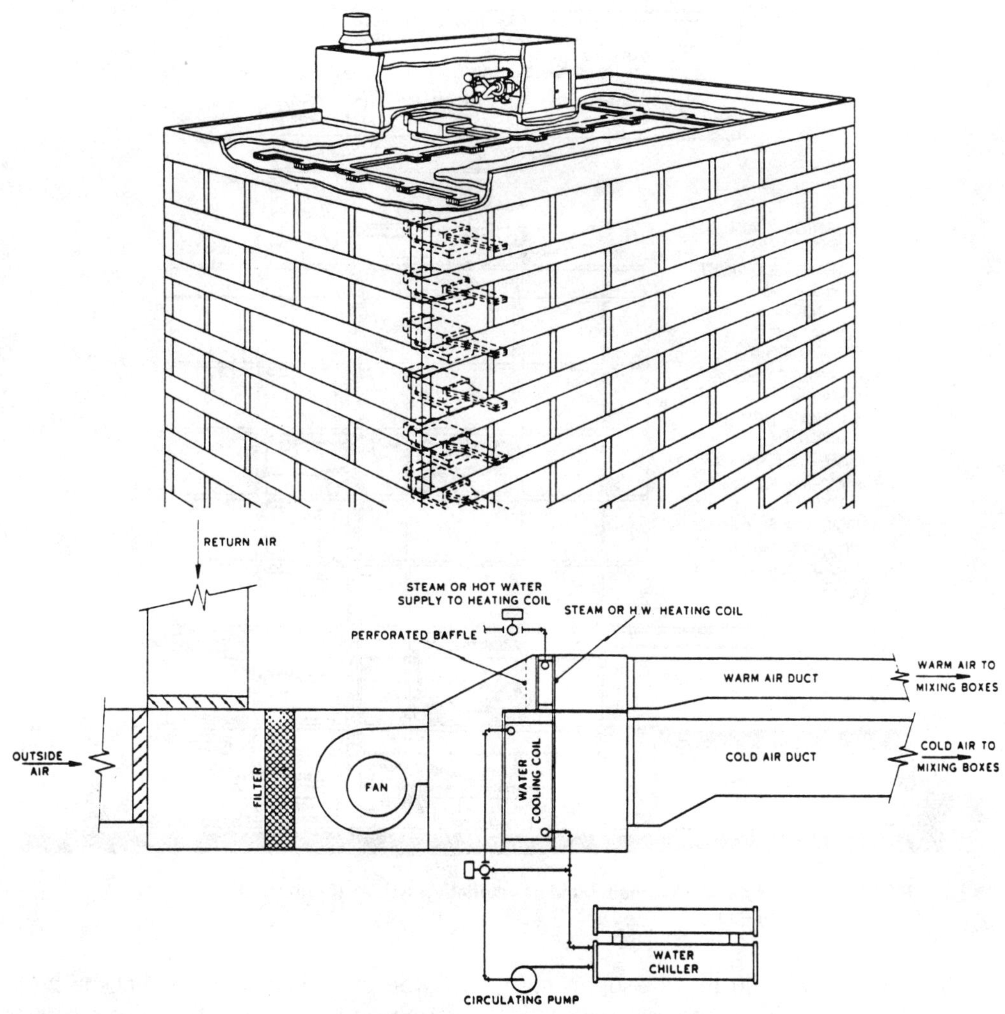

FIGURE 9-15 Typical dual-duct system. System with central fan, water cooling coil, steam or hot water coil, filters, double-duct air distribution, mixing boxes for conditioned spaces, refrigeration unit for chilling water, or a refrigeration compressor and direct expansion cooling coil for cooling air and controls. (Courtesy of The Trane Company.)

The cutaway drawing of a typical apartment building (Figure 9-16) shows the corridor air supply unit located at the top, but a second or third unit could be situated in other areas, depending on the size and design of the building. The number of units depends on the length of the corridors and on how much air is needed to pressurize them. (See "Quantities of Fresh Air Required," page 404).

The systems are designed by engineering consultants to eliminate many air related problems. The systems should be balanced by a knowledgeable engineer when they are

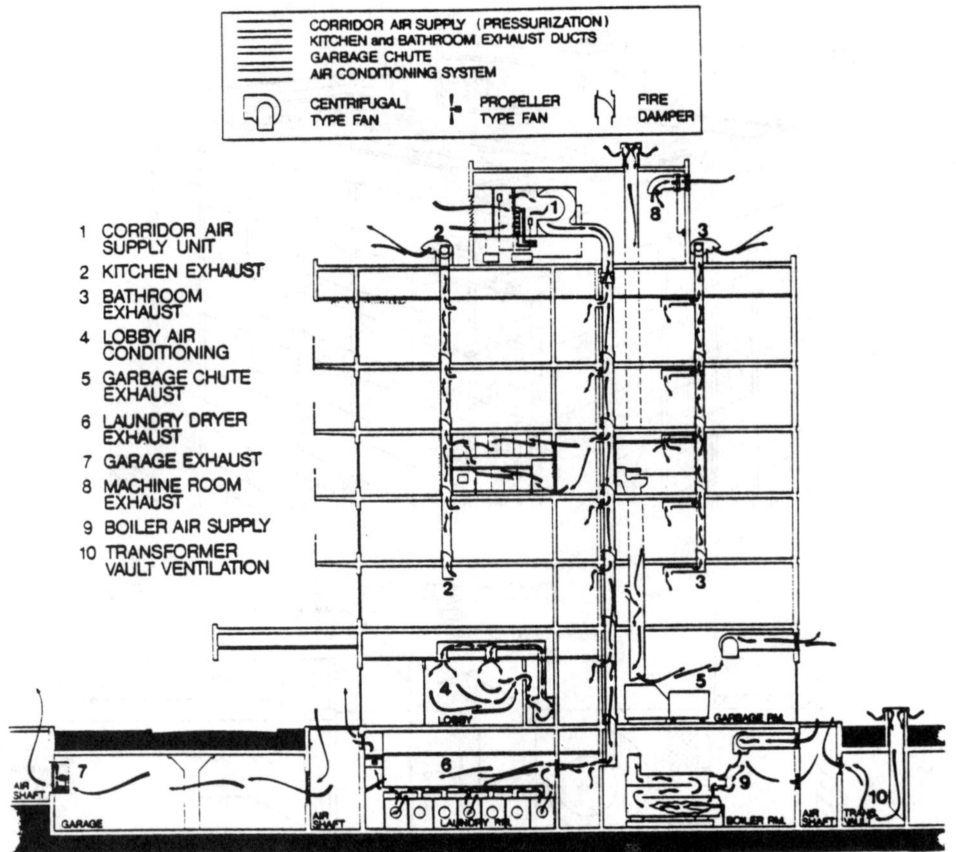

FIGURE 9-16 Typical apartment building ventilation system. (Courtesy of Cadillac Fairview Corporation, Limited.)

installed; this means adjusting the supply registers in each corridor to assure that air is properly distributed throughout the building. Methods of heating the corridor air supply are covered in Chapter 8, "Heating Systems."

Supply Register

The diffuser or supply register is decorative and is used to regulate the direction and the volume of air delivered to each area of the building. Do not install filters behind these registers as they will upset the balance of the system. Signs of dirt around the frame on the wall or ceiling indicate that the filter at the unit isn't doing its job. It also means that the frame is not installed properly.

Always ensure that the bird screens on the corridor air supply inlet are free of dirt. This is more of a problem on ground floor installations, where paper and leaves can accumulate.

Kitchen and Bathroom Exhaust

Notice that supply air enters each occupied unit around its entrance door. This air is then exhausted through the kitchen and bathroom exhaust grilles. BECAUSE OF THIS, THE ENTRANCE DOOR MUST NOT BE WEATHER-STRIPPED AND THE APARTMENT EXHAUST GRILLES MUST BE CLEAN. When these doors are weather-stripped, air infiltration is increased at exterior doors and windows. This causes drafts, allows dirt to enter, and wastes energy.

In many buildings centrifugal exhaust fans are situated on the roof over each series of apartments. In other buildings each unit has its own exhaust fans through the wall exhaust. The rooftop exhaust system is usually designed to exhaust 100 cfm per kitchen and 50 cfm per bathroom.

The dampers must never be altered unless the entire system is being professionally balanced.

Garage Exhaust

Garage exhaust fans are installed to remove automobile exhaust fumes from the garage and to prevent the fumes from entering the building.

The required air is supplied to the garage from screened air shafts. The screens must be kept free of paper, leaves, dirt, and if not kept clean, could cause flooding by plugging the drains.

Automatic Shutters on Fans or Back Draft Dampers

Shutters on propeller-type fans usually open on fan start and close by gravity when the motor stops. Adjustable shutters are used to direct air flow and remain as set (i.e., garage heaters). They must be cleaned and lubricated to open and close efficiently.

Elevator Machine Room Exhaust

To exhaust the hot air from the elevator machine room, most buildings use a propeller fan, which is controlled by a reverse acting thermostat. Fresh air is supplied by air inlet louvers that open when the fan is operating.

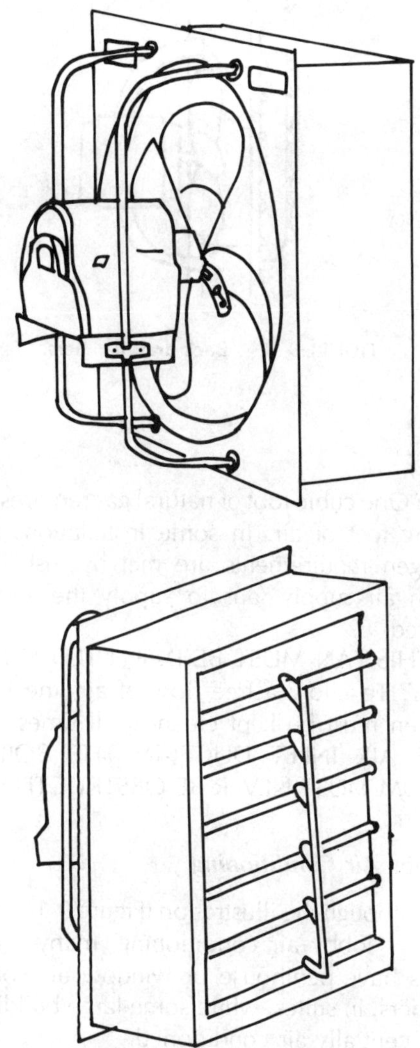

FIGURE 9-17 Propeller direct drive fan.

Boiler Room Air Supply

To assure combustion efficiency, the burner must be provided with sufficient oxy-

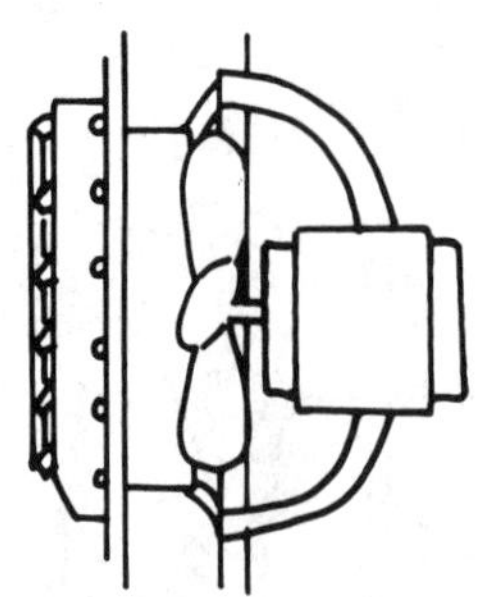

FIGURE 9-18 Back draft dampers.

gen. One cubic foot of natural gas requires 10 cubic feet of air. In some installations the oxygen requirements are met by installing fresh air supply fans to supply the air required.

THIS FAN MUST BE INSPECTED EVERY DAY. To allow a free flow of air, the inlet screen must be kept clean at all times and THE AIR INLET DUCT IN THE BOILER ROOM MUST NEVER BE OBSTRUCTED.

Lobby Air Conditioning

Although the illustration (Figure 9-16) only shows lobby air conditioning, many buildings have penthouse or window air conditioners, in suites, while some large buildings are centrally air conditioned.

The cooling and heating coils must be cleaned as often as required. Again, conditions and inspections will determine the frequency.

AIR FILTERS MUST BE KEPT CLEAN. Unless they are clean, the flow of air over the coils will be restricted and the coils will ice up. This icing could lead to very costly repairs such as a burned out compressor and a lack of air supply to the conditioned area.

Fans, motors, and controls should be inspected and serviced annually. Care should be exercised when lubricating fans to avoid allowing oil to run onto fan blades. The fan blades should also be checked for alignment. It is wise to do this maintenance during the off season when the unit is shut down, so it will be ready for start-up when needed the following season.

You should note that the unit illustrated on the system drawing only recirculates air within the lobby (see Figure 9-19).

Garbage Chute Exhaust

Because the garbage chute runs the full height of the building, it creates a "stack effect" or an "up draft." When this happens, garbage dust blows back into the face of anyone opening the chute. It also allows garbage odors to invade the garbage rooms and the corridors.

To offset the stack effect, a centrifugal fan is installed in the compactor room. The fan exhausts the air from the room, resulting in a down draft in the chute.

The compactor room doors must be closed if the exhaust system is to work efficiently. A fusible link damper is installed at the bottom of the chute. This link melts when a fire occurs, allowing the damper to close, sealing the chute. Heat sensitive sprinklers are generally installed every third floor. Spare sprinkler heads and fusible links should always be kept on hand.

Dryer Exhaust System

It should not be necessary to remind you that efficient operation of dryers requires adequate air supply and exhaust systems. To achieve this efficiency, each dryer must have available 150 cfm of air.

Generally, this air is supplied by the corridor air or by a fan installed for this purpose.

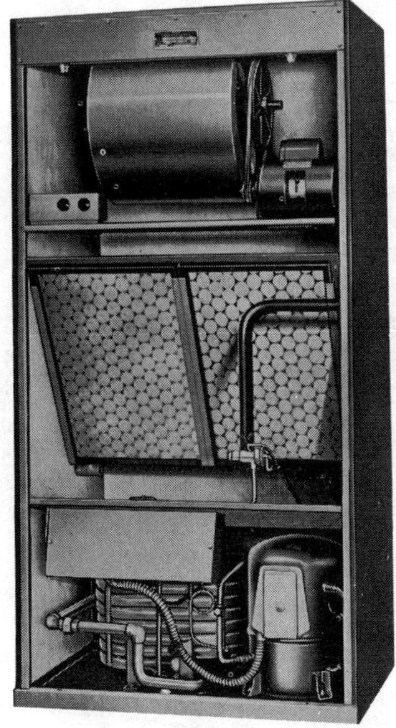

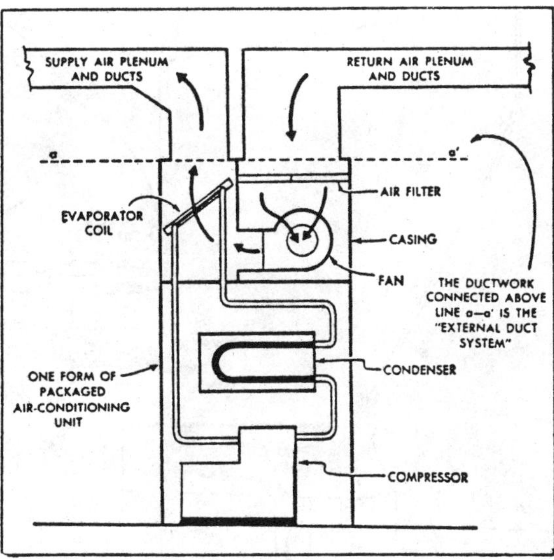

FIGURE 9-19 Unitary air conditioner for use with ducts.

Dryer Exhaust Maintenance Timer Setting —7:00 a.m. to 10:00 p.m. (Fig. 9-20.)

1. Clean or replace the removable lint screen daily.
2. The exhaust outlet louver and bird screen should be checked and cleaned as required. This louver should be hinged to allow easy access.
3. When servicing the exhaust fans, follow the electric motor lubrication instructions provided by the manufacturer.
4. Every six months the following service should be completed:
   (a) remove the backs of the dryers
   (b) change belts and lubricate
   (c) vacuum the backs of the machines
5. At the same time, a chimney cleaning service company should completely clean the dryer exhaust system from the ducts to the outside louver.
6. Any stripping, waxing, or painting required in the laundry room should be scheduled at the same time as the other maintenance.

Note of Caution It should be stressed that anything that interferes with the exhaust system in any suite, such as weather stripping of suite entrance doors or dirty, greasy exhaust grilles in kitchens and bathrooms, can have a negative effect on the performance of the whole system, upsetting any balancing that has been achieved.

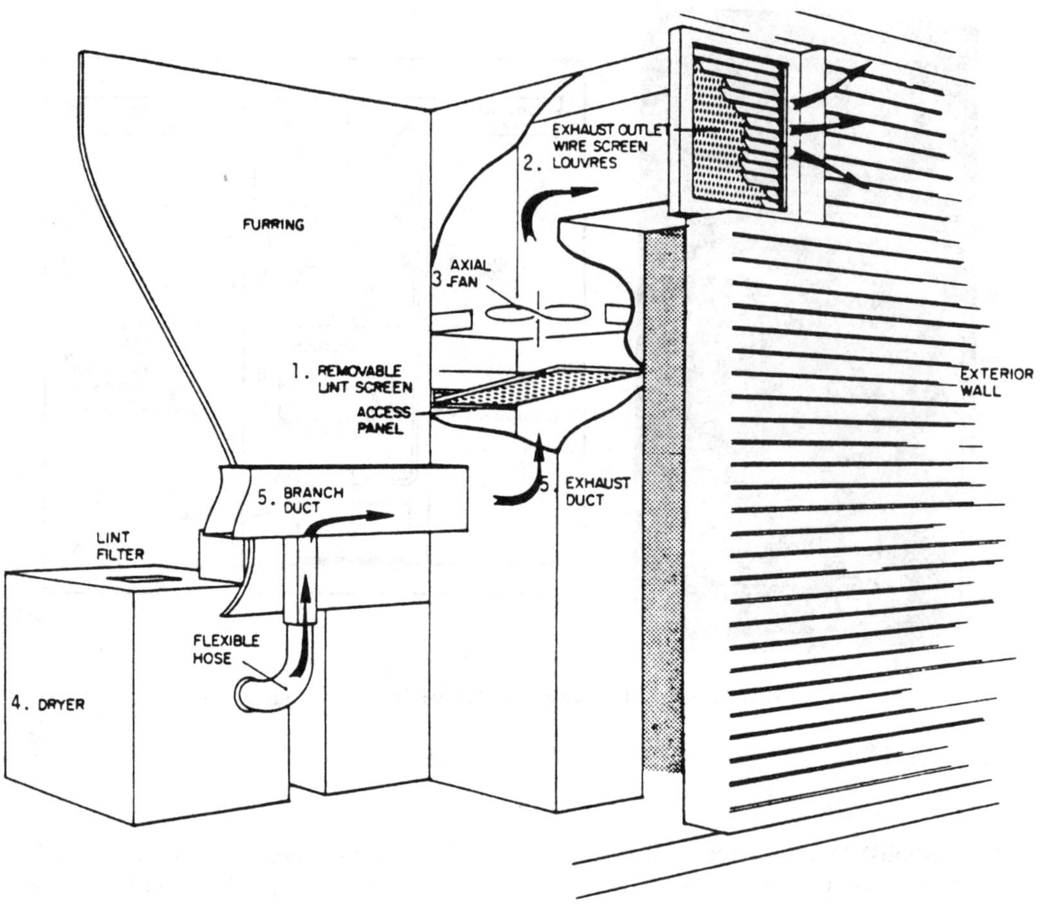

FIGURE 9-20 Typical laundry room exhaust system. (Courtesy of Cadillac Fairview Corporation, Limited.)

9-7 Balancing the System

AN OVERVIEW

As the cost of energy has escalated, engineers have become more aware of the importance of testing and balancing air conditioning systems. Many owners are now insisting upon reliable certification of equipment performance, quantities and quality of air, temperature and humidity control, and system stability. To assure these standards, the need for education about field measurement techniques, the instruments required and how to use them, and forms for gathering data all became essential.

The skilled balancing technician must understand fan operating characteristics, the theory of fluid flow, fan and pulley laws, how to use the instruments needed to take flow and pressure readings, how to adjust speed, flow, and pressure, as well as how to start-up test and balance the ventilation and air conditioning system. A skilled technician will translate these theories into actual operating conditions.

This text is only intended to make you aware of the importance of balancing, and of the need for a skilled technician.

BALANCING INSTRUMENTS AND TOOLS

Balancing technicians use several instruments and tools to test and balance an air conditioning or ventilation system.

1. A speed counter to measure the rpm.
2. A clamp-on volt-amp meter for measuring voltage and amperes.
3. Thermometers and psychrometers for measuring duct and space temperatures and relative humidity.
4. Rotating vane anemometer for measuring air flow at the coil face or large return air grille.
5. Swinging vane anemometer for measuring air flow at a grille or diffuser.
6. A Pitot tube to probe the air inside a duct. It is used in conjunction with an inclined manometer to read velocity pressure (Vp), static pressure (Sp), and total pressure (Tp) of fluid or gas inside of a duct.
7. An inclined manometer to measure air pressure inside of a duct; also known as a draft gauge, air meter, air velocity meter, or air gauge. It is a simple foolproof device, which responds directly to air pressure exerted against it (transmitted by the Pitot tube), and reads in inches of water.
8. A Magnahelic* pressure gauge to measure air pressure inside a duct. It is a diaphragm operated gauge that is much better than a liquid manometer.

STANDARD BALANCING PROCEDURE

The National Standards for field measurements and instrumentation was first published by the Associated Air Balance Council in 1967. To give you an overview of the balancing procedure, we will briefly summarize the procedure from that document.

1. All supply and return air duct dampers are set at full open position.

   All diffuser and side-wall grilles are set at full open position.

   Outside-air damper is set at minimum position.

   All controls are checked and set at full cooling cycle. Branch line splitter dampers are set to open positions.

   All extractors and distribution grilles are set in wide open positions.
2. Drill probe holes for static pressure readings, Pitot tube traverse readings, and temperature readings.

   Check motor electric current supply and rated running amperage of fan motors.

   Check fan and motor speeds.

   Check available adjustment tolerance.
3. Make first complete air distribution run throughout the entire system, recording first run statistics. Using Pitot tube traverse in all main ducts, branch ducts, and supply and return, proportion all air in required amounts to the various main duct and branch runs.

   Make a second complete air distribution run throughout entire system for check on proper proportion of air.
4. Using Pitot tube traverse, set all main line dampers to deliver proper amount of cfm

---

*MAGNAHELIC is not a generic term but is registered by the Dwyer Instrument Company.

to all areas. Using Pitot tube traverse, set all branch line dampers to deliver proper amount of cfm to diffusers and side-wall supply grilles in each zone.

Read cfm at each outlet and adjust to meet requirements.

Test and record all items as listed.

THE PITOT TUBE

For convenience and accuracy, the static and total pressure tubes are combined into one instrument known as a Pitot Tube. This tube consists of two tubes—one within the other, as shown in Figure 9-21. The inner

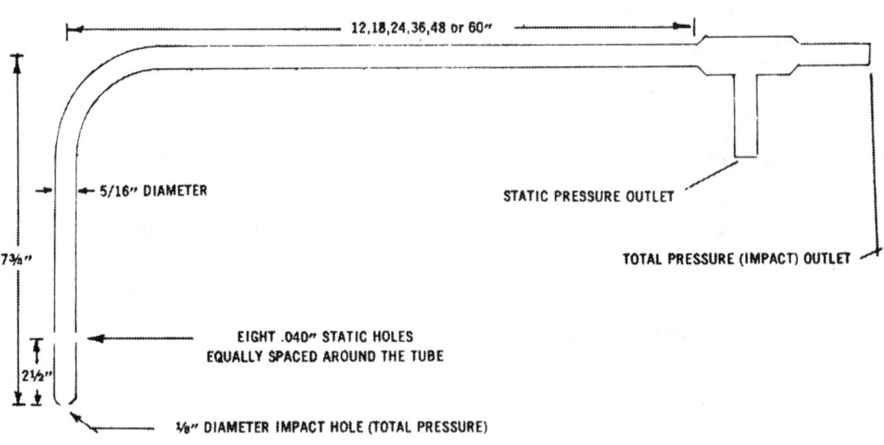

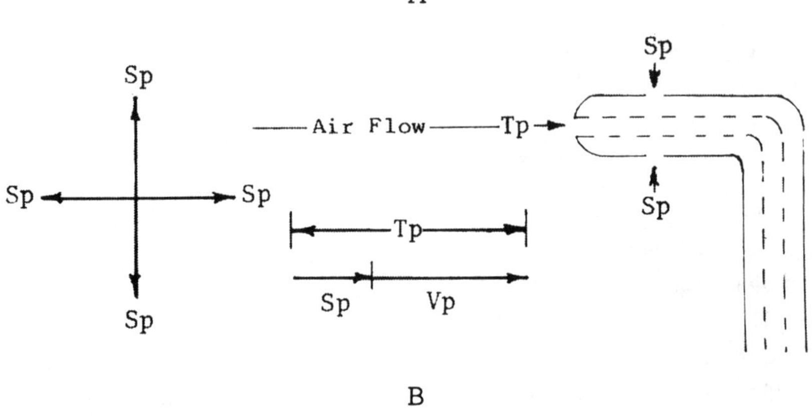

FIGURE 9-21 The Pitot tube. (a) Standard Pitot tube; (b) How pressure is exerted on the tube. (Reprinted by permission of Van Nostrand Reinhold Company, from *Air Conditioning Testing and Balancing* by John Gladstone, 1974.)

tube measures the total pressure. Eight holes 0.04 of an inch in diameter are drilled in the side of the outer tube for measuring the static pressure. Pitot tubes used with a standard manometer having a slope of 10 to 1 cannot be used to accurately measure air velocities of less than about 700 cfm. Ultrasensitive manometers will have to be used to accurately measure velocities below 700 cfm.

FAN PERFORMANCE

Commercial fan performance data are calculated from laboratory tests conducted in accordance with the present Air Moving and Conditioning Association's (AMCA) test code. The code establishes uniform testing methods to determine a fan's flow rate, pressure, power, speed of rotation, and efficiency.

When testing a fan, the Pitot tube makes a prescribed traverse of the cross section area of the duct measuring velocity pressure, static pressure, and total pressure. From the results of these tests and from the computations outlined by the AMCA code, fan performance may be completely established.

Fan Volume

The fan volume is defined as the volume of air in cubic feet per minute, passing through the fan outlet. In normal application the volume leaving the fan is equal to that entering, since the change in specific volume between fan inlet and outlet is negligible.

Fan Outlet Velocity

The outlet velocity of a fan is obtained by dividing the air volume by the fan outlet area. The fan outlet velocity is in reality a theoretical value: it is the velocity that would exist in the fan outlet if the velocity were uniform across the outlet area.

Fan Velocity Pressure

The fan velocity pressure is the pressure corresponding to the fan outlet velocity.

$$Pv = \left(\frac{V}{4005}\right)^2$$

Fan Total Pressure

The fan total pressure is the difference between the total pressure at the fan outlet and the total pressure at the fan inlet. The fan total pressure is a measure of the total mechanical energy added to the air or gas by the fan (measure as per Figure 9-23).

Fan Static Pressure

The fan static pressure is the fan total pressure less the fan velocity pressure. It can be calculated by subtracting the total pressure at the fan inlet from the static pressure at the fan outlet (measure as per Figure 9-24).

Fan Horsepower

The theoretical horsepower required to drive a fan is the power that would be required if there were no losses in the fan, that is, if its efficiency were 100 percent. The brake horsepower is the power actually required to drive a fan. The brake horsepower required to drive a fan is always larger than the theoretical horsepower because of energy losses in the fan. The brake horsepower required can only be determined by an actual test of the fan.

Fan Efficiency

After testing a fan and determining the brake horsepower, both the total and static efficiency can be computed.

SOUND PROBLEMS

Acoustical control is as important as temperature and humidity control. To cope with noise problems, a basic understanding of sound is needed, for noise is simply an unwanted sound. An air moving device must not be closer than 3 feet to any wall or major sound reflective surface. Equipment chosen to match the required air volume, properly installed and maintained, should not be a sound problem.

CHOOSING THE RIGHT FAN

First, the fan must deliver the necessary air volume to ventilate, heat, or cool the space being served. This must be done without increasing the sound level in the space. In order to select a fan to satisfy these requirements, the following factors must be known:

1. Air volume in cfm.
2. Fan static pressure.
3. Air density.
4. Type of application.
5. Size and shape of equipment room.
6. Normal sound level of conditioned space.
7. Proximity of equipment room to conditioned space and the distance between fan and first outlet.
8. Length of duct, number of elbows, and amount of acoustically lined duct.

MEASUREMENT OF AIR PRESSURE IN DUCTS

The pressure of air in sheet metal ducts, such as those ordinarily used in most air conditioning and ventilating systems, is very small. The air pressure in such systems seldom amounts to as much as 0.3 psi and more often is less than half this amount. Nevertheless, these pressures have a large influence on the performance of the fan and the delivery of the air through the various parts of the duct system.

Simple measuring devices that utilize a column of water were developed for field use. A pressure of 1.0 psi will support a column of water 2.31 feet high, or 27.7 inches. Gauges that utilize the elevation of a column of water to measure pressures are called manometers.

Originally, manometers were vertical and worked satisfactorily when measuring pressures of 1 inch or more. In air conditioning, work pressures as small as one-tenth of an inch of water or less must be measured. Such a small difference is difficult to measure accurately on the vertical tube and a different form of gauge, having an inclined (10 to 1) tube, is now commonly used. This instrument is called an inclined manometer (Figure 9-22).

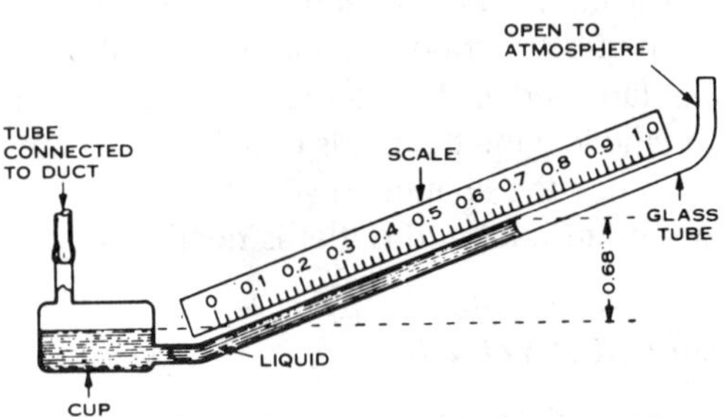

FIGURE 9-22 The inclined manometer. Manometers are gauges which utilize the elevation of a column of water to measure pressures. (Courtesy of The Trane Company.)

VELOCITY, STATIC, AND TOTAL PRESSURE

Velocity Pressure

In actual tests, the manometer can indicate the velocity pressure directly by connecting the total and static pressure tubes to the opposite end of the manometer, as shown in Figure 9-23.

Static Pressure

Any fluid, including air, will exert pressure on the walls of the duct in which it is confined. Thus, a gauge connected to a tank of compressed air will indicate what is called the "static pressure," or the outward push of the air against the walls. In a duct where the fluid is at rest because a damper at its outlet has been shut tightly, the static pressure of the air in the duct can be measured by means of a gauge connected to a tube that is inserted through the wall of the duct, as shown in Figure 9-24.

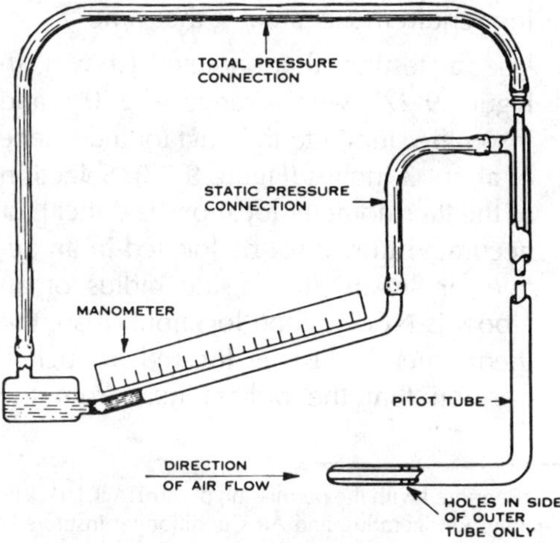

FIGURE 9-23 Pitot tube used to measure velocity pressure. (Courtesy of The Trane Company.)

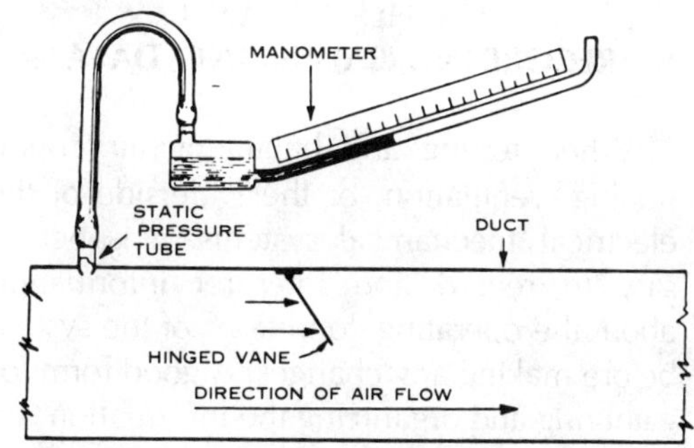

FIGURE 9-24 Measuring static pressure. (Courtesy of The Trane Company.)

Total Pressure

If a tube is inserted into the duct with its opening pointing towards the direction of the air movement (Figure 9-23), the pressure indicated by the gauge will be higher than when the static tube was used. The reason for this is apparent, because the open end of the tube faces the stream of air and the gauge would indicate the pressure of the moving air stream (velocity pressure) and the static pressure. In other words there are three pressures:

1. Static pressure
2. Velocity pressure
3. Total pressure

Actually, only the total and static pressure can be measured, and the velocity pressure is determined from the difference.

Symbols

V—velocity—fpm
v—specific volume
Pv—velocity pressure, inches of water
Pt—total pressure, inches of water
Ps—static pressure, inches of water

GATHERING AND RECORDING BALANCING DATA*

When testing and balancing air conditioning, ventilation, or the waterside of the electrical/mechanical systems, it is necessary to record and interpret information about the operating conditions of the system before making any changes. A good form for gathering and organizing the information is a prerequisite.

If the velocity of the air stream were uniform, then one reading at any point would be sufficient. However, the air moving along the duct wall loses speed because of friction, consequently (assuming there is no special turbulence motion), the velocity in the duct center will always be greater. Since the velocity pressure is seldom uniform, a series of pressure readings must be taken over an equal pattern across the duct section.

Four holes must be drilled in one wall of the duct in such a manner as to establish equal areas, and the Pitot tube must be marked with the same measurements so that four different positions will be read at each hole, giving a total of sixteen readings.

In a typical duct traverse reading, after taking sixteen velocity pressure (Pv) readings and sixteen velocity readings (fpm) and averaging them, we calculate the information shown in Figure 9-25.

The air handling test report (Figure 9-26) is a good example of a data recording form which organizes the information needed to complete the balancing exercise.

*Reprinted with permission from John Gladstone, *Air Conditioning Testing and Balancing*, Van Nostrand Reinhold Company.

9–8 Balancing Home Air Conditioning*

AIR TEMPERATURE RISE

Measuring the air temperature rise means measuring the temperature of the supply air and the return air and finding the difference.

However, before this can be done, the following actions are necessary:

1. Be sure all registers or diffuser shut-off dampers, as well as duct balancing dampers, are fully opened. If single use ducts for cooling only are part of the system, do not open these ducts.

   If the duct system has been balanced for cooling, be sure to mark these damper positions before changing.
2. Replace or clean dirty filters.
3. Set the fan control at the lowest possible temperature to insure continuous blower operation until reset. Do not use the cooling operation blower relay to operate the blower. Usually the cooling air and heating requirements are not the same.
4. Use a testing thermometer (shown in Figure 9-27), with a range of 240°F and insert the stem into the duct for a distance of about 3 inches (Figure 9-27). Selection of the thermometer locations is critical for accuracy; they must be located in an active air stream (the inside radius of an elbow is NOT a good location). Also, the thermometer must be located in such a position that the radiant heat from the

*Reprinted with the permission of Mr. T.A. Clark, The Heating, Refrigerating and Air Conditioning Institute of Canada.

BUILDING NAME & NO.____________________ SHEET NO._____OF_____

ADDRESS____________________________ ZONE______________

SYSTEM_____________________________ DATE______________

PREPARED BY__________________________

NO.	VELOCITY PRESSURE	VELOCITY	DUCT POSITION	NO	VELOCITY PRESSURE	VELOCITY	DUCT POSITION	NO.	VELOCITY PRESSURE	VELOCITY	DUCT POSITION
1A	.056	946		1B				1C			
2A	.068	1045		2B				2C			
3A	.028	670		3B				3C			
4A	.078	1119		4B				4C			
5A	.081	1140		5B				5C			
6A	.084	1161		6B				6C			
7A	.086	1175		7B				7C			
8A	.088	1188		8B				8C			
9A	.088	1188		9B				9C			
10A	.087	1181		10B				10C			
11A	.083	1154		11B				11C			
12A	.080	1133		12B				12C			
13A	.072	1075		13B				13C			
14A	.052	913		14B				14C			
15A	.062	913		15B				15C			
16A	.051	904		16B				16C			

1. TEST NUMBER 1 TRAVERSE STATION T-2
2. AIR TEMPERATURE 110 F CORRECTION FACTOR .93
3. ALTITUDE 1500 FT ABOVE SEA LEVEL. CORRECTION FACTOR .94
4. STATIC PRESSURE AT CENTER .086
5. GRAND TOTAL OF VELOCITIES 16905 / NUMBER OF READING POINTS 16 = 1056 FPM AVERAGE
6. DUCT WIDTH 30 x HEIGHT 12 = 360 SQ INCHES
7. SQ INCHES ÷ 144 = 2.5 SQ FEET
8. FPM AVERAGE (LINE 5) x CORRECTION FACTOR (LINES 2 AND 3) = 1056 x .87 = CORRECTED FPM 918
9. CORRECTED FPM 918 x 2.5 SQ FT (LINE 7) = 2297 CFM
10. ACTUAL CFM 2297 (LINE 9). DESIGN CFM 2300

FIGURE 9-25 Duct traverse readings. (Reprinted by permission of Van Nostrand Reinhold Company, from *Air Conditioning Testing and Balancing* by John Gladstone, 1974.)

heat exchanger does not strike the thermometer bulb.

Usually, the return air temperature can be taken by inserting the thermometer into the air filter if the filter is accessible via an access door.

5. With the thermometers in place, allow the unit to operate until the supply air temperature rises and levels out. This usually requires twenty to thirty minutes. To keep the unit operating, set the room thermostat to the top of the range. This will keep the anticipator in the thermostat from acting.
6. Read the thermometers and adjust the air quantity accordingly. This is done by blower speed adjustment. An increase in blower speed will result in delivery of more cfm and a reduced temperature rise. Conversely, a reduction in blower speed will reduce the cfm and increase the temperature rise. (Figs. 11-25 and 11-26.)

BUILDING NAME & NO.____________________ SHEET NO.______ OF____

ADDRESS________________________ ZONE____________

SYSTEM________________________ DATE____________

PREPARED BY________________

ITEM	SPECIFIED	FIELD TEST 1	FIELD TEST 2	FIELD TEST 3
Outside air cfm				
Total air cfm				
% outside air				
Discharge duct sq. ft.				
Discharge duct fpm				
Return duct sq. ft.				
Return duct fpm				
Return air cfm				
Manufacturer				
Fan size				
Arrangement				
Fan blade				
Fan sheave				
Motor sheave				
No. rows coil				
Filters				
Rpm				
Hp				
Bhp				
Volts				
Phase				
Cycle				
Full-load amps				
No-load amps				
Heaters: rated amps				
Suction sp				
Discharge sp				
Total sp				
Ent. DB temperature				
Ent. WB temperature				
Lvg. DB temperature				
Lvg. WB temperature				
Outside air temperature				
Gpm circulating H_2O				
Pressure drop				
Ent. water temperature				
Lvg. water temperature				

Remarks ________________________________

FIGURE 9-26 The air handler test report. (Reprinted by permission of Van Nostrand Reinhold Company, from *Air Conditioning Testing and Balancing* by John Gladstone, 1974.)

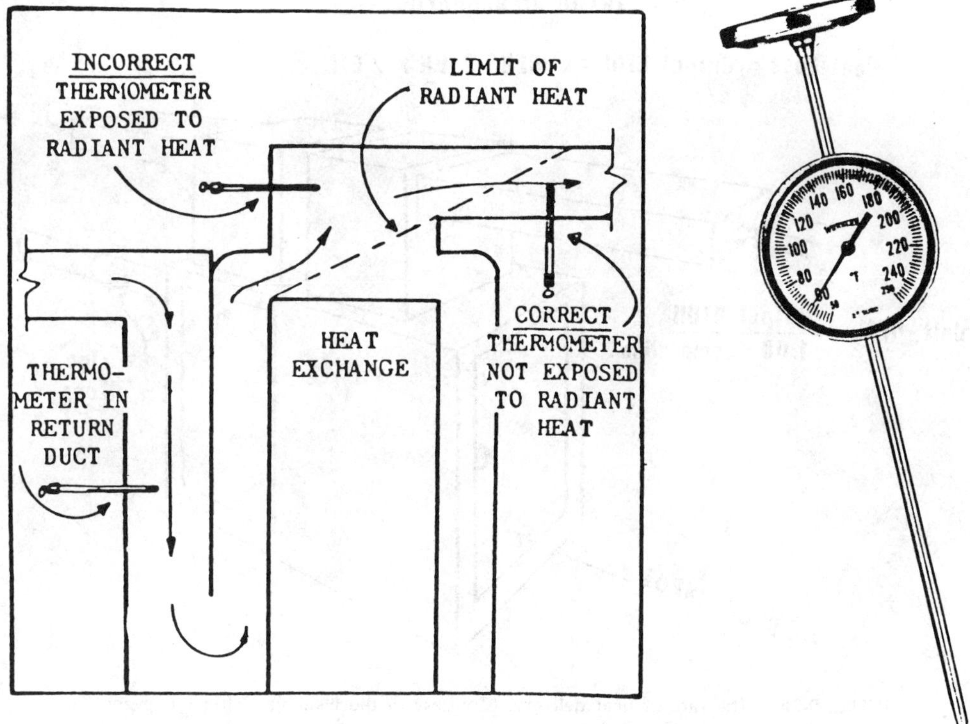

FIGURE 9-27 Air temperature thermometer reading locations.

THE HEAT OUTPUT CAPACITY AT THE BONNET

The heat output capacity rating of a heating unit is the rate of heat delivery (Btuh) at the bonnet when the unit is fired at the prescribed maximum rate of input. The rate of output is the difference between the rate of generation by the burner or heating element, and the rate of heat loss up the chimney flue. In other words, the heat output is dependent on the rate of heat input and the efficiency with which the unit transfers the heat to the air flowing over the heat exchanger.

An example: The heat output of an oil fired unit with an efficiency of 75 percent when fired at the rate of 1 gallon per hour may be calculated as follows:

$$\text{Heat Output} = \frac{75}{100} \times 168{,}000 \text{ (Btus)}$$
$$= 126{,}000 \text{ Btuh}$$

For each system installation it is generally understood that the bonnet output capacity (Btuh) of the heating unit must not be less than the calculated heat loss of the structure. It is obvious that the structure would not be heated to the required indoor temperature if the unit output is less than the calculated heat loss. On the other hand, it is also undesirable to operate the unit at a bonnet output greatly in excess of the heat loss. It is wise to set an

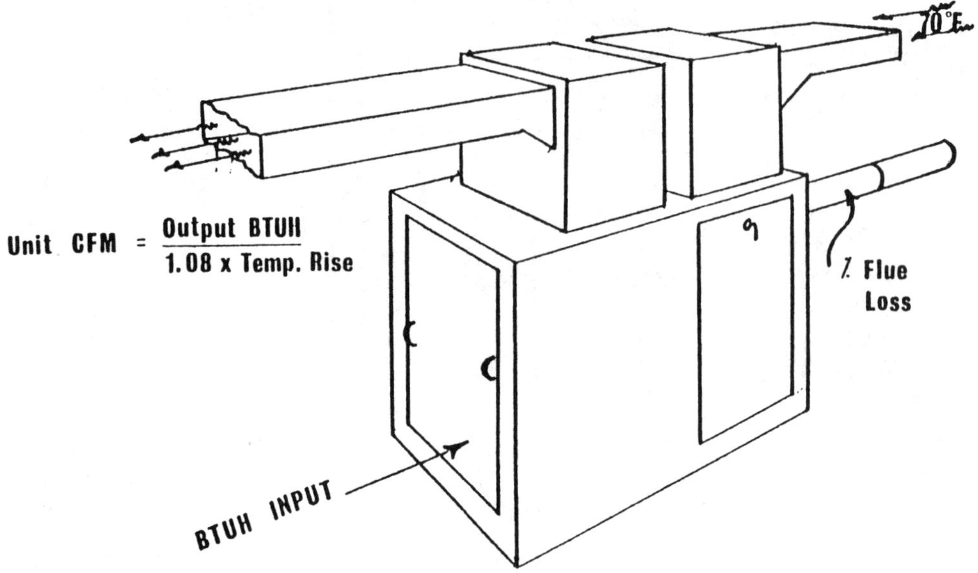

FIGURE 9-28 The rate of heat delivery. (Courtesy of the Heating, Refrigerating and Air Conditioning Institute of Canada.)

energy management comfort temperature goal of a maximum of 76°F or 24.4°C and endeavor to adjust the heating and cooling system to meet this goal. Once this goal is achieved, we can fine-tune the system to achieve further savings (if we are qualified to do this).

If the unit output exceeds the total heat loss, and is operated so that the blower is controlled by changes of bonnet air temperature, the system will function intermittently, and discomfort due to room air stratification may result.

If the system is well balanced and if the blower is set to run constantly on the summer switch, some excess bonnet capacity may be satisfactory since the thermostat controls the cycles of heat generation in the unit to suit the needs of the occupied space. In the selection of the heating unit, it is entirely satisfactory to choose a unit with a bonnet output rating about 10 percent or 15 percent in excess of the calculated heat loss, provided that the operation of the unit (firing rate) can be adjusted to suit the calculated heat loss.

Such a reduced firing rate, within the prescribed limits of the equipment manufacturer and the approvals authorities, may provide some additional economy of operation.

Bonnet Output Capacity (Btuh) =
Btuh Input × the percentage
combustion efficiency.

The combustion efficiency of approved

winter air conditioning units may be calculated at:

75% for Oil Fired Units –
1 gal. of #2 oil = 168,000 Btus
80% for Gas Fired Units –
1 MCF = 1,000,000 Btus
100% for Electric Units –
1 kWh = 3412 Btus

e.g. The Bonnet Output Capacity of a unit fired with 112 cubic feet of natural gas rated at 1,000 Btu/cu.ft. may be calculated as follows:

$$\text{Bonnet Output} = 112 \times 1000 \times 0.80 = 89{,}600 \text{ Btuh}$$

SUPPLY OUTLET HEAT DELIVERY

The rate of heat delivery (Btuh) through a supply diffuser or register may be estimated if the volume of air flow, the supply temperature, and the temperature of the air at the return intake grilles are known.

Using the method of air flow measurement illustrated in Figure 9-29, measure the outlet air volume. As the volume of air passes through the room, the rate of heat supplied to the room (Btuh) is directly proportional to the temperature change between the supply outlet and the return air intake. The temperature of the supply air may be measured by a thermometer inserted in the "Air Flow Unit" (Figure 9-29). Another thermometer, inserted

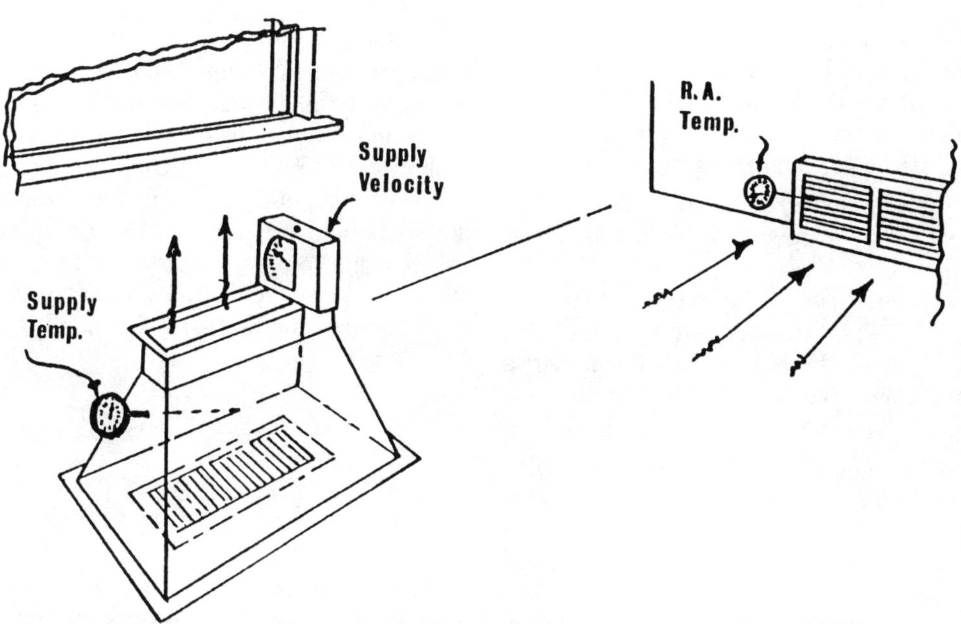

FIGURE 9-29 Heat delivery measurements. (Courtesy of the Heating, Refrigerating and Air Conditioning Institute of Canada.)

in the return intake grille, should be used to measure the temperature of the air as it leaves the space. The temperature change of the air is determined by deducting the temperature at the return intake from that measured at the supply outlet.

AIR VOLUME

The volume of air that a winter air conditioning unit can deliver is dependent on several factors, such as the size and speed of the blower, the horsepower of the blower motor, and the amount of resistance to air flow imposed by the supply and return duct systems.

The volume of air that the unit should deliver, however, must be related to the desired temperature rise of the air as it passes over the heat exchanger. It must, therefore, be related directly to the heat output capacity of the unit. If the required air temperature rise (bonnet outlet temperature minus return air temperature) and the bonnet heat output are known, the air volume of the unit may be calculated by the following equation:

$$\text{Btuh} = \text{cfm} \times 60 \times \text{density} \times \text{specific ht.} \times (\text{temperature rise})$$

$$\text{Btuh} = \text{cfm} \times (60 \times 0.075 \times 0.24) \times (\text{temperature rise})$$

$$\text{Btuh} = \text{cfm} \times 1.08 \times \text{temperature rise}$$

$$\text{and cfm} = \text{Btuh} / 1.08 \times \text{temperature rise}$$

As the air flows through the unit, it absorbs heat from the heat exchanger. The addition of heat to the air results in an increase in the temperature of the air. This increase in the temperature of the air is called the "temperature rise" of the unit. "Temperature rise" is the difference between the temperature of the air at the supply plenum outlet and the temperature of the air in the return plenum.

BONNET TEMP °F	TEMP RISE °F	cfm/mbh
110	40	23.2
120	50	18.5
130	60	15.4
140	70	13.2
150	80	11.6
160	90	10.3
170	100	9.3

UNIT AIR VOLUME = TEMP. RISE X cfm/Mbh

FIGURE 9-30 Calculating the required air volume. (Courtesy of the Heating, Refrigerating and Air Conditioning Institute of Canada.)

An example: Supply temperature 150°F
Return temperature is 70°F
Temperature rise = 150 − 70 or 80°F

The temperature rise of a unit is a function of the rate of heat output (Btuh) and the rate of air flow (cfm) through the unit. Figure 9-30 shows the number of cfm that each 1,000 Btuh (Mbh) of unit output can raise through a desired temperature rise to provide a required bonnet air temperature. Or it may calculate the volume of air that can be heated through a desired temperature change by the heat output of the unit.

9-9 The Refrigeration Cycle*

Refrigeration is a method of removing heat from air. A refrigeration system's capacity to

*Reprinted with permission of The Trane Company.

remove heat is usually expressed in tons. One ton of refrigeration removes 12,000 Btus per hour. Let us now explore the methods of producing refrigeration.

DEVELOPING A REFRIGERATION SYSTEM

Originally, ice was used as a refrigerant, but as we compare the amount of latent heat absorbed by 1 pound of ice (144 Btus) during melting, with the amount of latent heat required to evaporate 1 pound of water at atmospheric pressure (970.3 Btus), we note that water is a more effective refrigerant than ice. Water boils at 212°F (100°C), while other refrigerants such as Freon 22 boil at −41.4°F. This allows the refrigeration process to take place at temperatures well below that of melting ice. The advantage in using refrigerants such as Freon is that the process can be easily started and stopped, and the rate of cooling can be controlled within close limits.

FIGURE 9-31 What is refrigeration? (Courtesy of The Trane Company.)

FIGURE 9-32 A simple refrigeration system. (Courtesy of The Trane Company.)

A SIMPLE REFRIGERATION SYSTEM

A crude system connects a drum of liquid refrigerant to a coil (Figure 9-32). A valve, installed in the connecting pipe, regulates the flow rate of liquid refrigerant into the coil. If warm air (95°F) is blown across the coil, the boiling liquid refrigerant will absorb heat from the air. This reduces the air temperature and refrigeration is accomplished.

To improve the simple refrigeration system, a valve was added to regulate the flow rate of the liquid refrigerant. This made it possible to evaporate all the liquid refrigerant by the time it reached the open end of the coil. The completely evaporated refrigerant was then piped to the outdoors, which meant the continuous loss of the refrigerant. With the current cost of Freon, this would be very expensive.

ADDING RECOVERY EQUIPMENT

The next step in the development of the system was to provide a means of saving and re-using the refrigerant as well as a means of controlling its evaporating temperature. It was discovered that one good way to save the refrigerant was to put some sort of recovery

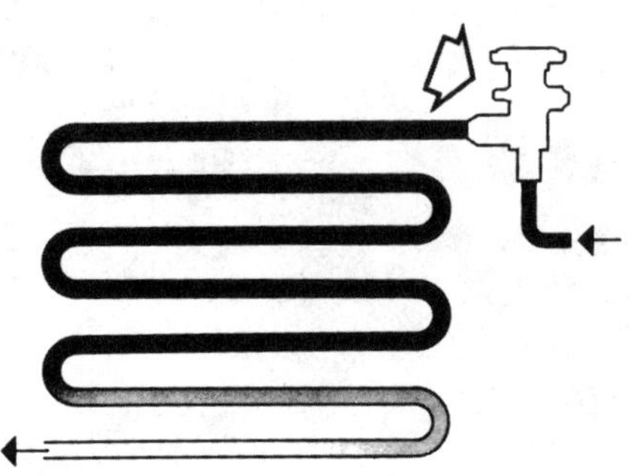

FIGURE 9-33 **A valve to regulate the flow rate.** (Courtesy of The Trane Company.)

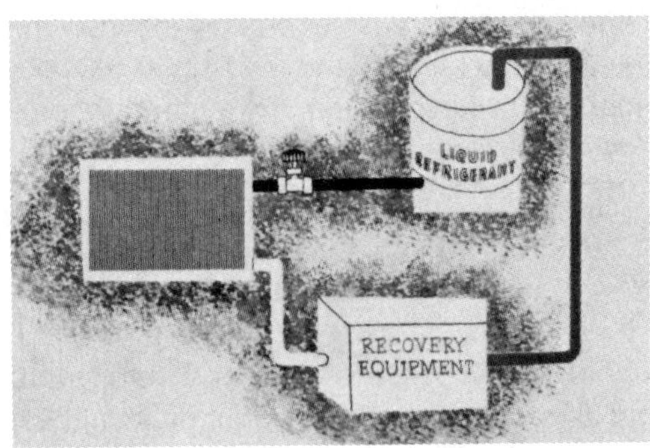

FIGURE 9-34 **Adding recovery equipment.** (Courtesy of The Trane Company.)

equipment near the open end of the coil. With this recovery apparatus in operation, the refrigerant can be used over and over again. It can be circulated from the drum, through the throttling valve, through the coil to the recovery equipment, and then back to the drum again. This is exactly what happens to the refrigerant in household refrigerators (Figure 9-34).

TYPICAL HOUSEHOLD REFRIGERATOR

In the typical household refrigerator, there is a freezing compartment or evaporator at the top, which consists of a plate-type coil with passages in which the liquid refrigerant evaporates and, in doing so, absorbs heat from the air inside the refrigerator. The evaporated refrigerant is drawn to the bottom of the refrigerator by a recovery unit and is reconverted to a high pressure liquid. The liquid refrigerant is then sent through a restriction, which acts like a throttling valve. It then flows back into the evaporator coil in the cabinet.

GAUGE AND ABSOLUTE PRESSURE

Pressures measured above atmospheric pressure are called gauge pressures. Absolute pressure is pressure registered by the gauge, plus the atmospheric pressure. Thus, 150 pound per square inch gauge pressure would be the equivalent to 150 + 14.7, or 164.7 pounds per square inch absolute pressure at sea level. Boiler steam gauges show gauge pressure, or pressure above atmospheric.

RECOVERING REFRIGERANT THROUGH "HEAT OF COMPRESSION"

Usually water boils at 212°F. If the "pressure" on the water is reduced below atmospheric pressure (which is roughly 14.7 pounds per square inch absolute at sea level), at 1/10 pounds per square inch absolute

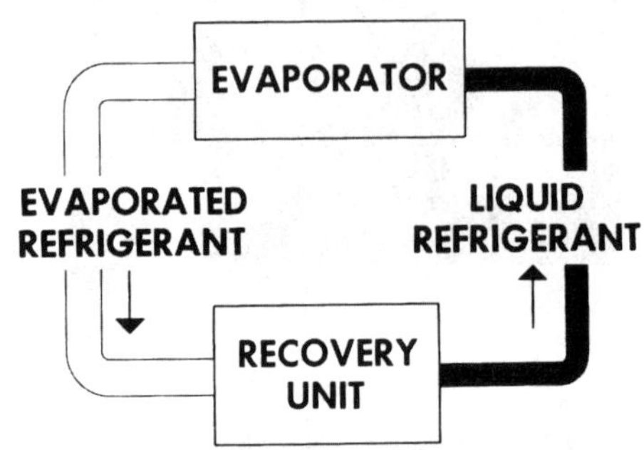

FIGURE 9-35 **Typical household refrigerator.** (Courtesy of The Trane Company.)

(psia), water can actually be made to boil at 35°F. The lower the pressure, the lower the boiling temperature. The refrigerants most commonly used for commercial air conditioning applications are Refrigerant-22 and Refrigerant-12. The chemical and physical properties of these two refrigerants are well suited to systems using the popular mechanical reciprocating compressor. Like water, the evaporation or condensing temperatures of these refrigerants can be varied by changing the pressure exerted upon them. At a higher pressure the refrigerant condenses at a higher temperature.

Figure 9-36 shows the temperatures at which Refrigerant-22 condenses at various pressures. When the pressure on liquid Refrigerant-22 is 69.02 psi gauge, it evaporates at a temperature of 40°F. If the pressure on the very same substance in its evaporated form is 197.9 psi gauge, it can be condensed back to a liquid at a temperature of 100°F.

THE PURPOSE OF THE COMPRESSOR

Figure 9-37 explains the purpose of the compressor in the refrigeration cycle. It takes the gas, which did some useful cooling in the process of evaporating, and compresses it to a higher pressure. The refrigerant is still a gas

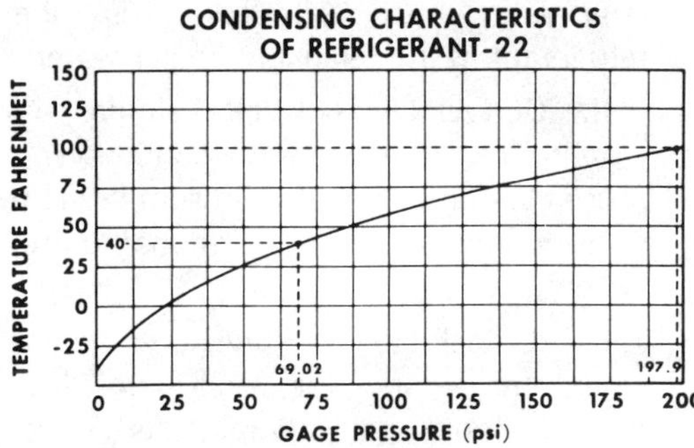

FIGURE 9-36 Condensing characteristics of refrigerant-22. (Courtesy of The Trane Company.)

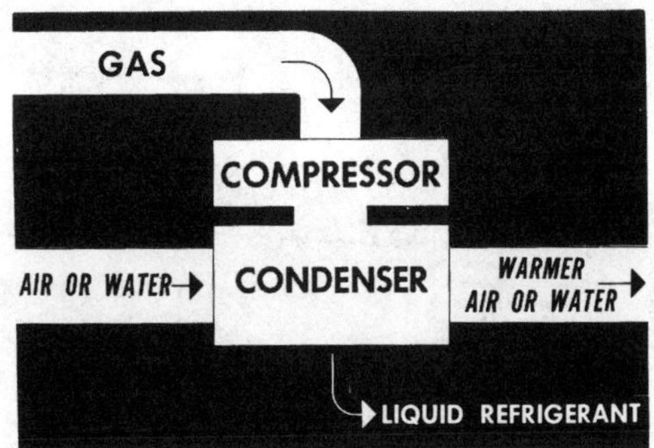

FIGURE 9-37 The purpose of the compressor. (Courtesy of The Trane Company.)

but its temperature is higher because it has absorbed much of the heat produced by the work required to compress it. This is known as the "heat of compression."

THE "HEAT OF COMPRESSION"

The refrigeration system compressor must raise the pressure of the gas to a level three or four times as high as it was when it first entered the compressor. Compressing the gas requires mechanical energy and this explains why a certain amount of horsepower is required to drive any refrigeration compressor. However, this mechanical energy does not simply disappear, but is converted into heat energy in the refrigerant and in the compressor (Figure 9-38).

CONDENSER HEAT REJECTION

To describe the situation of condenser heat rejection in a simple equation, the heat entering the refrigerant in the evaporator, plus the heat entering the refrigerant in the compressor, equals the heat that must be rejected from the refrigerant in the condenser (Figure 9-39). This equation neglects a small amount of heat gained or lost through con-

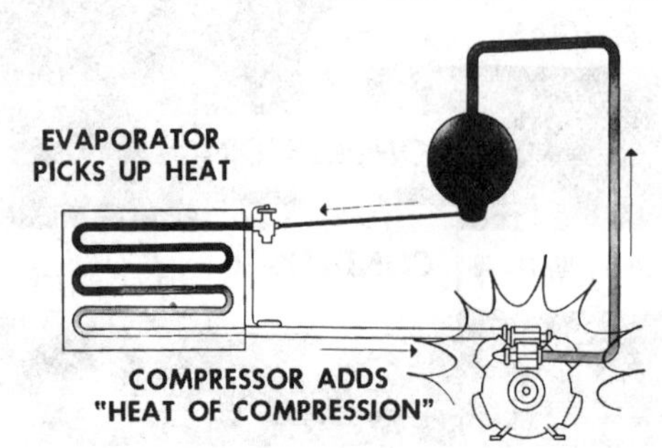

FIGURE 9-38 The heat of compression. (Courtesy of The Trane Company.)

necting piping or lost by heat radiation from the compressor.

THE AIR-COOLED CONDENSER

The modern air condenser is available with either propeller or centrifugal type fans for moving the air through the condenser coil. When the air condenser can be installed out of doors, the propeller fan type unit is generally used. If for some reason the condenser is to be installed indoors, with duct work to carry the air to and from the unit, the condenser with the centrifugal fan is more suitable. In addition, a centrifugal fan air-cooled condenser may be used to provide auxiliary heating or ventilation in certain applications.

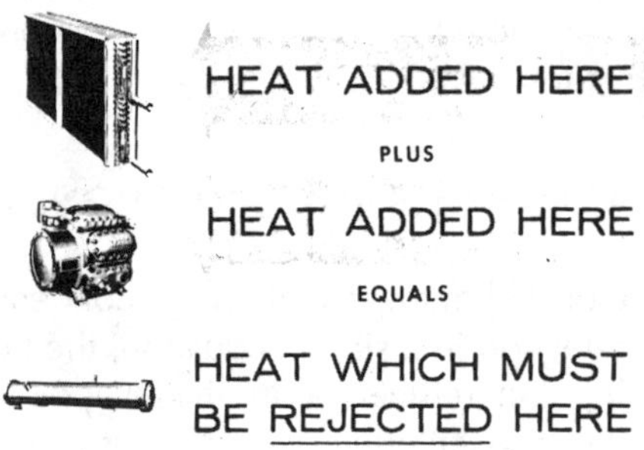

FIGURE 9-39 Condenser heat rejection. (Courtesy of The Trane Company.)

ROOFTOP AIR CONDITIONING UNITS

Self-contained rooftop air conditioning units are fairly new in design and application, but they are now extensively used in shopping centers, schools, workshops. The main advantages of the rooftop units are that they are mounted directly above the space to be conditioned so that virtually no valuable floor space is lost, and that supply and return duct systems can be kept to a minimum.

THE COMPONENTS OF THE REFRIGERATION CYCLE

1. THE REFRIGERANT—conversion of gas to liquid and recovery for recycle.
2. THE THROTTLING OR EXPANSION VALVE
3. THE CONDENSER—either water or air cooled. It condenses the refrigerant at high pressure and therefore it will condense at a high temperature. A source of water must be available at a temperature lower than the condensing temperature through the water-cooled condenser; heat will flow from the refrigerant to the relatively cooler water.
4. THE COOLING TOWER—similar in operation to an evaporative condenser. It is used to conserve water consumption by re-using the water in the air conditioning system.
5. THE COMPRESSOR—the refrigerant enters the evaporator as a cool low pressure liquid and evaporates. As it does, it absorbs heat from some other sub-

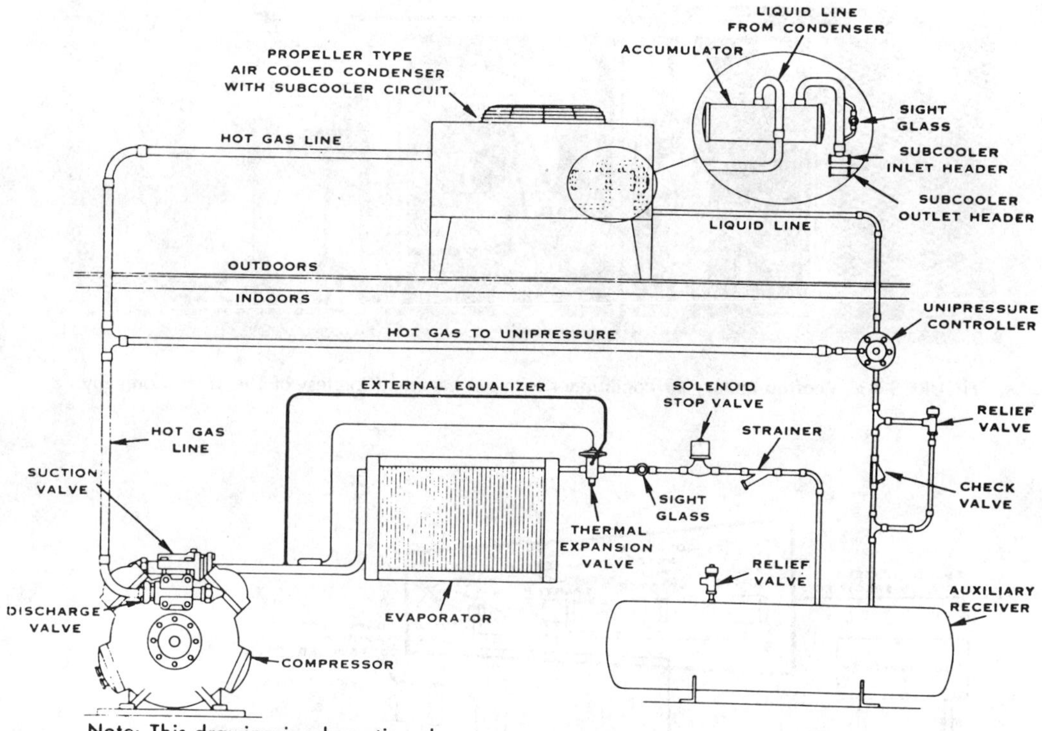

FIGURE 9-40 Typical system with air cooled condenser. (Courtesy of The Trane Company.)

stance, thereby accomplishing refrigeration. The refrigerant then leaves the evaporator as a cool low-pressure gas and proceeds to the compressor where its pressure and temperature are increased. It then leaves the compressor, as a gas, but at a much higher pressure and at a much higher temperature.

This hot refrigerant gas is then forced from the compressor into the condenser. In the condenser, the hot gas is cooled and condensed to a liquid. The condensing agent, usually water or air, is at a temperature lower than that at which the refrigerant condenses at this pressure. The refrigerant then flows from the condenser, as a high pressure liquid, to the expansion valve.

This is the basic refrigeration cycle. It is the foundation for a better understanding of refrigeration as it applies to air conditioning.

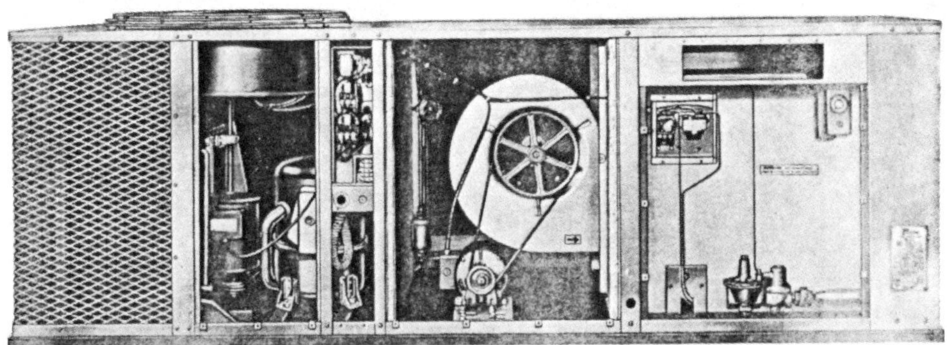

FIGURE 9-41 Rooftop unitary air conditioner with gas heating. (Courtesy of The Trane Company.)

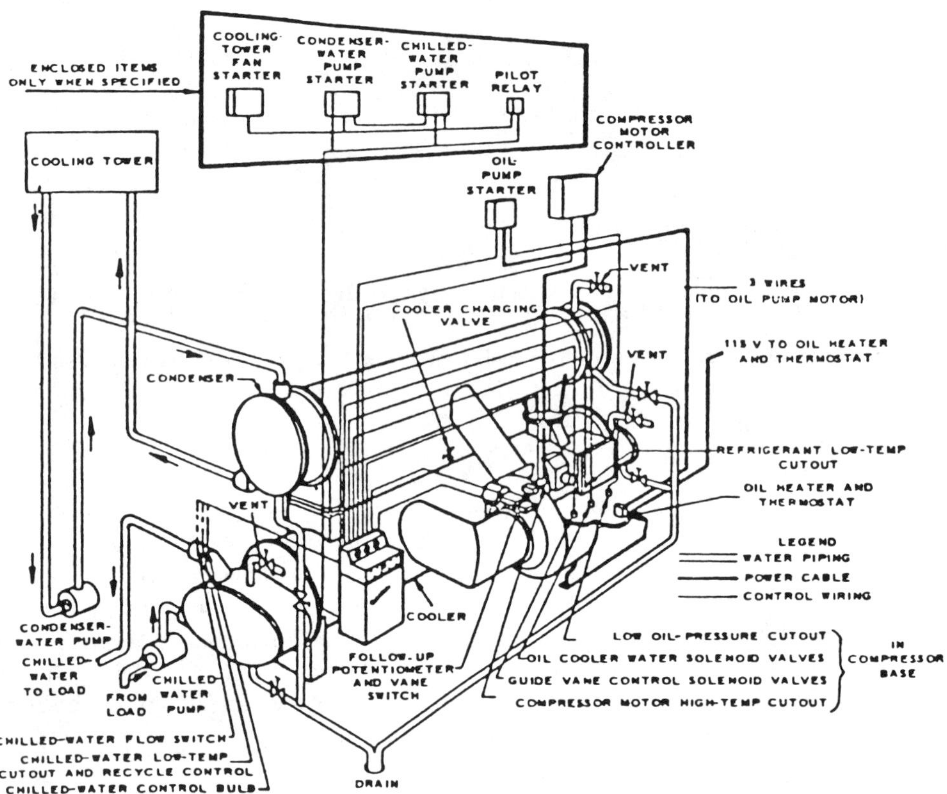

FIGURE 9-42 Automatic starting chilled water system.

9-10 The Cooling Tower *

ADVANTAGES AND LIMITATIONS OF COOLING TOWERS

The advantages and limitations of the cooling tower should be well understood before selecting a tower for a refrigeration system. Water, cooled by spraying in air, cannot be cooled below the prevailing wet-bulb temperature of the air. It is obvious, therefore, that the condensing temperature at which the system will operate must be somewhat above the wet-bulb temperature of the air. High efficiency forced or induced draft cooling towers will cool the condenser water to a point within 5 to 8 degrees of the prevailing wet-bulb temperature. Natural draft towers seldom approach closer than 10 or 12 degrees to the prevailing wet bulb.

It should be noted that the "design" wet-bulb temperature is sometimes exceeded by the actual wet-bulb temperature for appreciable lengths of time. Because of this it is common to increase the usual "design" wet-bulb temperature by 5 percent before selecting a cooling tower or forecasting its operation.

DISADVANTAGES OF COOLING TOWERS

Outdoor cooling towers are subject to other troubles. When the system must be operated during the winter, the quantity of air must be reduced to a point where the spray water will not freeze in the sump, on the packing, or at the tower discharge. Overflow and make-up water piping must be adequately protected. In severe climates it is sometimes necessary to provide an auxiliary tank within the heated part of the building in which reserve water is accumulated instead of in the tower sump. This auxiliary tank permits the spray water to drain from the tower immediately.

Indoor cooling towers eliminate some of the trouble due to freezing, but they still must be carefully tended during severe weather. The quantity of air handled must be carefully regulated so freezing temperatures are not reached at periods of light load.

In summer, algae or other organic slime may grow in the cooling tower and if permitted to develop will seriously foul the condenser tubes. This can be eliminated by proper water treatment (See Biological Fouling and Corrosion, Chapter One.)

WHY A COOLING TOWER?

The first water conservation idea was to employ the evaporation effect of water when rejecting condenser heat to the air. This was attractive because of the high latent heat of vaporization of water, approximately 1,000 Btus per pound evaporated. Spray ponds were one of the earliest devices used to obtain the evaporation effect. The removal of moisture-laden air from the spray pond area depended on natural air movement. Since winds are highly variable in most areas, spray ponds were not very practical. They required large open spaces to catch the slightest air movement, and they had to be sufficiently separated from populated areas because of the spray drift nuisance.

The next step was to enclose the spray pond to prevent or reduce windage losses

---

*Portions of this text reprinted with the permission of the Marley Co.

and spray drift nuisance. To be effective, this required some sort of stack or tower effect that would expose the maximum water surface area to the air. The result was the natural draft cooling tower, which overcame only a few of the spray pond problems.

When a fan that either pushed the air through the tower (forced draft design) or pulled the air through (induced draft design) was added to the cooling tower, the present concept of the cooling tower was reached.

Water from the sump or tank of the tower flows by gravity to the circulating pump. The circulating pump forces the water through the condenser where it picks up heat from the condensing refrigerant. The warm water from the condenser is carried to the sprays of the cooling tower where it is broken up into drops and falls over the slats or "packing" of the tower. The water, in its progress through the air and over the tower packing, is exposed to a blast of air induced by the cooling tower circulating fan. In this air stream part of the water evaporated, cooling the remaining water to a temperature satisfactory for condenser use. The cooled water collects in the sump and flows to the pump for re-use.

Since it takes approximately 1,000 Btus to evaporate 1 pound of water, the "pick-up" is 1,000 Btus per pound instead of 20. Therefore, 1 pound of water in a cooling tower theoretically does the equivalent work of 50 pounds of water in a conventional water-cooled condenser, or the cooling tower requires only 2 percent of the water required in a water-cooled condenser. In actual practice, this amount approaches 5 percent due to evaporation and intentional waste.

PRE-STARTING PROCEDURE

Cleaning

Remove dirt and trash that may have accumulated in the hot water distribution basins. Remove sediment from cold water basin, sump, and screens. Make sure there are no clogged nozzles. Use a water hose to flush basins.

Operate Water System

Circulate water over the tower continuously for several days before starting the mechanical equipment and putting the tower into continuous operation.

Inspection

It is imperative that all operating assemblies be inspected before they are placed in operation. The following list contains suggestions for components to be checked.

1. Check alignment of motor shaft, drive shaft, and gear reducer shaft. Realign if necessary.
2. Check tightness of bolts that attach fan support to the tower. Check tightness of fan cylinder anchor bolts and tie rods. Do not pull washers into the wood.
3. Tighten loose bolts at diagonals and columns, and at girts and columns.
4. Check tightness of the following bolted joints in the fan and drive assemblies:
   (a) Fan hub clamp bolts
   (b) Fan hub cover bolts
   (c) Gear reducer and motor mounting bolts
   (d) Drive shaft coupling and guard bolts.
5. Check gear reducer oil for sludge or water by draining off and testing a sample. Check gear reducer oil level at the fill plug or sight glass. Add oil as required. Check external sight glass for correct position of oil level placard. Use correct lubricant as listed in the manufacturer's service manual.
6. Rotate fan by hand to ensure free rotation and ample tip clearance.

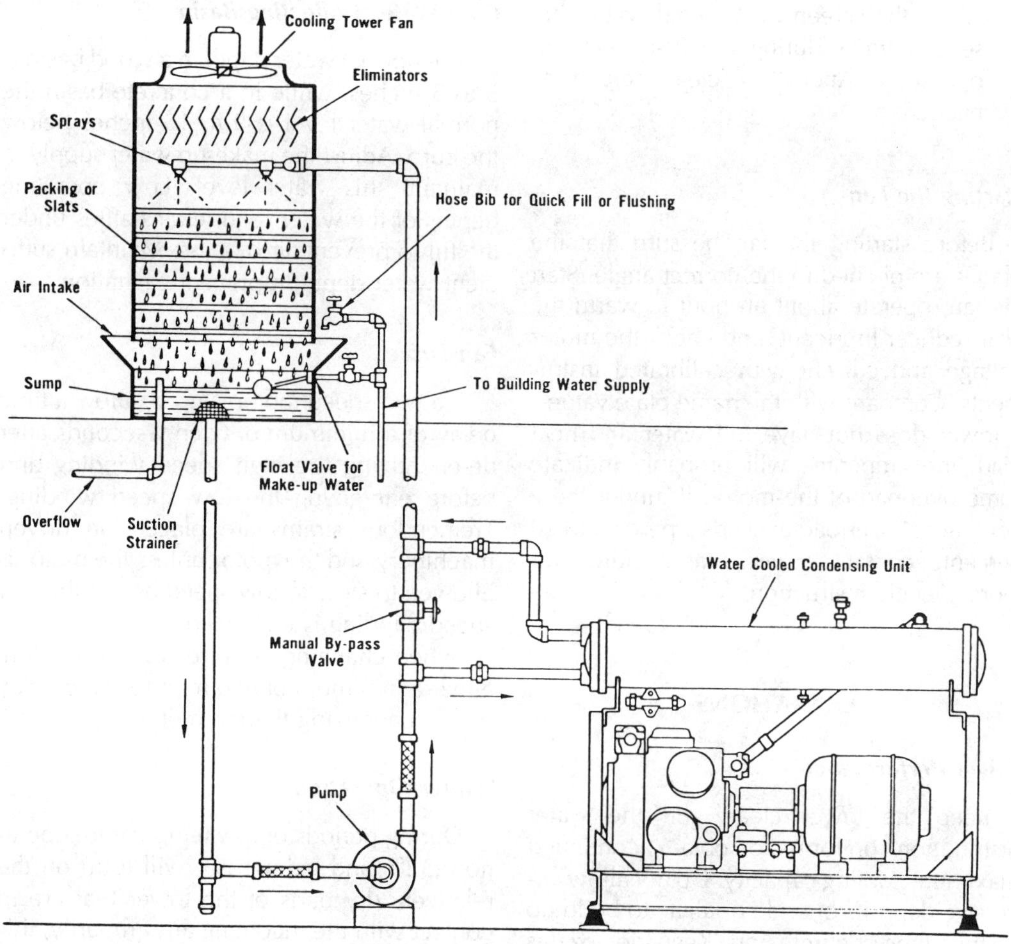

FIGURE 9-43 The cooling tower.

7. Check motor insulation with a megger.
8. Lubricate the motor according to motor manufacturer's instructions.
9. Test run fan separately for a short time. Check for excessive vibration or unusual noise. Be certain fan rotates in correct direction.
10. Check functioning of make-up water supply.
11. Make sure the blowdowns or bleed-off will carry the proper amount of water.

STARTING PROCEDURE

Filling the Water System

–Fill the cold water basin and circulating water system until the operating water level is reached.

–Open completely all hot water flow control valves, then prime and start the circulating water pumps. Adjust valves to equalize the hot water flow to each portion of the tower.

–Clean the screen in the cold water line several times during the first weeks of operation. After this, clean screen as needed.

Starting the Fan

Before starting the fan be sure that the blades are pitched to the correct angle. Start the fan, operate about an hour to warm the gear reducer lubricant, and check the motor voltage and current with calibrated instruments. Compare with the name plate values. If tower does not have full water and heat load, the amperage will probably indicate some overload of the motor. If, under these conditions, overload exceeds 5 percent to 10 percent, contact tower manufacturer for more specific instructions.

OPERATIONS

Tower Performance

Keep the tower clean and the water distribution uniform to obtain continued maximum cooling capacity. Do not allow excessive deposits of scale or algae to build up on the filling or eliminators. Keep the nozzles free of debris to assure correct distribution and cooling of water. The capacity of a tower to cool water to a given cold water temperature varies with the wet-bulb temperature and the heat load on the tower. As the wet-bulb temperature drops, the cold water temperature also drops. However, the cold water temperature does not drop as much as the wet-bulb temperature.

A tower does not control the heat load. The quantity of water circulated determines the cooling range for a given heat load. At a constant wet-bulb, the hot and cold water temperature increase with higher heat loads.

Cold Water Collecting Basin

The normal water depth in a wood basin is 5 to 8 inches, while in a concrete basin the normal water level is 9 to 15 inches below the curb. Adjust the make-up water supply to maintain this water level. Low operating depths of the water require air baffles under the fill to prevent air by-pass. Maintain sufficient water depth to prevent cavitation.

Fan Drive

If a two-speed motor is used, allow a time delay of a minimum of twenty seconds after de-energizing the high speed winding and before energizing the low speed winding. Tremendous strains are placed on driven machinery and the motor unless the motor is allowed to slow to low speed before the low speed winding is energized.

When changing fan direction of rotation, allow a minimum of two minutes time delay before energizing the fan motor.

Winter Operation

During periods of low temperature operation (32°F and below), ice will form on the relatively dry parts of the tower that are in contact with the incoming air. Primarily, this includes the louvers and adjacent structural framing.

Ice forming characteristics on any given tower will vary, depending on the velocity and direction of wind, circulating water rate, and heat load. Ice formation may be controlled by regulating air and water flow through the tower by one or more of the following procedures:

1. Shut the fan down; this reduces the cooling rate to a minimum and increases the quantity of warm water on the louvers to a maximum. Except for extreme cold conditions or extended freezing conditions,

this procedure will normally control ice formation. For automatic operation, a timer switch can be provided to shut down the fan for a few minutes each hour.

2. If the tower has two-speed motors, operate the fan at half speed forward; this reduces the cooling rate (heat transfer) and increases the quantity of warm water on the louvers.
3. Under extended extreme cold conditions, it may be necessary to operate the fan in reverse. This forces warm air out through the louvers, melting any accumulated ice. Reversal may be at either full or half speed; however, full speed is recommended. Reverse operation of the fan should only be used to eliminate ice, not to prevent it. REVERSE FAN OPERATION SHOULD NOT EXCEED FIFTEEN OR TWENTY MINUTES. Usually, much less time is required to melt accumulated ice.

UNIT MAINTENANCE

Well-maintained equipment gives the best operating results and the least maintenance cost. A regular inspection schedule is recommended to insure effective operation of the cooling tower. Use the schedule in Figure 9-44 to obtain the best continuous performance with the least tower maintenance. Keep a continuous lubrication and maintenance record for the tower.

Hot Water Basin

Metering orifices in the bottom of the hot water basin may be cleaned without shutting down any part of the tower. Remove dirt, algae, leaves, which may get in these basins or orifices. The metering orifices must be kept in place to assure proper water distribution.

Completely open and close flow control valves semi-annually to remove any scale on the threads. Grease the stainless steel stem to prevent scale forming. Lubricate the valves monthly with a lithium base NLGI #2 consistency grease.

Cold Water Collecting Basin

Inspect collecting basin occasionally for leaks, and repair if necessary. Minor leaks may appear in redwood basins when starting with a dry basin, but they will generally disappear after the wood becomes soaked. Keep cold water outlets clean and free of debris. Make-up and circulating water controls must operate freely and maintain the desired water quantity in the system.

Tower Framework

Keep framework bolts tight. Pay particular attention to bolts in the mechanical equipment supports.

Drive Shaft

Check drive shaft alignment and condition of couplings every six months.

Electric Motors

Lubricate and maintain each electric motor in accordance with the manufacturer's instructions. See Chapter 11, Mechanical Services, pages 528–530.

Fan

Inspect fan blade surfaces every six months.

Gear Reducer

Make weekly and monthly oil checks. Inspect internal parts during seasonal oil change. Refer to applicable manufacturer's manual for detailed maintenance instructions.

Painting

Periodically clean and paint all metal parts subject to corrosion.

Cooling Tower Wood Deterioration

Untreated wood in cooling towers can be damaged by decay anytime after the first few years of service. If decay is discovered and treated in its early stages, serious wood damage can be prevented. Routine inspections should be made to assure that decay is discovered before it becomes advanced.

ENERGY CONSERVATION TIPS

1. Keep the condenser water and evaporator water tubes clear by adequate water treatment, periodic physical observation, and cleaning of the tubes.
2. Reduce the temperature entering the condenser from the cooling tower.
3. Shut down completely during unoccupied times.
4. Reset the leaving chilled water temperature as the total heat content (enthalpy) of the outdoor air rises.

General Recommendations (More frequent inspection and maintenance may be desirable)	Fan	Motor	Drive Shaft	Gear Reducer	Eliminator	Wood Filling	Cold Water Basin	Hot Water Basin	Control Valves	Structural Members	Casing	Float Valve	Suction Screen	Fan Cylinder
1. Inspect for clogging								W						
2. Check for unusual noise or vibration	D	D	D	D						Y				
3. Inspect keys and keyways		S	S	S										
4. Make sure vents are open				S										
5. Lubricate (grease)		Q							S					
6. Check oil seals				S										
7. Check oil level				W										
8. Check oil for water and sludge				M										
9. Change oil, at least				S										
10. Check fan blade tip clearance	S													
11. Check water level							D	D						
12. Check for leakage				W				S				S		
13. Inspect general condition	S		S	S	Y	S	Y			S	Y	Y		
14. Tighten loose bolts and fan cylinder tie rods	S	S	S	S						Y	R			S
15. Clean	R	W	R	R	R	R	S	M	R			R	W	
16. Repaint	R	R	R	R							R			
17. Rebalance	R		R											
18. Completely open and close									S					

D–daily; W–weekly; M–monthly; Q–quarterly; S–semiannually; Y–yearly; R–as required.

FIGURE 9-44 Cooling tower inspection and maintenance schedule. (Courtesy of the Marley Company.)

5. Reduce the maximum cooling load as much as possible.

9-11 How To Budget The Necessary Funds

The information in this chapter emphasizes the complexity of the ventilation and air conditioning systems, as well as the knowledge required to design and install them, the understanding and monitoring required to assure that all the components operate as intended, and the importance of using trained personnel to operate the system efficiently.

As explained in Chapter One, Maintenance Programming, the planning process builds the program into a budget. This includes system start-up, tagging and gathering information about the equipment, and balancing the system. Workloads for the operating staff are developed around the necessary maintenance activities. These include daily "look, listen, and touch" inspections, lubrication, filter changes, belt changes, alignment, handling service requests, and non-routine repairs. Managers must be knowledgeable about these systems if they expect to hire and train competent operating staff and supply the tools, inventory, and equipment required for the job. They also must be qualified to make intelligent decisions about trades, suppliers, and service contracts.

All this information is then converted into dollars and detailed on the Budget Expense Schedules for these systems (Figure 9-45). Suitable inventory and equipment lists would be developed to control the purchases needed to maintain the system.

9-12 Terminology

Although almost all manufacturers of air conditioning equipment furnish application engineering charts, data, tables, graphs, or some rule-of-thumb information about air conditioning, the developers, designers, builders, and operators should become more knowledgeable about the fundamental principles and terms used in air conditioning. Everyone in the industry should be able to discuss the systems, know how to maintain them, and be able to recognize problems. Anyone who has attempted to install or operate air conditioning equipment without the proper knowledge has been responsible for poor operations and unsatisfactory experiences by the owners of the equipment. A person should know the terms used by architects and engineers in specifications as well as in discussions about the air conditioning systems and related problems.

British Thermal Unit The quantity of heat required to change the temperature of 1 pound of water 1 degree fahrenheit. It is also the quantity of heat required to change 55 cubic feet of air approximately 1 degree fahrenheit, under average conditions.

Dampers Automatic or manual adjustable metal plates installed inside of a duct to restrict, control volume, balance, or by-pass air, as required in an air conditioning system.

Damper-Louver A damper made up of several vanes operated by gravity or motor control. This type of damper is generally used to control the volume of outside air intake or exhaust to the atmosphere.

Damper—Splitter A damper used to change air flow from one duct to another.

Dehumidification The process of reducing the moisture content of air.

	ACCT. NOS.	SUB TOTALS	TOTAL
THE COOLING SYSTEM	51		

CHILLERS	511	
COOLING TOWERS	512	
CONDENSERS & COMPRESSORS	513	
EVAPORATORS	514	
FAN COIL UNITS	515	
FILTERS	516	
MOTORS & PUMPS	517	
PACKAGED OR INCREMENTAL UNITS	518	
PIPING, VALVES & CONTROLS	519	
WATER TREATMENT	5110	

THE VENTILATION SYSTEM	56	TOTAL	

BELTS & SHEAVES	561	
FANS-HOUSING-DUCTWORK-LOUVRES	562	
FILTERS	563	
HEAT RECOVERY	564	
MOTORS & THEIR CONTROLS	565	

FIGURE 9-45 **Summary of budget expense schedules, repair and maintenance categories; mechanical services.**

Dehumidifier A device that removes moisture from the air.

Design Conditions—Inside The dry-bulb and wet-bulb temperatures, or the dry-bulb temperature and relative humidity, specified to be produced inside at the time of occurrence of the design load.

Design Conditions—Outside The dry-bulb and wet-bulb temperatures, or the dry-bulb temperature and relative humidity, specified for design load conditions.

Design Load The capacity required to produce specified inside conditions when specified outside conditions of temperature and humidity prevail and when all sources of heat load taken at the maximum occur simultaneously.

Ducts Conveyors of air from one location of a system to another.

Evaporation The change of state from a liquid to a vapor. For example, when water changes to steam, the liquid water evaporates.

Evaporative Cooling The process of cooling by means of the evaporation of water into the air.

Heat A form of energy. Temperature, when measured with a thermometer, reveals the intensity of the energy in degrees. There are two types of heat in air conditioning and refrigeration: sensible and latent heat.

Heat—Latent The heat added to or taken from a substance to change its state, but not its temperature.

Heat—Sensible The heat which produces a temperature change, but does not induce a change of state.

Heat—Specific Using water as a standard (1 Btu per pound per 1°), the specific heat of a substance is the ratio of the heat required to raise the temperature of a substance 1° to that required to raise the same weight of water 1°. Under average conditions air has a specific heat of .241 Btus per pound per degree.

Heat—Total As applied to air conditioning, the sum of the sensible heat and the latent heat of a mixture of air and moisture. Total heat is also known as enthalpy.

Heat Transfer The movement of heat from a substance of a higher temperature to a substance of a lower temperature. In air conditioning, heat is transferred by conduction, convection, and radiation.

Humidification The process of adding moisture to air by the evaporation of water.

Humidifier A device that adds moisture to air.

Humidistat A control device sensitive to relative humidity.

Humidity The amount of water in the air. When the air holds all the moisture it can, it is 100 percent relative humidity, or saturated.

Humidity—Relative The ratio of the vapor pressure of the air to the vapor pressure of the air at the same temperature, saturated with moisture.

Infiltration The leakage of air into a building or space.

Sling Psychrometer An instrument equipped with both wet- and dry-bulb thermometers which, when whirled in the air using a handle attached, indicate simultaneously the wet- and dry-bulb temperatures.

Temperature The measurement of heat intensity, in degrees, as indicated on a thermometer, either fahrenheit or centigrade.

Temperature—Dew-Point The temperature at which a specified sample of air with no moisture added or removed would be completely saturated. It is sometimes described as the point at which moisture condenses out of the air onto a substance or material that is cooler than the surrounding atmosphere.

Temperature—Dry-Bulb The air temperature as indicated by a standard thermometer.

Temperature—Wet-Bulb The temperature of air measured by a thermometer with the bulb covered with a water-saturated wick.

Thermal Conduction The passage of heat from one point to another by transmission of molecular energy through a conductor from one particle to another particle.

Ventilation The process of supplying or removing the proper quantity of air from a given space by natural or mechanical means.

Chapter 10

ELECTRICAL SERVICES

10–1 An Overview

Until November 9, 1965, the availability of electrical energy was taken for granted. We really didn't give much thought to how electricity affected our daily life style. But on that date an unbelievable phenomenon occurred: All the lights went out in the northeastern part of the United States and Canada, and cities such as Toronto and New York were plunged into darkness. Subway trains stopped in their tunnels, elevators stopped in buildings, apartments and apartment corridors were blacked out, heat and water pumps stopped, stoves would not work, toilets would not flush, fire pumps would not supply water, and garbage piled up in garbage chutes because compactors would not work.

For many people, this was a rude awakening. First, electrical energy had an overwhelming effect on their daily life style. Second, this could be the warning of an impending shortage. The importance of electricity was suddenly brought to everyone's attention.

In this chapter, we hope to provide you with enough knowledge of electricity so that you will be able to

- –understand the fundamentals of electricity
- –recognize problems
- –know what to do and what not to do
- –treat electricity with the respect it deserves

To further your knowledge and allow you to complete certain electrical maintenance chores, you will need to attend a certified course conducted by a qualified electrician. *Remember, electricity kills!*

Electricity is the most versatile form of energy, but it is also the most mysterious; we can't see it; we can't smell it; we can't hear it.

Defining the word electricity is difficult because very little is known about its fundamental nature. However, through the years, scientists have discovered many things about electricity, harnessing and using it in accordance with certain behavior, or "laws."

The ancient Greeks used the word "electric" to describe the mysterious forces of attraction and repulsion exhibited by certain glass-like material when rubbed with a cloth.

One of the fundamental laws of electricity is that "like charges repel each other and unlike charges attract each other."

HYDRAULIC ANALOGY

The electric circuit can be compared with a water piping system, which may help you to more easily understand some of the fundamental principles.

In Figure 10-1, the pump corresponds to a generator or another source of electricity. The difference between the gauges A and B is the pressure on the system corresponding to the voltage of an electrical system. The pipe corresponds to the conductors, and the water flowing in the pipe corresponds to electric current. The coil might be part of a heating or air conditioning system such as a heating or cooling coil or condenser; in the electrical system, it could be a lamp bulb, an electric heater, or a motor.

The velocity of the water depends on the diameter of the pipe and also on its smoothness. However, there is a limit determined by the pressure in the pipe.

By replacing the water pipes with electric power lines we can better understand the similarity. Instead of water, we have a flow of current. The electricity is under "pressure." This pressure is called electromotive force (EMF) and is measured in volts.

In general, the larger the diameter of the wire, the greater the electric current. The conductivity of the material used to make the wire is similar to the smoothness of the water pipe. Good conductors have low resistance; current flows through copper much faster than through iron. The quantity of electric current is measured in amperes.

When a faucet is opened, water pours out. However, electricity does not pour out of a

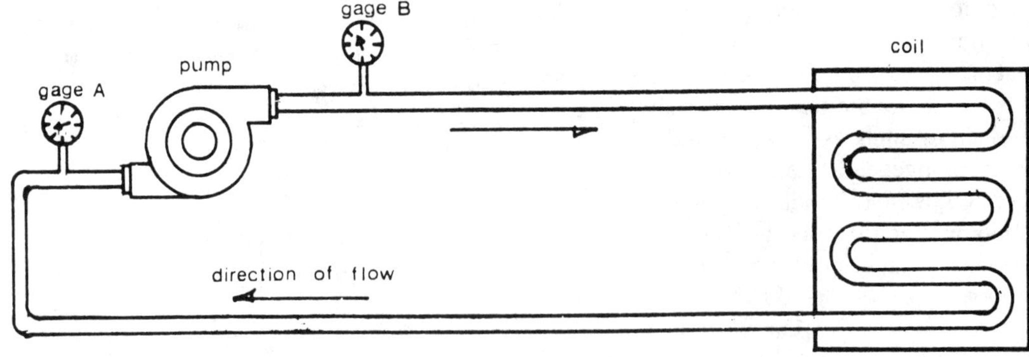

FIGURE 10-1 Hydraulic analogy. Water pumping system is similar to an electric circuit.

wall outlet or an empty lamp socket even when the switch is turned on.

Electricity or electric current flows only on a complete circuit.

ELECTRON THEORY

One of the oldest theories on the nature of electricity is called the "Electron Theory." This theory explains electricity by the existence of a tiny particle called the "electron." The entire study of electricity and the operation of electrical equipment is based on this theory.

Electricity is sometimes defined as "the force that moves electrons." Thus we describe the effect, not the force.

The electron theory assumes that all electrical effects are caused by the movement of the electrons from one point to another. This is more commonly referred to as electrical current or flow.

Electricity acts much like highway traffic. More cars can travel on a four lane highway than on a two lane highway. More electrons can travel in a large wire than in a small wire. Wire length, type of wire, and wire diameter have an effect. *Electricity is electrons in motion.* To give you an idea of the size of an electron, it takes six billion billion electrons to light a 100-watt bulb for a single second.

Electricity occurs in nature in the form of lightning, electric eels, and even in the small shock you sometimes get when you touch a doorknob.

An electric current travels with lightning speed at 20,000 miles per second along a copper wire—but individual electrons do not. They amble along at less than an inch per second. The current streaks through the wire because the electrons jostle each other all along the way.

The phenomenon can best be understood by imagining a pipe completely filled with golf balls. If an additional ball is pushed in at one end of the pipe, a ball will pop out almost instantly at the other end. Similarly, when a distant power plant forces electrons into one end of a wire, other electrons almost immediately come out the other end—to light a lamp, start a motor, or percolate the coffee.

HOW TO PRODUCE ELECTRICITY

Most of the electricity we use in our everyday lives is made in a power plant by spinning a magnet inside coils of wire. This puts electrons in motion and creates a flow of electricity.

When the wires move past a magnet within a generator, electricity is produced in the wires because of the magnetism.

Electricity can be produced in the following ways:

1. Pressure—piezoelectricity
2. Heat—thermoelectricity
3. Light—photoelectricity
4. Chemical Action—batteries
5. Magnetism
6. Static electricity

CONDUCTORS AND INSULATORS

Substances that allow the free motion or flow of electrons are called "conductors." These substances have such a structure that many "free electrons" exist in the atoms and can easily be moved from atom to atom inside the conductor.

The greater the number of electrons that can be made to move in a substance, under a given force, the better are the conductive qualities of that material. A good conductor has a low opposition or resistance to the electron or current flow.

A list of the best conductors and the best insulators, arranged in accordance with their respective abilities to conduct or resist the flow of electrons, follows:

Conductors	*Insulators*
Silver	Dry air
Copper	Glass
Aluminum	Mica
Zinc	Rubber
Brass	Asbestos
Iron	Bakelite
	Distilled water

RESISTANCE

Every material offers some resistance or opposition to current flow. Materials that offer little resistance are chosen for conductors, and those that offer high resistance are used for insulators. *The symbol R is used to indicate resistance in ohms.*

VOLTAGE

When producing electricity, the device or body becomes charged, or one part of the device or body has an excess of electrons compared to another part.

Electrons are particles with negative electric charges, therefore, the body or area having an excess of electrons is said to have a negative charge, and the body or area having a deficiency of electrons is said to have a positive charge. Since the negatively charged electrons are attracted to the positively charged body or area, this force of attraction represents a capability or potential to cause electrons to move.

The difference of potential is the force or pressure that causes electrons to move in a conductor as an electrical current; it is also called voltage. The unit used in measuring potential or pressure is the volt. Therefore, a volt measures the force that makes electricity flow.

ENERGY

In studying power, it is said that mechanically, work is performed when a force acts through a distance, and that electrically, work is performed when voltage causes current to flow in a closed circuit. Energy, either mechanical or electrical, is expended when work is done. Electrically the moving of a given quantity of electrons from one point to another represents a total amount of work done, or of energy expended. *Power is the rate at which the work is done; that is, energy expended per unit of time.* If we multiply the "energy expanded per unit of time" by the "number of time units during which the energy is expended," we will get the total energy expended. *The symbol E is used to indicate the energy expended or voltage in volts.*

WATTS

Watts are the third major measure of electricity, and measure the rate at which we consume electrical energy. The power consumption of many devices—lamps, irons, hair dryers—will be marked on them in watts. The unit of power was named to honor the memory of James Watt, the inventory of the steam engine. Other devices—fuses, motors—are rated by the current they carry; that is, by amperes. The units are related, however, so if you know one you can always figure out the other by using *"Ohm's Law Equations"* (Figure 10-2).

Total energy consumption, of course, depends on how long an appliance is kept

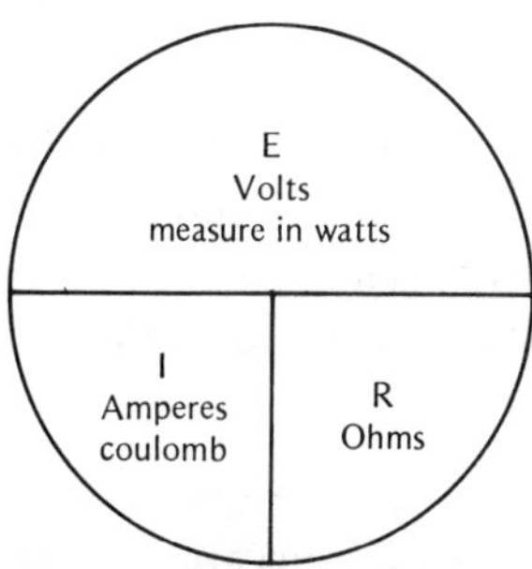

FIGURE 10-2 Ohm's circle law. To use this diagram, cover the unknown component and use the equation laws to determine the other circuit component.

running and is calculated by multiplying the power (expressed in 1,000 watt units called kilowatts and usually abbreviated by kW) by the time in hours. If we use a 1,000 watt appliance for one hour, it will consume exactly one kilowatt hour (kWh). This is recorded by the electric meter and will eventually figure in the electric bill.

POWER

The watt, which is the basic unit of electric power, is equal to the voltage multiplied by the current (or electrical force times a given quantity of electrons moved past a point in a second). This represents the rate at which work is being done in moving electrons through the circuit. *The symbol P is used to indicate electric power or watts.*

CURRENT

The flow of electrons through a conductor is called an electric current. Flow of electric current may be compared to the flow of water in a pipe. Water flowing past a given point is measured in "gallons per minute" or gpm.

AMPERE

In measuring electron flow, a unit called the ampere is used. In electricity, the term coulomb is a unit of quantity, meaning a definite number of electrons, and corresponds to the gallon as a quantity measure. The rate of flow of electric current would then be measured as "coulombs per second." (Fig. 10-1.)

However, instead of referring to coulombs per second, the term *AMPERE* is used. An ampere is the rate of electron flow past a given point in one second.

DIRECT AND ALTERNATING CURRENT

Current caused to flow by a battery is direct current (dc) because it flows in one direction only.

The generator that causes current to flow generates alternating current (ac). Alternating current reverses directions 120 times per second. This is called the 60-cycle current because it repeats itself 60 times per second. *The symbol I is used to indicate current flow, in amperes.*

OHM'S LAW

The amount of current flow around the circuit is governed by the voltage and the resistance of the circuit. If the resistance remains the same, but the voltage is increased, the current will increase. If the voltage is kept the same, but the resistance is increased, the current will decrease.

The mathematics of these relationships was proved by a German named George S. Ohm, who stated the principle in 1827. The principle is called Ohm's Law, and is the fundamental law or equation of electrical science.

Ohm's law is easy to apply mathematically because it follows a simple proportion; for example, if voltage is doubled, current is also doubled, or if resistance is doubled, then current is halved.

The unit for measuring resistance is the ohm. One ohm is the resistance of a circuit, or part of a circuit that permits a steady current of one ampere (one coulomb per second) to flow when a steady electromotive force (emf) of one volt is applied to the circuit.

Ohm's Law Symbols

E—means difference in potential, or *voltage* in volts.

I—means current flow, in amperes.

R—means *resistance* in ohms. The Greek letter Omega (Ω) is used as the symbol for ohms.

P—means power or watts.

Ohm's Law Equations

$$I = \frac{E}{R} \quad E = IR \quad R = \frac{E}{I} \quad P - EI$$

By knowing two of the three components we can determine the other circuit component. This information is essential if we are to solve electrical circuit problems or to plan proper electrical circuitry.

ELECTRICAL POWER TEST INSTRUMENTS

Voltage—measured by a *Voltmeter.*

Current—measured by an *Ammeter.*

Resistance—usually measured with an *Ohmeter.*

High Resistance—measured with a *Megohmmeter,* commonly called a megger, which measures resistance in megohms. (A megohm is a million ohms.)

Power—measured with a *Wattmeter.*

Energy—measured with a watt hour or *Kilowatt hour meter.*

Power Factor—measured with a *Power-factor meter.*

POWER DISTRIBUTION

Electricity is carried from the generating plant on electric lines that pass through step-up transformers at a very high voltage—from 15,000 volts to as much as 765,000 volts (Figure 10-3). This minimizes loss in the lines due to heat generated by the flow of electric current. The high line voltage must be reduced to about 2,300 volts for distribution, or before it can be used to operate lights and other electrical equipment inside a building. This is done with a step-down transformer which is generally mounted on a pole just outside the building.

If the service offered by the Electric Utility Company is 600V, it is reduced by step-down transformers to 120/240 or 120/208 volts for our use. If equipment requires 600 volts, it can be obtained straight from the mains.

Distribution Circuits

Electricity is distributed throughout a building by a number of circuits. *An electric circuit* (Figure 10-4) *is a complete physical pathway for current flow.* A closed loop of wire is not necessarily a circuit because a course of voltage must be included to make a circuit.

As long as the pathway is unbroken, there is a closed circuit and current will flow. However, if the path is broken at any point, it is said to be an open circuit and no current will flow.

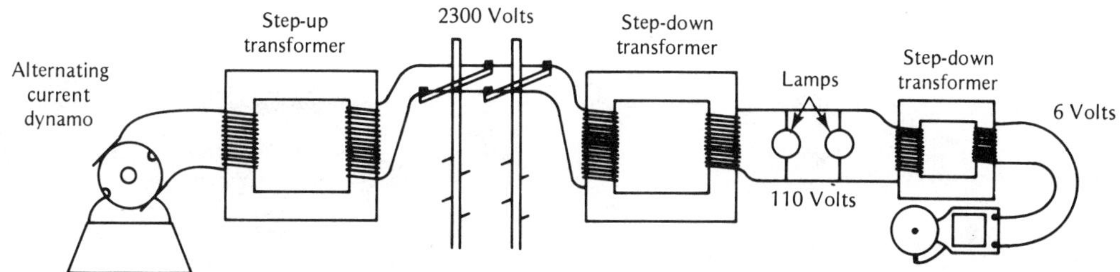

FIGURE 10-3 Power distribution. This diagram represents the essential devices and changes in electric current as electrical power is moved from the dynamo to a home.

WIRES, CABLES, CORDS, AND CONDUITS

Various methods are used to distribute electricity through a building, and various types of wire and cable are used for these circuits.

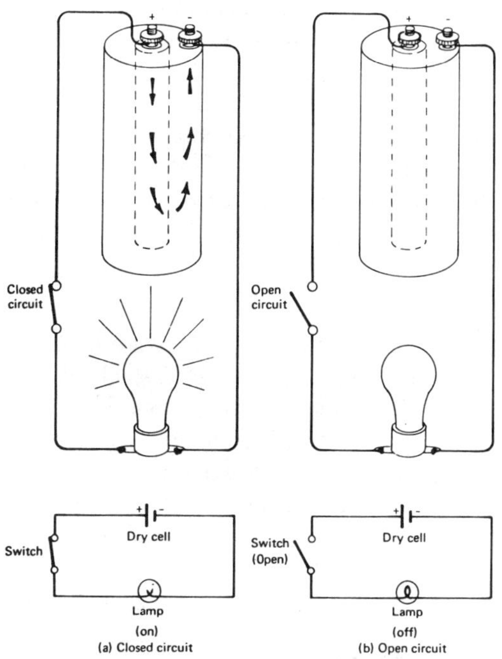

FIGURE 10-4 An electrical circuit. An electric circuit is a complete physical pathway for current flow. (Courtesy of Prentice-Hall, Inc.)

Electricity is conducted along circuits by wires grouped together in the form of cable or in some cases, contained in conduit. Cable consists of a preassembled combination of wires within a protective outer sheath made of metal or plastic. Conduit is simply piping of steel or plastic through which several wires are threaded after the pipe has been installed.

Wire is a single, solid strand and is the least flexible form of conductor.

The wires used in circuits are shown actual size in Figure 10-5. On larger sizes, wire diameter is indicated by a gauge number printed on the insulation and based on the American Wire Gauge (AWG) system—the smaller the number, the greater the diameter. Wire type is also marked. The smaller sizes—No. 18 and No. 16—are too small for printed identification.

Wire sizes No. 14 and No. 12 are used in standard 120-volt circuits for lighting and receptacles for televisions, clocks, and other small appliances. Size No. 10 is used in 120-volt circuits carrying electricity to major applicances such as dishwashers and clothes dryers. Wire sizes No. 8 and No. 6 are the most widely used in 240-volt circuits for electric ranges and central air conditioners. Wire sizes No. 18 and No. 16 are reserved for low-voltage systems like bells and intercoms; in stranded form, they are also used for lamp cord.

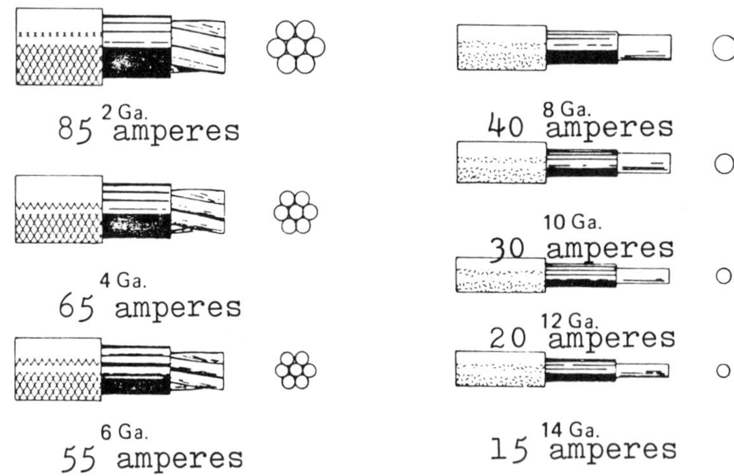

FIGURE 10-5 Various wire sizes. (Courtesy of Prentice-Hall, Inc.)

The maximum current that a wire of a given diameter can safely carry is stated in amperes and is known as the wire's ampacity. The smaller the wire, the greater its resistance to the flow of current and the greater the friction that generates heat, which could destroy insulation and even kindle a fire; thus large currents require large wires. The ampacities shown in Figure 10-5 are for copper wires, the most common wires in house circuits. Aluminum wire, which does not conduct electricity as efficiently as copper, has an ampacity approximately equal to that of copper wire two sizes smaller; for example, aluminum wire No. 12 has about the same ampacity as copper wire No. 14.

Matching Wire Size to Length and Amperage

All conductors have some resistance to the flow of electricity. This reduces the pressure (voltage) in long runs. This voltage drop reduces operating efficiency because the electric energy is wasted as heat in the wires.

Wires are sized to suit the voltage required for its end use. Therefore, there is a limit to the length of a circuit in relation to the voltage and amperage required. Exceeding these limits increases the possibility of overheating, fire, and burnout of equipment motors. All buildings and appliances are wired within the limits of the electrical code and *should not be changed.*

Flexible Armored Cable

In armored cable the wires are protected by a jacket of galvanized steel, wound spirally for flexibility. Each insulated conductor wire is further protected by a paper wrapping so the insulation will not be damaged when the outer casing is flexed; the ground wire, if any, is bare. *Because the steel jacket is subject to corrosion, armored cable—usually known as BX—may be used.*

Plastic-Sheathed Cable

Nonmetallic cable, usually called Romex (the name of its best known brand), is the

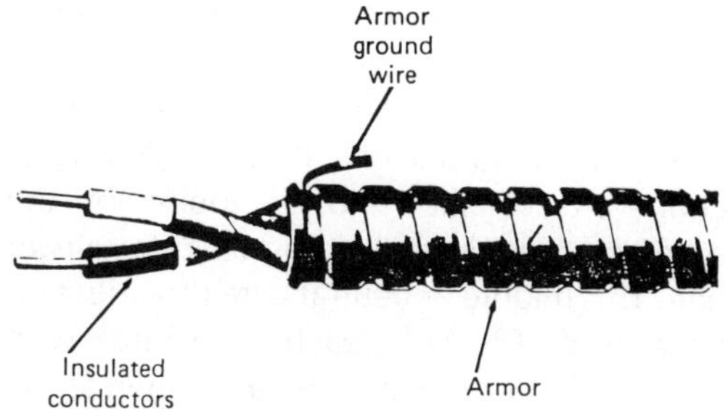

FIGURE 10-6 Flexible armored cable. (Courtesy of Prentice-Hall, Inc.)

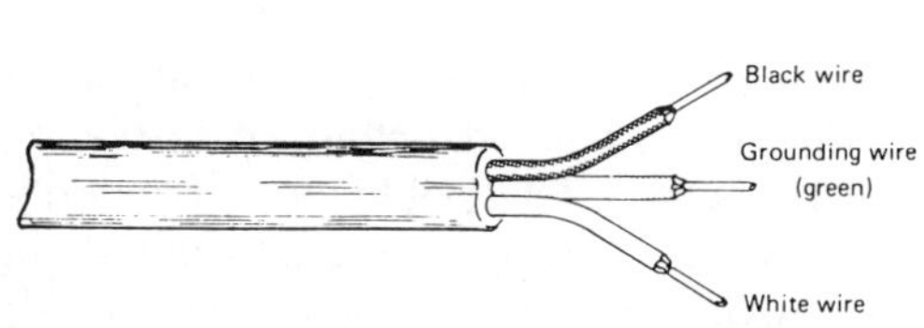

FIGURE 10-7 Plastic-sheathed cable. A ground wire in an NM (nonmetallic) sheathed cable. (Courtesy of Prentice-Hall, Inc.)

most common form of wiring used since 1960. It is the least expensive, and it also is the easiest to install because of its flexibility. The insulated hot and neutral wires and the uninsulated ground wire are enclosed in a protective sheath, generally of plastic.

Conduit

Many types of conduit are used to hold wires; the conduit most likely to be found in homes is a galvanized steel pipe known as thin-wall conduit. The piping protects wires from physical damage better than either armored or plastic-sheathed cable. Once the conduit is installed, additional wires may be threaded through. As many lengths of conduit as are needed can be joined to each other, or to cable, by connectors like the extension coupling and the "ell" corner joint shown in Figure 10-8. However, since thin-wall conduit does not have the flexibility of cable, it cannot be snaked behind walls and is therefore more difficult to install.

Other forms of conduit, sometimes preferred outdoors, include rigid conduit, a metal pipe more durable than the thin-walled variety and PVC (polyvinyl chloride), rigid plastic tubing that is more resistant to corrosion than metal. But PVC is more expensive than metal conduit and can be a hazard: It is combustible and emits toxic fumes when burning. Also PVC must be assembled to connectors with adhesive--once joined, the parts cannot be taken apart.

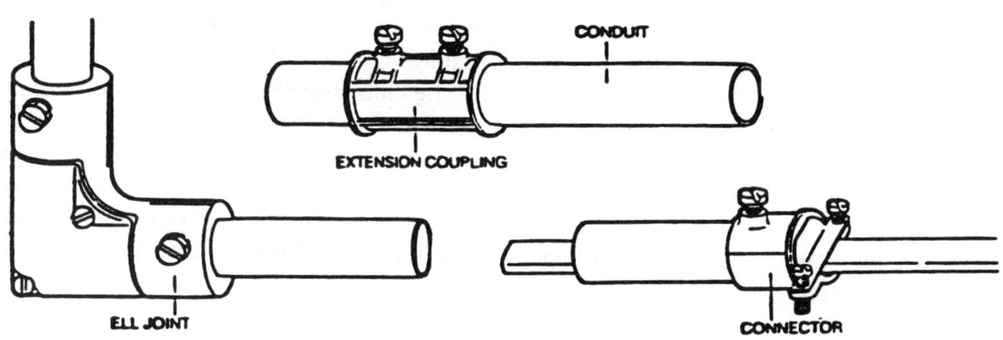

FIGURE 10-8 Conduits. Different conduits are used to hold different kinds of wires.

Cords

The cord's conductors are made of many strands of fine wire twisted together. The cord is made of two or more separately-insulated conductors assembled within an insulating jacket. It is the most flexible form of conductor and is used to supply current to hand-held appliances and portable tools. These cords sometimes have a third conductor (with green insulation) used for grounding.

Cord Fittings

Any electrical device that is designed to receive its electrical supply from a receptacle will be fitted with a line cord. Cord fittings attached to the line cord are used as a convenient method for connecting the device to the power source.

10-2 Understanding the Wiring Service

AN OVERVIEW

Electric power is supplied by the local utility company. Because there are so many appliances available today, two voltages are needed. Lighting and receptacles for small appliances, such as radios, toasters, tea kettles, frypans, and electric drills require 115 volt power. Large appliances, such as electric stoves, clothes dryers, some electric heaters, and air conditioners require 240 volts.

OBTAINING TWO VOLTAGES FROM THREE LINES

High tension (high voltage) lines supply the primary coil of the transformer with 2,300 or 2,400 volts (Figure 10-3). This transformer reduces the voltage on a 10 to 1 ratio (10 windings one side to one on the other), giving a secondary output of 240 volts. A wire is connected to the midway point of the secondary winding, dividing its 240 volts in half. This middle or neutral wire provides two voltages of 120 volts each on a three wire system. The two outer wires are known as the live wires. For safety purposes, the live wires are switch controlled and have fuses connected in series with them. The neutral wire is grounded at the transformer and in the residential switch box. (Fig. 10-12.)

THE IMPORTANCE OF THE ELECTRIC SERVICE ENTRANCE*

All present and future use of electric service depends upon the capacities of the electric service entrance wires and the electric service entrance equipment. If either one is too small, it may become necessary to replace the entire service entrance with larger wires and equipment when new major appliances are installed.

Electricity cannot be stored. It comes in only as it is used. No matter how large the electric service entrance is, no more current comes in than the lights and appliances require.

The following illustrations provide a rough guide for learning the capacity of the electric service entrance in a home. Both fuse-type and circuit breaker equipment are shown. One or the other, but not both, will be found in actual installations.

*Reprinted by permission of the Canadian Adequate Wiring Bureau, Toronto, Ontario.

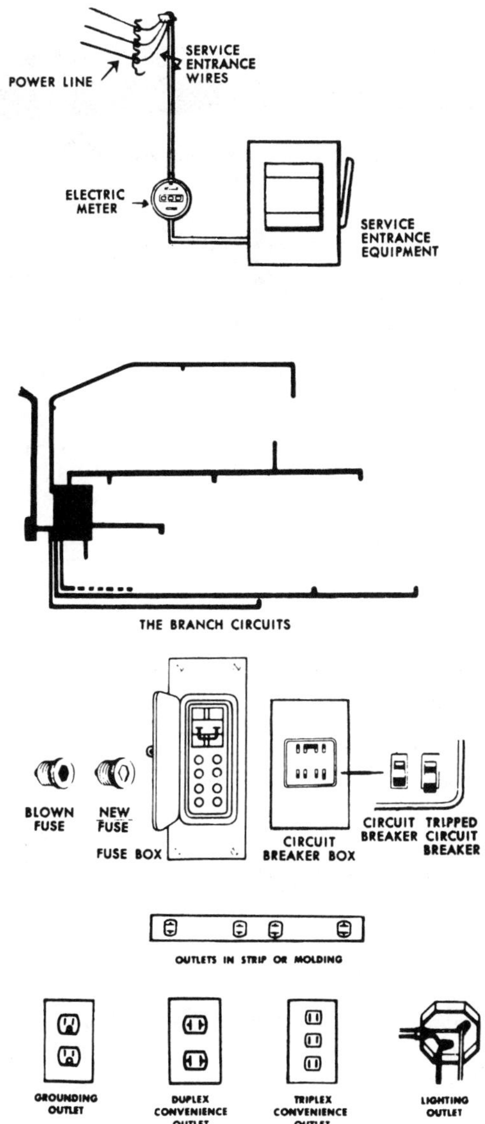

FIGURE 10-9 The home wiring system. (Courtesy of the Canadian Adequate Wiring Bureau.)

COMMON WIRE SERVICES

There are several wire services commonly used in buildings and it is useful to understand how they are wired. See Figures 10-11 through 10-14 for illustrations of the 110/220 Volt, single phase, three wire service, and the following:

120/240 Volt, Single Phase, 3 Wire System

This system is mostly used for a house service, temporary power, or services that feed lighting loads, receptacles and small motor loads.

120/208 Volt, 3 Phase, 4 Wire System

This system is frequently used in larger buildings with heavier motor loads (see Figures 10-13 and 10-14).

10-3 Understanding the System

FUNCTIONS OF THE HOME WIRING SYSTEM*

Brings Electricity from the Power Line into the Home

Electric service can be compared with water service in cities and towns. Electricity flows along the power lines, and then along the wires in the home, just as water flows through the public water mains and then through the home's plumbing system.

The wires which are connected to the outside power supply bring electricity into the house. In many areas, these wires are brought in through a pipe or conduit, or sometimes they are combined into a cable. They are called the "Service Entrance Wires."

*Reprinted by permission of the Canadian Adequate Wiring Bureau, Toronto, Ontario.

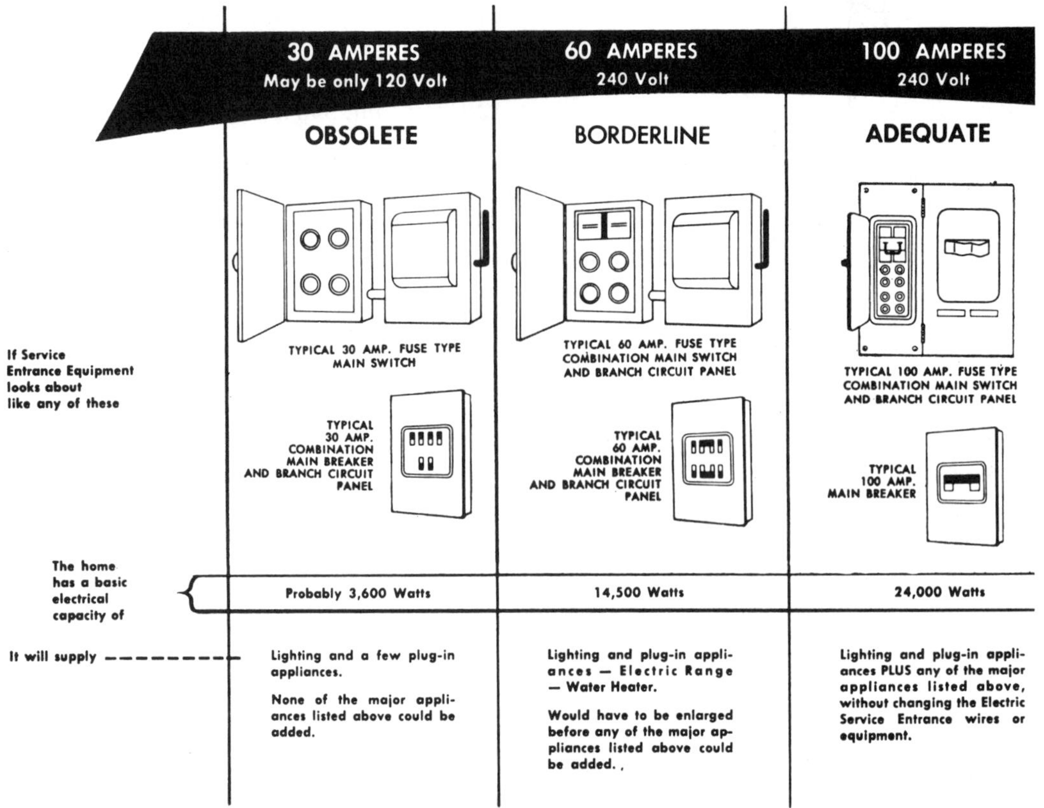

FIGURE 10-10 Overload protective devices. No branch circuit in a wiring system should have a current demand of more than 20 amperes and each branch circuit should be protected by an overcurrent device in the service panel. (Courtesy of the Canadian Adequate Wiring Bureau.)

Distributes Electricity Through the Home

The service entrance wires are connected to the main switch and fuse, or the main circuit breaker, which is called the "service entrance equipment." It serves as the junction point from which electricity is dispatched to various parts of the house. The service entrance equipment also can be used to disconnect the home's main flow of electricity.

After electricity has entered the house through the electric entrance equipment, it is distributed by a number of smaller wires called "branch circuits." The branch circuits carry electricity much in the same way plumbing pipes carry water.

Delivers Electricity to Lights and Appliances

Each branch circuit delivers electricity to one or more outlets to which appliances and lights are connected. Most branch circuits serve several outlets; some deliver electricity to individual major appliances.

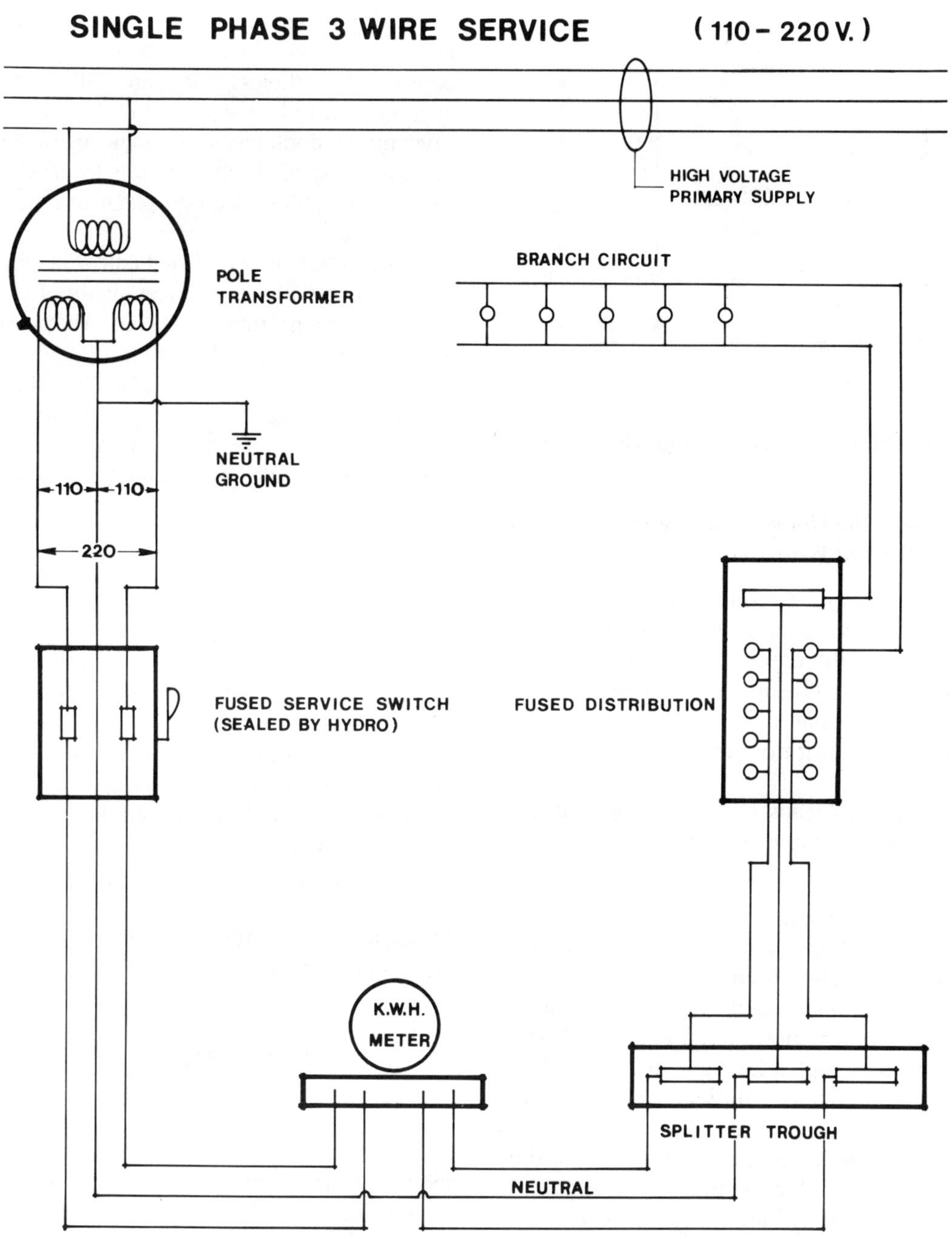

FIGURE 10-11 110/220 volt single phase 3 wire service. (Courtesy of Cadillac-Fairview Corporation, Limited.)

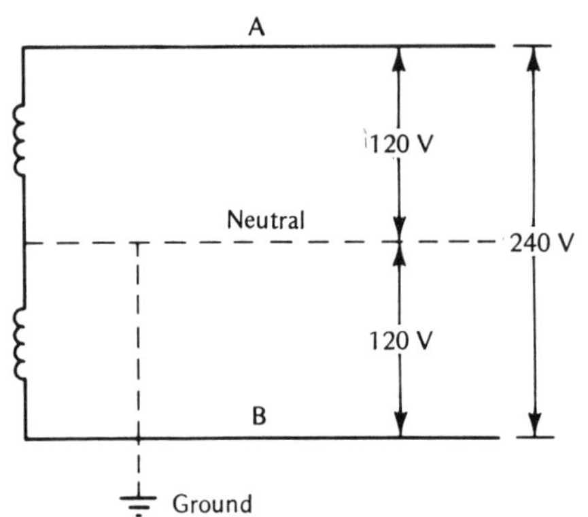

FIGURE 10-12 **120/240 volt single phase 3 wire service.**

Protects the Home from Fire Hazard Due to Overheated Wires.

Each branch circuit has its own protection in the form of a fuse or circuit breaker, located in the branch circuit box where the branch circuit begins. When a fuse blows, or a circuit breaker opens, the wiring system is protecting itself from overheating.

Provides a Means of Connecting and Controlling Lights and Appliances

The outlets in the wiring system correspond to the faucets in the plumbing system, except that the home requires many more electrical outlets than water faucets.

Convenience outlets are available in several forms, most common of which is the standard "Duplex Convenience Outlet." You can also obtain "Triplex" and two-circuit outlets, as well as a number of outlets assembled together on a strip or molding. Lamps and plug-in appliances should be plugged directly into the convenience outlet.

Special purpose outlets are the openings through which certain major appliances are connected to their individual branch circuits.

Lighting outlets are the openings for fixed lights. We seldom think of them as outlets because they are concealed behind lighting fixtures. Nevertheless, they are outlets for electricity, just like the special outlets which serve major appliances. In both cases, the outlet has a special job, which is to provide access to electricity for one piece of equipment.

Switches cut off or restore the flow of electricity to lights and appliances, without disconnecting them from the outlets. They also contribute to safety. When there are enough switches, properly located, you can "light your way" through dark rooms, and up and down stairways. A multiple switch control is a control of a single light source from two or more locations.

TYPICAL APARTMENT BUILDING ELECTRICAL SYSTEM

Figure 10-15 charts the four main electrical services in a typical apartment building. Each of these systems depends on electricity for the power to allow them to function. This power is distributed throughout the building by various circuits; the circuits may require anywhere from 150 amperes of current to 200 amperes. This power supply, after it passed the meter, enters service panels where the circuit connection originates.

TYPICAL APARTMENT ELECTRICAL SERVICE

In Figure 10-16 we show a 400 ampere service at the main switch. This load is then reduced into four 100 ampere services for the individual apartment units. In an apartment building there are also several other panels, or sub panels, and master and individual

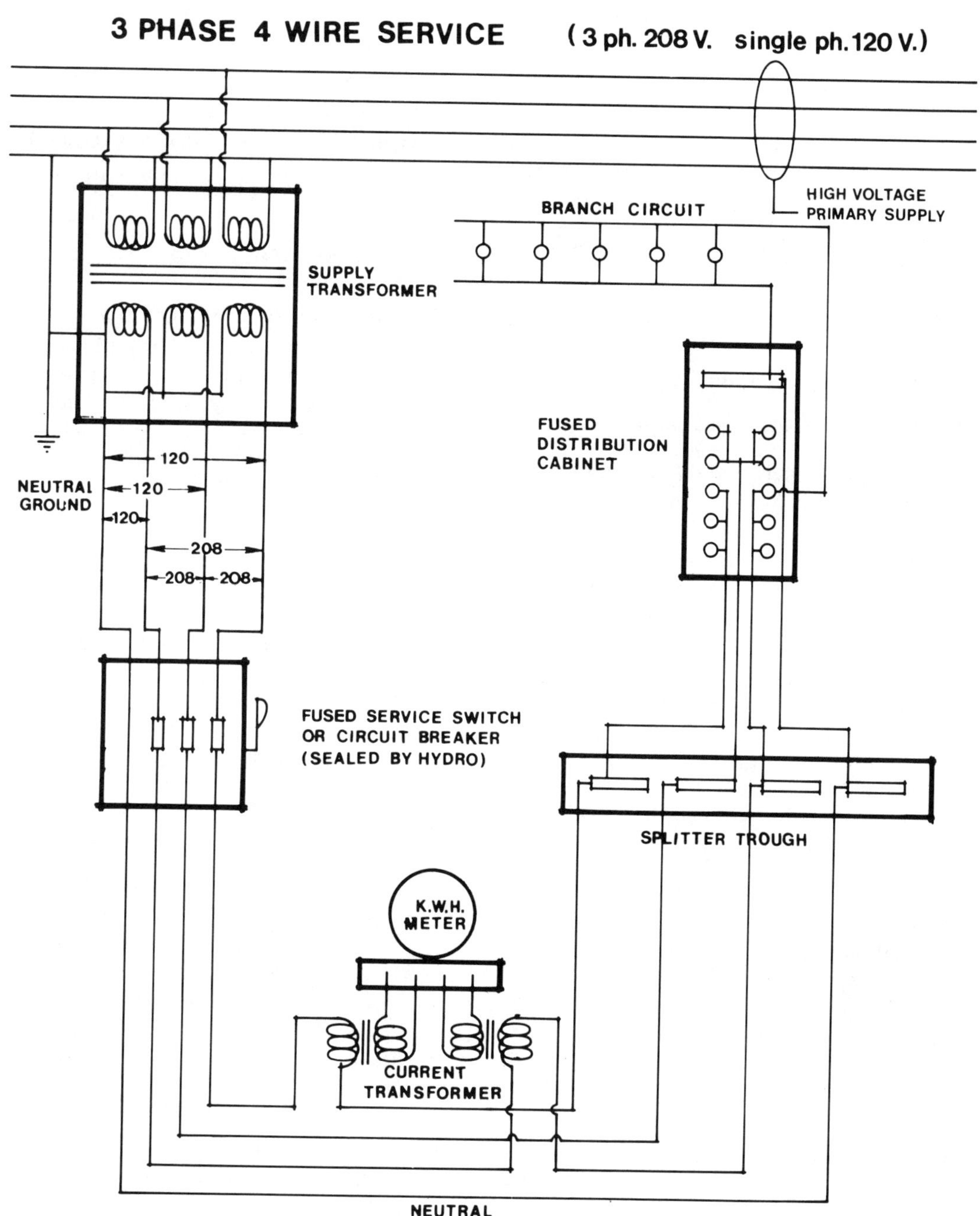

FIGURE 10-13 **120/208 volt 3 phase 4 wire service.** (Courtesy of Cadillac-Fairview Corporation, Limited.)

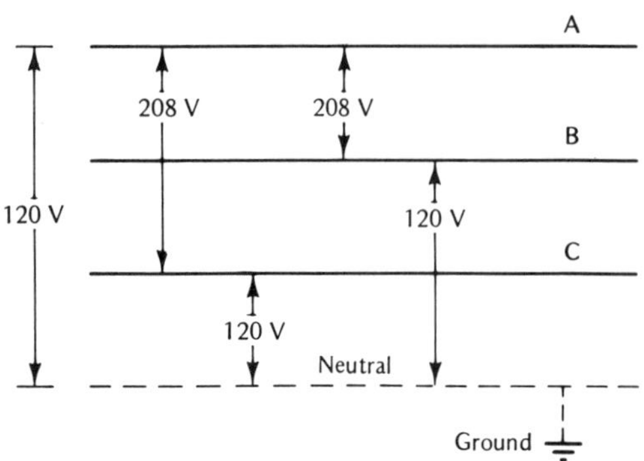

FIGURE 10-14 120/208 volt 3 phase 4 wire system.

breakers for other areas of the building which they serve, such as equipment, laundry, or pool.

To protect against fire or shock, every circuit includes one of two types of safety device: a fuse or a circuit breaker.

All of this equipment is fused in accordance with the local electrical code. Fuses can be replaced, but *never* with a fuse of a greater amperage than originally installed.

The fuses are the *safety valves* of the electrical system.

THE BRANCH CIRCUITS

Buildings should have enough branch circuits of proper size wires to accommodate all of the electrical equipment and lamps. Otherwise, each branch circuit will become overloaded from time to time. Then, instead of flowing smoothly, at full voltage, electricity is wasted through useless heating of the wires. Its voltage is reduced, just as water pressure is reduced when too many faucets are drawing water from one pipe.

The wiring system should contain three kinds of branch circuits, each having the correct size wire and fuse or circuit breaker. The sizes of fuses and circuit breakers are given in amperes, in Figure 10-10. Since appliances and lamps are generally rated in watts, however, the number of watts which you can connect simultaneously on a single circuit is also shown.

TYPICAL HOUSE CIRCUITS

There are a variety of voltages in a typical house circuit. A heavy-duty 240-volt circuit usually serves large appliances such as a clothes dryer, water heater, or electric range. These appliances are grounded with a grounding conductor.

THE KILOWATT-HOUR METER

When the power reaches the building, the supply lines pass through the kilowatt-hour meter, which runs faster or slower depending on how much current is entering the system. As the motor runs, it turns numbered indicators to register the cumulative total energy used.

TYPICAL APARTMENT ELECTRICAL CIRCUIT PLAN

It is wise to prepare an electrical circuit plan for each area or apartment. These circuit plans are useful for every multi-circuited areas. They can usually be taken from the electrical plan.

To prepare a plan, identify each outlet, receptacle, light fixture, or switch by the number assigned to the fuse or circuit breaker. Then sketch the plan as shown in Figure 10-18.

Such a sketch tells you which outlets will be affected if you cut off power to a circuit

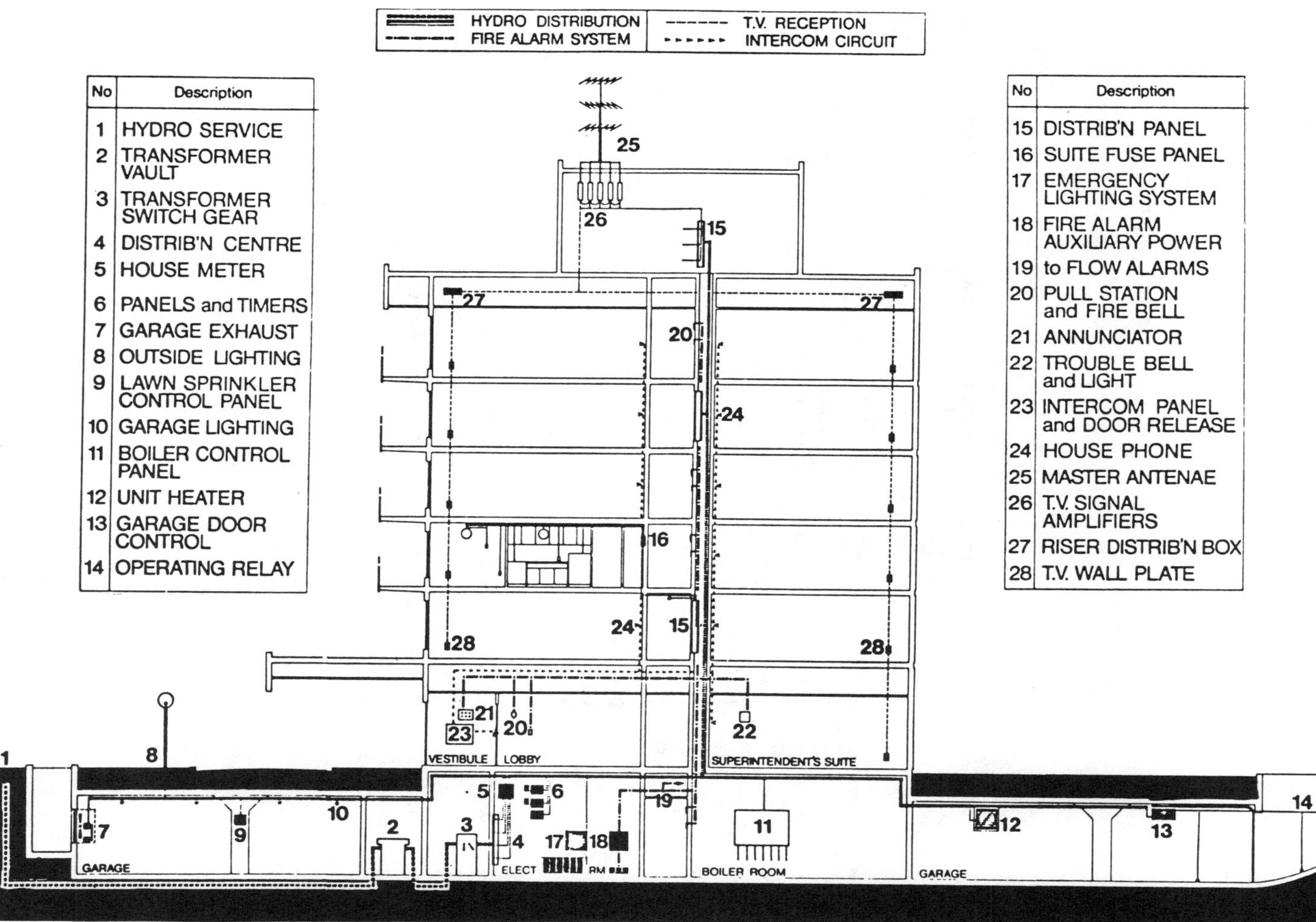

FIGURE 10-15 **Typical apartment building electrical system.** (Courtesy of Cadillac-Fairview Corporation, Limited.)

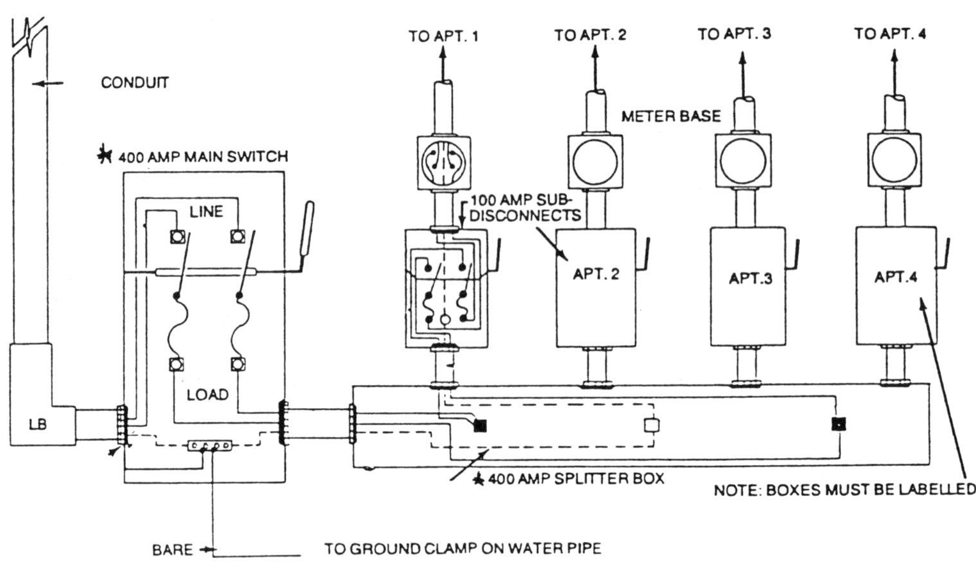

FIGURE 10-16 Typical apartment electrical service. (Reprinted with permission from *Applications of Electrical Construction* by Robert K. Clidero and Kenneth H. Sharpe, General Publishing Company, Limited.)

	They Serve	They Require	You Can Connect All at Once
GENERAL PURPOSE CIRCUITS	Lights all over the house and convenience outlets everywhere except in the kitchen, laundry and dining areas.	15-Ampere Fuse or Circuit Breaker 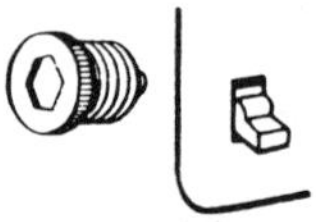	1650 Watts
	No. 14 wire, requiring a 15 Ampere protection, is found in most older homes. No. 12 wire is larger and is therefore recommended for present-day electrical systems for General Purpose and Small Appliance Circuits. Except under specially approved conditions, such circuits should be protected with 15 ampere fuses or circuit breakers to prevent damage to cords and appliances.		
SMALL APPLIANCE CIRCUITS	Only the convenience outlets – no lights – in the kitchen, laundry and dining areas, where portable appliances are most often used. (At least two appliance circuits are advisable; larger homes should have three.)	15-Ampere Fuse or Circuit Breaker 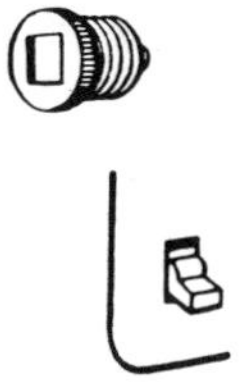	1650 Watts
	No. 12 wire is the smallest which should be used in Small Appliance Circuits.		
INDIVIDUAL CIRCUITS	One piece of major electrical equipment each.	Various sizes and types of fuses and circuit breakers, depending on the rating of the appliance. 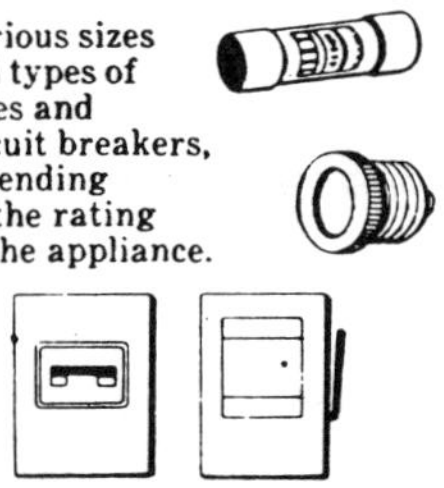	Nothing more than the appliance served by each circuit.
	An Individual Circuit seldom becomes overloaded, as no other appliance is connected to it.		

FIGURE 10-17 Typical house circuits. (Courtesy of the Canadian Adequate Wiring Bureau.)

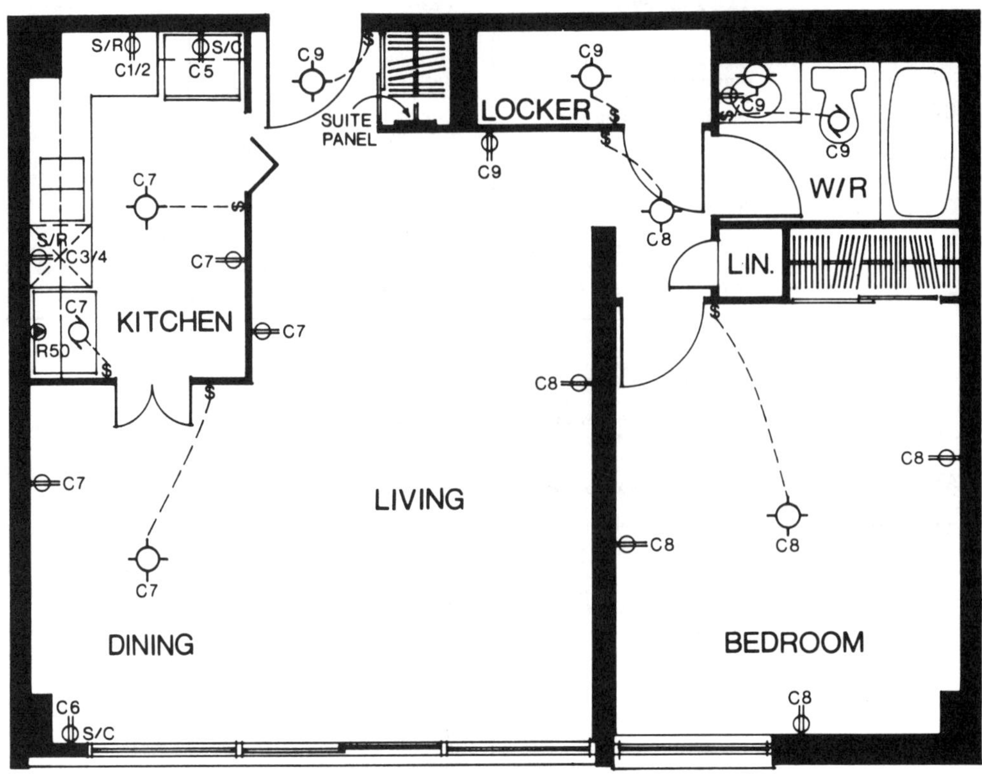

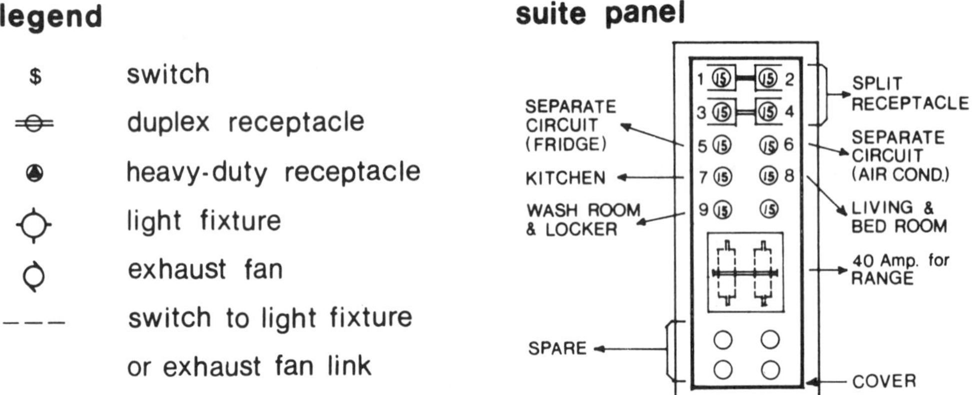

FIGURE 10-18 Typical apartment electrical circuit plan. (Courtesy of Cadillac-Fairview Corporation, Limited.)

and which fuse or circuit breaker to check when a circuit fails; thus, this plan becomes a valuable troubleshooting tool.

TYPICAL RECEPTACLES AND BLADE PATTERN

A receptacle is defined as a contact device installed at an outlet for the connection of an attachment plug. The outlet itself is a point on the wiring system at which current is taken to supply a load.

Today most receptacles are of the duplex type and accommodate two plugs, such as shown in Figure 10-19. Figure 10-20 illustrates the various blade patterns, but shows only half of the receptacle. Usually the two receptacles are connected in parallel. In better quality receptacles, however, a small metal strip can be broken out to permit isolation of the two sections.

With this arrangement, the top receptacle can be wired so that it is permanently live and convenient for supplying a temporary load, such as a vacuum cleaner. The bottom half can then be used for lamps and is switch controlled. Receptacles for the installment of portable cords must be rated at not less than 15A, 125V, or 10A, 250V.

PLUG CAPS

There are two main types of cord fittings: the male and the female plug cap. Both are produced with the same blade shapes.

The insulating disc of the male cap is a separate part fitted over the prongs where the cord has been connected. The purpose of the disc is to prevent loose strands or terminals from coming in contact with the cover plate of the receptacle. If the cover plate is made of metal and there is no insulating disc, a short-circuit flash can occur as the plug is inserted into the receptacle, burning the hand of the person plugging in the cap, and blowing the fuse.

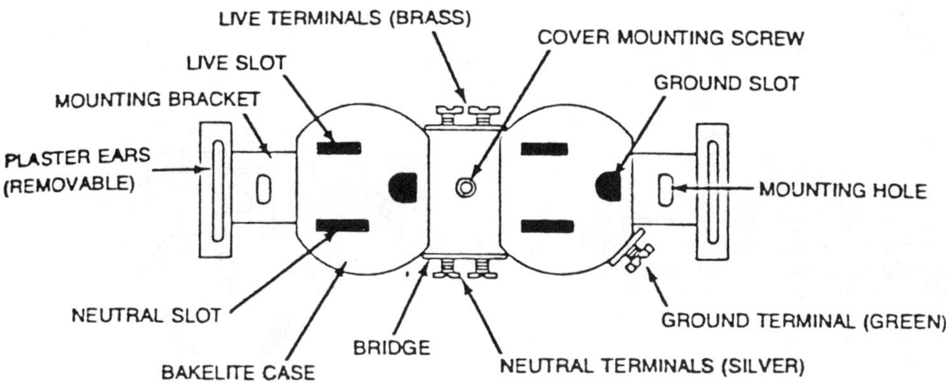

FIGURE 10-19 "U" ground receptacle. This receptacle accepts both the two-prong plug and the three-prong "U" ground plug. All wall plug caps should be the three-pronged type. *THESE SHOULD NEVER BE ALTERED TO FIT ANY OTHER WALL RECEPTACLE.* (Reprinted with permission from *Applications of Electrical Construction* by Robert K. Clidero and Kenneth H. Sharpe, General Publishing Company, Limited.)

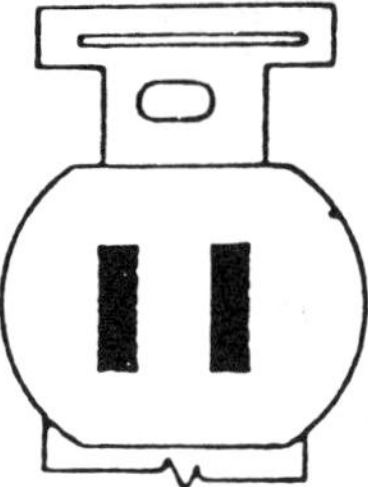

Old-style 2 prong: Many buildings constructed during the 1940s and 1950s were equipped with this unit. The main disadvantage is the lack of ground protection.

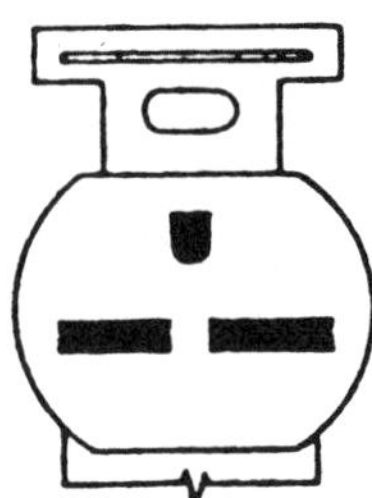

Tandem: Air conditioners, motors, and heaters of 230 volts use this unit. It is equipped with a ground prong and is used primarily on 230 volt circuits, where its blade shape prevents 115 volt units from being plugged in.

Twist-lock: This receptacle is available in 2, 3, and 4 prong units. Its major advantage is that the plug cannot be pulled out of the receptacle accidentally. The 3 and 4 prong units provide ground protection.

Direct-current: The main use for this receptacle is to keep the positive and negative conductors from being interchanged in D.C. systems. Some models have ground protection.

Crow's foot: This plug was an early attempt to provide ground protection in a receptacle. Unfortunately, the shape of the 2 prong plug could be modified with pliers, allowing it to be fitted into the receptacle. Also, the crow's-foot plug often had its ground prong removed and blades reshaped for use in standard 2 prong receptacles. Ground protection was lost in both cases, and it became obvious a change in design was needed.

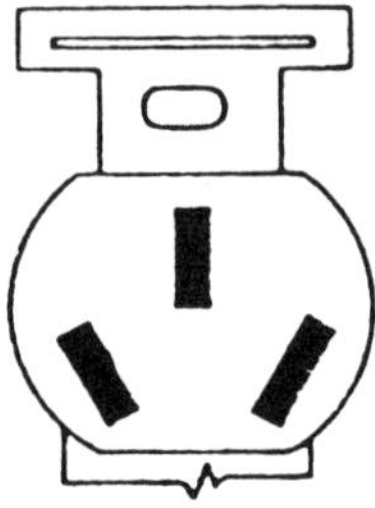

FIGURE 10-20 Typical receptacles and blade patterns. (Reprinted with permission from *Applications of Electrical Construction* by Robert K. Clidero and Kenneth H. Sharpe, General Publishing Company, Limited.)

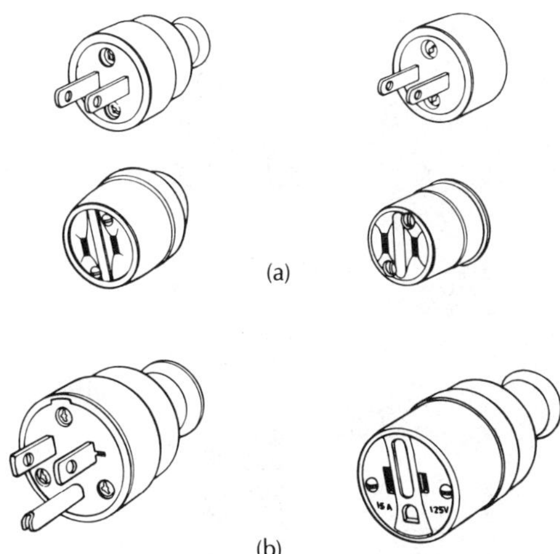

FIGURE 10-21 **Dead front caps and connectors.** (a) pole, 2 wire; (b) 2 pole, 3 wire. The illustrations show two types of male and female dead front caps and connectors (15 amp.). The male plug cap is designed to be inserted into the slots of a receptacle. It is usually attached to the end of line cords on electrical appliances, lamps, and power tools. The female plug cap is designed to receive the male plug cap. It is attached to one end of an extension cord, which has a male plug cap on the other end. Usually, both have the same blade pattern. (Courtesy of Smith and Stone Inc.)

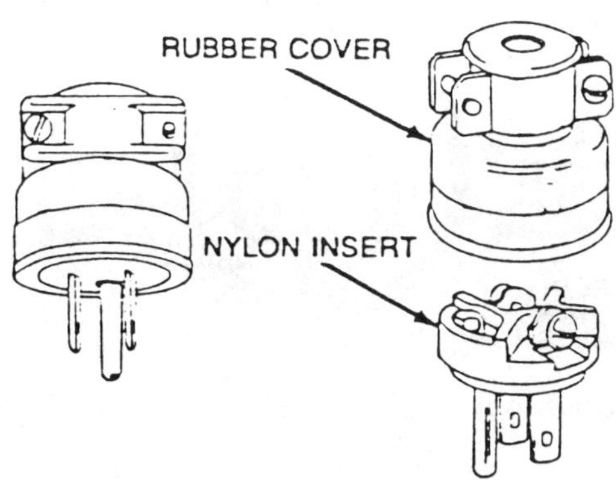

FIGURE 10-22 **Dead-front plug cap.** (Reprinted with permission from *Applications of Electrical Construction* by Robert K. Clidero and Kenneth H. Sharpe, General Publishing Company, Limited.)

Dead-Front Plug Caps

Dead-front plug caps, with the prongs and terminals assembled as a removable unit, are available. The cord connects to the rear of the unit. The front, which is the exposed portion of the plug cap, is free of terminals, conductors, and insulating disc.

Plug Cap Ratings

Plug caps are rated in volts and amps. The rating of the unit must be matched to the requirements of the circuit. If a light-duty unit is installed where a heavy-duty unit is needed, the plug will overheat. This can cause damage to the plug and/or receptacle and the conductor insulation. Look for the CSA or UL stamp on the cap: this is a guarantee that the manufacturer's ratings are correct.

Appliance Cap

Small portable appliances, such as tea kettles, frypans, and percolators, are often made with removable cord sets. These sets must have a plug that is easy to grip, provides strain relief for the cord, and resists heat.

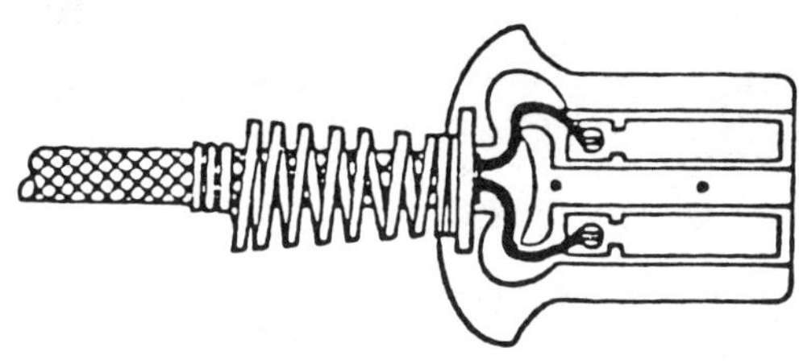

FIGURE 10-23 **Appliance cap.** (Reprinted with permission from *Applications of Electrical Construction* by Robert K. Clidero and Kenneth H. Sharpe, General Publishing Company, Ltd.)

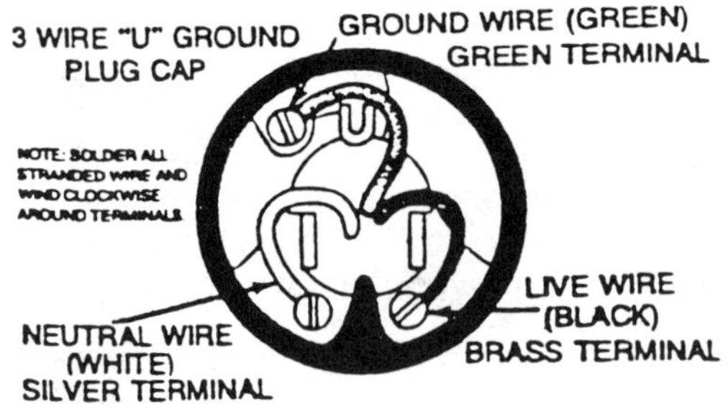

FIGURE 10-24 Plug cap connection. Many problems are created when plug caps are not properly connected. (Reprinted with permission from *Applications of Electrical Construction* by Robert K. Clidero and Kenneth H. Sharpe, General Publishing Company, Limited.)

Plug Cap Connection

Plug caps are often damaged by carelessness. For example, many people remove plugs from the receptacles by tugging on the cord. Figure 10-24 shows how line cords and plug caps are connected so that strain from pulling on the cord will be absorbed by the blades rather than by the terminals. To prevent loose strands of the flexible cord from slipping out of the terminal connection, the strands are twisted together and wound clockwise around the terminal screw. Soldering the groups of twisted strands before assembly also helps make the electrical connection secure.

Heavy Duty Plug Caps

Industrial or heavy-duty plug caps are now equipped with metal clamping devices to hold the cord in the plug cap (Figure 10-25). These devices are particularly useful on construction sites, where extension cords and caps are walked on, driven over, and treated roughly.

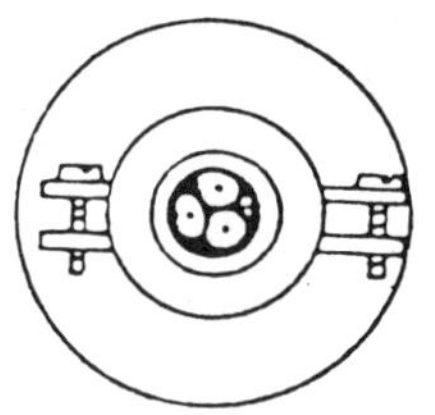

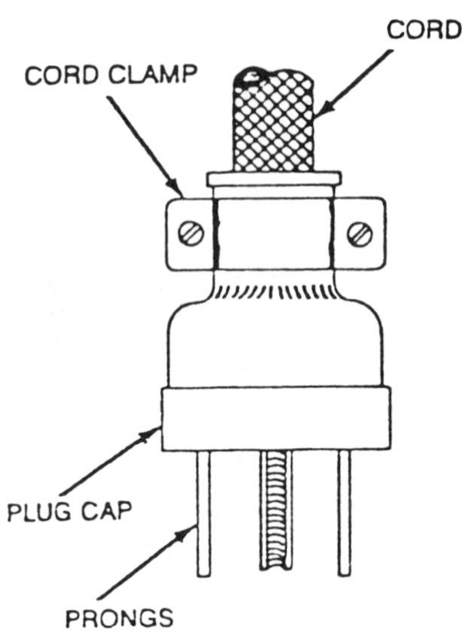

FIGURE 10-25 Industrial plug cap. A heavy-duty plug cap with cord clamp. (Reprinted with permission from *Applications of Electrical Construction* by Robert K. Clidero and Kenneth H. Sharpe, General Publishing Company, Limited.)

Heavy-Duty Range and Dryer Plug Cap and Cord Set

Each time an electric range or clothes dryer is connected to the cable in a house or apartment building, the cable is shortened slightly. Sometimes the cable is shortened to the point where it can no longer be used. The heavy-duty range and dryer plug and receptacle were designed to prevent that problem, as well as to allow the range and dryer to be pulled out from the wall for spring cleaning or simple removal. (Fig. 10-26.)

Some large stationary appliances, such as electric stoves and clothes dryers, are now being made with cord sets. This allows larger units to be pulled away from the wall for cleaning and to be quickly disconnected from the power source for servicing.

Mobile homes (trailers), electric stoves, and clothes dryers require heavy-duty cord caps for the power supply. In industry, cord fittings with current and voltage ratings other than the usual 10 to 15 amperes, 115 volt residential ratings are often required. Some examples are cord caps for welding machines, floor finishers, battery chargers, and marine shore lines.

THE IMPORTANCE OF GROUNDING

The words ground and earth mean the same thing. Thus, when any part of an electrical system is grounded, it is connected either directly or indirectly to earth. For reasons of safety, the neutral (white or gray) wire of all residential wiring systems is intentionally grounded.

In residential wiring, the grounded neutral wire is never interrupted by a fuse, circuit breaker, switch, or other device. The principal reason for system grounding is to limit the voltage to ground from rising above a safe value because of a fault outside the building. If, for example, outside wires are struck by lightning, the ground acts like a lightning rod to get rid of the very high electrical charge built up on the wires.

Equipment grounding is necessary to prevent electric shock to persons coming into contact with metallic objects that, either intentionally or accidentally, form part of the electrical system. If not grounded, a very serious shock hazard exists. Depending on the resistance of the person's body and the condition of the ground (dry, damp, or wet), the shock could even prove fatal.

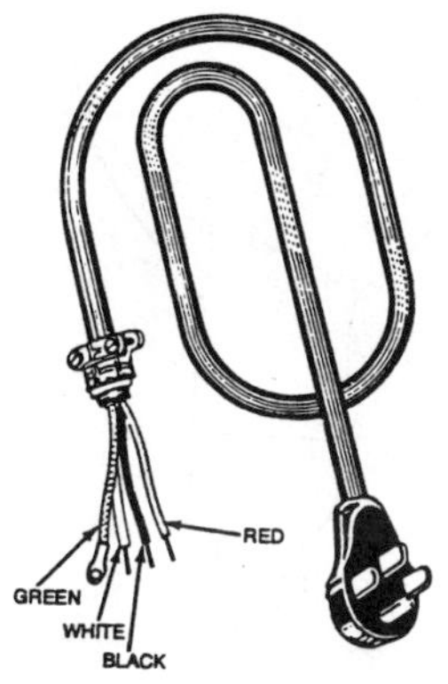

RANGE AND DRYER RECEPTACLE RATINGS 250 VOLTS 50 AMPS

FIGURE 10-26 Range and dryer plug cap and cord set. (Reprinted with permission from *Applications of Electrical Construction* by Robert K. Clidero and Kenneth H. Sharpe, General Publishing Company, Limited.)

10-4 Lighting

Incandescent lamps are used in fixtures that are designed for a particular lamp size and finish. For the most efficient results and proper light distribution, the correct lamp should be used. Reflectors are designed around the light centerlength of a particular lamp size.

In enclosed fixtures, the current trend to reduce lamp size has made it possible to now use higher wattage lamps. Excessive heat generated by these higher wattages can cause damage, and care should be exercised to conform to the wattage limitations of a particular fixture. (Fig. 10-27.)

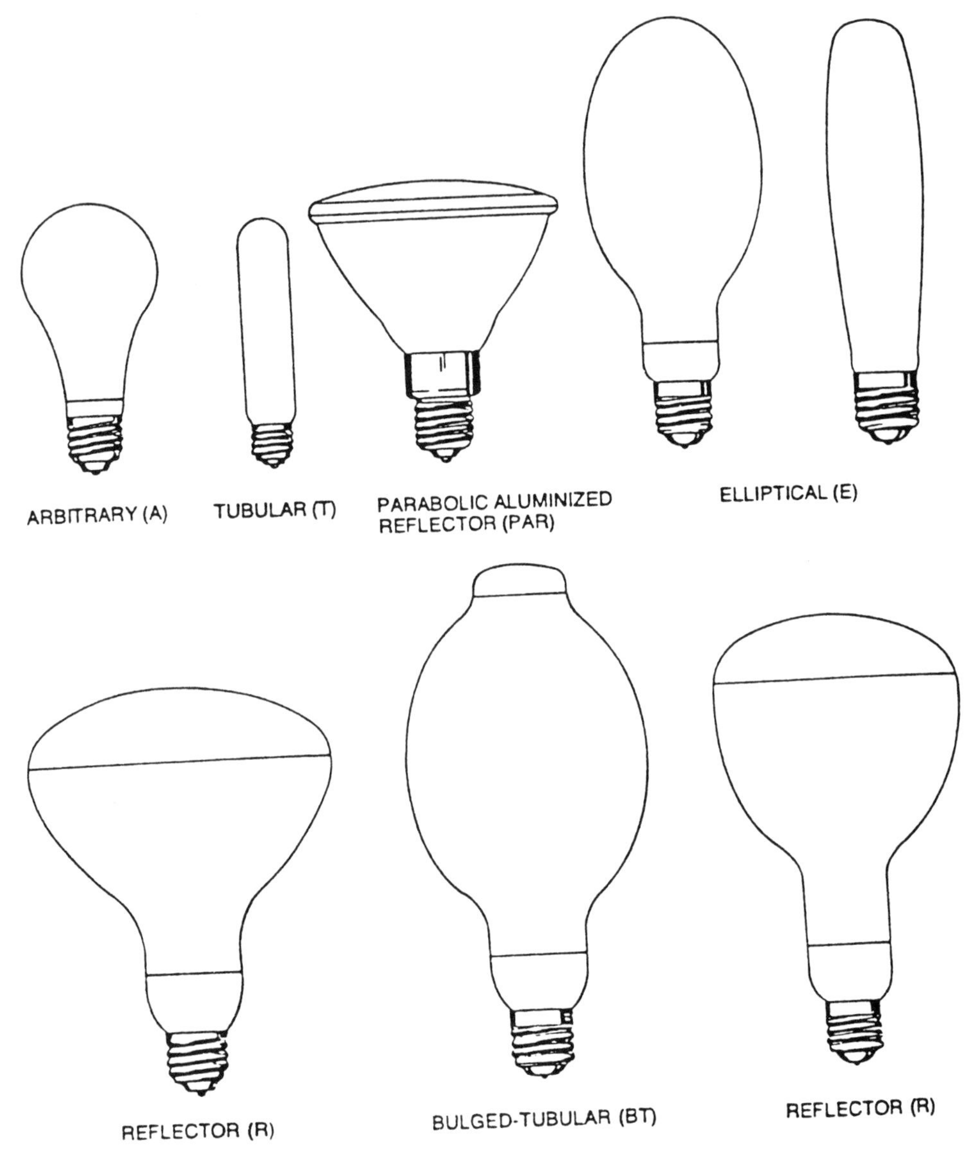

FIGURE 10-27 Typical incandescent lamps. (Courtesy of Canadian General Electric Company, Limited.)

INCANDESCENT LAMPS

Screw Base Sizes

Mogul base light bulbs range in size from 300 to 1,500 watts. Medium base is the common residential socket size from 7.5 to 300 watts. Intermediate base is used for outdoor Christmas lights (rating of 75 watts).

Candelabra base is used for indoor Christmas lights, as well as flame shaped lights. Miniature base is used for panel lights to illuminate dials. (Fig. 10-28.)

Voltage Ratings and Lamp Types

Voltage must also be taken into consideration when ordering general service lamps. Four separate voltage ratings are normally available. These are 115, 120, 125, and 130 volts. Incandescent lamps are designed to yield the maximum lighting economy when used on circuits of a voltage at or near their designed voltage, which is printed on the bulb. Under these conditions, the lamp will produce its rated values of life, watts, and light output.

Inside frosted lamps are used in most fixtures designed for lamps up to 100 watts in size. The frosted finish was developed to reduce lamp brightness, and does not appreciably reduce the light output.

Clear lamps are used in fixtures where control of light is required. Clear lamps should be used in reflectors having polished or etched reflecting surfaces and in enclosing globes or reflectors of prismatic glass to obtain the designed light distribution. This is particularly important where concentrating-type reflectors are mounted in high narrow bays.

White bowl lamps are used in reflector equipment of the dome type or the diffusing globe type where the lamp protrudes through the bottom of the fixture. The white bowl reduces the surface brightness and helps to reduce reflected glare from the working surfaces.

Silvered bowl lamps are designed principally for indirect lighting and for reflector equipment specially designed for it. Be sure that the fixture parts do not touch the lamp as the thermal stress may cause the bulb to crack and fail prematurely.

Reflector lamps are, in effect, a fixture in themselves. By putting the reflecting surface inside the lamp, the light can be controlled efficiently without depreciating due to the collection of dust and dirt. Flood (60°) and Spot (30°) beam spreads are available, together with a wide range of wattages, making these lamps useful in a wide variety of applications.

FIGURE 10-28 Screw base sizes. (Courtesy of Canadian General Electric Company.)

FLUORESCENT LIGHTING

Fluorescent lighting was first developed during the 1930s. The principle behind fluorescent lighting is simple, but it took years of research before it was developed into the familiar tube now used in modern lighting fixtures.

Fluorescent Tube Parts

The heart of the fluorescent fixture is the tube itself. The tube has several components.

Cathode: These small, oxide-coated filaments heat up and emit electrons into the tube. In some lamps, anodes are attached nearby to reduce the loss of wattage at the ends of the tube.

Mercury: Droplets of mercury are placed in the tube. They vaporize during the operation of the lamp and radiate light energy.

Filling Gas: A small amount of highly purified argon gas is also placed in the tube. This gas ionizes (producing electrical conductivity in gases) when sufficient voltage is applied, allowing current to flow readily through the tube.

Phosphor Coating: Much of the light energy produced by the mercury is ultraviolet and invisible to the naked eye. The phosphor coating reacts to the ultraviolet rays and turns the energy into visible light.

Fluorescent Starter

Some fluorescent fixtures need a small starting mechanism to establish an electron emission from the cathode (filament).

Preheat lamps use a starter in the circuit. This acts as a switch to close the circuit through the cathodes at each end of the lamp for a short period of time before an attempt is made to start the lamp. The resulting current flow through these cathodes causes them to heat up, and free electrons are emitted from the coating material on the cathodes. This action lowers the voltage necessary to start the lamp and when the starter switch opens, the voltage available from the ballast is sufficient to establish the arc through the lamp. In order to preheat the cathodes, a circuit through them must be available, so a bi-pin type of lamp base must be used.

Instant start or slimline lamp circuits use no starters. By applying a high open-circuit voltage across the lamp, electrons are ejected by field emission from the electrodes. These electrons flow through the lamp, ionize the gases, and initiate a mercury vapor discharge. Failure to preheat the cathode causes excessive wear on the coating material, and a more rugged triple wound coil is necessary. Since no preheating is required, a single pin base may be used with the lead wires joined together in the base pin.

Rapid start operation is a compromise between preheat and instant start. The rapid start principle of continuously heated cathodes allows a great deal of flexibility in lamp operation, such as dimming and flashing.

Fluorescent Lamp Colors

The popular demand for fluorescent lamps has necessitated an expansion of the available lamp colors. In order to meet the public demand for fluorescent light sources that would flatter specific areas of the color spectrum, the lamp industry has developed and is currently supplying seven shades of so-called white fluorescent light. These are Daylight, Cool White, Deluxe Cool White, White, Warm White, Deluxe Warm White, and Soft White. The light from each of these different colored light sources is flattering to a different portion of the color spectrum.

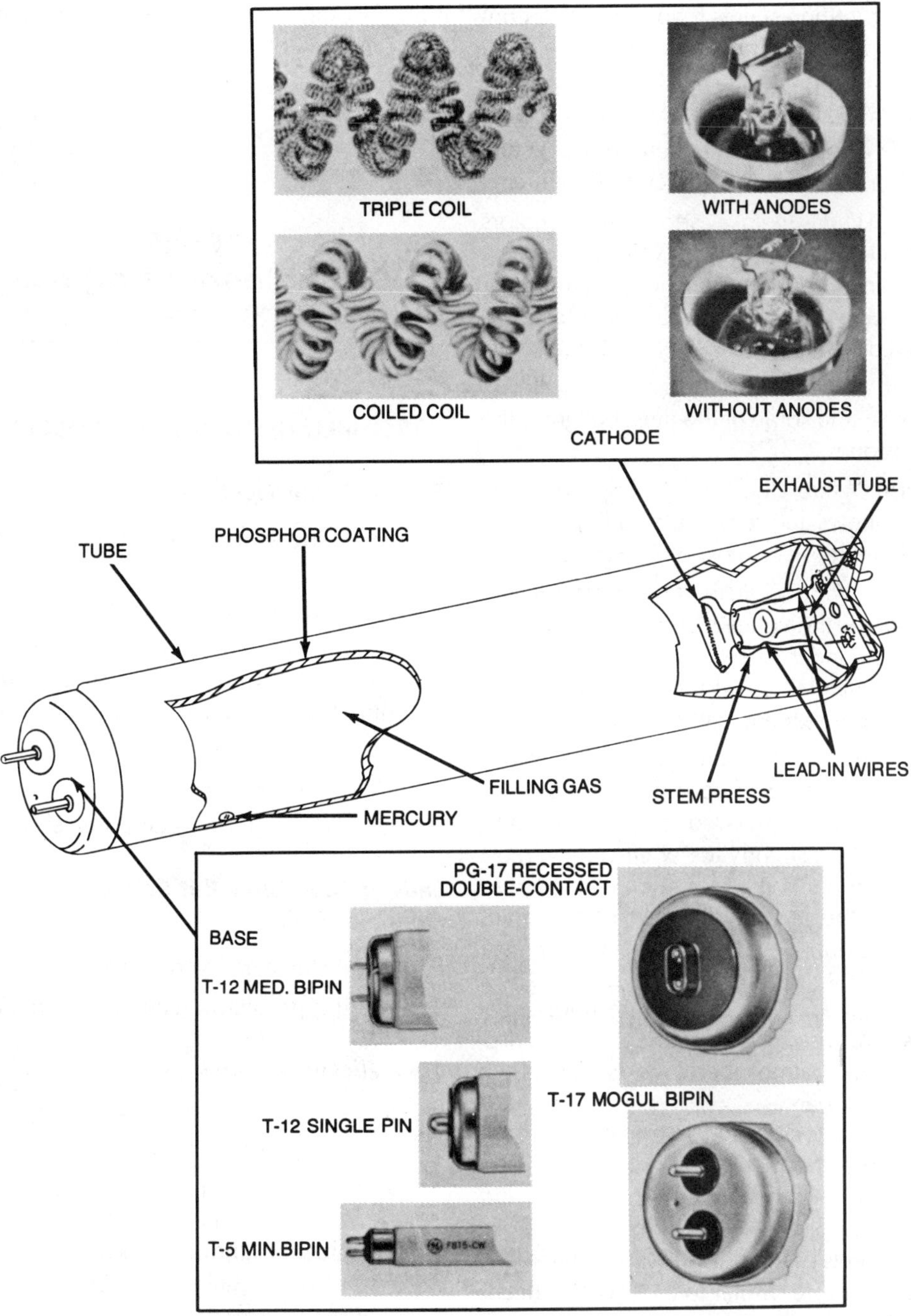

FIGURE 10-29 Typical fluorescent tube and components. (Courtesy of Canadian General Electric Company, Limited.)

Daylight fluorescents tend to create a cool atmosphere, but pale all colors except the blues and greens. They also emphasize the texture of many furs, however.

Cool White shows most colors without distortion, but has a tendency to gray them.

Cool White Deluxe shows most colors very clearly. Some of the yellows and reds appear as very warm. The greens appear light and clear. Some of the blues are grayed, while other blues are bright.

White tends to brighten the yellows, greens, and some of the tans, but grays the blue tones.

Warm White fluorescent lamps brighten the yellows and reds while adding warmth and clearness to most other colors.

Warm White Deluxe adds richness and brightens the yellows and reds. Blues and greens under these lamps will appear somewhat darker, while a slight yellowing of the blue-greens will be noted.

Soft White lamps have more red radiation than any other fluorescent lamps. Although the higher red output is accompanied by a slightly lower efficiency, most users are willing to sacrifice efficiency to obtain the desired natural look it gives complexions, merchandise, and displays.

Daylight and the cool white fluorescent lamps are used to create a cool, crisp, business-like atmosphere, as is desired in some factory areas.

The warm whites and soft white lamps are used more frequently in cafeterias, rest rooms, and theaters, where an intimate and restful atmosphere is desirable.

The effects of the deluxe warm white fluorescent lamp are similar to those of the incandescent lamp.

A colored material will always appear more favorable under a light that contains a high component of the same color.

10-5 Troubleshooting the System

TROUBLESHOOTING FLUORESCENTS

Tube Will Not Light

- –Fuse blown or circuit breaker switched off.
- –Tube burned out.
- –Tube pins not making contact with holders. For starter and rapid-start, rotate tube. For instant-start, make sure pins are firmly seated.
- –Defective starter—replace.
- –Defective ballast—call an electrician.

Ends of Tube Glow But Center Does Not Light:

- –Defective starter—replace.
- –If still a problem—call an electrician.

Tube Flickers or Blinks:

- –Normal with new tube. Should improve with use—if not, replace starter.
- –Tube pins not making proper contact with lamp holders. Rotate tube in holders for preheat and rapid-start types. For instant-start, make sure pins are fully seated in sockets.
- –Tube worn out—replace tube.

Fixture Hums or Buzzes:

–Call an electrician.

Brown or Grayish Bands About 2 Inches From Ends of Tube:

–Normal.

Dense Blackening at Ends of Tube:

–Tube worn out—replace tube. If tube is new, replace starter.

Slight Blackening at Ends of Tube:

–Tube nearly worn out—replace tube.

OVERLOADING A CIRCUIT

Plugging in an extra table lamp is unlikely to overload a circuit—such devices consume little electricity—but toasters, kettles, and irons are another matter. Before adding any heavy power user to a circuit, make sure it can bear the current it would carry.

Make an electrical circuit plan by listing lights and other devices, including any additions, that will operate simultaneously on the circuit, and total the wattage each consumes. The wattage is printed on incandescent bulbs and fluorescent tubes and on data plates of appliances. Then, *divide the total wattage by 120 to get the number of amperes of current.* The total amperage must not exceed the circuit capacity, which is marked on the fuse or circuit breaker.

The same calculation tells if an overload caused a tripped breaker or a blown fuse. Total the wattages of all devices in operation, and calculate the amperage to see if the circuit capacity was exceeded.

FUSES AND CIRCUIT BREAKERS

The fuses are the safety valves of the electrical system. Fuses of proper rating have been installed in accordance with the electrical code. They should not be replaced with fuses of a different rating. Usually a circuit has a maximum lighting load of 1,200 watts, and the fuses or circuit breakers are rated at 15 amperes for the circuit.

Fuses are actually metal resistors having very low resistance values. They are designed to "blow out" and thus open the circuit when the current exceeds the fuse's rated value. When the power consumed by the fuse raises the temperature of the metal too high, the metal melts and the fuse "blows." A fuse with too high of a rating may allow dangerously high currents to pass which may result in fire or death. (Fig. 10-10.)

DETECTING TROUBLE

A glance at a blown screw-in fuse often reveals that the circuit has been overloaded. An overload melts the strip, breaking the circuit. If the cause of a blown fuse is uncertain from observation, it will be necessary to calculate the amperage draw for the circuit by making an electrical circuit plan.

WHEN A FUSE BLOWS OR A CIRCUIT BREAKER GOES OUT

Dramatic evidence of overloaded circuits is seen when a fuse blows or a circuit breaker trips, causing a blackout. If there are enough circuits in the home wiring system, blackouts caused by overloading will seldom occur. Sometimes, however, a blackout occurs even in homes having plenty of branch circuits. These are usually caused by short circuits in

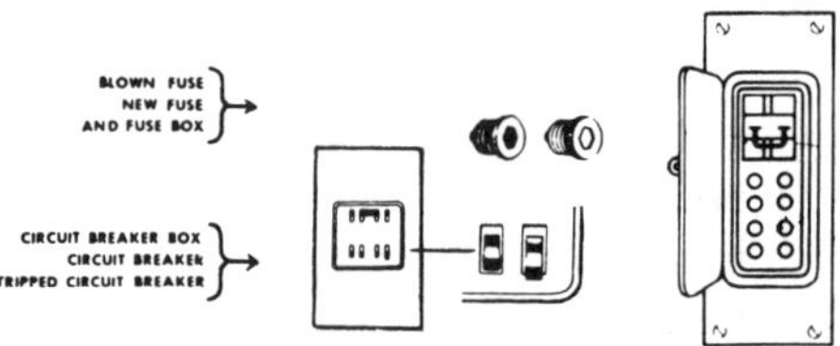

WHEN A FUSE BLOWS OR A CIRCUIT BREAKER GOES OUT

CHANGING A FUSE

1. Open Main Switch in the Service Entrance, to cut off current while you are working at the Branch Circuit Box.

2. Replace the blown fuse with a new one of proper size. They screw in and out just like light bulbs. Make sure your hands are dry, and stand on a dry board while doing this.

3. Close the Main Switch to restore service.

4. Throw away the blown fuse.

The fuse contains a metal link which will melt and cut off electricity from the Branch Circuit before the circuit wires become overheated from an overload or a short circuit. Electricity will remain "off" in that circuit until you have removed the cause of the difficulty and have replaced the fuse.

Be sure the new fuse is the correct size. Some people try to prevent fuse-blowing by replacing the original fuse with one of larger size. This is foolhardy. It eliminates the protection afforded by the correct size fuse. Fuses should blow, when an overload causes them to do so! That is your signal that something is wrong. When you permit an over-sized fuse to be used, you are risking permanent damage to the circuit wires within the walls, ceilings and floors of your home. Such damage may lead to fire!

RE-SETTING A CIRCUIT BREAKER

1. Push handle to extreme "off" position.

2. Return handle to "on" position.

The Circuit Breaker performs exactly the same function as the fuse, in a slightly different way. When an overload or a short circuit occurs in the Branch Circuit, the circuit breaker automatically trips open. No electricity will flow over that circuit until you have re-set the circuit breaker, after removing the cause of the difficulty.

FIGURE 10-30 **Fuses and circuit breakers.** (Courtesy of the Canadian Adequate Wiring Bureau.)

extension cords or appliances. Worn extension cords or faulty appliances are usually the cause of the short circuits.

TYPICAL FUSE PANEL

The typical fuse panel (see Figure 10-18) has the main fuses and two knife-blade fuses in the main pull-out block at the top of the panel.

Circuits for the lights and wall receptacles have 15 ampere fuses: the refrigerator has a 20 ampere fuse.

Each of the two pull-out blocks below the fuses contains a pair of ferrule-type cartridge fuses. These are used to protect the 240-volt kitchen range circuit.

Before removing any fuse to replace it, turn off all lights and devices on the circuit controlled by that fuse. To change a ferrule-type or knife-blade cartridge fuse, remove the appropriate block. For any other fuse, touch only the insulated outer rim to unscrew it. *Do not stand in a damp spot or put your hand on any object.*

WARNING

1. Always replace a blown 15 ampere fuse with only a new 15 ampere fuse. *Overfusing is dangerous.* Tighten fuses periodically to prevent overheating and blowing.
2. Never try to cheat the fuse system.
3. Don't remove the extra prong on a three-pronged plug to make it fit an existing outlet. The third prong provides grounding for your protection.

CARTRIDGE FUSE

Most cartridge fuses are time-delay. A blown cartridge fuse shows no visible sign of damage and must be checked with a continuity tester. The metal caps at the ends of a ferrule-type cartridge fuse (Figure 10-18) snap into spring-clip contacts in the fuse panel. Ferrule-type fuses are rated from 10 to 60 amperes and are generally used to protect separate circuits for individual large appliances, such as kitchen ranges. A cartridge fuse designed for more than 60 amperes, a so-called knife-blade fuse (Figure 10-32), has metal blades that snap into spring clips. In a home fuse panel such fuses are generally used in the main connection between the incoming power line and the branch circuits.

REMOVING A CARTRIDGE FUSE

Cartridge fuses are often used in auxiliary fuse boxes. To replace the fuses, open the box by moving the cutoff lever to the "off" position. Using the correct type of fuse puller, grasp the middle of the fuse and pull firmly to release it from the tight grip of the spring clips. If the circuit has just been in operation, be careful not to touch the metal end caps because they may be hot. Push the replacement fuse into the spring clips. When replacing a fuse in a panel block, pull the block out, then use the fuse puller.

TESTERS AND TOOLS

Essential to solving any kind of wiring problem are two inexpensive testers. The voltage tester has a neon bulb and two insulated wires that end in metal probes; its main purpose is to check that the current is off before you begin a job. It is also used with the power on, to check that voltage is available in wires.

Standard voltage testers can be used on circuits carrying 90 to 500 volts. There is also a low-voltage tester that looks similar, so be

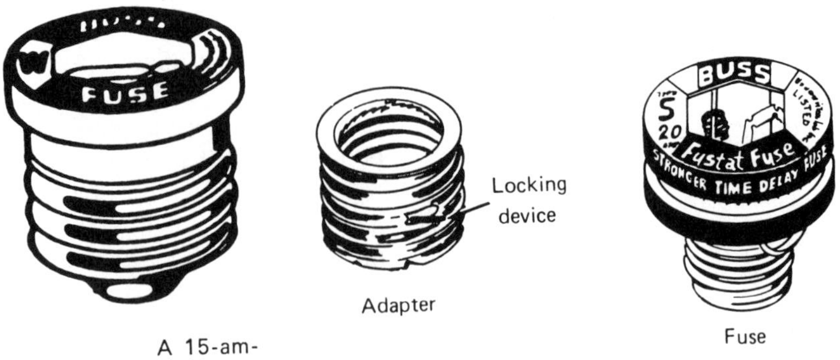

A 15-ampere plug-type fuse with Edison base and a window top

A Type S, or Fustat ® type of fuse

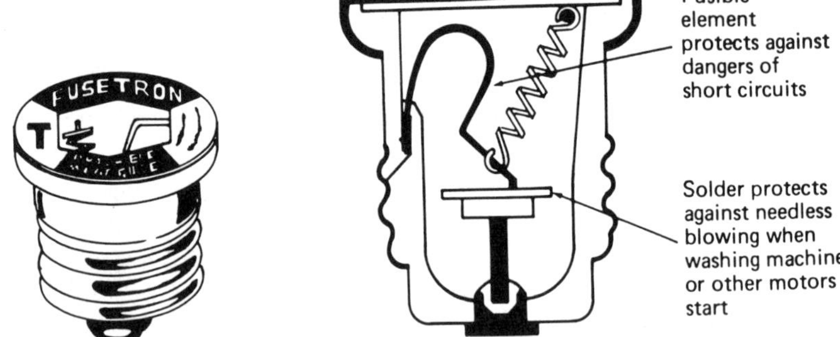

A typical time-lag fuse

FIGURE 10-31 Common screw-in type fuses. (Courtesy of Prentice-Hall, Inc.)

sure to check the rating on the package before you purchase one.

The continuity tester has its own source of power, a small battery, and is used only with the *power off* to pinpoint malfunctions in a wiring component—a broken switch or light socket, for instance.

Fuse Puller

If your service panel contains cartridge fuses, removing them for testing or replacement is done simply and safely with a fuse puller, which looks somewhat like pliers, but, for insulating purposes, is made entirely of a nonconducting material. Fuse pullers come in one size for cartridge fuses up to 60 amperes, and another for larger fuses.

Wall Receptacle Analyzer

To determine the condition of your electrical circuit, plug the analyzer into any single phase 125-volt 3 wire outlet. A combination of lighted and unlighted bulbs indicates circuit condition. This is not a comprehensive

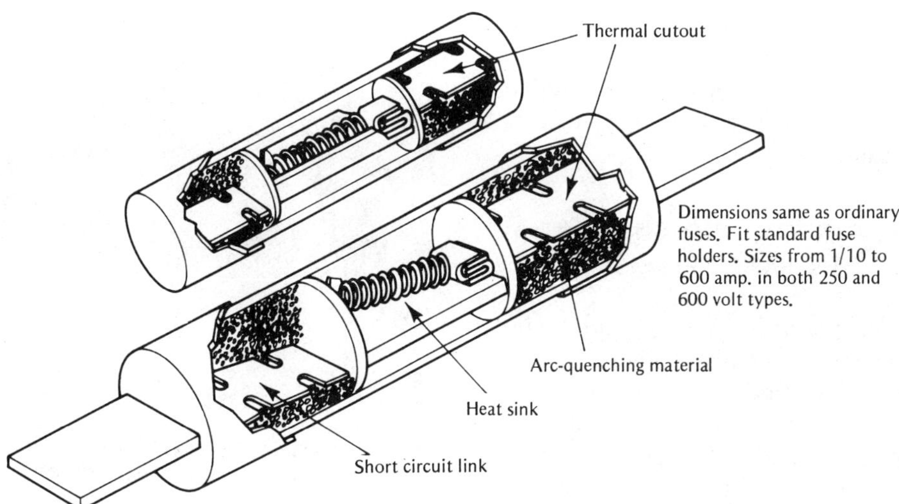

FIGURE 10-32 Cartridge fuses. Typical dual-element fuses are ideal for motor, heater, appliance, and lighting circuits. Have a time delay built in. (Courtesy of Bussmann Manufacturing Division, McGraw-Edison Company.)

diagnostic instrument. It indicates reversal of neutral and ground wire, quality of the ground path, and presence of multiple wiring errors. Refer faulty wiring indications to a qualified electrician for correction.

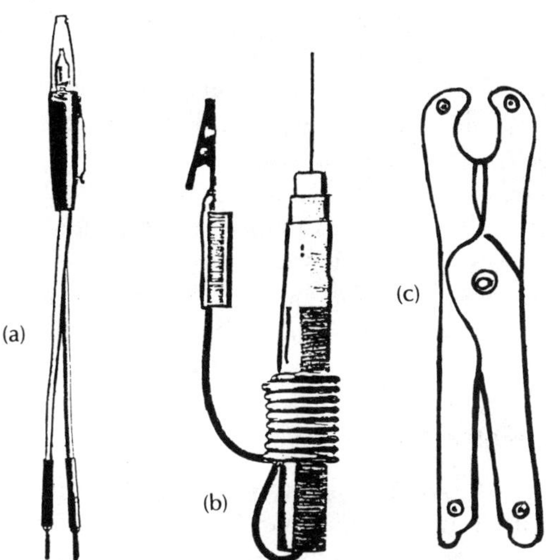

FIGURE 10-33 Testers and tools. (a) Voltage tester; (b) Continuity tester; (c) Fuse puller.

TESTING A CARTRIDGE FUSE

There is no external evidence of damage when a cartridge fuse blows, so if an appliance on a circuit protected by a cartridge fuse or fuses fails to operate, you have no way of knowing whether the fuse has blown or whether the appliance has simply failed. Remove the fuse and check it by touching a continuity tester to the metal end caps.

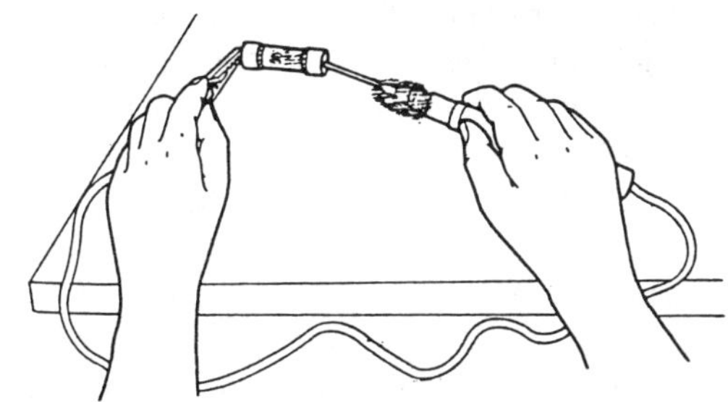

FIGURE 10-34 Testing a cartridge fuse.

(Figure 10-34) If the bulb lights, the fuse is good; the trouble is in the appliance. If the bulb does not light, the fuse is blown and needs replacement. If the appliance still does not work or the fuse blows again, call an electrician.

INTERCOM AND BUILDING ENTRANCE RELEASE*

The electric strike is wired into the building's intercom system and allows the tenants to control the front entrance door. In theory, only those people identified by the tenant should gain entrance. When properly specified, powered, and installed, the strike and the intercom have a long, maintenance-free life.

The fact that electric power is used for the strike's operation does not make it an electrical appliance. With few exceptions, the electrical circuit is designed to meet the needs of the strike and not the other way around. The strike should be selected and the electrician should provide the power at the point of installation. In a few cases, a strike must be selected to match an existing circuit.

For normal intermittent use the strike would require a 24-volt alternating current. Low voltage for electric strike operation is obtained by using a transformer to step down the normal 115 volt ac power to 12, 16, 24, or other low voltage.

When insufficient electrical power is suspected in a "weak" door release, a simple check can be made. Measure the voltage at the door release while the unit is activated. If the voltage is below that specified on the hardware schedule, the problem is in the circuit, probably due to an under-capacity transformer, if the current length is short. A long run may indicate both a transformer and a wire problem.

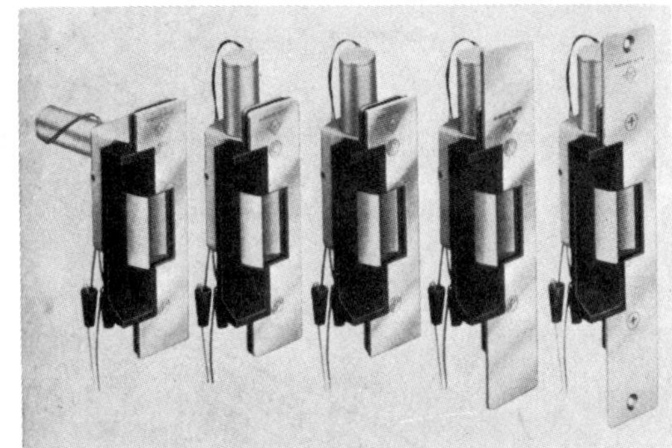

These five electric strikes are all designed to accept the same latch bolt, but differ in that they are designed for installation in different jambs. Left to right: wood, aluminum, hollow metal, aluminum (retrofit), and shallow wood.

FIGURE 10-35 Various electric strike designs. (Courtesy of Adams-Rite Manufacturing Company.)

OPERATION OF INTERCOM SYSTEM

Operation of the selected push button on the vestibule panel sounds a tone signal in the called apartment (the tone signal is also heard in the vestibule speaker). The tenant may talk and listen to the caller at the vestibule by depressing the TALK button. The tenant may open the door by pressing the DOOR button. A distinctive audible signal is provided at the vestibule to indicate door operation; holding the door button for a few seconds will allow the visitor ample time to enter.

Old Style System

The old style intercom system has two-button suite units. To get the best results with this system, visitors must speak close to the units.

*Adapted with permission from material provided by the Adams Rite Manufacturing Company.

Wall Mount Unit With a Telephone Receiver

To open the door, the tenant must depress the button on the receiver cradle. The receiver must be replaced vertically when the conversation is over. If the receiver is not properly placed in the holder, it will affect the operation of the rest of the system.

Three-Button System

One button is to talk, one is to listen, and one is to activate the door.

Two-Button System

One button is for communicating and the other button is for operating the door. Tenants must explain to their visitors that they cannot pause between words on this system or it will not work properly. This system is activated when a visitor starts talking, and will stop if the voice trails off.

If someone tapes down, or in some other manner depresses one of the buttons, it will affect the entire system.

All problems with these systems should be diagnosed and corrected by trained servicemen. Sometimes amateur repairmen only make the problems worse.

TELEVISION RECEPTION

By referring to the outline of the typical electrical system of an apartment building (Figure 10-15), you can trace the wiring circuit of the television system. The circuit originates with the antenna on the roof. The signal is amplified through strip amplifiers before being distributed to the individual apartments.

At the top of each series, the cable enters a "Riser Distribution Box" and is then wired to a vertical series of apartments to the individual wall plates. By following the drawing you can easily see why a problem with a wall plate in one apartment can affect the others on the same riser.

Cable Service

The difference between using an antenna and buying cable service is the substitution of the antenna for the antenna used by the cable company. The distribution cable, amplifiers, and wall plates used in buildings should be capable of giving the highest picture quality.

Television Complaints

By understanding the system you can follow a problem through to a logical resolution by asking the following questions:

1. Is the entire building experiencing a problem? You may have to contact various tenants in different locations in the building to find the answer. If they are all experiencing the problem, it is usually a problem with the antenna, the amplifier, or the cable company, depending on the system used.
2. If the entire building is not having the problem, visit the apartment with the problem. Check the following:
   —Is the set plugged in?
   —Is a flat lead wire being used? All wall plates must be connected to round coaxial cable.
   —Is the lead wire attached to the set? If not, secure the lead.
   —Make sure there are no other attachments that could be a problem.
3. Are complaints related to a specific channel?
4. Is there a relationship between the complaints and a vertical series of suites? If

yes, all suites on the riser must be checked, including vacant suites.

5. Does the person complaining understand how to operate and fine-tune the set?
6. Investigate and report all problems as soon as you have checked them. If you cannot correct them, a qualified technician must be called. *There is a tendency to hope the problem will go away.* As with other uncorrected problems, they only get worse.

A report outlining your investigation of the problem, explaining what you found during the initial investigation, will greatly assist the technician who is responding to the work order.

EMERGENCY POWER AND STANDBY BATTERIES

As apartment buildings became larger and more sophisticated, the need for emergency power became evident. Windowless corridors are completely dark without electricity.

Initially, the only standby power in a building was used to activate the fire alarm and control system. These systems used batteries as a power source. Today, we have standby generators, which power the fire alarm and control system, light up each floor, and power at least one elevator.

Power Source Systems

1. *Dry Cell Batteries:* Develop a direct current power of 120 volts for at least one half to one hour.
2. *Wet Cell Batteries:* Develop the same power as the dry cell battery but could provide up to two hours of power.
3. *Natural Gas-Fired Generator:* Battery ignited—activated automatically when the power is interrupted.
4. *Diesel Fuel-Fired Generator:* Battery ignited—activated automatically when the power is interrupted.

To ensure safety, all equipment and wiring must be CSA or UL approved. Each system should automatically switch the designed load from ac to dc upon failure or interruption of normal power.

All systems should be equipped with a battery charger and overcharge protection. The charger would automatically recharge the batteries when normal power is established.

Battery Test

Insert rubber tip of the hydrometer in the cell, hold the instrument in vertical position, squeeze the bulb, and draw up enough electrolyte to float the hydrometer freely, watching to see that the top of the hydrometer stem does not touch the rubber stopper at the top of the barrel. (Fig. 10-36.)

Read the specific gravity on the stem at the level of the liquid. Return electrolyte to the same cell from which it was taken. Rinse hydrometer thoroughly in water after each use.

Preventive Maintenance

1. Take specific gravity tests monthly and top up battery cells with distilled water when required.
2. Check for signs of battery corrosion and replace dry cell batteries immediately if they are corroded.
3. Electrical rooms should be properly ventilated.
4. Keep battery terminals clean—grease them for protection.
5. Replace any wet cell battery that does not hold a charge.
6. Once a month, activate the fast charge

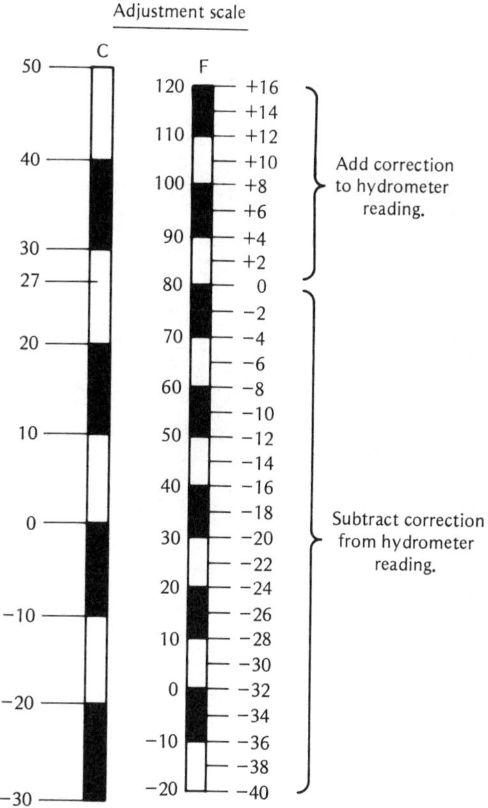

Automotive and radio batteries	
Full charged	1.285
Half charged	1.215
Discharged	1.150

Glass jar farm light batteries	
Full charged	1.225
Half charged	1.190
Discharged	1.160

FIGURE 10-36 Specific gravity readings at 80°F or 27°C.

unit for one hour and check to be sure that it is operating properly. *Be sure to turn off.*

7. Once a month, switch on the emergency power to ensure that it is operating properly and that the lights are not burned out or missing.

8. Under *no* circumstances should the emergency light be more than *25 watts* in each fixture. If we draw too much power, the batteries will not last. It should be noted that some fixtures may have one 60 watt bulb on the regular building power and one 25 watt bulb for emergency power.

9. The "Building Profile Statistics" (see Chapter 2) should have a listing of all equipment and fixtures wired to the emergency power.

10. Once a month, start the gas- or diesel-fired generators to ensure that they are operating properly and supplying the necessary power.

11. If the trouble light remains on without a power failure, call for service.

12. Specific gravity tests indicate when batteries are fully charged. If the green discs are down and the ampere meter shows no charging current, it indicates a fault in the charging equipment and a serviceman should be called.

GROUND FAULT DETECTORS

Since grounding is not considered complete protection, and to minimize the danger of electrocuting someone, we have, in addition to fuses or circuit breakers, ground fault interrupters. As little as 60 milliamperes of current can be fatal to a human. The ground fault device's job is to sense trouble the moment any current greater than 5 milliamperes starts to flow through ground, through a person, or through any other object not intended to carry the current. The device will snap the power off in twenty-five thousandths of a second.

Wherever these devices are installed (usually swimming pools and fountains), they must always be activated. Any problems with them must be considered an emergency and corrected immediately.

WARNING

The excess current that makes fuses blow can be caused by

—Plugging too many appliances into a circuit.

—Drawing so much electricity that resistance in the wire could produce enough heat to start a fire.

—A short circuit, perhaps caused by worn insulation that lets bare wires touch each other or the grounded frame of an appliance; this induces the danger of shock and produces a heavy heat generating surge of current.

Although circuit protectors will protect you from these consequences, they cannot cure an overload or short circuit. Before replacing a fuse, always find the cause of the trouble and correct it.

ELECTRIC HEATING

1. Check that all heating breakers are in the "ON" position (as need arises).
2. Check for overheated breakers at panel. If overheating at breakers occurs, engage an electrician for repairs.
3. Visually check driving ramp for operation.

10-6 Timers, Motors, and Their Controls

THE TWENTY-FOUR HOUR TIMER

Most timers use clock motors and work like clocks. The timer has no hands, and its face bears numerals covering twenty-four hours that rotate. Adjustable trippers (dogs) on the rim of the face start or stop motors operating various equipment.

Timers are also used to turn on and off morality lighting outside the building. Some buildings now use electric eye cells for this job, which are activated by darkness and light and do not need seasonal adjustment.

The dark areas on the timers indicate night, and light areas indicate daylight. Black trippers indicate the off tripper. White trippers are the on trippers.

It is wise to chart everything controlled by timers so that everyone is aware of the control and the times they are operated.

MOTOR CONTROLS*

The motor, machine, and motor controller are interrelated and need to be considered as

*Reprinted with permission from *Motor Control Fundamentals*, courtesy of Square D Company Canada, Limited.

a package when choosing a specific device for a particular application. First establish whether the service is direct current (dc) or alternating current (ac). If ac, determine the number of phases and frequency, and the voltage. The motor should be matched to the electrical service, and correctly sized for the machine load (horsepower rating). Other considerations include motor speed and torque. To select proper protection for the motor, its *full load current* rating, service factor, and time rating must be known.

The controller's main responsibility is to start and stop the motor, and protect the motor, machine, and operator. The controller might also be called on to provide supplementary functions, which could include reversing, jogging or inching, or plugging operating at several speeds, or at reduced levels of current and motor torque.

Controller enclosures serve to provide protection for operating personnel by preventing accidental contact with live parts. In certain applications, the controller itself must be protected from a variety of environmental conditions, including:

–Water, rain, snow, or sleet
–dirt or non-combustible dust
–cutting oils, coolants, or lubricants

Motor controls cover a broad classification of functions:

1. The means of connecting and disconnecting motors to and from their power supply; for large motors, to limit the initial in-rush of current upon starting.
2. A means of protecting motors from excessive heat due to abnormally high current flow.
3. The means for determining when a motor is to run and when it is to stop. This may be accomplished manually or it may be automatic, or it may be a combination of both.

Connecting and Disconnecting Motors

Each motor of any consequence will have its own branch feeder. The branch feeder usually is a smaller wire size than the circuit from which it is supplied. Each feeder, therefore, must have protection appropriate to the current-carrying capacity of its wires. This protection is provided by either a circuit breaker or fuse and switch. However, the branch circuit protection must carry the starting current of the motor and so must carry currents at least several times the normal running current of the motor. Sustaining this perhaps 20 percent excess of rated running current will damage the motor insulation.

An ordinary switch is, therefore, not used for normal motor starting and stopping, but only to de-energize the branch feeder and the motor for service purposes or for emergency use.

Knife-Switch or Safety Disconnect

Another aspect of disconnecting motors is the safety disconnect. The branch feeder switch or circuit breaker may not be in sight of the motor. If it is not, then another switch, normally a knife-switch, is required by electrical codes. This additional switch must be mounted in sight of the motor so that a person working on the motor, or the equipment it drives, will not be subjected to electrical or mechanical injury because of the closing of a remotely-located switch or breaker.

The knife-switch, or safety disconnect, should not be used as an operational switch, but should be opened only after the motor has been stopped by other means, or in the event of an emergency.

Warning

Experienced electricians usually do not stand in front of a knife-switch when it is being operated. The safest way is to keep the face and body off to one side and use the left hand to operate the switch. Enclosed knife-switches should only be operated with the doors closed.

Sequence Control

In systems having more than one motor-driven device (Figure 10-37), it is frequently desired that the system be put into operation when only one of the motors is manually started, as by pushing a start button.

Once the first motor runs, the other motors are to automatically run unless some safety devices associated with the subsequent motors are tripped. It is also desired that the subsequent motors not run unless the first motor is running.

An example of such an operation is the sequencing of the components of an air conditioning system shown in Figure 10-37.

Sequence Control in an Air Conditioning System

—The fan manually started and stopped.

—A thermal switch will shut the fan in the event of a fire in the building.

—When the fan runs, it is desired that the cooling equipment will run if the cooling switch is on, but the refrigerant compressor must not run unless the condenser water pump is running.

—The cooling tower fan is to run when the pump runs, except that it should stop if the cooling tower water is cooled sufficiently without operation of the fan.

MOTOR STARTERS

It is generally desired that some motors be operated automatically during their normal operational function. The device used for this purpose must be capable of repeatedly interrupting the motor current without damaging the motor. The motor must also operate automatically in response to the operation of a remote control device.

Because of the various sizes of motors and the variation of starting current, various types of motor starters are required (see Figures 10–38, 10–39, and 10–40). The type of starter is determined by the size of the motor.

Nearly all motors draw more current during the starting period than when rotating at

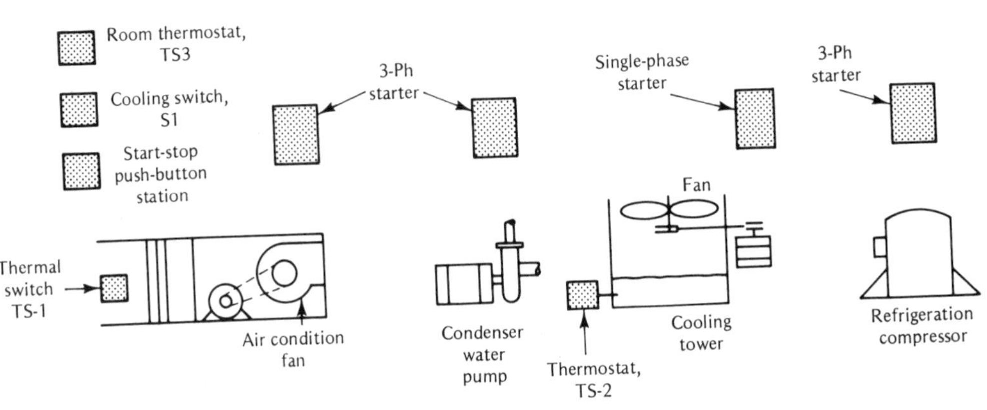

FIGURE 10-37 **Sequence control in an air conditioning system.**

operating speed. Motors are rated in horsepower (Hp). The higher the Hp rating of the motor, the higher the starting and running currents will be. Proper control of incoming current extends the life span of the motor. Excessive current draw will severely damage or burn the motor's windings. Most electric motors have a starting current that is three to five times the normal running current.

A motor starter, also called a motor controller, is a device that combines a contactor and thermal overload relays (Figure 10-43). There are two general classifications of motor starters:

1. *The across-the-line starter,* in which full line voltage is applied to the motor.
2. *The reduced voltage starters,* or starters using other principles to limit the starting current.

FIGURE 10-38 Motor starter. Typical remote push button start/stop control station. (Courtesy of Square D Company Canada, Limited.)

Across-the-Line Starters

The across-the-line starters may be either manual or magnetic. The manual starter is operated by pushing a button on the starter enclosure cover that mechanically operates the starter. Manual starters for single-phase motors are popular because they supply both motor protection and are used as a branch feeder disconnect.

Another important function of the control switch is to open the circuit, allowing the motor to stop. The switch or control device must have a very strong spring action to open the contacts quickly. Otherwise, there may be considerable damage to the switch.

Section 28 of the Canadian Electrical Code recommends that a control switch be located within sight of the motor. This allows the operator to check that there is no possible danger to equipment or persons before starting a motor.

Magnetic Motor Control

The second type of across-the-line motor starter is the magnetic controller. This very useful starter uses an electromagnet to activate the motor control switch. The main feature of this unit is the low voltage protection. There are three advantages to this type of control:

1. The loss of line voltage and the possible overheating of a motor allows the magnet to disengage and to open the motor circuit. It must be started again by an operator. This safety feature is useful in industrial plants.
2. A great variety of activating devices can be used, such as push buttons, limit, float, and pressure switches, and foot controls.

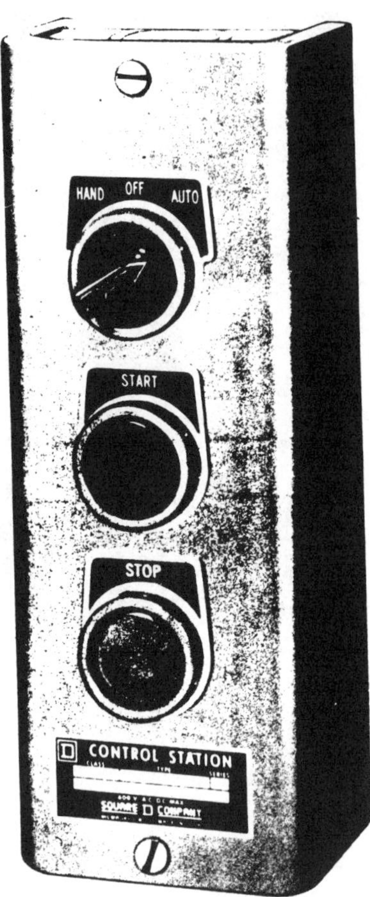

FIGURE 10-39 **Motor starter.** Typical push button control station for manual/automatic control. (Courtesy of Square D Company Canada, Limited.)

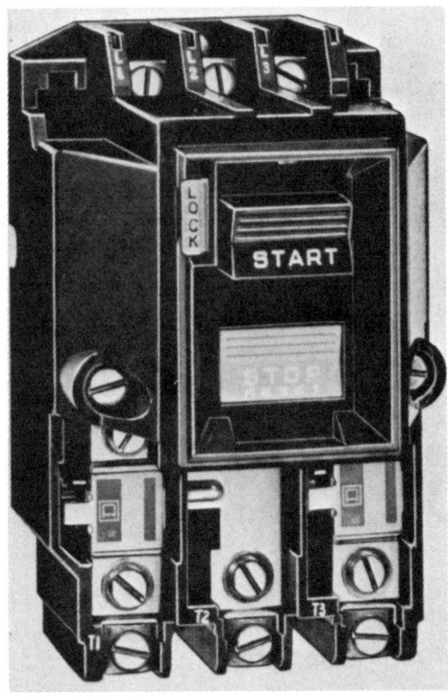

FIGURE 10-40 **Motor starters.** A more sophisticated 3 phase switch with thermal overload protection. This switch can control a 600 volt motor with ratings of up to 10 Hp. (Courtesy of Square D Company Canada, Limited.)

3. The use of low voltage in control circuits. Service and maintenance to the control circuit is less dangerous if 115 volts is used to control a 575-volt motor circuit.

MOTOR PROBLEMS

Even the best of the world's electric motors can develop occasional problems; many of them due to causes outside the motor itself. Like humans, motors usually give warning of their impending ills. If proper treatment is given at once, major damage and resultant stoppages can be averted.

Efficient motor maintenance requires the use of correct testing and regular inspections. Between inspections, alertness to the first signs of motor ailments can nip a problem in the bud.

There are symptoms that you can see, some that you can hear, and some that you can feel. Building operating staff should be trained to be alert to the problems listed. Most problems will be recognized and cor-

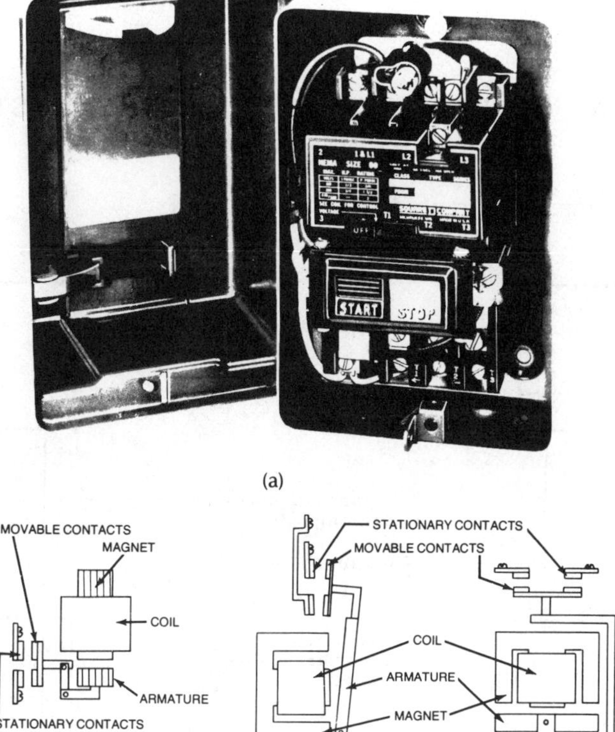

FIGURE 10-41 Motor starters. (a) Typical self-contained, 3 phase magnetic motor starter (with pilot light); (b) Three basic methods for operating magnetic motor starter contacts. (Courtesy of Square D Company Canada, Limited.)

rected during the daily "look, listen, and touch" inspections.

Overload

Motor Overload: This will cause motors to heat up and eventually to break down or burn out. Capacity is usually rated below their breaking point. Do not deliberately make a motor carry too great a mechanical load.

Causes of Motor Overload:

1. Error in application.
2. Obstruction in drive on the machine driven.
3. Excessive friction within the motor.
4. Efforts to obtain greater output from driven machine than motor is capable of carrying.

Results of Motor Overload:

1. Insulation will be damaged.
2. Soldered connections melted.
3. Burned out bearings.

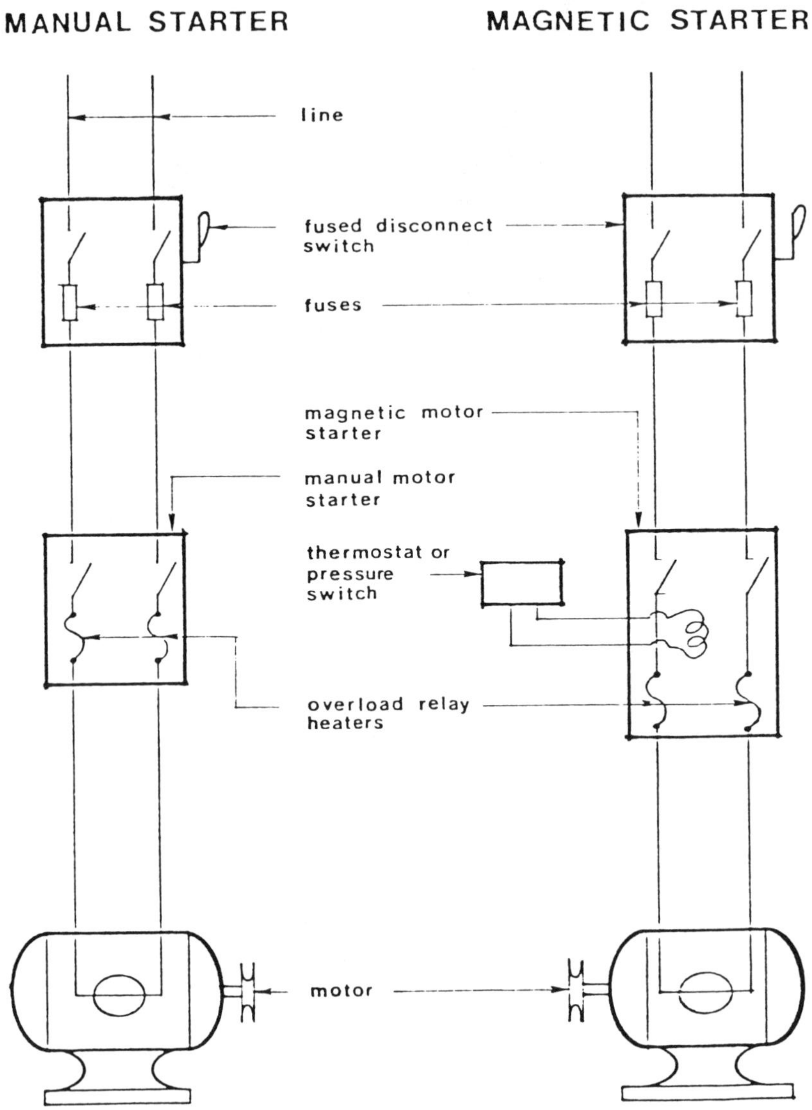

FIGURE 10-42 Magnetic motor control sequence. (Courtesy of Cadillac-Fairview Corporation, Limited.)

*Overload Protection**

An overload results in a rise in temperature in the motor windings. The larger the overload, the more quickly the temperature will increase to a point damaging to the insulation and lubrication of the motor. An inverse relationship, therefore, exists between current and time—the higher the current, the shorter the time before motor damage or "burn out" can occur.

All overloads shorten motor life by deteriorating the insulation. Relatively small overloads of short duration cause little damage, but, if sustained, can be just as harmful as overloads of greater magnitude.

Overload Relays

The overload relay is the heart of motor protection. Like the dual element fuse, the overload relay has inverse trip time characteristics, permitting it to hold in during the accelerating period (when inrush current is drawn), yet providing protection on small overloads when the motor is running. Unlike the fuse, the overload relay is renewable and can withstand repeated trip and reset cycles without need of replacement.

The overload relay consists of a current-sensing unit connected in the line to the motor, plus a mechanism, actuated by the sensing unit, which directly or indirectly serves to break the circuit. (Fig. 10-43.)

Underload

Underloading a motor is as improper as overloading it. Motors working only partly loaded will drop the "power factor" (ratio of power to total power), causing a higher energy cost.

To overcome a "low power factor" condition, the rated capacity of each induction motor and actual load should be determined and the data listed. This may indicate that a change in the motor is neccessary once the facts are gathered and assessed.

Service Record Label

–Tag number on the motor should be the same as the label equipment number.

–*All service* on the motor must be recorded on the label.

–If motor is replaced, the record label should go with the motor.

–A label should be attached to each new motor. (Fig. 10-44.)

How to Eliminate Motor Problems[1]

1. Daily "look, listen, and touch" inspections.
2. Keep motors wiped clean.
3. Regular, proper lubrication.
4. Report any unusual smells or noises—could be a sign of trouble.

10-7 Electrical Appliances

APPLIANCE PROBLEMS

Large appliances have become indispensable in the modern household. The energy they consume substitutes for the human

* Reprinted with permission from *Motor Control Fundamentals,* Courtesy of Square D Company Canada, Limited.

[1]See Chapter 11, "Mechanical Services" for details about motor service.

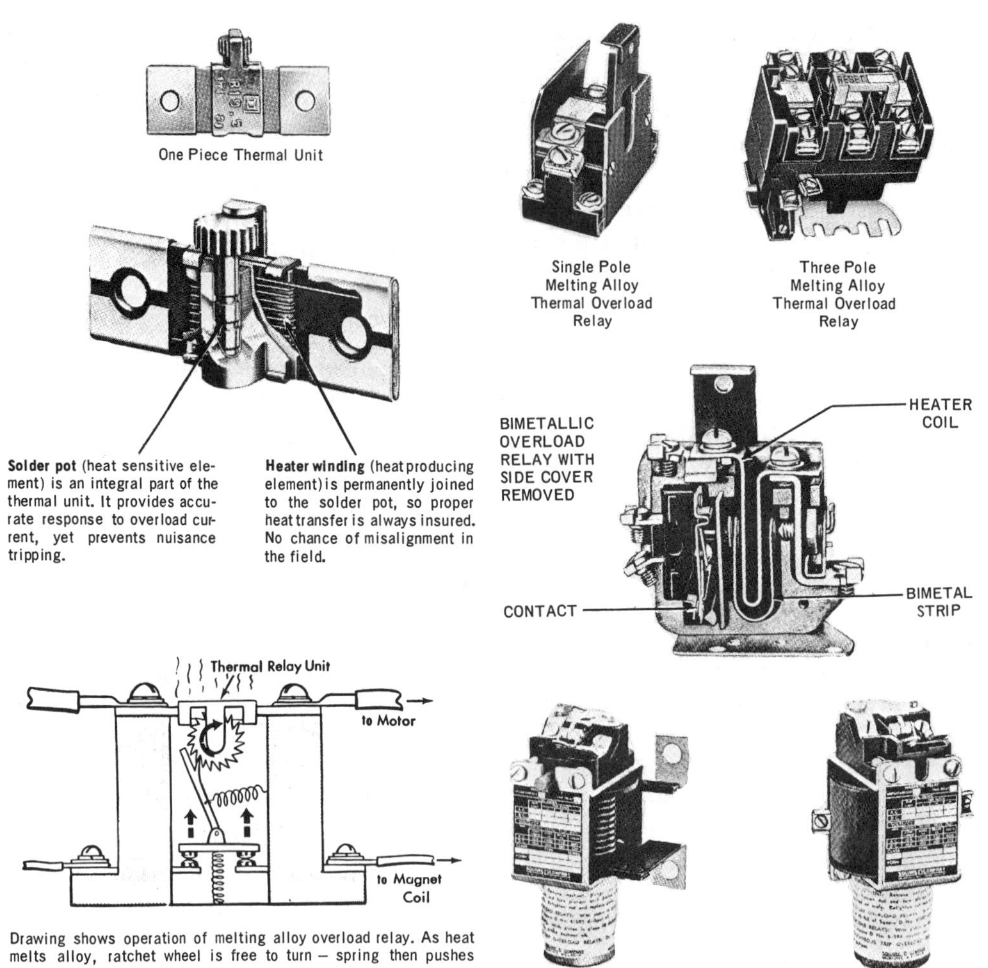

FIGURE 10-43 Overload relays. (Courtesy of Square D Company Canada, Limited.)

energy that hard manual labor once demanded—washing and drying clothes, hauling in ice, chopping wood or shoveling coal.

While these appliances have freed people from time-consuming household tasks, people, in turn, have become dependent on them. It is essential, therefore, that we understand how the appliances work and that we are able to diagnose problems and cut back on the downtime when they break down.

Failures are generally easily detected, through the senses:

–by smelling a motor burnout

–by hearing a funny or unfamiliar sound

The repair technician uses a systematic analysis to help him isolate the problem faster. Is it a mechanical or electrical problem?

Mechanical problems include

–motors

SERVICE RECORD FOR ________________ EQUIPMENT NO. ________

DATE	DESCRIPTION OF WORK COMPLETED	W/O #	SIGNATURE

FIGURE 10-44 Service record label. (Courtesy of Cadillac-Fairview Corporation, Limited.)

–pumps
–compressors
–valves
–heaters

Electrical problems include

–timers
–switches
–water level switches
–door interlocks
–thermostats
–heaters, fuses, etc.

When reporting a problem, always provide as much information as possible. Describe the appliance's failure symptoms and give the serviceman a head start.

TROUBLESHOOTING THE REFRIGERATOR

No Refrigeration:

Classified as a priority call and should be phoned in immediately and serviced as soon as possible.

Refrigerator Will Not Run:

Is interior light operating when door is opened? Check if unit is plugged in.

If light is operating when door is opened, check to see if cold control dial is turned to the "ON" position.

If no light, check for blown fuse or tripped breaker.

If bulb is burned out, replace bulb.

Power Has Failed:

Keep freezer door closed. (If power will be off for only four hours, no precautionary measures are necessary.)

If power will be off any longer than four hours, tenant should obtain dry ice and place in the freezer compartment or take food to the nearest food locker plant or to a friend.

Ice Cream Is Warm and Soft:

Is cold control turned to the cold position? (Advise tenant that ice cream does not have to be brick hard for preservation.)

Advise tenant to store ice cream on the

bottom of freezer compartment, and not on the freezer door inner panel shelf.

Advise that manual refrigerators will not keep all types of ice cream hard enough. (A one door manual defrost refrigerator does not have a true freezer area.)

Excessive Running Time:

Advise tenant that new model refrigerators are designed to maintain more even temperatures, and to do this, they must run a long time.

The food capacity of a new model refrigerator is greater, and so there is more heat to remove.

Door Operation:

If the tenant wants the door to close when he releases it, the refrigerator must be raised slightly at the front by turning down leveling legs.

Noisy:

Machine not level—adjust screw at base.

Odors:

Check defrost drain pan under refrigerator. (Advise resident to remove the lower panel to gain access to the defrost drain pan.)

Advise tenant that all food must be covered.

Advise tenant to wash out refrigerator with baking soda and water solution.

Advise tenant to place charcoal in the refrigerator, which helps to remove odors.

Excessive Frost Accumulation:

Unplug refrigerator for a couple of hours before serviceman arrives.

If too much ice, problem could be caused by the following:

–door open too often
–faulty door seal
–air humidity too high

TROUBLESHOOTING THE ELECTRIC RANGE

Oven Will Not Heat:

Is clock reset to "manual" position?
Check for blown fuse in oven circuit.
Is control set properly?

Oven Not Baking Properly:

Is oven control set at proper temperature for food being baked?

Did resident set control correctly? Modern ranges have automatic "preheat." If control was turned to "broil" and then turned back to the desired temperature position, only the broil element will be working. Advise tenant to turn control to the "off" position and select the desired temperature directly.

Are shelves covered with aluminum foil? This restricts heat circulation.

Keep baking pans in center of oven.

If more than one pan, arrange pans to allow free circulation of air. Pans and cooking sheets that are too large will cause burning on edges.

Automatic Oven Cooking:

Push in start knob and set to when you want food to start cooking.

Push in stop knob and set to when you want food to stop cooking.

Turn oven control to desired temperature.

Elements:

If no elements are heating, check the fuse or circuit breaker and replace defective fuse.

If one element is not working, replace defective fuse.

If there is not sufficient heat, check cartridge fuse.

Check plug in element with a continuity tester. If circuit O.K., plug in new element.

If unable to correct, call for service.

TROUBLESHOOTING THE GAS RANGE

Top Burner Will Not Light:

If pilot light out, re-light pilot.

If ports in burners are clogged, clean with a pin; if necessary, use a wirebrush.

Pilot Light Goes Out:

Partially close mixer plate, and adjust pilot to three-quarters of an inch.

Gas Odor:

Shut off main gas valve.

Call the gas company immediately.

Do not use the range until it has been checked.

TROUBLESHOOTING THE CLOTHES DRYER

Machine Won't Run:

Is the cord plugged in?

Check fuses or circuit breakers.

Door open or defective door switch—call for service.

Machine Runs But Won't Heat:

Defective thermostat or element—call for service.

Check fuses or circuit breakers.

Machine Runs But Does Not Dry Clothes:

Blocked lint trap or exhaust duct—clean the duct.

Machine overloaded—insufficient drying time.

Drum Will Not Rotate:

Broken belt or tension spring.

Dryer Runs With Door Open:

Defective door switch—call for service.

TROUBLESHOOTING THE AUTOMATIC WASHER

Machine Won't Run:

Is the cord plugged in?

Are house fuses blown or breakers kicked off?

Machine Runs But Water Will Not Enter Tub:

If machine makes buzzing sound when it should be filling, one or both of the water faucets may be closed. Both hot and cold water faucets must be open.

New plumbing: Sand or plumbing compound can accumulate in hose screens at faucets or machine. Remove hoses from faucets and clean screens in hoses and water inlet valve.

No Hot Water:

Is hot water supply depleted?

Fill hoses may be reversed (hot to cold, cold to hot). Usually this only occurs on a new installation or when some plumbing work has been done and machine has been disconnected.

Water Keeps Draining From Machine:

Has drain hose fallen or dropped lower than water level in machine? If so, water will siphon out of washer. Minimum height of a standpipe should be 34 inches from the floor.

Vibrates on the Spin Cycle:

Load may be out of balance. Stop washer and balance load, then proceed with cycle. Small loads tend to bunch to one side.

Small throw rugs, bedspreads, mattress covers, and blankets become out of balance very easily. Always wash two small throw rugs, as one may throw the machine off balance.

Machine Fails to Spin:

Washer will not spin with lid open.

Too many suds can cause a "suds lock" and can interfere with good spinning and rinsing action. If spin speed appears very slow, and excess suds are indicated, put load through a second cycle.

Noisy During Agitation Cycle:

If noise occurs just at start of wash or rinse period after it fills, it is gear case shifting into agitation.

10-8 How to Budget the Necessary Funds

The funds for electrical services are basically meant for appliances, wiring distribution, fire protection, and the television system.

To decide about the funds needed to maintain the appliances in an apartment building, it is helpful to review the kind of problems that may appear and the cost to repair them, the age of the equipment, and their condition. Some plan of replacement should be established so that these costs can be handled from the revenue generated by the building. *Do not replace them in an ad hoc manner.*

Inventory lists should be made from the spare parts on hand at the building. This should include spare parts for appliances, fuses, fixtures, and light bulbs.

Naturally, equipment records should be available for the appliances, emergency lighting, intercom, F.M., or the television system. Review the cable contract if there is one. This should articulate the monthly rate and the responsibility and cost for maintaining the distribution system.

10-9 Safety Tips

1. Whenever there is a possible danger to eyes or hands, *wear safety glasses and gloves. Safety shoes,* with rubber soles and heels, should also be worn.
2. *Do not wear loose clothing* near motors or belts.
3. *Use circuit testers* only as directed on page 483-486.
4. *Never touch* parts of the plumbing system or gas piping when checking electrical problems or while using an electrical appliance.
5. *Do not stand on a damp floor* when working with wiring. When using an appliance, be sure your hands are dry.

APPLIANCES	ACCOUNT NUMBERS 47	SUB TOTALS	TOTAL
DISHWASHERS	471		
DRYERS	472		
FLOOR POLISHERS	473		
REFRIGERATORS	474		
STOVES	475		
VACUUM CLEANERS	476		

WIRING DISTRIBUTION	48	TOTAL	
EMERGENCY LIGHTING	481		
F.M. RADIO	482		
FIXTURES & LIGHT BULBS	483		
FUSES & PANELS	484		
WIRING	485		

FIGURE 10-45 Summary of budget expense schedules, repair and maintenance categories; electrical services.

Dry skin resists electricity 500 times better than wet skin. Wear rubber soles and heels.

6. Always unplug a lamp or appliance before working on it. Pull the plug itself—*do not pull on the cord.* Replace any frayed cords or broken plugs promptly.
7. Be careful when putting up a steel or wooden fence or patio screen. Any tool cutting through an underground power line can be extremely dangerous—and could black out power to an entire area. *Before digging, check the building's as-built plot plan and stake-out underground power lines, telephone lines, television cable, gas main, and fuel lines.*
8. When painting eavestrough or working around the roof, keep ladders away from the service entrance mast and incoming power lines.

	ACCOUNT NUMBERS	SUB TOTALS	TOTAL
*FIRE PROTECTION SYSTEM	49		
ALARMS	491		
BATTERIES	492		
HOSES & EXTINGUISHERS	493		
MOTORS & PUMPS	494		
PIPING, VALVES & CONTROLS	495		
SPRINKLER SYSTEM	496		
TESTING	497		
TELEVISION SYSTEM	50	TOTAL	
CABLE CONTRACT	501		
WIRING DISTRIBUTION	502		

FIGURE 10-46 Summary of budget expense schedules, repair and maintenance categories; electrical services. *See Chapter 3, "Security, Safety and Fire Protection," for information about the fire protection system.

9. Never attempt to touch a downed wire—call the local utility company; the line crew will repair the power lines.
10. If a tree is interfering with power wires, call the local utility and ask for their free tree trimming service. Remember, a live tree can become a live wire if it touches a power line. *Leave the job to the experts and live long enough to enjoy the tree.*
11. If you receive a shock from an appliance, *do not use it again* until it has been serviced by a repairman.
12. You must constantly keep in mind that *electricity can kill!* Do not attempt any electrical maintenance job unless you are qualified to do it.
13. Before you buy any appliance or electrical equipment, ask the salesman to show you the Underwriters' Laboratories (UL) or Canadian Standards Association (CSA) Seal of Approval. To earn CSA approval, an appliance, wire, outlet box, or any electrical product must undergo rigid testing by the Canadian Standards

Association. *Only when* it is deemed "100 percent Electrically Safe" will the product be released on the market. The United States equivalent is approved by the Underwriters' Laboratory (UL).

14. Always use a fuse puller to remove cartridge fuses.
15. Use only one hand to remove screw-in fuses, and touch only the knurled glass rim of the fuse. *Do not touch anything with the other hand.*
16. Electricity can be dangerous. The danger is controlled if you follow the safety rules.

Chapter 11

MECHANICAL SERVICES

11-1 An Overview

When planning a book about building maintenance, one of the most important considerations was the organization of the material into logical, easy-to-refer-to chapters.

The various mechanical systems provided the key to organizing most of the information. However, certain equipment did not fit into a specific system: garbage compactors, elevators, motors, pumps, couplings, bearings, seals, valves.

To resolve this, a chapter on Mechanical Services was created. This chapter includes everything mentioned above, along with lubrication, troubleshooting, and preventive maintenance.

Mechanical services account for about 25 percent of the initial cost of the various systems and thus become a very important factor in the cost of maintaining a building. Whether a building shows a profit or loss, the dollars spent on this equipment has a great bearing on the results. To minimize a building's operating expenses, the electrical/mechanical equipment must be in excellent condition, and must perform at peak efficiency.

In the past the initial cost of the mechanical equipment was only important because it affected the cost to develop and build the building. The low bid usually got the contract. High energy and maintenance costs should make the case for quality and efficiency more important. The only true way to decide is to add the operational costs over the life span of the equipment to the initial cost. In this way, values can be more realistically evaluated.

In the United States, when contractors are bidding on heating, ventilation, and air conditioning systems for new government buildings, the bids are set up with a life factor of forty. In other words, the bidder must furnish the initial cost of installation, plus the operational factors over a forty-year life cycle span. The manufacturers of cheap inefficient equipment should not be able to effectively compete with those offering highly efficient equipment.

11-2 Elevators*

When James Watt developed the steam engine, and when the owner of a coal mine later put it to use around 1800 for lifting coal up the mine shafts, power other than "muscle" was considered for use with hoisting devices. Since then, three common types of elevators have been developed.

HYDRAULIC ELEVATORS

The hydraulic elevator is used extensively in low-rise buildings of up to five floors and has speeds rarely exceeding 150 feet per minute. The elevator is mounted on a piston, inside a cylinder that extends into the ground to a depth equal to the height the elevator will rise.

Relatively simple in design, the system uses only an electric pump to force oil into the cylinder, displacing the piston, to give the elevator a controlled ascent. Electrically controlled valves release the oil for a controlled descent.

*My special thanks to Mr. Ray Scanlan of the Otis Elevator Company for his assistance in preparing most of the elevator material. Reprinted courtesy of the Otis Elevator Company.

GEARLESS ELECTRIC TRACTION ELEVATORS

This type of elevator is used in high-rise buildings and it travels at speeds from 400 to 1,800 feet per minute. The elevator uses a large, slow-speed electric motor directly connected to a large, grooved drive sheave (pulley). The "hoist" ropes are connected to the car and counterweight (similar to a geared traction elevator), although sometimes the cables are double wrapped around the sheave to achieve desired traction.

Elevators are designed so that the electric lifting motor uses no electricity at all when an almost full elevator is coming down. In fact, the motor then acts as an electric generator, which adds power back into the system.

GEARED ELECTRIC TRACTION ELEVATORS

This type of elevator is used in low- and medium-rise buildings and has speeds from 25 to 350 feet per minute. The elevator is powered by a high speed motor driving a worm and gear reduction unit, which drives the hoisting sheave (grooved pulley).

One end of the "hoist ropes" (actually steel cables) is attached to the top of the elevator car, and is then wrapped around the drive sheave in the grooves. The other end of the cables is attached to a counterweight that slides up and down the shaftway on its own guide rails. With this weight and traction, lifting power is gained by the pressure of the cables on the sheave grooves. The full weight of the car and about one-half of its passenger load is balanced out by the counterweight, which is going down as the car moves up. The electric motor, therefore, does not have to lift the full weight. Many heavy-duty freight elevators utilize the geared electric traction machine.

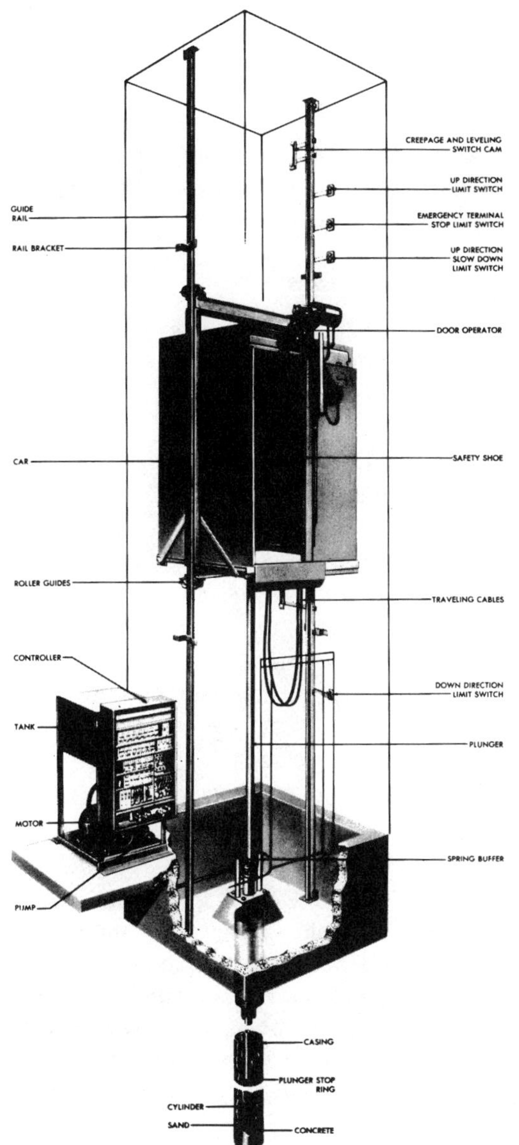

FIGURE 11-1 Hydraulic elevator. (Courtesy of the Otis Elevator Company.)

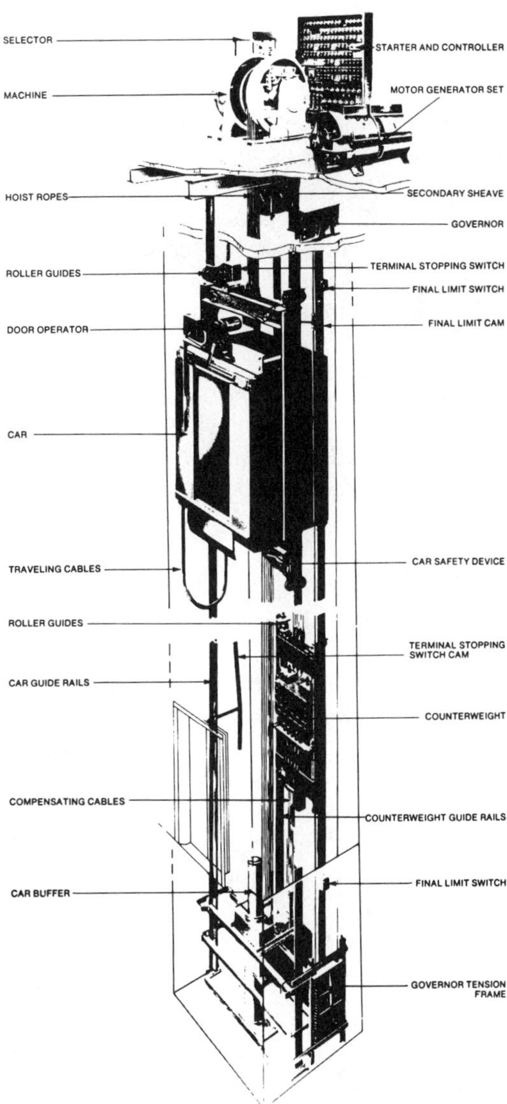

FIGURE 11-2 Gearless traction elevator. (Courtesy of the Otis Elevator Company.)

ELEVATOR SAFETY FEATURES

Brake

Each traction machine includes an electrically released, spring activated brake. Braking action to a suitable pulley is applied whenever the power to the brake is interrupted, not only assuring brake operation during normal use of the elevator, but also upon failure of the power supply.

Safety Clamp

A mechanical device acting upon the elevator guide rails for stopping the descent of the car if it exceeds a designated speed.

Governor

A mechanical device measuring the speed of the car and at predetermined speeds, initiates a variety of operations. In normal operation the governor may control electric circuits to regulate the speed of the elevator. When the downward speed becomes excessive, the governor may cut off power to the elevator motor, applying the brake. If the downward speed continues to increase to a predetermined critical value, the governor actuates the safety mechanism.

Door Interlock

A locking device to prevent each hoistway door from being opened from the corridor side unless the car is at that particular landing; also an electrical device so related to the controls that the car cannot run unless every door is *closed* and *locked.*

Safety Shoe

Used with electric door operators for automatic operation. It is a movable leading edge to the car door, which activates the stopping and reversal of the car door whenever it strikes a passenger or obstacle.

Emergency Stop Switch

A switch mounted in the car operating panel to actuate an emergency stop and prevent motion of the car in either direction.

Final Limit Switches

Switches that actuate an emergency stop if the car overruns the terminal landing by a designated distance.

ELEVATOR CONTROL

The three basic functions of elevator control are

1. POWER CONTROL—involves starting, stopping, accelerating, deceleration, braking and reversing, elevator drive machinery, as well as opening and closing the elevator doors.
2. ELEVATOR OPERATION—deals with the movement and position of the car in response to passenger calls.
3. GROUP SUPERVISION—used with groups or banks of elevators, automatically coordinates the "dispatching" of all cars to meet building traffic demands such as the morning peak, up and down at noon, morning and afternoon coffee breaks, and down in the evening peak.

Elevator Power Control System

There are three methods used to control the speed of electric traction elevators:

1. Resistance control
2. Unit multi-voltage or variable voltage control (UMV)
3. Silicon-controlled rectifiers (SCR)

Resistance Control In resistance control, the external power supply (usually alternating current) is applied directly to the elevator motor subject to resistances in the power circuit.

Unit Multi-Voltage Control With unit multi-voltage control, a separate motor generator set is used, whose driving motor is subject to the external power supply (usually alternating current) and whose generator applies direct current power to the elevator motor. The performance of the elevator is controlled basically through the generator fields.

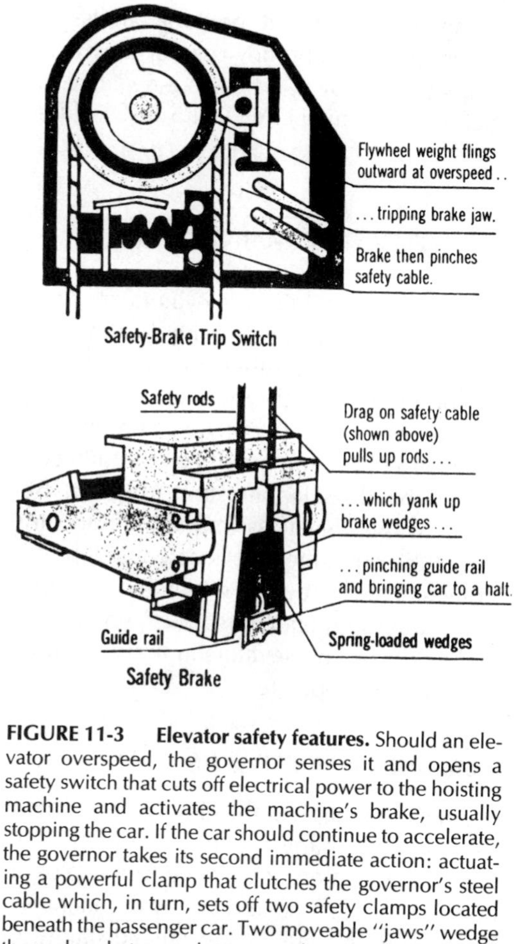

Flywheel weight flings outward at overspeed . .

. . . tripping brake jaw.

Brake then pinches safety cable.

Safety-Brake Trip Switch

Safety rods

Drag on safety cable (shown above) pulls up rods . . .

. . . which yank up brake wedges . . .

. . . pinching guide rail and bringing car to a halt.

Guide rail

Spring-loaded wedges

Safety Brake

FIGURE 11-3 Elevator safety features. Should an elevator overspeed, the governor senses it and opens a safety switch that cuts off electrical power to the hoisting machine and activates the machine's brake, usually stopping the car. If the car should continue to accelerate, the governor takes its second immediate action: actuating a powerful clamp that clutches the governor's steel cable which, in turn, sets off two safety clamps located beneath the passenger car. Two moveable "jaws" wedge themselves between the two guideway rails until sufficient force is exerted to bring the car to a smooth, sliding stop. The elevator is slowed gradually to prevent injuries to passengers that would be caused by a sudden stop. (Courtesy of the Otis Elevator Company.)

Silicon-Controlled Rectifier Control The motor generator set used to produce direct current for the drive machine is replaced with a solid state direct drive system called a power converter (which uses silicon-controlled rectifiers). This high-power semiconductor electrical device converts ac to dc and can be turned off at appropriate times in order to regulate the dc voltage.

Elevator Leveling Automatic two-way leveling is a control feature whereby accurately regulated slow speed is available for stopping the platform level with the landing, and for maintaining this relationship under all conditions of changing load or stretch of the hoist ropes. With resistance control, automatic leveling is achieved through a slow-speed winding of the elevator motor. On UMV control, automatic leveling is always supplied and is obtained through control of the generator field called the "WARD-LEONARD SYSTEM." It is based on the principle that the speed of an elevator motor is directly proportional to the voltage impressed on its armature and takes advantage of the electrical fact that the output voltage of a dc generator can easily be made to build up smoothly and gradually.

Since the speed of the elevator is proportional to the voltage applied to the elevator motor, and since the voltage is smoothly varied, this virtually stepless operation naturally results in smooth elevator operation, which explains why UMV control has been used in most medium and high-rise buildings. SCR control draws power only when an elevator moves and is a very energy efficient system.

Operation

The operation is the method available to the user of the elevator to activate its motion in the hoistway. Modern automatic elevators use a "Collective Operation" as a base.

- A set of buttons, one for each floor, located in the car.
- A single hall button at each terminal landing and two buttons at each intermediate landing.
- The passenger is instructed to press the button corresponding to the direction in which he wishes to travel.
- All calls are recorded until answered.
- Car travel is subject alternatively to "up and down" calls traveling as far as is necessary in each direction; to answer all calls registered in advance of the car, for the direction in which the car is traveling, calls are answered irrespective of the order in which they were placed.

Group Supervisory System

Until the 1960s, elevator control systems were primarily electromechanical in design with controllers using relays and switches. Direct current (dc) power needed to run the hoisting machine was provided by a motor generator set, which was operated on alternating current (ac) power as a primary power source. Floor positioning was accomplished by an electromechanical selector device.

With the rapid growth in power electronics, microelectronics, and computer technology, elevator control systems began to bring solid state electronics into play. By the mid 1970s, several manufacturers introduced solid state control systems employing discreet logic and minicomputers with microcomputers. The fully integrated microcomputer system controls every aspect of elevator operation. Velocity, position, direction, passenger travel, waiting time, door operations, car assignment, energy use, and system diagnostics are all part of a totally integrated, software-based elevator control system.

The designers of elevator systems have gone to great lengths to combine the correct motors, machines, drive sheaves, hoist ropes, and control systems to achieve efficient and reliable elevator operation. The smallest amount of dissatisfaction with elevator performance—whether it be long waits, improper leveling, a bumpy ride, or at worst, a complete shutdown—creates a negative image for a building. ELEVATORS ARE IMPORTANT.

ELEVATOR MAINTENANCE

In high-rise buildings, elevators are probably as important as plumbing, heating, and ventilation; however, they are the most visible and controversial system in the building. The choice of elevators (type, number, and speed) is a vital decision and is carefully considered by the planners and builders. Because of the elevator's importance and the cost of the equipment, it is essential that it is protected by a preventive maintenance program. Building operators must understand the basic types of elevators in their buildings and how they operate.

Equipment and Building Life

An examination of the elevator equipment room reveals many electrical cabinets filled with relays, timers, resistance tubes, plug-in boards, as well as motors and machines. Because of the highly specialized nature of elevator equipment, a maintenance program is required.

Approximately 60 percent to 70 percent of

an elevator system's parts are subject to wear. Major wearing parts may have a life expectancy of 20 to 25 years, while the estimated useful life of buildings range from

- Apartment buildings—50 years
- Office buildings—40–60 years
- Shopping centers—30–45 years
- Industrial buildings—25–50 years

Preventive maintenance keeps the elevators operating in a "like new" condition, thus delivering the daily service, safety, and performance the passenger expects, and at the same time, protecting the large investment for the life span of the building.

Maintenance Contracts

A full maintenance contract from the manufacturer of the equipment installed in the building assures that they take full responsibility for the equipment identified by such a contract. In theory, all equipment should be in as good an operating condition, after many years of service, as it was when new. All electrical signals should operate, rotating components be free and in good repair, motors operating as designed, relays functioning perfectly.

Objective of Elevator Maintenance

The objective of elevator maintenance is to ensure that the elevator system provides safe, dependable operation with maximum efficiency and minimum wear. By examining the elevator mileage in a typical building, we should get some idea of what we mean by wear.

An example: An elevator in a 25-story building, after ten hours of operation, uses 85 kWh of electricity. Using a cost of 3¢ per kWh for electrical energy, the cost of elevator operation for the day would be $2.55.

The wear and tear on the elevator could be detailed as follows: The average round trip with five stops in each direction would be approximately three minutes, giving the elevator the capability of twenty round trips per hour, and thus in ten hours per day:

- 10 stops every three minutes, which includes door openings and closings, acceleration-deceleration, braking, etc.
- 10 × 20 trips = 200 operations per hour.
- 200 × 10 hours = 2,000 operations per day.
- 2,000 × 5 days = 10,000 operations per week.
- 10,000 × 52 weeks = 520,000 operations per year.
- Elevator travel during this period would be approximately 7000 miles.

Mechanical / electrical equipment that operates one-half million cycles per year is certainly subject to wear. Many vital smaller parts, like contacts and commutator brushes, wear out much sooner than the twenty to twenty-five year life cycle of the major wearing parts. Wearing of minor parts results in less than optimum performance and can set off a chain reaction causing major subsystems to fail. For example, if a bearing on a gearless machine is allowed to wear out, an expensive armature could eventually need replacement. A worn selector device, on the other hand, can affect brake-to-brake time, making it difficult for the elevator to hold the floor at the proper speed, causing a potential safety hazard.

Scope of Elevator Maintenance

A preventive maintenance contract should include

- Examinations
- Lubrication

- Cleaning
- Adjustments
- Parts replacement

"Hands On" Housekeeping Inspection This represents 75 percent of the total time spent by a good elevator serviceman. Potential troubles and worn parts are detected while performing these chores, which include lubrication, cleaning, and adjusting. Cleaning requires an intimate contact with all component parts and often reveals potential troubles that may be the cause of future faulty operation.

The other 25 percent of the serviceman's time is spent on repairs and replacement of parts, which include all major and minor wearing parts, motors, gears, hoisting cables, control equipment.

Liability Under the contract, the safe operation of the elevators is the joint responsibility of the maintenance company and the owner.

Equipment in the machine room or elevator hoistway is the responsibility of the service company. Problems caused by excessive heat, water, or electrical complications are the responsibility of the owner.

Problems of vandalism or misuse of equipment are the owner's responsibility. The building operators are on site all the time, while the service people are only there periodically.

Maintenance in the elevator cab—including floor coverings, tile or carpet, wall furnishings, ceiling grid replacement, and light bulbs—is the responsibility of the owner.

Overtime Call Backs All normal work should be performed during the regular working hours of the elevator servicemen. As with all other operating problems, a call for service should not be made before a problem is checked out. This is especially true after regular working hours. Overtime call backs are charged at very high rates. "Look and listen" inspections will make you aware of potential troubles. Call for service early, and avoid breakdowns after hours.

BUILDING MANAGER'S VISUAL SERVICE CHECK

At various times during the day, stand in the lobby area near the elevator entrances and observe the traffic. Listen for the comments of riders waiting for the elevators. The best time to observe is when the elevators are busy. You will get a great deal of insight into the general health of the system and how well it is serving the building's needs. In effect, you are taking the "pulse" and "temperature" of the building.

Check The "Reflexes"

With a stop watch, you can get a reading on how well your elevator system is performing. Check the reaction time of the equipment. Here are some of the symptoms to look for:

1. Can you detect negative passenger reactions about the elevator service?
2. Are large groups of people trying to crowd on cars with still more people left waiting for a second or third car?
3. Are passengers being soundly "bumped" by closing doors?
4. Are the passengers waiting longer for an elevator than you (or they) think they should? A rough estimate of the time passengers are willing to wait without complaining is

Hospital	20–35 seconds
Office building	25–35 seconds
Department store	30–50 seconds
Hotel or motel	30–50 seconds
Apartment building	40–60 seconds

IT IS IMPORTANT, ON EVERY VISIT, THAT THE ITEMS IN GUIDE BELOW RECEIVE SYSTEMATIC ATTENTION.

MACH., SELECTORS, MG SETS, CONTROLLERS	General inspection of mach., sheaves, worm & gear, motor, brake, also selectors or floor controllers when used, lub. as reqd.
	Empty drip pan. NOTE: Oil should not be reused.
	Observe brake oper., check brake linings, adj. brake when necessary.
	Inspect & lub. mach. automatic, contacts, linkage & gearing.
	Clean coll. rings, brush rigging, commutators & undercutting as reqd.
	Clean & lub. contr. contacts, connectors & holders, as reqd.
OVER-HEAD	Lub. bearings, remove grease from around sheaves, bearing boxes.
	Inspect governor working parts & lubrication, check gov. switch.
	Clean & lub. signal drive mechanism when used.
CAR	Check car flooring for wear that would create tripping hazard.
	Check door operation.
	Check car gate contacts for operation, when used.
	Lubricate car & cwt. sheave bearings when used.
	Check condition of car switch handle, replace emergency release glasses if required.
HOIST-WAY	If rails are lubricated, check condition and lubrication.
	Check governor & tape tension sheave lubrication.
HOISTWAY ENTRANCES	Inspect. gate ropes or cables, gate body, tracks, posts.
	Observe operation of door locks, contacts, checks, Rixson hinges, if used.
	Check for any broken or worn pull straps on bi-parting doors.
	Check oper. of car call bell system when used.
MISC.	Check battery for emergency lighting and executone.

ON EVERY VISIT . . . . It is essential that the following be properly executed (items 1-8)

1. SEE CUSTOMER OR HIS REPRESENTATIVE; CONTACT STARTER & OPERATOR.
2. RIDE CAR, OBSERVING STARTING AND STOPPING OPERATION OF DOORS & GATES, ELECTRONIC DECTOR OR REVERSAL DEVICES; CHECK FOR UNUSUAL NOISES.
3. INSPECT ALL EQUIPMENT IN MACHINE ROOM PAYING PARTICULAR ATTENTION TO CONTACTS, CONNECTORS, REVERSE PHASE RELAY.
4. MAKE CORRECTIONS AS INDICATED BY THESE INPECTIONS OR COMPLAINTS RECEIVED. REPORT REQUIRED REPAIRS OR WORK NOT COVERED BY ABSTRACT OF CONTRACT TO OFFICE.
5. CLEAN MACHINE ROOM AND FLOOR WHEN NECESSARY.
6. CHECK CONDITION OF PIT AND CLEAN FLOOR AND BOTTOM OF CAR IF NECESSARY.
7. KEEP CAR TOP CLEAN.
8. USE PERSONAL PROTECTIVE EQUIPMENT AS REQUIRED.

FIGURE 11-4 "Hands on" serviceman inspection guide. (Courtesy of the Otis Elevator Company.)

FIGURE 11-5 Visual service check. (Courtesy of the Otis Elevator Company.)

It is important to check consistency of service, since people dislike unexpectedly long waits.

If you determine from your observations that riders are waiting for service longer than they should, the next step is to try to find out what is causing the slow service.

Door Timing

5. Does the timing for the elevator doors exceed the following acceptable limits?

Width and Type of Doors	*Opening Time*	*Closing Time*
3′6″ Center Opening	1.1 to 1.5 sec.	2.3 to 2.5 sec.
3′0″ Single Slide	1.7 to 2.3 ″	3.3 to 3.5 ″
4′0″ Two Speed	2.1 to 2.7 ″	4.0 to 4.2 ″

The doors should be adjusted to stay open long enough for people to enter and leave without wasting time. This will vary with each building.

6. Do the doors close before people have a chance to enter and leave the elevator?
7. Do the doors stay open longer than necessary after a passenger has entered and registered a call?

Door Reversal Stand in the center of the door opening:

8. If equipped with a rubber safety shoe, do the doors continue to close after the safety shoe touches you?
9. If equipped with electronic detectors or light rays, do the doors strike you before reversing?

Car Start Time

10. After the doors are fully closed, does it take longer than one second before the car starts to move?

Start To Stop Time

11. Are there differences in the run times between elevators in the same bank, and are the run times longer than in competitive buildings?

    Inadequate maintenance procedures can result in sluggish, slow performance in any of these "reflex" areas. Don't forget that passenger comfort is also very important. So, the next step in your examination is to take a ride and . . .

Listen to the "Heartbeat"

You may ride your elevators dozens of times each week, but because of habit or familiarity, you don't notice the sounds and motions and you probably don't detect small changes in the quality of the ride. Like the human body, an elevator continuously undergoes wear and tear from the minute it begins to operate.

Take a ride with all of your senses tuned. One way to amplify what you hear is to ride with your eyes shut. You'll be surprised how much more conscious you are of sound and motion. The same trick works when you ride with your ears covered. Your sense of sight and awareness of motion are much more acute.

FIGURE 11-6 Listen to the "heartbeat." (Courtesy of the Otis Elevator Company.)

Riding Comfort and Convenience

12. Is starting and stopping abrupt or uncomfortable?
13. Do you hear squeaks, scrapes, or feel vibrations when the elevators are running?
14. Are any of the floor indicators or overhead lights not working?
15. Is the ventilation system not functioning?

Safety

16. At floor stops, could someone trip because the car isn't level with the floor?
17. Have you received any repair or adjustment directives from your local authorities or insurance inspectors?
18. Is the emergency alarm bell inoperative?
19. If your equipment has an intercom or telephone hookup, is it out of order?
20. If you have an emergency lighting system, does it fail to operate during a simulated power shutdown?

Maintenance Housekeeping

21. Check the housekeeping of all equipment. There should be no accumulation of dirt and lint in the control cabinets, hoist machinery, or motors. Materials should be neatly stored in cabinets; wiping cloths should be stored in metal cans; the floor should be free of debris and oil.

Wiring Diagrams

The wiring diagrams are the electrical road maps that makes future troubleshooting and problem solving possible. The wiring diagrams help to provide independence from the manufacturer relative to maintenance of the system. The wiring diagram of each elevator installation should be kept on file with other plans of the building. It is essential that these wiring diagrams are available when an elevator serviceman needs to trace a problem.

Signing The Work Order

The building operator should not sign the serviceman's work order unless he is satisfied with the service.

Evaluating Elevator Service

The maintenance contractor should carry out his work following an organized and documented program of preventive maintenance. An example of this is the check chart shown in Figures 11-4 and 11-7. These charts indicate work functions and the yearly quarter each function is to be carried out. A program should also document the work that should be carried out on each visit.

Check Charts and Programs

It is wise for building managers to determine if the elevator service company has an organized maintenance program, and if the company's servicemen use a formal check chart. The company should be willing to explain its program to you. Some routines may be upset by unforeseen circumstances,

THIS CHECK LIST MAY BE USED FOR 1 TO 5 ELEVATORS OF SAME TYPE LOCATED IN SAME BUILDING

NOTE: Insert Building Identification Car Numeral, Letter or Location of Elevators Covered

INDICATE WITH A ✓ MARK PERIOD IN WHICH EACH ANN.& SEMI-ANN.ITEM IS TAKEN CARE OF

When check list form is filled, sign, date and return it to the office for a replacement.

CAR ____ QUARTER 1 2 3 4 | CAR ____ QUARTER 1 2 3 4 | CAR ____ QUARTER 1 2 3 4 | CAR ____ QUARTER 1 2 3 4 | CAR ____ QUARTER 1 2 3 4

	Item	Months
MACHS.	Remove, clean & lubricate brake cores on DC brakes, clean linings if necessary, check wear.	(1)
	Seal small leaks.	(2-8)
MOTORS GEN. EXCITERS	Clean armatures, motors with blower or vacuum.	(2)
	Check armature & rotor clearances.	(2)
	Check all connections & loop circuite.	(2)
	Change oil in bearings & seal small leaks.	(2)
CONTR.	Clean w/blower, check align.of sws.,lub.hinge pins.	(3-9)
	Check all condensers, resistance tubes & grids.	(3-9)
	Check oil in overload relays, settings & oper.	(3-9)
	Clean & check fuses & holders;check contr.conns.	(3)
SEL.	Check traveling nut & gears for wear, and chains.	(5-11)
SHEAVES	See that sheaves are tight on shafts, sound spokes and rim with hammer for cracks.	(4)
TAPE DR.	Check hitches & broken tape switch.	(2-8)
CAR	Check stile channels for bends or cracks, also carframe, cams & support and steadier plates.	(6-12)
	Check Alarm, Emerg. Light. Telephone and intercom.	(3-6-9-12)
	Check safety clearance and guide shoe gib wear.	(6)
DOOR OPER.	Check shaft brgs.,tapered pins, alignment, oper. of cams, rollers.	(5-11)
	Clean electronic detector chassis (cold cathode type).	(5)
D. CL'SER	Check fastenings, operation of checks,interlocks.	(5-11)
C.O. BOX	Check contacts,switches,clean & lub.car oper.box.	(2-8)
ROPES	Check all ropes hitches,shackles,equal rope tension.	(5-11)
G. SHOES	Lubricate guide shoe stems & check gib wear.	(3)
R. GUIDE	(Car & cwt.) lubricate roller guide pivots.	(6-12)
HOIST-WAY	Clean & check guide rails,cams & fstngs.,also cwt.	(7)
	Inspect limit & term. stop sws., lub.pins & rollers.	(7)
TRAV. CABLE	Check wear,insul.,hanging,inspect junc.box conns.	(8)
BI-PART DOORS	Clean chains, tracks,sheaves,lubricate as reqd.	(4-10)
	Check door contacts.	(4-10)
HOIST-WAY DOORS	Clean,lub.,tracks,h'gers,ch'k upthrust & adj.if nec.	(10)
	Fill & adjust checks. Check Spirators.	(10)
	Check bottom gibs, struts, sills, headers, fastenings, adjust door contacts.	(10)
HALL	Check hall button contacts, springs, wiring, clean & lubricate as required.	(5)
MISC.	Lubricate indicator dials & pulleys.	(1-7)
	Check SES, (if possible with EP where used)	(1-7)
	Check load weigh. devices & dispatch time set'gs.	(1-7)
PIT	Lubricate compensating sheave & check hitches.	(4-10)
	Check oil level in oil buffers.	(4-10)
	Check governor & tape tension sheave fastenings.	(4-10)

FIGURE 11-7 A check list guide for elevator servicemen. The numbers following the item indicate the months in which the work is scheduled. Cross out those items that do not apply. (Courtesy of the Otis Elevator Company.)

necessitating deviation from the plan; however, you should evaluate the overall program. Major repairs should be anticipated, and work orders for men and materials should be arranged so that you can schedule them at times that will upset the occupants of the building as little as possible.

EMERGENCIES

Building managers and operators should be prepared to handle elevator emergencies. When confronted with fire, power blackouts, and passengers trapped in stalled elevators, the building manager must know how to handle the situation and who to call for assistance. He should not be expected to and should not attempt to carry out the emergency rescue of trapped passengers or to operate the elevators in an abnormal manner.

Fire

Elevators should be equipped for "Firemen's Service" or "Emergency Service," which entails special controls, and in some cases, automatic return to street level. You should know

- What special controls do your elevators have and are they properly identified?
- How do the special controls operate and how are they initiated, and tested?
- Where are the special keys located?
- What will happen if the power is disrupted at the same time you are using the special controls?
- Are signs in place restricting use of elevators during fire?

Loss of Power

Many buildings are equipped with Emergency Power supplies. These include provisions to operate elevators in many different ways, and you should know

- Which elevators, if any, will operate during a power failure?
- Do the elevators switch over to emergency power automatically or manually?
- Do the elevators automatically return to the main floor?
- Who has been instructed to initiate the manual switching and / or re-call if this is the case?
- Where are the various switches located and are they identified?
- Who has the keys, or where are they located?
- Is there a written procedure?
- When was the whole system last tested?
- Do the elevators have battery-operated emergency lighting units?
- Is the "Emergency Call" button arranged to operate on the battery power supply?

In some buildings the hydraulic elevators are equipped with a battery-operated unit that will automatically open the "lowering valve" in the event of a power failure, allowing the elevator to return to the lowest floor and to open the doors, thus preventing passengers from becoming trapped.

Emergency Recall

The emergency recall will capture passenger elevators instantly and return them to the street level.

This action can be initiated manually with a key switch located at the street level, or automatically with a sensing device. The key should be located where the building staff or the fire department can locate it. It should be covered and marked "Emergency Recall."

When the emergency recall device is activated, the following occurs:

1. All hall and car calls are canceled instantly.
2. All door re-opening devices are rendered inoperative (safety shoe, light ray, electronic detectors).
3. Elevators parked at a floor other than the street floor will return non-stop to the street level.
4. Elevators traveling away from the street level will reverse and return to the street level, non-stop.
5. Elevators on independent service will be given an audible signal to close the doors and will return to the street level, non-stop.
6. The emergency stop switch will be rendered inoperative.

Normal Operation is restored by turning the "emergency recall" key switch to the "off" position.

FIGURE 11-8 A 1912 elevator inspection team. It wasn't until 1924 that the Otis sales organization began to offer maintenance service to its customers, officially merging sales and service. (Courtesy of the Otis Elevator Company.)

In-Car Emergency Service

The in-car emergency service allows the firefighters to use the elevators for fighting the fire.

This service can be initiated by using a key switch, which is located in or adjacent to the car operating panel, and is marked "Emergency—On-Off."

When the key is activated, the following occurs:

1. The elevator can only be operated by the person in the car and will not answer any hall calls.
2. The elevator will operate when one or more calls are registered. Constant pressure on the "Door Close" or any car call button will close the doors. Pressure release on the button before the door closes will allow the doors to immediately open.
3. Any error in car call can be canceled by momentary operation of the emergency key switch to the "off" position.
4. After the door closes, the car will run to the car call floor and stop with the doors closed. Doors can be opened by putting constant pressure on the "door open" button. If pressure is released, the doors will reclose immediately.
5. Once fully opened, the doors will remain open until closing is initiated manually.

FIGURE 11-9 First class main floor cab entrance. (Courtesy of the Otis Elevator Company.)

Normal operation is restored by turning the "emergency" key switch to the "off" position.

Trapped Passengers

Building managers are often asked what procedure to follow when a passenger is trapped in a stuck elevator. The following list of Dos and Don'ts will help you to handle this situation.

- Do phone the elevator service company.
- Do take a minute to provide all the details: name, phone, building name and address, and elevator involved.
- Do maintain constant communication with the passengers and reassure them that help is definitely on the way and that they are safe.
- Do try to identify the position to the nearest floor.
- Do ask the passengers questions such as "Can you push the 'Door open' button?"

FIGURE 11-10 "Elevonic" 401 car operating panel. A technician at Otis Elevator's research center in Farmington, Connecticut, checks microcomputer operation of their latest car operation panel. (Courtesy of the Otis Elevator Company.)

ELEVATORS	ACCT. NOS.	SUB TOTALS	TOTAL
	52		

INSPECTIONS	521	
LICENSES	522	
OVERTIME	523	
REPAIRS	524	
SERVICE CONTRACT	525	

FIGURE 11-11 Summary of budget expense schedules, repair and maintenance categories; mechanical services.

or "Can you pull out the 'Emergency Stop' button?"

- Do instruct the passengers to stay put unless they can walk out normally.
- Don't (under any circumstances) attempt to remove the passenger through the entrance if the elevator is not at floor level.
- Don't allow anyone to attempt rescue operations.
- Remember that the trapped passenger is safe inside the elevator, that there is sufficient air by natural ventilation, that there is no danger, and that help is on the way.

11-3 Overhead Doors

Mechanically operated overhead doors serve two purposes. They maintain a degree of security and keep the exterior elements out of the garage area. The main components include the following:

1. The key switch or pressure hose that activates the operator.
2. Electric door openers.
3. Torsion springs.
4. Horizontal track.
5. Lift cables.

PREVENTIVE MAINTENANCE

1. A building operator, during his daily "look, listen, and touch" routine, activates the door using the key switch and the pressure hose. The door should be square when closed and should lift in the same manner.
2. If he finds that the door does not roll freely, he should recheck the track spacing. A properly fitting door should have about ¼-inch side play.
3. Once the lift cables begin to fray, *both cables* should be changed as soon as possible. If one of the cables snaps, the door will hang by one cable and twist everything out of shape.
4. If one of the cables is slack when the door is in the open position, the building operator should check to see that the door is

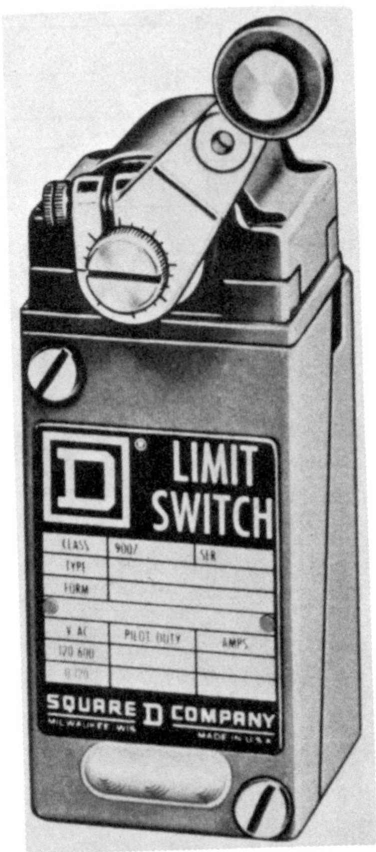

FIGURE 11-12 Typical limit switch. A limit switch is used to control such things as the up and down movement of a garage door. (Courtesy of Square D Company Canada, Limited.)

level when closed, that the tops of the vertical tracks are an equal distance from the top of the door, and that the horizontal tracks are parallel and square with the door.

5. When lubricating the working parts of the door, use a multipurpose grease. Check for a special wax type of spray for the torsion springs and the horizontal tracks at the curve. As the track rollers move in the tracks, they will become lubricated and cause the door to run more smoothly. Before applying the film of wax be sure that the tracks are cleaned. Ask the manufacturer for specific instructions for their product.
6. The V-belt should be checked regularly and replaced at the first sign of cracking.

TROUBLESHOOTING OVERHEAD DOORS

1. Determine if the problem is electrical or mechanical. When reporting a problem, always describe what actually happened, such as "door would not open," or "door is stuck half-way."
2. It may be necessary to open the door manually and leave it that way until the problem is corrected. Checking the door every day reduces the probability of unforeseen failure. This should be done early in the day so that problems can be corrected the same day. This eliminates leaving the door open all night, especially during the cold weather.

11-4 Garbage Compactor Maintenance

The following is a list of garbage compactor problems and the probable causes. The items marked with an asterisk * may be corrected by the building operator. Other repairs should be done by a specialist. It is a wise practice to wear a hard hat, safety glasses, and safety shoes when working in the compactor room.

Unit Keeps Running

*1. Dirty glass on the electric eye
2. Electric eye out of alignment
*3. Defective or weak bulb
4. Open circuit in photo cell wiring
5. Relay stuck
6. Dirt in relay
7. Micro switch out of adjustment

Motor Keeps Running—Ram Does Not Move

1. Low oil
2. Defective relay
3. Broken valve assembly
4. Broken hydraulic hose

Unit Stops Running

*1. Faulty fuse
2. Faulty on/off switch
3. Dirty and/or faulty mechanical latch

No Automatic Operation (Manual Only)

1. Faulty micro switch

Unit Jammed In Full Forward Position

1. Shorted micro switch
*2. Foreign matter under ram
3. Faulty power unit
4. Stuck relay
5. Pressure switch defective or out of adjustment

Unit Jammed In Rear Position

1. Micro switch out of alignment
2. Sides and bottom of ram need lubrication

Fuses Keep Blowing

*1. Check circuit breaker—reset button
*2. Improper size fuse at unit
*3. Improper size fuse at main unit
4. Faulty power unit

11-5 Motors

In general, motors are classified by the type of power used and by the motor's principle of operation.

Single-phase motors are used in locations where polyphase power is not available or where the required motor output is so low that single-phase motors prove to be more economical than polyphase motors. Practically all motors used in the home and on most farms are single-phase motors. These are used to drive domestic appliances, heating and cooling equipment, water pumps, hoists, conveyors, shop tools, and other equipment.

Single-phase motor types are manufactured only in small fractional horsepower ratings, usually 1/20 to 1/2 horsepower, and are not normally found in industrial applications.

The word "polyphase" means more than one phase. In practice, most of these motors that we are likely to encounter will be three-phase motors.

CHOOSING THE CORRECT MOTOR

There are three basic factors to be considered in the selection of the correct motor for a particular application:

1. The mechanical characteristics of the load the motor is to drive.
2. The environmental characteristics of the area in which the motor is to operate.
3. The electrical characteristics of the available power supply.

MOTOR CHARACTERISTICS*

AC Squirrel Cage Motor

The workhorse of industry is the ac squirrel cage motor. Of the thousands of motors used today in general applications, the vast majority are of the squirrel cage type. Squirrel cage motors are simple in construction and operation—merely connect three power lines to the motor and it will run. The squirrel cage motor gets its name because of its rotor construction, which resembles a squirrel cage and has no wire winding (Figure 11-13).

* Reprinted with permission from *Motor Control Fundamentals*, Courtesy of Square D Company Canada, Limited.

Full Load Current (FLC)

The current required to produce full load torque at the rated speed.

Locked Rotor Current (LRC)

During the acceleration period at the moment a motor is started, it draws a high current, called the "inrush" current. When the motor is connected directly to the line (so that full line voltage is applied to the motor) the inrush current is called the locked rotor or stalled rotor current. The locked rotor current can be from four to ten times the motor full load current. The vast majority of motors have a LRC of about six times FLC, and therefore this figure is generally used. The "six times" value is often expressed as 600 percent of FLC.

Motor Speed

The speed of a squirrel cage motor depends on the number of poles of the motor's winding. On 60 cycles, a 2-pole motor runs at about 3450 rpm, a 4-pole runs at 1725

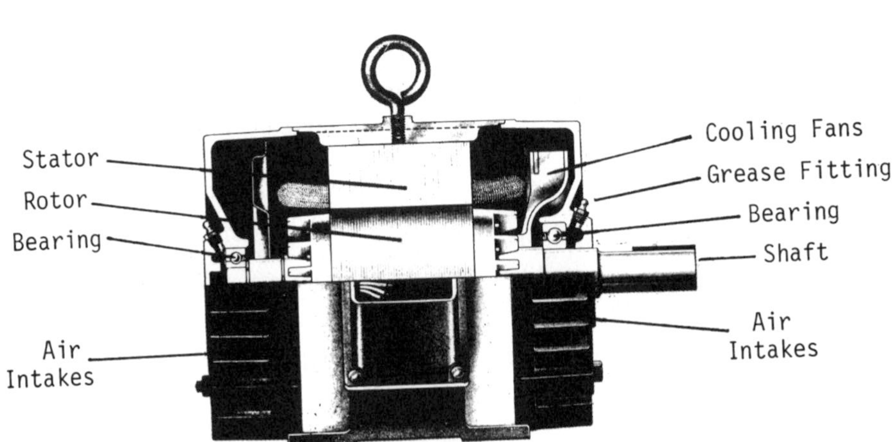

FIGURE 11-13 3-phase squirrel-cage motor. Understanding motor terminology is important for managers and operators. (Courtesy of the Canadian General Electric Company, Limited.)

rpm, and a 6-pole runs at 1150 rpm. Although motor nameplates are usually marked with their actual full load speeds, motors are often referred to by their "synchronous speeds"—3600, 1800, and 1200 rpm, respectively.

Torque

Torque is the "turning" or "twisting" force of the motor and is usually measured in pound-feet. Except when the motor is accelerating up to speed, the torque is related to the motor Hp by the formula:

$$\text{Torque in pound-feet} = \frac{\text{Hp} \times 5252}{\text{rpm}}$$

The torque of a 25 Hp motor, running at 1725 rpm, would be computed as follows:

$$\text{Torque} = \frac{25 \times 5252}{1725} = \text{approx. } 76$$

pound-feet

If 90 pound-feet were required to drive a particular load, the above motor would be overloaded and would draw a current in excess of full load current.

Ambient Temperature

The temperature of the air where a piece of equipment is situated is called the ambient temperature. Most controllers are enclosed and the ambient temperature is the temperature of the air outside the enclosure, not inside. Similarly, if a motor is said to be in an ambient temperature of 30°C (86°F), this is the air's temperature outside of the motor, not inside.

Temperature Rise

Current passing through the windings of a motor results in an increase in the motor temperature. The difference between the winding temperature of the running motor and the ambient temperature is called the temperature rise. The temperature rise produced at full load is not harmful, provided the motor ambient temperature does not exceed 40°C (104°F).

Higher temperature caused by increased current or higher ambient temperatures produces a deteriorating effect on motor insulation and lubrication. A general rule states that, for each increase of 10° above the rated temperature, motor life is cut in half.

Time (Duty) Rating

Most motors have a continuous duty rating, permitting indefinite operation at rated load. Intermittent duty ratings are based on a fixed operating time (5, 15, 30, 60 minutes), after which the motor must be allowed to cool.

Motor Service Factor

If the manufacturer has given a motor a "service factor," it means that the motor can be allowed to develop more than its rated or nameplate HP, without causing undue deterioration of the insulation. The service factor is a margin of safety. If, for example, a 10 Hp motor has a service factor of 1.15, the motor can be allowed to develop 11.5 Hp. The service factor depends on the motor design.

Jogging (Inching)

Jogging refers to the repeated starting and stopping of a motor at frequent intervals for short periods of time. A motor would be jogged when a piece of driven equipment has to be positioned fairly closely—for example, when positioning the table of a horizontal boring mill during set-up. If jogging is to occur more frequently than 5 times per minute,

CEMA standards require that the starter be derated.

A CEMA size 1 starter has a normal duty rating of 7½ Hp at 230 V, polyphase. On jogging application, this same starter has a maximum rating of 3 Hp.

Plugging

Plugging occurs when a motor running in one direction is momentarily reconnected to reverse direction, rapidly bringing it to rest. If a motor is plugged more than 5 times per minute, derating of the controller is necessary, owing to the heating of the contacts. Plugging can only be used if the driven machine and its load will not be damaged by reversing the motor torque.

MOTOR CONTROL

When we consider motor controls it is useful to understand something about the power that makes them operate. The early power systems were direct current (dc), the first motors were dc types. With the advent of alternating current (ac) power systems, the popularity of the dc power motor declined. It never disappeared entirely because it is still most suitable for smooth, efficient, wide-range speed control, such as in elevators.

Electrical utilities usually deliver alternating current energy and this meant that an ac motor was needed to drive a dc generator, which would in turn supply a dc motor. With the advent of solid-state diodes and silicon-controlled rectifiers (SCR), the need for dc generators was eliminated. This made dc motor drives more versatile and more popular than ever.

To operate the motors, we must have a convenient way to start and stop them, and sometimes there is a need to reverse the direction of rotation and/or control the speed. The switching devices used to perform these tasks are known as motor starters and controllers, and manually operated switches are commonly used.

Electrically operated switches, known as relays or contactors, are more suitable for starting large motors, or for switching operations requiring more than one step, and they are absolutely essential if the motor is to be controlled automatically or by a computer (Figure 11-14).

With very few exceptions, all motors must be provided with overload protection. For this reason we will include an example of one of these devices to help you understand how they operate and how they are reactivated (Figure 11-16).

MOTOR MAINTENANCE

Dust in Motors

Dust is probably the most natural enemy of a motor. Dust is constantly settling on motors, housings, windings, and slip rings, trying to work its way into the bearings.

On windings dust acts as a layer of insulation confining heat until it may reach dangerous temperatures. Dust also plugs ventilation spaces, which further interferes with proper cooling. Dust will act as an abrasive and insulator on slip rings, multiplying the wear and blocking full passage of current. Once inside bearings, dust can be as harmful as sandpaper to the highly polished surfaces. If it is allowed to fill the open spaces in a winding, it turns the entire wound section into a sponge for soaking up harmful soil, moisture, and acid fumes. Dust is the main reason for painting mechanical rooms and equipment and for keeping the mechanical rooms as clean as possible.

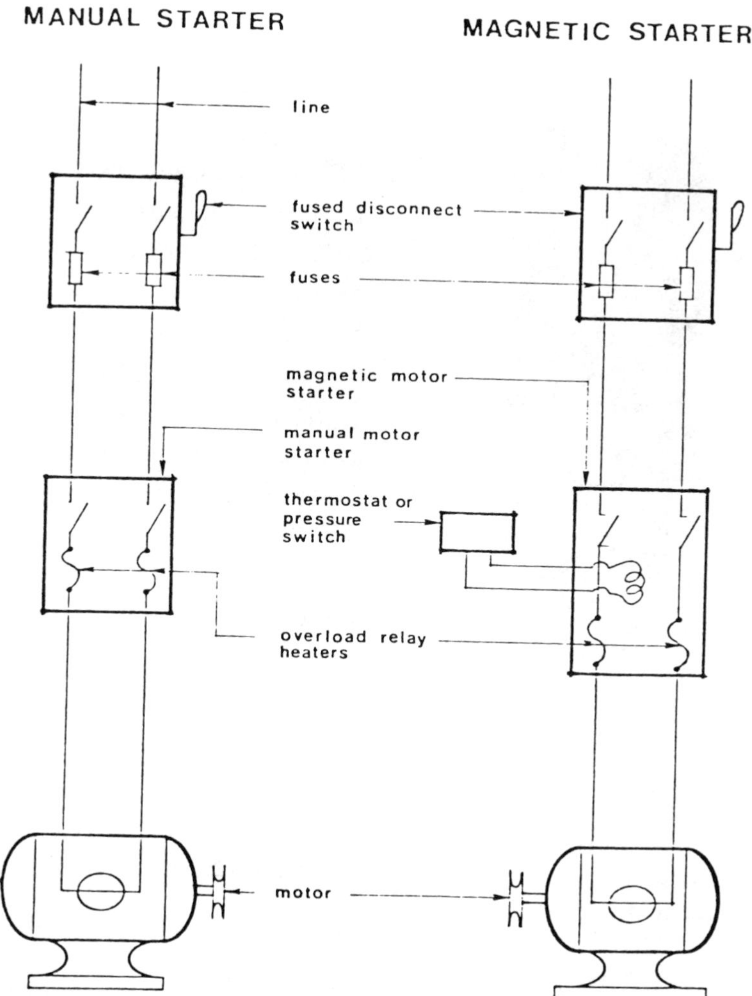

FIGURE 11-14 Switching devices for motors. (Courtesy of Cadillac-Fairview Corporation, Limited.)

Methods of Cleaning

The time to catch dust in motors is before it has a chance to unite with water or oil to form a gummy mass.

This means wiping off motors on a regular basis. They should be wiped off as soon as dust is noticed. At least once a week, all motors must be wiped clean. Oil filler caps must be kept closed at all times and dust seals and gaskets must be kept in good condition.

Worn or rotted seals must be replaced; their replacement is much easier than a burned out bearing.

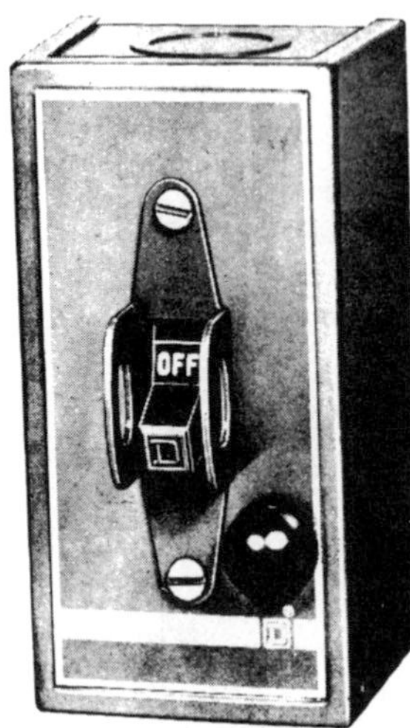

FIGURE 11-15 Typical manual motor starter—3-pole 3-phase with pilot light. 3-phase systems required 3-pole switches capable of opening all 3 live conductors of the circuit. The pilot light shows whether the switch is on and the circuit alive. It has no overload protection. (Courtesy of Square D Company Canada, Limited.)

Moisture

If a motor acquires moisture, remove the moisture as quickly as possible because

- It takes time for moisture to soak and soften insulation.
- Moisture on a motor is usually pure water at first. At that point, it is at its least dangerous stage. Every hour water stays in a motor it has time to absorb harmful compounds.

Vibration

The causes of motor vibration are

1. Misalignment
2. Vibration in driven machinery:
   (a) rotors out of balance
   (b) loose motor mounting bolts
   (c) worn bearings
   (d) mismatched coupling

Misalignment Problems

1. Sprung or broken shafts
2. Burned out bearings
3. Overload failure

Causes of Misalignment

1. Improper installation
2. Base off level (settlement)
3. Heavy loading
4. Excessive bearing wear
5. Loose mounting bolts

Warning of Misalignment

1. Excessing temperature caused by bearing overload
2. Increased vibration
3. Whirling or grinding sounds

Correcting Misalignment (Belt Drive Only)

1. Loosen mounting bolts—experiment with position—retighten.
2. Place shims under motor legs as required.

MOTOR APPLICATIONS

Manufacturers make a wide range of multipurpose motors. Some cases demand that a motor be specifically designed to meet the needs of a particular type of application.

Vertical pump motors are designed to meet the requirements of the vertical turbine pump, while elevator motors incorporate special high-resistance rotors to provide high-starting torque required for elevator service.

Crane and hoist motors incorporate special bracing of the rotor stator coils and extra strong shafts, bearings, and rotor components to withstand the vibration, shock, and overloads inherent in crane service.

Gear motors are designed to operate at speeds far below the synchronous speeds of

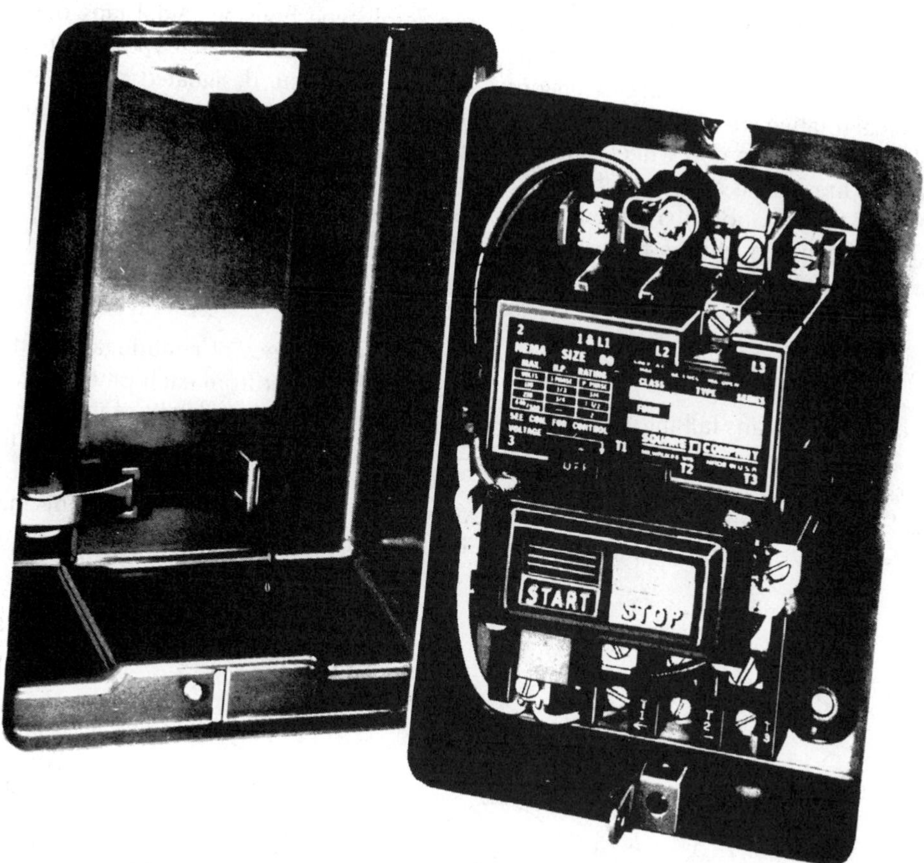

FIGURE 11-16 Typical 3-phase magnetic motor starter, self-contained with pilot light. This useful type of starter uses an electromagnet to activate the motor control switch. It has a low voltage protection feature and the operator must press the start button to re-start. (Courtesy of Square D Company Canada, Limited.)

induction motors. It is necessary, therefore, to provide some means of speed reduction between the machine and the motor. A belt chain or a separate gear reducer can be used.

Propeller fan motors are a totally enclosed and nonventilated squirrel cage induction type for propeller and axial-flow fans. There are basically two types of fans, a propeller fan and a centrifugal fan.

11-6 Fans

WHAT IS A FAN?

A fan is a gas flow producing machine that operates on the same basic principles as a centrifugal pump or compressor. A fan is similar to these machines in that they all convert mechanical rotative energy, applied at their shafts, to gas (or fluid) energy. The conversion of mechanical rotative energy to gas energy is accomplished by means of a wheel that imparts a spin to the gas. As a result of this spin, and provided there is no entering spin, the tendency of the gas is always to leave the wheel with a forward spiral motion.

TYPES OF FANS

Most commercial fans fall into one of two general classifications: centrifugal fans or axial fans. Centrifugal fans have flow within the wheel that is substantially parallel to the shaft (Figure 11-19). Centrifugal fans operate in a scroll type housing. Axial fans operate within a cylindrical or ring-type housing.

Fans are often designated as boosters, blowers, or exhausters. As they are considered here, a booster is a fan with ducts connected to both inlet and discharge; a blower has a discharge duct only; an exhauster has an inlet duct only.

Centrifugal Fans

The various types of centrifugal fans that are available differ from each other in structural details and in the details of their design and assembly. But the principal feature that distinguishes one type of centrifugal fan from another is the inclination of blades. This inclination of the blades determines the perfor-

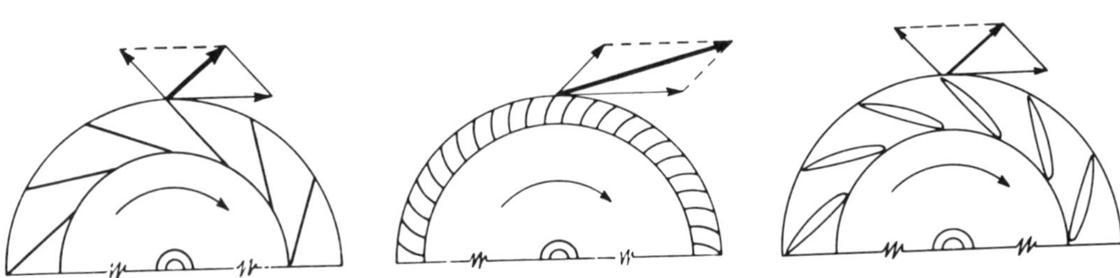

(ABOVE) DIRECTION OF AIR LEAVING VARIOUS FAN BLADE DESIGNS
(BELOW) EACH TYPE OF BLADE SHOWN INCORPORATED IN A FAN WHEEL

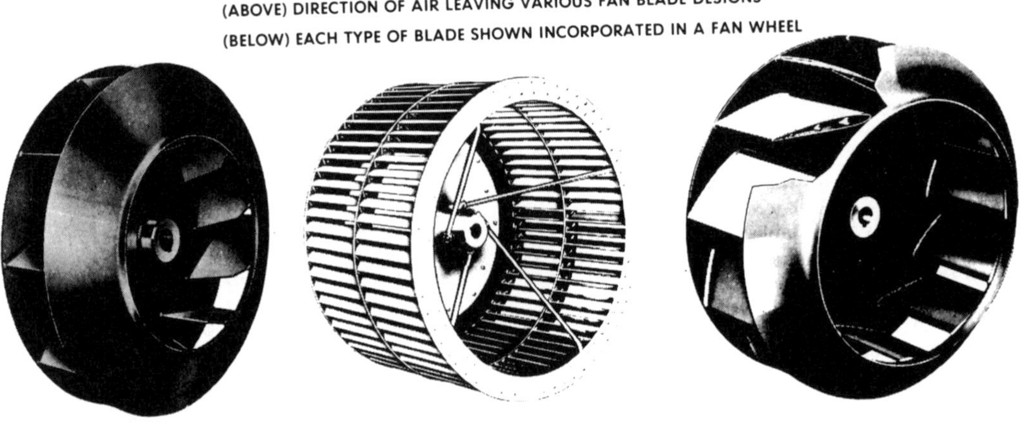

FIGURE 11-17 Different types of centrifugal fans. (Courtesy of the Trane Company.)

mance characteristics of the fan. The three different types of centrifugal fans used in heating, ventilating, and air conditioning are the forward curved blade fan, the backward inclined blade fan with plate blades, and the backward inclined blade fan incorporating an airfoil shaped blade design. These three types of fan blades are illustrated in Figure 11-17 in both a vector example of the air leaving the blade and an illustration of each type blade incorporated in a fan wheel.

Centrifugal Fan Designations

In order to designate the direction in which a fan wheel shall rotate, the designations clockwise and counterclockwise are used. To determine the direction in which the wheel of a double inlet fan wheel shall rotate, the fan should be viewed from the pulley end of the shaft. To determine the direction in which the wheel of a single inlet fan shall rotate, the fan should be viewed from the side opposite the inlet.

There are also a series of terms used in designating the air discharge of a fan. Fan discharge is designated as horizontal if the air leaves in a horizontal direction; as a blast if the air is discharged vertically upward from the fan; and a down blast if the air discharges vertically downward from the fan.

Centrifugal fans also have standardized nomenclature according to the arrangement of the drive. These arrangements are illustrated in Figure 11-18. For ventilation and general air conditioning work, the belt drive arrangements are usually preferred. This eliminates the necessity of selecting a direct-drive fan for a definite motor speed. The modern V-belt drive is inexpensive and reliable. Also, it permits fan speed adjustment on the installation if an adjustable pitch sheave is used. Even with a fixed speed drive, adjustments of speed can be made to meet chang-

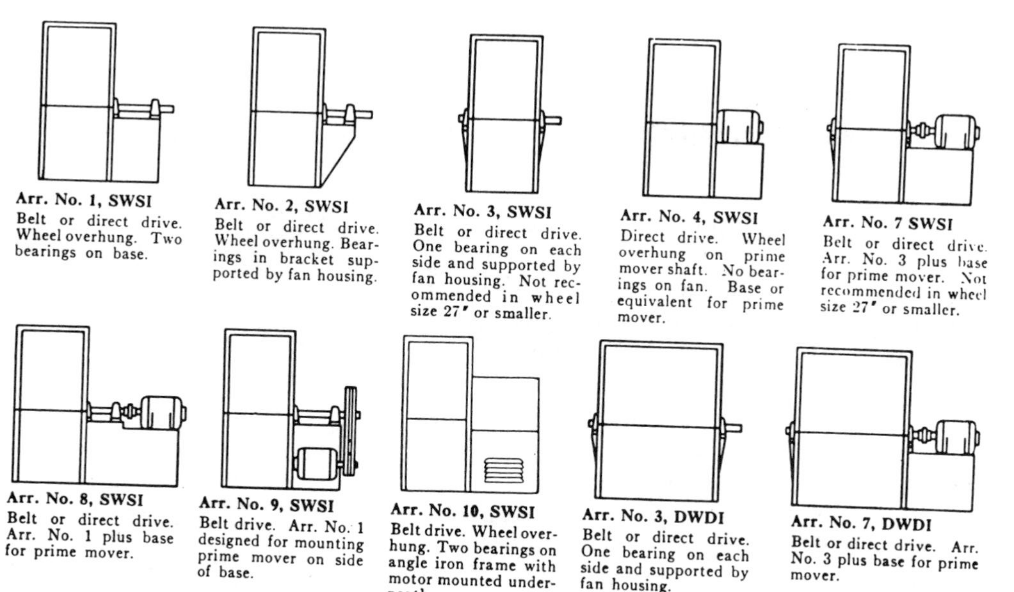

FIGURE 11-18 Drive nomenclature. (Courtesy of the Trane Company.)

ing conditions by substituting sheaves of a different size.

How a Centrifugal Fan Works

The outer shell of a centrifugal fan is a volute curve that increases the air space in the direction of rotation, delivering large volumes of air without creating a noise problem.

You should know that reversing rotation does not reverse air flow. It actually drastically reduces air flow and increases noise (siren effect). The impeller sucks in air at the wheel center, which it discharges at the required velocity. Velocity that is measured in feet per minute is critical in high volume equipment and should be controlled if air noise and duct vibration is to be minimal. The volume of air handled by any fan is measured in cubic feet of air per minute (cfm) at the fan outlet.

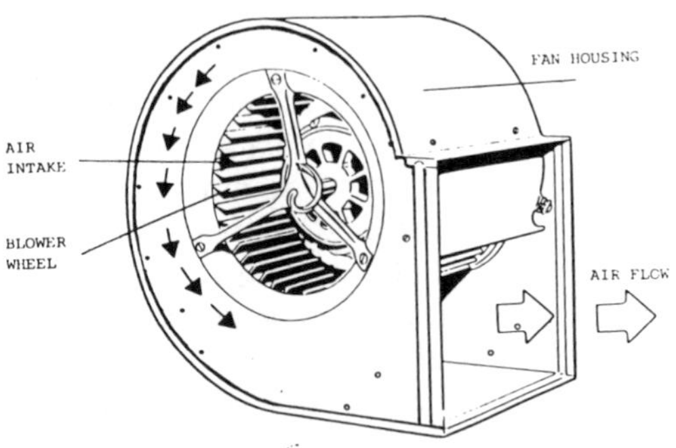

FIGURE 11-19 Typical centrifugal fan. In operation, air is drawn through the intake into the center space of a bladed wheel. Within the wheel, the air stream diverges into the rotating blades, which accelerates it. The accelerated air leaves the trailing edge of the blades and follows the inside wall of the fan scroll to the discharge opening. (Courtesy of Cadillac-Fairview Corporation, Limited.)

11-7 Maintenance of Air Handling Equipment

AN OVERVIEW

The maintenance requirements for most air handling equipment are similar. The frequency at which maintenance is required may vary from unit to unit depending on the cleanliness of the surroundings and the number of hours the unit is operated.

Any air handling system is balanced to delivery a certain cfm against a certain static pressure. Anything that contributes to changing the original design static pressure, such as dirty filters, dirty coils, or improperly operated air side dampers, causes the system to change its balance point. In some cases it is possible to force the fan to operate on an undesirable part of its performance curve, resulting in noisy operation. Therefore, cleanliness of all devices within the system's air stream is a key maintenance consideration.

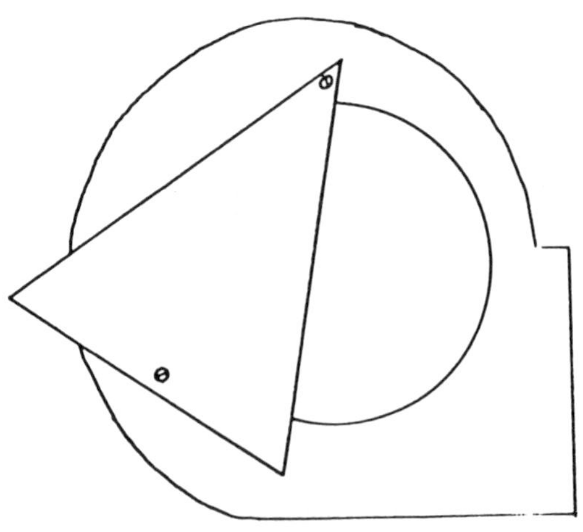

FIGURE 11-20 Air adjustment direct drive blower assembly. This illustration shows the shape and positioning of the adjustor. It adjusts the return air resistance and affects the performance of the blower by changing the load on the blower and motor.

Speed Control of Direct Drive Blowers

There are several ways to control the speed of direct drive blowers:

1. Multi-Speed Motor
   A popular way to control the speed of later model units is to install a multi-speed motor. This is often done on furnaces that have cooling systems.
2. Reactor Control
   To control the operating speed of some units, multi-tap reactors that control the voltage can be attached to a single speed motor.
3. No Speed Control
   If a direct drive blower assembly does not have a means of speed control, a single speed motor can be substituted with a multi-speed motor.

Insufficient Adjustment Range
Occasionally a system will have very little resistance to air flow and the lowest blower speed will still supply more air than is required, resulting in too low a temperature rise. To overcome this, a wedge-shaped piece of galvanized metal can be placed over the dead side of the blower (side opposite the opening containing the blower motor). (Fig. 11-20.)

V-Belt Drives (Tension—Alignment—Adjustment)

Drive sets for fans and blowers consist of a driver pulley on the motor shaft, a driven pulley on the blower shaft, and a belt or set of matched belts to transmit the power. (Figure 11-21). Such transmissions of power using a V-belt are commonly applied to sheave ratios

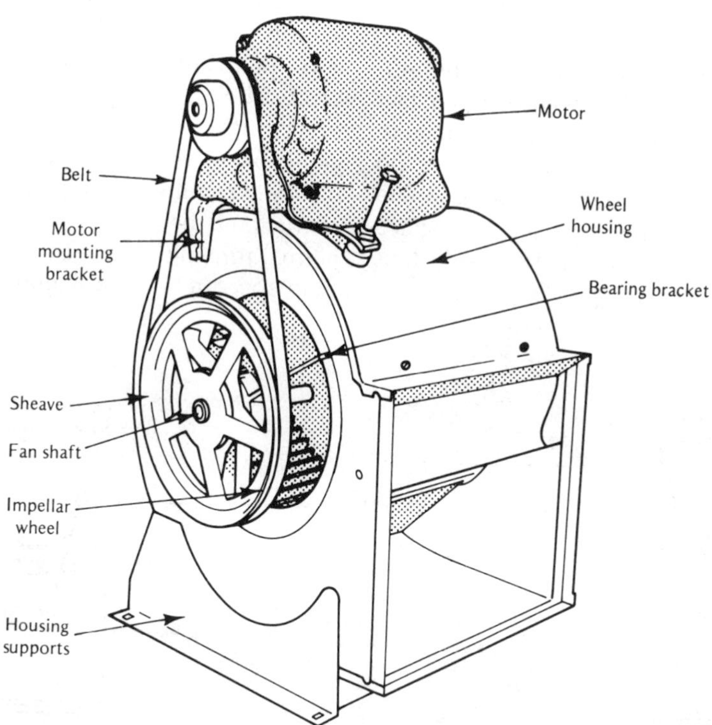

FIGURE 11-21 Belt drive centrifugal fan. The basic parts of the fan and housing. (Courtesy of Cadillac-Fairview Corporation, Limited.)

varying from 1 to 1 up to 7½ to 1. While most people understand the term "pulley," the term "sheave" could be confusing. A sheave is grooved to take a V-belt.

Common V-Belt Uses

V-belts provide a compact resilient transmission and are used extensively on drives for fans, generators, compressors, and water pumps. Speed ratio is the speed of the motor related to the speed of the driven object. The relationship between the diameter of the "driver" and the "driven" and their speed can be determined from standard basic pulley laws. This information allows the mechanic to choose the correct motor size related to the speed of the driven object and the correct size for the driver.

Belt Sizes

For maximum efficiency only the 40° angular side of a V-belt should be in contact with the sides of the sheave groove (Figure 11-22). The belt should ride flush with the top of the sheave and the sheave groove should be deep enough to provide a clearance space at the bottom of about 1/8" × 3/16", thus ensuring belt contact.

Correct V-Belt Tension

Power transmission is effected by the action of friction between the belt's sides and the sheaves around which they pass. The necessary contact pressure between the belt and the sheave is ensured by appropriate tightening of the belt.

Literally thousands of field investigations prove that incorrect drive belt tension and alignment is the major cause of bearing and belt failure. An easy means of checking belt tension is illustrated in Figure 11-27. When the belt is grasped as shown, you should obtain approximately 1 inch for every 36 inches between shaft centers deflection (total) when "finger" pressure is applied.

Excessive Deflection is an indication of too little tension, leading to belt failure through wear and loss of wheel speed.

Too Little Deflection indicates excessive tension, and will surely lead to noisy operation, premature bearing failure, and decreased belt life.

Bearings and shafting can fail simply because excessive belt tension destroyed the oil film between the bearing and the shaft. Tension should be applied until slip ceases at normal running speed. This can be checked from speed-ratio data (Figure 11-24). When

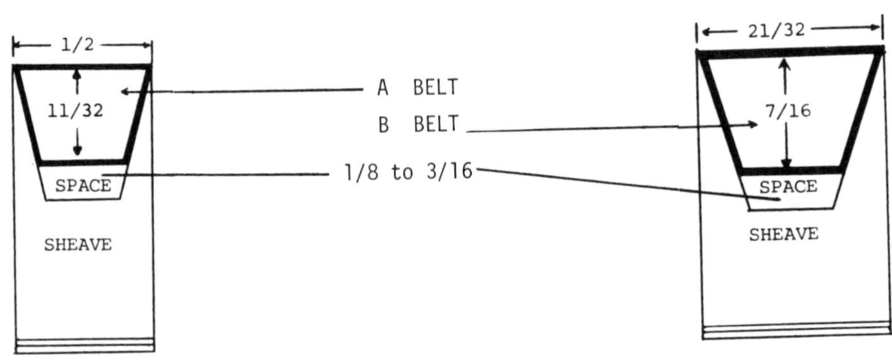

FIGURE 11-22 Belt and sheave size cross section.

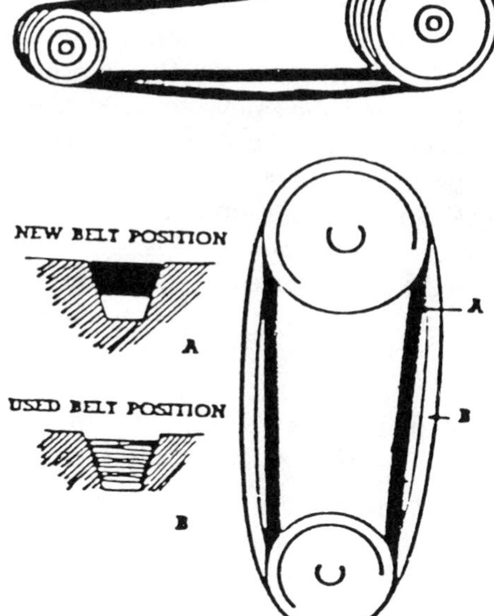

FIGURE 11-23 **Tips concerning fan belts.** *Matching V-belts*—Matched belt sets must only be ordered from the manufacturer as a matched set. *Don't mix new and used belts—the new belts will be overloaded.* Care should be taken to ensure the selection of the proper-size belts for their respective companion-size sheaves.

the drive is idle the belts should appear snug; when in motion a slight sag will be noticed in the direction away from the driving sheave.

Run-In Period

Following the initial tension adjustment, additional tension may be needed during the forty-eight hour run-in period. During this period two things take place:

1. The initial stretch is taken out of the belt.
2. The soft rubber surface of the outer envelope is abraded and the belt is seated at a slightly lower position in the sheave, permitting the belt to run slack.

Unless new belts are taken up, there is likely to be considerable slipping, burning, or other irreparable damage done to the belt.

Speed Control of Belt Driven Blowers

With V-belt drive blowers, the blower speed (cfm) can be adjusted by changing the width of the sheave on the motor. This shifts the position of the belt in the sheave and

PULLEY - R.P.M. CHART

Using Die Cast Single Drive Pulleys

MOTOR PULLEY	BLOWER PULLEY	0 TURN OPEN	1 TURN OPEN	2 TURNS OPEN	3 TURNS OPEN	4 TURNS OPEN	5 TURNS OPEN	6 TURNS OPEN	7 TURNS OPEN
3¼ x ½" & 3¼ x ⅝" 3.25" Dia.	5"	1130	1087	1044	1000	956	912	873	830
	6"	943	905	868	830	792	755	712	670
	7"	810	777	745	713	680	648	612	575
	8"	700	672	644	616	588	560	528	497
	9"	625	600	575	550	525	500	472	444
	10"	577	556	534	511	490	468	446	425
	12"	477	460	443	427	410	392	375	357
3½ x ½" & 3½ x ⅝" 3.50" Dia.	5"	1195	1154	1109	1065	1021	982	939	895
	6"	1012	977	937	898	864	826	792	754
	7"	869	842	806	779	743	715	682	653
	8"	755	732	703	679	651	621	597	568
	9"	665	640	616	592	568	543	519	495
	10"	611	592	568	543	524	505	480	461
	12"	514	495	475	461	441	422	403	388

FIGURE 11-24 **Sheave adjustment chart.** (Courtesy of T.A. Clark and the Heating, Refrigerating and Air-Conditioning Institute of Canada.)

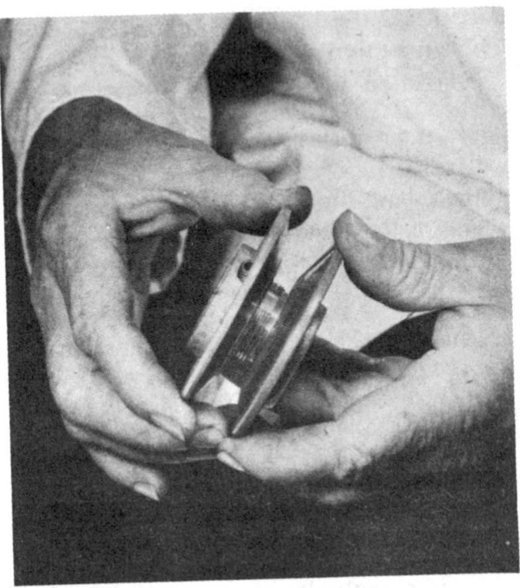

FIGURE 11-25 **Adjusting sheave speed, the slow-running position.** (Courtesy of the Department of Energy, Mines, and Resources, Canada.)

alters the speed. An "A" sheave is still used with an "A" belt; and a "B" sheave with a "B" belt. DO NOT TRY TO ADJUST AN "A" SHEAVE FOR A "B" BELT. Allowing the belt to ride lower in the groove changes the effective diameter of the sheave, which changes the speed of the driven equipment, fan pump, etc. Motor amperage must be checked to insure that full load amperage is not exceeded when the blower speed is increased. (Figures 11-22 to 11-26.)

PROBLEMS CAUSED BY INCORRECT BELT ADJUSTMENT

1. Slack belts cause sheave and belt wear and loss of speed due to running slippage.
2. Belt running slippage glazes the belt surfaces, and the friction heat causes cracks in the belt.

FIGURE 11-26 **Adjusting sheave speed, the fast-running position.** (Courtesy of the Department of Energy, Mines, and Resources, Canada.)

FIGURE 11-27 **Correct tension is important.** (Courtesy of Cadillac-Fairview Corporation, Limited.)

3. Tight belts wear out bearings by overloading.
4. Cracks in belts cause sheave wear and if unattended, often break the sheave or other parts of the driven object.

Basic Pulley Laws

1. Rpm of driven =
$$\frac{\text{diameter of driver} \times \text{rpm}}{\text{diameter of driven}}$$
2. Rpm of driver =
$$\frac{\text{diameter of driven} \times \text{rpm}}{\text{diameter of driver}}$$
3. Diameter of driven =
$$\frac{\text{diameter of driver} \times \text{rpm}}{\text{rpm of driven}}$$
4. Diameter of driver =
$$\frac{\text{diameter of driven} \times \text{rpm}}{\text{rpm of driver}}$$

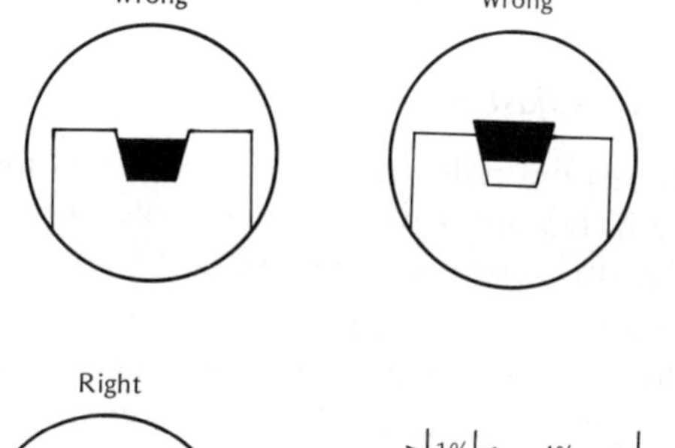

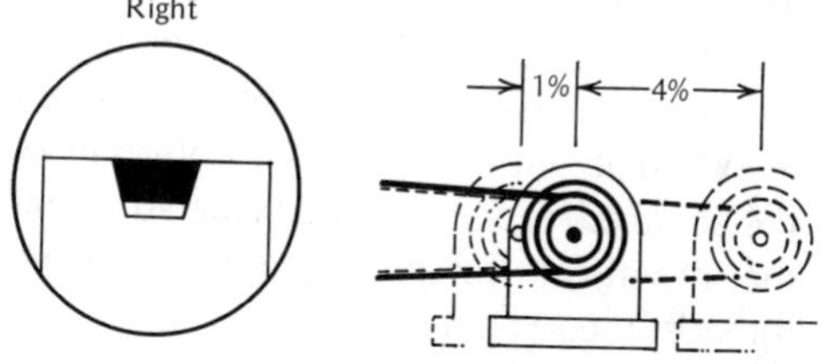

FIGURE 11-28 Tips concerning fan belts. To assist in the application of new belts without undue strain, the motor takeup should be sufficient to handle 5% variation in belt length and normal takeup due to wear and stretch. The motor should be positioned so that one-fifth of the takeup is toward the driven unit to allow for ease of application while the remaining four-fifths are available for takeup purposes.

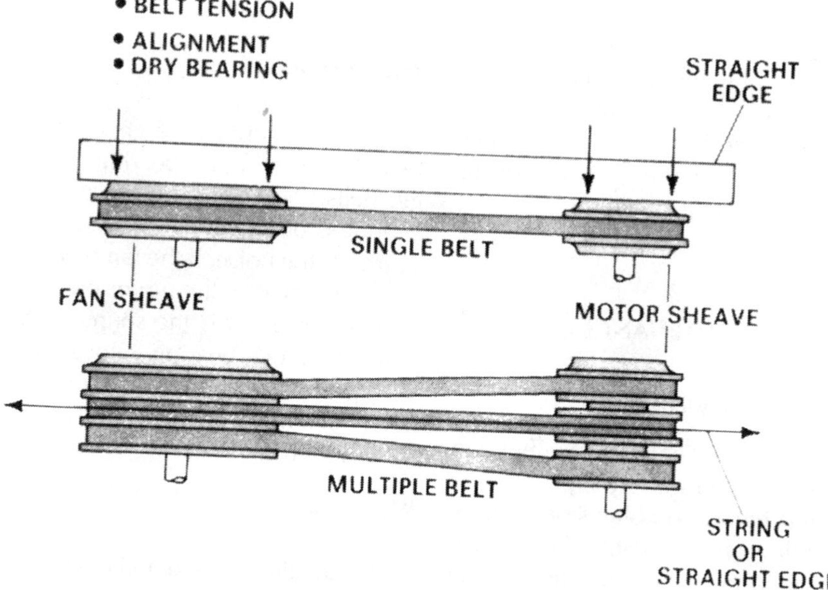

FIGURE 11-29 Belt alignment. A squealing sound can be immediately attributed to loose or misaligned fan belts or dry bearings. (Courtesy of the Trane Company.)

SHEAVES

How to Adjust Sheave Speed

1. Open the switch supplying power to the unit. Do not depend on fan switch or relays to keep power from the blower motor.
2. Adjust the variable pitch motor sheave for lower speeds (higher temperature rise) by widening the space between the sheave halves. It is wise to limit each adjustment to one-half turn of the adjustable half of the sheave (Figure 11-25). Make sure that the set screw is not adjusted on the sheave threads. (See Fig. 11-24.)
3. Close the switch supplying the power to the unit and allow the unit to operate until the system has again reached balance.

Replacing the Sheaves

It should be noted that the sheaves on the driven object are specially sized by the manufacturer and should NEVER be replaced with a different one. All changes will only be made, if necessary, to the motor sheave. Suitable ratios can only be determined by a qualified mechanic who understands fan operation characteristics, fan and pulley laws, and the use of a variety of instruments that assure accurate adjustments.

FAN MAINTENANCE

Air Side System Analysis

The air side system analysis is confined to analyzing noise sources at the fan, resulting from either mechanical problems or changes in system air flow characteristics. The course of action to follow when analyzing a noise problem is dictated by the nature of the sound.

Vibration

Fan vibration is usually caused by an out-of-balance fan wheel. This condition is statically checked by removing the belts from the fan sheave, cleaning the fan blades, and then rotating the fan wheel by hand. When the fan wheel slows to a stop, it should remain stationary. If it reverses direction and comes to rest in another position, the wheel is obviously out of balance. Another possible cause of fan vibration is cracked or fraying belts, bent shaft, worn bearings, or dirt on the rotor blade. Unless corrected immediately, one or more of the following problems will be encountered:

1. Noise
2. Worn or burned out bearings
3. Weakening of the fan's supports
4. Loosening of the piping
5. Springing of the shaft or damaging the wheel
6. Defective belts

Rumbling Sounds

Rumbling sounds are generally attributed to faulty fan or motor bearings. First, remove the belts and rotate the fan by hand. Each bearing is observed in an effort to isolate the source of the noise. If the fan bearings appear to be satisfactory, the motor operation is observed to see if it is the source of the noise. Once the faulty bearing is located, it should be replaced as soon as possible. Complete failure of a noisy bearing is only a matter of a short period of time.

Squealing

A squealing sound may be immediately attributed to either loose or misaligned fan belts, or a dry bearing.

Normally, the fan belts may squeal for a short period of time when the fan is started. If a loud squealing sound continues after the fan comes up to speed, the belt tension and alignment should be checked.

As mentioned before, the drive side of the belts should form a straight line with a small amount of bow on the slack side. If the bow on the slack side appears excessive, or a bowing of the belts appears on the drive side, the belts are too loose. Misalignment of the fan and motor sheaves may also be responsible for noisy operation. Sheave alignment may be checked in one of two ways, depending on the type of sheave in use. With the smaller or double groove sheaves, a straight edge of string is held tightly across the faces of the sheave (Figure 11-29). Alignment is correct when the straight edge touches the sheaves at the four points shown.

If excessive slack or misalignment has caused one or more of the belts to become frayed, the entire belt set should be replaced. It is not possible to properly tension a belt set when old and new belts are used together. The diameter of the old belt will normally be greater than that of the new one. (Fig. 11-23.)

Pulsation

Pulsation, which is normally heard as a rumbling sound within the air stream, is the result of excessive static pressure within the system.

Since abnormal static pressure conditions are the result of some kind of air blockage within the system, the condition that generally precedes pulsation is loss of fan capacity.

The first and most likely causes for an air blockage are dirty filters and coils. If cleaning fails to correct the condition, the investigation should be extended to the unauthorized closing of outdoor, return, or other air control dampers in the system.

FILTERS

All air used in an air conditioning system must be filtered to maintain a clear atmosphere in the conditioned space. Outside air always contains a number of contaminants, such as bacteria, pollens, insects, soot, ash, dust, and dirt. Return air also has contaminants, such as house dirt, lint, soot, and ash. The type of filter used will be determined by the degree of cleanliness expected and the concentration of contaminants.

Types of Filters

The infinite variety of contaminants makes it impossible to design one type of air cleaner that will be ideal for all applications. As a result, many types of air filters, or cleaners, have been designed to meet the needs of various applications. These filters can be divided into three classifications:

1. Viscous impingement type
2. Dry type (sieve or strainer)
3. Electronic air cleaners

Viscous Impingement Filter

The most common type of filter is the viscous impingement unit. This type includes the disposable furnace filter, the metal washable filter, the automatic oil bath filter, and the automatic roll filter.

The principle of viscous impingement has two basic components. First, the air stream and entrained dust particles change direction vigorously as they pass through the filtering material. Second, a sticky coating is applied to the individual fibers or members of the filter material and the constant change of direction causes the dirt particles to collide with the fibers or strands of filter material. The sticky coating holds the particles to prevent them from bouncing or sliding on through. (Fig. 11-30.)

Sieve or Strainer

The sieve, or strainer, principle of filtration operates exactly as its name implies. It essentially relies on a filtering medium that will allow air to pass, but because of its porous structure, will not allow dirt particles to pass.

In a sieve-type filter the interstices, or openings in the filtering medium, are given depth and irregular shape to allow the dirt particles to become trapped inside. (Figure 11-31.)

Electronic Filters

Electrostatic precipitation is probably the most interesting principle of dust collecting since it is effective in the high efficiency ranges, and since it relies on a controllable physical action and reaction. By imposing an electrostatic charge on a dirt particle, it can be attracted to a field having the opposite charge as it is carried along the air stream.

The particle is then carried between parallel plates, one charged positively, and one grounded negatively. The positively charged particle is attracted to the negative plate. (Figure 11-32.)

Filter Maintenance

Air filters are by their nature a disagreeable and unattractive component of the air con-

FIGURE 11-30 Viscous impingement filter. Viscous impingement filters can be used for the home furnace or in large buildings, and in industry, as in this illustration. (Courtesy of American Air Filter, Limited.)

ditioning system when considered from the maintenance standpoint. This unattractiveness is well overshadowed by the high values they have in protecting the other system components, and by the desired end product of clean, conditioned air. A filter is designed to catch dirt and therefore, it is going to get dirty.

There are three basic maintenance methods for air filters, as well as the mechanical and electrical details for automatic and/or electronic types. The filter can be maintained by replacement, by cleaning, or by the particular requirement of an automatic machine.

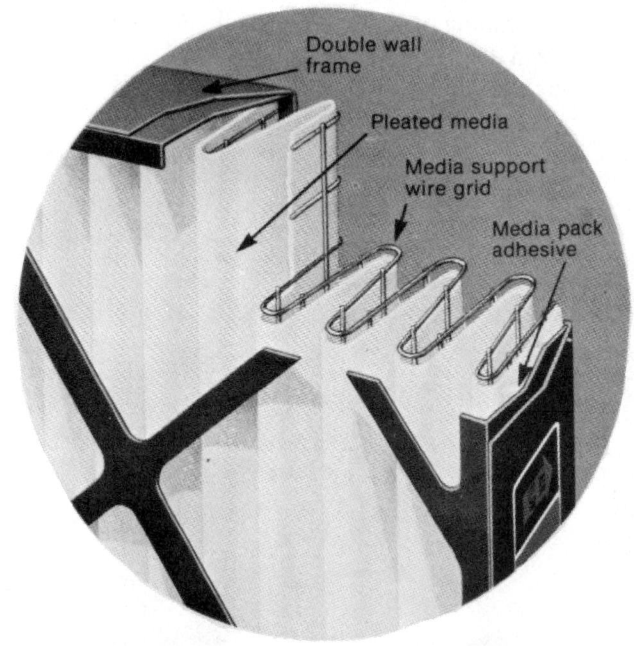

FIGURE 11-31 Sieve or strainer filter. (Courtesy of American Air Filter, Limited.)

COIL MAINTENANCE

Coil cleanliness is checked as frequently as necessary to assure efficient system performance. As mentioned previously, restricted air flow destroys the system design balance. In addition, dirt insulates the coil surfaces reducing heat transfer efficiency. Therefore, the coils must be kept as clean as possible at all times.

Steam, applied to the coil through a suitable nozzle, is an effective cleaning method. If the coil is extremely dirty, a detergent may be applied through the nozzle with steam.

If steam is available, or a refrigerant coil is to be cleaned, a strong detergent solution may be applied to the coil with a long bristle paint brush. If a detergent is used, the coil must be rinsed thoroughly after cleaning.

Normally, annual coil cleaning is satisfactory for the smaller air handling units, such as a fan coil unit. Since these units are generally located in occupied spaces where cleaning fluids may damage decorated surfaces, a wet pick-up vacuum would be recommended for use while doing the job.

FIGURE 11-32 Electronic air cleaner. American Air Filter's "Dri-Pak" fillers are used in the storage section to collect the large particles created by the agglomerator section of the "Electro-Pak" electronic air cleaner. (Courtesy of American Air Filter, Limited.)

FIGURE 11-33 Filter with disposable pad. (Courtesy of the American Air Filter, Limited.)

While steam cleaning is satisfactory for hot water, chilled water, and steam coils, it is not recommended for refrigerant coils because the heat may cause excessively high pressures to develop within the coil or system, causing possible damage.

INSPECTION

Annual Inspection

An annual inspection of all air handling equipment is recommended. At this time, the fan shaft and bearing setscrews are tightened to the torques recommended by the manufacturer. The fan blades, scroll, and air handling casings are cleaned. Any rust or corrosion is removed and the affected area repainted.

In addition, all damper bearings and linkages, except nylon bushings, are lubricated with light machine oil.

Daily/Weekly Fan Inspections

Fans operating properly run smoothly. Anything other than a smooth, quiet operation should be considered a problem.

Supply Fans

1. Check damper and shutter operation.
2. Check manometer and filter—change as required.
3. Wipe off fan housings, motors, etc.—clean equipment rooms.
4. Check holding bolts and fan housing.
5. Check for abnormal sound.
6. Check belts for tension, cracks, and frays.
7. Check sheaves and screws.
8. Check air intake bird screens and clean as required.

Exhaust Fans

1. Check belts for tension, fraying, and cracks.
2. Wipe off fan housing, motors, etc.
3. Check holding bolts.
4. Check flexible joints between fan and duct.
5. Check bird screen; clean as required.
6. Check for abnormal sound, vibration.
7. Check operation of back draft damper.

11-8 Lubrication

WHY WE NEED LUBRICATION

Friction is the force that resists the sliding motion between surfaces in contact with each other. To overcome this resistance, a film of lubricant is used to separate the surfaces. The lubricant creates a "fluid friction" within itself; the only friction is from the motion within the fluid.

Roller friction is any system of rolling elements that reduces friction considerably.

Sliding friction is created when one solid body is pulled or pushed across the surface of another with adhesion—such as a shaft revolving in a bearing with no lubricant to separate the surfaces. With lubrication we overcome "sliding friction" and create a "fluid friction" situation.

There are two types of lubricant in common use. Oil is a liquid of either high or low viscosity. Grease is a solid semi-fluid product composed of oil and a thickening agent. Therefore, the difference between oil and grease is in the consistency. Grease does not run like oil and therefore tends to remain where it is put. Grease also has a much higher adhesive property than oil.

ADVANTAGES OF OIL

1. Oil is the lowest price maintenance cost.
2. Oil is easier to drain and refill.
3. The amount used is easier controlled.
4. If bearings operate under high temperature, conditions favor oil.
5. Viscosity is by far an oil's most important property. Oil with a high viscosity won't flow as easily as oil with a low viscosity.

CAUTION

1. Never use oil in a grease fitting or vice versa.
2. Oil is harmful to taped and varnished insulation of winding.
3. Once a winding is thoroughly oil soaked, the motor is in immediate danger of a burnout or breakdown.

ADVANTAGES OF GREASE

1. Greased bearings do not need replenishing as often as oiled bearings.
2. Grease forms an effective seal that prevents entrance of dirt into the bearing. It stays put and only the simplest seals are needed. Grease gives better bearing protection.

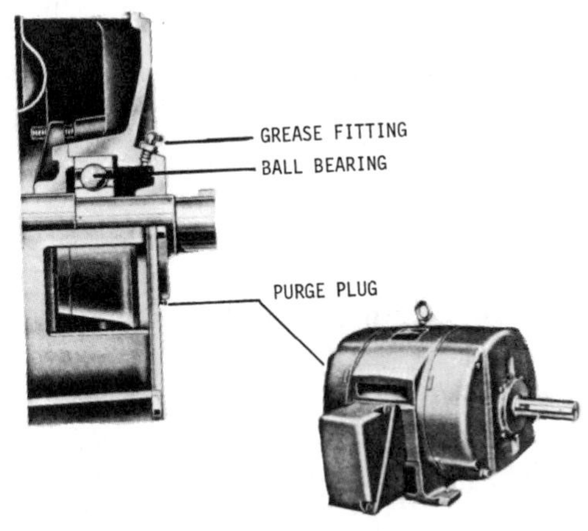

FIGURE 11-34 Greasing a motor. (Courtesy of the Canadian General Electric Company, Limited.)

3. Proper grease quantity is easily confined in the housing; this simplifies the design of bearing enclosures.
4. No need for high pressure equipment to apply.
5. Grease must be added while motor is running to force out excess lubrication.
6. The risk of losing the grease and eventually the bearing from grease leakage through seals is a point often raised. The melting and dropping point of grease is 350° to 480°F, eliminating this problem.

HOW TO GREASE A MOTOR

1. Remove the purge plug.
2. Clear out any hardened grease from the purge opening.
3. Inject grease at the grease fitting until an excess of new grease is expelled from purge plug opening.
4. After greasing, allow motor to run for about ten minutes before replacing purge plug.

11-9
Bearings

WHAT IS A BEARING?

Ball and roller bearings are collectively referred to as "anti-friction bearings." They are usually comprised of two components:

- the rollers or balls in an inner or outer race
- the cage for retaining them, with possibly seals or shields

The function of the cage is to maintain the balls or rollers in their correct relative positions so that they do not touch one another, and also to provide a certain amount of guidance for the rolling elements.

TYPES OF BEARINGS COMMONLY USED

1. Cylindrical roller
2. Taper roller
3. Ball or roller thrust bearing
4. Sleeve bearings

BEARING FEATURES

1. Low frictional loss when starting
2. Long service life
3. Low lubricant consumption

INSTALLATION AND MAINTENANCE

Proper precaution during installation and maintenance can greatly prolong the life of a bearing, avoiding premature failure and costly replacement.

Probably the most important single factor to keep in mind is CLEANLINESS. Dust, dirt, or any form of abrasive material is an anti-friction bearing's greatest enemy.

Except in the case of completely sealed bearings, dirty working conditions in the area where bearings are installed or maintained could easily lead to serious contamination and early failure. KEEP BEARINGS CLEAN—DIRT MEANS DAMAGE!

COMMON BEARING PROBLEMS

1. Overheating
2. Vibration
3. Loose on shaft
4. Hard turning shaft
5. Forcing bearings on to oversize or out of round shafting
6. Incorrect substitution

BEARING TYPES AND THEIR FUNCTIONS

Designers have a wide variety of bearing types from which to choose. Each bearing has characteristics which make it the best choice for a certain application. Therefore, a replacement should be made with the same type of bearing.

BEARING PROBLEMS

Noise (Call for Service)	*Probable Cause*
High pitch, steady tone	Excessive axial or radial load or misalignment.
Low pitch, continuous or intermittent	Too much clearance, or raceways pitted.
Intermittent squeal or high pitch noise	Balls skidding, or shaft rubbing housing.
Intermittent rumbles, rattles, clicks	Too much clearance in bearings; dirt in bearings; loose machine parts.

BEARING PROBLEMS

Excessive Vibration (Call for Service)	*Probable Cause*
During acceleration or deceleration periods	Critical speeds of machine's components.
During operation at fixed speeds	Unbalanced rotating parts; shaft bent; cams, gears, or linkage; misalignment.
Runout (Call for Service)	***Probable Cause***
Shaft does not run true Shaft binds when rotated by hand	Shaft bent; bearing misaligned; bearings rings out of square; dirt; machine deflection.
Temperature	***Probable Cause***
High after first start	Grease distribution. Stop; allow to cool; restart.
Continuously high	Churning of lubricant. Use lower oil level, less grease, stiffer grease. Add lubricant. Excessive axial load. Excessive radial load. Bearing misaligned. Excessive seal drag.

BEARING REPLACEMENT

Any of the following defects will cause unusual noise or vibration and should be serviced by a trained mechanic as soon as possible.

1. Broken or cracked rings.
2. Dented seals or shields.
3. Broken or cracked cages.
4. Broken or cracked balls or roller.
5. Bearings that have overheated. These bearings are generally darkened to brownish-blue or blue-black color.
6. Flaked areas on balls, rollers, or raceways.

Self-aligning ball bearings: The self-aligning ball bearing, with two rows of balls rolling on the spherical surface of the outer ring, compensates for angular misalignment resulting from errors in mounting, shaft deflection and distortion of the foundation. It is impossible for this bearing to exert any bending influence on the shaft, a most important consideration in applications requiring extreme accuracy, at high speeds. Self-aligning ball bearings are recommended for radial loads and moderate thrust loads in either direction.

Single row, deep groove ball bearings: The single row, deep groove ball bearing will sustain, in addition to radial load, a substantial thrust load in either direction, even at very high speeds. This advantage results from the intimate contact existing between the balls and the deep, continuous groove in each ring. When using this type of bearing, careful alignment between the shaft and housing is essential. This bearing is also available with seals and shields, which serve to exclude dirt and retain lubricant.

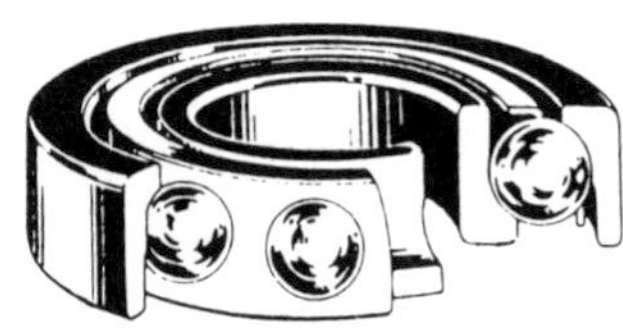

Angular contact ball bearings: The angular contact ball bearing supports a heavy thrust load in one direction, sometimes combined with a moderate radial load. A steep contact angle, assuring the highest thrust capacity and axial rigidity, is obtained by a high thrust supporting shoulder on the inner ring and a similar high shoulder on the opposite side of the outer ring. These bearings can be mounted singly, or when the sides are flush ground, in tandem for constant thrust in one direction; and mounted in pairs, also when sides are flush ground, for a combined load, either face-to-face or back-to-back.

FIGURE 11-35 Bearing types and functions. (Courtesy of SKF Canada, Ltd.)

Double row, deep groove ball bearings: The double row, deep groove ball bearing embodies the same principle of design as the single row bearing. However, the grooves for the two rows of balls may be so positioned that the load lines through the balls have either an outwardly converging or an inwardly converging contact angle. This bearing has a lower axial displacement than occurs in the single row design, substantial thrust capacity in either direction, and high radial capacity due to the two rows of balls.

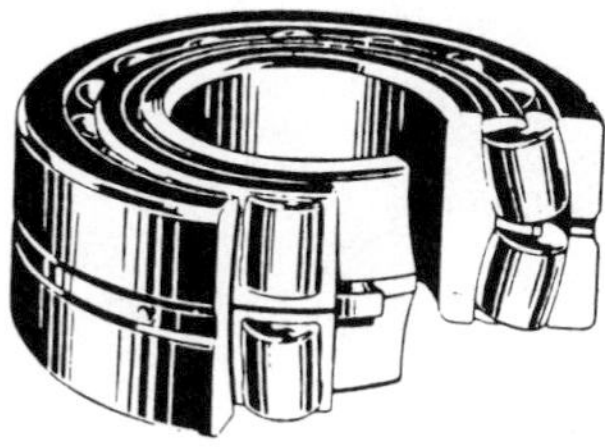

Spherical roller bearings: The spherical roller bearing, due to the number, size and shape of the rollers and the accuracy with which they are guided, has unexcelled capacity. Since the bearing is inherently self-aligning, angular misalignment between the shaft and housing has no detrimental effect and the full capacity is always available for useful work. The design and proportion are such, that in addition to radial load, heavy thrust load may be carried in either direction.

Cylindrical roller bearings: The cylindrical roller bearing has high radial capacity and provides accurate guiding of the rollers, resulting in a close approach to true rolling. Consequent low friction permits operation at high speed. Those types which have flanges on one ring only allow a limited free axial movement of the shaft in relation to the housing. They are easy to dismount even when both rings are mounted with a tight fit. The double row type assures maximum radial rigidity and is particularly suitable for machine tool spindles.

FIGURE 11-36 Bearing types and functions. (Courtesy of SKF Canada, Ltd.)

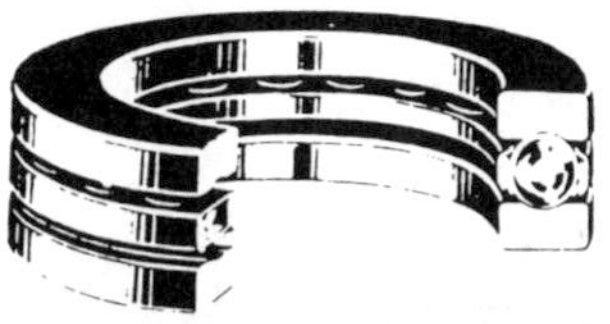

Ball thrust bearings: The ball thrust bearing is designed for thrust load in one direction only. The load line through the balls is parallel to the axis of the shaft, resulting in high thrust capacity and minimum axial deflection. Flat seats are preferred, particularly where the load is heavy or where close axial positioning of the shaft is essential; as for example, in machine tool spindles.

Spherical roller thrust bearings: The spherical roller thrust bearing is designed to carry heavy thrust loads or combined loads which are predominantly thrust. This bearing has a single row of rollers which roll on a spherical outer race with full self-alignment. The cage, centered by an inner ring sleeve, is constructed so that lubricant is pumped directly against the inner ring's usually high guide flange. This insures good lubrication between the roller ends and the guide flange. The spherical roller thrust bearing operates best with relatively heavy oil lubrication.

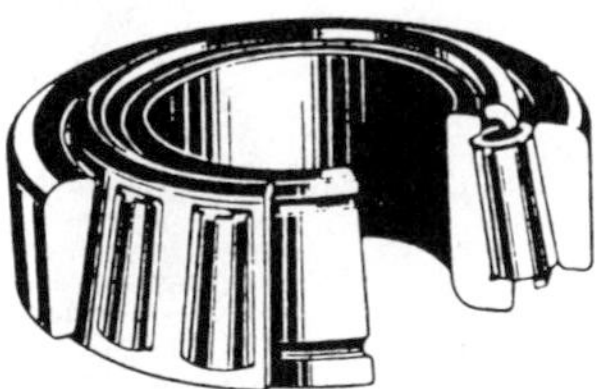

Tapered roller bearings: Since the axes of its rollers and raceways form an angle with the shaft axis, the tapered roller bearing is especially suitable for carrying radial and axial loads acting simultaneously. A bearing of this type usually must be adjusted toward another bearing capable of carrying thrust loads in the opposite direction. Tapered roller bearings are separable—their cones (inner rings) with rollers and their cups (outer rings) are mounted separately.

FIGURE 11-37 Bearing types and functions. (Courtesy of SKF Canada, Ltd.)

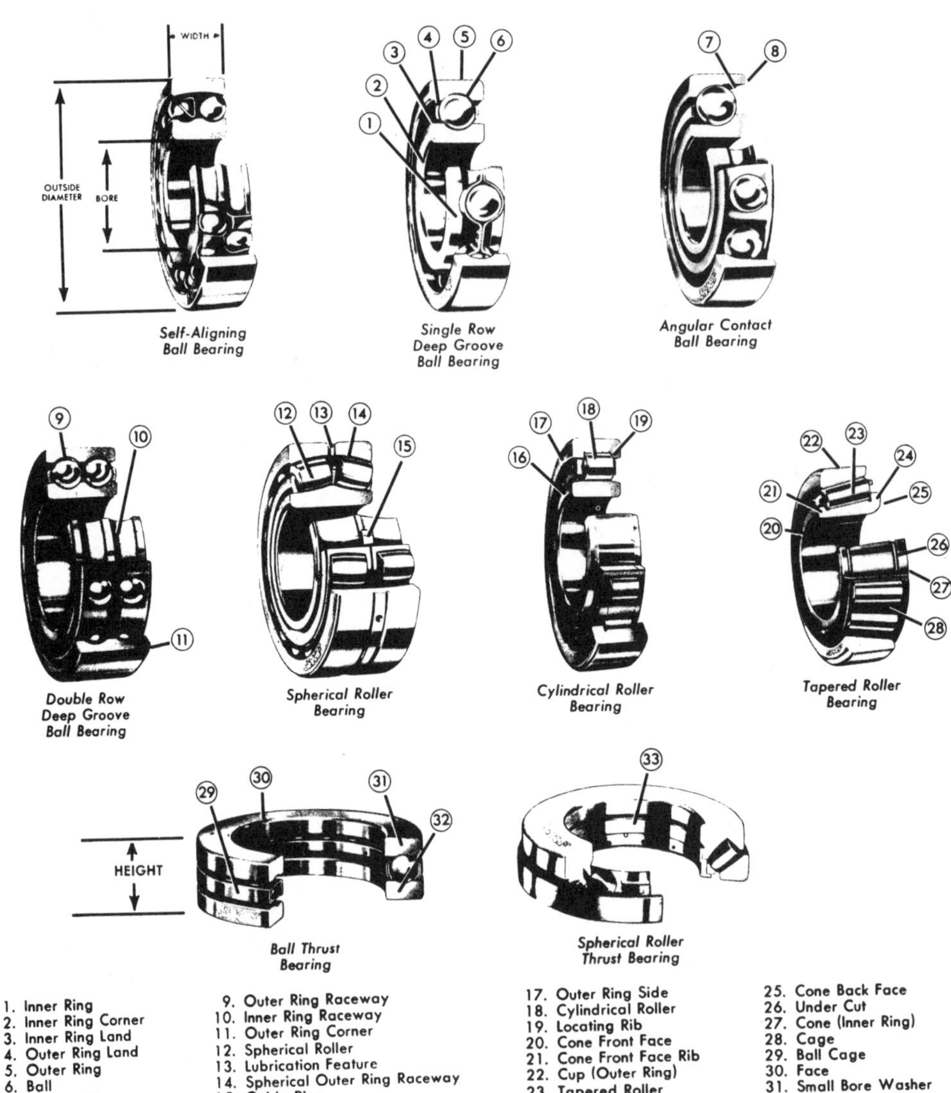

FIGURE 11-38 Bearing nomenclature. The illustrations below identify the bearing parts of the nine basic bearing types. The terms used conform with the terminology section of the Anti-Friction Bearing Manufacturers Association, Inc. Standards and are mutually accepted by the anti-friction bearing manufacturers. (Courtesy of SKF Canada, Ltd.)

7. Bearings whose raceways are indented or "brinelled" by balls or rollers being impressed into the races.

NOTE: When bearings are changed, ensure that the complete set of bearings is changed at both ends of the shaft.

11-10 Pumps

WHAT IS A PUMP?

Pumps circulate or move water from one location to another, either in a closed system where the water is used over and over again (as in heating and cooling), or in an open system where water is consumed or replaced (as in a sump pump or domestic water pump).

PUMP USAGE

A *boiler feedwater pump* supplies the boiler with feedwater as required. It must be capable of forcing this water into the boiler against the pressure existing in the boiler.

A *fuel oil pump* is used with oil-fired boilers to pump fuel oil to the burners.

A *circulating pump* is used to circulate heated or chilled water through the various heating and cooling systems of a building.

A *cooling water pump* circulates water from the cooling tower to the condenser of the refrigerating unit and back.

A *lubricating oil pump* supplies oil to the bearings of large refrigerating compressors and pumps.

A *chemical feed pump* supplies small, measured quantities of chemicals to boilers, circulating systems, and cooling towers.

A *domestic water pump* supplies domestic water to various parts of the building in which it is installed.

A *fire pump* supplies water to the standpipe, the hose, and the sprinkler system.

A *sump pump* is used to empty sumps that cannot be drained to gravity.

TYPES OF PUMPS

There are several types of pumps found in buildings:

1. IN-LINE CIRCULATORS, which are mounted in the pipe line.
2. BASE MOUNTED, which have pump and motor mounted on a common base and connected through a coupling. These pumps may be vertical or horizontal split case; may be single or double suction; and may have suction and discharge openings located in the end, side, or top.
3. CLOSE-COUPLED or built-together pumps, which have the impeller located on the end of an extended motor shaft.

SAFETY

Pumps should be treated like any other piece of rotating machinery. All exposed rotating parts should have a guard. When performing any maintenance other than lubrication, the local controls, as well as the main power disconnect, should be turned off and tagged.

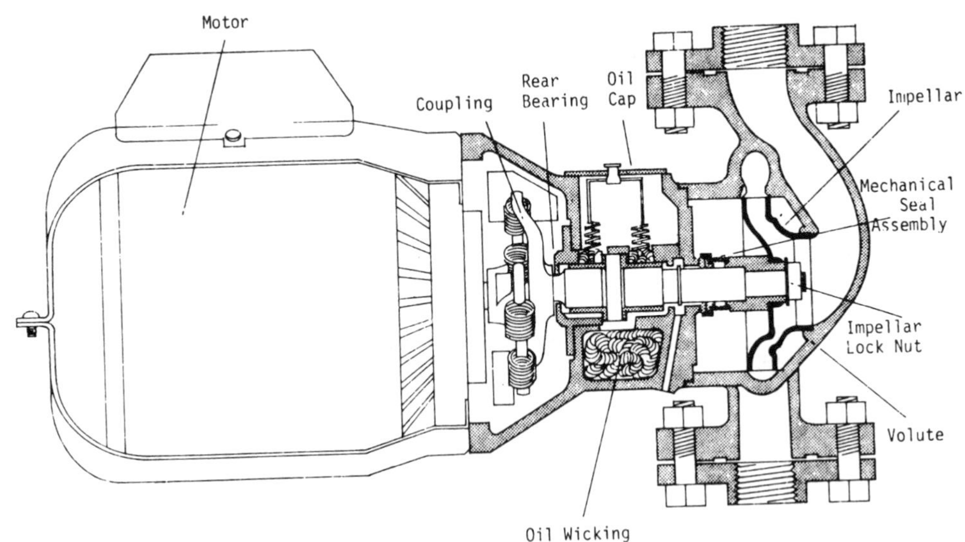

FIGURE 11-39 "In line" circulating pump (equipped with sleeve bearings). Oil should only be applied to the pump through the oil fill cap which is located on the top of the bearing housing. The level of the oil can be established easily by checking the oil level cup located on the side of the oil well (if one is installed). *Note:* The oil level cup should be only used for the purpose of checking the oil level. IT IS NOT A FILL LOCATION. (Courtesy of Cadillac-Fairview Corporation, Limited.)

COMMON PROBLEMS

All equipment should be maintained in accordance with instructions outlined in the manufacturer's manual. Regular "look, listen, and touch" inspections will alert you to problems before they become serious.

Vibration

1. Misalignment of motor and pump shaft.
2. Loose pump and motor base mountings.
3. Pump base inadequately grouted.
4. Pipe strain on either suction or discharge connections.
5. Pump coupler:
   - broken or worn springs or arms on flexible coupler;
   - worn discs in solid-type coupler;
   - worn motor bearings;
   - worn pump bearings.

Squealing

May be caused by lack of lubrication on either pump or motor. It may mean bearing or seal trouble. If squealing comes from the stuffing box, there may be too tight an adjustment on the gland.

Motor Failure

If the motor will not start and the fuses are okay, CALL FOR SERVICE.

Mechanical Failure

1. A frozen shaft on a pump may be caused by lack of bearing lubrication; by a foreign

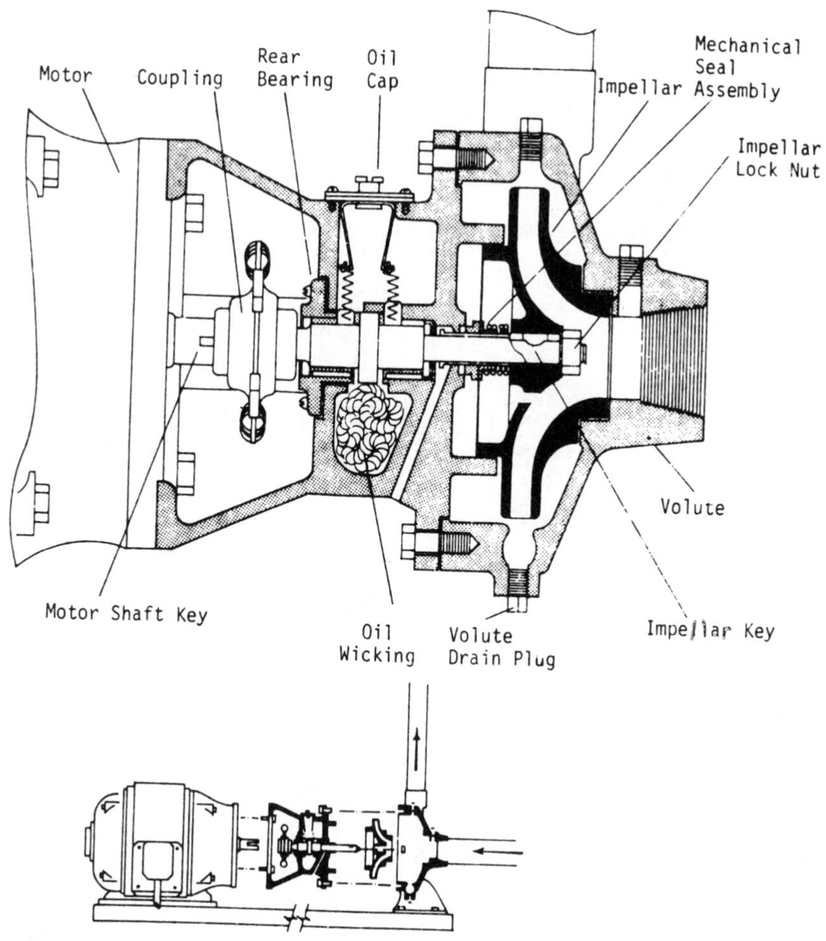

FIGURE 11-40 Base mounted circulating pump. *Note:* Change the oil in the oil well every time a new seal is installed, or at least once a year. (Courtesy of Cadillac-Fairview Corporation, Limited.)

object caught in the impeller; or by corrosion around the seal or impeller. TO CORRECT, CALL FOR SERVICE.

2. If you are experiencing flow problems, check that valves are open, and check couplings. If a centrifugal base mounted pump operates but does not circulate water, it may be air locked. Open small petcock to bleed out air.
3. When seals or spring couplings are changed, it is wise to also change motor resilient rubber ring mounts. This extends their life by properly lining up the motor.
4. Leaking mechanical seals and gaskets must be changed immediately. CALL FOR SERVICE.

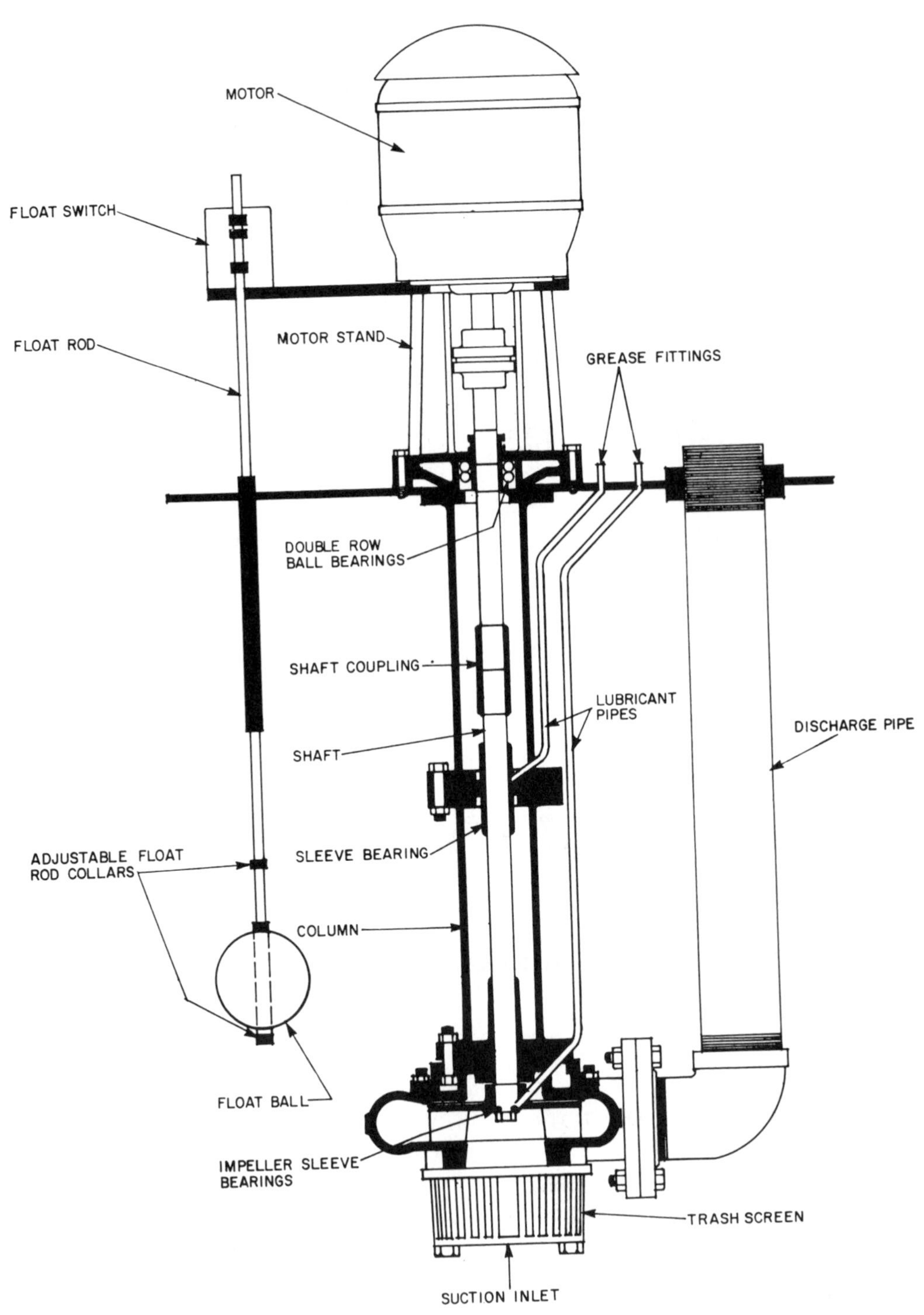

FIGURE 11-41 Sump pump. (Courtesy of Cadillac-Fairview Corporation, Limited.)

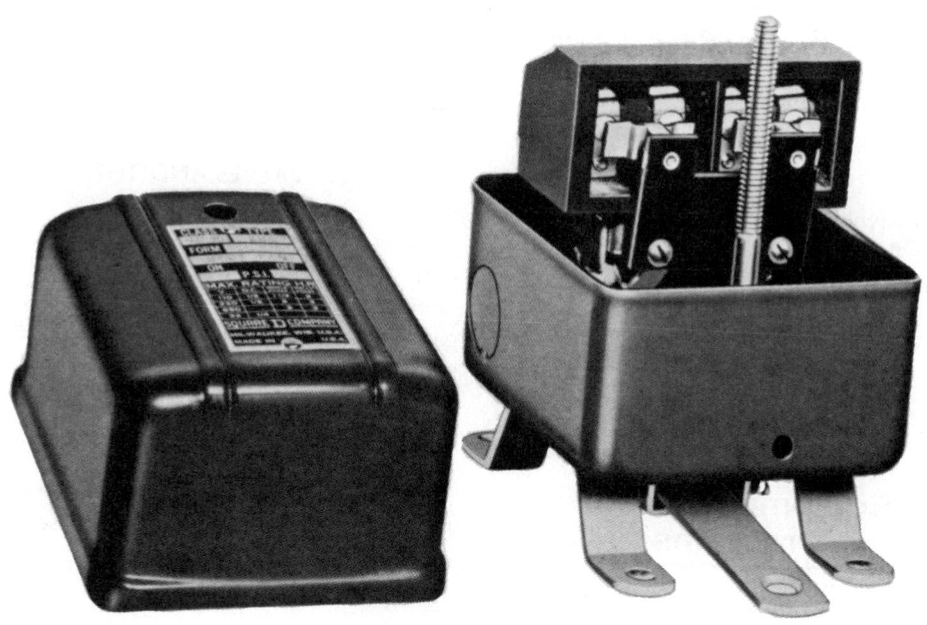

FIGURE 11-42 Typical float switch. Float switches control the level of the water in a sump pit. (Courtesy of Square D Company Canada, Limited.)

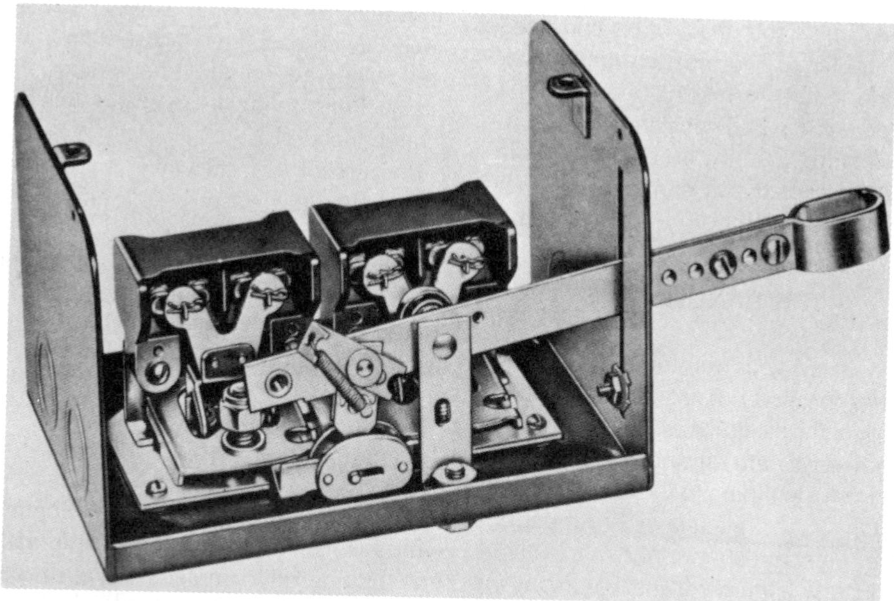

FIGURE 11-43 Typical dual-action pump control switch. (Courtesy of Square D Company Canada, Limited.)

Reasons for Mechanical Seal Failures

1. Improper installation of seal or pump.
2. Operating dry or partially dry.
3. Suspended solids in circulating water.
4. Excessively high water temperature. To date there is no conclusive evidence that connects seal failure to a particular water treatment.

11–11 Equipment Noise Problems

Noise and vibration problems are among the most common and most difficult to correct complaints faced by the building operator or by other troubleshooting specialists.

Many such problems can be traced to installation oversights that, once corrected, end the problems. The most common oversight is the failure to mount operating machinery on some type of isolation spring, or separate floating pad. To be effective, isolation must be such that it eliminates 90 percent to 99 percent of the sound vibration.

PIPE HANGERS

As the concrete is reinforced with steel bars, noises or vibrations are carried throughout their lengths. The use of pipe hangers is therefore necessary to eliminate carrying the problem from the piping to the concrete slab.

Pipe hangers include a layer of rubber between the spring and the supports. As with all other isolators, alignment and balancing of the piping network is critical and requires special attention.

11–12 Valves

TYPES OF VALVES AND THEIR USES

Valves control the flow of liquids. They start, stop, direct, regulate, or throttle the volume and rate of flow of water, steam, or gases. There is no universal valve to accomplish all these purposes, but there are several basic designs generally found in buildings: gate, globe, butterfly, ball, disc, diaphram, check, and cock or plug valves.

Each basic design has numerous modifications to meet special needs. It is essential to understand the mechanics of the particular valve under inspection or repair.

VALVE MAINTENANCE

With a minimum maintenance effort, thousands of dollars in valve replacement can be saved each year. Most manual valves need to operate only in emergencies. A little care will ensure proper operation when desperately needed.

Because of this, all valves should be accessible and tagged for ease in identification (see Chapter 2, Figure 2-17).

Valves that are usually left open should never be left completely open. The stem should be turned at least a half turn shut so that corrosion will not seal it in the open position.

Valve Leaks

Leaking is the major problem encountered with valves. A valve can leak internally by not shutting off completely when required. More obvious are external valve leaks at various connections, such as where the pipe joins the valve or flange, around the stuffing box, or where the body and bonnet connect.

Frequent and regular inspections are the best valve maintenance. *WHEN A LEAK IS FOUND, IT SHOULD BE CORRECTED, AS TIME WILL ONLY MAKE IT WORSE, NOT BETTER.*

Caution

When opening a closed valve, do it slowly. Surge pressure or rapid temperature change can easily damage piping or equipment downstream of the valve. The condition created is sometimes called "water hammer."

WHEN VALVES THAT ARE NORMALLY OPEN ARE CLOSED, THEY MUST BE TAGGED UNTIL THEY ARE OPENED AGAIN. (Figure 11-44).

Testing

Proper maintenance can prevent a number of valve problems. A routine schedule of valve maintenance is essential to ensure elimination of leaks and that the valves can be opened and closed when necessary.

A frozen valve stem may indicate a corrosion problem.

Records of the various types of valves, along with locations and code tags, should be assembled and used to organize regular inspections and maintenance (see Figure 2-17, Chapter Two).

BLENDING VALVES

The success or failure of our energy conservation effort dictates that the blending valves operate efficiently. The operator or controller positions or repositions the valve stem, which changes the proportion of the hotter or cooler water entering each of the two inlets. The result is a change in the water temperature leaving the outlet and going to the system (see Chapter 8, Figure 8-45).

TROUBLESHOOTING BLENDING VALVES

1. Check the power supply and fuses.
2. Check the position of the valve stem to make certain it moves when the motor operates.
3. Make sure the packing is not leaking. Excessive leaking will wear out the valve stem, making repacking difficult.

RECORD OF VALVE CLOSURES

LOCATION OF VALVE OR NO.	AREA CONTROLLED	TIME & DATE CLOSED	TURNS TO CLOSE	TIME & DATE OPENED	TURNS TO OPEN	LOCKED OPEN		DRAIN TEST		SIGNED BY
						YES	NO	STATIC	RESID.	

FIGURE 11-44 Record of valve closures. Used for fire sprinkler lines only. (Courtesy of the Factory Mutual Insurance Company.)

4. If the valves are air operated, air pressure closes the valve and spring pressure opens it. Check the air pressure (Chapter 8, Figure 8-42).
5. If the problem cannot be corrected, open the by-pass and call for the service of a qualified mechanic.

BASIC VALVE DESIGNS

Globe Valve

The construction of the globe valve is designed to regulate the flow of fluids. Seat and disc can be quickly and conveniently reseated or replaced. This feature makes them ideal for lines that require frequent valve maintenance. Also, shorter "disc travel" saves operator's time when valves are operated frequently.

Angle Valve

Angle valves have the same operating characteristics as globe valves. They are used when making a 90° turn in the line. An angle valve reduces the number of joints and saves make-up time. It also gives less restriction to flow than the elbow and globe valve that would otherwise have to be used.

Lift Check Valve

The check valve is placed in the circuit to prevent backflow. The pressure of flow opens the valve, and backflow closes it again when the flow pressure abates. Since check valves only operate "positively" in one direction, care must be taken to install them correctly. A check valve installed "backwards" will result in cutting the flow through the line. The lift check valve, because of its design, causes the flow to move through the body in a changing course—as in globe and angle valves. For this reason lift checks are particularly suitable to prevent backflow of gases or fluids where the flow velocities are high. Unlike the swing check valve, lift check valves depend on gravity in order to operate; they cannot, therefore, be used in a vertical line.

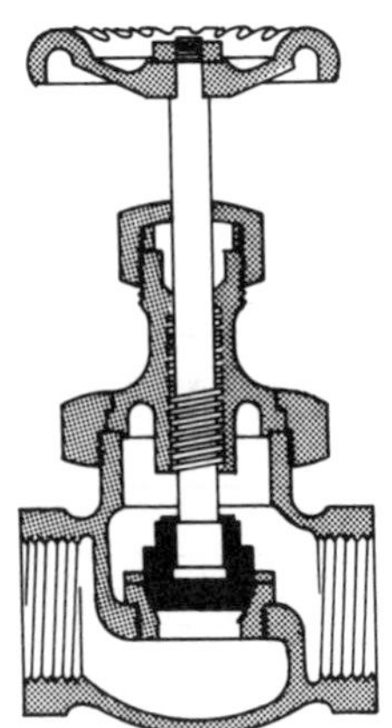

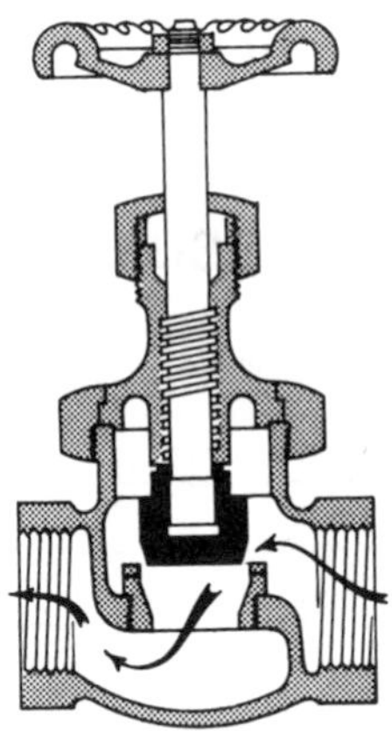

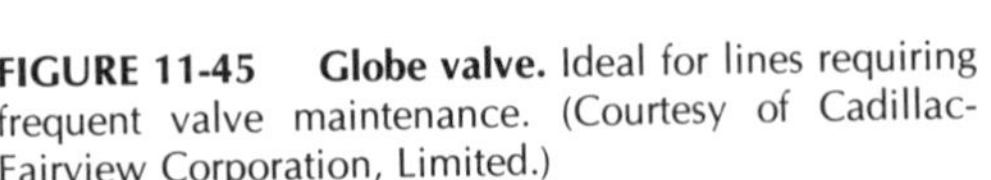

FIGURE 11-45 **Globe valve.** Ideal for lines requiring frequent valve maintenance. (Courtesy of Cadillac-Fairview Corporation, Limited.)

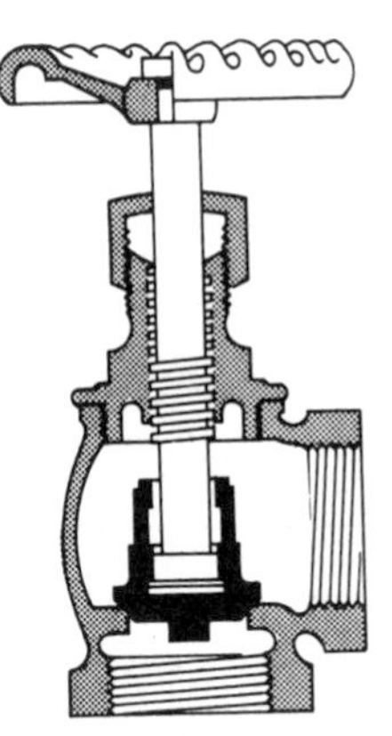

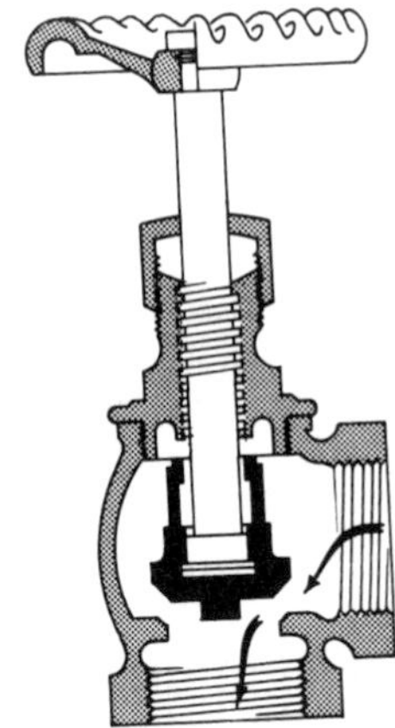

FIGURE 11-46 **Angle valve.** Used when making a 90° turn in a line. (Courtesy of Cadillac-Fairview Corporation, Limited.)

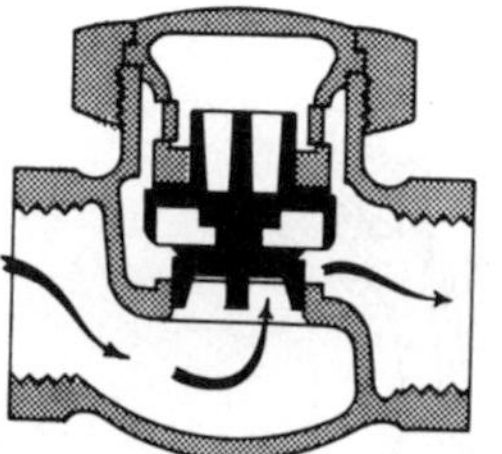
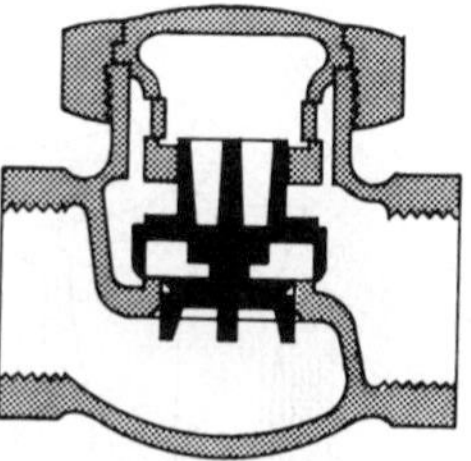

FIGURE 11-47 **Lift check valve.** Used in a line to prevent back flow.

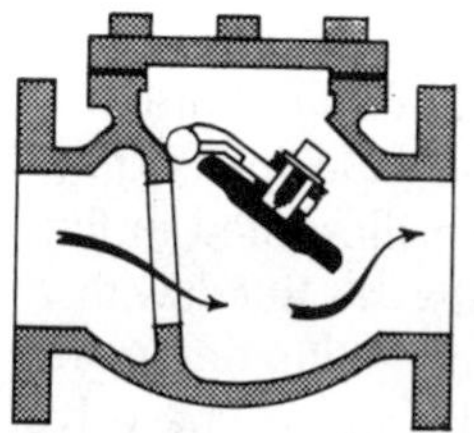
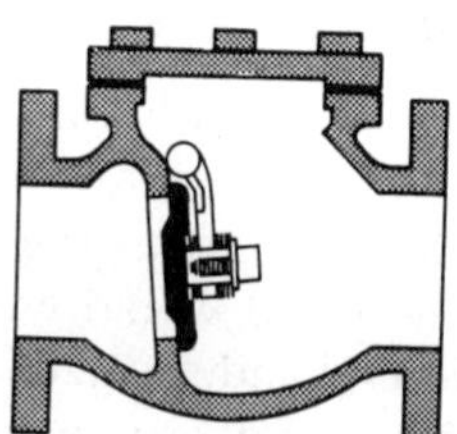

FIGURE 11-48 **Swing check valve.** Recommended on lines carrying fluids where flow velocities are low. (Courtesy of Cadillac-Fairview Corporation, Limited.)

Swing Check Valve

The swing check valve operates on the same principle as the lift check and the same basic characteristics apply to both valves. The alternative "swing" design does, however, offer certain differences. The flow moves through the swing check valve in approximately a straight line, comparable to that in a gate valve and, as a general rule, are recommended on lines carrying fluids where flow velocities are low. Also, swing check valves should not be used on lines with pulsating flow because of destructive "pounding" effects.

Ball Valve

Ball valves are generally used when a quick-acting, low profile valve is necessary to fit into a confined space. A 90° turn of the valve handle quickly opens and closes the valve, and the direction of the handle indicates whether the valve is open or closed. When a standard ball valve is fully open, it offers little resistance to flow. If the ball has what is known as a full internal port, then it offers almost no resistance to flow in the open position. Under noncritical conditions, ball valves may be used to regulate flow. A major advantage of the ball valve is the ease with which the design lends itself to repair.

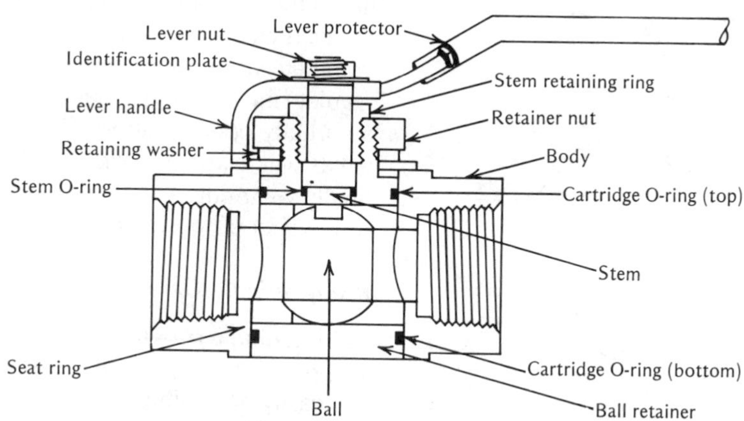

FIGURE 11-49 **Ball valve.** A quick acting, low profile valve.

Butterfly Valve

The butterfly valve features a flat disc that can be rotated 90° from the wide open to fully closed position. The valve illustrated in Figure 11-50 would normally be fitted with a lever, handwheel, or a pneumatic or electric operator depending on the size of the valve and its application.

In buildings, this valve is commonly used as a stop valve in various water supply and circulating systems and as a control valve in the gas supply lines to the burners of boilers and water heaters.

Some of the advantages of the butterfly valve are ease of operation, relatively small size and light weight, little restriction to flow, and absence of sliding parts.

Stop Cock

The stop cock is a mechanically simple, fast acting shut-off valve that requires only a simple 90° turn in either direction to form a complete seal. Although "fast acting," this does not mean that the valve should be shut off quickly, since this is likely to cause "hammering." The direction of the open flow position is indicated on the stem head by a stamped rib or groove. The valve's principal purpose is that of a main stop or shut-off valve on gas lines, but it is also used on "fluid" lines where the fluid flow is not under pressure.

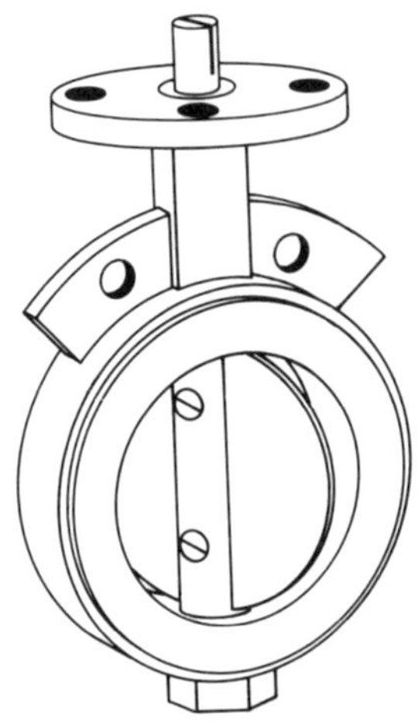

FIGURE 11-50 Butterfly valve. Can be fitted with a hand lever or with an electric or pneumatic operator.

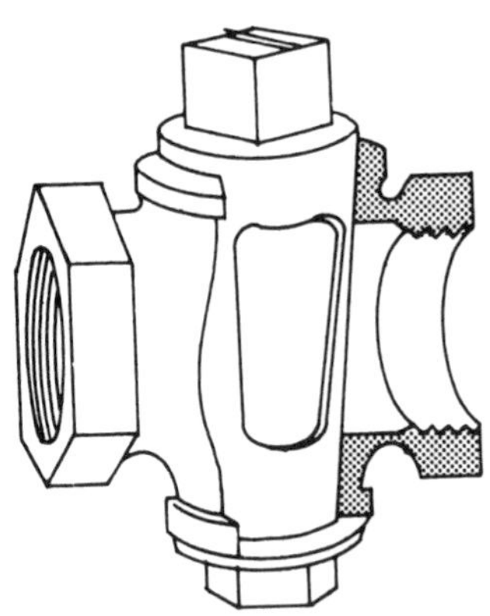

FIGURE 11-51 Stop cock. Main purpose is that of a main stop or shut-off for natural gas lines. (Courtesy of Cadillac-Fairview Corporation, Limited.)

Gate Valve

Gate valves act as a shut-off control for steam, water, oil, or gas. The disc (or gate) lifts at the turn of the handle to allow full and unobstructed flow, and lowers to stop flow completely. The gate valve is not intended to regulate the flow and should never be used in a partially open position. This misuse of the valve will cause the disc to "chatter" and finally wear out. A worn disc is likely to leak in the shut-off position.

Rising Spindle Gate Valve

The spindle rises through the yoke sleeves; its operating threads are outside where they are easily accessible and where they cannot be affected by the corrosive effects of fluids in the line. The rising spindle gate valve requires

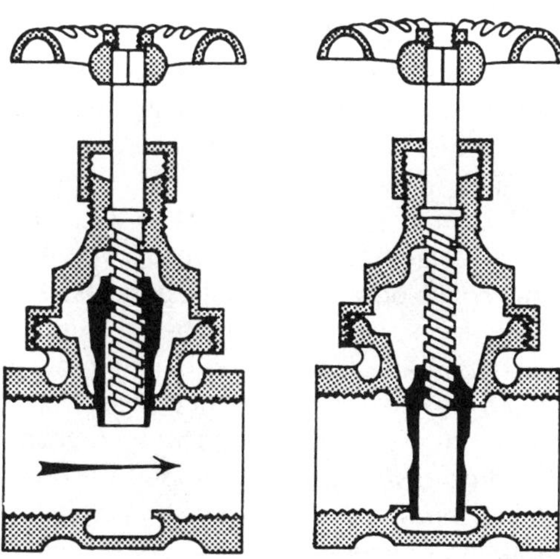

FIGURE 11-52 **Gate valve.** Used as a shut-off control for steam, water, oil, or gas. (Courtesy of Cadillac-Fairview Corporation, Limited.)

cleaning and lubrication on the spindle threads.

The height of the spindle also indicates what position the valve is in, whether open or closed.

Note the difference in handle mechanisms in Figure 11-53. The choice of handle is dictated by accessibility. These valves are used on all fire sprinkler lines as the main shut-off valves.

11-13 Budgeting the Funds

Throughout the various chapters of this book you will find references to inspections and maintenance. Each chapter includes a "Zero-Base" budget expense chart that allocates funds for maintenance and operations expenses related to the expense classification explained in that chapter.

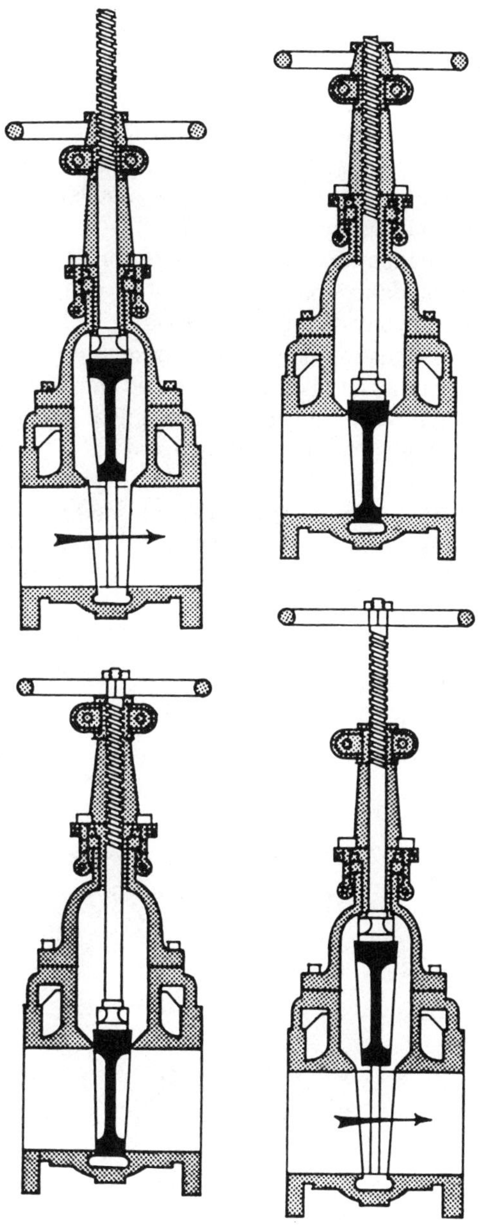

FIGURE 11-53 **Rising spindle gate valve.** the height of the spindle serves as an indicator as to what position the valve is in, whether open or closed. (Courtesy of Cadillac-Fairview Corporation, Limited.)

The mechanical services workload covers the daily, weekly, monthly, quarterly, and annual inspections and the maintenance required to efficiently operate the electrical/mechanical systems, elevator, garage doors, garbage compactor, motors, the belts, filters, bearings, pumps, and valves.

Chapter One explains how to organize the maintenance programs for the equipment, how to organize the workload to include all the housekeeping, groundskeeping, and structural services activities and the maintenance of the electrical/mechanical systems. All these activities are organized into a "master action plan" to assure that everything is planned, completed, and controlled.

As mechanical services include all of the electrical/mechanical systems, it is not necessary to detail the budget expense classifications for them in this chapter. It should be noted that motors, pumps, fans, filters, and valves are used in all the systems and are detailed in those chapters.

By summarizing the items that wear out or need replacing, you will identify the things that could possibly be bulk purchased and drop shipped in the quantities required for each building. Individual building owners could also take advantage of these savings by using this system in concert with other small building owners. These people are usually linked through a trade association such as the Building Owners and Managers Association (BOMA), or other similar groups.

Chapter 12

ENERGY MANAGEMENT

12–1 An Overview

WHY AN ENERGY MANAGEMENT PROGRAM?

In 1970, the operations staff at Cadillac Development were faced with an unbelievable problem when the in-suite heating convector valves (Figure 8-56) seized in either the open or shut position. By inserting a magnetic tipped probe into the body of the valve, it was discovered that the black substance picked up by the probe was actually ferrous iron oxide. These metal filings were the reason why the valves were seizing, and were evidence of corrosion in the heating system.

To overcome the problems of electrolysis and corrosion a chemical called "Nutek" was introduced into the system. To offset the high cost of this chemical they looked into ways to improve the efficiency of the heating system operations and, through this action to save fuel consumption. This was the beginning of Cadillac Development's energy management program. To be successful, it meant improving their competence, identifying problems with the structure and the electrical/mechanical equipment, setting operations goals, and keeping records of their results.

Fortunately, previous records of utility consumption and operational expenditures were available up to that point in time. It took some time to develop the program, introduce the water treatment, correct leaks, set up a system of testing the water, overcome resistance to change, and obtain support for the program.

In 1973, the cost of oil soared and triggered increases in other forms of energy and in the cost of maintenance. In 1973, the cost of one MCF of natural gas in Toronto was 65¢. By the end of 1981 the cost had risen to $3.50 and the Canadian government announced that this cost would double by 1986. It also meant that the savings would double. The benefits of the program were now really showing results. The water treatment put the iron oxide back in solution, it pacified the electrolysis that created the problem in the first place, leaks in the systems were corrected, valves and controls operated properly, and the fuel and maintenance costs were reduced substantially. The competance of the operations staff improved as they received "in-class" and "hands-on" training to overcome their previous lack of training.

WHAT IS ENERGY?

The dictionary defines energy as the power or capacity to be active; strength of body or mind to think or to work; natural power vigorously exerted; or the capacity for performing work. Energy originates with the sun and can be converted from one form to another. The efficiency with which these energies are converted results in operational savings.

Electrical energy can be converted to illumination of light and to mechanical energy, such as in motors. Chemical energy (fuel) can be converted to heat.

ENERGY USE IN BUILDINGS

The energy used in buildings varies greatly in residential, commercial, and institutional buildings. A residential building or hospital is in use virtually twenty-four hours per day, 365 days a year, while a school or office building is only in use part of the day. In these buildings equipment can be turned off when not in use, but in hospitals or apartment buildings, it is more difficult to shut things down. Control of the staff and the equipment is the key to a successful energy management program. A successful program needs the participation of everyone on the management team.

PARTICIPATION AND COOPERATION

Many buildings were designed and built without considering the cost of energy, so we must be knowledgeable enough to analyze the present status of the building and to improve or change things if they are feasible. The maintenance programming system explained in Chapter 1 is ideal for gathering information that can be used to support recommendations for an energy management program.

Regardless of how efficiently a building is constructed, it cannot operate effectively without the full cooperation and understanding of the operating personnel. It is hoped that the information in this book will make you and your staff more aware of the potential available. By improving the knowledge and dedication of your staff, you will be able to derive full benefits from the program. If an employee does not understand or accept the mode of operation, he can literally cause the program to fail.

OBJECTIVES OF THE PROGRAM

We could summarize energy management objectives as the ability to maintain an inside comfort temperature for the occupants irrespective of the outside weather conditions. Figure 12-1 illustrates some environmental comfort parameters that affect how we feel. Comfort is also explained further in Chapter 8 and in Chapter 9.

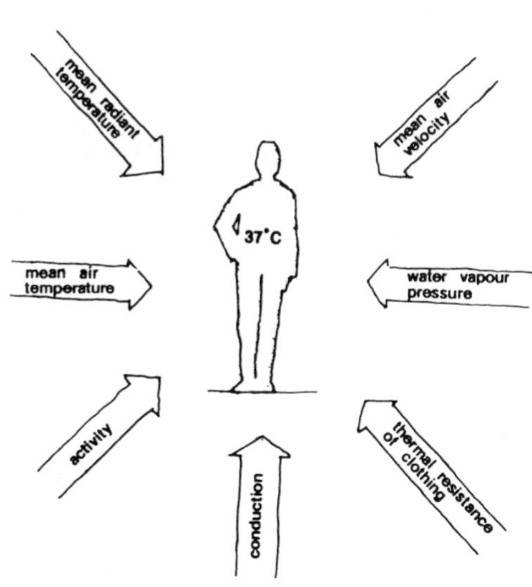

FIGURE 12-1 Environmental comfort parameters. Happy and healthy human life is possible as long as the human thermo-regulatory system can maintain a body temperature of around 37°C. A requirement for this condition is the maintenance of a thermal equilibrium in which heat lost to the environment is replaced at the same rate by heat resulting from the metabolic processes.

A successful energy management program should reduce the consumption of energy to its lowest possible level, without making the occupants feel uncomfortable.

Comfort is achieved when people are not aware of a room's temperature. In other words, they are not too hot or too cold, nor are they influenced by drafts.

WHY WE NEED HEATING AND COOLING

Basically, a building needs heating when the outside temperature falls below the desired inside temperature and cooling when the outside temperature rises above the desired inside temperature. In other words, it needs heat if internal gains, minus the shell or building loss, is negative. It needs cooling when heat gains inside and from outside are positive and not adequately controlled by natural or mechanical ventilation.

Some buildings, mostly office buildings, or buildings where the activities within the building generate heat, do not require as much energy as a building that is not self-heating. This varies the point at which a building requires heat. It is wise to experiment to find the point in time when a building needs heat. The blended heating water supply temperature chart (Figure 12-2) shows the commonly used design parameters for engineers that are used in many apartment buildings.

If you study the chart, you will find that when the outside temperature is 60°F, or around 15°C, a blended water temperature of 110°F, or around 43°C, is required.

INTERNAL HEAT GAIN

In effect, we could say that the internal heat gain should be determined before setting the controls. The resistance to heat loss by the building envelope (double glazing, insulation) and the amount of heat gain generated by the people, equipment, and activities within the building could alter the point when a building would need heating or cooling. It is wise to determine precisely when a building needs heat, rather than to set a 60°F outside temperature as a point for heating and a 75°F outside temperature for cooling.

In buildings that generate internal heat gain, more air conditioning is needed to offset the heat gained through the building envelope and the internal heat gain.

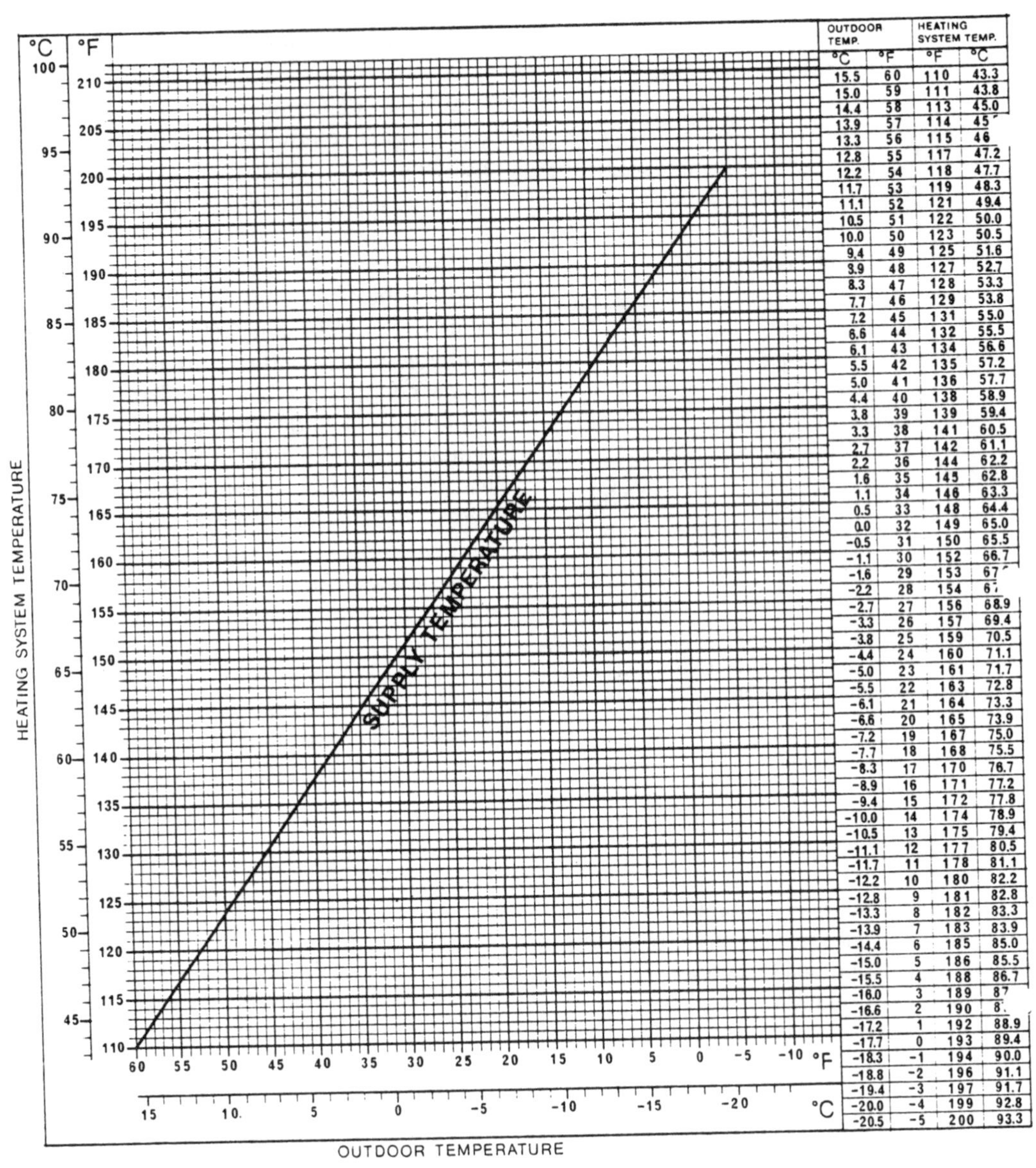

OUTDOOR TEMP.		HEATING SYSTEM TEMP.	
°C	°F	°F	°C
15.5	60	110	43.3
15.0	59	111	43.8
14.4	58	113	45.0
13.9	57	114	45
13.3	56	115	46
12.8	55	117	47.2
12.2	54	118	47.7
11.7	53	119	48.3
11.1	52	121	49.4
10.5	51	122	50.0
10.0	50	123	50.5
9.4	49	125	51.6
8.9	48	127	52.7
8.3	47	128	53.3
7.7	46	129	53.8
7.2	45	131	55.0
6.6	44	132	55.5
6.1	43	134	56.6
5.5	42	135	57.2
5.0	41	136	57.7
4.4	40	138	58.9
3.8	39	139	59.4
3.3	38	141	60.5
2.7	37	142	61.1
2.2	36	144	62.2
1.6	35	145	62.8
1.1	34	146	63.3
0.5	33	148	64.4
0.0	32	149	65.0
-0.5	31	150	65.5
-1.1	30	152	66.7
-1.6	29	153	67
-2.2	28	154	6
-2.7	27	156	68.9
-3.3	26	157	69.4
-3.8	25	159	70.5
-4.4	24	160	71.1
-5.0	23	161	71.7
-5.5	22	163	72.8
-6.1	21	164	73.3
-6.6	20	165	73.9
-7.2	19	167	75.0
-7.7	18	168	75.5
-8.3	17	170	76.7
-8.9	16	171	77.2
-9.4	15	172	77.8
-10.0	14	174	78.9
-10.5	13	175	79.4
-11.1	12	177	80.5
-11.7	11	178	81.1
-12.2	10	180	82.2
-12.8	9	181	82.8
-13.3	8	182	83.3
-13.9	7	183	83.9
-14.4	6	185	85.0
-15.0	5	186	85.5
-15.5	4	188	86.7
-16.0	3	189	87
-16.6	2	190	8
-17.2	1	192	88.9
-17.7	0	193	89.4
-18.3	-1	194	90.0
-18.8	-2	196	91.1
-19.4	-3	197	91.7
-20.0	-4	199	92.8
-20.5	-5	200	93.3

FIGURE 12-2 The blended heating water supply temperature. (Courtesy of Cadillac-Fairview Corporation, Limited.)

DETERMINING THE INTERNAL HEAT GAIN

A simple way to determine the internal heat gain is to study the spring and fall consumption for heating and cooling. The spring and fall are used because the least amount of energy is consumed in these months. The consumption figures could then be used to identify the approximate heat gain statistics. After converting to fuel/degree day figures, this energy could be deducted or added when determining a building's heating and cooling energy requirements.

INSULATION

In buildings with a low internal heat gain, the better insulated the building, the more you gain. This is not true in buildings with a high internal heat gain. It is also true that good insulation prevents excess gain from outside. "What is good for the heat is good for the cold."

Because of the heat generated internally, the insulation that is installed to keep the heat out when it is 90° or 100°F outside, also keeps the internally generated heat from leaking out when it is 50° or 60°F outside. If that internally generated heat cannot leak out of the building, it will have to be removed using mechanical energy, either with fan energy or air conditioning energy.

DESIGN PARAMETERS

There is also a relationship between the temperatures in various locations in a city and, more important, in different parts of a country. If the temperature varied between 30°F and 70°F for 75 percent of the time, then 75 percent of a building's energy would also be consumed in that time span.

If you study Figure 12-2, you will note that the design engineers supply 200°F water in the heating systems when the outside temperature is −5°F. It is not unusual for engineers to design for the extreme weather rather than for the more moderate temperatures that prevail for 75 percent of the time.

12-2 A Building Energy Analysis

BUILDING ENERGY USE

A building's components that affect energy consumption can be classified into the following:

1. The Building Envelope (weather sensitive)
2. The Ventilation System (weather and occupant sensitive)
3. The Electrical/Mechanical Equipment (weather sensitive)
4. Lighting, appliances and other user-related sources (occupant sensitive)
5. Hot Water (occupant sensitive)

LOAD REQUIREMENTS

A substantial portion of the energy waste associated with the boilers and chillers is due to part load performance. Heating and air conditioning systems operate at less than full load for a considerable time during an annual operating cycle. This is critical when we also consider that most of the equipment is oversized. The trend now is to smaller progressive-use equipment with controls for staging start-up when required.

The information gathered by an energy audit should determine the load requirements for a building. Units can thus be shut down when they are not required. When this is done, the equipment on the line should operate at its rated capacity.

In schools or office buildings the need for heating domestic water is very small compared to a hospital or an apartment building. Unless the building has a separate water heating system for this purpose, the space heating boiler is run at a very low fraction of its capacity all summer.

HEAT LOSS AND HEAT GAIN

One of the factors which affect the rate at which a structure loses heat is its construction. This includes not only the material used, but also the air leakage between the inside of the structure and the outdoors. Another important factor affecting heat loss rates is the difference between indoor and outdoor temperature. An additional factor in heat loss is the wind velocity. For most locations, designers consider a 15 mph wind a suitable allowance for wind velocity.

It should be understood that, during the heating season, extreme temperatures are of short duration, occur late at night, and have minimal impact on occupant comfort. On the other hand, during the cooling season, extreme outdoor temperatures span longer periods of time. Because they occur during the working day, they have a greater impact on occupant comfort. A good average indoor comfort goal temperature is 75°F for summer and winter.

If we study local degree day records, we would find that we can maintain this comfort temperature for most of the year. During extreme weather conditions, however, this goal may not be achievable and may need to be raised or lowered. The important thing to remember is that someone should have the responsibility of monitoring and adjusting the inside temperature goal to a comfortable level for the occupants. This action will save energy and money without making the occupants feel uncomfortable.

Because most structures were built before the energy crisis it is necessary to conduct an energy audit to determine the building's existing thermal characteristics if we expect to establish realistic winter and summer energy goals for a building. This audit will help determine the amount of energy the electrical/mechanical equipment consumes to offset the "heat loss" in the winter and "heat gain" in the summer. The operating staff should be trained to operate the heating and cooling systems so they achieve the energy management goals for their buildings.

Most surfaces used in a building are a composite of several materials. The rate at which heat flows through this combination of materials is called the "U" value, or overall coefficient of heat transfer. The resistance to heat loss, through roofs, walls, windows, doors, is referred to as an "R" value (Figures 12-6 and 12-7). The more energy we lose, the more we need to replace the loss. This energy is measured in British Thermal Units (Btus) (Figure 12-3).

The conduction heat loss in Btus for a wall, window, ceiling, door, or floor exposed to outdoor temperatures is the product of the design temperature difference times the "U" factor times the area of each building component. Heat loss is shown mathematically as follows: $H = U \times A \times (t_i - t_o)$, where H = heat loss; A = area of surface; t_i = inside temperature; and t_o = outside temperature. Heat gain is shown mathematically as follows: $H = U \times A \times (t_o - t_i)$. In existing structures, actual measurements can be taken or building plans can be used to find lengths, widths, and heights.

FIGURE 12-3 British thermal unit (Btu). A Btu is the amount of heat which must be added to one pound of water to raise the temperature of that pound of water one degree fahrenheit. The quantity of heat in an object is altogether different. Quantity is not the same as intensity. A gallon of water may contain more heat than a quart of water yet the temperature of the quart of water may be higher because its heat energy is more concentrated or intense. (Courtesy of The Trane Company.)

So far, we have considered the ways in which a building loses heat by conduction or transmission of the heat through the outside shell of the structure. A building can also lose heat by having cold outside air enter and displace warm air. When this air leakage occurs through cracks and is not under control, it is called infiltration. When air is brought in or exhausted through openings designed for this purpose—usually by controlled methods—it is called ventilation.

Infiltration occurs mainly around windows, doors, frames, and between foundation walls and sill plates. In a double-hung home window, air might leak in at 20 cubic feet per hour per foot of crack if the wind is blowing at 15 miles per hour.

AN ENERGY AUDIT

An energy audit is the gathering of information that could affect energy use in a building. The information can be fed into a computer or manually calculated. This should be done on a building-by-building basis to determine the following information:

1. The heat loss and infiltration (the thermal characteristics about a building).
2. The heating degree days (the average daily outside temperature below 18°C or 65°F relative to the building's location). This provides a means of calculating annual heating demand.
3. The electrical energy used (kWh's used by motors, lights, etc.).
4. The internal heat gain (the heat generated by lights, equipment, and people).
5. The water consumption (how it is used and why).

DEGREE DAYS

To compare "apples to apples" we use a heating degree day balance temperature. The idea of using a heating degree day was first established by the U.S. government in 1936 and we have been using it ever since. It was determined that a house would require heat when the average daily outside temperature dropped below 18°C, or 65°F. This is the degree day base.

Degree day records are kept by the weather bureau and are almost directly related to the heating or cooling needs of a building. If a building is using fuel consistently, the fuel consumption/degree day figure on the consumption records (Figures 12-27 and 12-28) should be fairly constant on a month-to-month basis. If a building has a large internal heat gain, an adjustment should be made to the fuel/degree day figure.

The energy usage of a building per degree day is proportional to the weather (which is constantly varying), and could also show up as an electrical/mechanical or operations problem when two identical buildings are not showing the same fuel/degree day figures.

THE Btu FACTORS

We have used natural gas in our recordkeeping illustration. However, by knowing the Btu factors for fuel oil, electricity, or coal, you can develop a suitable recordkeeping form, based on our example, for any of the energy sources.

Comparisons of one building to another in Btu per square foot terms, or per square meter, can also reveal differences and identify problems that can be investigated and corrected.

If the facts gathered are used intelligently, we will know precisely how many Btus per hour we will need, on a building-by-building basis, to achieve the building's comfort temperature goal. The energy analysis system should group similar buildings together, as well as compare the Btus per hour consumption against the targets calculated from the energy audit. It is not uncommon to find great variations in consumption between similar buildings. Being able to identify and correct the variations can help overcome problems and contribute to the energy management program.

THE HEAT OUTPUT

If we know the volume of MCF for natural gas, gallons for fuel oil, or kilowatt hours for electricity consumed, we can calculate the dollar cost or compare consumption to predetermined goals. Listed below are the most commonly used factors.

1 gallon of #2 fuel oil = 168,000 Btus—Residential

1 gallon of #4 fuel oil = 173,000 Btus—Light Industrial

1 gallon of #5 fuel oil = 180,000 Btus—Medium Industrial

1 gallon of #6 fuel oil = 180,000 Btus—Medium Industrial (with less than 1 percent sulphur)

1 gallon of #6 fuel oil = 182,000 Btus—Heavy Industrial (with a maximum of 2 percent sulphur)

100 cubic feet of natural gas (1 therm) = 100,000 Btus

1 MCF = 1,030,000 Btus (see Figure 12-9)

1 kilowatt hour = 3,412 Btus

Chilled water—calculate 1 Btu per pound per degree fahrenheit

1 ton of refrigeration = 12,000 Btus per hour

1 ton of coal = 25,200,000 Btus

THE FLOW OF HEAT

Heat can be transferred to other substances, such as air or water, but cannot be destroyed.

To designate a rate of flow, the term Btu per hour is used. This term indicates the amount of heat that flows from one substance to another in one hour.

12-3 A Building's Weather Sensitive Components

THE THERMAL CHARACTERISTICS

To know the thermal characteristics of a building, we must determine the amount of

FIGURE 12-4 The flow of heat. (Courtesy of The Trane Company.)

window, the amount of wall, and the amount of insulation. Unless we gather and study all the relevant data about a building, our decisions concerning energy will be based on assumptions, and not on facts.

As an example, most people think that an all glass high-rise office building is energy inefficient. In fact, the opposite may be true, because the internally generated heat from equipment and people is allowed to leak out through the glass, thus lowering the air conditioning load.

THERMAL CHARACTERISTICS DATA

(To calculate in sq. meters, multiply sq. feet by 0.093)

DATE ____________

BUILDING NO. ___
BUILDING ADDRESS ____________

HEIGHT ______ WIDTH ______ LENGTH ______
NO. OF FLOORS ______ NO. OF BALCONIES ______
NO. OF SUITES ______ SQUARE FOOTAGE ______

ROOF (TOPSIDE AND UNDERSIDE)
TYPE ______ INSULATION ______ DECK ______
GYPSUM BOARD ______ PLASTER ______
AIR SPACE ______ LENGTH ______
WIDTH ______ AREA ______

WALLS
TYPE: CURTAIN ______ BEARING ______
SLAB EDGE ______
CLADDING: BRICK: FACE ___ COMMON ___
CONCRETE ______
OTHER ______
AIR SPACE ______
INTERIOR: GYPSUM BOARD ______
PLASTER ______ FURRING ______
REFLECTIVE AIR SPACE ______
INSULATION ______
AIR SPACES ______
BLOCK ______
VAPOR BARRIER ______
AREA: HEIGHT ______ WIDTH ______
TOTAL ______ GLASS ______
(HEIGHT × WIDTH = AREA × NO. OF WALLS)
TOTAL AREA MINUS GLASS AREA = WALL AREA

OUTSIDE DOORS: TYPE ______ SIZE ______
NO. ___ TOTAL DOOR AREA ______
WINDOWS: STEEL ______ ALUMINUM ______
SINGLE GLAZE ______
DOUBLE GLAZE ______
SIZE ______ NUMBER ______
TOTAL WINDOW AREA ______

VENTILATION
EXHAUST: cfm PER FAN PER SUITE = TOTAL cfm ______
cfm PER FAN PER SQUARE FOOT = TOTAL cfm ______
SUPPLY: HEATED ___ UNHEATED ______
RECLAIM ___
cfm PER FAN × NO. OF FANS = TOTAL cfm ______

HEAT LOSS VALUES

Ventilation "U" Values

Total suite exhaust air	1.95 Btuh/cfm
Total corridor air supply	1.95 Btuh/cfm heated
Total corridor air supply	1.95 Btuh/cfm unheated
Garage exhaust air	1.95 Btuh/cfm

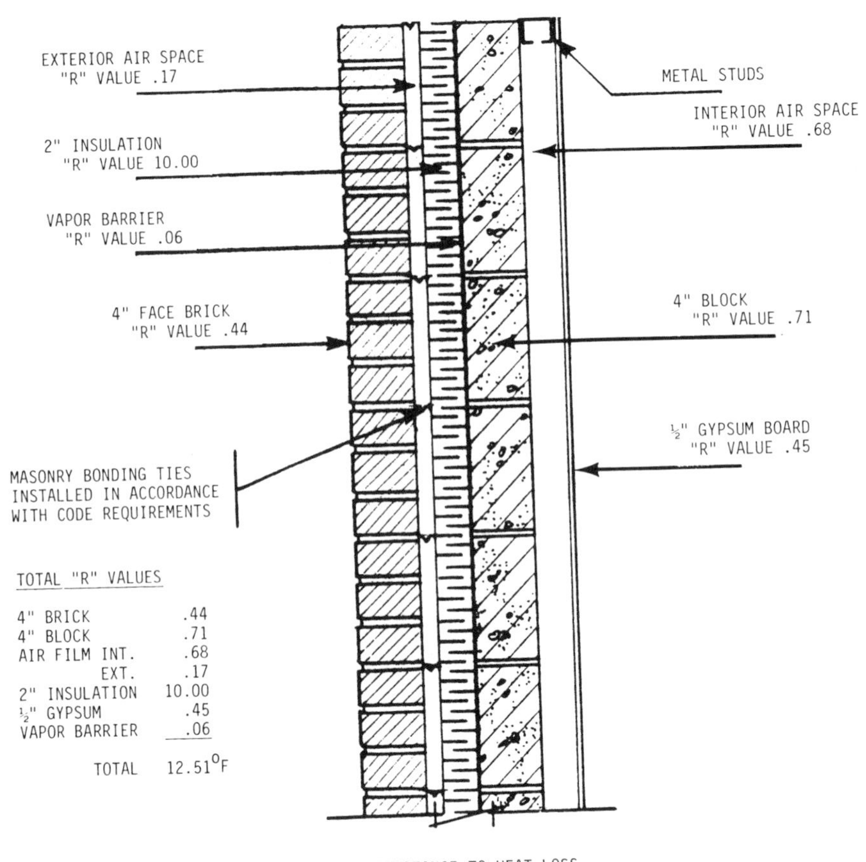

FIGURE 12-5 **Thermal resistance "R" Values.** Exterior brick and block wall.

CALCULATING THE MCF PER DAY FUEL CONSUMPTION GOAL

1. Total the square footage for each structural component in column 1 in Figure 12-9 and enter the figures.
2. Enter the resistance to heat loss values (R values) opposite each structural component (see Figures 12-6 and 12-7 for the R values).
3. Multiply the square footage by the R values and enter the figures in column 3.
4. Calculate the heat loss (Btuh) or U values for each of the components by dividing the R values into 1. Enter these figures in column 4.
5. Multiply the U values by 24 hours to give you the Btuh per day heat loss figures for each of the components.
6. Total column 5 to give you the total daily heat loss for that building.
7. Divide this total by 1,030,000 to give you the MCF per day fuel consumption goal for that building.

ROOF COMPONENTS "R" VALUES	°F	°C
EXTERIOR AIR FILM	0.17	0.09
BUILT UP ROOF	0.33	0.18
INVERTED ROOF	0.33	0.18
EXTRUDED POLYSTYRENE 1"	5.00	2.78
EXTRUDED POLYSTYRENE 2"	10.00	5.56
FIBREBOARD 1"	3.00	1.67
FIBREBOARD 2"	6.00	3.33
CONCRETE SLAB 4"	0.32	0.18
CONCRETE SLAB 8"	0.64	0.36
CEILING SPACE	0.93	0.52
GYPSUM BOARD 1/2"	0.45	0.25
PLASTER	0.13	0.07
INTERIOR AIR FILM	0.61	0.34

FIGURE 12-6 Thermal resistance values. To calculate the "U" values or the heat loss in Btuh, divide 1 by the "R" values.

8. To establish the fuel consumption per degree day goal for any month, determine the number of reading days from the utility bill for that month, and multiply the daily fuel consumption goal by that number. Dividing the degree days for that month by the consumption figure gives the consumption per degree day goal, which is calculated each month and entered in column 10 in Figure 12-28. Variances should be followed up and investigated immediately.

Deduct the Energy Used to Heat the Domestic Water

During the months that the building heating is off, determine the MCF consumption figures from the utility bills. Calculate the MCF per day to give you the energy used to heat the domestic water. Multiply this daily consumption figure by the number of reading days to give the consumption goal for heating the domestic water each month during the year.

WALL COMPONENTS "R" VALUES	°F	°C
EXTERIOR AIR FILM	0.17	0.09
FACE BRICK	0.44	0.24
COMMON BRICK	0.80	0.44
AIR SPACE 2"	1.02	0.57
MORTAR 1"	0.20	0.11
CONCRETE BLOCK 4"	0.71	0.39
CONCRETE BLOCK 8"	1.11	0.62
EXTRUDED POLYSTYRENE 1"	5.00	2.78
EXTRUDED POLYSTYRENE 2"	10.00	5.56
AIR SPACE 1/2"	0.91	0.51
AIR SPACE 1"	1.00	0.56
INTERIOR AIR FILM	0.68	0.38
POURED CONCRETE 4"	0.32	0.17
POURED CONCRETE 8"	0.64	0.36
VAPOUR BARRIER	0.06	0.03
FURRING 1"	0.94	0.52
PLASTER 1/2"	0.13	0.07
PLASTER 3/4"	0.15	0.08
GYPSUM BOARD 3/8"	0.32	0.17
GYPSUM BOARD 1/2"	0.45	0.25
REFLECTIVE AIR SPACE	1.83	1.02

FIGURE 12-7 Thermal resistance values. To calculate the "U" values or the heat loss in Btuh, divide 1 by the "R" values.

WINDOWS Btuh/sq.ft. ("U" VALUES)	°F	°C
SINGLE GLAZED		
STEEL SASH	1.13	2.03
ALUMINUM SASH	1.24	2.23
BALCONY DOORS - ALUMINUM	1.24	2.23
DOUBLE GLAZED		
STEEL SASH	0.73	1.31
ALUMINUM SASH	0.79	1.42
WOOD	0.64	1.15
STORM DOORS	0.39	0.70

FIGURE 12-8 Thermal resistance values.

As this is an "occupant sensitive" energy user and not "weather sensitive," this consumption figure is deducted from the building's energy consumption (Figure 12-28).

THE VENTILATION SYSTEM

Ventilation is defined as the intentional introduction of outside air into a building for removing fumes and odors and for providing oxygen for the occupants. Infiltration is defined as the introduction of unwanted air into a building.

During moderate weather, many operators shut down the air conditioning system and bring in cooler outside air so they can enjoy some free cooling. Controlling the introduction of outside air in this manner can provide energy saving benefits. In buildings that generate a lot of internal "heat gain," controlling the ventilation system to provide only the air required to keep the occupants comfortable will also provide energy saving benefits. The key to success is *CONTROL. Knowledgeable workers are needed for control.*

Many heating, ventilating and air conditioning (HVAC) systems use a large percentage of their total fuel consumption to heat and cool ventilation air. A heat recovery system can provide substantial savings. Such systems as heat wheels, glycol systems, heat pipes, and air-to-air recuperators should be investigated to determine the savings potential for your situation.

BUILDING NO. ____ BUILDING NAME ____________ ADDRESS ____________

TOWNSHIP ________ NO. OF SUITES ________ SQ. FOOTAGE ________ SQ. METERS ________

METEOROLOGICAL AREA ____________

$$\text{* Btuh Heat Loss ("U" Values)} = \frac{1}{\text{Resistance to Heat Loss ("R" Values)}}$$

** Btuh Per Day Heat Loss = "U" Values x 24 hours

*** To convert square footage to square meters, multiply by 0.093

	***1 x	2 =	3	*4	**5
STRUCTURAL AREA	AREA SQ. FOOTAGE	"R" VALUES	TOTAL "R" VALUES	"U" VALUES	Btuh/DAY HEAT LOSS
BEARING WALL					
EXHAUST AIR					
GLASS					
EXPOSED CONCRETE					
OUTSIDE DOORS					
OUTSIDE WALLS					
ROOF					
				TOTAL DAILY HEAT LOSS	

$$\frac{\text{TOTAL DAILY HEAT LOSS}}{1{,}030{,}000} = \text{TOTAL MCF PER DAY CONSUMPTION GOAL \_\_\_\_\_\_}$$

To calculate the monthly degree day fuel consumption goal, multiply the daily goal by the number of reading days shown on your utility bill. Multiply this figure by the monthly degree days and enter this number in column 10 in Figure 12-28.

FIGURE 12-9 Calculating the daily fuel consumption goal.

HEATING AND AIR CONDITIONING SYSTEMS

Depending on the climate, the influence of heating on the energy bill can be as little as 10 percent and as much as 50 percent, and the influence of cooling can be 10 percent to 40 percent. In the south the predominance would be for cooling, while in the north it would be for heating.

In a residential building, most of the energy is used for the purpose of maintaining internal occupant comfort. In an office building, much of the energy is used to remove the heat generated by lighting, office equipment, fans, and pumps.

THE DISTRIBUTION OF ENERGY

Because heating and cooling equipment is not usually in the same room where the comfort condition is required, energy is moved by wires, ducts or pipes to the areas where it is needed. Besides the space it takes up in a building, a ducted air conditioning system uses more energy to distribute energy than one that has a piped system.

For example, to move 100 tons of cooling it takes a 4-inch diameter pipe or a 56-inch diameter air duct. There is also more heat loss from a ducted system than from a piped system because of the surface area of the ducts. A further loss occurs because 10 percent to 20 percent of the air never makes it to the last outlet.

The air furnace in most homes has a ¼ horsepower fan motor on it, whereas a residential hot water heating system could operate with a ¼ or ⅓ circulating pump, using about 10 percent less energy.

Experience has shown that the more suites heated or cooled by a central system, the lower the energy consumption. When several buildings are added to a single heating plant, the costs are reduced significantly.

A system that can be shut off when not needed can make a significant difference to the energy consumption in a building. To take full advantage of this savings, a knowledgeable operator or an automatic control system is needed that will shut down electrical/mechanical equipment when not required.

CONTROLS

Because control is so important, there have been many studies done on thermostats, outside-inside sensors, computer controls, blend valves, and variable speed devices for motors. A specific example of this is the installation of a night set-back thermostat in a house. The thermostat automatically lowers the temperature during the night.

Although the home is heated by a forced air furnace, a heat loss problem in one of the bedrooms was overcome by installing an electric baseboard heater under the windows. The house was built with two supply registers in the room that were not located under the windows. Once the heat loss was offset, the other two supply registers, were shut, and the room was comfortable even during the most extreme weather.

This points out the advantage of zone heating and heating areas on an as-required basis. Experiments have shown that by being able to control each area separately, the living and sleeping area consumption can be reduced by 10 percent to 15 percent.

Individual control on hot water heating radiators should further reduce consumption. In apartment buildings, the systems were zoned and thermostats added to each individual suite to help reduce energy costs. The benefits of this kind of control are minimized when the zoning is not suited to the building orientation. The sunny or shaded side should always be zoned separately from the cooler side of the building.

Air conditioning systems such as multi-zone, dual duct, and reheat are rated as very high energy users, while induction, fan coil, individual units, and heat pumps are rated lower.

12-4 A Building's Occupant Sensitive Components

LIGHTING AND ELECTRIC POWER

The lighting energy in a building is either function related as in a commercial or institutional building or nonfunction related for residential buildings. Nonfunction related lighting can be defined as the lighting used in parking lots, lobbies, corridors, stairwells, and mechanical rooms. Function related lighting would include such things as office space, merchandizing areas, work areas, or classrooms.

MANAGING ELECTRICAL ENERGY

The specific goal of electrical energy management is to reduce the waste of electrical energy consumption to its lowest possible level while maintaining reasonable occupant comfort.

A building's electrical system basically consists of lighting and motor loads. Lighting should provide the illumination required by the occupants for their daily activities and should shut down when not required. Motor loads are required to power the components of the plumbing, heating, ventilation, and air conditioning systems.

A successful energy management program would reduce electrical energy by controlling manually or automatically the following:

1. Lighting
2. Power factor of motors
3. Re-use of heat generated by people, lights, equipment, appliances
4. Controls
   - –on-off energy users when not required
   - –optimizes usage system
   - –gives a warning of problems

To be successful, the entire management team must acquire an understanding of electrical / mechanical efficiencies and heat recovery techniques. To monitor progress, a system of recordkeeping must be developed and maintained.

LIGHTING

The electrical energy consumed by lighting in a building can range from 20 percent to as high as 50 percent depending on the building. Because many apartment buildings are bulk metered, the incentive for tenants to turn off lights or to reduce wattage is removed because the landlord pays the bills.

In commercial buildings, the selection of lighting is often made for aesthetic rather than practical purposes. To overcome this problem energy audits must be developed that would study ways to reduce the wattage. Further substantial savings can be achieved by shutting down lighting and equipment when not required.

It has been shown that the electrical energy cost for lighting constitutes the greatest share of the overall total electrical energy costs. These costs break down as follows:

–70 percent for the utility company

–20 percent for maintenance (replacing bulbs, cleaning)

–10 percent for the cost of bulbs

How to Reduce Operating Costs

The first step in reducing operating costs is to reduce lighting levels where they exceed the requirements for the area by initiating any or all of the following actions:

1. Use task lighting where practical.
2. Remove fixtures that are not required.
3. Remove the lamps and/or disconnect the ballast.
4. Use lower wattage lamps.
5. Install dummy fluorescent lamps.
6. In buildings with large glass areas, use photoelectric switches to control the lights near the perimeter where the sun is bright and is supplying an overabundance of light.

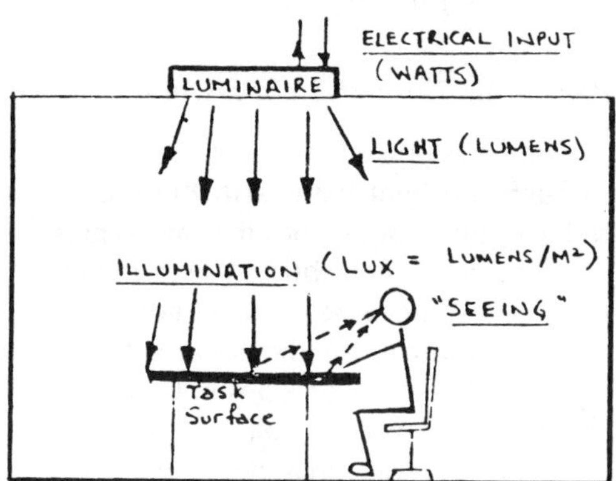

FIGURE 12-10 Task lighting. Lux is a unit of illumination equal to the direct illumination on a surface that is one meter from a uniform source of one candle, or equal to one lumen per square meter.

A Guide for Reasonable Light Levels

Always use a light meter to test levels of illumination—don't guess.

–Office Work Stations—55–65 foot candles, higher for intricate work

–General Office—25–35 foot candles

–Halls and Corridors—20 foot candles or less

Quality of Illumination

To upgrade the quality of illumination to meet the building's requirements, a knowledge of the most efficient sources that are available is required.

1. High pressure sodium vapor—100 lumens/watt
2. Metal Halide—74 lumens/watt
3. Fluorescent—67 lumens/watt
4. Mercury vapor—46 lumens/watt
5. Incandescent—17 lumens/watt

Importance of Painting, Cleaning, and Control

Unless fixtures and lamps are properly maintained, 50 percent of the illumination produced and 50 percent of the electricity going through the meter is wasted.

Proper maintenance of a lighting fixture includes cleaning and washing fixtures and lamps as well as surrounding walls and ceilings. Lighting fixtures become less efficient as fine dirt collects on them and losses of 10 percent to 25 percent are not uncommon. Fluorescent tubes must be dusted as often as necessary. Proper maintenance also includes repair or replacement of defective components of the lighting system.

If surrounding walls and ceilings are unpainted concrete, the reflectance of light is very low. To overcome this and also to make cleaning easier, the walls and ceilings of underground garages, public areas, and equipment rooms should be painted. Painting will increase the reflectivity by 80 percent. In offices, nonreflecting colors should be used as this will increase the amount of reflection light from the fixture's reflector.

Natural light should be used whenever possible. Photo cells, timers, and better switching systems should be utilized to turn off lights in unused areas and after hours. Electronic systems of programmable lighting are now being marketed that efficiently control this problem.

Cleaning and security staff operations should be arranged so that all lighting, except security lighting, is switched off whenever an area is unoccupied. Cleaning time for each area should be as short as possible, and the amount of lighting switched on during cleaning held to a minimum.

Lamp Life

As a rule, operating an incandescent bulb rated 130V will double the life of a bulb.

A six-hour burning cycle for a fluorescent tube will extend its life 25 percent. A twelve-hour burning cycle will extend its life 60 percent.

Group Re-Lamping

Group re-lamping is recommended because it organizes the bulb replacing effort and saves labor costs. It also eliminates the need to have a large number of spares on hand, which is very costly.

To gain as much use out of the old bulbs as possible:

—Replace lamps in the usual way until 20 percent have been replaced. *Then change them all.* Long-life incandescent bulbs that are rated for 130V service should be used.

—4 foot, 40-watt fluorescents will need changing every three years, as they should last 30,000 hours if they burn continuously.

—When you do the first group re-lamp of an older installation you will lose half the life of all the lamps. To help defray the cost, the bulbs removed could be used to replace burned out bulbs in vacant units.

—Other than at the time of group re-lamping, you should date the base of each bulb when it is changed. In this way you will know exactly how long the bulb lasted.

—Keep the newest bulbs for use in the building; throw away bulbs that have been used for 80 percent or 85 percent of their life expectancy.

Return Air Through Light Fixtures

Some systems allow the return air to pass through the light fixtures in the room. This reduces the amount of air flow required to cool the room and thus reduces overall fan horsepower because a large percentage of the heat never enters the conditioned space. The building energy consumption can be reduced even more if the heat extracted from the lights is recovered and re-used to satisfy a heating need in the building.

In a contemporary office building both sensible and latent heat are generated within an occupied space by people, lights,

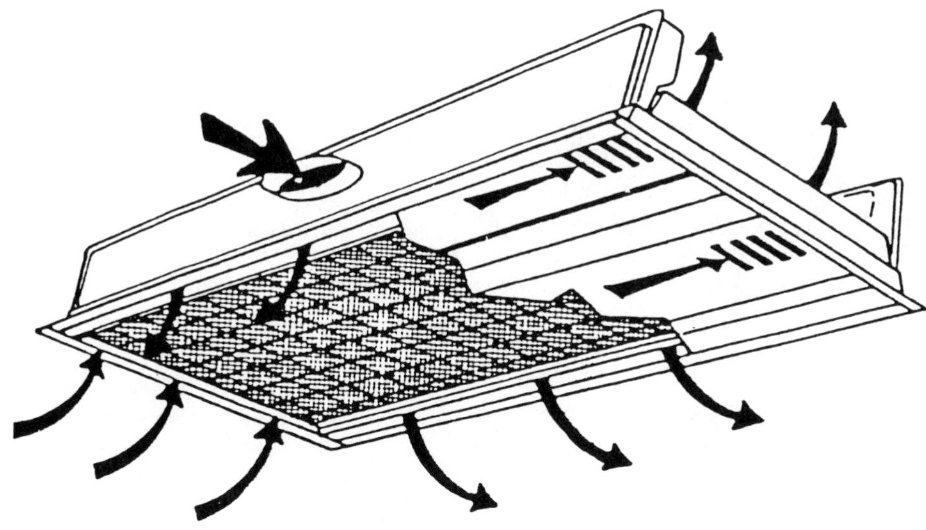

FIGURE 12-11 Return air through light fixtures.

equipment. People generate about 75 watts/person as sensible heat and 60 watts/person as latent heat. In an air conditioned building, the equipment heat should be collected and mixed with the return air during the heating season. Ideally, during the cooling season it should be rejected directly to the outside.

Lights are especially wasteful of energy because both the lights themselves and the air conditioning equipment needed to remove the heat from the lights consume electrical energy.

Fluorescent Lamps

Fluorescent lamps are a widely used source of artificial illumination because they are efficient, economical to operate, and readily available.

The main factors affecting the luminous efficiency of a fluorescent lamp are

- –Design
- –Materials used in its construction
- –Reflector used in the lamp
- –Method of installation
- –Ambient temperature
- –Voltage and frequency of the electrical input
- –Cleaning and maintenance

APPLIANCE CONSUMPTION

There are several reasons why it is useful to know the power consumed by various electrical appliances:

1. To conserve energy—as energy is measured by a watt hour meter, and since many appliances are rated in amps, it will be necessary to convert amperes to watts to calculate the energy used. *This is done by multiplying the amps drawn by the voltage.*
2. To properly wire a circuit.

3. To resolve electrical problems (blown fuses).

The name plates on electrical devices will usually give you sufficient information so that you can calculate power consumption or the current carried.

Unnecessary consumption adds up quickly in any building. Making people aware of consumption should alert them to saving energy by turning off lights and by not using appliances. or running motors unnecessarily.

Using a cost rate of 3¢ per kWh, the following listing can be used as an approximate guide to estimated annual kWh appliance consumption:

Appliance	*kWh*	*Cost*
Air conditioner (6,000 Btu)	500	15.00
Car block heater	456	13.68
Clock	18	.54
Clothes dryer	900	27.00
Coffee maker	100	3.00
Dehumidifier	400	12.00
Dishwasher (not including hot water)	300	9.00
Electric blanket	125	3.75
Electric kettle	150	4.50
Electric shaver	1	
Electric stove	1200	36.00
Electric water heater	4000	120.00
Food waste disposer	25	.75
Fryer, deep fat	70	2.10
Frying pan	180	5.40
Grill (sandwich)	30	.90
Fan (furnace)	800	24.00
Hair dryer	15	.45
Humidifier	200	6.00
Iron	120	3.60
Kitchen fan	50	1.50
Mixmaster	15	.45
Radio (tube type)	100	3.00
(solid state)	10	.30
Refrigerator (12 cubic feet)	850	25.50
(frost free)	1200	36.00
Freezer (14 cubic feet)	1200	36.00
(frost free)	1600	48.00
Sewing machine	10	.30
Television		
(black and white tube)	400	12.00
(black and white solid state)	350	10.50
(color solid state)	450	13.50
Toaster	40	1.20
Vacuum cleaner	40	1.20
Washing machine		
(not including hot water)	50	1.50
automatic (not including hot water)	90	2.70

MOTOR LOADS

A motor does not use 100 horsepower just because the name plate says that is is a 100 Hp motor. Its actual use of power is based on the motor's driven load. A 100 Hp motor may use a fraction of its name plate rating. Most motors have more capability than the load to which they are connected. As loads are reduced during a building's unoccupied periods, this over capacity becomes even greater.

THE POWER FACTOR

A motor also has another characteristic that affects power consumption. A motor uses up to 30 percent of its name plate rating without any load just to provide the required magnetization of the windings to operate the motor. Thus, when using a 100 Hp motor, 30 Hp is used to give off unwanted heat to the motor's windings. As 1 Hp uses 746 kW, 30 Hp [(746 × 30) ÷ 1000] consumes 22.38 kW per day needlessly. This unnecessary consumption multiplied by all the motors in a building could be a factor in high power demand charges on your electric bill. If the motor could be reduced to 75 Hp from 100 Hp and still carry the load, only 22.5 Hp would be used instead of 30 Hp. *MATCH*

THE MOTOR TO THE DRIVEN LOAD TO SAVE ENERGY.

LOAD FACTOR

Load factor could be defined as the number of hours of use. How long lights burn or motors run would determine the load factor. In most businesses records are kept on a monthly cycle over a twelve-month period, including records concerning energy consumption. This allows all of the seasonal variations that take place over the course of a year to be considered.

Load factor is important because we must know, for example, how long a motor is used and how much it is used. A 1 Hp motor that is used with a 100 percent load factor is going to consume more energy than a 10 Hp motor used with a 5 percent load factor. Therefore, when analyzing a building's use of electrical energy, the circulating pump motor is more critical than the motor on the garage door operator.

EFFICIENCY OF MOTORS

Motors sizes under 20 Hp and installed in buildings in the past twenty-five years are not very efficient. Today, most motor manufacturers make "High Efficiency" motors. It usually pays to replace motors that are sized under 20 Hp and that have annual *HIGH LOAD FACTORS* with new high efficiency motors.

Another concern with motors is that their part load efficiency is poor, especially at less than 25 percent capacity. Many motors used in buildings are larger than needed, resulting in operation at light loads. It may even be worth considering moving the motors to equipment closer to their rated capacity.

USEFUL CONVERSION FACTORS

I = Ampere, a unit of current
E = Volt, a unit of pressure
W = Watt, a measure of power
R = Ohm, a unit of resistance
kW = 1,000 Watts, a measure of power
Hp = Horsepower; 1 Hp = 0.746 kW.

When measuring the operating efficiency of a motor, record the name plate data; the manufacturer; the horsepower (Hp); the voltage (E); the amperage (I); and what the motor powers.

ENERGY EFFICIENCY FORMULA (eff)

$$\frac{\text{Energy output}}{\text{Energy input}} \times 100 = \%\ \text{efficiency}$$

$$1\ \text{kW} = 1.35\ \text{Hp} = 3{,}413\ \text{Btu}$$

$$1\ \text{Hp} = .746\ \text{kW} = 2{,}544\ \text{Btu}$$

e.g. Motor output is 2.5 Hp; motor input is 2.25 kW.

$$\text{Efficiency} = \frac{2.5\ \text{Hp}}{2.25\ \text{kW} \times 1.35\ \text{Hp}}$$

$$= \frac{2.5\ \text{Hp}}{3.00\ \text{Hp}} \times 100 = 82.5\%$$

The motor data records gathered as recommended in Chapter 2 (The Building Profile) will give you the energy output in each of the electrical/mechanical systems. The energy input would require the use of an ammeter to check the actual power (voltage and amperage).

The Power Factor (pf) is the ratio of the actual power to the apparent power. Where the efficiency (eff) is unknown, use 85 percent.

To find the power factor:

$$\text{Single-phase circuits: pf} = \frac{W}{E \times I}$$

$$\text{Two-phase circuits: pf} = \frac{W}{E \times I \times 2}$$

$$\text{Three-phase circuits: pf} = \frac{W}{E \times I \times 1.73}$$

To find amps where Hp is known:

$$\text{Single-phase circuits: } I = \frac{Hp \times 746}{E \times eff \times pf}$$

Three-phase circuits:

$$I = \frac{Hp \times 746}{1.73 \times E \times eff \times pf}$$

To find Hp where amps are known:

$$\text{Single-phase circuits: Hp} = \frac{I \times E \times eff \times pf}{746}$$

Three-phase circuits:

$$Hp = \frac{I \times E \times eff \times pf \times 1.73}{746}$$

UNDERSTANDING YOUR ELECTRIC BILL

If you do not understand your electric bill, you cannot possibly establish a successful energy management program. One of the most costly and misunderstood billing concepts is the "demand charge." We will try and explain this part of your electric bill first.

Power Demand

Many electric utility companies have specific demand provisions in their rates. Controlling peak demand can mean a substantial savings.

If we ignore the effect of power factor, the energy consumption characteristics of any electrical device may be expressed in terms of the device's steady-state kW rating. By assuming steady-state conditions, we temporarily ignore the power surge experienced during the start-up of many motor driven devices. Some building engineers are concerned about the starting surge of a large piece of equipment. They believe that it somehow "peaks out" on the demand meter and causes a high demand charge on the next bill. That is not the case.

Kilowatt Demand

Any electrical device has a kW rating simply because of its power consumption characteristics. The situation changes whenever we connect the kW rated device to a source of electrical power. The device will only exert a kW demand equal to its kW rating as soon as it has operated at its rated load for twenty minutes. The demand meter does not register until that point in time.

Minimize Demand Charges

Demand charges cannot be eliminated. They are the real cost for the utility, but they can be minimized. Minimizing demand is to the utility's and the customer's benefit alike, and the building owner will obtain more electrical energy per dollar if the peak demand is reduced.

Demand charge revenue is used by the utility company to recover its fixed asset investment in generators, transmission, and distribution lines. As these demand charges make up a substantial part of some customer's bills, it is obviously very important that all building owners, managers, and operators have an understanding about how these charges are calculated.

From a common 100-watt light bulb to a

huge, 1,000-ton centrifugal chiller, every electrical device that consumes power has a kW rating. The kW rating of power-consuming electrical equipment is equal to its steady-state power consumption expressed in watts and divided by 1,000 watts/kW. For the light bulb, the kW rating would be 100 watts divided by 1,000 watts/kW or .1kW. For the chiller (at about .8 kW/ton with auxiliaries), the kW rating would be 1,000 tons times .8 kW/ton or 800 kW. Notice that we still do not have kW demand, only kW rating, ignoring the power factor and under steady-state operating conditions. Any electrical device will exhibit a kW demand equal to its kW rating as soon as it is operated at its rated load for twenty minutes (five minutes per hour).

The Demand Meter

Except for loads supplied on a "flat-rate" basis, the use of demand indicating kilowatt hour meters for commercial and industrial buildings is practically universal. These are really two meters in one—a kilowatt hour (kWh) meter that "counts up" the energy used and a (thermal) demand meter that indicates both the present and peak load that has occurred during a billing period.The demand meter is reset each time the kWh meter is read.

Demand meters usually have a (90 percent) rise time of about twenty minutes; that is, from a cold start the meter will rise to 90 percent of the true load value in twenty minutes, 99 percent of the true load in forty minutes, and 99.9 percent in one hour. They are, therefore, not affected by surging motor starting currents, which usually last for one minute.

In a typical building there is a wide spread between the amount of power used in optimum operation and the maximum demands that will be made for short periods on the supplying utility's facilities. The impact that demand has on the electric bill may not be fully realized from a cursory inspection of the billing rate structure.

The 1977 typical electrical utility's commercial/industrial rate was as follows:

Demand Charge	@ \$2.20 per kilowatt
First 100 × Demand kW Hours	@ 4.57 ¢ per kW
Second 100 × Demand kW Hours	@ 1.9 ¢ per kW
Remainder of kW Hours	@ 1.12 ¢ per kW

Billing Demand—1,728 kW shown on the bill (Figure 12-14)
kWh Consumed—707,200

Demand Charge	1,728 × \$2.20	= \$ 3,801.60
1st Energy Charge	100 × 1,728 × 4.57 ¢	= 7,896.96
2nd Energy Charge	100 × 1,728 × 1.9 ¢	3,283.20
Balance of Energy		
707,200 − 2 (100 × 1,728) = 361,600 × 1.12 ¢		= 4,049.92
	GROSS AMOUNT	\$19,031.68

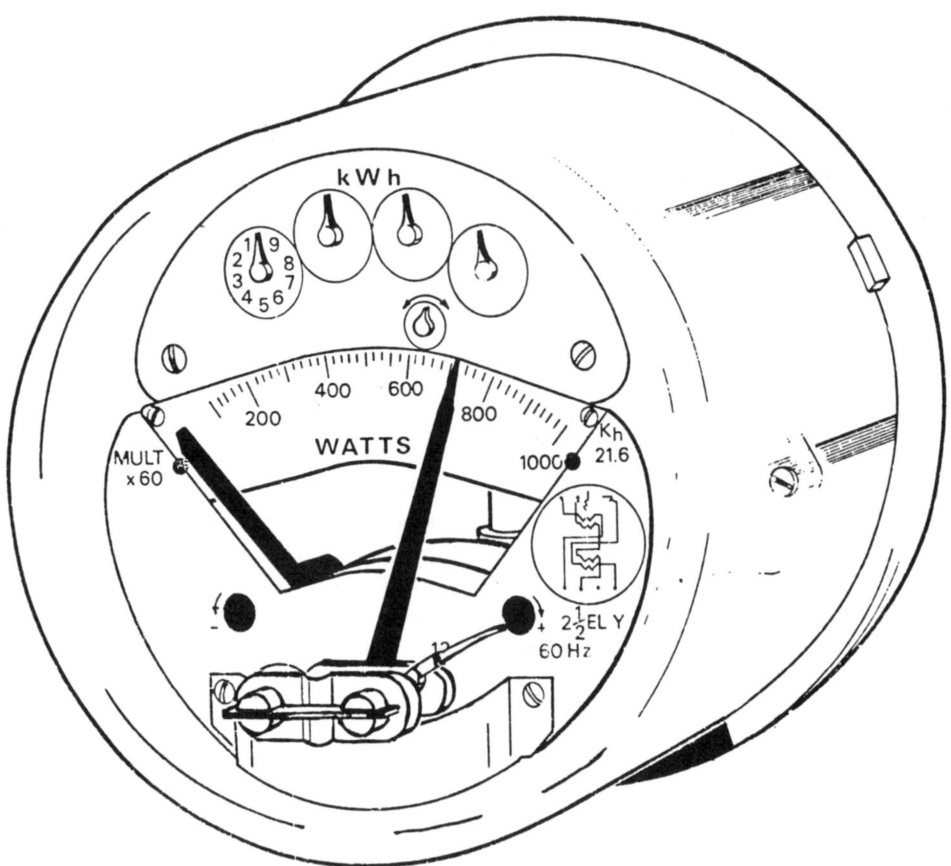

FIGURE 12-12 The demand meter. (Courtesy of Ontario Hydro.)

CUTTING DOWN ELECTRICITY BILLS

Whichever way the building is metered, it is important that the electrical energy is not wasted. Every effort must be made to minimize waste.

1. Explain conservation to staff and tenants.
2. Turn off unnecessary lights and equipment. Set timers properly.
3. Do not use higher wattage bulbs than necessary. Regularly clean walls, ceilings, bulbs, and fixtures to ensure maximum reflectivity.
4. Use a single bulb of higher wattage rather than several low-watt bulbs; two 60-watt bulbs produce less light than one 100-watt bulb, although they consume about 20 percent more energy.
5. Use lampshades that are wide at both ends.

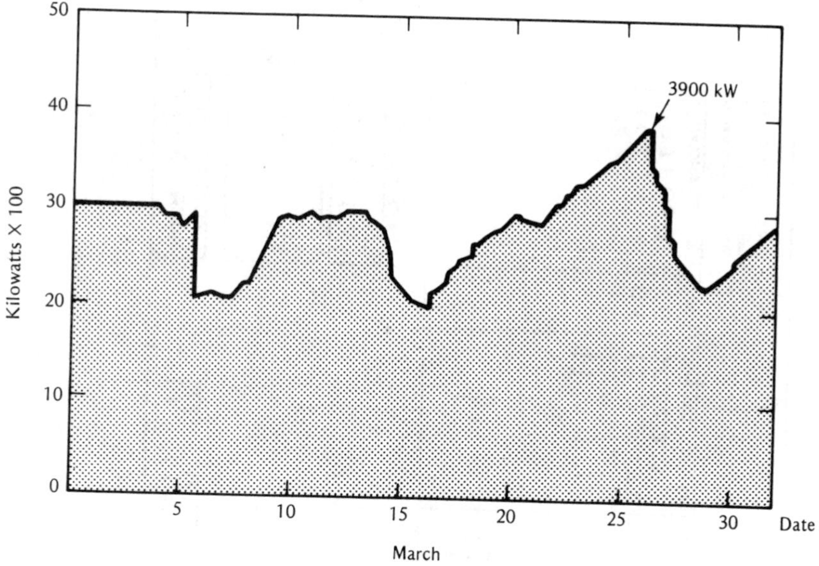

FIGURE 12-13 Typical demand recording. (Courtesy of Ontario Hydro.)

6. If necessary, use switches with a pilot light where an out of the way light or equipment may be forgotten.
7. When buying appliances, compare the wattage consumption. Buy the one that consumes less power.
8. Dirt and dust in controls, valves, pumps, motor bearings, and fans could cause failures that are very costly to repair. The waste of energy because an appliance cannot function efficiently is obvious.
9. Investigate peak shedding, load cycling, and power factor improvement as possible methods of reducing the cost of electricity. Reviewing your bills with the local utility company will reveal any penalties being paid for low power factor.
10. Analyze building energy consumption to determine what equipment contributes to peak demand and what can be rescheduled to off-peak periods. Demand control is the most lucrative field for cost reduction.
11. Use a "total energy balance" approach for maximum energy utilization and savings, rather than concentrating on a single area.
12. Reduce or eliminate decorative lighting and replace (incandescent) lamps with lower wattage lamps where practical.

MONTHLY CONSUMPTION FIGURES

By means of a small motor that runs faster or slower depending on how much current is entering, the meter registers the amount of electricity that is consumed. As the motor runs, it turns numbered indicators to register

Keep this stub for your record

MONTHS	CODE	GROSS AMOUNT
10	07	1903188
10	15	161
10	11	420

D	READING DATE FEB 11 77
METER READING	4624
KW HRS CONSUMED	707200
BT 1	BILLING DEMAND 17280

GROSS AMOUNT	1903749
10% DISCOUNT	190358
NET AMOUNT	1713391

DISCOUNT DATE	ACCOUNT NUMBER
MAR 09 77	

Please return this portion of bill with payment and include account number on all cheques

MONTHS	READING	BILLING DEMAND	K W HRS CONSUMED	CODE	GROSS AMOUNT
10	4624	17280	707200	07	1903188
10			TAX 11	15	161
10				11	420

FOR CODE EXPLANATION SEE OVER

1903749	GROSS AMOUNT
190358	10% PROMPT PAYMENT DISCOUNT
1713391	NET AMOUNT IF PAID BEFORE DISCOUNT DATE

ACCOUNT NUMBER	READING DATE	BT	DISCOUNT DATE
	FEB 11 77	1	MAR 09 77

FIGURE 12-14 Typical electric utility bill.

BUILDING NO.________ BUILDING NAME__________________ ADDRESS_______________

TOWNSHIP______________ NO. OF SUITES_________________ SQ. FOOTAGE___________

UTILITY ACCOUNT NO.______________ PRESENT RATES: DEMAND__________

RATE CLASSIFICATION______________ 1st CHARGE__________

METER NUMBER_____________________ 2nd CHARGE__________

DATES OF RATE INCREASES______________________________ 3rd CHARGE__________

YEAR		NO.OF	KILOWATT HOUR CONSUMPTION					TOTAL	Kwh/	COST
DATE READ	FOR THE MONTH OF	DAYS	DEMAND	1st CHGE	2nd CHGE	3rd CHGE	BALANCE	Kwh's	Sq.Ft.	Kwh/ Sq. Ft.
	JANUARY									
	FEBRUARY									
	MARCH									
	APRIL									
	MAY									
	JUNE									
	JULY									
	AUGUST									
	SEPT									
	OCTOBER									
	NOVEMBER									
	DECEMBER									

FIGURE 12-15 Monthly electrical consumption records.

the cumulative total energy used. The indicator numbers show kilowatt hours, usually abbreviated kWh, and these are the figures that appear on the billing. One kWh is equivalent to 1,000 watts consumed over a one hour time span.

MONITORING ELECTRICITY CONSUMPTION

To monitor the success of your electrical management program, it is wise to chart the consumption figures. The entry cycles would match the billing habits of your local utility company, either monthly or every other month.

12-5 Domestic Hot Water

HEATING THE DOMESTIC WATER

In hospitals and residential buildings the energy used to satisfy the needs of the occupants can run from 10 percent to 30 percent of the total energy consumption. In retail stores and office buildings it is often less than 5 percent.

In most recirculating hot water systems, more energy is consumed to keep the piping and storage tanks hot than is used to heat the hot water used by the occupants. Because of this, it is wise to install a night set back controller on the storage tanks to reduce the temperature at night or during low use periods.

CONTROLLING THE TEMPERATURE

Tests have shown that reductions in hot water temperature provide proportional reductions in hot water energy consumption. While it has been thought that lower hot water temperatures would result in higher hot water consumption, experience has shown that this is not the case.

The hot water consumption does not change as the temperature changes, because most people use hot water at whatever temperature it may be set.

SERVICING THE STORAGE TANK

Problems encountered with the temperature of the domestic hot water (DHW) resulted in the opening of a storage tank to see if there was a problem inside. Once we saw the condition of the tanks (Figures 12-16 and 12-17) we decided to open all of them on a regular basis. At that time we cleaned and cement-washed the tank (Figure 12-20), and most important, cleaned the heating coil, both inside and outside.

The coils are removed and taken back to the maintenance depot, where they are immersed in a bath of hot water (Figures 12-18 and 12-19) into which the chemical "Nutek" had been added. While the service men eat their lunch, the coils soak in the bath until they are completely cleaned.

There are three benefits from this program:

1. Complaints about hot water disappeared.
2. The cement washing protected the tank, thus prolonging its life.
3. The temperature of the DHW was reduced from 140°F to 120°F. The temperatures were set back even further during low use periods.

In some buildings with two storage tanks, you will be able to eliminate one tank without experiencing any problem with a shortage of hot water, if you service the tank being used on a regular basis.

FIGURE 12-16 Condition of heat exchange coil before cleaning. (Photo by A. Zuliani.)

FIGURE 12-17 Material removed from a domestic hot water storage tank. (Photo by A. Zuliani.)

In other buildings, with two storage tanks of the same pressure, you can repipe the tanks in series so that one tank stores the hot water while the other is used for heating and storing. All of these actions will reduce your energy bills for heating the domestic water substantially.

LEAKING FAUCETS ARE EXPENSIVE

It is important to remind you about the waste caused by leaks, especially leaking taps and toilets. You should have a supply of the proper sized washers and seats on hand and arrange to change them on a regular basis. When we consider that 10 percent to 30 percent of the energy consumed in an apartment building is spent to heat the domestic water, letting it drip down the drain must be the worst thing that we can allow to

FIGURE 12-18 The heating coil cleaning bath. (Photo by A. Zuliani.)

FIGURE 12-19 The black water is evidence of corrosion. (Photo by A. Zuliani.)

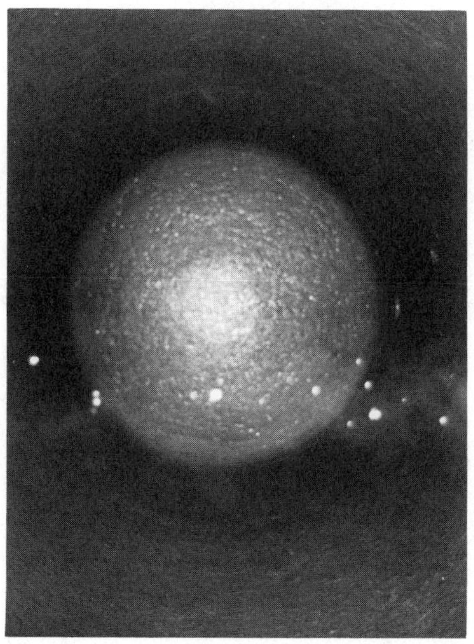

FIGURE 12-20 Condition of tank after cleaning. (Photo by A. Zuliani.)

happen. Leaks can also occur in valve packing glands, pump seals, pipes. The loss of water chart shows how serious a problem this can be.

COPPER PIPE HEAT LOSSES

When considering the waste of energy in a building, one factor that should not be overlooked is the heat loss from bare piping. This heat loss can be substantially overcome by adding insulation.

The amount of heat loss and the potential savings can easily be determined by referring to Figure 12- 22 and using a 1½-inch pipe as an example. We find that

—we lose 45 Btuh per linear foot of bare pipe, at 1¢ per kWh it costs $107.22.

—if we add 1 inch of asbestos insulation, it only costs $53.61.

—if we add 1 inch of fiberglass, it only costs $30.92, saving $76.30.

LOSS OF WATER

One drop per second:	1 day loss	= 1 gal. & 1 pt.	(4.26 liters)
	1 week loss	= 8 gallons	(30.28 liters)
	1 month loss	= 34 gallons	(128.69 liters)
Two drops per second:	1 day loss	= 3 2/3 gallons	(13.88 liters)
	1 week loss	= 26 gallons	(98.41 liters)
	1 month loss	= 100 gallons	(378.5 liters)
Drops to stream:	1 day loss	= 24 gallons	(90.84 liters)
	1 week loss	= 175 gallons	(662.38 liters)
	1 month loss	= 700 gallons	(2,649.50 liters)
1/16" stream:	1 day loss	= 64 gallons	(317.94 liters)
	1 week loss	= 575 gallons	(2,176.38 liters)
	1 month loss	= 2,500 gallons	(9,462.50 liters)
1/8" stream:	1 day loss	= 260 gallons	(984.10 liters)
	1 week loss	= 1,800 gallons	(6,813.00 liters)
	1 month loss	= 7,800 gallons	(29,523.00 liters)
3/16" stream:	1 day loss	= 425 gallons	(1,608.62 liters)
	1 week loss	= 3,000 gallons	(11,355.60 liters)
	1 month loss	= 12,750 gallons	(48,258.75 liters)
1/4" stream:	1 day loss	= 925 gallons	(3,501.13 liters)
	1 week loss	= 6,500 gallons	(24,602.50 liters)
	1 month loss	= 27,750 gallons	(105,033.75 liters)

BUILDING NO._______ BUILDING NAME______________ ADDRESS_____________

TOWNSHIP____________ NO. OF SUITES_______ RATE CLASSIFICATION______

UTILITY ACCOUNT NO._______________METER NUMBER______________________

DATES OF RATE INCREASES____

YEAR		NO OF DAYS	METER READING #1	METER READING #2	MONTHLY CONSUMP. PER M	PRESENT RATE	MONTHLY COST	GAL/ SUITE/ PER DAY
DATE READ	FOR THE MONTH OF							
	JANUARY							
	FEBRUARY							
	MARCH							
	APRIL							
	MAY							
	JUNE							
	JULY							
	AUGUST							
	SEPT.							
	OCTOBER							
	NOVEMBER							
	DECEMBER							

FIGURE 12-21 Monthly water consumption cost records.

	BARE PIPE			ASBESTOS INSULATION				GLASS FIBER INSULATION			
Pipe Size	BTUH/ Linear Ft.	Bare Pipe	Approx. $/Year	1/2"	Approx. $/Year	1"	Approx. $/Year	1/2"	Approx. $/Year	1"	Approx. $/Year
1/2"	22	650 W	$ 56.94	520 W	$ 45.55	260 W	$ 22.77	300 W	$ 26.28	150 W	$13.14
3/4"	30	885 W	$ 77.52	710 W	$ 62.19	355 W	$ 27.90	408 W	$ 35.74	204 W	$17.87
1"	37	1090 W	$ 95.48	876 W	$ 76.73	438 W	$ 38.36	506 W	$ 44.32	253 W	$22.16
1-1/4"	45	1325 W	$116.70	1060 W	$ 92.85	530 W	$ 46.42	610 W	$ 53.43	305 W	$26.71
1-1/2"	52	1530 W	$134.02	1224 W	$107.22	612 W	$ 53.61	706 W	$ 61.84	353 W	$30.92
2"	66	1940 W	$169.94	1550 W	$135.78	775 W	$ 67.89	892 W	$ 78.13	446 W	$39.06
2-1/2"	78	2290 W	$200.60	1830 W	$160.30	915 W	$ 80.15	1056 W	$ 92.50	528 W	$46.25
3"	92	2700 W	$236.52	2160 W	$182.21	1080 W	$ 94.60	1246 W	$109.14	623 W	$54.52
3-1/2"	104	3060 W	$268.05	2450 W	$214.62	1225 W	$107.31	1410 W	$123.51	705 W	$61.75
4"	118	3470 W	$303.97	2770 W	$242.65	1385 W	$121.32	1600 W	$140.16	800 W	$70.08

FIGURE 12-22 Copper pipe heat losses: Loss in watts per 100 linear feet and loss per year at 1¢ per kWh. Heat losses from bare tarnished copper tube—the loss may be much greater with steel. *Temperature differential:* 150°F (WATER); 70°F (AIR) = 80°F. (Courtesy of ASHRAE.)

As today's rates in Toronto, Ontario, Canada are 3¢ per kWh, heat loss from bare pipes is expensive. In Toronto this rate may double in the next few years and makes the case for insulating domestic hot water piping more attractive in new buildings. In existing buildings, long runs of exposed piping could be insulated.

12-6 Monitoring Efficiency

AN OVERVIEW

Regular inspections of the electrical/mechanical systems, keeping records of the temperatures and pressure readings, and completing preventive maintenance chores, are vital to a successful energy management program.

It was for this reason that the electrical/mechanical logs (Figures 12-23, 12-24, and 12-25) were developed. These logs lay out in a logical sequence the information needed to monitor the efficiency of the heating and ventilating systems and to alert us to problems. Someone conducting "look, listen, and touch" inspections, would also look for structural defects or other signs of possible problems. It is wise to *record everything and to correct any problems uncovered.*

BOILER AND PUMP LOGS

A brief explanation of the three logs illustrated in Figures 12-23, 12-24, and 12-25, will help you understand them.

#1–For buildings with one or two heating zones and one or two boilers.

#2–For buildings with up to four boilers and four heating zone pumps. This log must be combined with log #3 to complete all the readings required.

#3–This log includes

- –corridor air supply—heat exchangers and glycol coils;
- –up to four domestic hot water heat exchangers;
- –up to four domestic hot water storage tanks;
- –fire pumps, sump pumps, booster pump; plus
- –four more zone pumps. This form supplements form #2.

Studying the normal temperature and pressure readings for equipment in a building will help train the operator to immediately recognize an abnormal situation. Anything beyond the ability of the operator to correct must be reported as soon as discovered so that skilled technicians can be called to correct the situation.

THREE-WAY BLEND VALVE EFFICIENCY

To help monitor the efficiency of the three-way blend valve, which controls the temperature of the heating system supply water, plot the "Heating Performance Graph" (Figure 12-26).

The following information is needed:

1. The daily outdoor temperature.
2. The blended water temperature required to comfortably heat the building relative to the outdoor temperature. This is the "design blended supply water temperature" (Figure 12-2).
3. The actual operating temperatures.

DAILY LOG

BUILDING NO:__________

\- BOILERS AND PUMPS -

BUILDING ADDRESS____________________ WEEK ENDING ____________________

REPORT ALL LEAKS AND UNUSUAL READINGS TO THE PROPERTY MANAGER IMMEDIATELY

	BOILER Nº				BOILER Nº				METER READINGS			
	PRESS	SUPPLY TEMP	RETURN TEMP	STACK TEMP	PRESS	SUPPLY TEMP	RETURN TEMP	STACK TEMP	OUTSIDE TEMP	TIME LOG TAKEN	GAS / OIL	WATER
SUN												
MON												
TUES												
WED												
THUR												
FRI												
SAT												

	_____ ZONE PUMP			_____ ZONE PUMP			GARAGE HEATING PUMP			DOMESTIC HOT WATER		
	PRESS DIFF	BLEND TEMP	RETURN TEMP	PRESS DIFF	BLEND TEMP	RETURN TEMP	PRESS DIFF	SUPPLY TEMP	RETURN TEMP	HTR ON / OFF	SUPPLY TEMP	RETURN TEMP
SUN												
MON												
TUES												
WED												
THUR												
FRI												
SAT												

	DOMESTIC HOT WATER TANKS				DOMESTIC HOT WATER TANK HEAT EXCHANGERS						COLD WATER BOOSTER PUMP PRESS.
	TANK Nº 1		TANK Nº 2		Nº 1			Nº 2			
	SUPPLY TEMP	RETURN TEMP	SUPPLY TEMP	RETURN TEMP	SUPPLY TEMP	RETURN TEMP.	PUMP ON / OFF	SUPPLY TEMP	RETURN TEMP	PUMP ON / OFF	
SUN											
MON											
TUES											
WED											
THUR											
FRI											
SAT											

	RAMP HEATING				
	HEAT EXCHANGERS			RAMP GLYCOL	
	SUPPLY TEMP	RETURN TEMP	PUMP ON / OFF	SUPPLY TEMP	RETURN TEMP
SUN					
MON					
TUES					
WED					
THUR					
FRI					
SAT					

COMMENTS:

WEEKLY MECHANICAL INSPECTION COMPLETED YES _____ NO _____

EMERGENCY BATTERIES–WATER LEVELS FULL _____ WATER ADDED __________

HYDROMETER READING __________

CUSHION TANK LEVELS 1/4 _____ 1/2 _____ 3/4 _____ FULL __________

CORRIDOR AIR SUPPLY FILTERS CHANGED–DATE __________

DOMESTIC HOT WATER RECIRCULATING LINE BLOWN DOWN–DATE(S) __________

MAINTENANCE REQUESTS - HEATING ATTENDED TO DURING THE WEEK MUST BE ATTACHED TO FORM Nº 170 OF THE DAILY LOGS.

WHITE – ENGINEERING SERVICES
PINK – MANAGEMENT OFFICE
BLUE – BOILER LOG – SUPT.

Prepared By:

CFRM 170 REV. 7/79

FIGURE 12-23 **Daily log.** (Courtesy of Cadillac-Fairview Corporation, Limited.)

DAILY LOG

BUILDING NO: ____________

-BOILERS AND PUMPS-

BUILDING ADDRESS ______________________________ WEEK ENDING ____________________

REPORT ALL LEAKS AND UNUSUAL READINGS TO THE PROPERTY MANAGER IMMEDIATELY

	BOILER No				BOILER No				BOILER No				BOILER No			
	PRESS	SUPPLY TEMP	RETURN TEMP	STACK TEMP	PRESS	SUPPLY TEMP	RETURN TEMP	STACK TEMP	PRFSS	SUPPLY TEMP	RETURN TEMP	STACK TEMP	PRESS	SUPPLY TEMP	RETURN TEMP	STACK TEMP
SUN																
MON																
TUES																
WED																
THUR																
FRI																
SAT																

	______ ZONE PUMP			______ ZONE PUMP			______ ZONE PUMP			______ ZONE PUMP		
	PRESS DIFF	BLEND TEMP	RETURN TEMP	PRESS DIFF	BLEND TEMP	RETURN TEMP	PRESS DIFF	BLEND TEMP	RETURN TEMP	PRESS DIFF	BLEND TEMP	RETURN TEMP
SUN												
MON												
TUES												
WED												
THUR												
FRI												
SAT												

			RAMP HEATING					RAMP HEATING				
			HEAT EXCHANGERS			RAMP GLYCOL		HEAT EXCHANGERS			RAMP GLYCOL	
	OUTSIDE TEMP	TIME LOG TAKEN	SUPPLY TEMP	RETURN TEMP	PUMP ON / OFF	SUPPLY TEMP	RETURN TEMP	SUPPLY TEMP	RETURN TEMP	PUMP ON OFF	SUPPLY TEMP	RETURN TEMP
SUN												
MON												
TUES												
WED												
THUR												
FRI												
SAT												

	METER READINGS		PRIMARY PUMP No			PRIMARY PUMP No			PRIMARY PUMP No		
	GAS OIL	WATER	PRESS DIFF	SUPPLY TEMP	RETURN TEMP	PRESS DIFF	SUPPLY TEMP	RETURN TEMP	PRESS DIFF	SUPPLY TEMP	RETURN TEMP
SUN											
MON											
TUES											
WED											
THUR											
FRI											
SAT											

WEEKLY MECHANICAL INSPECTION COMPLETED YES______ NO______

EMERGENCY BATTERIES–WATER LEVELS FULL______ WATER ADDED ____________

HYDROMETER READING ____________

CUSHION TANK LEVELS 1/4_____ 1/2_____ 3/4_____ FULL ____________

CORRIDOR AIR SUPPLY FILTERS CHANGED–DATE ____________

DOMESTIC HOT WATER RECIRCULATING LINE BLOWN DOWN–DATE(S) ____________

MAINTENANCE REQUESTS–HEATING ATTENDED TO DURING THE WEEK MUST BE ATTACHED TO FORM NO 170A OF THE DAILY LOGS.

Prepared By:

WHITE – ENGINEERING SERVICES
PINK – MANAGEMENT OFFICE
BLUE – BOILER LOG – SUPT

CFRM_170A REV. 7/79

FIGURE 12-24 **Daily log.** (Courtesy of Cadillac-Fairview Corporation, Limited.)

DAILY LOG

BUILDING NO. __________

- BOILERS AND PUMPS -

BUILDING ADDRESS __________ WEEK ENDING __________

	CORRIDOR AIR SUPPLY No. ______							CORRIDOR AIR SUPPLY No. ______				
		HEAT EXCHANGER			GLYCOL COIL			HEAT EXCHANGER			GLYCOL COIL	
	DISCH AIR TEMP	SUPPLY TEMP	RETURN TEMP	BLEND TEMP	SUPPLY TEMP	RETURN TEMP	DISCH AIR TEMP	SUPPLY TEMP	RETURN TEMP	BLEND TEMP	SUPPLY TEMP	RETURN TEMP
SUN												
MON												
TUES												
WED												
THUR												
FRI												
SAT												

	DOMESTIC HOT WATER TANK HEAT EXCHANGERS											
	Nº1			Nº2			Nº3			Nº4		
	SUPPLY TEMP	RETURN TEMP	PUMP ON/OFF	SUPPLY TEMP	RETURN TEMP	PUMP ON OFF	SUPPLY TEMP	RETURN TEMP	PUMP ON OFF	SUPPLY TEMP	RETURN TEMP	PUMP ON OFF
SUN												
MON												
TUES												
WED												
THUR												
FRI												
SAT												

	DOMESTIC HOT WATER TANKS								FIRE PUMP PRESS	SUMP PUMPS CHECKED	COLD WATER BOOSTER PUMP PRESS
	Nº1 TANK TEMP		Nº2 TANK TEMP		Nº3 TANK TEMP		Nº4 TANK TEMP				
	SUPPLY	RETURN	SUPPLY	RETURN	SUPPLY	RETURN	SUPPLY	RETURN			
SUN											
MON											
TUES											
WED											
THUR											
FRI											
SAT											

	______ ZONE PUMP			______ ZONE PUMP			______ ZONE PUMP			______ ZONE PUMP		
	PRESS DIFF	BLEND TEMP	RETURN TEMP	PRESS DIFF	BLEND TEMP	RETURN TEMP	PRESS DIFF	BLEND TEMP	RETURN TEMP	PRESS DIFF	BLEND TEMP	RETURN TEMP
SUN												
MON												
TUES												
WED												
THUR												
FRI												
SAT												

REPORT ALL MECHANICAL PROBLEMS AND LEAKS IN COMMENT SECTION

COMMENTS __________

MAINTENANCE REQUESTS HEATING ATTENDED TO DURING THE WEEK MUST BE ATTACHED TO FORM Nº 170 B OF THE DAILY LOGS

Prepared By:

WHITE – ENGINEERING SERVICES
PINK – MANAGEMENT OFFICE
BLUE – BOILER LOG – SUPT

CFRM 170 B 7/79

FIGURE 12-25 Daily log. (Courtesy of Cadillac-Fairview Corporation, Limited.)

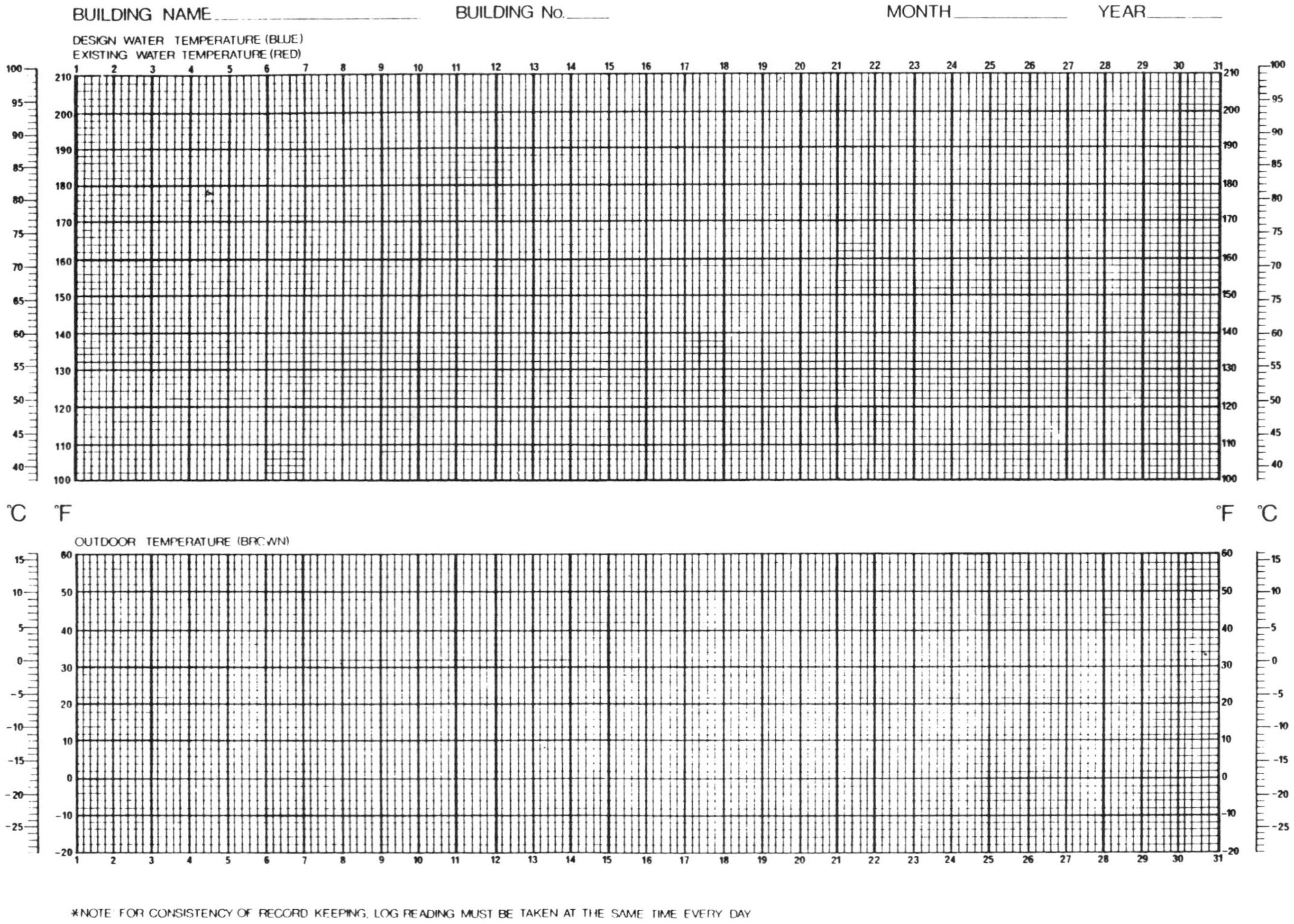

BUILDING NAME________ BUILDING No.____ MONTH________ YEAR______

DESIGN WATER TEMPERATURE (BLUE)
EXISTING WATER TEMPERATURE (RED)

°C °F °F °C

OUTDOOR TEMPERATURE (BROWN)

*NOTE: FOR CONSISTENCY OF RECORD KEEPING, LOG READING MUST BE TAKEN AT THE SAME TIME EVERY DAY

FIGURE 12-26 **Heating performance graph.** (Courtesy of Cadillac-Fairview Corporation, Limited.)

By plotting this information on the "Heating Performance Graph," you can instantly detect deviation from design and bring the system back on the efficiency track.

The systems are designed to give 193°F blended water when the outside temperature is 0°F. *A drop of 1°F outside requires an increase of 1.5°F to the blended water temperature.*

In the past engineers have been known to add 10 percent to their calculations to assure positive results. Operating at 10 percent below design would therefore not be a problem.

MONTHLY FUEL CONSUMPTION COST REPORT (NATURAL GAS)

To keep a monthly record of consumption and dollar cost, use Figure 12-27. Record the following information from the utility bill on the chart.

BUILDING NO.________ BUILDING NAME____________ ADDRESS____________

TOWNSHIP________ NO. OF SUITES____________ SQ. FOOTAGE____________

UTILITY ACCOUNT NO.____________ METER NO.____________ RATE CLASS________

PRESENT RATE________ DATE CONTRACT EXPIRES____________ MIN. CONS.________

DATES OF RATE INCREASES________________________

NAME OF COMPANY____________ ADDRESS____________ CONTACT____________

YEAR DATE READ	FOR THE MONTH	NO OF DAYS	METER READING	CONSUMP. PER MCF	VOLUME PER MCF	RATE PER MCF	COST PER MONTH
	JANUARY						
	FEBRUARY						
	MARCH						
	APRIL						
	MAY						
	JUNE						
	JULY						
	AUGUST						
	SEPT.						
	OCTOBER						
	NOVEMBER						
	DECEMBER						

FIGURE 12-27 **Monthly fuel consumption report—natural gas.**

- –year
- –reading date
- –meter reading
- –consumption in MCF
- –volume if stated on the bill
- –dollar cost per month, and
- –verify that the rate charged agrees with the contracted price

MONTHLY FUEL CONSUMPTION PER HEATING DEGREE DAY REPORT

1. Enter columns 1 to 5 as per Figure 12-27.
2. Using the average fuel consumption figure from the previous months of June, July and August (when the building is not heated) as the cost for heating the domestic water (DHW), enter this figure in every month in column 6.
3. Each month the cost of heating the DHW is deducted from the MCF volume of fuel required to heat the building. Column 6 is deducted from column 5 and the answer is entered in column 7.
4. Enter the monthly degree days in column 8. This information is obtained from your local Meteorological Bureau report.
5. Divide the volume of fuel in MCF consumed by the degree days for the month to give you the actual MCF per degree day consumption. This figure is entered in column 9.
6. Compare the actual consumption per degree day (column 9) with the consumption per degree day goal and enter the results in column 11.
7. Unfavorable variances should be immediately investigated to determine the cause of overconsumption and to correct the problem.

12-7 Summing Up

TIPS FOR OPERATING PERSONNEL

- –Carry out daily "look, listen, and touch" inspections.
- –Record data on operating logs every day.
- –Report all abnormal conditions.
- –Keep mechanical rooms clean.
- –Carry out a proper lubrication program.
- –Make sure that all time clocks are properly set.
- –Keep temperature control settings as directed.
- –Keep belts, sheaves, and drives operating properly.
- –Regularly check the condition of bearings.
- –Change filters as required.
- –Monitor boiler and burner efficiency.
- –Monitor cooling system efficiency.
- –Keep lighting intensities at proper levels.
- –Carry out strainer maintenance as required.
- –Check the exterior of the building for structural problems.
- –Understand the mechanical systems (how they were designed and the performance expected so that they can make sure that the systems are continually operated as designed)
- –Keep the systems balanced to reflect occupant needs

BUILDING NO._____ BUILDING NAME____________________ ADDRESS__________________________

TOWNSHIP ________ METEOROLOGICAL AREA______________ TYPE OF ENERGY USED_____________

To compare buildings by size, use square feet or square meters. To calculate the actual heating fuel consumption in MCF per degree day, divide column 7 by column 8.

1	2	3	4	5 −	6 =	7 /	8 =	9	10	11
YEAR DATE READ	FOR THE MONTH OF	NO OF DAYS	CONSUMP. PER MCF	VOLUME PER MCF	LESS DHW/MCF GOAL	HEATING VOLUME PER MCF	MONTHLY DEGREE DAYS	ACTUAL MCF/DD CONSUMP.	MCF/DD CONSUMP. GOAL	OVER OR UNDER GOAL
	JANUARY									
	FEBRUARY									
	MARCH									
	APRIL									
	MAY									
	JUNE						0000			
	JULY						0000			
	AUGUST						0000			
	SEPT.									
	OCTOBER									
	NOVEMBER									
	DECEMBER									

There are zero degree days during the months of June, July and August because no heat is required in those months.

FIGURE 12-28 Monthly fuel consumption per heating degree day report. Heating degree days are a measurement of heating requirements and are expressed as the average number of degree days Centigrade each 24 hour period is below 18°C; i.e. on a day when the average temperature is 1°C for a 24 hour period, there are 18 − 1 or 17 degree days.

ANNUAL IN-SUITE APARTMENT MAINTENANCE

The following maintenance should be carried out in each apartment suite at least once a year.

–Make sure that heating baseboard convectors are not blocked.

–Check shut-off valves for leaks.

–Replace all tap washers and "O" rings in faucets.

–Tap washer seats are to be inspected and replaced as required.

–Replace swing spout "O" rings, as leaks in them are the major cause of countertop deterioration. If any sign of deterioration is detected, have it corrected immediately.

–Water closet tanks should be inspected for float adjustment, water level, and defective ball and flapper valves.

–Clean shower heads and aerators.

—Shower heads that are scaled with lime should be changed and the old head soaked in a de-liming solution to clean.

—Check bathroom wall tile for hairline cracks, soggy grout, or faulty caulking. Arrange for re-grouting if a problem is detected. A straightened paper clip is ideal for probing for signs of softening due to water penetration.

ENERGY ACTIONS RECOMMENDED BY ASHRAE*

Questions to Ask When Doing an Energy Survey

1. What does it** do?
2. When does it run? (time of day and/or season of the year)
3. When is it off? (what happens when it is off?)
4. When is it occupied? (by how many?)

The answers to these questions will help you make meaningful decisions about adding such things as programmable lighting or other programmable shut-down or start-up systems.

ASHRAE "Quick Fix" Suggestions

1. Reduce lighting.
2. Stop equipment.
3. Reduce fresh air.
4. Minimize exhaust.
5. Insulate.
6. Seal cracks.
7. Adjust controls.
8. Reduce hot water temperature.
9. Use space efficiently.
10. Reduce water use.
11. Review maintenance.

"Quick fix" is the first priority in an energy management program. It is merely "doing the right thing right," and does not involve any cash outlay.

---

*The American Society of Heating, Refrigeration and Air Conditioning Engineers.

**Any piece of energy using equipment or occupied space.

FIGURE 12-29 Original atmospheric heaters. Installation before removal. Heaters were inefficient and wasted money. (Photo by A. Zuliani.)

FIGURE 12-30 Original fresh air supply heaters. Prior to removal. (Photo by A. Zuliani.)

FIGURE 12-31 Empty rooftop boiler room. Hole in boiler room wall for removal of old and installation of new equipment. (Photo by A. Zuliani.)

Success for this part of the energy management program depends on knowledgeable and dedicated operating personnel. Feedback to the building personnel of information about consumption and cost of maintenance is essential if they are expected to become a part of the program.

Everyone should keep in mind that any missed opportunity to save automatically becomes a loss. Also, the operating staff should not attempt to adjust or change any piece of electrical/mechanical equipment if they are not qualified to do so. As an example, the more sophisticated equipment such as burners and their controls, electronic controls for heatng, air conditioning systems, and elevators should not be serviced by the building staff.

The purchase of special manufacturer's service contracts for this type of equipment is recommended, as any adjustment would then be made by skilled technicians. Knowing how to recognize a problem and who to call to correct it is the mark of a good operator.

FIGURE 12-32 **New exhaust air heat recuperators.** Heat is now recovered from warm exhaust air. (Photo by A. Zuliani.)

FIGURE 12-33 **Hoisting new watertube boiler.** Boiler room on eighteenth floor makes replacement difficult. (Photo by A. Zuliani.)

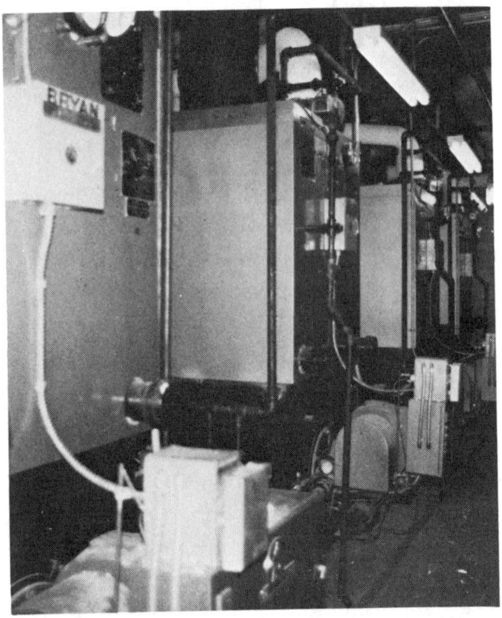

FIGURE 12-34 **Four new watertube boilers.** Three watertube boilers replaced 23 atmospheric heaters. One of the boilers was removed after the first year of operation because it was not needed. (Photo by A. Zuliani.)

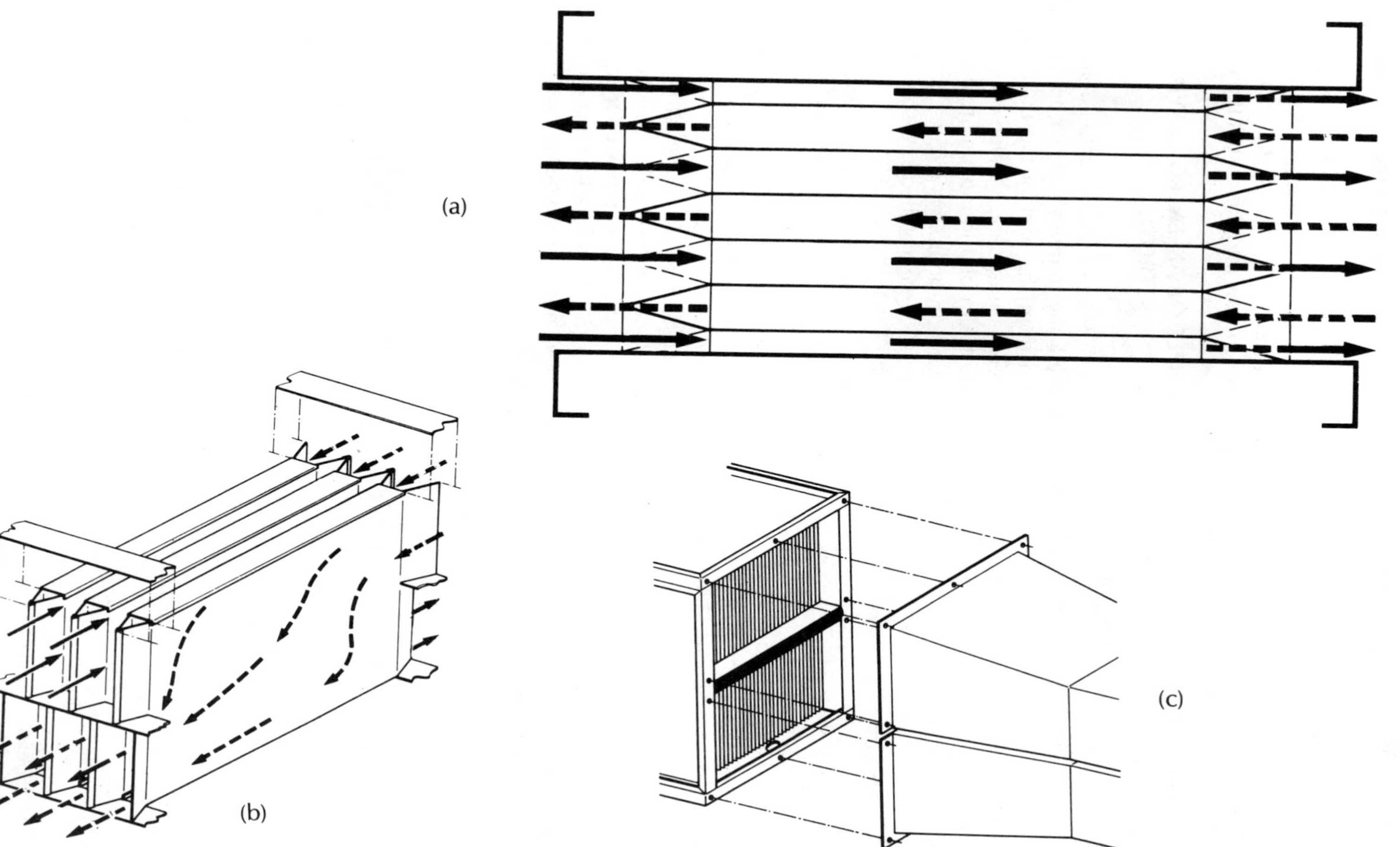

FIGURE 12-35 How a recuperator works. (a) The cold outside air (solid arrows) enters from the left end above the partition and flows towards the right end. The warm and cold air passages are alternated so that the heat from the warm exhaust air can be picked up without cross contamination between the two streams. (b) The warm air enters above the center partition. Since the exits above the partition are closed, the air is forced to leave the recuperator below the partition. (c) Shows how the recuperator is fitted into the duct. Courtesy of Indusco Sales, Ltd., Canada.)

ASHRAE Retrofit Suggestions

1. Add zone demand reset to multizone and dual duct systems.
2. Convert multizone and dual duct systems to variable volume systems.
3. Use fresh air for cooling when practical.
4. Add heat recovery to exhaust system.
5. Isolate off-line chillers, boilers, and other equipment.
6. Modify lighting systems or add programmable lighting.
7. Use central control systems.

Tips for Selling Retrofits to Owners

When analyzing the merits of a retrofit

1. Consider the year prior to the retrofit as a loss and the first year as a gain. Recovering the loss opportunity gives you a double savings in the first year, shortening the pay back period.
2. Use the building's cash flow figures as a base. Deduct from the cash flow the losses each year if you do not do the retrofit. Add the savings to the cash flow if you do the retrofit. The losses compound downward and the savings compound up, thus showing a much faster payback than the simple payback formula of dividing the savings each year into the cost of the job.

AN EXAMPLE OF AN ENERGY SAVING RETROFIT

Figures 12-29 to 12-35 illustrate a retrofit that involved the removal of a complete boiler room from the roof of the building. Twenty-three atmospheric heaters (Figure 12-29) were taken off the roof and replaced with three water-tube boilers (Figure 12-34). "Recuperators" were installed to recover the heat from the exhausted air (Figure 12-35).

The payback for this costly renovation was predicted to be five years. At the time of the replacement, the cost of energy escalated dramatically and the payback was achieved in four years. All of these savings increased the cash flow substantially during this time. *As the fuel costs increase in the future, the savings and the cash flow will automatically go up*. Inefficient use of manpower or equipment eats up profits, while efficiency automatically puts money into your pockets on a continuing basis.

INDEX

Air (see Heating, Ventilating, and Air conditioning)
  supply and exhaust air, 418-421
Air conditioning, 399
  air passage in a duct system, 409
  air pressure problems, 405
  air purity, 404
  air volume, 434
  balancing homes, 428-430
  balancing procedure, 423
  budget (see Cooling System)
  diffusers, 414
  energy conservation tips, 436
  fresh air requirements, 404
  lobby, 420
  measuring the property of air, 401
  methods of air distribution, 407, 411-422
  refrigeration cycle, 434-440
  rooftop units, 438
  room air flow, 414
  system examples, 74, 75
  window room cooler, 408
Air handling equipment (see Fans)
Alarms
  annunciator panel, 115
  fire, 115
  life system audit, 133
  manual, 115
  records, 68
  system illustration, 114
Ampere (see Electricity)
Appliances
  energy consumption, 582
  laundry room dryer exhaust, 421
  problems, 497-502
  refrigerators, 68, 436
  safety, 103
  stoves, 68

Batteries (see Electricity)
Bearings, 547-551
Belts
  alignment, 539
  basic pulley laws, 539
  incorrect belt adjustment, 539
  run-in period, 537
  sizes, 536
  speed control of belt drive blowers, 538
  V-belts drives, 535-536
Boilers, 349
  classification, 349
  data records, 72
  efficiency test report, 341
  firebox, 350
  firetube, 350
  gas flow patterns, 353
  maintenance, 357
  tube failure, 353-356
  watertube, 357
Brickwork
  bond between brick and mortar, 240
  design and detailing, 241
  faulty brickwork, 237
  faulty mortar, 237, 238, 240
  quality of workmanship, 241
  taping and grouting, 240
British thermal unit (see Heating)
Budgeting, 23-24
  building hardware, 134
  cooling system, 448
  electrical system, 503
Budgeting *(Contd.)*
  elevators, 523
  fire protection system, 134, 504
  groundskeeping, 215, 217
  heating system, 391-393
  housekeeping services, 179-181
  key expense items, 9-18
  plumbing system, 321, 322
  security system, 134
  structural services, 280-284
  television system, 504
  ventilation system, 448
  zero-base, 23
Building hardware
  door closers, 272, 273
  hinges, 269-271
  keys, 94-96
  lever passage latch, 276
  locks, 274-279
  panic exit devices, 277-279
  security, 96
Building profile, 89-92
Burners
  air atomizing oil, 343
  atmospheric, 345
  combustion efficiency, 337, 339
  data records, 73
  efficiency test report, 341
  gas, 345
  maintenance, 347-349
  mechanical forced draft, 346
  mechanical or pressure atomizing, 343
  oil, 342
  ring type forced draft (gas/oil), 348
  rotary cup oil, 344
  start-up, 342
  troubleshooting pilot lights, 380

Cables, cords, and conduits (see Electricity)
Carpets, 167
  care, 164-170
  fabrication, 165
  padding, 167
  spot and stain removal, 169
  type of backing, 166
  vacuuming, 168
  walk-off, 166
Caulking, 235, 240
Ceilings, 63, 65, 66, 142
Charts
  air supply glycol inspection, 372
  air supply heat exchanger inspections, 372
  blowers, furnace, 379
  boiler maintenance inspection, 357
  bulb planting data, 215
  burners, furnace, troubleshooting, 37, 379
  color coordination, 207
  combustion air, effect, 338
  combustion air, requirements, 337
  comfort chart, occupants, 329
  contracts, services and suppliers, 91
  cooling system, 71
  cooling tower inspection, 446
  copper pipe heat losses, 595
  domestic water heat exchanger inspections, 372
  domestic water storage tank inspections, 374
  electrical demand recording, 587
  exterior elements, 57
  fire control system, 68
Charts *(Contd.)*
  fire extinguishers, types and uses, 126
  freon, condensing characteristics, 437
  fuel consumption goal, 576
  furnaces, forced air, troubleshooting, 381
  groundskeeping, work classifications, 187
  heating performance graph, 600
  heating system, 60
  heating water, blended supply temperature, 566
  heating zone pump inspection, 360
  heat pump capacities, 334
  housekeeping time estimates, 34
  interior elements, 62
  life cycle costs, percentages, 5
  life system audit, 131
  landscape "as-built" plan, 60, 61
  liquid measures, 190
  maintenance programming, 36
  metric conversions, 56, 330
  "O" ring sizing chart, 299
  pH scale of H-ion concentration, 40, 189
  pilot lights, troubleshooting, 380
  plan information, 59
  plumbing and drainage system, 78
  project consultants, 58
  ramp glycol heat exchanger inspection, 371
  ramp glycol system inspection, 37
  roof inspection chart, 268
  room finish schedules, 65, 66
  "R" values, 572, 573, 574
  resources, occupant services and operations, 3
  sheave adjustment chart, 587
  soil analysis, 188
  stain removal chart, 171
  thermal shock, roofs, 264
  thermostats, troubleshooting, 583
  tool kit, typical, 84
  "U" values, 571, 575
  valve shut-off chart, 79
  ventilation system, 71
  water, potable standards, 289
  washer sizing chart, 296, 297
Chemicals
  chemical control, 189
  floor sealers, 158
  safety tips, 191
  spraying tips, 190, 191
  spray materials, 213
Circuit breakers
  fires, 113
  fuses, 104, 481, 482, 483, 484, 485
  fuses, why they blow, 490
  ground fault detectors, 490
  motor overload protection, 497
  overloading a circuit, 481
  overload protective devices, 462, 498
Closers (see Building Hardware)
Combustion
  chemical terms and symbols, 335
  chemistry, 336
  draft control, 346
  effect of combustion air on boiler performance, 338
  efficiency, 337, 339, 433
  flue gas analysis, 338
  pilot lights, 380
  theoretical air requirement, 337
Comfort, 326, 329
  air temperature and body heat, 327

Comfort *(Contd.)*
comfortable temperature goal, 400-432
comfort and effective temperature, 399
comfort and indoor-outdoor temperatures, 328
comfort chart, 329
environmental comfort parameters, 565
space conditions affecting comfort, 327
transfer of body heat, 326, 327
Communications
budgets as communication tools, 23
feedback as a channel of communication, 30
(see Forms)
Compressors, 437
air compressor maintenance, 366
typical pneumatic control system, 366, 367
Condensation, 242
causes, 243
curing problems, 243
dew point, 242, 403
humidification and dehumidification, 403
relative humidity, 242, 401
Condenser
air-cooled, 438
heat rejection, 437
(see Cooling Tower)
Consultants, 38, 58
Cooling
budget, 448
records, 71
system examples, 74, 75
tower, 441-446
(see Refrigeration)
Corrosion, 41-44, 46
aqua feeders, 288
boiler tubes, 353, 355, 356
cathodic protection, 47
the pH scale, 40
Cracks, 230-234
Cultivation, 196, 197
Cushion tank, 389, 390

Degree days, 569
Diagnosis, 221
Diffusers
(see Heating, Ventilation, Air Conditioning, Registers)
Doors
bevel of, 271
handling of, 271, 272
overhead, 523, 524
residential entrance, 275
(see Building Hardware)
Drains, 307-310
cleaning, 311
clogged basin and sink, 314
clogged toilets, 311
grease traps, 315
roof drain fittings, 315
storm water, 315
water closet flush designs, 313
Ducts
double or dual duct, 415, 416
ducting air, 407
ducts and fittings, 377
duct traverse readings, 429
heat distributor, 377
systems in buildings, 379, 408-411
systems in homes, 411-415
Dusting
furniture, 143
mopping, 153, 155
storing mops, 156
types of mops, 153

Electrical current (see Electricity)
Electricity
auxiliary power, 114
demand meter, 586
demand recording chart, 587
distribution circuits, 457
door release strikes, 486
electrical energy, 578
electric conductors and insulators, 453
electric current, 455
electron theory, 453
emergency power and standby batteries, 488
grounding, 475
ground fault detectors, 490

Electricity *(Contd.)*
home wiring systems, 461-470
Ohm's law, 455, 456
overload protection (see Circuit Breakers)
plug caps, 473, 474
power distribution, 456, 457
receptacles, wall, 471, 472
shock, 104, 105
transformer vault, 113
voltage, 454
watts, 454
wires, cables, cords and conduits, 457-460
wiring service, 460, 461
Elevators
budget expenses, 523
control, 510
emergencies, 111, 519
geared electric traction, 508
gearless traction, 508
hydraulic, 508
life system audit, 132
maintenance, 512-518
safety features, 510
Emergencies
boilers, 101
elevators, 100, 110, 111, 115, 132, 518-523
emergency power, 111, 488
evacuation, 109, 110
exits, 112, 113
fire, 113, 116, 119
first aid, 104-108
ground fault detectors, 490
poison control, 101
procedures, 133
shock, 101, 104, 120
smoke, 113, 116, 119
staff responsibilities, 113-115
Energy
appliance consumption, 582
Ashrae, 604-608
conservation, 446, 586
consumption records (see Forms)
design parameters, 567
distribution, 577
electrical, 454
forms of energy, 330
heating domestic water, 590
heating water, blend valve efficiency, 596
motors, 582, 583
operating personnel tips, 602
retrofits, selling the owners, 608
solar heating, 331
thermal characteristics data, 571
Equipment
brooms and brushes, 153
budgeting additions and replacements, 9
dust mops, 153
fire extinguishers, 120-126
floor stripping, 156, 157
garbage compactor, 139
gardening list, 204
lists, 70, 85
plumbing lists, 79-82
pool, 317, 318
saunas, 141
sprinkler heads, 130
vacuum cleaners, 168, 169

Fans, 531
(see Belts)
equipment records, 77
furnace blowers, 379
gathering and recording balancing data, 428-430
how a centrifugal fan works, 534
maintenance, 534-545
speed control of direct drive blowers, 535
types, 532
Fertilizers, 192
application tips, 193, 194, 195
fertilizing trees, shrubs and hedges, 195
Filters, 541-542
dryer lint screen, 421
maintenance, 543
Fire protection
alarm system, 110, 111, 114, 133
battery maintenance, 488
Canadian code, 107-109
combustible materials, 109-112

Fire protection *(Contd.)*
control system, 114
detectors, 116-118
electrical hazards, 102-104
emergency power, 488
fire doors, 111, 114
fire extinguishers, 70, 111, 114, 120-127
fire hoses, 114, 128, 129
fire pumps, 69, 107, 114
frostproof hydrants, 127
life system audit, 131-133
safety features, 107, 110, 111
safety in high-rise buildings, 107
smoke, 111, 113, 116, 119
sprinkler systems, 110, 114, 129-131
standpipe system, 107, 114, 127, 128, 287
system records, 68, 69
Fires
classifications, 119, 120
detectors, 116
electrical, 113
elevator fireman service, 518-523
extinguishers, 126
fire triangle, 113, 115, 119
kitchen, 118
First aid
artificial respiration, 105
burns, 105
cardio pulmonary resuscitation, 105
electric shock, 104
mouth-to-mouth resuscitation, 105
poison, 101
Floors, 146
brick, 148
ceramic tile, 150
choosing a floor, 145
concrete, 148
coverings, 62, 65, 66
hardwood, 151
maintenance, 152
marble; slate; stone, 148
terrazzo, 147
Fluorescents (see Lighting)
Forms
air handler test report, 430
appliance expenses, 503
bitting list summary, 96
boiler and pump logs, 596-599
boiler-burner efficiency report, 341
burner data records, 73
brickwork and structural expenses, 282
building hardware records, 67, 134, 282
burner data records, 73
capitalized expenses, 9, 282
caulking expenses, 282
computer printout account summary, 16-18
cooling system expenses, 448
counter tops and cupboards expenses, 283
door expenses, 283
duct traverse reading, 429
electrical/mechanical expenses, 12
electricity consumption (monthly), 589
elevator serviceman's check list, 518
elevator system expenses, 523
equipment lists, 85, 204, 266
exterior painting expenses, 283
fan equipment records, 77
faucets, identifying them, 80
fire hose cabinet inspection, 70
fire protection system expenses, 134, 504
floor expenses, 283
fuel consumption cost, 601
fuel consumption goal (daily), 576
fuel consumption per degree day, 603
groundskeeping expenses, 10, 217
groundskeeping inspection report, 216
groundskeeping workload diary, 35
heating system expenses, 393
housekeeping expenses, 10, 180, 181
lamp bulb inventory, 69
maintenance request, 20
maintenance request (heating), 388
major expense record form, 87
miscellaneous expenditures, 13, 14
parking allocations, 63, 64
parts and inventory lists, 85, 205, 213, 214
paving expenses, 284
plant materials, 208-212
plumbing accessories, 82

Forms (*Contd.*)
plumbing and drainage expenses, 322
pool operations expenses, 322
pump equipment records, 76
rain infiltration (maintenance request), 239
renovation proposal form, 88
roofing expenses, 284
security services, 134
staff salary expenses, 11
structural expenses, 11
suppliers and services guide, 84
valve closures, 132
ventilation expenses, 448
walls and ceiling expenses, 284
water closet tank fittings, 81
water consumption and cost (monthly), 594
water treatment test control, 50
window expenses, 284
wiring distribution expenses, 503
work order, 22
Fountains (see Pools)
Fuels
chemical terms and symbols, 335
coal, 331
consumption (see Energy)
electricity, 330
gas, 331
heat output, 570
oil, 331
oil pump, 344
solar, 331
Furnace
air volume, 434
air temperature (reading locations), 431
combustion efficiency, 433
forced air furnace, 374, 375
heat delivery measurements, 433
rate of heat delivery, 432
Fuses (see Circuit Breakers)

Grounding (see Electricity)
Groundskeeping
architectural components, 206
bulbs, corms and tubers, 205
chemical control, 189
cultivation, 196
design planning, 185
fertilizers, 192, 194, 195
gardening equipment lists, 204, 205
groundskeeping workload, 186
insect and pest control, 191, 193
lawn care, 199, 200
pruning, 197, 198
service (in-house or outside), 186
soil analysis, 188
spraying tips, 190
trees and shrubs, 206
watering, 199-203
weed control, 188
work classifications, 187

Hazards, 101-104
Heat exchanger
coil maintenance, 544
domestic water, 293, 373
furnace, 377
heat pump, 332
maintenance, 371, 372, 591-593
pools, 318
solar, 331
types, 369, 373
Heat gain, internal, 565
Heating
air distribution in high-rise buildings, 415-422
air supply (boiler room), 419
apartment system, 368, 391
balancing (home air conditioning), 423, 428-430
blend valve efficiency, 596
boiler and pump logs, 596-599
British thermal unit, 400
combustion efficiencies, 433
corridor air, 605-607
diffusers, 414
distribution, 358-374
domestic water, 292, 293, 375
electric heating maintenance, 490
electric on-off boiler operation, 367
flow of heat, 570

Heating (*Contd.*)
furnace air volume, 434
furnace heat loss, 432
heat delivery measurements, 433
heat gain, 402, 403
heat output, 570
home, 374-381
operator's responsibility, 385-387
output capacity at the bonnet, 431
pool water, 318, 373
records, 70
room air flow, 414
sensible and latent heat, 401, 435
systems, 74, 75, 573
solar, 331
temperature control, 362, 378, 382, 383, 385
transfer, 400
Heat loss, 568, 592-596
Heat pump, 332
ground-to-air, 334
heating capacities, 334
water-to-air, 334
Hinges, 269-271
Housekeeping
apartments, 143
contracts (in-house versus outside), 37
dusting, 143
dust mopping, 153
floors, 148-164
germicidal cleaning, 139
graffiti removal, 142
inspections, 28
laundry rooms, 142
lights and fixtures, 143
metal cleaning, 144
saunas, 141
showers and washrooms, 140, 141
spot cleaning, 142
venetian blinds, 141
wall washing, 141
work organization, 30
Human resources
feedback as a channel of communications, 30
organizing work and people, 29, 30
performance evaluation, 37
staffing to fit the hours, 31
waste in labor productivity, 29
Humidity (see Condensation)

Infiltration (see Ventilation)
Inspections, 25, 27
building takeover, 8, 54
electrical/mechanical, 28
elevator (visual check), 514-518
fans (daily/weekly), 545
filters, 543
grounds, 216
housekeeping, 28
inventory and equipment, 27
locks (checking daily), 277-279
piping systems, 286
roofs, 265-267
staff (operating), 26
structure, 220-240
Insects, 191
garden, 193
household, 172-175
Insulation
heat gain (how it affects it), 567
piping, 287, 595
roofs, 257
wall and roof section, 257
Intercoms
intercom and building entrance release, 486, 487
operation, 486
system records, 68
Inventory
bitting list (key control), 96
building hardware, 67
equipment lists, 85
faucets, 80
fire hose cabinets, 70
gardening accessories, 205
lamp bulbs, 69
landscape architectural components, 206
parts and inventory form, 85
plumbing accessories, 82

Inventory (*Contd.*)
soils, fertilizers and chemicals, 213
tool kit, 84
water closet tank fittings, 81
watering equipment, 213

Keys, 94-96

Lawns, 199-200
Leaks, 230
condensation, 242
investigation, 220, 239
rainwater infiltration, 239
water penetration, 236
Lighting
cleaning lights and fixtures, 143
electric power, 578
emergency, 113
exit signs, 112
fluorescents, 478-481, 581
guide for reasonable light levels, 579
incandescents, 475-477
lamp bulb inventory, 69
life system audit, 131, 132
quality of illumination, 579
task lighting, 579
Locks, 274
checking, 277-279
deadlocking plunger, 280
grip handle entrance, 276
hand of a lock, 279, 280
keying, 94-97, 274
lubricating, 277
mortice rim cylinders, 276
security, 274
selection, 276
tubular dead bolt, 274
tumbler key in knob set, 275
Lubrication, 546

Maintenance programming
air compressors, 366
air handling equipment, 534-545
batteries, 488
boilers, 357
burners, 347, 379
cooling towers, 445, 446
dryer exhausts, 421
electric heating, 421
elevators, 512
filters and coils, 542
master action plan, 19
specialized services, 9
troubleshooting
appliances, 497-502
blending valves, 369, 384
fluorescents, 480
furnaces, 379-381
fuses or circuit breakers, 482
garbage compactors, 524
heating complaints, 387, 388
motors, 494-497
television reception, 487
thermostats, 383
overhead doors, 523
Management theory, 3-8, 25
Metric
conversion table, 56
temperature conversion, 330
Mopping (see Housekeeping)
Mortar (see Brickwork)
Motors
applications, 528
characteristics, 526
choosing the correct motor, 525
controls, 490-496, 528
efficiency, 583
loads, 582

Ohm's law (see Electricity)
Overload relays (see Circuit Breakers)

Painting, 247
exterior, 249
interior, 248, 249
prepainting considerations, 248
Paving, 245-247
Pests
birds, 177
common garden pests, 193

Pests *(Contd.)*
common household pests, 172
control, 172
rodents, 177
services, 172
wood-destroying pests, 177
Piping
copper pipe heat losses, 595
corrosion due to dissimilar metal, 44
fire control system, 114, 133
heating system schematic, 391
hot and cold water distribution, 287, 292, 293
lawn sprinkler lines, 288
leaking, 298
piping systems, 286, 361, 363, 364, 365, 368
pool recirculation system, 316, 318
siamese connection, 114
Planning
basic management activities, 7
budget as a planning tool, 23
building takeover, 8
converting operations expenses to income, 11
use of consultants, 38
Plants
annual flower plantings, 212
bulbs, corms, tubers, 205, 215
perennials, 208-211
trees and shrubs, 206
Plaster
cracks, 234
deterioration, 234
popping, 234
squash, handball, racquetball courts, 235
Plumbing
accessories, 82
aerators, 298
drainage, 307, 309
auger, how to use it, 313
plunger, how to use it, 313
pop-up drain operation, 311
servicing the lines, 312
faucets, 80, 295, 298, 302
leaking, 294
packing and "O" ring replacement, 296
replacing the faucets, 298
replacing the washer, 296
washer and "O" ring sizing charts, 296, 297, 299
system records, 78
tub and shower assembly, 298, 300, 301
water closet
removing, 311
repairing, 300, 304-306
tank fittings, 81
Pools (swimming and fountains)
filtration and heating, 316
filter pump, 319, 320
major components, 317
pool operating instructions, 319-321
recirculation system, 316, 318
safety equipment, 317
Power (see Electricity)
Pressure, gauge and absolute, 436
Pruning, 197-198
Pumps, 551
base-mounted booster, 289
equipment records, 69, 76
fire booster, 114
fuel oil pump, 345
maintenance, 552-556
pool filter pump, 320
Purchasing
in-house versus outside contractor, 37, 186
suppliers and services guide, 83

Receptacles (*see* Electricity)
Recordkeeping
building hardware, 67
cooling system, 71
electrical services, 68
equipment list, 85
importance, 20, 86
landscape "as built" plan, 60, 61
maintenance requests, 20, 388
major expense record form, 86
parking, 63, 64

Recordkeeping *(Contd.)*
parts and inventory form, 85
plans, 59
plumbing and drainage system, 78
renovation proposal form, 88
ventilation system, 71
work order, 21, 22
Refrigeration
coil maintenance, 544
refrigeration cycle, 434-440
ton of refrigeration, 401, 435
Renovations, 9, 88
Retrofits (*see* Energy)
Roofing, 251
flashing and counter flashing detail, 253-256
function, 252
inspections, 265-267
maintenance considerations, 267, 269
problems, 258-261
roofing felts, 255
scale drawing, typical, 268
types of roofs, 253, 254, 256, 257

Safety
boiler low water cut-off switch, 353
boiler relief safety valve, 353
boilers, 101
electrical hazards, 102-104
elevators, 100, 101
evacuation, 109, 110
features, 110
fuses and circuit breakers, 481-485
garbage compactors, 98
household products, 101
ladders, 98, 99
lifting and carrying, 97, 98
window cleaners, 98
Security
bitting list, 95, 96
building hardware, 96
building manager's responsibility, 277
life system audit, 131-133
lighting, 112, 131, 132
loss prevention tips, 111-113
master keys, 95
pass system, 96
security service, 97
Sheaves, 539-540
Shelf angle, 227
Slab edge, 226
Snow removal
budget, 217
inventory and equipment list, 213
Soils, chemicals and fertilizers
inventory list, 213
pH scale, 188, 189
soil analysis, 188
spraying tips, 190, 191
Solar energy, 331-332
Sprinklers
fire control, 114
lawn sprinkler heads, 203
life system audit, 133
Staffing
basic management activities, 7
budgeting operations staff salaries, 15
operator's responsibility, 385, 387
Stains, removal, 163, 169, 170, 171
Starters (*see* Motors)
Sweeping, 153
Swimming pools (*see* Pools)
Switches
fire alarm, 115
low water cut-off, 353

Thermal transmission
heat gained through glass, 404
heat gained through walls, floors and ceilings, 402
thermal characteristics, 571-576
Thermostat, 382-383
Timers (*see* Motors)
Tools
air balancing instruments and tools, 423
electric power test instruments, 456
plumbing tools, 294
safety, 111
testers and tools, 483
wall receptacle analyzer, 484

Television
handling complaints, 487
reception, 487
system records, 68

Vacuuming, 168
Valves, 556-561
backflow preventers, 290, 355
color coding and tagging, 78
controlling a three-way blend valve, 369-371
fire control, 114
gas supply shut-off valve, 342
maintenance, 556-558
pressure regulating valve (prv), 259, 351, 354
how a prv works, 291
piping arrangement, 291
shut-off, 113, 114, 131
swimming pools, 318
water relief safety valve, 353, 356
Vapor barrier
air vapor barriers, 243, 244
avoiding moisture problems, 245
details of house construction, 228
Ventilation, 243
air distribution in high-rise buildings, 415-422
air handler test report, 430
air pressure problems, 405
attic ventilation in a home, 245
boiler room air supply, 419
corridor air supply, 416, 605-607
diffusers, 414
eliminating drafts, 376
forced air system components, 377
fresh air requirements, 404
heat loss values, 571
how a building affects wind flow, 405
infiltration, 406
maintenance of laundry room exhaust, 421
records, 71, 406, 416
return air through light fixtures, 581
stack effect, 405
standard balancing procedure, 423
system budget, 448
systems, 417, 418
Voltage (*see* Electricity)

Walls
coverings, 63
graffiti removal, 142
washing, 142
Waste disposal
cleaning, 139-140
garbage compactor maintenance, 524
garbage room storage and washdown, 293
Water, domestic
contamination, 289
controlling the temperature, 590
heating, 292, 293, 373, 375
loss of water, 593
potable water, 288, 289
supply, 289
Watering, 199
equipment inventory list, 214
how much to water, 202
lawn sprinkler lines, 288
loss of water, 201
penetration, 199
sprinkler heads, 203
wetting pattern, 203
Water treatment
algae, 48
bacteria, 49
chlorine, 49
corrosion of heating systems, 592
swimming pool water, 316
testing control, 49
Watts (*see* Electricity)
Weeds, 188-190
Windows
interior glass cleaning, 140
locks, 251
preventive maintenance, 250
washing, 140, 251
Wires and wiring service (*see* Electricity)